PRAISE FOR

My Life

"By a generous measure, the richest American presidential autobiography—no other book tells us as vividly or fully what it is like to be president of the United States. . . . And he can write."
—Larry McMurtry,
The New York Times Book Review

"*My Life* is, without question, the best written U.S. presidential tome of all time."
—Douglas Brinkley, *Financial Times*

"A hell of a good story."
—Frank McCourt, *Entertainment Weekly*

"Consistently fascinating." —*The Seattle Times*

"Clinton talks with disarming frankness [and] writes with grace and fluidity. . . . He is also a born storyteller." —*The New Republic*

"Might just be the perfect representation of the man himself." —*The Plain Dealer*

"Clinton has many tales to tell, particularly a rich, sometimes moving account of his years before the public life."
—*The Nation*

"A rags-to-riches tale full of the stuff of human frailty, with a cast of hundreds, complete with low-life villains and high-minded heroes and, as such stories require, an upbeat ending."
—*The Star-Ledger* (Newark)

"He manages to create the distinct impression that he is sitting in the living room talking to the reader. . . . Anyone who is genuinely interested in American politics will find his insights and anecdotes fascinating. . . . The book helps to elucidate the question of 'how he did it.'"
—*Deseret Morning News*

"Tremendously interesting and entertaining. . . . Clinton's is a truly American story to which the average person can relate. . . . Future politicians will find it a must-read, and average Americans will identify with the highs and lows we all experience as we make our way through life."
—*Chattanooga Times Free Press*

"It's an almost voluptuous pleasure to read Clinton when he's recounting and analyzing a political race or a legislative battle, whether it's one of his own or somebody else's."
—*The New Yorker*

"A reading of *My Life* is a necessity for lovers of good autobiography. It reads like a down-home history of a life and, thus, anchors Clinton as a superb storyteller. . . . Candid. . . . Honest. . . . Stimulating."
—*The Huntsville Times*

Bill Clinton

My Life

THE EARLY YEARS

VINTAGE BOOKS
A Division of Random House, Inc.
New York

ISBN: 1-4000-9671-5

Book design by Christopher M. Zucker

www.vintagebooks.com
www.clintonfoundation.org

Printed in the United States of America
10 9 8 7 6 5 4 3 2 1

PHOTOGRAPH CREDITS

Photo insert researched, edited, and designed by Vincent Virga,
with the assistance of Carolyn Huber.
Every effort has been made to identify copyright holders;
in case of oversight, and upon notification to the publisher,
corrections will be made in subsequent printings.

Unless otherwise noted, all photos are from the author's collection.
AP/Wide World Photos: page 15, lower right.
Arkansas Democrat-Gazette: page 5, top right; page 6, top left; page 10,
top right; page 15, top.
Arsenio Hall Show, courtesy Paramount Pictures: page 15, lower left.
PF BENTLEY Archive, Center for American History, UT-Austin: page 13,
center left and right; page 14, center right and bottom.
PF Bentley/PFPIX.com: page 13, bottom.
Donald R. Broyles/Office of Governor Clinton: page 9, center left.
Clinton Presidential Materials Project: page 14, top left, top right,
and upper left.
Tipper Gore: page 13, top.
Morning News of Northwest Arkansas: page 7, top.
Jim Perry, *The Hope Star*: page 3, lower right.
Brooke Shearer: page 6, lower left.
Joseph Sohm/visionsofamerica.com: page 15, top right.
Jerry Staley: page 16, center right and bottom.

To my mother, who gave me a love of life

To Hillary, who gave me a life of love

To Chelsea, who gave joy and meaning to it all

And to the memory of my grandfather,
who taught me to look up to people others looked down on,
because we're not so different after all

PREFACE

AFTER THE PUBLICATION of *My Life* in June 2004, I traveled across America and to many other countries to promote it. I was astonished and grateful when so many people waited long hours, sometimes overnight, to get their books signed, as more than 60,000 people now have. In book signings, interviews, and chance encounters, people made very specific and widely diverse observations about what they took away from reading my story, further evidence that we all absorb information through the prism of our own experiences, interests, and needs.

Most people's comments fell into three categories: how the account of my early years struck a chord with them; how they had been affected by something I did as President; and how the book had increased their understanding of modern politics and policy issues. Of course, a fair number of people kidded me about the book's length and weight. Many were kind enough just to say they enjoyed it, including, most recently, a young member of the Florida A&M University band as former President Bush and I were walking onto the field for the pre-game show at the Super Bowl to salute our military forces.

For the first several weeks after the book came out, most people talked to me about my childhood and how reading about it caused them to reflect back on their own early years. A woman Hillary and I met in a Colorado bookstore and a European television interviewer both spoke openly about their own troubled childhoods and said reading my story had helped them to better understand their own, including problems they wrestled with well into adulthood. Many young readers, often immigrants or foreign exchange students, said they read my story to get guidance about how they, too, could live their dreams.

Many people at the book signings spoke briefly or handed me letters of thanks for the Family and Medical Leave Law, the extra help to go to college, the chance to move from welfare to work, the opportunity to serve in AmeriCorps, or the benefits they received from our economic policies. People from Ireland, Bosnia, Kosovo, Haiti, Mexico, Colombia, Vietnam, Korea, the Middle East, and Africa thanked me for trying to help their homelands and for telling the story of the struggles going on there. A Secret Service agent who had served in the U.S. Army Special Forces in Somalia during the days of "Black Hawk Down" thanked me for explaining the errors that I and others had made and for defending the soldiers in the field and their commander.

As the presidential election approached and passed, more and more readers wanted to talk to me about politics, about my own political philosophy, my account of the rise of the Republican Right over the last forty years, and whether recent Democratic losses signaled a long-term decline in our party's fortunes. One day shortly after the election, I was ordering take-out lunch at Susan Lawrence's in Chappaqua, New York, where I live now. Four of my neighbors came up to me. They were distraught about our loss and wanted to know what could be done about it. As I was trying to reassure them that all was not lost, a man standing near enough to overhear our conversation broke in and said, "If people would just read your book, they'd know what to do!" I don't know if he's right, since Hillary is in the arena now and I am more removed from it; still it was nice to hear.

When I saw how many people of modest means came to the book signings, I worried about my long and heavy book also being too expensive. I can't change the length, but I hope the paperback edition, in reducing the weight and cost, will make *My Life* accessible to a new round of readers.

My Life

THE EARLY YEARS

PROLOGUE

WHEN I WAS A YOUNG MAN just out of law school and eager to get on with my life, on a whim I briefly put aside my reading preference for fiction and history and bought one of those how-to books: *How to Get Control of Your Time and Your Life*, by Alan Lakein. The book's main point was the necessity of listing short-, medium-, and long-term life goals, then categorizing them in order of their importance, with the A group being the most important, the B group next, and the C the last, then listing under each goal specific activities designed to achieve them. I still have that paperback book, now almost thirty years old. And I'm sure I have that old list somewhere buried in my papers, though I can't find it. However, I do remember the A list. I wanted to be a good man, have a good marriage and children, have good friends, make a successful political life, and write a great book.

Whether I'm a good man is, of course, for God to judge. I know that I am not as good as my strongest supporters believe or as I hope to become, nor as bad as my harshest critics assert. I have been graced beyond measure by my family life with Hillary and Chelsea. Like all families' lives, ours is not perfect, but it has been wonderful. Its flaws, as all the world knows, are mostly mine, and its continuing promise is grounded in their love. No person I know ever had more or better friends. Indeed, a strong case can be made that I rose to the presidency on the shoulders of my personal friends, the now legendary FOBs.

My life in politics was a joy. I loved campaigns and I loved governing. I always tried to keep things moving in the right direction, to give more people a chance to live their dreams, to lift people's spirits, and to bring them together. That's the way I kept score.

As for the great book, who knows? It sure is a good story.

ONE

EARLY ON THE MORNING OF AUGUST 19, 1946, I was born under a clear sky after a violent summer storm to a widowed mother in the Julia Chester Hospital in Hope, a town of about six thousand in southwest Arkansas, thirty-three miles east of the Texas border at Texarkana. My mother named me William Jefferson Blythe III after my father, William Jefferson Blythe Jr., one of nine children of a poor farmer in Sherman, Texas, who died when my father was seventeen. According to his sisters, my father always tried to take care of them, and he grew up to be a handsome, hardworking, fun-loving man. He met my mother at Tri-State Hospital in Shreveport, Louisiana, in 1943, when she was training to be a nurse. Many times when I was growing up, I asked Mother to tell me the story of their meeting, courting, and marriage. He brought a date with some kind of medical emergency into the ward where she was working, and they talked and flirted while the other woman was being treated. On his way out of the hospital, he touched the finger on which she was wearing her boyfriend's ring and asked her if she was married. She stammered "no"—she was single. The next day he sent the other woman flowers and her heart sank. Then he called Mother for a date, explaining that he always sent flowers when he ended a relationship.

Two months later, they were married and he was off to war. He served in a motor pool in the invasion of Italy, repairing jeeps and tanks. After the war, he returned to Hope for Mother and they moved to Chicago, where he got back his old job as a salesman for the Manbee Equipment Company. They bought a little house in the suburb of Forest Park but couldn't move in for a couple of months, and since Mother was pregnant with me, they decided she should go home to Hope until they could get into the new house. On May 17, 1946, after moving their furniture into their new home, my father was driving from Chicago to Hope to fetch his wife. Late at night on Highway 60 outside of Sikeston, Missouri, he lost control of his car, a 1942 Buick, when the right front tire blew out on a wet road. He was thrown clear of the car but landed in, or crawled into, a drainage ditch dug to reclaim swampland. The ditch held three feet of water. When he was found, after a two-hour search, his hand was grasping a branch above the waterline. He had tried but failed to pull himself out. He drowned, only twenty-eight years old, married two years and eight months, only seven months of which he had spent with Mother.

That brief sketch is about all I ever really knew about my father. All my life I have been hungry to fill in the blanks, clinging eagerly to every photo or story or scrap of paper that would tell me more of the man who gave me life.

When I was about twelve, sitting on my uncle Buddy's porch in Hope, a man walked up the steps, looked at me, and said, "You're Bill Blythe's son. You look just like him." I beamed for days.

In 1974, I was running for Congress. It was my first race and the local paper did a feature story on my mother. She was at her regular coffee shop early in the morning discussing the article with a lawyer friend when one of the breakfast regulars she knew only casually came up to her and said, "I was there, I was the first one at the wreck that night." He then told Mother what he had seen, including the fact that my father had retained enough consciousness or survival instinct to try to claw himself up and out of the water before he died. Mother thanked him, went out to her car and cried, then dried her tears and went to work.

In 1993, on Father's Day, my first as President, the *Washington Post* ran a long investigative story on my father, which was followed over the next two months by other investigative pieces by the Associated Press and many smaller papers. The stories confirmed the things my mother and I knew. They also turned up a lot we didn't know, including the fact that my father had probably been married three times before he met Mother, and apparently had at least two more children.

My father's other son was identified as Leon Ritzenthaler, a retired owner of a janitorial service, from northern California. In the article, he said he had written me during the '92 campaign but had received no reply. I don't remember hearing about his letter, and considering all the other bullets we were dodging then, it's possible that my staff kept it from me. Or maybe the letter was just misplaced in the mountains of mail we were receiving. Anyway, when I read about Leon, I got in touch with him and later met him and his wife, Judy, during one of my stops in northern California. We had a happy visit and since then we've corresponded in holiday seasons. He and I look alike, his birth certificate says his father was mine, and I wish I'd known about him a long time ago.

Somewhere around this time, I also received information confirming news stories about a daughter, Sharon Pettijohn, born Sharon Lee Blythe in Kansas City in 1941, to a woman my father later divorced. She sent copies of her birth certificate, her parents' marriage license, a photo of my father, and a letter to her mother from my father asking about "our baby" to Betsey Wright, my former chief of staff in the governor's office. I'm sorry to say that, for whatever reason, I've never met her.

This news breaking in 1993 came as a shock to Mother, who by then had been battling cancer for some time, but she took it all in stride. She said young people did a lot of things during the Depression and the war that people in another time might disapprove of. What mattered was that my father was the love of her life and she had no doubt of his love for her. Whatever the facts, that's all she needed to know as her own life moved toward its end. As for me, I wasn't quite sure what to make of it all, but given the life I've led, I could hardly be surprised that my father was more complicated than the idealized pictures I had lived with for nearly half a century.

In 1994, as we headed for the celebration of the fiftieth anniversary of D-day, several newspapers published a story on my father's war record, with a snapshot of him in uniform. Shortly afterward, I received a letter from Umberto

Baron of Netcong, New Jersey, recounting his own experiences during the war and after. He said that he was a young boy in Italy when the Americans arrived, and that he loved to go to their camp, where one soldier in particular befriended him, giving him candy and showing him how engines worked and how to repair them. He knew him only as Bill. After the war, Baron came to the United States, and, inspired by what he had learned from the soldier who called him "Little GI Joe," he opened his own garage and started a family. He told me he had lived the American dream, with a thriving business and three children. He said he owed so much of his success in life to that young soldier, but hadn't had the opportunity to say good-bye then, and had often wondered what had happened to him. Then, he said, "On Memorial Day of this year, I was thumbing through a copy of the New York *Daily News* with my morning coffee when suddenly I felt as if I was struck by lightning. There in the lower left-hand corner of the paper was a photo of Bill. I felt chills to learn that Bill was none other than the father of the President of the United States."

In 1996, the children of one of my father's sisters came for the first time to our annual family Christmas party at the White House and brought me a gift: the condolence letter my aunt had received from her congressman, the great Sam Rayburn, after my father died. It's just a short form letter and appears to have been signed with the autopen of the day, but I hugged that letter with all the glee of a six-year-old boy getting his first train set from Santa Claus. I hung it in my private office on the second floor of the White House, and looked at it every night.

Shortly after I left the White House, I was boarding the US Airways shuttle in Washington for New York when an airline employee stopped me to say that his stepfather had just told him he had served in the war with my father and had liked him very much. I asked for the old vet's phone number and address, and the man said he didn't have it but would get it to me. I'm still waiting, hoping there will be one more human connection to my father.

At the end of my presidency, I picked a few special

places to say good-bye and thanks to the American people. One of them was Chicago, where Hillary was born; where I all but clinched the Democratic nomination on St. Patrick's Day 1992; where many of my most ardent supporters live and many of my most important domestic initiatives in crime, welfare, and education were proved effective; and, of course, where my parents went to live after the war. I used to joke with Hillary that if my father hadn't lost his life on that rainy Missouri highway, I would have grown up a few miles from her and we probably never would have met. My last event was in the Palmer House Hotel, scene of the only photo I have of my parents together, taken just before Mother came back to Hope in 1946. After the speech and the good-byes, I went into a small room where I met a woman, Mary Etta Rees, and her two daughters. She told me she had grown up and gone to high school with my mother, then had gone north to Indiana to work in a war industry, married, stayed, and raised her children. Then she gave me another precious gift: the letter my twenty-three-year-old mother had written on her birthday to her friend, three weeks after my father's death, more than fifty-four years earlier. It was vintage Mother. In her beautiful hand, she wrote of her heartbreak and her determination to carry on: "It seemed almost unbelievable at the time but you see I am six months pregnant and the thought of our baby keeps me going and really gives me the whole world before me."

My mother left me the wedding ring she gave my father, a few moving stories, and the sure knowledge that she was loving me for him too.

My father left me with the feeling that I had to live for two people, and that if I did it well enough, somehow I could make up for the life he should have had. And his memory infused me, at a younger age than most, with a sense of my own mortality. The knowledge that I, too, could die young drove me both to try to drain the most out of every moment of life and to get on with the next big challenge. Even when I wasn't sure where I was going, I was always in a hurry.

TWO

I WAS BORN on my grandfather's birthday, a couple of weeks early, weighing in at a respectable six pounds eight ounces, on a twenty-one-inch frame. Mother and I came home to her parents' house on Hervey Street in Hope, where I would spend the next four years. That old house seemed massive and mysterious to me then and still holds deep memories today. The people of Hope raised the funds to restore it and fill it with old pictures, memorabilia, and period furniture. They call it the Clinton Birthplace. It certainly is the place I associate with awakening to life—to the smells of country food; to buttermilk churns, ice-cream makers, washboards, and clotheslines; to my "Dick and Jane" readers, my first toys, including a simple length of chain I prized above them all; to strange voices talking over our "party line" telephone; to my first friends, and the work my grandparents did.

After a year or so, my mother decided she needed to go back to New Orleans to Charity Hospital, where she had done part of her nursing training, to learn to be a nurse anesthetist. In the old days, doctors had administered their own anesthetics, so there was a demand for this relatively new work, which would bring more prestige to her and more money for us. But it must have been hard on her, leaving me. On the other hand, New Orleans was an amazing place after the war, full of young people, Dixieland music, and over-the-top haunts like the Club My-Oh-My, where men in drag danced and sang as lovely ladies. I guess it wasn't a bad place for a beautiful young widow to move beyond her loss.

I got to visit Mother twice when my grandmother took me on the train to New Orleans. I was only three, but I remember two things clearly. First, we stayed just across Canal Street from the French Quarter in the Jung Hotel, on one of the higher floors. It was the first building more than two stories high I had ever been in, in the first real city I had ever seen. I can remember the awe I felt looking out over all the city lights at night. I don't recall what Mother and I did in New Orleans, but I'll never forget what happened one of the times I got on the train to leave. As we pulled away from the station, Mother knelt by the side of the railroad tracks and cried as she waved good-bye. I can see her there still, crying on her knees, as if it were yesterday.

For more than fifty years, from that first trip, New Orleans has always had a special fascination for me. I love its music, food, people, and spirit. When I was fifteen, my family took a vacation to New Orleans and the Gulf Coast, and I got to hear Al Hirt, the great trumpeter, in his own club. At first they wouldn't let me in because I was under-age. As Mother and I were about to walk away, the door-man told us that Hirt was sitting in his car reading just around the corner, and that only he could let me in. I found him—in his Bentley, no less—tapped on the window, and made my case. He got out, took Mother and me into the club, and put us at a table near the front. He and his group played a great set—it was my first live jazz experience. Al Hirt died while I was President. I wrote his wife and told her the story, expressing my gratitude for a big man's long-ago kindness to a boy.

When I was in high school, I played the tenor saxophone solo on a piece about New Orleans called *Crescent City Suite*. I always thought I did a better job on it because I played it with memories of my first sight of the city. When I was twenty-one, I won a Rhodes scholarship in New Orleans. I think I did well in the interview in part because I felt at home there. When I was a young law professor, Hillary and I had a couple of great trips to New Orleans for conventions, staying at a quaint little hotel in the French Quarter, the Cornstalk. When I was governor of Arkansas, we played in the Sugar Bowl there, losing to Alabama in one of the legendary Bear Bryant's last great victories. At least he was born and grew up in Arkansas! When I ran for President, the people of New Orleans twice gave me overwhelming victory margins, assuring Louisiana's electoral votes for our side.

Now I have seen most of the world's great cities, but New Orleans will always be special—for coffee and beignets at the Morning Call on the Mississippi; for the music of Aaron and Charmaine Neville, the old guys at Preservation Hall, and the memory of Al Hirt; for jogging through the French Quarter in the early morning; for amazing meals at a host of terrific restaurants with John Breaux, Sheriff Harry Lee, and my other pals; and most of all, for those first memories of my mother. They are the magnets that keep pulling me down the Mississippi to New Orleans.

While Mother was in New Orleans, I was in the care of my grandparents. They were incredibly conscientious about me. They loved me very much; sadly, much better than they were able to love each other or, in my grandmother's case, to love my mother. Of course, I was blissfully unaware of all this at the time. I just knew that I was loved. Later, when I became interested in children growing up in hard circumstances and learned something of child development from Hillary's work at the Yale Child Study Center, I came to realize how fortunate I had been. For all their own demons, my grandparents and my mother always made me feel I was the most important person in the world to them. Most children will make it if they have just one person who makes them feel that way. I had three.

My grandmother, Edith Grisham Cassidy, stood just over five feet tall and weighed about 180 pounds. Mammaw was bright, intense, and aggressive, and had obviously been pretty once. She had a great laugh, but she also was full of anger and disappointment and obsessions she only dimly understood. She took it all out in raging tirades against my grandfather and my mother, both before and after I was born, though I was shielded from most of them. She had been a good student and ambitious, so after high school she took a correspondence course in nursing from the Chicago School of Nursing. By the time I was a toddler she was a private-duty nurse for a man not far from our house on

Hervey Street. I can still remember running down the side-walk to meet her when she came home from work.

Mammaw's main goals for me were that I would eat a lot, learn a lot, and always be neat and clean. We ate in the kitchen at a table next to the window. My high chair faced the window, and Mammaw tacked playing cards up on the wooden window frame at mealtimes so that I could learn to count. She also stuffed me at every meal, because conventional wisdom at the time was that a fat baby was a healthy one, as long as he bathed every day. At least once a day, she read to me from "Dick and Jane" books until I could read them myself, and from *World Book Encyclopedia* volumes, which in those days were sold door-to-door by salesmen and were often the only books besides the Bible in working people's houses. These early instructions probably explain why I now read a lot, love card games, battle my weight, and never forget to wash my hands and brush my teeth.

I adored my grandfather, the first male influence in my life, and felt pride that I was born on his birthday. James Eldridge Cassidy was a slight man, about five eight, but in those years still strong and handsome. I always thought he resembled the actor Randolph Scott.

When my grandparents moved from Bodcaw, which had a population of about a hundred, to the metropolis Hope, Papaw worked for an icehouse delivering ice on a horse-drawn wagon. In those days, refrigerators really were ice-boxes, cooled by chunks of ice whose size varied according to the size of the appliance. Though he weighed about 150 pounds, my grandfather carried ice blocks that weighed up to a hundred pounds or more, using a pair of hooks to slide them onto his back, which was protected by a large leather flap.

My grandfather was an incredibly kind and generous man. During the Depression, when nobody had any money, he would invite boys to ride the ice truck with him just to get them off the street. They earned twenty-five cents a day. In 1976, when I was in Hope running for attorney general, I had a talk with one of those boys, Judge John Wilson. He grew up to be a distinguished, successful lawyer, but he still had vivid memories of those days. He told me that at the end of one day, when my grandfather gave him his quarter, he asked if he could have two dimes and a nickel so that he could feel he had more money. He got them and walked home, jingling the change in his pockets. But he jingled too hard, and one of the dimes fell out. He looked for that dime for hours to no avail. Forty years later, he told me he still never walked by that stretch of sidewalk without trying to spot that dime.

It's hard to convey to young people today the impact the Depression had on my parents' and grandparents' generation, but I grew up feeling it. One of the most memorable stories of my childhood was my mother's tale of a Depression Good Friday when my grandfather came home from work and broke down and cried as he told her he just couldn't afford the dollar or so it would cost to buy her a new Easter dress. She never forgot it, and every year of my childhood I had a new Easter outfit whether I wanted it or not. I remember one Easter in the 1950s, when I was fat and self-conscious. I went to church in a light-colored short-sleeved shirt, white linen pants, pink and black Hush Puppies, and a matching pink suede belt. It hurt, but my mother had been faithful to her father's Easter ritual.

When I was living with him, my grandfather had two jobs that I really loved: he ran a little grocery store, and he supplemented his income by working as a night watchman at a sawmill. I loved spending the night with Papaw at the sawmill. We would take a paper bag with sandwiches for supper, and I would sleep in the backseat of the car. And on clear starlit nights, I would climb in the sawdust piles, taking in the magical smells of fresh-cut timber and sawdust. My grandfather loved working there, too. It got him out of the house and reminded him of the mill work he'd done as a young man around the time of my mother's birth. Except for the time Papaw closed the car door on my fingers in the dark, those nights were perfect adventures.

The grocery store was a different sort of adventure. First, there was a huge jar of Jackson's cookies on the counter, which I raided with gusto. Second, grown-ups I didn't know came in to buy groceries, for the first time exposing me to adults who weren't relatives. Third, a lot of my grandfather's customers were black. Though the South was completely segregated back then, some level of racial interaction was inevitable in small towns, just as it had always been in the rural South. However, it was rare to find an uneducated rural southerner without a racist bone in his body. That's exactly what my grandfather was. I could see that black people looked different, but because he treated them like he did everybody else, asking after their children and about their work, I thought they were just like me. Occasionally, black kids would come into the store and we would play. It took me years to learn about segregation and prejudice and the meaning of poverty, years to learn that most white people weren't like my grandfather and grandmother, whose views on race were among the few things she had in common with her husband. In fact, Mother told me one of the worst whippings she ever got was when, at age three or four, she called a black woman "Nigger." To put it mildly, Mammaw's whipping her was an unusual reaction for a poor southern white woman in the 1920s.

My mother once told me that after Papaw died, she found some of his old account books from the grocery store with lots of unpaid bills from his customers, most of them black. She recalled that he had told her that good people who were doing the best they could deserved to be able to feed their families, and no matter how strapped he was, he never denied them groceries on credit. Maybe that's why I've always believed in food stamps.

After I became President, I got another firsthand account of my grandfather's store. In 1997, an African-American woman, Ernestine Campbell, did an interview for her hometown paper in Toledo, Ohio, about her grandfather buying groceries from Papaw "on account" and bringing her with him to the store. She said that she remembered playing with me, and that I was "the only white boy in that neighborhood who played with black kids." Thanks to my grandfather, I didn't know I was the only white kid who did that.

Besides my grandfather's store, my neighborhood provided my only other contact with people outside my family. I experienced a lot in those narrow confines. I saw a house burn down across the street and learned I was not the only person bad things happened to. I made friends with a boy who collected strange creatures, and once he invited me over to see his snake. He said it was in the closet. Then he opened the closet door, shoved me into the darkness, slammed the door shut, and told me I was in the dark alone with the snake. I wasn't, thank goodness, but I was sure scared to death. I learned that what seems funny to the strong can be cruel and humiliating to the weak.

Our house was just a block away from a railroad underpass, which then was made of rough, tar-coated timbers. I liked to climb on the timbers, listen to the trains rattle overhead, and wonder where they were going and whether I would ever go there.

And I used to play in the backyard with a boy whose yard adjoined mine. He lived with two beautiful sisters in a bigger, nicer house than ours. We used to sit on the grass for hours, throwing his knife in the ground and learning to make it stick. His name was Vince Foster. He was kind to me and never lorded it over me the way so many older boys did with younger ones. He grew up to be a tall, handsome, wise, good man. He became a great lawyer, a strong supporter early in my career, and Hillary's best friend at the Rose Law Firm. Our families socialized in Little Rock, mostly at his house, where his wife, Lisa, taught Chelsea to swim. He came to the White House with us, and was a voice of calm and reason in those crazy early months.

There was one other person outside the family who influenced me in my early childhood. Odessa was a black woman who came to our house to clean, cook, and watch me when my grandparents were at work. She had big buckteeth, which made her smile only brighter and more beautiful to me. I kept up with her for years after I left Hope. In 1966, a friend and I went out to see Odessa after visiting my father's and grandfather's graves. Most of the black people in Hope lived near the cemetery, across the road from where my grandfather's store had been. I remember our visiting on her porch for a good long while. When the time came to go, we got in my car and drove away on dirt streets. The only unpaved streets I saw in Hope, or later in Hot Springs when I moved there, were in black neighborhoods, full of people who worked hard, many of them raising kids like me, and who paid taxes. Odessa deserved better.

The other large figures in my childhood were relatives: my maternal great-grandparents, my great-aunt Otie and great-uncle Carl Russell, and most of all, my great-uncle Oren—known as Buddy, and one of the lights of my life—and his wife, Aunt Ollie.

My Grisham great-grandparents lived out in the country in a little wooden house built up off the ground. Because Arkansas gets more tornadoes than almost any other place in the United States, most people who lived in virtual stick houses like theirs dug a hole in the ground for a storm cellar. Theirs was out in the front yard, and had a little bed and a small table with a coal-oil lantern on it. I still remember peering into that little space and hearing my great-grandfather say, "Yes, sometimes snakes go down there too, but they won't bite you if the lantern's lit." I never found out whether that was true or not. My only other memory of my great-grandfather is that he came to visit me in the hospital when I broke my leg at age five. He held my hand and we posed for a picture. He's in a simple black jacket and a white shirt buttoned all the way up, looking old as the hills, straight out of *American Gothic*.

My grandmother's sister Opal—we called her Otie—was a fine-looking woman with the great Grisham family laugh, whose quiet husband, Carl, was the first person I knew who grew watermelons. The river-enriched, sandy soil around Hope is ideal for them, and the size of Hope's melons became the trademark of the town in the early fifties when the community sent the largest melon ever grown up to that time, just under two hundred pounds, to President Truman. The better-tasting melons, however, weigh sixty pounds or less. Those are the ones I saw my great-uncle Carl grow, pouring water from a washtub into the soil around the melons and watching the stalks suck it up like a vacuum cleaner. When I became President, Uncle Carl's cousin Carter Russell still had a watermelon stand in Hope where you could get good red or the sweeter yellow melons.

Hillary says the first time she ever saw me, I was in the Yale Law School lounge bragging to skeptical fellow students about the size of Hope watermelons. When I was President, my old friends from Hope put on a watermelon feed on the South Lawn of the White House, and I got to tell my watermelon stories to a new generation of young people who pretended to be interested in a subject I began to learn about so long ago from Aunt Otie and Uncle Carl.

My grandmother's brother Uncle Buddy and his wife, Ollie, were the primary members of my extended family. Buddy and Ollie had four children, three of whom were gone from Hope by the time I came along. Dwayne was an executive with a shoe manufacturer in New Hampshire. Conrad and Falba were living in Dallas, though they both came back to Hope often and live there today. Myra, the youngest, was a rodeo queen. She could ride like a pro, and she later ran off with a cowboy, had two boys, divorced, and moved home, where she ran the local housing authority. Myra and Falba are great women who laugh through their tears and never quit on family and friends. I'm glad they are still part of my life. I spent a lot of time at Buddy and Ollie's house, not just in my first six years in Hope, but for forty more years until Ollie died and Buddy sold the house and moved in with Falba.

Social life in my extended family, like that of most people of modest means who grew up in the country, revolved around meals, conversation, and storytelling. They couldn't afford vacations, rarely if ever went to the movies, and didn't have television until the mid- to late 1950s. They went out a few times a year—to the county fair, the watermelon festival, the occasional square dance or gospel singing. The men hunted and fished and raised vegetables and watermelon on small plots out in the country that they'd kept when they moved to town to work.

Though they never had extra money, they never felt poor as long as they had a neat house, clean clothes, and enough food to feed anyone who came in the front door. They worked to live, not the other way around.

My favorite childhood meals were at Buddy and Ollie's, eating around a big table in their small kitchen. A typical weekend lunch, which we called dinner (the evening meal was supper), included ham or a roast, corn bread, spinach or collard greens, mashed potatoes, sweet potatoes, peas, green beans or lima beans, fruit pie, and endless quantities of iced tea we drank in large goblet-like glasses. I felt more grown-up drinking out of those big glasses. On special days we had homemade ice cream to go with the pie. When I was there early enough, I got to help prepare the meal, shelling the beans or turning the crank on the ice-cream maker. Before, during, and after dinner there was constant talk: town gossip, family goings-on, and stories, lots of them. All my kinfolks could tell a story, making simple events, encounters, and mishaps involving ordinary people come alive with drama and laughter.

Buddy was the best storyteller. Like both of his sisters, he was very bright. I often wondered what he and they would have made of their lives if they had been born into my generation or my daughter's. But there were lots of people like them back then. The guy pumping your gas might have had an IQ as high as the guy taking your tonsils out. There are still people like the Grishams in America, many of them new immigrants, which is why I tried as President to open the doors of college to all comers.

Though he had a very limited education, Buddy had a fine mind and a Ph.D. in human nature, born of a lifetime of keen observation and dealing with his own demons and those of his family. Early in his marriage he had a drinking problem. One day he came home and told his wife he knew his drinking was hurting her and their family and he was never going to drink again. And he never did, for more than fifty years.

Well into his eighties, Buddy could tell amazing stories highlighting the personalities of dogs he'd had five or six decades earlier. He remembered their names, their looks, their peculiar habits, how he came by them, the precise way they retrieved shot birds. Lots of people would come by his house and sit on the porch for a visit. After they left he'd have a story about them or their kids—sometimes funny, sometimes sad, usually sympathetic, always understanding.

I learned a lot from the stories my uncle, aunts, and grandparents told me: that no one is perfect but most people are good; that people can't be judged only by their worst or weakest moments; that harsh judgments can make hypocrites of us all; that a lot of life is just showing up and hanging on; that laughter is often the best, and sometimes the only, response to pain. Perhaps most important, I learned that everyone has a story—of dreams and nightmares, hope and heartache, love and loss, courage and fear, sacrifice and selfishness. All my life I've been interested in other people's stories. I've wanted to know them, understand them, feel them. When I grew up and got into politics, I always felt the main point of my work was to give people a chance to have better stories.

Uncle Buddy's story was good until the end. He got lung cancer in 1974, had a lung removed, and still lived to be ninety-one. He counseled me in my political career, and if I'd followed his advice and repealed an unpopular car-tag increase, I probably wouldn't have lost my first gubernatorial reelection campaign in 1980. He lived to see me elected President and got a big kick out of it. After Ollie died, he kept active by going down to his daughter Falba's doughnut shop and regaling a whole new generation of kids with his stories and witty observations on the human condition. He never lost his sense of humor. He was still driving at eighty-seven, when he took two lady friends, aged ninety-one and ninety-three, for drives separately once a week. When he told me about his "dates," I asked, "So you like these older women now?" He snickered and said, "Yeah, I do. Seems like they're a little more settled."

In all our years together, I saw my uncle cry only once. Ollie developed Alzheimer's and had to be moved to a nursing home. For several weeks afterward, she knew who she was for a few minutes a day. During those lucid intervals, she would call Buddy and say, "Oren, how could you leave me in this place after fifty-six years of marriage? Come get me right now." He would dutifully drive over to see her, but by the time he got there, she would be lost again in the mists of the disease and didn't know him.

It was during this period that I stopped by to see him late one afternoon, our last visit at the old house. I was hoping to cheer him up. Instead, he made me laugh with bawdy jokes and droll comments on current events. When darkness fell, I told him I had to go back home to Little Rock. He followed me to the door, and as I was about to walk out, he grabbed my arm. I turned and saw tears in his eyes for the first and only time in almost fifty years of love and friendship. I said, "This is really hard, isn't it?" I'll never forget his reply. He smiled and said, "Yeah, it is, but I signed on for the whole load, and most of it was pretty good." My uncle Buddy taught me that everyone has a story. He told his in that one sentence.

THREE

AFTER THE YEAR in New Orleans, Mother came home to Hope eager to put her anesthesia training into practice, elated at being reunited with me, and back to her old fun-loving self. She had dated several men in New Orleans and had a fine time, according to her memoir, *Leading with My Heart*, which I'm sure would have been a bestseller if she had lived to promote it.

However, before, during, and after her sojourn in New Orleans, Mother was dating one man more than anyone else, the owner of the local Buick dealership, Roger Clinton. She was a beautiful, high-spirited widow. He was a handsome, hell-raising, twice-divorced man from Hot Springs, Arkansas' "Sin City," which for several years had been home to the largest illegal gambling operation in the United States. Roger's brother Raymond owned the Buick dealership in Hot Springs, and Roger, the baby and "bad boy" of a family of five, had come to Hope to take advantage of the war activity around the Southwestern Proving Ground and perhaps to get out of his brother's shadow.

Roger loved to drink and party with his two best buddies from Hot Springs, Van Hampton Lyell, who owned the Coca-Cola bottling plant across the street from Clinton Buick, and Gabe Crawford, who owned several drugstores in Hot Springs and one in Hope, later built Hot Springs' first shopping center, and was then married to Roger's gorgeous niece, Virginia, a woman I've always loved, who was the very first Miss Hot Springs. Their idea of a good time was to gamble, get drunk, and do crazy, reckless things in cars or airplanes or on motorcycles. It's a wonder they didn't all die young.

Mother liked Roger because he was fun, paid attention to me, and was generous. He paid for her to come home to see me several times when she was in New Orleans, and he probably paid for the train trips Mammaw and I took to see Mother.

Papaw liked Roger because he was nice both to me and to him. For a while after my grandfather quit the icehouse because of severe bronchial problems, he ran a liquor store. Near the end of the war, Hempstead County, of which Hope is the county seat, voted to go "dry." That's when my grandfather opened his grocery store. I later learned that Papaw sold liquor under the counter to the doctors, lawyers, and other respectable people who didn't want to drive the thirty-three miles to the nearest legal liquor store in Texarkana, and that Roger was his supplier.

Mammaw really disliked Roger because she thought he was not the kind of man her daughter and grandson should be tied to. She had a dark side her husband and daughter lacked, but it enabled her to see the darkness in others that they missed. She thought Roger Clinton was nothing but trouble. She was right about the trouble part, but not the "nothing but." There was more to him than that, which makes his story even sadder.

As for me, all I knew was that he was good to me and had a big brown and black German shepherd, Susie, that he brought to play with me. Susie was a big part of my childhood, and started my lifelong love affair with dogs.

Mother and Roger got married in Hot Springs, in June 1950, shortly after her twenty-seventh birthday. Only Gabe and Virginia Crawford were there. Then Mother and I left her parents' home and moved with my new stepfather, whom I soon began to call Daddy, into a little white wooden house on the south end of town at 321 Thirteenth Street at the corner of Walker Street. Not long afterward, I started calling myself Billy Clinton.

My new world was exciting to me. Next door were Ned and Alice Williams. Mr. Ned was a retired railroad worker who built a workshop behind his house filled with a large sophisticated model electric-train setup. Back then every little kid wanted a Lionel train set. Daddy got me one and we used to play with it together, but nothing could compare to Mr.

Ned's large intricate tracks and beautiful fast trains. I spent hours there. It was like having my own Disneyland next door.

My neighborhood was a class-A advertisement for the post–World War II baby boom. There were lots of young couples with kids. Across the street lived the most special child of all, Mitzi Polk, daughter of Minor and Margaret Polk. Mitzi had a loud, roaring laugh. She would swing so high on her swing set the poles of the frame would come up out of the ground, as she bellowed at the top of her lungs, "Billy sucks a bottle! Billy sucks a bottle!" She drove me nuts. After all, I was getting to be a big boy and I did no such thing.

I later learned that Mitzi was developmentally disabled. The term wouldn't have meant anything to me then, but when I pushed to expand opportunities for the disabled as governor and President, I thought often of Mitzi Polk.

A lot happened to me while I lived on Thirteenth Street. I started school at Miss Marie Purkins' School for Little Folks kindergarten, which I loved until I broke my leg one day jumping rope. And it wasn't even a moving rope. The rope in the playground was tied at one end to a tree and at the other end to a swing set. The kids would line up on one side and take turns running and jumping over it. All the other kids cleared the rope.

One of them was Mack McLarty, son of the local Ford dealer, later governor of Boys State, all-star quarterback, state legislator, successful businessman, and then my first White House chief of staff. Mack always cleared every hurdle. Luckily for me, he always waited for me to catch up.

Me, I didn't clear the rope. I was a little chunky anyway, and slow, so slow that I was once the only kid at an Easter egg hunt who didn't get a single egg, not because I couldn't find them but because I couldn't get to them fast enough. On the day I tried to jump rope I was wearing cowboy boots to school. Like a fool, I didn't take the boots off to jump. My heel caught on the rope, I turned, fell, and heard my leg snap. I lay in agony on the ground for several minutes while Daddy raced over from the Buick place to get me.

I had broken my leg above the knee, and because I was growing so fast, the doctor was reluctant to put me in a cast up to my hip. Instead, he made a hole through my ankle, pushed a stainless steel bar through it, attached it to a stainless steel horseshoe, and hung my leg up in the air over my hospital bed. I lay like that for two months, flat on my back, feeling both foolish and pleased to be out of school and receiving so many visitors. I took a long time getting over that leg break. After I got out of the hospital, my folks bought me a bicycle, but I never lost my fear of riding without the training wheels. As a result, I never stopped feeling that I was clumsy and without a normal sense of balance until, at the age of twenty-two, I finally started riding a bike at Oxford. Even then I fell a few times, but I thought of it as building my pain threshold.

I was grateful to Daddy for coming to rescue me when I broke my leg. He also came home from work a time or two to try to talk Mother out of spanking me when I did something wrong. At the beginning of their marriage he really tried to be there for me. I remember once he even took me on the train to St. Louis to see the Cardinals, then our nearest major league baseball team. We stayed overnight and came home the next day. I loved it. Sadly, it was the only trip the two of us ever took together. Like the only time we ever went fishing together. The only time we ever went out into the woods to cut our own Christmas tree together. The only time our whole family took an out-of-state vacation together. There were so many things that meant a lot to me but were never to occur again. Roger Clinton really loved me and he loved Mother, but he couldn't ever quite break free of the shadows of self-doubt, the phony security of binge drinking and adolescent partying, and the isolation from and verbal abuse of Mother that kept him from becoming the man he might have been.

One night his drunken self-destructiveness came to a head in a fight with my mother I can't ever forget. Mother wanted us to go to the hospital to see my great-grandmother, who didn't have long to live. Daddy said she couldn't go. They were screaming at each other in their bedroom in the back of the house. For some reason, I walked out into the hall to the doorway of the bedroom. Just as I did, Daddy pulled a gun from behind his back and fired in Mother's direction. The bullet went into the wall between where she and I were standing. I was stunned and so scared. I had never heard a shot fired before, much less seen one. Mother grabbed me and ran across the street to the neighbors. The police were called. I can still see them leading Daddy away in handcuffs to jail, where he spent the night.

I'm sure Daddy didn't mean to hurt her and he would have died if the bullet had accidentally hit either of us. But something more poisonous than alcohol drove him to that level of debasement. It would be a long time before I could understand such forces in others or in myself. When Daddy got out of jail he had sobered up in more ways than one and was so ashamed that nothing bad happened for some time.

I had one more year of life and schooling in Hope. I went to first grade at Brookwood School; my teacher was Miss Mary Wilson. Although she had only one arm, she didn't believe in sparing the rod, or, in her case, the paddle, into which she had bored holes to cut down on the wind resistance. On more than one occasion I was the recipient of her concern.

In addition to my neighbors and Mack McLarty, I became friends with some other kids who stayed with me for a lifetime. One of them, Joe Purvis, had a childhood that made mine look idyllic. He grew up to be a fine lawyer, and when I was elected attorney general, I hired Joe on my staff. When Arkansas had an important case before the U.S. Supreme Court, I went, but I let Joe make the argument. Justice Byron "Whizzer" White sent me a note from the bench saying that Joe had done a good job. Later, Joe became the first chairman of my Birthplace Foundation.

Besides my friends and family, my life on Thirteenth Street was marked by my discovery of the movies. In 1951 and 1952, I could go for a dime: a nickel to get in, a nickel for a Coke. I went every couple of weeks or so. Back then, you got a feature film, a cartoon, a serial, and a newsreel.

The Korean War was on, so I learned about that. Flash Gordon and Rocket Man were the big serial heroes. For cartoons, I preferred *Bugs Bunny, Casper the Friendly Ghost*, and *Baby Huey*, with whom I probably identified. I saw a lot of movies, and especially liked the westerns. My favorite was *High Noon*—I probably saw it half a dozen times during its run in Hope, and have seen it more than a dozen times since. It's still my favorite movie, because it's not your typical macho western. I loved the movie because from start to finish Gary Cooper is scared to death but does the right thing anyway.

When I was elected President, I told an interviewer that my favorite movie was *High Noon*. At the time, Fred Zinnemann, its director, was nearly ninety, living in London. I got a great letter from him with a copy of his annotated script and an autographed picture of himself with Cooper and Grace Kelly in street clothes on the *High Noon* set in 1951. Over the long years since I first saw *High Noon*, when I faced my own showdowns, I often thought of the look in Gary Cooper's eyes as he stares into the face of almost certain defeat, and how he keeps walking through his fears toward his duty. It works pretty well in real life too.

FOUR

IN THE SUMMER after my first-grade year, Daddy decided he wanted to go home to Hot Springs. He sold the Buick dealership and moved us to a four hundred–acre farm out on Wildcat Road a few miles west of the city. It had cattle, sheep, and goats. What it didn't have was an indoor toilet. So for the year or so we lived out there, on the hottest summer days and the coldest winter nights, we had to go outside to the wooden outhouse to relieve ourselves. It was an interesting experience, especially when the nonpoisonous king snake that hung around our yard was peering up through the hole at me when I had to go. Later, when I got into politics, being able to say I had lived on a farm with an outhouse made a great story, almost as good as being born in a log cabin.

I liked living on the farm, feeding the animals, and moving among them, until one fateful Sunday. Daddy had several members of his family out to lunch, including his brother Raymond and his children. I took one of Raymond's daughters, Karla, out into the field where the sheep were grazing. I knew there was one mean ram we had to avoid, but we decided to tempt fate, a big mistake. When we were about a hundred yards away from the fence, the ram saw us and started to charge. We started running for the fence. Karla was bigger and faster and made it. I stumbled over a big rock. When I fell I could see I wasn't going to make the fence before the ram got to me, so I retreated to a small tree a few feet away in the hope I could keep away from him by running around the tree until help came. Another big mistake. Soon he caught me and knocked my legs out from under me. Before I could get up he butted me in the head. Then I was stunned and hurt and couldn't get up. So he backed up, got a good head start, and rammed

me again as hard as he could. He did the same thing over
and over and over again, alternating his targets between my
head and my gut. Soon I was pouring blood and hurting
like the devil. After what seemed an eternity my uncle
showed up, picked up a big rock, and threw it hard, hitting
the ram square between the eyes. The ram just shook his
head and walked off, apparently unfazed. I recovered, left
with only a scar on my forehead, which gradually grew into
my scalp. And I learned that I could take a hard hit, a lesson that I would relearn a couple more times in my childhood and later in life.

A few months after we moved to the farm, both my folks
were going to town to work. Daddy gave up on being a
farmer and took a job as a parts manager for Uncle Raymond's Buick dealership, while Mother found more anesthesia work in Hot Springs than she could handle. One day,
on the way to work, she picked up a woman who was walking to town. After they got acquainted, Mother asked her if
she knew anyone who would come to the house and look
after me while she and Daddy were at work. In one of the
great moments of good luck in my life, she suggested herself.
Her name was Cora Walters; she was a grandmother with
every good quality of an old-fashioned countrywoman. She
was wise, kind, upright, conscientious, and deeply Christian. She became a member of our family for eleven years.
All her family were good people, and after she left us, her
daughter Maye Hightower came to work for Mother and
stayed thirty more years until Mother died. In another age,
Cora Walters would have made a fine minister. She made me
a better person by her example, and certainly wasn't responsible for any of my sins, then or later. She was a tough old
gal, too. One day she helped me kill a huge rat that was
hanging around our house. Actually, I found it and she
killed it while I cheered.

When we moved out to the country, Mother was concerned about my going to a small rural school, so she
enrolled me in St. John's Catholic School downtown, where
I attended second and third grade. Both years my teacher

was Sister Mary Amata McGee, a fine and caring teacher but no pushover. I often got straight As on my six-week report card and a C in citizenship, which was a euphemism for good behavior in class. I loved to read and compete in spelling contests, but I talked too much. It was a constant problem in grade school, and as my critics and many of my friends would say, it's one I never quite got over. I also got in trouble once for excusing myself to go to the bathroom and staying away too long during the daily rosary. I was fascinated by the Catholic Church, its rituals and the devotion of the nuns, but getting on my knees on the seat of my desk and leaning on the back with the rosary beads was often too much for a rambunctious boy whose only church experience before then had been in the Sunday school and the summer vacation Bible school of the First Baptist Church in Hope.

After a year or so on the farm, Daddy decided to move into Hot Springs. He rented a big house from Uncle Raymond at 1011 Park Avenue, in the east end of town. He led Mother to believe he'd made a good deal for it and had bought the house with his income and hers, but even with their two incomes, and with housing costs a considerably smaller part of the average family's expenses than now, I can't see how we could have afforded it. The house was up on a hill; it had two stories, five bedrooms, and a fascinating little ballroom upstairs with a bar on which stood a big rotating cage with two huge dice in it. Apparently the first owner had been in the gambling business. I spent many happy hours in that room, having parties or just playing with my friends.

The exterior of the house was white with green trim, with sloping roofs over the front entrance and the two sides. The front yard was terraced on three levels with a sidewalk down the middle and a rock wall between the middle and ground levels. The side yards were small, but large enough for Mother to indulge her favorite outdoor hobby, gardening. She especially loved to grow roses and did so in all her homes until she died. Mother tanned easily and deeply, and she got most of her tan while digging dirt around her flowers in a tank top and shorts. The back had a gravel driveway with a four-car garage, a nice lawn with a swing set, and, on both sides of the driveway, sloping lawns that went down to the street, Circle Drive.

We lived in that house from the time I was seven or eight until I was fifteen. It was fascinating to me. The grounds were full of shrubs, bushes, flowers, long hedges laced with honeysuckle, and lots of trees, including a fig, a pear, two crab apples, and a huge old oak in the front.

I helped Daddy take care of the grounds. It was one thing we did do together, though as I got older, I did more and more of it myself. The house was near a wooded area, so I was always running across spiders, tarantulas, centipedes, scorpions, wasps, hornets, bees, and snakes, along with more benign creatures like squirrels, chipmunks, blue jays, robins, and woodpeckers. Once, when I was mowing the lawn, I looked down to see a rattlesnake sliding along with the lawn mower, apparently captivated by the vibrations. I didn't like the vibes, so I ran like crazy and escaped unscathed.

Another time I wasn't so lucky. Daddy had put up a huge three-story birdhouse for martins, which nest in groups, at the bottom of the back driveway. One day I was mowing grass down there and discovered it had become a nesting place not for martins but for bumblebees. They swarmed me, flying all over my body, my arms, my face. Amazingly, not one of them stung me. I ran off to catch my breath and consider my options. Mistakenly, I assumed they had decided I meant them no harm, so after a few minutes I went back to my mowing. I hadn't gone ten yards before they swarmed me again, this time stinging me all over my body. One got caught between my belly and my belt, stinging me over and over, something bumblebees can do that honeybees can't. I was delirious and had to be rushed to the doctor, but recovered soon enough with another valuable lesson: tribes of bumblebees give intruders one fair warning but not two. More than thirty-five years later, Kate Ross,

the five-year-old daughter of my friends Michael Ross and
Markie Post, sent me a letter that said simply: "Bees can
sting you. Watch out." I knew just what she meant.

My move to Hot Springs gave my life many new experiences: a new, much larger and more sophisticated city; a
new neighborhood; a new school, new friends, and my
introduction to music; my first serious religious experience
in a new church; and, of course, a new extended family in
the Clinton clan.

The hot sulfur springs, for which the city is named, bub-
ble up from below ground in a narrow gap in the Ouachita
Mountains a little more than fifty miles west and slightly
south of Little Rock. The first European to see them was
Hernando de Soto, who came through the valley in 1541,
saw the Indians bathing in the steaming springs, and, legend
has it, thought he had discovered the fountain of youth.

In 1832, President Andrew Jackson signed a bill to protect four sections of land around Hot Springs as a federal
reservation, the first such bill Congress ever enacted, well
before the National Park Service was established or Yellowstone became our first national park. Soon more hotels
sprang up to house visitors. By the 1880s, Central Avenue,
the main street, snaking a mile and a half or so through the
gap in the mountains where the springs were, was sprouting
beautiful bathhouses as more than 100,000 people a year
were taking baths for everything from rheumatism to paral-
ysis to malaria to venereal disease to general relaxation. In
the first quarter of the twentieth century, the grandest bathhouses were built, more than a million baths a year were
taken, and the spa city became known around the world.
After its status was changed from federal reservation to
national park, Hot Springs became the only city in America
that was actually in one of our national parks.

The city's attraction was amplified by grand hotels, an
opera house, and, beginning in the mid-nineteenth century,
gambling. By the 1880s, there were several open gambling
houses, and Hot Springs was on its way to being both an

attractive spa and a notorious town. For decades before and
during World War II, it was run by a boss worthy of any big
city, Mayor Leo McLaughlin. He ran the gambling with the
help of a mobster who moved down from New York, Owen
Vincent "Owney" Madden.

After the war, a GI ticket of reformers headed by Sid
McMath broke McLaughlin's power in a move that, soon
after, made the thirty-five-year-old McMath the nation's
youngest governor. Notwithstanding the GI reformers,
however, gambling continued to operate, with payoffs to
state and local politicians and law-enforcement officials,
well into the 1960s. Owney Madden lived in Hot Springs as
a "respectable" citizen for the rest of his life. Mother once
put him to sleep for surgery. She came home afterward and
laughingly told me that looking at his X-ray was like visiting a planetarium: the twelve bullets still in his body
reminded her of shooting stars.

Ironically, because it was illegal, the Mafia never took
over gambling in Hot Springs; instead, we had our own
local bosses. Sometimes the competing interests fought, but
in my time, the violence was always controlled. For example, the garages of two houses were bombed, but at a time
when no one was home.

For the last three decades of the nineteenth century and
the first five of the twentieth, gambling drew an amazing
array of characters to town: outlaws, mobsters, military
heroes, actors, and a host of baseball greats. The legendary
pool shark Minnesota Fats came often. In 1977, as attorney
general, I shot pool with him for a charity in Hot Springs.
He killed me in the game but made up for it by regaling me
with stories of long-ago visits, when he played the horses by
day, then ate and gambled up and down Central Avenue all
night, adding to his pocketbook and his famous waistline.

Hot Springs drew politicians too. William Jennings
Bryan came several times. So did Teddy Roosevelt in 1910,
Herbert Hoover in 1927, and Franklin and Eleanor Roo-
sevelt for the state's centennial in 1936. Huey Long had a
second honeymoon with his wife there. JFK and Lyndon
Johnson visited before they were Presidents. So did Harry

Truman, the only one who gambled—at least the only one who didn't hide it.

The gambling and hot-water attractions of Hot Springs were enhanced by large, brightly lit auction houses, which alternated with gambling spots and restaurants on Central Avenue on the other side of the street from the bathhouses; by Oaklawn racetrack, which offered fine Thoroughbred racing for thirty days a year in the spring, the only legal gambling in the city; by slot machines in many of the restaurants, some of which even kids were allowed to play if they were sitting on their parents' laps; and by three lakes near the city, the most important of which was Lake Hamilton, where many of the city's grandees, including Uncle Raymond, had large houses. Thousands of people flocked to the lake's motels for summer vacation. There was also an alligator farm in which the largest resident was eighteen feet long; an ostrich farm, whose residents sometimes paraded down Central Avenue; Keller Breland's IQZoo, full of animals and featuring the alleged skeleton of a mermaid; and a notorious whorehouse run by Maxine Harris (later Maxine Temple Jones), a real character who openly deposited her payoffs in the local authorities' bank accounts and who in 1983 wrote an interesting book about her life: "*Call Me Madam*": *The Life and Times of a Hot Springs Madam*. When I was ten or eleven, on a couple of occasions my friends and I entertained ourselves for hours by calling Maxine's place over and over, tying up her phone and blocking calls from real customers. It infuriated her and she cursed us out with salty and creative language we'd never before heard from a woman, or a man, for that matter. It was hilarious. I think she thought it was funny, too, at least for the first fifteen minutes or so.

For Arkansas, a state composed mostly of white Southern Baptists and blacks, Hot Springs was amazingly diverse, especially for a town of only 35,000. There was a good-sized black population and a hotel, the Knights of the Pythias, for black visitors. There were two Catholic churches and two synagogues. The Jewish residents owned some of the best stores and ran the auction houses. The best toy store in town was Ricky's, named by the Silvermans after their son, who was in the band with me. Lauray's, the jewelry store where I bought little things for Mother, was owned by Marty and Laura Fleishner. And there was the B'nai B'rith's Leo N. Levi Hospital, which used the hot springs to treat arthritis. I also met my first Arab-Americans in Hot Springs, the Zorubs and the Hassins. When David Zorub's parents were killed in Lebanon, he was adopted by his uncle. He came to this country at nine, unable to speak any English, and eventually became valedictorian of his class and governor of Boys State. Now he is a neurosurgeon in Pennsylvania. Guido Hassin and his sisters were the children of the World War II romance of a Syrian-American and an Italian woman; they were my neighbors during high school. I also had a Japanese-American friend, Albert Hahm, and a Czech classmate, René Duchac, whose émigré parents owned a restaurant, The Little Bohemia. There was a large Greek community, which included a Greek Ortho-dox church and Angelo's, a restaurant just around the cor-ner from Clinton Buick. It was a great old-fashioned place, with its long soda fountain–like bar and tables covered with red-and-white checked tablecloths. The house specialty was a three-way: chili, beans, and spaghetti.

My best Greek friends by far were the Leopoulos family. George ran a little café on Bridge Street between Central Avenue and Broadway, which we claimed was the shortest street in America, stretching all of a third of a block. George's wife, Evelyn, was a tiny woman who believed in reincarnation, collected antiques, and loved Liberace, who thrilled her by coming to her house for dinner once while he was performing in Hot Springs. The younger Leopoulos son, Paul David, became my best friend in fourth grade and has been like my brother ever since.

When we were boys, I loved to go with him to his dad's café, especially when the carnival was in town, because all the carnies ate there. Once they gave us free tickets to all the rides. We used every one of them, making David happy and me dizzy and sick to my stomach. After that I stuck to bumper cars and Ferris wheels. We've shared a lifetime of ups and downs, and enough laughs for three lifetimes.

That I had friends and acquaintances from such a diverse group of people when I was young may seem normal today, but in 1950s Arkansas, it could have happened only in Hot Springs. Even so, most of my friends and I led pretty normal lives, apart from the occasional calls to Maxine's bordello and the temptation to cut classes during racing season, which I never did, but which proved irresistible to some of my classmates in high school.

From fourth through sixth grades, most of my life ran up and down Park Avenue. Our neighborhood was interesting. There was a row of beautiful houses east of ours all the way to the woods and another row behind our house on Circle Drive. David Leopoulos lived a couple of blocks away. My closest friends among the near neighbors were the Crane family. They lived in a big old mysterious-looking wooden house just across from my back drive. Edie Crane's Aunt Dan took the Crane kids, and often me, everywhere—to the movies, to Snow Springs Park to swim in a pool fed by very cold springwater, and to Whittington Park to play miniature golf. Rose, the oldest kid, was my age. Larry, the middle child, was a couple of years younger. We always had a great relationship except once, when I used a new word on him. We were playing with Rose in my backyard when I told him his epidermis was showing. That made him mad. Then I told him the epidermises of his mother and father were showing too. That did it. He went home, got a knife, came back, and threw it at me. Even though he missed, I've been leery of big words ever since. Mary Dan, the youngest, asked me to wait for her to grow up so that we could get married.

Across the street from the front of our house was a collection of modest businesses. There was a small garage made of tin sheeting. David and I used to hide behind the oak tree and throw acorns against the tin to rattle the guys who worked there. Sometimes we would also try to hit the hubcaps of passing cars and, when we succeeded, it made a

loud pinging noise. One day one of our targets stopped suddenly, got out of the car, saw us hiding behind a bush, and
rushed up the driveway after us. After that, I didn't lob so
many acorns at cars. But it was great fun.

Next to the garage was a brick block that contained a
grocery, a Laundromat, and Stubby's, a small family-run
barbeque restaurant, where I often enjoyed a meal alone,
just sitting at the front table by the window, wondering
about the lives of the people in the passing cars. I got my
first job at thirteen in that grocery store. The owner, Dick
Sanders, was already about seventy, and, like many people
his age back then, he thought it was a bad thing to be left-
handed, so he decided to change me, a deeply left-handed
person. One day he had me stacking mayonnaise right-
handed, big jars of Hellmann's mayonnaise, which cost
eighty-nine cents. I misstacked one and it fell to the floor,
leaving a mess of broken glass and mayo. First I cleaned it
up. Then Dick told me he'd have to dock my pay for the lost
jar. I was making a dollar an hour. I got up my courage and
said, "Look, Dick, you can have a good left-handed grocery
boy for a dollar an hour, but you can't have a clumsy right-
handed one for free." To my surprise, he laughed and
agreed. He even let me start my first business, a used-comic-
book stand in front of the store. I had carefully saved two
trunkloads of comic books. They were in very good condition and sold well. At the time I was proud of myself,
though I know now that if I'd saved them, they'd be valuable collectors' items today.

Next to our house going west, toward town, was the
Perry Plaza Motel. I liked the Perrys and their daughter
Tavia, who was a year or two older than I. One day I was visiting her just after she'd gotten a new BB gun. I must have
been nine or ten. She threw a belt on the floor and said if I
stepped over it she'd shoot me. Of course, I did. And she shot
me. It was a leg hit, so it could have been worse, and I resolved
to become a better judge of when someone's bluffing.

I remember something else about the Perrys' motel. It
was yellow-brick—two stories high and one room wide,
stretching from Park Avenue to Circle Drive. Sometimes

people would rent rooms there, and at other motels and rooming houses around town, for weeks or even months at a time. Once a middle-aged man did that with the backmost room on the second floor. One day the police came and took him away. He had been performing abortions there. Until then, I don't think I knew what an abortion was.

Farther down Park Avenue was a little barbershop, where Mr. Brizendine cut my hair. About a quarter mile past the barbershop, Park Avenue runs into Ramble Street, which then led south up a hill to my new school, Ramble Elementary. In fourth grade I started band. The grade school band was composed of students from all the city's elementary schools. The director, George Gray, had a great, encouraging way with little kids as we squawked away. I played clarinet for a year or so, then switched to tenor saxophone because the band needed one, a change I would never regret. My most vivid memory of fifth grade is a class discussion about memory in which one of my classmates, Tommy O'Neal, told our teacher, Mrs. Caristianos, he thought he could remember when he was born. I didn't know whether he had a vivid imagination or a loose screw, but I liked him and had finally met someone with an even better memory than mine.

I adored my sixth-grade teacher, Kathleen Schaer. Like a lot of teachers of her generation, she never married and devoted her life to children. She lived into her late eighties with her cousin, who made the same choices. As gentle and kind as she was, Miss Schaer believed in tough love. The day before we had our little grade school graduation ceremony, she held me after class. She told me I should be graduating first in my class, tied with Donna Standiford. Instead, because my citizenship grades were so low—we might have been calling it "deportment" by then—I had been dropped to a tie for third. Miss Schaer said, "Billy, when you grow up you're either going to be governor or get in a lot of trouble. It all depends on whether you learn when to talk and when to keep quiet." Turns out she was right on both counts.

When I was at Ramble, my interest in reading grew and I discovered the Garland County Public Library, which was downtown, near the courthouse and not far from Clinton Buick Company. I would go there for hours, browsing among the books and reading lots of them. I was most fascinated by books about Native Americans and read children's biographies of Geronimo, the great Apache; Crazy Horse, the Lakota Sioux who killed Custer and routed his troops at Little Bighorn; Chief Joseph of the Nez Percé, who made peace with his powerful statement, "From where the sun now stands, I will fight no more forever"; and the great Cherokee Sequoyah, who developed a written alphabet for his people. I never lost my interest in Native Americans or my feeling that they had been terribly mistreated.

My last stop on Park Avenue was my first real church, Park Place Baptist Church. Though Mother and Daddy didn't go except on Easter and sometimes at Christmas, Mother encouraged me to go, and I did, just about every Sunday. I loved getting dressed up and walking down there. From the time I was about eleven until I graduated from high school, my teacher was A. B. "Sonny" Jeffries. His son Bert was in my class and we became close friends. Every Sunday for years, we went to Sunday school and church together, always sitting in the back, often in our own world. In 1955, I had absorbed enough of my church's teachings to know that I was a sinner and to want Jesus to save me. So I came down the aisle at the end of Sunday service, professed my faith in Christ, and asked to be baptized. The Reverend Fitzgerald came to the house to talk to Mother and me. Baptists require an informed profession of faith for baptism; they want people to know what they are doing, as opposed to the Methodists' infant-sprinkling ritual that took Hillary and her brothers out of hell's way.

Bert Jeffries and I were baptized together, along with several other people on a Sunday night. The baptismal pool was just above the choir loft. When the curtains were opened, the congregation could see the pastor standing in a white robe, dunking the saved. Just ahead of Bert and me in the line was a woman who was visibly afraid of the water. She trembled down the steps into the pool. When the preacher held her nose and dunked her, she went completely rigid. Her right leg jerked straight up in the air and came to rest on the narrow strip of glass that protected the choir loft from splashes. Her heel stuck. She couldn't get it off, so when the preacher tried to lift her up, he couldn't budge her. Since he was looking at her submerged head, he didn't see what had happened, so he just kept jerking on her. Finally he looked around, figured it out, and took the poor woman's leg down before she drowned. Bert and I were in stitches. I couldn't help thinking that if Jesus had this much of a sense of humor, being a Christian wasn't going to be so tough.

Besides my new friends, neighborhood, school, and church, Hot Springs brought me a new extended family in the Clintons. My step-grandparents were Al and Eula Mae Cornwell Clinton. Poppy Al, as we all called him, came from Dardanelle, in Yell County, a beautiful wooded place seventy miles west of Little Rock up the Arkansas River. He met and married his wife there after her family migrated from Mississippi in the 1890s. We called my new grandmother Mama Clinton. She was one of a huge Cornwell family that spread out all over Arkansas. Together with the Clintons and my mother's relatives, they gave me kinfolk in fifteen of Arkansas' seventy-five counties, an enormous asset when I started my political career in a time when personal contacts counted more than credentials or positions on the issues.

Poppy Al was a small man, shorter and slighter than Papaw, with a kind, sweet spirit. The first time I met him we were still living in Hope and he dropped by our house to see his son and his new family. He wasn't alone. At the time, he was still working as a parole officer for the state and he was taking one of the prisoners, who must have been out on furlough, back to the penitentiary. When he got out of the car to visit, the man was handcuffed to him. It was a hilarious sight, because the inmate was huge; he must have been twice Poppy Al's size. But Poppy Al spoke to him gently and respectfully and the man seemed to respond in kind. All I know is that Poppy Al got his man safely back on time.

Poppy Al and Mama Clinton lived in a small old house up on top of a hill. He kept a garden out back, of which he was very proud. He lived to be eighty-four, and when he was over eighty, that garden produced a tomato that weighed two and a half pounds. I had to use both hands to hold it.

Mama Clinton ruled the house. She was good to me, but she knew how to manipulate the men in her life. She always treated Daddy like the baby of the family who could do no wrong, which is probably one reason he never grew up. She liked Mother, who was better than most of the other family members at listening to her hypochondriacal tales of woe and at giving sensible, sympathetic advice. She lived to be ninety-three.

Poppy Al and Mama Clinton produced five children, one girl and four boys. The girl, Aunt Ilaree, was the second-oldest child. Her daughter Virginia, whose nickname was Sister, was then married to Gabe Crawford and was a good friend of Mother's. The older she got, the more of an idiosyncratic character Ilaree became. One day Mother was visiting her and Ilaree complained she was having trouble walking. She lifted up her skirt, revealing a huge growth on the inside of her leg. Not long afterward, when she met Hillary for the first time, she picked up her skirt again and showed her the tumor. It was a good beginning. Ilaree was the first of the Clintons to really like Hillary. Mother finally convinced her to have the tumor removed, and she took the first flight of her life to the Mayo Clinic. By the time they cut the tumor off it weighed nine pounds, but miraculously it had not spread cancer cells to the rest of her leg. I was told the clinic kept that amazing tumor for some time for study. When jaunty old Ilaree got home, it was clear she had been more afraid of her first flight than of the tumor or the surgery.

The oldest son was Robert. He and his wife, Evelyn, were quiet people who lived in Texas and who seemed sensibly happy to take Hot Springs and the rest of the Clintons in small doses.

The second son, Uncle Roy, had a feed store. His wife, Janet, and Mother were the two strongest personalities outside the blood family, and became great friends. In the early fifties Roy ran for the legislature and won. On election day, I handed out cards for him in my neighborhood, as close to the polling station as the law would allow. It was my first political experience. Uncle Roy served only one term. He was very well liked but didn't run for reelection, I think because Janet hated politics. Roy and Janet played dominoes with my folks almost every week for years, alternating between our home and theirs.

Raymond, the fourth child, was the only Clinton with any money or consistent involvement in politics. He had been part of the GI reform effort after World War II, although he wasn't in the service himself. He had three children, all supporters of mine. Raymond Jr., "Corky," was not only younger than I, he was also brighter. He literally became a rocket scientist, with a distinguished career at NASA.

Mother always had an ambiguous relationship with Raymond, because he liked to run everything and because, with Daddy's drinking, we often needed his help more than she wanted it. When we first moved to Hot Springs, we even went to Uncle Raymond's church, First Presbyterian, though Mother was at least a nominal Baptist. The pastor back then, the Reverend Overholser, was a remarkable man who produced two equally remarkable daughters: Nan Keohane, who became president of Wellesley, Hillary's alma mater, and then the first woman president of Duke University; and Geneva Overholser, who was editor of the *Des Moines Register* and endorsed me when I ran for President, and who later became the ombudsman for the *Washington Post*, where she aired the legitimate complaints of the general public but not the President.

Notwithstanding Mother's reservations, I liked Raymond. I was impressed with his strength, his influence in town, and his genuine interest in his kids, and in me. His egocentric foibles didn't bother me much, though we were as different as daylight and dark. In 1968, when I was giving pro–civil rights talks to civic clubs in Hot Springs, Raymond was supporting George Wallace for President. But in 1974, when I launched an apparently impossible campaign for Congress, Raymond and Gabe Crawford co-signed a

$10,000 note to get me started. It was all the money in the world to me then. When his wife of more than forty-five years died, Raymond got reacquainted with a widow he had dated in high school and they married, bringing happiness to his last years. For some reason I can't even remember now, Raymond got mad at me late in his life. Before we could reconcile he got Alzheimer's. I went to visit him twice, once in St. Joseph's Hospital and once in a nursing home. The first time I told him I loved him, was sorry for whatever had come between us, and would always be grateful for all he'd done for me. He might have known who I was for a minute or two; I can't be sure. The second time, I know he didn't know me, but I wanted to see him once more anyway. He died at eighty-four, like my aunt Ollie, well after his mind had gone.

Raymond and his family lived in a big house on Lake Hamilton, where we used to go for picnics and rides in his big wooden Chris-Craft boat. We celebrated every Fourth of July there with lots of fireworks. After his death, Raymond's kids decided with sadness that they had to sell the old house. Luckily my library and foundation needed a retreat, so we bought the place and are renovating it for that purpose, and Raymond's kids and grandkids can still use it. He's smiling down on me now.

Not long after we moved to Park Avenue, in 1955 I think, my mother's parents moved to Hot Springs to a little apartment in an old house on our street, a mile or so toward town from our place. The move was motivated primarily by health concerns. Papaw's bronchiectasis continued to advance and Mammaw had had a stroke. Papaw got a job at a liquor store, which I think Daddy owned a part of, just across from Mr. Brizendine's barbershop. He had a lot of free time, since even in Hot Springs most people were too conventional to frequent liquor stores in broad daylight, so I often visited him there. He played a lot of solitaire and taught me how. I still play three different kinds, often when I'm thinking through a problem and need an outlet for nervous energy.

Mammaw's stroke was a major one, and in the aftermath she was racked by hysterical screaming. Unforgivably, to calm her down, her doctor prescribed morphine, lots of it. It was when she got hooked that Mother brought her and Papaw to Hot Springs. Her behavior became even more irrational, and in desperation Mother reluctantly committed her to the state's mental hospital, about thirty miles away. I don't think there were any drug-treatment facilities back then.

Of course I didn't know anything about her problem at the time; I just knew she was sick. Then Mother drove me over to the state hospital to see her. It was awful. It was bedlam. We went into a big open room cooled by electric fans encased in huge metal mesh to keep the patients from putting their hands into them. Dazed-looking people dressed in loose cotton dresses or pajamas walked around aimlessly, muttering to themselves or shouting into space. Still, Mammaw seemed normal and glad to see us, and we had a good talk. After a few months, she had settled down enough to come home, and she was never again on morphine. Her problem gave me my first exposure to the kind of mental-health system that served most of America back then. When he became governor, Orval Faubus modernized our state hospital and put a lot more money into it. Despite the damage he did in other areas, I was always grateful to him for that.

FIVE

IN 1956, I finally got a brother, and our family finally got a television set. My brother, Roger Cassidy Clinton, was born on July 25, his father's birthday. I was so happy. Mother and Daddy had been trying to have a baby for some time (a couple of years earlier she'd had a miscarriage). I think she, and probably he too, thought it might save their marriage. Daddy's response was not auspicious. I was with Mammaw and Papaw when Mother delivered by cesarean section. Daddy picked me up and took me to see her, then brought me home and left. He had been drinking for the last few months, and instead of making him happy and responsible, the birth of his only son prompted him to run back to the bottle.

Along with the excitement of a new baby in the house was the thrill of the new TV. There were lots of shows and entertainers for kids: cartoons, *Captain Kangaroo* and *Howdy Doody*, with Buffalo Bob Smith, whom I especially liked. And there was baseball: Mickey Mantle and the Yankees, Stan Musial and the Cardinals, and my all-time favorite, Willie Mays and the old New York Giants.

But strange as it was for a kid of ten years old, what really dominated my TV viewing that summer were the Republican and Democratic conventions. I sat on the floor right in front of the TV and watched them both, transfixed. It sounds crazy, but I felt right at home in the world of politics and politicians. I liked President Eisenhower and enjoyed seeing him renominated, but we were Democrats, so I really got into their convention. Governor Frank Clement of Tennessee gave a rousing keynote address. There was an exciting contest for the vice-presidential nomination between young Senator John F. Kennedy and the eventual victor, Senator Estes Kefauver, who served Tennessee in the Senate with Al Gore's father. When Adlai

Stevenson, the nominee in 1952, accepted his party's call to run again, he said he had prayed "this cup would pass from me." I admired Stevenson's intelligence and eloquence, but even then I couldn't understand why anyone wouldn't want the chance to be President. Now I think what he didn't want was to lead another losing effort. I do understand that. I've lost a couple of elections myself, though I never fought a battle I didn't first convince myself I could win.

I didn't spend all my time watching TV. I still saw all the movies I could. Hot Springs had two old-fashioned movie houses, the Paramount and the Malco, with big stages on which touring western stars appeared on the weekends. I saw Lash LaRue, all decked out in cowboy black, do his tricks with a bullwhip, and Gail Davis, who played Annie Oakley on TV, give a shooting exhibition.

Elvis Presley began to make movies in the late fifties. I loved Elvis. I could sing all his songs, as well as the Jordanaires' backgrounds. I admired him for doing his military service and was fascinated when he married his beautiful young wife, Priscilla. Unlike most parents, who thought his gyrations obscene, Mother loved Elvis, too, maybe even more than I did. We watched his legendary performance on *The Ed Sullivan Show* together, and laughed when the cameras cut off his lower body movements to protect us from the indecency. Beyond his music, I identified with his small-town southern roots. And I thought he had a good heart. Steve Clark, a friend of mine who served as attorney general when I was governor, once took his little sister, who was dying of cancer, to see Elvis perform in Memphis. When Elvis heard about the little girl, he put her and her brother in the front row, and after the concert he brought her up onstage and talked to her for a good while. I never forgot that.

Elvis's first movie, *Love Me Tender*, was my favorite and remains so, though I also liked *Loving You*, *Jailhouse Rock*, *King Creole*, and *Blue Hawaii*. After that, his movies got more saccharine and predictable. The interesting thing about *Love Me Tender*, a post–Civil War western, is that Elvis, already a national sex symbol, got the girl, Debra

Paget, but only because she thought his older brother, whom she really loved, had been killed in the war. At the end of the film, Elvis gets shot and dies, leaving his brother with his wife.

I never quite escaped Elvis. In the '92 campaign, some members of my staff nicknamed me Elvis. A few years later, when I appointed Kim Wardlaw of Los Angeles to a federal judgeship, she was thoughtful enough to send me a scarf Elvis had worn and signed for her at one of his concerts in the early seventies, when she was nineteen. I still have it in my music room. And I confess: I still love Elvis.

My favorite movies during this time were the biblical epics: *The Robe, Demetrius and the Gladiators, Samson and Delilah, Ben-Hur,* and especially *The Ten Commandments,* the first movie I recall paying more than a dime to see. I saw *The Ten Commandments* when Mother and Daddy were on a brief trip to Las Vegas. I took a sack lunch and sat through the whole thing twice for the price of one ticket. Years later, when I welcomed Charlton Heston to the White House as a Kennedy Center honoree, he was president of the National Rifle Association and a virulent critic of my legislative efforts to keep guns away from criminals and children. I joked to him and the audience that I liked him better as Moses than in his present role. To his credit, he took it in good humor.

In 1957, my grandfather's lungs finally gave out. He died in the relatively new Ouachita Hospital, where Mother worked. He was only fifty-six years old. Too much of his life had been occupied with economic woes, health problems, and marital strife, yet he always found things to enjoy in the face of his adversity. And he loved Mother and me more than life. His love, and the things he taught me, mostly by example, including appreciation for the gifts of daily life and the problems of other people, made me better than I could have been without him.

Nineteen fifty-seven was also the year of the Little Rock Central High crisis. In September, nine black kids, supported by Daisy Bates, the editor of the *Arkansas State Press*, Little Rock's black newspaper, integrated Little Rock Central High School. Governor Faubus, eager to break Arkansas' tradition of governors serving only two terms, abandoned his family's progressive tradition (his father had voted for Eugene Debs, the perpetual Socialist candidate for President) and called out the National Guard to prevent the integration. Then President Dwight Eisenhower federalized the troops to protect the students, and they went to school through angry mobs shouting racist epithets. Most of my friends were either against integration or apparently unconcerned. I didn't say too much about it, probably because my family was not especially political, but I hated what Faubus did. Though Faubus had inflicted lasting damage to the state's image, he had assured himself not only a third two-year term but another three terms beyond that. Later he tried comebacks against Dale Bumpers, David Pryor, and me, but the state had moved beyond reaction by then.

The Little Rock Nine became a symbol of courage in the quest for equality. In 1987, on the thirtieth anniversary of the crisis, as governor I invited the Little Rock Nine back. I held a reception for them at the Governor's Mansion and took them to the room where Governor Faubus had orchestrated the campaign to keep them out of school. In 1997, we had a big ceremony on the lawn of Central High for the fortieth anniversary. After the program, Governor Mike Huckabee and I held open the doors of Central High as the nine walked through. Elizabeth Eckford, who at fifteen was deeply seared emotionally by vicious harassment as she walked alone through an angry mob, was reconciled with Hazel Massery, one of the girls who had taunted her forty years earlier. In 2000, at a ceremony on the South Lawn of the White House, I presented the Little Rock Nine with the Congressional Gold Medal, an honor initiated by Senator Dale Bumpers. In that late summer of 1957, the nine helped to set all of us, white and black alike, free from the dark shackles of segregation and discrimination. In so doing, they did more for me than I could ever do for them. But I hope that what I did do for them, and for civil rights, in the years afterward honored the lessons I learned more than fifty years ago in my grandfather's store.

In the summer of 1957 and again after Christmas that year, I took my first trips out of Arkansas since going to New Orleans to see Mother. Both times I got on a Trailways bus bound for Dallas to visit Aunt Otie. It was a luxurious bus for the time, with an attendant who served little sandwiches. I ate a lot of them.

Dallas was the third real city I had been in. I visited Little Rock on a fifth-grade field trip to the state Capitol, the highlight of which was a visit to the governor's office with the chance to sit in the absent governor's chair. It made such an impression on me that years later I often took pictures with children sitting in my chair both in the governor's office and in the Oval Office.

The trips to Dallas were remarkable to me for three reasons, beyond the great Mexican food, the zoo, and the most beautiful miniature golf course I'd ever seen. First, I got to meet some of my father's relatives. His younger brother, Glenn Blythe, was the constable of Irving, a suburb of Dallas. He was a big, handsome man, and being with him made me feel connected to my father. Sadly, he also died too young, at forty-eight, of a stroke. My father's niece, Ann Grigsby, had been a friend of Mother's since she married my father. On those trips she became a lifetime friend, telling me stories about my father and about what Mother was like as a young bride. Ann remains my closest link to my Blythe family heritage.

Second, on New Year's Day 1958, I went to the Cotton Bowl, my first college football game. Rice, led by quarterback King Hill, played Navy, whose great running back Joe Bellino won the Heisman Trophy two years later. I sat in the end zone but felt as if I were on a throne, as Navy won 20–7.

Third, just after Christmas I went to the movies by myself on an afternoon when Otie had to work. I think *The Bridge on the River Kwai* was showing. I loved the movie, but I didn't like the fact that I had to buy an adult ticket even though I wasn't yet twelve. I was so big for my age, the ticket seller didn't believe me. It was the first time in my life someone refused to take my word. This hurt, but I learned an important difference between big impersonal cities and small towns, and I began my long preparation for life in Washington, where no one takes your word for anything.

I started the 1958–59 school year at the junior high school. It was right across the street from Ouachita Hospital and adjacent to Hot Springs High School. Both school buildings were dark red brick. The high school was four stories high, with a great old auditorium and classic lines befitting its 1917 vintage. The junior high was smaller and more pedestrian but still represented an important new phase of my life. The biggest thing that happened to me that year, however, had nothing to do with school. One of the Sunday-school teachers offered to take a few of the boys in our church to Little Rock to hear Billy Graham preach in his crusade in War Memorial Stadium, where the Razorbacks played. Racial tensions were still high in 1958. Little Rock's schools were closed in a last-gasp effort to stop integration, its kids dispersed to schools in nearby towns. Segregationists from the White Citizens Council and other quarters suggested that, given the tense atmosphere, it would be better if the Reverend Graham restricted admission to the crusade to whites only. He replied that Jesus loved all sinners, that everyone needed a chance to hear the word, and therefore that he would cancel the crusade rather than preach to a segregated audience. Back then, Billy Graham was the living embodiment of Southern Baptist authority, the largest religious figure in the South, perhaps in the nation. I wanted to hear him preach even more after he took the stand he did. The segregationists backed down, and the Reverend Graham delivered a powerful message in his trademark twenty minutes. When he gave the invitation for people to come down onto the football field to become Christians or to rededicate their lives to Christ, hundreds of blacks and whites came down the stadium aisles together, stood together, and prayed together. It was a powerful counterpoint to the racist politics sweeping across the South. I loved Billy Graham for doing that. For months after that I regularly sent part of my small allowance to support his ministry.

Thirty years later, Billy came back to Little Rock for another crusade in War Memorial Stadium. As governor, I was honored to sit on the stage with him one night and even more to go with him and my friend Mike Coulson to visit my pastor and Billy's old friend W. O. Vaught, who was dying of cancer. It was amazing to listen to these two men of God discussing death, their fears, and their faith. When Billy got up to leave, he held Dr. Vaught's hand in his and said, "W. O., it won't be long now for both of us. I'll see you soon, just outside the Eastern Gate," the entrance to the Holy City.

When I became President, Billy and Ruth Graham visited Hillary and me in the White House residence. Billy prayed with me in the Oval Office, and wrote inspiring letters of instruction and encouragement in my times of trial. In all his dealings with me, just as in that crucial crusade in 1958, Billy Graham lived his faith.

Junior high school brought a whole new set of experiences and challenges, as I began to learn more about my mind, my body, my spirit, and my little world. I liked most of what I learned about myself but not all of it. And some of what came into my head and life scared the living hell out of me, including anger at Daddy, the first stirrings of sexual feelings toward girls, and doubts about my religious convictions, which I think developed because I couldn't understand why a God whose existence I couldn't prove would create a world in which so many bad things happened.

My interest in music grew. I was now going to junior high band practices every day, looking forward to marching at football game halftimes and in the Christmas parade, to the concerts, and to the regional and state band festivals, at which judges graded the bands as well as solo and ensemble performances. I won a fair number of medals in junior high, and when I didn't do so well, it was invariably because I tried to perform a piece that was too difficult for me. I still have some of the judges' rating sheets on my early solos, pointing out my poor control in the lower register, bad phrasing, and puffy cheeks. The ratings got better when I grew older, but I never quite cured the puffy cheeks. My favorite solo in this period was an arrangement of *Rhapsody in Blue*, which I loved to try to play and once performed for guests at the old Majestic Hotel. I was nervous as could be, but determined to make a good impression in my new white coat, with red plaid bow tie and cummerbund.

My junior high band directors encouraged me to improve and I decided to try. Arkansas had a number of summer band camps back then on university campuses and I wanted to go to one of them. I decided to attend the camp at the main University of Arkansas campus in Fayetteville because it had a lot of good teachers and I wanted to spend a couple of weeks on the campus where I assumed I'd go to college one day. I went there every summer for seven years, until the summer after high school graduation. It proved to be one of the most important experiences in my growing up. First, I played and played. And I got better. Some days I would play for twelve hours until my lips were so sore I could hardly move them. I also listened to and learned from older, better musicians.

Band camp also proved an ideal place for me to develop political and leadership skills. The whole time I was growing up, it was the only place being a "band boy" instead of a football player wasn't a political liability. It was also the only place being a band boy wasn't a disadvantage in the adolescent quest for pretty girls. We all had a grand time, from the minute we got up for breakfast at a university dining hall until we went to bed in one of the dorms, all the while feeling very important.

I also loved the campus. The university is the oldest land-grant college west of the Mississippi. As a high school junior I wrote a paper on it and as governor I supported an appropriation to restore Old Main, the oldest building on campus. Built in 1871, it is a unique reminder of the Civil

War, marked by two towers, with the northern one higher than its southern counterpart.

The band also brought me my best friend in junior high, Joe Newman. He was a drummer, and a good one. His mother, Rae, was a teacher in our school, and she and her husband, Dub, always made me feel welcome in their big white wood-frame house on Ouachita Avenue, near where Uncle Roy and Aunt Janet lived. Joe was smart, skeptical, moody, funny, and loyal. I liked to play games or just talk with him. I still do—we've stayed close over the years.

My main academic interest in junior high was math. I was lucky enough to be among the first group in our town to take algebra in the eighth, not the ninth, grade, which meant I'd have a chance to take geometry, algebra II, trigonometry, and calculus by the time I finished high school. I loved math because it was problem-solving, which always got my juices flowing. Although I never took a math class in college, I always thought I was good at it until I had to give up helping Chelsea with her homework when she was in ninth grade. Another illusion bites the dust.

Mary Matassarin taught me algebra and geometry. Her sister, Verna Dokey, taught history, and Verna's husband, Vernon, a retired coach, taught eighth-grade science. I liked them all, but even though I was not particularly good at science, it was one of Mr. Dokey's lessons that stayed with me. Though his wife and her sister were attractive women, Vernon Dokey, to put it charitably, was not a handsome man. He was burly, a bit heavy around the waist, wore thick glasses, and smoked cheap cigars in a cigar holder with a small mouthpiece, which gave his face a peculiar pinched look when he sucked on it. He generally affected a brusque manner, but he had a great smile, a good sense of humor, and a keen understanding of human nature. One day he looked out at us and said, "Kids, years from now you may not remember anything you learned about science in this class, so I'm going to teach you something about human nature you should remember. Every morning when I wake up, I go into my bathroom, splash water on my face, shave, wipe the shaving cream off, then look in the mirror and say, 'Vernon, you're beautiful.' You remember that, kids. Everybody wants to feel like they're beautiful." And I have remembered, for more than forty years. It's helped me understand things I would have missed if Vernon Dokey hadn't told me he was beautiful, and I hadn't come to see that, in fact, he was.

I needed all the help I could get in understanding people in junior high school. It was there that I had to face the fact that I was not destined to be liked by everyone, usually for reasons I couldn't figure out. Once when I was walking to school and was about a block away, an older student, one of the town "hoods," who was standing in the gap between two buildings smoking a cigarette, flicked the burning weed at me, hitting the bridge of my nose and nearly burning my eye. I never did figure out why he did it, but after all, I was a fat band boy who didn't wear cool jeans (Levi's, preferably with the stitching on the back pockets removed).

Around that same time, I got into an argument about something or other with Clifton Bryant, a boy who was a year or so older, but smaller than I was. One day my friends and I decided to walk home from school, about three miles. Clifton lived in the same end of town, and he followed us home, taunting me and hitting me on the back and shoulders over and over. We walked like that all the way up Central Avenue to the fountain and the right turn to Park Avenue. For more than a mile I tried to ignore him. Finally I couldn't take it anymore. I turned, took a big swing, and hit him. It was a good blow, but by the time it landed he had already turned to run away, so it caught him only in the back. As I said, I was slow. When Clifton ran away home, I yelled at him to come back and fight like a man. He kept on going. By the time I got home, I had calmed down and the "attaboys" I got from my buddies had worn off. I was afraid I might have hurt him, so I made Mother call his house to make sure he was okay. We never had any trouble after that. I had learned I could defend myself, but I hadn't enjoyed hurting him and I was a little disturbed by my anger, the currents of which would prove deeper and stronger in the years ahead. I now know that my anger on that day was a normal and healthy response to the way I'd been treated. But because of the way Daddy behaved when he was angry and drunk, I associated anger with being out of control and I was determined not to lose control. Doing so could unleash the deeper, constant anger I kept locked away because I didn't know where it came from.

Even when I was mad I had sense enough not to take on every challenge. Twice in those years, I took a pass, or, if you're inclined to be critical, a dive. Once I went swimming with the Crane kids in the Caddo River, west of Hot Springs, near a little town called Caddo Gap. One of the local country boys came up to the riverbank near where I was swimming and shouted some insult at me. So I mouthed off back at him. Then he picked up a rock and threw it at me. He was twenty yards or so away, but he hit me right in the head, near the temple, and drew blood. I wanted to get out and fight, but I could see he was bigger, stronger, and tougher than I, so I swam away. Given my experiences with the ram, Tavia Perry's BB gun, and similar mistakes I still had ahead of me, I guess I did the right thing.

The second time I took a pass in junior high I know I did the right thing. On Friday nights there was always a dance in the gym of the local YMCA. I loved rock-and-roll music and dancing and went frequently, starting in eighth or ninth grade, even though I was fat, uncool, and hardly popular with the girls. Besides, I still wore the wrong jeans.

One night at the Y, I strolled into the poolroom next to the gym, where the Coke machine was, to get something to drink. Some older high school boys were shooting pool or standing around watching. One of them was Henry Hill, whose family owned the old bowling alley downtown, the Lucky Strike Lanes. Henry started in on me about my jeans, which, that night, were especially raunchy. They were carpenter's jeans, with a right side loop to hang a hammer in. I was insecure enough without Henry grinding on me, so I sassed him back. He slugged me in the jaw as hard as he could. Now, I was big for my age, about five nine, 185 pounds. But Henry Hill was six foot six with an enormous reach. No way was I going to hit back. Besides, to my amazement, it didn't hurt too badly. So I just stood my ground and stared at him. I think Henry was surprised I didn't go down or run off, because he laughed, slapped me on the back, and said I was okay. We were always friendly after that. I had learned again that I could take a hit and that there's more than one way to stand against aggression.

By the time I started ninth grade, in September 1960, the presidential campaign was in full swing. My homeroom and English teacher, Ruth Atkins, was also from Hope and, like me, a stomp-down Democrat. She had us read and discuss Dickens's *Great Expectations*, but left lots of time for political debate. Hot Springs had more Republicans than most of the rest of Arkansas back then, but their roots were far less conservative than the current crop. Some of the older families had been there since the Civil War and became Republicans because they were against secession and slavery. Some families had Republican roots in Teddy Roosevelt's progressivism. Others supported Eisenhower's moderate conservatism.

The Arkansas Democrats were an even more diverse group. Those in the Civil War tradition were Democrats because their forebears had supported secession and slavery. A larger group swelled the ranks of the party in the Depression, when so many unemployed workers and poor farmers saw FDR as a savior and later loved our neighbor from Missouri, Harry Truman. A smaller group were immigrant Democrats, mostly from Europe. Most blacks were Democrats because of Roosevelt, and Truman's stand for civil rights, and their sense that Kennedy would be more aggressive than Nixon on the issue. A small group of whites felt that way too. I was one of them.

In Miss Atkins's class most of the kids were for Nixon. I remember David Leopoulos defending him on the grounds that he had far more experience than Kennedy, especially in foreign affairs, and that his civil rights record was pretty good, which was true. I didn't really have anything against Nixon at this point. I didn't know then about his Red-baiting campaigns for the House and Senate in California against Jerry Voorhis and Helen Gahagan Douglas, respectively. I liked the way he stood up to Nikita Khrushchev. In 1956, I had admired both Eisenhower and Stevenson, but by 1960, I was a partisan. I had been for LBJ in the primaries because of his Senate leadership, especially in passing a civil rights bill in 1957, and his poor southern roots. I also liked Hubert Humphrey, because he was the most passionate advocate for civil rights, and Kennedy, because of his youth, strength, and commitment to getting the country moving again. With Kennedy the nominee, I made the best case I could to my classmates.

I badly wanted him to win, especially after he called Coretta King to express his concern when her husband was jailed, and after he spoke to the Southern Baptists in Houston, defending his faith and the right of Catholic Americans to run for President. Most of my classmates, and their parents, disagreed. I was getting used to it. A few months earlier, I had lost the student council president's race to Mike Thomas, a good guy, who would be one of four classmates to be killed in Vietnam. Nixon carried our county, but Kennedy squeaked by in Arkansas with 50.2 percent of the vote, despite the best efforts of Protestant fundamentalists to convince Baptist Democrats that he would be taking orders from the pope.

Of course, the fact that he was a Catholic was one of the reasons I wanted Kennedy to be President. From my own experiences at St. John's School and my encounters with the nuns who worked with Mother at St. Joseph's Hospital, I liked and admired Catholics—their values, devotion, and social conscience. I was also proud that the only Arkansan ever to run for national office, Senator Joe T. Robinson, was the running mate of the first Catholic candidate for President, Governor Al Smith of New York, in 1928. Like Kennedy, Smith carried Arkansas, thanks to Robinson.

Given my affinity for Catholics, it's ironic that, besides music, my major extracurricular interest from ninth grade on was the Order of DeMolay, a boys' organization sponsored by the Masons. I always thought the Masons and DeMolays were anti-Catholic, though I didn't understand why. DeMolay was, after all, a pre-Reformation martyr who died a believer at the hands of the Spanish Inquisition. It was not until I was doing research for this book that I learned that the Catholic Church had condemned Masons going back to the early eighteenth century as a dangerous authority-threatening institution, while the Masons don't ban people of any faith and, in fact, have had a few Catholic members.

The purpose of DeMolay was to foster personal and civic virtues and friendship among its members. I enjoyed the camaraderie, memorizing all the parts of the rituals, moving up the offices to be master counselor of my local chapter, and going to the state conventions, with their vigorous politics and parties with the Rainbow Girls, DeMolay's sister organization. I learned more about politics by participating in the state DeMolay election, though I never ran myself. The cleverest man I supported for state master counselor was Bill Ebbert of Jonesboro. Ebbert would have made a great mayor or congressional committee chairman in the old days when seniority ruled. He was funny, smart, tough, and as good at deal making as LBJ. Once he was barreling down an Arkansas highway at ninety-five miles per hour when a state police car, with siren screaming, gave chase. Ebbert had a shortwave radio, so he called the police to report a serious car wreck three miles behind. The police car got the message and quickly changed direction, leaving the speeding Ebbert home free. I wonder if the policeman ever figured it out.

Even though I enjoyed DeMolay, I didn't buy the idea that its secret rituals were a big deal that somehow made our lives more important. After I graduated out of DeMolay, I didn't follow a long line of distinguished Americans going back to George Washington, Benjamin Franklin, and Paul Revere into Masonry, probably because in my twenties

I was in an anti-joining phase, and I didn't like what I mistakenly thought was Masonry's latent anti-Catholicism, or the segregation of blacks and whites into different branches (though when I was exposed to black Prince Hall Masonic conventions as governor, the members seemed to be having more fun on their own than the Masons I had known).

Besides, I didn't need to be in a secret fraternity to have secrets. I had real secrets of my own, rooted in Daddy's alcoholism and abuse. They got worse when I was fourteen and in the ninth grade and my brother was only four. One night Daddy closed the door to his bedroom, started screaming at Mother, then began to hit her. Little Roger was scared, just as I had been nine years earlier on the night of the gunshot. Finally, I couldn't bear the thought of Mother being hurt and Roger being frightened anymore. I grabbed a golf club out of my bag and threw open their door. Mother was on the floor and Daddy was standing over her, beating on her. I told him to stop and said that if he didn't I was going to beat the hell out of him with the golf club. He just caved, sitting down in a chair next to the bed and hanging his head. It made me sick. In her book, Mother says she called the police and had Daddy taken to jail for the night. I don't remember that, but I do know we didn't have any more trouble for a good while. I suppose I was proud of myself for standing up for Mother, but afterward I was sad about it, too. I just couldn't accept the fact that a basically good person would try to make his own pain go away by hurting someone else. I wish I'd had someone to talk with about all this, but I didn't, so I had to figure it out for myself.

I came to accept the secrets of our house as a normal part of my life. I never talked to anyone about them—not a friend, a neighbor, a teacher, a pastor. Many years later when I ran for President, several of my friends told reporters they never knew. Of course, as with most secrets, some people did know. Daddy couldn't be on good behavior with everyone but us, though he tried. Whoever else knew—family members, Mother's close friends, a couple of policemen—didn't mention it to me, so I thought I had a real secret and kept quiet about it. Our family policy was "don't ask, don't tell."

The only other secret I had in grade school and junior high was sending part of my allowance to Billy Graham after his Little Rock crusade. I never told my parents or friends about that, either. Once when I was on my way to the mailbox near our driveway off Circle Drive with my money for Billy, I saw Daddy working in the backyard. To avoid being seen, I went out the front down to Park Avenue, turned right, and cut back through the driveway of the Perry Plaza Motel next door. Our house was on a hill. Perry Plaza was on flat land below. When I got about halfway through the drive, Daddy looked down and saw me anyway with the letter in my hand. I proceeded to the mailbox, put the letter in, and came home. He must have wondered what I was doing, but he didn't ask. He never did. I guess he had enough secrets of his own to carry.

The question of secrets is one I've thought about a lot over the years. We all have them and I think we're entitled to them. They make our lives more interesting, and when we decide to share them, our relationships become more meaningful. The place where secrets are kept can also provide a haven, a retreat from the rest of the world, where one's identity can be shaped and reaffirmed, where being alone can bring security and peace. Still, secrets can be an awful burden to bear, especially if some sense of shame is attached to them, even if the source of the shame is not the secret holder. Or the allure of our secrets can be too strong, strong enough to make us feel we can't live without them, that we wouldn't even be who we are without them.

Of course, I didn't begin to understand all this back when I became a secret-keeper. I didn't even give it much thought then. I have a good memory of so much of my childhood, but I don't trust my memory to tell me exactly what I knew about all this and when I knew it. I know only that it became a struggle for me to find the right balance between secrets of internal richness and those of hidden fears and shame, and that I was always reluctant to discuss with anyone the most difficult parts of my personal life, including a major spiritual crisis I had at the age of thirteen, when my faith was too weak to sustain a certain belief in God in the face of what I was witnessing and going through. I now know this struggle is at least partly the result of growing up in an alcoholic home and the mechanisms I developed to cope with it. It took me a long time just to figure that out. It was even harder to learn which secrets to keep, which to let go of, which to avoid in the first place. I am still not sure I understand that completely. It looks as if it's going to be a lifetime project.

SIX

I DON'T KNOW how Mother handled it all as well as she did. Every morning, no matter what had happened the night before, she got up and put her game face on. And what a face it was. From the time she came back home from New Orleans, when I could get up early enough I loved sitting on the floor of the bathroom and watching her put makeup on that beautiful face.

It took quite a while, partly because she had no eyebrows. She often joked that she wished she had big bushy ones that needed plucking, like those of Akim Tamiroff, a famous character actor of that time. Instead, she drew her eyebrows on with a cosmetic pencil. Then she put on her makeup and her lipstick, usually a bright red shade that matched her nail polish.

Until I was eleven or twelve, she had long, dark wavy hair. It was really thick and beautiful, and I liked watching her brush it until it was just so. I'll never forget the day she came home from the beauty shop with short hair, all her beautiful waves gone. It was not long after my first dog, Susie, had to be put to sleep at age nine, and it hurt almost as badly. Mother said short hair was more in style and more appropriate for a woman in her mid-thirties. I didn't buy it, and I never stopped missing her long hair, though I did like it when, a few months later, she stopped dyeing the gray streak that had run through the middle of her hair since she was in her twenties.

By the time she finished her makeup, Mother had already run through a cigarette or two and a couple of cups of coffee. Then, after Mrs. Walters got there, she'd head off to work, sometimes dropping me at school when our starting times were close enough. When I got home from school, I'd keep busy playing with my friends or with Roger. I loved having a little brother, and all my pals liked having him around, until he got big enough to prefer his own friends.

Mother usually got home by four or five, except when the racetrack was open. She loved those races. Though she rarely bet more than two dollars across the board, she took it seriously, studying the racing form and the tout sheets, listening to the jockeys, trainers, and owners she got to know, debating her options with her racetrack friends. She made some of the best friends of her life there: Louise Crain and her husband, Joe, a policeman who later became chief and who used to drive Daddy around in his patrol car when he was drunk until his anger died down; Dixie Seba and her husband, Mike, a trainer; and Marge Mitchell, a nurse who staffed the clinic at the track for people who had health problems while there and who, along with Dixie Seba, and later Nancy Crawford, Gabe's second wife, probably came as close as anyone ever did to being Mother's real confidante. Marge and Mother called each other "Sister."

Shortly after I came home from law school I had the chance to repay Marge for all she'd done for Mother and for me. When she was dismissed from her job at our local community mental-health center, she decided to challenge the decision and asked me to represent her at the hearing, where even my inexperienced questioning made it obvious that the termination was based on nothing but a personal conflict with her supervisor. I tore the case against her to shreds, and when we won I was thrilled. She deserved to get her job back.

Before I got Mother into politics, most of her friends were involved in her work—doctors, nurses, hospital personnel. She had a lot of them. She never met a stranger, worked hard to put her patients at ease before surgery, and genuinely enjoyed the company of her co-workers. Of course, not everybody liked her. She could be abrasive with people she thought were trying to push her around or take advantage of their positions to treat others unfairly. Unlike me, she actually enjoyed making some of these people mad. I tended to make enemies effortlessly, just by being me, or, after I got into politics, because of the positions I took and the changes I tried to make. When Mother really didn't like people, she worked hard to get them foaming at the mouth. Later in her career, it cost her, after she had fought for years to avoid going to work for an MD anesthesiologist and had some problems with a couple of her operations. But most people did like her, because she liked them, treated them with respect, and obviously loved life.

I never knew how she kept her energy and spirit, always filling her days with work and fun, always being there for my brother, Roger, and me, never missing our school events, finding time for our friends, too, and keeping all her troubles to herself.

I loved going to the hospital to visit her, meeting the nurses and doctors, watching them care for people. I got to watch an actual operation once, when I was in junior high, but all I remember about it is that there was a lot of cutting and a lot of blood and I didn't get sick. I was fascinated by the work surgeons do and thought I might like to do it myself one day.

Mother took a lot of interest in her patients, whether they could pay or not. In the days before Medicare and Medicaid there were a lot who couldn't. I remember one poor, proud man coming to our door one day to settle his account. He was a fruit picker who paid Mother with six bushels of fresh peaches. We ate those peaches for a long time—on cereal, in pies, in homemade ice cream. It made me wish more of her patients were cash poor!

I think Mother found enormous relief from the strains of her marriage in her work and friends, and at the races. There must have been many days when she was crying inside, maybe even in physical pain, but most people didn't have a clue. The example she set stood me in good stead when I became President. She almost never discussed her troubles with me. I think she figured I knew about all I needed to know, was smart enough to figure out the rest, and deserved as normal a childhood as possible under the circumstances.

When I was fifteen, events overtook the silent strategy.

Daddy started drinking and behaving violently again, so
Mother took Roger and me away. We had done it once
before, a couple of years earlier, when we moved for a few
weeks into the Cleveland Manor Apartments on the south
end of Central Avenue, almost to the racetrack. This time, in
April 1962, we stayed about three weeks at a motel while
Mother searched for a house. We looked at several houses
together, all much smaller than the one we lived in, some still
out of her price range. Finally, she settled on a three-
bedroom, two-bath house on Scully Street, a one-block-long
street in south Hot Springs about a half mile west of Central
Avenue. It was one of the new, all-electric Gold Medallion
houses with central heat and air—we had window-unit air
conditioners back on Park Avenue—and I think it cost
$30,000. The house had a nice living room and dining room
just left of the front entrance. Behind it was a large den that
connected to the dining area and kitchen, with a laundry
room off it just behind the garage. Beyond the den was a
good-sized porch we later glassed in and outfitted with a
pool table. Two of the bedrooms were to the right of the hall;
to the left was a large bathroom, and, behind it, a bedroom
with a separate bathroom with a shower. Mother gave me
the big bedroom with the shower, I think because she wanted
the big bathroom with its larger makeup area and mirror.
She took the next biggest bedroom in the back, and Roger
got the small one.

Though I loved our house on Park Avenue, the yard I
worked hard to keep up, my neighbors and friends and
familiar haunts, I was glad to be in a normal house and to
feel safe, maybe more for Mother and Roger than for me.
By then, even though I knew nothing of child psychology, I
had begun to worry that Daddy's drinking and abusive
behavior would scar Roger even more than it would scar
me, because he'd lived with it all his life and because Roger
Clinton was his natural father. Knowing my father was
someone else, someone I thought of as strong, trustworthy,
and reliable, gave me more emotional security and the space
necessary to see what was happening with some detach-
ment, even sympathy. I never stopped loving Roger Clinton,

never stopped pulling for him to change, never stopped enjoying being with him when he was sober and engaged. I was afraid even then that little Roger would come to hate his father. And he did, at a terrible cost to himself.

As I relate these events from long ago, I see how easy it is to fall into the trap Shakespeare's Marc Antony spoke of in his eulogy for Julius Caesar: allowing the evil that men do to live after them, while the good is interred with their bones. Like most alcoholics and drug addicts I've known, Roger Clinton was fundamentally a good person. He loved Mother and me and little Roger. He had helped Mother to see me when she was finishing school in New Orleans. He was generous to family and friends. He was smart and funny. But he had that combustible mix of fears, insecurities, and psychological vulnerabilities that destroys the promise of so many addicts' lives. And as far as I know, he never sought help from those who knew how to give it.

The really disturbing thing about living with an alcoholic is that it isn't always bad. Weeks, sometimes even whole months, would pass while we'd enjoy being a family, blessed with the quiet joys of an ordinary life. I'm grateful that I haven't forgotten all those times, and when I do, I've still got a few postcards and letters Daddy sent to me and some I sent to him to remind me.

Some of the bad times tend to be forgotten, too. When I recently reread my deposition in Mother's divorce filings, I saw that in it I recounted an incident three years earlier when I called her attorney to get the police to take Daddy away after a violent episode. I also said he'd threatened to beat me the last time I stopped him from hitting her, which was laughable, because by that time I was bigger and stronger than he was sober, much less drunk. I'd forgotten both instances, perhaps out of the denial experts say families of alcoholics engage in when they continue to live with them. For whatever reason, those particular memories remained blocked after forty years.

Five days after we left, on April 14, 1962, Mother filed for divorce. Divorce can happen quickly in Arkansas, and she certainly had grounds. But it wasn't over. Daddy was desperate to get her, and us, back. He fell apart, lost a lot of weight, parked for hours near our house, even slept on our concrete front porch a couple of times. One day he asked me to take a ride with him. We drove up behind our old house on Circle Drive. He stopped at the bottom of our back driveway. He was a wreck. He hadn't shaved in three or four days, though I don't think he'd been drinking. He told me he couldn't live without us, that he had nothing else to live for. He cried. He begged me to talk to Mother and ask her to take him back. He said he would straighten up and never hit her or scream at her again. When he said it, he really believed it, but I didn't. He never understood, or accepted, the cause of his problem. He never acknowledged that he was powerless in the face of liquor and that he couldn't quit all by himself.

Meanwhile, his entreaties were beginning to get to Mother. I think she was feeling a little uncertain about her ability to take care of us financially—she didn't make really good money until Medicaid and Medicare were enacted a couple of years later. Even more important was her old-school view that divorce, especially with kids in the house, was a bad thing, which it often is if there's no real abuse. I think she also felt that their problems must be partly her fault. And she probably did trigger his insecurities; after all, she was a good-looking, interesting woman who liked men and worked with a lot of attractive ones who were more successful than her husband. As far as I know, she never carried on with any of them, though I couldn't blame her if she had, and when she and Daddy were apart, she did see a dark-haired handsome man who gave me some golf clubs I still have.

After we had been on Scully Street just a few months and the divorce had been finalized, Mother told Roger and me that we needed to have a family meeting to discuss Daddy. She said he wanted to come back, to move into our new house, and she thought it would be different this time, and then she asked what we thought. I don't remember what Roger said—he was only five and probably confused. I told her that I was against it, because I didn't think he could change, but that I would support whatever decision she made. She said that we needed a man in the house and that she would always feel guilty if she didn't give him another chance. So she did; they remarried, which, given the way Daddy's life played out, was good for him, but not so good for Roger or for her. I don't know what effect it had on me, except that later, when he got ill, I was very glad to be able to share his last months.

Although I didn't agree with Mother's decision, I understood her feelings. Shortly before she took Daddy back, I went down to the courthouse and had my name changed legally from Blythe to Clinton, the name I had been using for years. I'm still not sure exactly why I did it, but I know I really thought I should, partly because Roger was about to start school and I didn't want the differences in our lineage ever to be an issue for him, partly because I just wanted the same name as the rest of my family. Maybe I even wanted to do something nice for Daddy, though I was glad Mother had divorced him. I didn't tell her in advance, but she had to give her permission. When she got a call from the courthouse, she said okay, though she probably thought I had slipped a gear. It wouldn't be the last time in my life that my decisions and my timing were open to question.

The deterioration of my parents' marriage, the divorce and reconciliation, took up a lot of my emotional energy at the end of junior high and through my sophomore year in the old high school just up the hill.

Just as Mother threw herself into work, I threw myself into high school, and into my new neighborhood on Scully Street. It was a block full of mostly newer, modest houses. Just across the street was a completely empty square block, all that was left of the Wheatley farm, which had covered a much larger area not long before. Every year Mr. Wheatley planted the whole block with peonies. They brightened the spring and drew people from miles around, who waited patiently for him to cut them and give them away.

We lived in the second house on the street. The first house, on the corner of Scully and Wheatley, belonged to the Reverend Walter Yeldell, his wife, Kay, and their kids, Carolyn, Lynda, Deborah, and Walter. Walter was pastor of Second Baptist Church and later president of the Arkansas Baptist Convention. He and Kay were wonderful to us from the first day. I don't know how Brother Yeldell, as we called him, who died in 1987, would have fared in the harshly judgmental environment of the Southern Baptist Convention of the nineties, when wrong-thinking "liberals" were purged from the seminaries and the church hardened its positions rightward on every social issue but race (it apologized for the sins of the past). Brother Yeldell was a big, broad man who weighed well over 250 pounds. Beneath a shy demeanor, he had a terrific sense of humor and a great laugh. So did his wife. They didn't have a pompous bone between them. He led people to Christ through instruction and example, not condemnation and ridicule. He wouldn't have been a favorite of some of the recent Baptist overlords or today's conservative talk-show hosts, but I sure liked talking to him.

Carolyn, the oldest Yeldell child, was my age. She loved music, had a wonderful voice, and was an accomplished pianist. We spent countless hours around her piano singing. She also accompanied my saxophone solos from time to time, probably not the first time an accompanist was better than the soloist. Carolyn soon became one of my closest friends and a part of our regular gang, along with David Leopoulos, Joe Newman, and Ronnie Cecil. We went to movies and school events together, and spent lots of time playing cards and games or just goofing off, usually at our house. In 1963, when I went to American Legion Boys Nation and took the now famous photo with President Kennedy, Carolyn was elected to Girls Nation, the only time that ever happened to hometown neighbors. Carolyn went to Indiana University and studied voice. She wanted to be an opera singer but didn't want the lifestyle. Instead she married Jerry Staley, a fine photographer, had three kids, and became a leader in the field of adult literacy. When I became governor I put her in charge of our adult literacy program, and she and her family lived in a great old house about three blocks from the Governor's Mansion, where I often visited for parties, games, or singing the way we did in the old days. When I became President, Carolyn and her family moved to the Washington area, where she went to work for, and later led, the National Institute for Literacy. She stayed on for a while after I left the White House, then followed her father into the ministry. The Staleys are still a good part of my life. It all started on Scully Street.

The house on the other side of us belonged to Jim and Edith Clark, who had no kids of their own but treated me like theirs. Among our other neighbors were the Frasers, an older couple who always supported me when I got into politics. But their greatest gift to me came by accident. Over the holidays in 1974, after I lost a heartbreaking race for Congress and was still feeling pretty low, I saw the Frasers' little granddaughter, who must have been five or six. She had a severe medical condition that made her bones weak and was in a body cast up to her chest that also splayed her legs outward to take the pressure off her spine. It was very awkward for her to navigate with her crutches, but she was a tough little girl with that total lack of self-consciousness that secure young children have. When I saw her I asked if she knew who I was. She said, "Sure, you're still Bill Clinton." I needed to be reminded of that just then.

The Hassins, the Syrian-Italian family I mentioned earlier, were packed, all six of them, in a tiny little house at the end of the street. They must have spent all their money on food. Every Christmas and on several other occasions during the year they fed the whole block huge Italian meals. I can still hear Mama Gina saying, "A-Beel, a-Beel, you gotta eat some more."

And then there were Jon and Toni Karber, who were both book readers and the most intellectual people I knew, and their son Mike, who was in my class. And Charley Housley—a man's man who knew about hunting, fishing, and fixing things, the things that matter to small boys—who took Roger under his wing. Though our new house and yard were smaller than our old one, and the immediate surroundings less beautiful, I came to love my new home and neighborhood. It was a good place for me to live out my high school years.

SEVEN

HIGH SCHOOL WAS a great ride. I liked the schoolwork, my friends, the band, DeMolay, and my other activities, but it bothered me that Hot Springs' schools still weren't integrated. The black kids still went to Langston High School, which claimed as its most famous alumnus the legendary Washington Redskins back Bobby Mitchell. I followed the civil rights movement on the evening news and in our daily paper, the *Sentinel-Record*, along with Cold War events like the Bay of Pigs and the U-2 incident with Francis Gary Powers. I can still see Castro riding into Havana at the head of his ragtag but victorious army. But as with most kids, politics took a backseat to daily life. And apart from Daddy's occasional relapses, I liked my life a lot.

It was in high school that I really fell in love with music. Classical, jazz, and band music joined rock and roll, swing, and gospel as my idea of pure joy. For some reason I didn't get into country and western until I was in my twenties, when Hank Williams and Patsy Cline reached down to me from heaven.

In addition to the marching and concert bands, I joined our dance band, the Stardusters. I spent a year dueling for first chair on tenor sax with Larry McDougal, who looked as if he should have played backup for Buddy Holly, the rocker who died tragically in a bad-weather plane crash in 1959 along with two other big stars, the Big Bopper and seventeen-year-old Richie Valens. When I was President I gave a speech to college students in Mason City, Iowa, near where Holly and his pals had played their last gig. Afterward I drove to the site, the Surf Ballroom, in neighboring Clear Lake, Iowa. It's still standing and ought to be turned into a shrine for those of us who grew up on those guys.

Anyway, McDougal looked and played as if he belonged with them. He had a ducktail hairdo, crew cut on top, long hair greased back on the sides. When he stood for a solo, he gyrated and played with a blaring tone, more like hard-core rock and roll than jazz or swing. I wasn't as good as he was in 1961, but I was determined to get better. That year we entered a competition with other jazz bands in Camden in south Arkansas. I had a small solo on a slow, pretty piece. At the end of the performance, to my astonishment, I won the prize for "best sweet soloist." By the next year, I had improved enough to be first chair in the All-State Band, a position I won again as a senior, when Joe Newman won on drums.

In my last two years I played in a jazz trio, the 3 Kings, with Randy Goodrum, a pianist a year younger and light-years better than I was or ever could be. Our first drummer was Mike Hardgraves. Mike was raised by a single mom, who often had me and a couple of Mike's other friends over for card games. In my senior year Joe Newman became our drummer. We made a little money playing for dances, and we performed at school events, including the annual Band Variety Show. Our signature piece was the theme from *El Cid*. I still have a tape of it, and it holds up pretty well after all these years, except for a squeak I made in my closing riff. I always had problems with the lower notes.

My band director, Virgil Spurlin, was a tall, heavyset man with dark wavy hair and a gentle, winning demeanor. He was a pretty good band director and a world-class human being. Mr. Spurlin also organized the State Band Festival, which was held over several days every year in Hot Springs. He had to schedule all the band performances and hundreds of solo and ensemble presentations in classrooms in the junior and senior high school buildings. He scheduled the days, times, and venues for all the events on large poster boards every year. Those of us who were willing stayed after school and worked nights for several days to help him get the job done. It was the first large organizational effort in which I was ever involved, and I learned a lot that I put to good use later on.

At the state festivals, I won several medals for solos and ensembles, and a couple for student conducting, of which I was especially proud. I loved to read the scores and try to get the band to play pieces exactly as I thought they should sound. In my second term as President, Leonard Slatkin, conductor of the Washington National Symphony, asked me if I would direct the orchestra in Sousa's "Stars and Stripes Forever" at the Kennedy Center. He told me all I had to do was wave the baton more or less in time and the musicians would do the rest. He even offered to bring me a baton and show me how to hold it. When I told him that I'd be delighted to do it but that I wanted him to send me the score of the march so I could review it, he almost dropped the phone. But he brought the score and the baton. When I stood before the orchestra I was nervous, but we got into it, and away we went. I hope Mr. Sousa would have been pleased.

My only other artistic endeavor in high school was the junior class play, *Arsenic and Old Lace*, a hilarious farce about two old maids who poison people and stash them in the house they share with their unsuspecting nephew. I got the role of the nephew, which Cary Grant played in the movie. My girlfriend was played by a tall, attractive girl, Cindy Arnold. The play was a big success, largely because of two developments that weren't part of the script. In one scene, I was supposed to lift up a window seat, find one of my aunts' victims, and feign horror. I practiced hard and had it down. But on play night, when I opened the seat, my friend Ronnie Cecil was crammed into it, looked up at me, and said, "Good evening," in his best vampire voice. I lost it. Luckily, so did everyone else. Something even funnier happened offstage. When I kissed Cindy during our only love scene, her boyfriend—a senior football player named Allen Broyles, who was sitting in the front row—let out a loud comic groan that brought the house down. I still enjoyed the kiss.

My high school offered calculus and trigonometry, chemistry and physics, Spanish, French, and four years of Latin, a range of courses many smaller schools in Arkansas lacked. We were blessed with a lot of smart, effective teachers and a remarkable school leader, Johnnie Mae Mackey, a tall, imposing woman with thick black hair and a ready smile or a stern scowl as the occasion demanded. Johnnie Mae ran a tight ship and still managed to be the spark plug of our school spirit, which was a job in itself, because we had the losingest football team in Arkansas, back when football was a religion, with every coach expected to be Knute Rockne. Every student from back then can still remember Johnnie Mae closing our pep rallies leading the Trojan yell, fist in the air, dignity discarded, voice roaring, "Hullabloo, Ke-neck, Ke-neck, Hullabloo, Ke-neck, Ke-neck, Wo-Hee, Wo-Hi, We win or die! Ching Chang, Chow Chow! Bing Bang, Bow Wow! Trojans! Trojans! Fight, Fight, Fight!" Fortunately, it was just a cheer. With a 6–29–1 record in my three years, if the yell had been accurate, our mortality rate would have been serious.

I took four years of Latin from Mrs. Elizabeth Buck, a delightful, sophisticated woman from Philadelphia who had us memorize lots of lines from Caesar's *Gallic Wars*. After the Russians beat us into space with *Sputnik*, President Eisenhower and then President Kennedy decided Americans needed to know more about science and math, so I took all the courses I could. I was not very good in Dick Duncan's chemistry class, but did better in biology, though I remember only one remarkable class, in which the teacher, Nathan McCauley, told us we die sooner than we should because our bodies' capacity to turn food into energy and process the waste wears out. In 2002, a major medical study concluded that older people could increase their life span dramatically by sharply decreasing food intake. Coach McCauley knew that forty years ago. Now that I am one of those older people, I am trying to take his advice.

My world history teacher, Paul Root, was a short, stocky man from rural Arkansas who combined a fine mind with a homespun manner and an offbeat, wicked sense of humor. When I became governor, he left his teaching position at Ouachita University to work for me. One day in 1987, I came upon Paul in the state Capitol talking to three state legislators. They were discussing Gary Hart's recent downfall after the story broke about Donna Rice and the *Monkey Business*. The legislators were all giving Gary hell in their most sanctimonious voices. Paul, a devout Baptist, director of his church choir, and certified straight arrow, listened patiently while the legislators droned on. When they stopped for breath, he deadpanned, "You're absolutely right. What he did was awful. But you know what else? It's amazing what being short, fat, and ugly has done for my moral character." The legislators shut up, and Paul walked off with me. I love that guy.

I enjoyed all my English courses. John Wilson made Shakespeare's *Julius Caesar* come alive to Arkansas fifteen-year-olds by having us put the meaning of the play in ordinary words and asking us repeatedly whether Shakespeare's view of human nature and behavior seemed right to us. Mr. Wilson thought old Will had it about right: life is comedy and tragedy.

In junior honors English class, we had to write an autobiographical essay. Mine was full of self-doubt I didn't understand and hadn't admitted to myself before. Here are some excerpts:

> I am a person motivated and influenced by so many diverse forces I sometimes question the sanity of my existence. I am a living paradox—deeply religious, yet not as convinced of my exact beliefs as I ought to be; wanting responsibility yet shirking it; loving the truth but often times giving way to falsity. . . . I detest selfishness, but see it in the mirror every day. . . . I view those, some of whom are very dear to me, who have never learned how to live. I desire and struggle to be different from them, but often am almost an exact likeness. . . . What a boring little word—I! I, me, my, mine . . . the only things that enable worthwhile uses of these words are the universal good qualities which we are not too often able to place with them—faith, trust, love, responsibility, regret, knowledge. But the acronyms to these symbols of

what enable life to be worth the trouble cannot be
escaped. I, in my attempts to be honest, will not be
the hypocrite I hate, and will own up to their ominous presence in this boy, endeavoring in such
earnest to be a man. . . .

My teacher, Lonnie Warneke, gave me a grade of 100,
saying the paper was a beautiful and honest attempt to go
"way down inside" to fulfill the classic demand to "know
thyself." I was gratified but still unsure of what to make of
what I'd found. I didn't do bad things; I didn't drink,
smoke, or go beyond petting with girls, though I kissed a
fair number. Most of the time I was happy, but I could never
be sure I was as good as I wanted to be.

Miss Warneke took our small class on a field trip to
Newton County, my first trip into the heart of the Ozarks in
north Arkansas, our Appalachia. Back then it was a place of
breathtaking beauty, hardscrabble poverty, and rough, all-
consuming politics. The county had about six thousand
people spread over more than a couple of hundred square
miles in hills and hollows. Jasper, the county seat, had a little more than three hundred people, a WPA-built courthouse, two cafés, a general store, and one tiny movie
theater, where our class went one night to watch an old
Audie Murphy western. When I got into politics I came to
know every township in Newton County, but I fell in love
with it at sixteen, as we navigated the mountain roads,
learning about the history, geology, flora, and fauna of the
Ozarks. One day we visited the cabin of a mountain man
who had a collection of rifles and pistols dating back to the
Civil War, then explored a cave the Confederates had used
for munitions storage. The guns still fired, and remnants of
the arsenal were still in the cave, visible manifestation of
how real a century-old conflict was in places where time
passed slowly, grudges died hard, and handed-down memories hung on and on. In the mid-seventies, when I was attorney general, I was invited to give the commencement
address at Jasper High School. I urged the students to keep
going in the face of adversity, citing Abraham Lincoln and

all the hardships and setbacks he'd overcome. Afterward, the leading Democrats took me out into a bright starlit Ozark night and said, "Bill, that was a fine speech. You can give it down in Little Rock anytime. But don't you ever come up here and brag on that Republican President again. If he'd been that good, we wouldn't have had the Civil War!" I didn't know what to say.

In Ruth Sweeney's senior English class, we read *Macbeth* and were encouraged to memorize and recite portions of it. I made it through a hundred lines or so, including the famous soliloquy that begins, "Tomorrow, and tomorrow, and tomorrow creeps in this petty pace from day to day, to the last syllable of recorded time" and ends, "Life's but a walking shadow, a poor player that struts and frets his hour upon the stage and then is heard no more. It is a tale told by an idiot, full of sound and fury, signifying nothing." Almost thirty years later, when I was governor, I happened to visit a class in Vilonia, Arkansas, on a day the students were studying *Macbeth*, and I recited the lines for them, the words still full of power for me, a dreadful message I was always determined would not be the measure of my life.

The summer after my junior year, I attended the annual weeklong American Legion Boys State program at Camp Robinson, an old army camp with enough primitive wooden barracks to house a thousand sixteen-year-old boys. We were organized by cities and counties, divided equally into two political parties, and introduced as candidates and voters to local, county, and state politics. We also developed platforms and voted on issues. We heard addresses from important figures, from the governor on down, and got to spend one day at the state Capitol, during which the Boys State governor, the other elected officials and their "staffs," and the legislators actually got to occupy the state offices and legislative chambers.

At the end of the week, both parties nominated two candidates for the Boys Nation program, to be held toward the end of July at the University of Maryland in College Park, near the nation's capital. An election was held, and the top two vote-getters got to go as Arkansas' senators. I was one of them.

I went to Camp Robinson wanting to run for Boys Nation senator. Though the most prestigious post was governor, I had no interest in it then, or in the real job itself, for years thereafter. I thought Washington was where the action was on civil rights, poverty, education, and foreign policy. Besides, I couldn't have won the governor's election anyway, since it was, in the Arkansas vernacular, "saucered and blowed"— over before it started. My longtime friend from Hope, Mack McLarty, had it in the bag. As his school's student-council president, a star quarterback, and a straight-A student, he had begun lining up support all across the state several weeks earlier. Our party nominated Larry Taunton, a radio announcer with a wonderful silken voice full of sincerity and confidence, but McLarty had the votes and won going away. We were all sure he would be the first person our age to be elected governor, an impression reinforced four years later when he was elected student body president at the University of Arkansas, and again just a year after that when, at twenty-two, he became the youngest member of the state legislature. Not long after that, Mack, who was in the Ford business with his father, devised a then-novel leasing scheme for Ford trucks, which eventually made him and Ford Motor Company a fortune. He gave up politics for a business career that led him to the presidency of Arkansas-Louisiana Gas Company, our largest natural gas utility. But he stayed active in politics, lending leadership and fund-raising skills to many Arkansas Democrats, especially David Pryor and me. He stayed with me all the way to the White House, first as chief of staff, then as special envoy to the Americas. Now he is Henry Kissinger's partner in a consulting business and owns, among other things, twelve car dealerships in São Paulo, Brazil.

Though he lost the governor's race, Larry Taunton got a big consolation prize: as the only boy besides McLarty with 100 percent name recognition, he was a lock cinch for one of the two Boys Nation slots; he had only to file. But there was a problem. Larry was one of two "stars" in his hometown delegation. The other was Bill Rainer, a bright, handsome multi-sport athlete. They had come to Boys State agreeing that Taunton would run for governor, Rainer for Boys Nation. Now, though both were free to run for Boys Nation, there was no way two boys from the same town were going to be elected. Besides, they were both in my party and I had been campaigning hard for a week. A letter I wrote to Mother at the time recounts that I had already won elections for tax collector, party secretary, and municipal judge, and that I was running for county judge, an important position in real Arkansas politics.

At the last minute, not long before the party met to hear our campaign speeches, Taunton filed. Bill Rainer was so stunned he could hardly get through his speech. I still have a copy of my own speech, which is unremarkable, except for a reference to the Little Rock Central High turmoil: "We have grown up in a state ridden with the shame of a crisis it did not ask for." I did not approve of what Faubus had done, and I wanted people from other states to think better of Arkansas. When the votes were counted, Larry Taunton finished first by a good margin. I was second with a pretty good cushion. Rainer finished well back. I had come to really like Bill, and I never forgot the dignity with which he bore his loss.

In 1992, when Bill was living in Connecticut, he contacted my campaign and offered to help. Our friendship, forged in the pain of youthful disappointment, enjoyed a happy renewal.

Larry Taunton and I defeated our opponents from the other party after another day of campaigning, and I arrived in College Park on July 19, 1963, eager to meet the other delegates, vote on important issues, hear from cabinet members and other government officials, and visit the White House, where we hoped to see the President.

The week passed quickly, the days packed with events and legislative sessions. I remember being particularly impressed by Secretary of Labor Willard Wirtz and completely caught up in our debates over civil rights. Many of the boys were Republicans and supporters of Barry Goldwater, who they hoped would defeat President Kennedy in 1964, but there were enough progressives on civil rights, including four of us from the South, for our legislative proposals to carry the day.

Because of my friendship with Bill Rainer and my more liberal views on civil rights, I had a tense relationship with Larry Taunton the whole week of Boys Nation. I'm glad that, after I became President, I got to meet the grown-up Larry Taunton and his children. He seemed to be a good man who'd built a good life.

On Monday, July 22, we visited the Capitol, took pictures on the steps, and met our state's senators. Larry and I had lunch with J. William Fulbright, chairman of the Foreign Relations Committee, and John McClellan, chairman of the Appropriations Committee. The seniority system was alive and well, and no state had more power from it than Arkansas. In addition, all four of our congressmen held important positions: Wilbur Mills was chairman of the Ways and Means Committee; Oren Harris, chairman of the Commerce Committee; "Took" Gathings, ranking member of the Agriculture Committee; and Jim Trimble, who had been in Congress "only" since 1945, a member of the powerful Rules Committee, which controls the flow of legislation to the House floor. Little did I know that within three years I would be working for Fulbright on the Foreign Relations Committee staff. A few days after the lunch, Mother got a letter from Senator Fulbright saying that he had enjoyed our lunch and that she must be proud of me. I still have that letter, my first encounter with good staff work.

On Wednesday, July 24, we went to the White House to meet the President in the Rose Garden. President Kennedy walked out of the Oval Office into the bright sunshine and made some brief remarks, complimenting our work, especially our support for civil rights, and giving us higher marks than the governors, who had not been so forward-leaning in their annual summer meeting. After accepting a Boys Nation T-shirt, Kennedy walked down the steps and began shaking hands. I was in the front, and being bigger and a bigger supporter of the President's than most of the others, I made sure I'd get to shake his hand even if he shook only two or three. It was an amazing moment for me, meeting the President whom I had supported in my ninth-grade class debates, and about whom I felt even more strongly after his two and a half years in office. A friend took a photo for me, and later we found film footage of the handshake in the Kennedy Library.

Much has been made of that brief encounter and its impact on my life. My mother said she knew when I came home that I was determined to go into politics, and after I became the Democratic nominee in 1992, the film was widely pointed to as the beginning of my presidential aspirations. I'm not sure about that. I have a copy of the speech I gave to the American Legion in Hot Springs after I came home, and in it I didn't make too much of the handshake. I thought at the time I wanted to become a senator, but deep down I probably felt as Abraham Lincoln did when he wrote as a young man, "I will study and get ready, and perhaps my chance will come."

I had some success in high school politics, getting elected president of the junior class, and I wanted to run for president of the student council, but the accrediting group that oversaw our high school decided that Hot Springs students were not allowed to be involved in too many activities and ordered restrictions. Under the new rules, since I was the band major, I was ineligible to run for student council or class president. So was Phil Jamison, the captain of the foot-ball team and the odds-on favorite to win.

Not running for high school student-council president didn't hurt me or Phil Jamison too much. Phil went on to the Naval Academy, and after his naval career he did important work in the Pentagon on arms control issues. When I was President, he was involved in all our important work with Russia, and our friendship gave me a close account of our efforts from an operational level, which I would not have received had I not known him.

In one of the dumber political moves of my life, I allowed my name to be put up for senior class secretary by a friend who was angry about the new activity restrictions.

My next-door neighbor Carolyn Yeldell defeated me handily, as she should have. It was a foolish, selfish thing for me
to do, and proof positive of one of my rules of politics:
Never run for an office you don't really want and don't have
a good reason to hold.

Notwithstanding the setbacks, sometime in my sixteenth year I decided I wanted to be in public life as an
elected official. I loved music and thought I could be very
good, but I knew I would never be John Coltrane or Stan
Getz. I was interested in medicine and thought I could be a
fine doctor, but I knew I would never be Michael DeBakey.
But I knew I could be great in public service. I was fascinated by people, politics, and policy, and I thought I could
make it without family wealth, or connections, or establishment southern positions on race and other issues. Of course
it was improbable, but isn't that what America is all about?

EIGHT

ONE OTHER MEMORABLE EVENT happened to me in the summer of 1963. On August 28, nine days after I turned seventeen, I sat alone in a big white reclining chair in our den and watched the greatest speech of my lifetime, as Martin Luther King Jr. stood in front of the Lincoln Memorial and spoke of his dream for America. In rhythmic cadences reminiscent of old Negro spirituals, his voice at once booming and shaking, he told a vast throng before him, and millions like me transfixed before television sets, of his dream that "one day on the red hills of Georgia, the sons of former slaves and the sons of former slave owners will be able to sit down together at the table of brotherhood," and that "my four little children will one day live in a nation where they will not be judged by the color of their skin but by the content of their character."

It is difficult to convey more than forty years later the emotion and hope with which King's speech filled me; or what it meant to a nation with no Civil Rights Act, no Voting Rights Act, no open housing law, no Thurgood Marshall on the Supreme Court; or what it meant in the American South, where schools were still mostly segregated, the poll tax was used to keep blacks from voting or to round them up to vote as a bloc for the status quo crowd, and the word "nigger" was still used openly by people who knew better.

I started crying during the speech and wept for a good while after Dr. King finished. He had said everything I believed, far better than I ever could. More than anything I ever experienced, except perhaps the power of my grandfather's example, that speech steeled my determination to do whatever I could for the rest of my life to make Martin Luther King Jr.'s dream come true.

A couple of weeks later, I started my senior year in high

school, still on a high from Boys Nation, and determined to enjoy my last shot at childhood.

The most challenging course I took in high school was calculus. There were seven of us in the class; it had never been offered before. I recall two events with clarity. One day the teacher, Mr. Coe, handed back an exam on which I had all the right answers but a grade reflecting that I'd missed one. When I asked about it, Mr. Coe said I hadn't worked the problem properly and therefore must have gotten the correct answer by accident, so he couldn't give me credit for it; in the textbook, the problem required several more steps than I had used. Our class had one true genius, Jim McDougal (no, not the Whitewater one), who asked if he could see my paper. He then told Mr. Coe he should give me credit because my solution was as valid as the one in the textbook, indeed better, because it was shorter. He then volunteered to demonstrate the validity of his opinion. Mr. Coe was just as much in awe of Jim's brain as the rest of us, so he told him to go ahead. Jim then proceeded to fill two full blackboards with symbolic mathematical formulas analyzing the problem and demonstrating how I had improved on the textbook solution. You could have fooled me. I had always liked solving puzzles, still do, but I was just clawing my way through a maze. I didn't have a clue about what Jim was saying, and I'm not sure Mr. Coe did either, but at the end of his bravura performance I got my grade changed. That incident taught me two things: that in problem-solving, sometimes good instincts can overcome intellectual inadequacy; and that I had no business pursuing advanced mathematics any further.

Our class met at fourth period, just after lunch. On November 22, Mr. Coe was called out of class to the office. When he returned, he was white as a sheet and could hardly speak. He told us President Kennedy had been shot and probably killed in Dallas. I was devastated. Just four months before, I had seen him in the Rose Garden, so full of life and strength. So much of what he did and said—the inaugural address; the Alliance for Progress in Latin America; the cool handling of the Cuban Missile Crisis; the Peace

Corps; the stunning line from the "Ich bin ein Berliner" speech: "Freedom has many difficulties, and democracy is not perfect, but we have never had to put a wall up to keep our people in"—all these embodied my hopes for my country and my belief in politics.

After class, all the students in the annex where our class met walked back to the main building. We were all so sad, all of us but one. I overheard an attractive girl who was in the band with me say that maybe it was a good thing for the country that he was gone. I knew her family was more conservative than I was, but I was stunned and very angry that someone I considered a friend would say such a thing. It was my first exposure, beyond raw racism, to the kind of hatred I would see a lot of in my political career, and that was forged into a powerful political movement in the last quarter of the twentieth century. I am thankful that my friend outgrew it. When I was campaigning in Las Vegas in 1992, she came to one of my events. She had become a social worker and a Democrat. I treasured our reunion and the chance it gave me to heal an old wound.

After I watched President Kennedy's funeral and was reassured by Lyndon Johnson's sober assumption of the presidency with the moving words "All that I have I would have given gladly not to be standing here today," I slowly returned to normal life. The rest of senior year passed quickly with DeMolay and band activities, including a senior band trip to Pensacola, Florida, and another trip to All-State Band; and lots of good times with my friends, including lunches at the Club Café, with the best Dutch apple pie I've ever had, movies, dances at the Y, ice cream at Cook's Dairy, and barbeque at McClard's, a seventy-five-year-old family place with arguably the best barbeque and unquestionably the best barbeque beans in the whole country.

For several months that year, I dated Susan Smithers, a girl from Benton, Arkansas, thirty miles east of Hot Springs on the highway to Little Rock. Often on Sundays, I would go to Benton to church and lunch with her family. At the end of the meal Susan's mother, Mary, would put a pile of peach or apple fried pies on the table, and her father, Reese,

and I would eat them until I practically had to be carried
away. One Sunday after lunch, Susan and I went for a drive
to Bauxite, a town near Benton named for the ore used to
make aluminum, which was dug out of open pit mines
there. When we got to town we decided to drive out to see
the mines, going off the road onto what I thought was hard
clay soil, right up to the edge of a huge open pit. After walking around the site, we got back in the car to go home, and
our mood took a sharp downward turn. My car's wheels
had sunk deep into the soft, wet ground. The wheels turned
over and over, but we didn't move an inch. I found some old
boards, dug down behind the wheels, and put them in the
space for traction. Still no luck. After two hours, I had
burned all the tread off the tires, it was getting dark, and we
were still stuck. Finally I gave up, walked to town, asked for
help, and called Susan's parents. Eventually help came and
we were towed out of the huge ruts, my tires as smooth as a
baby's behind. It was way past dark when I got Susan home.
I think her folks believed our story, but her dad sneaked a
look at my tires just to be sure. In that more innocent time,
I was mortified.

As my senior year drew to a close, I became increasingly
anxious about college. For some reason, I never even considered applying to any Ivy League school. I knew just where I
wanted to go, and I applied only there: the Georgetown University School of Foreign Service. I didn't want to go into the
foreign service and I had never even seen the Georgetown
campus when I was at Boys Nation, but I wanted to go back
to Washington; Georgetown had the best academic reputation in the city; the intellectual rigor of the Jesuits was legendary and fascinating to me; and I felt that I needed to
know all I could about international affairs, and that somehow I would absorb all I could learn about domestic issues
just by being in Washington in the mid-sixties. I thought I
would get in, because I was fourth in my class of 327, my
College Board scores were pretty good, and Georgetown
tried to have at least one student from every state (an early
affirmative action program!). Still, I was worried.

I had decided that if I got turned down at Georgetown, I'd go to the University of Arkansas, which had an open admissions policy for Arkansas high school graduates, and where the smart money said aspiring politicians should go anyway. In the second week of April, my acceptance notice from Georgetown arrived. I was happy, but by then I'd begun to question the wisdom of going. I didn't get a scholarship and it was so expensive: $1,200 for tuition and $700 for room and fees, plus books, food, and other expenses. Although we were a comfortable middle-class family by Arkansas standards, I was worried that my folks couldn't afford it. And I was worried about being so far away and leaving Mother and Roger alone with Daddy, though age was slowing him down. My guidance counselor, Edith Irons, was adamant that I should go, that it was an investment in my future that my parents should make. Mother and Daddy agreed. Also, Mother was convinced that once I got there and proved myself I'd get some financial help. So I decided to give it a shot.

I graduated from high school on the evening of May 29, 1964, in a ceremony at Rix Field, where we played our football games. As fourth-ranked student, I got to give the benediction. Subsequent court decisions on religion in public schools, had they been law then, might have taken us prayer leaders off the program. I agree that tax money should not be used to advance purely religious causes, but I was honored to get in the last word at the end of my high school years.

My benediction reflected my deep religious convictions as well as a little politics as I prayed that God would "leave within us the youthful idealism and moralism which have made our people strong. Sicken us at the sight of apathy, ignorance, and rejection so that our generation will remove complacency, poverty, and prejudice from the hearts of free men. . . . Make us care so that we will never know the misery and muddle of life without purpose, and so that when we die, others will still have the opportunity to live in a free land."

I know that some nonreligious people may find all this

offensive or naïve but I'm glad I was so idealistic back then, and I still believe every word I prayed.

After graduation, I went with Mauria Jackson to our senior party at the old Belvedere Club, not far from our Park Avenue house. Since Mauria and I were both unattached at the time and had been in grade school together at St. John's, it seemed like a good idea, and it was.

The next morning, I headed into my last summer as a boy. It was a typical, good, hot Arkansas summer, and it passed quickly, with a sixth and final trip to the university band camp, and a return to Boys State as a counselor. That summer I helped Daddy for a couple of weeks with the annual inventory at Clinton Buick, something I had done a few times before. It's hard to remember today, when records are computerized and parts can be ordered from efficient distribution centers, that in those days we kept parts in stock for cars more than ten years old, and counted them all by hand every year. The small parts were in little cubbyholes in very tall shelves set close together, making the back of the parts department very dark, in stark contrast to the bright showroom in front, which was only large enough to accommodate one of the new Buicks.

The work was tedious, but I liked doing it, mostly because it was the only thing I did with Daddy. I also enjoyed being at the Buick place, visiting with Uncle Raymond, with the salesmen on the car lot full of new and used cars, and with the mechanics in the back. There were three men back there I especially liked. Two were black. Early Arnold looked like Ray Charles and had one of the greatest laughs I ever heard. He was always wonderful to me. James White was more laid-back. He had to be: he was trying to raise eight kids on what Uncle Raymond was paying him and what his wife, Earlene, earned by working at our house for Mother after Mrs. Walters left. I lapped up James's armchair philosophy. Once, when I remarked on how quickly my high school years had flown by, he said, "Yeah, time's goin' by so fast, I can't hardly keep up with my age." Then I thought it was a joke. Now it's not so funny.

The white guy, Ed Foshee, was a genius with cars and

later opened his own shop. When I went away to school, we sold him the Henry J I drove, one of six badly burned cars Daddy had repaired at the Buick dealership in Hope. I hated to part with that car, leaking hydraulic brakes and all, and I'd give anything to get it back now. It gave my friends and me a lot of good times, and one not-so-good one. One night, I was driving out of Hot Springs on Highway 7 on slick pavement, just behind a black car. As we were passing Jessie Howe's Drive-In, the car in front stopped dead in its tracks, apparently to see what was showing on the big screen. One of its brake lights was out, and I didn't see it stop until it was too late. The combination of inattention, slow reflexes, and iffy brakes plowed me right into the back of the black car, driving my jaw into the steering wheel, which promptly broke in half. Luckily, no one was seriously hurt, and I had insurance to cover the other car's damage. The guys at Clinton Buick fixed the Henry J as good as new, and I was grateful that the steering wheel had broken instead of my jaw. It didn't hurt any worse than when Henry Hill had slugged me a few years earlier, and not nearly as badly as when the ram had almost butted me to death. By then I was more philosophical about such things, with an attitude rather like the wise man who said, "It does a dog good to have a few fleas now and then. It keeps him from worrying so much about being a dog."

NINE

THE SUMMER ENDED too quickly, as all childhood summers do, and on September 12 Mother and I flew to Washington, where we would spend a week sightseeing before I started freshman orientation. I didn't know exactly what I was getting into, but I was full of anticipation.

The trip was harder on Mother than on me. We were always close, and I knew that when she looked at me, she often saw both me and my father. She had to be worried about how she was going to raise little Roger and deal with big Roger without me to help out on both fronts. And we were going to miss each other. We were enough alike and enough different that we enjoyed being together. My friends loved her, too, and she loved having them at our house. That would still happen, but usually only when I was home at Christmas or in the summer.

I couldn't have known then as I know now how much she worried about me. Recently, I came across a letter she wrote in December 1963 as part of my successful application for the Elks Leadership Award, which was given to one or two high school seniors each year in towns with Elks Clubs. She wrote that her letter "relieves in a small way a guilt complex I have about Bill. Anesthesia is my profession and it has always taken time that I felt rightfully belonged to him. And, because of this, the credit for what he is and what he has done with his life actually belongs to him. Thus, when I look at him I see a 'self-made' man." Was she ever wrong about that! It was she who taught me to get up every day and keep going; to look for the best in people even when they saw the worst in me; to be grateful for every day and greet it with a smile; to believe I could do or be anything I put my mind to if I were willing to make the requisite effort; to believe that, in the end, love and kindness would prevail over cruelty and selfishness. Mother was not conventionally religious then, though she grew to be as she aged. She saw so many people die that she had a hard time believing in life after death. But if God is love, she was a godly woman. How I wish I'd told her more often that I was the furthest thing in the world from a self-made man.

Despite all the apprehension about the big changes in our lives, Mother and I were both giddy with excitement by the time we got to Georgetown. Just a couple of blocks away from the main campus was the so-called East Campus, which included the School of Foreign Service and other schools that had women and were religiously and racially more diverse. The college was founded in 1789, George Washington's first year as President, by Archbishop John Carroll. A statue of him anchors the grand circle at the entrance to the main campus. In 1815, President James Madison signed a bill granting Georgetown a charter to confer degrees. Although our university has from the beginning been open to people of all faiths, and one of the greatest Georgetown presidents, Father Patrick Healy, was from 1874 to 1882 the first African-American president of a predominantly white university, the Yard was all male, almost all Catholic, and all white. The School of Foreign Service was founded in 1919 by Father Edmund A. Walsh, a staunch anti-Communist, and when I got there the faculty was still full of professors who had fled from or suffered from Communist regimes in Europe and China and who were sympathetic to any anti-Communist activity by the U.S. government, including in Vietnam.

The politics weren't all that was conservative at the Foreign Service School. So was the curriculum, the rigor of which reflected the Jesuit educational philosophy, the *Ratio Studiorum*, developed in the late sixteenth century. For the first two years, six courses a semester were required, totaling eighteen or nineteen hours of class time, and there were no electives until the second semester of the junior year. Then there was the dress code. In my freshman year, men were still required to wear dress shirt, jacket, and tie to class. Synthetic-fabric "drip-dry" shirts were available, but they felt awful, so I went to Georgetown determined to fit the five-dollar-a-week dry-cleaning bill for five shirts into my

twenty-five-dollar-a-week allowance for food and other
expenses. And there were the dorm rules: "Freshmen are
required to be in their rooms and studying weeknights, and
must have their lights out by midnight. On Friday and Saturday evenings, freshmen must return to their rooms for the
night by 12:30 a.m. . . . Absolutely no guests of the opposite
sex, alcoholic beverages, pets, or firearms are allowed in
University dormitories." I know things have changed a bit
since then, but when Hillary and I took Chelsea to Stanford
in 1997, it was still somewhat unsettling to see the young
women and men living in the same dorm. Apparently the
NRA hasn't yet succeeded in lifting the firearms restriction.

One of the first people I met when Mother and I went
through the front gate was the priest in charge of freshman
orientation, Father Dinneen, who greeted me by saying
Georgetown couldn't figure out why a Southern Baptist with
no foreign language except Latin would want to go to the
Foreign Service School. His tone indicated that they also
couldn't quite figure out why they had let me in. I just
laughed and said maybe we'd figure it out together in a year
or two. I could tell Mother was concerned, so after Father
Dinneen went on to other students, I told her that in a little
while they'd all know why. I suspect I was bluffing, but it
sounded good.

After the preliminaries, we went off to find my dorm
room and meet my roommate. Loyola Hall is at the corner
of Thirty-fifth and N streets just behind the Walsh Building,
which houses the Foreign Service School and is connected to
it. I was assigned Room 225, which was right over the front
entrance on Thirty-fifth and overlooked the house and
beautiful garden of Rhode Island's distinguished senator
Claiborne Pell, who was still in the Senate when I became
President. He and his wife, Nuala, became friends of
Hillary's and mine, and thirty years after staring at the exterior of their grand old house, I finally saw the inside of it.

When Mother and I got to the door of my dorm room, I
was taken aback. The 1964 presidential campaign was in
full swing, and there, plastered on my door, was a Goldwater sticker. I thought I'd left them all behind in Arkansas! It

belonged to my roommate, Tom Campbell, an Irish Catholic from Huntington, Long Island. He came from a staunch conservative Republican family, and had been a football player at Xavier Jesuit High School in New York City. His father was a lawyer who won a local judgeship running on the Conservative Party line. Tom was probably more surprised than I was by his assigned roommate. I was the first Southern Baptist from Arkansas he'd ever met, and to make matters worse, I was a hard-core Democrat for LBJ.

Mother wasn't about to let a little thing like politics stand in the way of good living arrangements. She started talking to Tom as if she'd known him forever, just as she always did with everyone, and before long she won him over. I liked him too and figured we could make a go of it. And we have, through four years of living together at Georgetown and almost forty years of friendship.

Soon enough, Mother left me with a cheerful, stiff-upper-lip parting, and I began to explore my immediate surroundings, beginning with my dorm floor. I heard music coming from down the hall—"Tara's Theme" from *Gone with the Wind*—and followed it, expecting to find another southerner, if not another Democrat. When I came to the room where the music was playing, I found instead a character who defied categories, Tommy Caplan. He was sitting in a rocking chair, the only one on our floor. I learned that he was an only child from Baltimore, that his father was in the jewelry business, and that he had known President Kennedy. He spoke with an unusual clipped accent that sounded aristocratic to me, told me he wanted to be a writer, and regaled me with Kennedy tales. Though I knew I liked him, I couldn't have known then that I had just met another person who would prove to be one of the best friends I'd ever have. In the next four years Tommy would introduce me to Baltimore; to his home on Maryland's Eastern Shore; to the Episcopal church and its liturgy; in New York to the Pierre Hotel and its great Indian curry, to the Carlyle Hotel and my first experience with expensive room service, and to the "21" Club, where several of us celebrated his twenty-first birthday; and to Massachusetts and Cape Cod, where I nearly drowned after failing to hold on to a barnacle-covered rock in an effort that shredded my hands, arms, chest, and legs. Trying desperately to get back to shore, I was saved by a fortuitous long, narrow sandbar and a helping hand from Tommy's old school friend, Fife Symington, later Republican governor of Arizona. (If he could have foreseen the future, he might have had second thoughts!) In return, I introduced Tommy to Arkansas, southern folkways, and grassroots politics. I think I made a good trade.

Over the next several days, I met other students and started classes. I also figured out how to live on twenty-five dollars a week. Five dollars came off the top for the required five dress shirts, and I decided to eat on a dollar a day Monday through Friday, and allocate another dollar to weekend meals, so that I'd have fourteen dollars left to go out on Saturday night. In 1964, I could actually take a date to dinner for fourteen dollars, sometimes a movie too, though I had to let the girl order first to make sure our combined order plus a tip didn't go over my budget. Back then there were a lot of good restaurants in Georgetown where fourteen dollars would go that far. Besides, in the first few months I didn't have a date every Saturday, so I was often a little ahead on my budget.

It wasn't too hard to get by on a dollar a day the rest of the time—I always felt I had plenty of money, even enough to cover the extra cost of a school dance or some other special event. At Wisemiller's Deli, just across Thirty-sixth Street from the Walsh Building, where most of my classes were, I got coffee and two doughnuts for twenty cents every morning, the first time in my life I ever drank coffee, a habit I still try to lick now and then, with limited success. At lunch, I splurged to thirty cents. Half of it bought a Hostess fried pie, apple or cherry; the other half went for a sixteen-ounce Royal Crown Cola. I loved those RCs and was really sad when they quit producing them. Dinner was more expensive, fifty cents. I usually ate at the Hoya Carry Out, a couple of blocks from our dorm, which despite its name had a counter where you could enjoy your meal. Eating there was half the fun. For fifteen cents, I got another big soft drink, and for thirty-five cents, a great tuna fish sandwich on rye, so big you could barely get your mouth around it. For eighty-five cents you could get a roast beef sandwich just as big. Once in a while, when I hadn't blown the whole fourteen dollars the previous Saturday night, I would get one of those.

But the real attractions of the Hoya Carry Out were the proprietors, Don and Rose. Don was a husky character with a tattoo on one of his bulging biceps, back when tattoos were a rarity rather than a common sight on the bodies of rock stars, athletes, and hip young people. Rose had a big beehive hairdo, a nice face, and a great figure, which she showed off to good effect in tight sweaters, tighter pants, and spiked heels. She was a big draw for boys with small budgets and large imaginations, and Don's good-natured but vigilant presence guaranteed that all we did was eat. When Rose was at work, we ate slowly enough to ensure good digestion.

In my first two years, I rarely ventured beyond the confines of the university and its immediate surroundings, a small area bordered by M Street and the Potomac River to the south, Q Street to the north, Wisconsin Avenue to the east, and the university to the west. My favorite haunts in Georgetown were the Tombs, a beer hall in a cellar below the 1789 Restaurant, where most of the students went for beer and burgers; Billy Martin's restaurant, with good food and atmosphere within my budget; and the Cellar Door, just down the hill from my dorm on M Street. It had great live music. I heard Glenn Yarborough, a popular sixties folksinger; the great jazz organist Jimmy Smith; and a now forgotten group called the Mugwumps, who broke up shortly after I came to Georgetown. Two of the men formed a new, more famous band, the Lovin' Spoonful, and the lead singer, Cass Elliot, became Mama Cass of the Mamas and the Papas. Sometimes the Cellar Door opened on Sunday afternoon, when you could nurse a Coke and listen to the Mugwumps for hours for just a dollar.

Though occasionally I felt cooped up in Georgetown, most days I was happy as a clam, absorbed in my classes and friends. However, I was also grateful for my few trips out of the cocoon. Several weeks into my first semester, I went to the Lisner Auditorium to hear Judy Collins sing. I can still see her, standing alone on the stage with her long blond hair, floor-length cotton dress, and guitar. From that day on, I was a huge Judy Collins fan. In December 1978, Hillary and I were on a brief vacation to London after the first time I was elected governor. One day as we window-shopped down King's Road in Chelsea, the loudspeaker of a store blared out Judy's version of Joni Mitchell's "Chelsea Morning." We agreed on the spot that if we ever had a daughter we'd call her Chelsea.

Though I didn't leave the Georgetown environs often, I did manage two trips to New York my first semester. I went home with Tom Campbell to Long Island for Thanksgiving. LBJ had won the election by then, and I enjoyed arguing politics with Tom's father. I goaded him one night by asking if the nice neighborhood they lived in had been organized under a "protective" covenant, under which homeowners committed not to sell to members of proscribed groups, usually blacks. They were common until the Supreme Court ruled them unconstitutional. Mr. Campbell said yes, the area they lived in had been established under a covenant, but it ran not against blacks but Jews. I lived in a southern town with two synagogues and a fair number of anti-Semites who referred to Jews as "Christ killers," but I was surprised to find anti-Semitism alive and well in New York. I guess I should have been reassured to know the South didn't have a corner on racism or anti-Semitism, but I wasn't.

A few weeks before the Thanksgiving trip, I got my first bite at the Big Apple when I traveled to New York City with the Georgetown band, pretty much a ragtag outfit. We practiced only once or twice a week, but we were good enough to be invited to play a concert at a small Catholic school, St. Joseph's College for Women, in Brooklyn. The concert went fine, and at the mixer afterward I met a student who invited me to walk her home and have a Coke with her and her mother. It was my first foray into one of the endless apartment buildings that house the vast majority of New Yorkers, poor to rich. There was no elevator, so we had to walk up several flights to reach her place. It seemed so small to me then, accustomed as I was to Arkansas' one-story houses with yards, even for people of modest means. All I remember about the encounter is that the girl and her mother seemed incredibly nice, and I was amazed that you could develop such outgoing personalities living in such confined spaces.

After I said good night, I was on my own in the big city. I hailed a cab and asked to go to Times Square. I had never seen so many bright neon lights. The place was loud, fast, and throbbing with life, some of it on the seamy side. I saw my first streetwalker, hitting on a hapless archetype: a pathetic-looking guy wearing a dark suit, crew cut, and thick black horn-rimmed glasses and carrying a briefcase. He was both tempted and terrified. Terror won out. He walked on; she smiled, shrugged, and went back to work. I checked out the theaters and storefronts, and one bright sign caught my eye—Tad's Steaks—advertising big steaks for $1.59.

It seemed too good to pass up, so I went in, got my steak, and found a table. Sitting near me were an angry boy and his heartbroken mother. He was giving her a verbal beating with the words, "It's cheap, Mama. It's cheap." She kept saying the salesman had told her it was nice. Over the next few minutes I pieced the story together. She had saved up enough money to buy her son a record player that he wanted badly. The problem was that it was a standard high-fidelity system, called "hi-fi," but he wanted one of the new stereo systems that had much better sound, and apparently more status among fashion-conscious kids. With all her scrimping, his mother couldn't afford it. Instead of being grateful, the kid was screaming at her in public, "Everything we have is cheap! I wanted a nice one!" It made me sick. I wanted to slug him, to scream back at him that he was lucky to have a mother who loved him so much, who put food on his plate and clothes on his back with what was almost certainly a deadly dull job that paid too little. I got up and walked out in disgust, without finishing my bargain steak. That incident had a big impact on me, I guess because of what my own mother had done and endured. It made me more sensitive to the daily struggles of women and men who do things we want someone else to do but don't want to pay much for. It made me hate ingratitude more and resolve to be more grateful myself. And it made me even more determined to enjoy life's lucky breaks without taking them too seriously, knowing that one turn of fate's screw could put me back to square one or worse.

Not long after I got back from New York, I left the band to concentrate on my studies and student government. I won the election for freshman class president in one of my better campaigns, waged to an electorate dominated by Irish and Italian Catholics from the East. I don't remember how I decided to go for it, but I had a lot of help and it was exciting. There were really no issues and not much patronage, so the race boiled down to grassroots politics and one speech. One of my campaign workers wrote me a note showing the depth of our canvassing: "Bill: problems in New Men's; Hanover picking up lots of votes. There are possibilities on 3rd (Pallen's) floor Loyola—down at the end towards the pay phone. Thanks to Dick Hayes. See you tomorrow. Sleep well Gentlemen. King." King was John King, a five-foot-five dynamo who became the coxswain of the Georgetown crew team and study partner of our classmate Luci Johnson, the President's daughter, who once invited him to dinner at the White House, earning our admiration and envy.

On the Tuesday before the election, the class gathered to hear our campaign speeches. I was nominated by Bob Billingsley, a gregarious New Yorker whose Uncle Sherman had owned the Stork Club and who told me great stories of all the stars who had come there from the twenties on. Bob said I had a record of leadership and was "a person who will get things done, and done well." Then came my turn. I raised no issue and promised only to serve "in whatever capacity is needed at any time," whether I won or lost, and to give the election "a spirit which will make our class a little bit stronger and a little bit prouder when the race is over." It was a modest effort, as it should have been; as the saying goes, I had much to be modest about.

The stronger of my two opponents tried to inject some gravity into an inherently weightless moment when he told us he was running because he didn't want our class to fall "into the bottomless abyss of perdition." I didn't know much about that—it sounded like a place you'd go for collaborating with Communists. This bottomless remark was over the top, and was my first big break. We worked like crazy and I was elected. After the votes were counted, my friends collected a lot of nickels, dimes, and quarters so that I could call home on the nearest pay phone and tell my family I had won. It was a happy conversation. I could tell there was no trouble on the other end of the line, and Mother could tell I was getting over my homesickness.

Though I enjoyed student government, the trips to New York, and just being in the Georgetown area, my classes were the main event of my freshman year. For the first time I had to work to learn. I had one big advantage: all six of my courses were taught by interesting, able people. We all had to study a foreign language. I chose German because I was interested in the country and impressed by the clarity and precision of the language. Dr. von Ihering, the German professor, was a kindly man who had hidden from the Nazis in the loft of a farmhouse after they began burning books, including the children's books he wrote. Arthur Cozzens, the geography professor, had a white goatee and a quaint professional manner. I was bored in his class until he told us that, geologically, Arkansas was one of the most interesting places on earth, because of its diamond, quartz crystal, bauxite, and other mineral deposits and formations.

I took logic from Otto Hentz, a Jesuit who had not yet been ordained as a priest. He was bright, energetic, and concerned about the students. One day he asked me if I'd like to have a hamburger with him for dinner. I was flattered and agreed, and we drove up Wisconsin Avenue to a Howard Johnson's. After a little small talk, Otto turned serious. He asked me if I had ever considered becoming a Jesuit. I laughed and replied, "Don't I have to become a Catholic first?" When I told him I was a Baptist and said, only half in jest, that I didn't think I could keep the vow of celibacy even if I were Catholic, he shook his head and said, "I can't believe it. I've read your papers and exams. You write like a Catholic. You think like a Catholic." I used to tell this story to Catholic groups on the campaign trail in Arkansas, assuring them I was the closest thing they could get to a Catholic governor.

Another Jesuit professor, Joseph Sebes, was one of the most remarkable men I've ever known. Lean and stoop-shouldered, he was a gifted linguist whose primary interest was Asia. He had been working in China when the Communists prevailed, and spent some time in captivity, much of it in a small hole in the ground. The abuse damaged his stomach, cost him a kidney, and kept him in poor health for much of the rest of his life. He taught a course called Comparative Cultures. It should have been entitled Religions of the World: we studied Judaism, Islam, Buddhism, Shintoism, Confucianism, Taoism, Hinduism, Jainism, Zoroastrianism, and other faiths. I loved Sebes and learned a lot from him about how people the world over defined God, truth, and the good life. Knowing how many of the students came from foreign countries, he offered everyone the chance to take the final exam orally—in nine languages. In the second semester I got an A, one of only four that were given, and one of my proudest academic achievements.

My other two teachers were real characters. Robert Irving taught English to freshmen who were unprepared for his rapid-fire, acid commentary on the propensity of freshmen to be verbose and imprecise. He wrote withering comments in the margins of essays, calling one of his students "a capricious little bilge pump," responding to another's expression of chagrin with "turned into a cabbage, did you?" My papers received more pedestrian rebukes: in the margins or at the end, Dr. Irving wrote "awk" for awkward, "ugh," "rather dull, pathetic." On one paper I saved, he finally wrote "clever and thoughtful," only to follow it by asking me to "next time be a sport" and write my essay on "better paper"! One day Dr. Irving read aloud an essay one of his former students had written on Marvell to illustrate the importance of using language with care. The student noted that Marvell loved his wife even after she died, then added the unfortunate sentence, "Of course physical love, for the most part, ends after death." Irving roared, "For the most part! For the most part! I suppose to some people, there's nothing better on a warm day than a nice cold corpse!" That was a little rich for a bunch of eighteen-year-old Catholic school kids and one Southern Baptist. Wherever he is today, I dread the thought of Dr. Irving reading this book, and can only imagine the scorching comments he's scribbling in the margins.

The most legendary class at Georgetown was Professor Carroll Quigley's Development of Civilizations, a requirement for all freshmen, with more than two hundred people in each class. Though difficult, the class was wildly popular because of Quigley's intellect, opinions, and antics. The antics included his discourse on the reality of paranormal phenomena, including his claim to have seen a table rise off the floor and a woman take flight at a séance, and his lecture condemning Plato's elevation of absolute rationality over observed experience, which he delivered every year at the end of the course. He always closed the lecture by ripping apart a paperback copy of Plato's *Republic*, then throwing it across the room, shouting, "Plato is a fascist!"

The exams were filled with mind-bending questions like "Write a brief but well-organized history of the Balkan Peninsula from the start of the Würm Glacier to the time of Homer" and "What is the relationship between the process of cosmic evolution and the dimension of abstraction?"

Two of Quigley's insights had a particularly lasting impact. First, he said that societies have to develop organized instruments to achieve their military, political, economic, social, religious, and intellectual objectives. The problem, according to Quigley, is that all instruments eventually become "institutionalized"—that is, vested interests more committed to preserving their own prerogatives than to meeting the needs for which they were created. Once this

happens, change can come only through reform or circum-
vention of the institutions. If these fail, reaction and decline
set in.

His second lasting insight concerned the key to the
greatness of Western civilization, and its continuing capacity for reform and renewal. He said our civilization's success
is rooted in unique religious and philosophical convictions:
that man is basically good; that there is truth, but no finite
mortal has it; that we can get closer to the truth only by
working together; and that through faith and good works,
we can have a better life in this world and a reward in the
next. According to Quigley, these ideas gave our civilization
its optimistic, pragmatic character and an unwavering belief
in the possibility of positive change. He summed up our ide-
ology with the term "future preference," the belief that "the
future can be better than the past, and each individual has a
personal, moral obligation to make it so." From the 1992
campaign through my two terms in office, I quoted Professor Quigley's line often, hoping it would spur my fellow
Americans, and me, to practice what he preached.

By the end of my first year, I had been dating my first long-
term girlfriend for a few months. Denise Hyland was a tall,
freckle-faced Irish girl with kind, beautiful eyes and an
infectious smile. She was from Upper Montclair, New Jersey, the second of six children of a doctor who was studying
to be a priest before he met her mother. Denise and I broke
up at the end of our junior year, but our friendship has
endured.

I was glad to be going home, where at least I'd have old
friends and my beloved hot summer. I had a job waiting for
me at Camp Yorktown Bay, a Navy League camp for poor
kids mostly from Texas and Arkansas, on Lake Ouachita,
the largest of Hot Springs' three lakes and one of the clean-
est in America. You could see the bottom clearly at a depth
of more than thirty feet. The man-made lake was in the
Ouachita National Forest, so development around it, with
the attendant pollution runoff, was limited.

For several weeks, I got up early every morning and

drove out to the camp, twenty miles or so away, where I supervised swimming, basketball, and other camp activities. A lot of the kids needed a week away from their lives. One came from a family of six kids and a single mother and didn't have a penny to his name when he arrived. His mother was moving and he didn't know where he'd be living when he got back. I talked with one boy who tried unsuccessfully to swim and was in bad shape when he was pulled out of the lake. He said it was nothing: in his short life, he'd already swallowed his tongue, been poisoned, survived a bad car wreck, and lost his father three months earlier.

The summer passed quickly, full of good times with my friends and interesting letters from Denise, who was in France. There was one last terrible incident with Daddy. One day he came home early from work, drunk and mad. I was over at the Yeldells', but luckily, Roger was home. Daddy went after Mother with a pair of scissors and pushed her into the laundry room off the kitchen. Roger ran out the front door and over to the Yeldells' screaming, "Bubba, help! Daddy's killing Dado!" (When Roger was a baby he could say "Daddy" before he could say "Mother," so he created the term "Dado" for her, and he used it for a long time afterward.) I ran back to the house, pulled Daddy off Mother, and grabbed the scissors from him. I took Mother and Roger to the living room, then went back and reamed Daddy out. When I looked into his eyes I saw more fear than rage. Not long before, he had been diagnosed with cancer of the mouth and throat. The doctors recommended radical, and disfiguring, surgery, but he refused, so they treated him as best they could. This incident took place early in the two-year period leading to his death, and I think it was his shame at the way he'd lived and his fear of dying that drove him to what would be his last bad outburst. After that, he still drank, but he became more withdrawn and passive.

This incident had a particularly devastating effect on my brother. Almost forty years later, he told me how humiliated he'd felt running for assistance, how helpless he felt that he couldn't stop his father, how irrevocable his hatred was

after that. I realized then how foolish I'd been, in the immediate aftermath of the episode, to revert to our family policy
of just pretending nothing had happened and going back to
"normal." Instead, I should have told Roger that I was very
proud of him; that it was his alertness, love, and courage
that had saved Mother; that what he did was harder than
what I had done; that he needed to let go of his hatred,
because his father was sick, and hating his father would
only spread the sickness to him. Oh, I often wrote to Roger
and called him a lot when I was away; I encouraged him in
his studies and activities and told him I loved him. But I
missed the deep scarring and the trouble it would inevitably
bring. It took Roger a long time and a lot of self-inflicted
wounds to finally get to the source of the hurt in his heart.

Though I still had some concerns about Mother's and
Roger's safety, I believed Daddy when he promised he was
through with violence, and besides, he was losing the capacity to generate it, so I was ready when the time came to go
back to Georgetown for my second year. In June, I had been
awarded a $500 scholarship, and the requirement to wear
tie and shirt to class had been scrapped, so I was looking
forward to a more affluent existence on my twenty-five dollars a week. I also had been reelected president of my class,
this time with a real program concentrating on campus
issues, including nondenominational religious services and a
community-service initiative we took over from the outgoing senior class: GUCAP, the Georgetown University Community Action Program, which sent student volunteers into
poor neighborhoods to help kids with their studies. We also
tutored adults working for high school diplomas through an
extension program, and did whatever else we could to help
families struggling to get by. I went a few times, although
not as often as I should have. Along with what I knew from
growing up in Arkansas, I saw enough of inner-city Washington to convince me that volunteer charity alone would
never be enough to overcome the grinding combination of
poverty, discrimination, and lack of opportunity that held
so many of my fellow citizens back. It made my support for

President Johnson's civil rights, voting rights, and anti-poverty initiatives even stronger.

My second year, like the first, was primarily focused on class work, really for the last time. From then on, through my final two years at Georgetown, the stay in Oxford, and law school, my formal studies increasingly fought a losing battle with politics, personal experiences, and private explorations.

For now, there was more than enough to hold my attention in the classroom, starting with second-year German, Mary Bond's absorbing course on major British writers, and Ulrich Allers's History of Political Thought. Allers was a gruff German who noted these few words on a paper I wrote on the ancient Athenian legal system: "Plodding but very decent." At the time, I felt damned with faint praise. After I had been President a few years, I would have killed to be called that.

I made a C in Joe White's microeconomics class first semester. Professor White also taught macroeconomics second semester, and I got an A in that class. I suppose both grades were harbingers, since as President I did a good job with the nation's economy and a poor job with my personal economic situation, at least until I left the White House.

I studied European history with Luis Aguilar, a Cuban expatriate who had been a leader of the democratic opposition to Batista before he was overthrown by Castro. Once, Aguilar asked me what I intended to do with my life. I told him that I wanted to go home and get into politics but that I was becoming interested in a lot of other things too. He replied wistfully, "Choosing a career is like choosing a wife from ten girlfriends. Even if you pick the most beautiful, the most intelligent, the kindest woman, there is still the pain of losing the other nine." Though he loved teaching and was good at it, I had the feeling that for Professor Aguilar, Cuba was those other nine women rolled into one.

My most memorable class sophomore year was Professor Walter Giles's U.S. Constitution and Government, a course he taught largely through Supreme Court cases. Giles was a redheaded, crew-cut confirmed bachelor whose life was filled by his students, his love for the Constitution and social justice, and his passion for the Washington Redskins, win or lose. He invited students to his house for dinners, and a lucky few even got to go with him to see the Redskins play. Giles was a liberal Democrat from Oklahoma, not common then and rare enough today to place him under the protection of the Endangered Species Act.

I think he took an interest in me partly because I was from a state that bordered his own, though he liked to kid me about it. By the time I got to his class I had embraced my lifelong affinity for sleep deprivation and had developed the sometimes embarrassing habit of falling asleep for five or ten minutes in class, after which I'd be fine. I sat in the front row of Giles's big lecture class, a perfect foil for his biting wit. One day as I was napping, he noted loudly that a certain Supreme Court ruling was so crystal clear anyone could understand it, "unless, of course, you're from some hick town in Arkansas." I awoke with a start to peals of laughter from my classmates and never fell asleep on him again.

TEN

AFTER MY SOPHOMORE YEAR I went home without a job but with a clear idea of what I wanted to do. It was the end of an era in Arkansas—after six terms, Orval Faubus wasn't running for reelection as governor. Finally our state would have a chance to move beyond the scars of Little Rock and the stains of cronyism that also tainted his later years. I wanted to work in the governor's race, both to learn about politics and to do what little I could to put Arkansas on a more progressive course.

The pent-up ambitions from the Faubus years propelled several candidates into the race, seven Democrats and one very big Republican, Winthrop Rockefeller, the fifth of the six children of John D. Rockefeller Jr., who left his father's empire to oversee the charitable efforts of the Rockefeller Foundation; left his father's conservative, anti-labor politics under the influence of his more liberal wife, Abby, and the great Canadian liberal politician Mackenzie King; and, finally, left his father's conservative religious views to found the interdenominational Riverside Church in New York City with Harry Emerson Fosdick.

Winthrop had seemed destined to be the black sheep of the family. He was expelled from Yale and went to work in the Texas oil fields. After distinguished service in World War II, he married a New York socialite and reacquired his reputation as a hard-partying dilettante. In 1953, he moved to Arkansas, partly because he had a wartime buddy from there who interested him in the possibilities of setting up a ranching operation, and partly because the state had a thirty-day divorce law and he was eager to end his brief first marriage. Rockefeller was a huge man, about six feet four, weighing about 250 pounds. He really took to Arkansas, where everybody called him Win, not a bad name for a politician. He always wore cowboy boots and a white Stetson hat, which became his trademark. He bought a huge chunk of Petit Jean Mountain, about fifty miles west of Little Rock, became a successful breeder of Santa Gertrudis cattle, and married his second wife, Jeannette.

As he settled into his adopted state, Rockefeller worked hard to shed the playboy image that had dogged him in New York. He built up the small Arkansas Republican Party and worked to bring industry to our poor state. Governor Faubus appointed him chairman of the Arkansas Industrial Development Commission, and he brought in a lot of new jobs. In 1964, impatient with Arkansas' backward image, he challenged Faubus for governor. Everybody appreciated what he had done, but Faubus had an organization in every county; most people, especially in rural Arkansas, still supported his segregationist position over Rockefeller's pro–civil rights stance; and Arkansas was still a Democratic state.

Also, the painfully shy Rockefeller was a poor speaker, a problem aggravated by his legendary drinking habits, which also made him so late so often that he made me look punctual. Once, he arrived inebriated and more than an hour late to address the chamber of commerce banquet in Wynne, county seat of Cross County, in eastern Arkansas. When he got up to speak, he said, "I'm glad to be here in—" When he realized he didn't know where he was, he whispered to the master of ceremonies, "Where am I?" The man whispered back, "Wynne." He asked again and got the same answer. Then he boomed out, "Damn it, I know my name! Where am I?" That story crossed the state like wildfire, but was usually told good-naturedly, because everybody knew Rockefeller was an Arkansan by choice and had the state's best interests at heart. In 1966, Rockefeller was running again, but even with Faubus gone, I didn't think he could make it.

Besides, I wanted to back a progressive Democrat. My sentimental favorite was Brooks Hays, who had lost his seat in Congress in 1958 for supporting the integration of Little Rock Central High. He was defeated by a segregationist optometrist, Dr. Dale Alford, in a write-in campaign, which succeeded partly because of the use of stickers with his name on them that could be plastered on ballots by voters who couldn't write but were "smart" enough to know that blacks and whites shouldn't go to school together. Hays was a devout Christian who had served as president of the Southern Baptist Convention before the majority of my fellow Baptists decided that only conservatives could lead them, or the country. He was a marvelous man, bright, humble, funny as all get-out, and kind to a fault, even to his opponent's young campaign workers.

Ironically, Dr. Alford was in the race for govenor, too, and he couldn't win either, because the racists had a far more fervent champion in Justice Jim Johnson, who had risen from humble roots in Crossett, in southeast Arkansas, to the state supreme court on rhetoric that won the endorsement of the Ku Klux Klan in the governor's race. He thought Faubus was too soft on civil rights; after all, he had appointed a few blacks to state boards and commissions. With Faubus, who had genuine populist impulses, racism was a political imperative. He preferred improving schools and nursing homes, building roads, and reforming the state mental hospital to race-baiting. It was just the price of staying in office. With Johnson, racism was theology. He thrived on hate. He had sharp features and bright, wild eyes, giving him a "lean and hungry" look that would have made Shakespeare's Cassius green with envy. And he was a savvy politician who knew where his voters were. Instead of going to the endless campaign rallies where the other candidates spoke, he traveled all over the state on his own, with a country-and-western band, which he used to pull in a crowd. Then he would whip them into a frenzy with tirades against blacks and their traitorous white sympathizers.

I didn't see it at the time, but he was building strength among people the other candidates couldn't reach: people upset with federal activism in civil rights, scared by the Watts riots and other racial disturbances, convinced the War on Poverty was socialist welfare for blacks, and frustrated with their own economic conditions. Psychologically, we're all a complex mixture of hopes and fears. Each day we wake up with the scales tipping a bit one way or the other. If they go too far toward hopefulness, we can become naïve and unrealistic. If the scales tilt too far the other way, we can get consumed by paranoia and hatred. In the South, the dark side of the scales has always been the bigger problem. In 1966, Jim Johnson was just the man to tip them in that direction.

The best candidate with a good shot at winning was another supreme court justice and a former attorney general, Frank Holt. He had the support of most of the courthouse crowd and the big financial interests, but he was more progressive on race than Faubus, and completely honest and decent. Frank Holt was admired by just about everybody who knew him (except those who thought he was too easygoing to make any real change), had wanted to be governor all his life, and also wanted to redeem his family's legacy: his brother, Jack, who was more of an old-fashioned southern populist, had lost a hot Senate race to our conservative senior senator, John McClellan, a few years before.

My uncle Raymond Clinton was a big supporter of Holt's and told me he thought he could get me on the campaign. Holt already had secured the support of a number of student leaders from Arkansas colleges, who called themselves the "Holt Generation." Before long I got hired at fifty dollars a week. I think Uncle Raymond paid my way. Since I had been living on twenty-five dollars a week at Georgetown, I felt rich.

The other students were a little older and a lot better connected than I was. Mac Glover had been president of the University of Arkansas student body; Dick King was president of the student body at Arkansas State Teachers College; Paul Fray was president of the Young Democrats at Ouachita Baptist; Bill Allen was a former Arkansas Boys State governor and student leader at Memphis State, just across the Mississippi River from Arkansas; Leslie Smith was a beautiful, smart girl from a powerful political family who had been Arkansas Junior Miss.

At the start of the campaign, I was definitely a second stringer in the Holt Generation. My assignments included nailing "Holt for Governor" signs on trees, trying to get people to put his bumper stickers on their cars, and handing out his brochures at rallies around the state. One of the most important rallies, then and later when I became a candidate, was the Mount Nebo Chicken Fry. Mount Nebo is a beautiful spot overlooking the Arkansas River in Yell County, in western Arkansas, where the Clintons originally settled. People would show up for the food, the music, and a long stream of speeches by candidates, beginning with those running for local office and ending with those running for governor.

Not long after I got there and began working the crowd, our opponents started to arrive. Judge Holt was running late. When his opponents began speaking, he still wasn't there. I was getting worried. This was not an event to miss. I went to a pay phone and somehow tracked him down, which was a lot harder before cell phones. He said that he just couldn't get there before the speeches were over, and that I should speak for him. I was surprised and asked if he was sure. He said I knew what he stood for and I should just tell the people that. When I told the event organizers Judge Holt couldn't make it and asked if I could speak in his place, I was scared to death; it was much worse than speaking for myself. After I finished, the people gave me a polite reception. I don't remember what I said, but it must have been okay, because after that, along with my sign and bumper-sticker duties, I was asked to stand in for Judge Holt at a few smaller rallies he couldn't attend. There were so many, no candidate could make them all. Arkansas has seventy-five counties, and several counties held more than one rally.

After a few weeks, the campaign decided that the judge's wife, Mary, and his daughters, Lyda and Melissa, should go on the road to cover places he couldn't. Mary Holt was a tall, intelligent, independent woman who owned a fashionable dress shop in Little Rock; Lyda was a student at Mary Baldwin College in Staunton, Virginia, where Woodrow Wilson was born; Melissa was in high school. They were all attractive and articulate, and they all adored Judge Holt and

were really committed to the campaign. All they needed was
a driver. Somehow I was chosen.

We crisscrossed the state. We were gone a week at a time,
coming back to Little Rock to wash our clothes and recharge
for another lap. It was great fun. I really got to know the
state and learned a lot from hours of conversation with
Mary and her daughters. One night we went to Hope for a
rally on the courthouse steps. Because my grandmother was
in the crowd, Mary graciously invited me to speak to the
hometown folks, though Lyda was supposed to do it. I think
they both knew I wanted the chance to show that I'd grown
up. The crowd gave me a good listen and I even got a nice
write-up in the local paper, the *Hope Star*, which tickled
Daddy because when he had the Buick dealership in Hope,
the editor disliked him so much he got an ugly mongrel dog,
named him Roger, and frequently let the dog loose near the
Buick place so that he could go down the street after him
shouting, "Come here, Roger! Here, Roger!"

That night I took Lyda to see the house where I had
spent my first four years and the wooden railroad overpass
where I'd played. The next day we went out to the cemetery
to visit the graves of Mary Holt's family, and I showed them
my father's and grandfather's graves.

I treasure the memories of those road trips. I was used to
being bossed around by women, so we got along well, and I
think I was useful to them. I changed flat tires, helped a family get out of a burning house, and got eaten alive by mos-
quitoes so big you could feel them puncture your skin. We
passed the hours of driving by talking about politics, people, and books. And I think we got some votes.

Not long before the Hope rally, the campaign decided to
put on a fifteen-minute TV program featuring the students
who were working for Judge Holt; they thought it would
position him as the candidate of Arkansas' future. Several of
us spoke for a couple of minutes about why we were supporting him. I don't know if it did any good, but I enjoyed
my first TV appearance, though I didn't get to watch it. I
had to speak at yet another rally in Alread, a remote community in Van Buren County, in the mountains of north-

central Arkansas. The candidates who made it way up there usually got the votes, and I was beginning to realize that we needed all we could get.

As the hot summer weeks passed, I saw more and more evidence that the Old South hadn't given up the ghost, and the New South wasn't yet powerful enough to chase it away. Most of our schools were still segregated, and resistance remained strong. One county courthouse in the Mississippi Delta still had "white" and "colored" designations on the doors of the public restrooms. When I asked one elderly black lady in another town to vote for Judge Holt, she said she couldn't because she hadn't paid her poll tax. I told her that Congress had eliminated the poll tax two years earlier and all she had to do was register. I don't know if she did.

Still, there were signs of a new day. While campaigning in Arkadelphia, thirty-five miles south of Hot Springs, I met the leading candidate for the south Arkansas congressional seat, a young man named David Pryor. He was clearly a progressive who thought if he could just meet enough people he could persuade most of them to vote for him. He did it in 1966, did it again in the governor's race in 1974, and again in the Senate race in 1978. By the time he retired, much to my dismay, from the Senate in 1996, David Pryor was the most popular politician in Arkansas, with a fine progressive legacy. Everybody thought of him as their friend, including me.

The kind of retail politics Pryor mastered was important in a rural state like Arkansas, where more than half the people lived in towns with fewer than five thousand people, and tens of thousands just lived "out in the country." We were still in the days before television ads, especially negative ones, assumed the large role in elections they have now. Candidates mostly bought television time to look into the camera and talk to voters. They also were expected to visit the courthouses and main businesses in every county seat, go into the kitchen of every café, and campaign in sale barns, where livestock are auctioned. The county fairs and pie suppers were fertile territory. And, of course, every

weekly newspaper and radio station expected a visit and an
ad or two. That's how I learned politics. I think it works
better than TV air wars. You could talk, but you had to listen, too. You had to answer voters' tough questions face-to-
face. Of course, you could still be demonized, but at least
your adversaries had to work harder to do it. And when you
took a shot at your opponent, you had to take it, not hide
behind some bogus committee that expected to make a
killing from your time in office if its attacks destroyed the
other candidate.

Though the campaigns were more personal, they were
far from just personality contests. When there were big
issues at stake, they had to be addressed. And if a strong tide
of public opinion was rolling in, and you couldn't go with
the flow in good conscience, you had to be tough, disciplined, and quick to avoid being washed away.

In 1966, Jim Johnson—or "Justice Jim," as he liked to
be called—was riding the tide and making big, ugly waves.
He attacked Frank Holt as a "pleasant vegetable," and
implied that Rockefeller had had homosexual relations
with black men, a laughable charge considering his earlier
well-earned reputation as a ladies' man. Justice Jim's message was simply the latest version of an old southern song
sung to white voters in times of economic and social uncertainty: You're good, decent, God-fearing people; "they're"
threatening your way of life; you don't have to change, it's
all their fault; elect me and I'll stand up for you just as you
are and kick the hell out of them. The perennial political
divide, Us versus Them. It was mean, ugly, and ultimately
self-defeating for the people who bought it, but as we still
see, when people feel discontented and insecure it often
works. Because Johnson was so extreme in his rhetoric, and
largely invisible on the traditional campaign trail, most
political observers thought it wouldn't work this time. As
election day neared, Frank Holt refused to answer his
attacks, or the attacks from other candidates, who assumed
he was way ahead and also began to hit him for being the
"old-guard machine" candidate. We didn't have many polls

back then and most people didn't put much stock in the few that floated around.

Holt's strategy sounded good to the idealistic young people around him, like me. He simply replied to all charges with a statement that he was completely independent, that he wouldn't respond to unsubstantiated attacks or attack his opponents in return, and that he wanted to win on his own merits "or not at all." I finally learned that phrases like "or not at all" are often used by candidates who forget that politics is a contact sport. The strategy can work when the public mood is secure and hopeful and when the candidate has a platform of serious, specific policy proposals, but in the summer of 1966 the mood was mixed at best, and the Holt platform was too general to inspire much intense feeling. Besides, those who most wanted a candidate who simply embodied opposition to segregation could vote for Brooks Hays.

Despite the attacks on him, most people thought Frank Holt would lead the ticket, but without a majority, and then would win the runoff two weeks later. On July 26, the people spoke, more than 420,000 of them. The results surprised the pundits. Johnson led with 25 percent of the vote, Holt was second with 23 percent, Hays was third with 15 percent, Alford got 13 percent, and the other three split the rest.

We were shocked but not without hope. Judge Holt and Brooks Hays had gotten slightly more votes between them than the segregationist combo of Johnson and Alford. Also, in one of the more interesting legislative races, a long-serving old-guard House member, Paul Van Dalsem, was defeated by a young, progressive, Yale-educated lawyer, Herb Rule. A couple of years earlier Van Dalsem had infuriated supporters of the rising women's movement by saying women should be kept at home, "barefoot and pregnant." That got Herb, later Hillary's partner at the Rose Law Firm, an army of female volunteers, who dubbed themselves "Barefoot Women for Rule."

The outcome of the runoff election was very much up in

the air, because runoffs are about voter turnout, about
which candidate will do a better job of getting his own voters back to the polls, and a better job of persuading those
who voted for candidates who were eliminated or people
who didn't vote the first time to support him. Judge Holt
tried hard to make the runoff a choice between the Old
South and the New South. Johnson didn't exactly undermine that framing of the race when he went on TV to tell
the voters that he stood "with Daniel in the lion's den" and
"with John the Baptist in Herod's court" in opposing god-
less integration. I think somewhere in that talk Justice Jim
even got on Paul Revere's horse.

Though the Holt strategy was smart and Johnson was
willing to fight it out as Old versus New, there were two
problems with Holt's approach. First, the Old South voters
were highly motivated to vote and they were sure Johnson
was their champion, while the New South voters weren't so
sure about Holt. His refusal to really take the gloves off
until late in the race reinforced their doubts and reduced
their incentive to vote. Second, an undetermined number of
Rockefeller supporters wanted to vote for Johnson because
they thought he'd be easier than Holt for their man to beat,
and anyone, Republican or Democrat, could vote in the
Democratic runoff as long as he or she hadn't voted in the
Republican primary. Only 19,646 people had done that,
since Rockefeller was unopposed. On runoff election day,
only 5,000 fewer people voted than in the first primary.
Each candidate got twice as many votes as the first time, and
Johnson won by 15,000 votes, 52 to 48 percent.

I was sick about the outcome. I had come to care deeply
about Judge Holt and his family, to believe he would have
been a better governor than he was a candidate, and to dislike what Justice Jim stood for even more. The only bright
spot was Rockefeller, who actually had a chance to win. He
was a better-organized candidate the second time around.
He spent money as if it was going out of style, even buying
hundreds of bicycles for poor black kids. In the fall he won
with 54.5 percent of the vote. I was very proud of my state.
I had gone back to Georgetown by then and didn't watch

the campaign unfold firsthand, but a lot of people commented that Johnson seemed less animated in the general election. Perhaps it was because his financial support was limited, but there was also a rumor that he might have gotten some "encouragement" from Rockefeller to cool it. I have no idea if that was true or not.

Except for a brief interregnum in the Carter years, when I was President Carter's point man in Arkansas, and when he wanted a federal appointment for his son, Jim Johnson remained way out there on the right, where he grew more and more hostile toward me. In the 1980s, like so many southern conservatives he became a Republican. He ran again for the supreme court and lost. After that, he made his mischief in the background. When I ran for President, he planted ingenious stories, directly and indirectly, with anyone gullible enough to believe them, and got some surprising takers among the so-called eastern liberal media he loved to revile, especially for Whitewater tales. He's a canny old rascal. He must have had a great time conning them, and if the Republicans in Washington had succeeded in running me out of town, he'd have had a good claim to the last laugh.

After the campaign I got to wind down by taking my first trip to the West Coast. A regular customer of Uncle Raymond's wanted a new Buick he didn't have in stock. Uncle Raymond found one at a dealership in Los Angeles, where it was being used as a "demonstrator," a car prospective customers could test-drive to see how they liked it. Dealers often swapped these cars or sold them to one another at a discount. My uncle asked me to fly out to L.A. and drive the car back, along with Pat Brady, whose mother was his secretary, and who had been in my high school class and the band. If we both went, we could drive straight through. We were eager to go, and back then student fares were so cheap Raymond could fly us out for nearly nothing and still make a profit on the car.

We flew into LAX, got the car, and headed home, but not in a straight line. Instead, we took a minor detour to Las

Vegas, a place we thought we'd never have another chance to see. I still remember driving across the flat desert at night with the windows down, feeling the warm, dry air and seeing the bright lights of Vegas beckoning in the distance.

Las Vegas was different then. There were no big theme hotels like the Paris or the Venetian, just the Strip, with its gambling and entertainment. Pat and I didn't have much money, but we wanted to play the slot machines, so we picked a place, got a roll of nickels each, and went to work. Within fifteen minutes I had hit one jackpot and Pat had pulled two. This did not go unnoticed by the regular hostages to the one-armed bandits. They were convinced we were good luck, so every time we left a machine without hitting, people rushed to it, jostling for the right to pull up the jackpot we had left waiting for them. We couldn't understand it. We were convinced that we'd completely used up years of luck in those few minutes, and we didn't want to squander it. We got back on the road with most of our winnings still bulging in our pockets. I don't think anyone carries that many nickels anymore.

After we turned the car in to Uncle Raymond, who didn't seem to mind the side trip, I had to get ready to go back to Georgetown. At the end of the campaign, I had spoken to Jack Holt about my interest in going to work for Senator Fulbright, but I didn't know if anything would come of it. I had written Fulbright for a job the previous spring and had received a letter back saying there were no vacancies but they'd keep my letter on file. I doubted things had changed, but a few days after getting back to Hot Springs, I got a call early in the morning from Lee Williams, Fulbright's administrative assistant. Lee said Jack Holt had recommended me and there was a job opening as an assistant clerk on the Foreign Relations Committee. He said, "You can have a part-time job for $3,500 or a full-time job for $5,000." Even though I was sleepy, I couldn't miss that one. I said, "How about two part-time jobs?" He laughed and said I was just the kind of person he was looking for and I should report for work Monday morning. I was so excited I could have popped. The Foreign Relations Committee under Fulbright had become the center of national debate over foreign policy, especially the escalating war in Vietnam. Now I would witness the drama unfold firsthand, albeit as a flunky. And I would be able to pay for college without any help from Mother and Daddy, taking the financial burden off them and the guilt burden off me. I had worried about how in the world they could afford Daddy's medical treatments on top of the costs of Georgetown. Though I never told anyone at the time, I was afraid I'd have to leave Georgetown and come home, where college was so much less expensive. Now, out of the blue, I had the chance to stay on at Georgetown and work for the Foreign Relations Committee. I owe so much of the rest of my life to Jack Holt for recommending me for that job, and to Lee Williams for giving it to me.

ELEVEN

A COUPLE OF DAYS after Lee Williams called I was packed and ready to drive back to Washington in a gift. Since my new job required me to get to Capitol Hill every day, Mother and Daddy gave me their "old car," a three-year-old white convertible Buick LeSabre with a white and red leather interior. Daddy got a new car every three years or so and turned the old one in to be sold on the used-car lot. This time I replaced the used-car lot and I was ecstatic. It was a beautiful car. Though it got only seven or eight miles to the gallon, gas was cheap, dropping under thirty cents per gallon when there was a "gas war" on.

On my first Monday back in Washington, as instructed, I presented myself in Senator Fulbright's office, the first office on the left in what was then called the New Senate Office Building, now the Dirksen Building. Like the Old Senate Office Building across the street, it is a grand marble edifice, but much brighter. I had a good talk with Lee, then was taken upstairs to the fourth floor, where the Foreign Relations Committee had its offices and hearing room. The committee also had a much grander space in the Capitol building, where the chief of staff, Carl Marcy, and a few of the senior staff worked. There was also a beautiful conference room where the committee could meet privately.

When I arrived at the committee office, I met Buddy Kendrick, the documents clerk, who would be my supervisor, fellow storyteller, and provider of homespun advice over the next two years; Buddy's full-time assistant, Bertie Bowman, a kind, bighearted African-American who moonlighted as a cabdriver and also drove Senator Fulbright on occasion; and my two student counterparts, Phil Dozier from Arkansas and Charlie Parks, a law student from Anniston, Alabama.

I was told I would be taking memos and other materials back and forth between the Capitol and Senator Fulbright's office, including confidential material for which I would have to receive proper government clearance. Beyond that, I would do whatever was required, from reading newspapers and clipping important articles for the staff and interested senators to answering requests for speeches and other materials, to adding names to the committee's mailing list. Keep in mind that this was before computers and e-mail, even before modern copying machines, though while I was there we did graduate from copies made on carbon paper while typing or writing to rudimentary "Xerox" copies. Most of the newspaper articles I clipped were never copied; they were simply put into a big folder every day with a routing sheet that had the names of the committee staff from the chairman on down. Each person would receive and review them, check off his or her name on the sheet, and pass them along. The main mailing lists were kept in the basement. Each name and address was typed onto a small metal plate; then the plates were stored in alphabetical order in file cabinets. When we sent a mailing out, the plates were put into a machine that inked them and stamped the imprints on envelopes as they passed through.

I enjoyed going to the basement to type new names and addresses on plates and put them in file drawers. Since I was always exhausted, I often took a nap down there, sometimes just leaning against the file cabinets. And I really loved reading the newspapers and clipping articles for the staff to read. For nearly two years, every day, I read the *New York Times*, the *Washington Post*, the now defunct *Washington Star*, the *Wall Street Journal*, the *Baltimore Sun*, and the *St. Louis Post-Dispatch*, the last because it was thought the committee should see at least one good "heartland" newspaper. When McGeorge Bundy was President Kennedy's national security advisor, he remarked that any citizen who read six good newspapers a day would know as much as he did. I don't know about that, but after I did what he recommended for sixteen months, I did know enough to survive my Rhodes scholarship interview. And if Trivial Pursuit had been around back then, I might have been national champion.

We also handled requests for documents. The committee produced a lot of them: reports on foreign trips, expert testimony in hearings, and full hearing transcripts. The deeper we got into Vietnam, the more Senator Fulbright and his allies tried to use the hearing process to educate Americans about the complexities of life and politics in North and South Vietnam, the rest of Southeast Asia, and China.

The document room was our regular workplace. In the first year I worked my half day in the afternoon from one to five. Because the committee hearings and other business often ran beyond that, I often stayed after five o'clock and never begrudged it. I liked the people I worked with, and I liked what Senator Fulbright was doing with the committee.

It was easy to fit the job into my daily schedule, partly because in junior year only five courses were required instead of six, partly because some classes started as early as 7 a.m. Three of my requirements—U.S. History and Diplomacy, Modern Foreign Governments, and Theory and Practice of Communism—complemented my new work. Scheduling was also easier because I didn't run again for president of the class.

Every day, I looked forward to the end of classes and the drive to Capitol Hill. It was easier to find parking then. And it was a fascinating time to be there. The vast majority that had carried Lyndon Johnson to his landslide victory in 1964 was beginning to unravel. In a few months the Democrats would see their majorities in the House and Senate diminish in the 1966 midterm elections, as the country moved to the right in reaction to riots, social unrest, and the rise of inflation, and President Johnson escalated both domestic spending and our involvement in Vietnam. He claimed our country could afford both "guns and butter," but the people were beginning to doubt it. In his first two and a half years as President, Johnson had enjoyed the most stunning legislative successes since FDR: the Civil Rights Act of 1964, the

Voting Rights Act of 1965, sweeping anti-poverty legislation, and Medicare and Medicaid, which at last guaranteed medical care for the poor and elderly.

Now, more and more, the attention of the President, the Congress, and the country was turning to Vietnam. As the death toll mounted with no victory in sight, rising opposition to the war took many forms, from protests on campuses to sermons from pulpits, from arguments in coffee shops to speeches on the floor of Congress. When I went to work for the Foreign Relations Committee, I didn't know enough about Vietnam to have a strong opinion, but I was so supportive of President Johnson that I gave him the benefit of the doubt. Still, it was clear that events were conspiring to undermine the magic moment of progress ushered in by his landslide election.

The country was dividing over more than Vietnam. The Watts riots in Los Angeles in 1965 and the rise of militant black activists pushed their sympathizers to the left and their opponents to the right. The Voting Rights Act, of which LBJ was particularly and justifiably proud, had a similar effect, especially as it began to be enforced. Johnson was an uncommonly shrewd politician. He said when he signed the voting rights legislation that he had just killed the Democratic Party in the South for a generation. In fact, the so-called Solid South of the Democrats had been far from solid for a long time. The conservative Democrats had been falling away since 1948, when they recoiled at Hubert Humphrey's barn-burning civil rights speech at the Democratic convention and Strom Thurmond bolted the party to run for President as a Dixiecrat. In 1960, Johnson helped Kennedy hold enough southern states to win, but Kennedy's commitment to enforcing court-ordered integration of southern public schools and universities drove more conservative whites into the Republican fold. In 1964, while losing in a landslide, Goldwater carried five southern states.

However, in 1966 a lot of the white segregationists were still southern Democrats, people like Orval Faubus and Jim Johnson and Governor George Wallace of Alabama. And the Senate was full of them, grand characters like Richard

Russell of Georgia and John Stennis of Mississippi and some others who had no grandeur at all, just power. But President Johnson was right about the impact of the Voting Rights Act and the other civil rights efforts. By 1968, Richard Nixon and George Wallace, running for President as an independent, would both outpoll Humphrey in the South, and since then, the only Democrats to win the White House were two southerners, Jimmy Carter and me. We won enough southern states to get in, with huge black support and a few more white voters than a non-southerner could have gotten. The Reagan years solidified the hold of the Republican Party on white conservative southerners, and the Republicans made them feel welcome.

President Reagan even went so far as to make a campaign speech defending states' rights and, by implication, resistance to federal meddling in civil rights, in Philadelphia, Mississippi, where civil rights workers Andrew Goodman, Michael Schwerner, and James Chaney, two whites and one black, were martyred to the cause in 1964. I always liked President Reagan personally and wished he hadn't done that. In the 2002 midterm elections, even with Colin Powell, Condi Rice, and other minorities holding prominent positions in the Bush administration, Republicans were still winning elections on race, with white backlashes in Georgia and South Carolina over Democratic governors removing the Confederate flag from the Georgia State flag and from the South Carolina Capitol building. Just two years earlier, George W. Bush had campaigned at the notoriously right-wing Bob Jones University in South Carolina, where he declined to take a stand on the flag issue, saying it was a matter for the state to decide. When a Texas school insisted on hoisting the Confederate flag every morning, Governor Bush said it was not a state but a local issue. And they called me slick! President Johnson foresaw all this in 1965, but he did the right thing anyway, and I'm grateful he did.

In the summer of 1966, and even more after the elections that fall, all the foreign and domestic conflicts were apparent in the deliberations of the U.S. Senate. When I went to work there, the Senate was full of big personalities and high drama. I tried to absorb it all. The president pro tempore, Carl Hayden of Arizona, had been in Congress since his state entered the Union in 1912 and in the Senate for forty years. He was bald, gaunt, almost skeletal. Senator Fulbright's brilliant speechwriter Seth Tillman once cracked that Carl Hayden was "the only ninety-year-old man in the world who looks twice his age." The Senate majority leader, Mike Mansfield of Montana, had enlisted to fight in World War I at fifteen, then had become a college professor with a specialty in Asian affairs. He held the post of majority leader for sixteen years, until 1977, when President Carter appointed him ambassador to Japan. Mansfield was a fitness fanatic who walked five miles a day well into his nineties. He was also a genuine liberal and, behind his taciturn façade, something of a wit. He had been born in 1903, two years before Senator Fulbright, and lived to be ninety-eight. Shortly after I became President, Mansfield had lunch with Fulbright. When he asked Fulbright his age and Fulbright said he was eighty-seven, Mansfield replied, "Oh, to be eighty-seven again."

The Republican leader, Everett Dirksen of Illinois, had been essential to passing some of the President's legislation, providing enough liberal Republican votes to overcome the opposition of segregationist southern Democrats. Dirksen had an amazing face, with a large mouth and lots of wrinkles, and an even more amazing voice. Deep and full, it boomed out one pithy phrase after another. Once he hit Democratic spending habits with this ditty: "A billion here, a billion there, pretty soon you're talking about real money." When Dirksen talked it was like hearing the voice of God or a pompous snake-oil salesman, depending on your perspective.

The Senate looked a lot different then from how it looks today. In January 1967, after the Democrats had lost four seats in the midterm elections, they still had a margin of sixty-four to thirty-six—a far more lopsided group than what we usually find today. But the differences then were deep, too, and the lines were not only drawn on party affiliation. A few things have not changed: Robert Byrd of West

Virginia still serves in the Senate. In 1966, he was already the authoritative voice on the rules and history of the body.

Eight states of the Old South still had two Democratic senators each, down from ten before the 1966 elections, but most of them were conservative segregationists. Today, only Arkansas is represented by two Democrats. Oklahoma had two Democrats, California two Republicans. Today it's the reverse. In the inter-mountain West, now solidly Republican, Utah, Idaho, and Wyoming each had one progressive Democratic senator. Indiana, a conservative state, had two liberal Democratic senators, one of whom, Birch Bayh, is the father of current senator Evan Bayh, a gifted leader who might be President someday, but who's not as liberal as his dad was. Minnesota was represented by the brilliant but diffident intellectual Gene McCarthy and future vice president Walter Mondale, who succeeded Hubert Humphrey when he became President Johnson's vice president. Johnson picked Humphrey over Connecticut senator Tom Dodd, one of the chief prosecutors of Nazis at the Nuremberg War Crimes Tribunal. Dodd's son, Chris, now represents Connecticut in the Senate. Al Gore's father was in his last term and was a hero to young southerners like me because he and his Tennessee colleague, Estes Kefauver, were the only two southern senators who refused to sign the so-called Southern Manifesto in 1956, which called for resistance to court-ordered school integration. The fiery populist Ralph Yarborough represented Texas, though the rightward future of the state was emerging with the election in 1961 of a Republican senator, John Tower, and a young Republican congressman from Houston, George Herbert Walker Bush. One of the most interesting senators was Oregon's Wayne Morse, who started out as a Republican, then became an independent, and was by 1966 a Democrat. Morse, who was long-winded but smart and tough, and Democrat Ernest Gruening of Alaska were the only two senators to oppose the Tonkin Gulf resolution in 1964, which LBJ claimed gave him authority to wage the war in Vietnam. The only woman in the Senate was a Republican who smoked a pipe, Margaret Chase Smith of Maine. By 2004, there were fourteen women senators, nine Democrats and five Republicans. Back then there were also a number of influential liberal Republicans, alas, a virtually extinct group today, including Edward Brooke of Massachusetts, the Senate's only African-American; Mark Hatfield of Oregon; Jacob Javits of New York; and George Aiken of Vermont, a crusty old New Englander who thought our Vietnam policy was nuts and tersely suggested we should simply "declare victory and get out."

By far the most famous first-term senator was Robert Kennedy of New York, who joined his brother Ted in 1965, after defeating Senator Kenneth Keating for the seat Hillary now holds. Bobby Kennedy was fascinating. He radiated raw energy. He's the only man I ever saw who could walk stoop-shouldered, with his head down, and still look like a coiled spring about to release into the air. He wasn't a great speaker by conventional standards, but he spoke with such intensity and passion it could be mesmerizing. And if he didn't get everyone's attention with his name, countenance, and speech, he had Brumus, a large, shaggy Newfoundland, the biggest dog I ever saw. Brumus often came to work with Senator Kennedy. When Bobby walked from his office in the New Senate Building to the Capitol to vote, Brumus would walk by his side, bounding up the Capitol steps to the revolving door on the rotunda level, then sitting patiently outside until his master returned for the walk back. Anyone who could command the respect of that dog had mine too.

John McClellan, Arkansas' senior senator, was not merely an ardent conservative. He was also tough as nails, vindictive when crossed, a prodigious worker, and adept at obtaining power and using it, whether to bring federal money home to Arkansas or to pursue people he saw as evildoers. McClellan led a life of ambition and anguish, the difficulties of which bred in him an iron will and deep resentments. The son of a lawyer and farmer, at age seventeen he became the youngest person ever to practice law in Arkansas, when he passed an oral examination with honors after reading law books he had checked out of the traveling library of the Cumberland Law School. After he served in

World War I, he returned home to find that his wife had become involved with another man, and he divorced her, a rare occurrence in Arkansas that long ago. His second wife died of spinal meningitis in 1935, when he was in the House of Representatives. Two years later, he married his third wife, Norma, who was with him for forty years until he died. But his sorrows were far from over. Between 1943 and 1958 he lost all three of his sons: the first to spinal meningitis, the next in a car accident, the last in a small-plane crash.

McClellan lived an eventful but difficult life, the sorrows of which he drowned in enough whiskey to float the Capitol down the Potomac River. After a few years, he decided drunkenness was inconsistent with both his values and his self-image and he gave up liquor completely, sealing the only crack in his armor with his iron will.

By the time I got to Washington, he was chairman of the powerful Appropriations Committee, a position he used to get our state a great deal of money for things like the Arkansas River Navigation System. He served another twelve years, a total of six terms, dying in 1977 after announcing he would not seek a seventh. When I worked on the Hill, McClellan seemed a remote, almost forbidding figure, which is how he wanted to be perceived by most people. After I became attorney general in 1977, I spent quite a bit of time with him. I was touched by his kindness and his interest in my career, and wished he had been able to show the side of him I saw to more people and to reflect it more in his public work.

Fulbright was as different from McClellan as daylight from dark. His childhood had been more carefree and secure, his education more extensive, his mind less dogmatic. He was born in 1905 in Fayetteville, a beautiful Ozark Mountain town in north Arkansas where the University of Arkansas is located. His mother, Roberta, was the outspoken progressive editor of the local paper, the *Northwest Arkansas Times*. Fulbright went to the hometown university, where he was a star student and quarterback of the Arkansas Razorbacks. When he was twenty, he went to

Oxford on a Rhodes scholarship. When he returned two years later, he was a committed internationalist. After law school and a brief stint in Washington as a government lawyer, he came home to teach at the university with his wife, Betty, a delightful, elegant woman who turned out to be a better retail politician than he was and who kept his morose side in check through more than fifty years of marriage, until she died in 1985. I'll never forget one night in 1967 or '68. I was walking alone in Georgetown when I saw Senator and Mrs. Fulbright leaving one of the fashionable homes after a dinner party. When they reached the street, apparently with no one around to see, he took her in his arms and danced a few steps. Standing in the shadows, I saw what a light she was in his life. At thirty-four, Fulbright was named president of the University of Arkansas, the youngest president of a major university in America. He and Betty seemed headed for a long and happy life in the idyllic Ozarks. But after a couple of years, his apparently effortless rise to prominence was abruptly interrupted when the new governor, Homer Adkins, fired him because of his mother's sharply critical editorials.

In 1942, with nothing better to do, Fulbright filed for the open congressional seat in northwest Arkansas. He won, and in his only term in the House of Representatives, he sponsored the Fulbright Resolution, which presaged the United Nations in its call for American participation in an international organization to preserve peace after the end of World War II. In 1944, Fulbright ran for the U.S. Senate and for a chance to get even. His main opponent was his nemesis, Governor Adkins. Adkins had a flair for making enemies, a hazardous trait in politics. Besides getting Fulbright fired, he had made the mistake of opposing John McClellan just two years earlier, going so far as to have the tax returns of McClellan's major supporters audited. As I said, McClellan never forgot or forgave a slight. He worked hard to help Fulbright defeat Adkins, and Fulbright did it. They both got even.

Despite the thirty years they served together in the Senate, Fulbright and McClellan were never particularly close. Neither was prone to personal relationships with other politicians. They did work together to advance Arkansas' economic interests, and voted with the southern bloc against civil rights; beyond that, they didn't have much in common.

McClellan was a pro-military, anti-Communist conservative who wanted to spend tax dollars only on defense, public works, and law enforcement. He was bright but not subtle. He saw things as black or white. He spoke in blunt terms, and if he ever had any doubts about anything, he never revealed them for fear of looking weak. He thought politics was about money and power.

Fulbright was more liberal than McClellan. He was a good Democrat who liked and supported President Johnson until they fell out over the Dominican Republic and Vietnam. He favored progressive taxation, social programs to reduce poverty and inequality, federal aid to education, and more generous American contributions to international institutions charged with alleviating poverty in poor countries. In 1946, he sponsored legislation creating the Fulbright program for international education exchange, which has funded the education of hundreds of thousands of Fulbright scholars from the United States and sixty other countries. He thought politics was about the power of ideas.

On civil rights, Fulbright never spent much time defending his voting record on the merits. He simply said he had to vote with the majority of his constituents on issues like civil rights, areas about which they knew as much as he did, which is just a euphemistic way of saying he didn't want to get beat. He signed the Southern Manifesto after he watered it down a little, and didn't vote for a civil rights bill until 1970, during the Nixon administration, when he also took a leading role in defeating President Nixon's anti–civil rights nominee to the Supreme Court, G. Harrold Carswell.

Despite his civil rights stance, Fulbright was far from gutless. He hated sanctimonious demagogues parading as patriots. When Senator Joe McCarthy of Wisconsin was terrorizing innocent people with his blanket accusations of Communist ties, he intimidated most politicians into silence, even those who loathed him. Fulbright cast the only vote in the Senate against giving McCarthy's special investigative subcommittee more money. He also co-sponsored the resolution censuring McCarthy, which the Senate finally passed after Joseph Welch exposed him to the whole country for the fraud he was. McCarthy came along too soon— he would have been right at home in the crowd that took over the Congress in 1995. But back in the early fifties, a period so vulnerable to anti-Communist hysteria, McCarthy was the nine hundred–pound gorilla. Fulbright took him on before his other colleagues would.

Fulbright didn't shy away from controversy in foreign affairs, either, an area in which, unlike civil rights, he knew more than his constituents did or could know. He decided just to do what he thought was right and hope he could sell it to the voters. He favored multilateral cooperation over unilateral action; dialogue with, not isolation from, the Soviet Union and Warsaw Pact nations; more generous foreign assistance and fewer military interventions; and the winning of converts to American values and interests by the force of our example and ideas, not the force of arms.

Another reason I liked Fulbright was that he was interested in things besides politics. He thought the purpose of politics was to enable people to develop all their faculties and enjoy their fleeting lives. The idea that power was an end in itself, rather than a means to provide the security and opportunity necessary for the pursuit of happiness, seemed to him stupid and self-defeating. Fulbright liked to spend time with his family and friends, took a couple of vacations a year to rest and recharge his batteries, and read widely. He liked to go duck hunting, and he loved golf, shooting his age when he was seventy-eight. He was an engaging conversationalist with an unusual, elegant accent. When he was relaxed, he was eloquent and persuasive. When he got impatient or angry, he exaggerated his speech patterns in a tone of voice that made him seem arrogant and dismissive.

Fulbright had supported the Tonkin Gulf resolution in August 1964, giving President Johnson the authority to respond to apparent attacks on American vessels there, but by the summer of 1966, he had decided our policy in Vietnam was misguided, doomed to fail, and part of a larger pattern of errors that, if not changed, would bring disastrous consequences for America and the world. In 1966, he published his views on Vietnam and his general critique of American foreign policy in his most famous book, *The Arrogance of Power.* A few months after I joined the committee staff, he autographed a copy for me.

Fulbright's essential argument was that great nations get into trouble and can go into long-term decline when they are "arrogant" in the use of their power, trying to do things they shouldn't do in places they shouldn't be. He was suspicious of any foreign policy rooted in missionary zeal, which he felt would cause us to drift into commitments "which though generous and benevolent in content, are so far reaching as to exceed even America's great capacities." He also thought that when we brought our power to bear in the service of an abstract concept, like anti-communism, without understanding local history, culture, and politics, we could do more harm than good. That's what happened with our unilateral intervention in the Dominican Republic's civil war in 1965, where, out of fear that leftist President Juan Bosch would install a Cuban-style Communist government, the United States supported those who had been allied with General Rafael Trujillo's repressive, reactionary, often murderous thirty-year military dictatorship, which ended with Trujillo's assassination in 1961.

Fulbright thought we were making the same mistake in Vietnam, on a much larger scale. The Johnson administration and its allies saw the Vietcong as instruments of Chinese expansionism in Southeast Asia, which had to be stopped before all the Asian "dominoes" fell to communism. That led the United States to support the anti-Communist, but hardly democratic, South Vietnamese government. As South Vietnam proved unable to defeat the Vietcong alone, our support was expanded to include military advisors, and finally to a massive military presence to defend what Fulbright saw as "a weak, dictatorial government which does not command the loyalty of the South Vietnamese people." Fulbright thought Ho Chi Minh, who had been an admirer of Franklin Roosevelt for his opposition to colonialism, was primarily interested in making Vietnam independent of all foreign powers. He believed that Ho, far from being a Chinese puppet, shared the historic Vietnamese antipathy for, and suspicion of, its larger neighbor to the north. Therefore, he did not believe we had a national interest sufficient to justify the giving and taking of so many lives. Still, he did not favor unilateral withdrawal. Instead, he supported an attempt to "neutralize" Southeast Asia, with American withdrawal conditioned on agreement by all parties to self-determination for South Vietnam and a referendum on reunification with North Vietnam. Unfortunately, by 1968, when peace talks opened in Paris, such a rational resolution was no longer possible.

As nearly as I could tell, everyone who worked on the committee staff felt the way Fulbright did about Vietnam. They also felt, increasingly, that the political and military leaders of the Johnson administration consistently overstated the progress of our military efforts. And they set out systematically to make the case for a change in policy to the administration, the Congress, and the country. As I write this, it seems reasonable and straightforward. But Fulbright, his committee colleagues, and the staff were in fact walking a high political tightrope across dangerous rocks. War hawks in both parties accused the committee, and Fulbright in particular, of giving "aid and comfort" to our enemies, dividing our country, and weakening our will to fight on to victory. Still, Fulbright persevered. Though he endured harsh criticism, the hearings helped to galvanize anti-war sentiment, especially among young people, more and more of whom were participating in anti-war rallies and "teach-ins."

In the time I was there, the committee held hearings on such subjects as attitudes of Americans toward foreign policy, China-U.S. relations, possible conflicts between U.S. domestic goals and foreign policy, the impact of the dispute between China and the Soviet Union on the Vietnam conflict, and the psychological aspects of international relations. Distinguished critics of our policy appeared, people like Harrison Salisbury of the *New York Times*; George Kennan, former ambassador to the USSR and author of the idea of "containment" of the Soviet Union; Edwin Reischauer, former ambassador to Japan; distinguished historian Henry Steele Commager; retired general James Gavin; and professor Crane Brinton, an expert on revolutionary movements. Of course, the administration sent up its witnesses, too. One of the most effective was Undersecretary of State Nick Katzenbach, who had a leg up with me at least, because of his civil rights work in President Kennedy's Justice Department. Fulbright also met privately with Secretary of State Dean Rusk, usually for early-morning coffee in Fulbright's office.

I found the dynamics between Rusk and Fulbright fascinating. Fulbright himself had been on Kennedy's short list for secretary of state. Most people thought he was eliminated because of his anti–civil rights record, especially his signing of the Southern Manifesto. Rusk was also a southerner, from Georgia, but he was sympathetic to civil rights and had not faced the political pressure Fulbright had, since he was not in Congress but a member of the foreign policy establishment. Rusk saw the Vietnam conflict in simple, stark terms: It was the battleground of freedom and communism in Asia. If we lost Vietnam, communism would sweep through Southeast Asia with devastating consequences.

I always thought the dramatically different ways Fulbright and Rusk viewed Vietnam were due in part to the very different times when they were young Rhodes scholars in England. When Fulbright went to Oxford in 1925, the Treaty of Versailles ending World War I was being implemented. It imposed harsh financial and political burdens on Germany, and redrew the map of Europe and the Middle East after the collapse of the Austro-Hungarian and Ottoman empires. The humiliation of Germany by the victorious European powers, and the postwar isolationism and protectionism of the United States, reflected in the Senate's rejection of the League of Nations and the passage of the Smoot-Hawley Tariff Act, led to an ultra-nationalist backlash in Germany, the rise of Hitler, and then World War II. Fulbright was loath to make that mistake again. He rarely saw conflicts in black and white, tried to avoid demonizing adversaries, and always looked for negotiated solutions first, preferably in a multilateral context.

By contrast, Rusk was at Oxford in the early thirties, when the Nazis came to power. Later, he followed the hopeless attempts of Prime Minister Neville Chamberlain of Great Britain to negotiate with Hitler, an approach given one of history's most stinging rebukes: appeasement. Rusk equated Communist totalitarianism with Nazi totalitarianism, and despised it as much. The movement of the Soviet Union to control and communize Central and Eastern Europe after World War II convinced him communism was a disease that infected nations with a hostility to personal freedom and an unquenchable aggressiveness. And he was determined not to be an appeaser. Thus, he and Fulbright came to Vietnam from different sides of an unbridgeable intellectual and emotional divide, formed decades before Vietnam appeared on America's radar screen.

The psychological divide was reinforced on the pro-war side by the natural tendency in wartime to demonize one's adversary and by the determination Johnson, Rusk, and others had not to "lose" Vietnam, thus doing lasting damage to America's prestige, and to their own. I saw the same compulsion at work in peacetime when I was President, in my ideological battles with the Republican Congress and their allies. When there is no understanding, respect, or trust, any compromise, much less an admission of error, is seen as weakness and disloyalty, a sure recipe for defeat.

To the Vietnam hawks of the late sixties, Fulbright was the poster boy of gullible naïveté. Naïveté is a problem all well-meaning people have to guard against. But hardheadedness has its own perils. In politics, when you find yourself in a hole, the first rule is to quit digging; if you're blind to the possibility of error or determined not to admit it, you just look for a bigger shovel. The more difficulties we had in Vietnam, the more protests mounted at home, the more troops we sent in. We topped out at more than 540,000 in 1969, before reality finally forced us to change course.

I watched all this unfold with amazement and fascination. I read everything I could, including the material stamped "confidential" and "secret" that I had to deliver from time to time, which showed clearly that our country was being misled about our progress, or lack of it, in the war. And I saw the body count mount, one at a time. Every day Fulbright got a list of the boys from Arkansas who had been killed in Vietnam. I got in the habit of dropping by his office to check the list, and one day I saw the name of my friend and classmate Tommy Young. Just a few days before he was to return home, his jeep ran over a mine. I was so sad. Tommy Young was a big, smart, ungainly, sensitive guy who I thought would grow up to have a good life. Seeing his name on the list, along with others I was sure had more to give and get in life, triggered the first pangs of guilt I felt about being a student and only touching the deaths in Vietnam from a distance. I briefly flirted with the idea of dropping out of school and enlisting in the military—after all, I was a democrat in philosophy as well as party; I didn't feel entitled to escape even a war I had come to oppose. I talked to Lee Williams about it. He said that I'd be crazy to quit school, that I should keep doing my part to end the war, that I wouldn't prove anything by being one more soldier, perhaps one more casualty. Rationally, I could understand that and I went on about my business, but I never felt quite right about it. After all, I was the child of a World War II veteran. I respected the military, even if I thought many of those in charge were clueless, with more guts than brains. So began my personal bout with guilt, one that was fought by many thousands of us who loved our country but hated the war.

Those long-distant days are not easy to re-create for those who didn't live through them. For those who did, little needs to be said. The war took its toll at home, too, even on its most self-confident opponents. Fulbright liked and admired President Johnson. He enjoyed being part of a team he thought was moving America forward, even on civil rights, where he couldn't help. He always wore his game face to work, but he hated being a reviled, isolated outsider. Once, coming to work early in the morning, I saw him walking alone down the corridor toward his office, lost in sadness and frustration, actually bumping into the wall a time or two as he trudged to his damnable duty.

Although the Foreign Relations Committee had to concern itself with other things, Vietnam overshadowed everything else for the committee members and for me. In my first two years at Georgetown, I saved virtually all my class notes, papers, and exams. From my third year, about all I have are two not at all impressive Money and Banking papers. In the second semester I even withdrew from the only course I ever dropped at Georgetown, Theory and Practice of Communism. I had a good reason, though it had nothing to do with Vietnam.

In the spring of 1967, Daddy's cancer had returned, and he went to the Duke Medical Center in Durham, North Carolina, for several weeks of treatment. Every weekend I would drive the 266 miles from Georgetown to see him, leaving Friday afternoon, returning late Sunday night. I couldn't do it and make the communism course, so I bagged it. It was one of the most exhausting but important times of my young life. I would get into Durham late Friday night, then go get Daddy and spend Saturday with him. We'd spend Sunday morning and early afternoon together, then I'd head back to school and work.

On Easter Sunday, March 26, 1967, we went to church in the Duke Chapel, a grand Gothic church. Daddy had never been much of a churchgoer, but he really seemed to enjoy this service. Maybe he found some peace in the message that Jesus had died for his sins, too. Maybe he finally believed it when we sang the words to that wonderful old hymn "Sing with All the Sons of Glory": "Sing with all the sons of glory, sing the resurrection song! Death and sorrow, Earth's dark story, to the former days belong. All around the clouds are breaking, soon the storms of time shall cease; In God's likeness man, awaking, knows the everlasting peace." After church, we drove over to Chapel Hill, home of the University of North Carolina. The place was in full bloom, awash in the dogwoods and redbuds. Most southern springtimes are beautiful; this one was spectacular and remains my most vivid Easter memory.

On those weekends, Daddy talked to me in a way he never had before. Mostly it was small talk, about my life and his, Mother and Roger, family and friends. Some of it was deeper, as he reflected on the life he knew he would be leaving soon enough. But even with the small stuff, he spoke with an openness, a depth, a lack of defensiveness I'd never heard before. On those long, languid weekends, we came to terms with each other, and he accepted the fact that I loved and forgave him. If he could only have faced life with the same courage and sense of honor with which he faced death, he would have been quite a guy.

TWELVE

ALONG TOWARD THE END of my junior year, it was election time again. I had decided a year or so earlier that I would run for president of the student council. Though I had been away from campus a lot, I'd kept up with my friends and activities, and given my earlier successes, I thought I could win. But I was more out of touch than I knew. My opponent, Terry Modglin, was vice president of our class. He had been preparing for the race all year, lining up support and devising a strategy. I presented a specific but conventional platform. Modglin tapped into the growing sense of discontent on college campuses across America, and the specific opposition many students were expressing to the rigidity of Georgetown's academic requirements and campus rules. He called his campaign the "Modg Rebellion," a takeoff on "The Dodge Rebellion," the slogan of the automobile company. He and his supporters portrayed themselves in white hats fighting against the Jesuit administration and me. Because of my good relations with the school administrators, my job and car, my orthodox campaign, and my glad-handing manner, I became the establishment candidate. I worked hard, and so did my friends, but I could tell we were in trouble from the intensity of Modglin and his workers. For example, our signs were disappearing at an alarming rate. In retaliation, one night close to the election, some of my guys tore down Modglin's signs, put them in the back of a car, then drove off and dumped them. They would be caught and reprimanded.

That sealed it. Modglin beat the hell out of me, 717–570. He deserved to win. He had outthought, outorganized, and outworked me. He also wanted it more. Looking back, I see I probably shouldn't have run in the first place. I disagreed with the majority of my classmates about the need for relaxing the required curriculum; I liked it the way it was. I had

lost the singular focus on campus life that had provided the
energy for my victories in the earlier races for class president.
And my daily absence from campus made it easier to portray
me as an establishment backslapper gliding his way through
the turmoil of the time. I got over the loss soon enough and
by the end of the year was looking forward to staying in
Washington for the summer, working for the committee and
taking some courses. I couldn't know that the summer of '67
was the calm before the storm, for me and for America.

Things slow down in the summer in Washington, and
the Congress is usually in recess all of August. It's a good
time to be there if you're young, interested in politics, and
don't mind the heat. Kit Ashby and another of my classmates, Jim Moore, had rented an old house at 4513
Potomac Avenue, just off MacArthur Boulevard, a mile or
so behind the Georgetown campus. They invited me to live
with them and to stay on for senior year, when we would be
joined by Tom Campbell and Tommy Caplan. The house
overlooked the Potomac River. It had five bedrooms, a small
living room, and a decent kitchen. It also had two decks off
the second-floor bedrooms, where we could catch some sun
in the daytime and, on occasion, sleep at night in the soft
summer air. The house had belonged to a man who wrote
the national plumbing code back in the early 1950s. There
was still a set of those fascinating volumes on the living-
room bookshelves, incongruously kept upright by a book-
end of Beethoven at his piano. It was the only interesting
artifact in the whole house. My roommates bequeathed it to
me, and I still have it.

Kit Ashby was a doctor's son from Dallas. When I
worked for Senator Fulbright, he worked for Senator Henry
"Scoop" Jackson of Washington State, who, like LBJ, was a
domestic liberal and a Vietnam hawk. Kit shared his views
and we had a lot of good arguments. Jim Moore was an
army brat who had grown up all over. He was a serious historian and genuine intellectual whose views on Vietnam fell
somewhere between Kit's and mine. In that summer and the
senior year that followed, I formed a lasting friendship with
both of them. After Georgetown, Kit went into the Marine

Corps, then became an international banker. When I was President, I appointed him ambassador to Uruguay. Jim Moore followed his father into the army, then had a very successful career managing state pension investments. When a lot of states got in trouble with them in the 1980s, I got some good free advice from him on what we should do in Arkansas.

We all had a great time that summer. On June 24, I went to Constitution Hall to hear Ray Charles sing. My date was Carlene Jann, a striking girl I had met at one of the numerous mixers the area girls' schools held for Georgetown boys. She was nearly as tall as I was and had long blond hair. We sat near the back of the balcony and were among the tiny minority of white people there. I had loved Ray Charles since I heard his great line from "What'd I Say": "Tell your mama, tell your pa, I'm gonna send you back to Arkansas." By the end of the concert Ray had the audience dancing in the aisles. When I got back to Potomac Avenue that night, I was so excited I couldn't sleep. At 5 a.m., I gave up and went for a three-mile run. I carried the ticket stub from that concert in my wallet for a decade.

Constitution Hall had come a long way since the 1930s, when the Daughters of the American Revolution had denied the great Marian Anderson permission to sing there because she was black. But a lot of younger blacks had moved way beyond wanting access to concert halls. Rising discontent over poverty, continuing discrimination, violence against civil rights activists, and the disproportionate number of blacks fighting and dying in Vietnam had sparked a new militancy, especially in America's cities, where Martin Luther King Jr. was competing for the hearts and minds of black America against the much more militant idea of "Black Power."

In the mid-sixties, race riots of varying size and intensity swept through non-southern ghettos. Before 1964, Malcolm X, the Black Muslim leader, had rejected integration in favor of black-only efforts to fight poverty and other urban problems, and predicted "more racial violence than white Americans have ever experienced."

In the summer of 1967, while I was enjoying Washington, there were serious riots in Newark and Detroit. By the end of the summer there had been more than 160 riots in American cities. President Johnson appointed a National Advisory Commission on Civil Disorders, chaired by Otto Kerner, the governor of Illinois, which found that the riots were the result of police racism and brutality, and the absence of economic and educational opportunities for blacks. Its ominous conclusion was summed up in a sentence that became famous: "Our nation is moving toward two societies, one black, one white—separate and unequal."

Washington was still fairly quiet in that troubled summer, but we got a small taste of the Black Power movement when, every night for several weeks, black activists took over Dupont Circle, not far from the White House, at the intersection of Connecticut and Massachusetts avenues. A friend of mine got to know a few of them and took me down one night to hear what they had to say. They were cocky, angry, and sometimes incoherent, but they weren't stupid, and though I disagreed with their solutions, the problems at the root of their grievances were real.

Increasingly, the lines between the militancy of the civil rights movement and that of the anti-war movement were beginning to blur. Though the anti-war movement began as a protest of middle-class and affluent white college students and their older supporters among intellectuals, artists, and religious leaders, many of its early leaders also had been involved in the civil rights movement. By the spring of 1966, the anti-war movement had outgrown its organizers, with large demonstrations and rallies all across America, fueled in part by popular reaction to the Fulbright hearings. In the spring of 1967, 300,000 people demonstrated against the war in New York City's Central Park.

My first exposure to serious anti-war activists came that summer when the liberal National Student Association (NSA) held its convention at the University of Maryland campus, where I had attended Boys Nation just four years earlier. The NSA was less radical than the Students for a Democratic Society (SDS) but firmly anti-war. Its credibility had been damaged the previous spring when it was revealed that for years the organization had been taking money from the CIA to finance its international operations. Despite this, it still commanded the support of a lot of students all over America.

One night I went out to College Park to the convention to see what was going on. I ran into Bruce Lindsey, from Little Rock, whom I had met in the 1966 governor's campaign when he was working for Brooks Hays. He had come to the meeting with Southwestern's NSA delegate, Debbie Sale, also an Arkansan. Bruce became my close friend, advisor, and confidant as governor and President—the kind of friend every person needs and no President can do without. Later, Debbie helped me get a foothold in New York. But at the NSA convention in 1967, we were just three conventional-looking and conventional-acting young Arkansans who were against the war and looking for company.

The NSA was full of people like me, who were uncomfortable with the more militant SDS but still wanted to be counted in the ranks of those working to end the war. The most notable speech of the convention was given by Allard Lowenstein, who urged the students to form a national organization to defeat President Johnson in 1968. Most people at the time thought it was a fool's errand, but things were changing quickly enough to make Al Lowenstein a prophet. Within three months, the anti-war movement would produce 100,000 protesters at the Lincoln Memorial. Three hundred of them turned in their draft cards, which were presented to the Justice Department by two older anti-warriors, William Sloane Coffin, the chaplain of Yale University, and Dr. Benjamin Spock, the famous baby doctor.

Interestingly, the NSA also had a history of opposing strict totalitarianism, so there were representatives of the Baltic "captive nations" there, too. I had a conversation with the woman representing Latvia. She was a few years older than I, and I had the feeling that going to these kinds of meetings was her career. She spoke with conviction about her belief that one day Soviet Communism would fail and

Latvia would again be free. At the time I thought she was three bricks shy of a full load. Instead, she turned out to be as prophetic as Al Lowenstein.

Besides my work for the committee and my occasional excursions, I took three courses in summer school—in philosophy, ethics, and U.S. Diplomacy in the Far East. For the first time I read Kant and Kierkegaard, Hegel and Nietzsche. In the ethics class I took good notes, and one day in August another student, who was smart as a whip but seldom attended class, asked me if I'd take a few hours and go over my notes with him before the final exam. On August 19, my twenty-first birthday, I spent about four hours doing that, and the guy got a B on the test. Twenty-five years later, when I became President, my old study partner Turki al-Faisal, son of the late Saudi king, was head of Saudi Arabia's intelligence service, a position he held for twenty-four years. I doubt his philosophy grade had much to do with his success in life, but we enjoyed joking about it.

The professor for U.S. Diplomacy, Jules Davids, was a distinguished academic who later helped Averell Harriman write his memoirs. My paper was on Congress and the Southeast Asia resolution. The resolution, more commonly known as the Tonkin Gulf resolution, was passed on August 7, 1964, at the request of President Johnson, after two U.S. destroyers, the USS *Maddox* and the USS *C. Turner Joy*, allegedly were attacked by North Vietnamese vessels on August 2 and 4, 1964, and the United States retaliated with attacks on North Vietnamese naval bases and an oil storage depot. It authorized the President to "take all necessary measures to repel any armed attack against the forces of the United States and to prevent further aggression" and "to take all necessary steps, including the use of armed force," to assist any nation covered by the SEATO Treaty "in defense of its freedom."

The main point of my paper was that, except for Senator Wayne Morse, no one had seriously examined or even questioned the constitutionality, or even the wisdom, of the resolution. The country and the Congress were hopping mad and wanted to show we wouldn't be pushed around or run out of Southeast Asia. Dr. Davids liked my paper and said it was worthy of publication. I wasn't so sure; there were too many unanswered questions. Beyond the constitutional ones, some distinguished journalists had questioned whether the attacks had even occurred, and at the time I finished the paper, Fulbright was asking the Pentagon for more information on the incidents. The committee's review of Tonkin Gulf ran into 1968, and the investigations seemed to confirm that at least on the second date, August 4, the U.S. destroyers were not fired upon. Seldom in history has a nonevent led to such huge consequences.

Within a few months, those consequences would come crashing down on Lyndon Johnson. The swift and nearly unanimous passage of the Tonkin Gulf resolution became a painful example of the old proverb that life's greatest curse is the answered prayer.

THIRTEEN

MY SENIOR YEAR was a strange combination of interesting college life and cataclysmic personal and political events. As I look back on it, it seems weird that anyone could be absorbed in so many big and little things at the same time, but people inevitably search for the pleasures and deal with the pain of normal life under difficult, even bizarre circumstances.

I took two particularly interesting courses, an international law seminar and a European history colloquium. Dr. William O'Brien taught the international law course, and he permitted me to do a paper on the subject of selective conscientious objection to the draft, examining other nations' conscription systems as well as America's, and exploring the legal and philosophical roots of the conscientious-objection allowances. I argued that conscientious objection should not be confined to those with a religious opposition to all wars, because the exception was grounded not in theological doctrine but in personal moral opposition to military service. Therefore, though judging individual cases would be difficult, the government should allow selective conscientious objection if its assertion was determined to be genuine. The end of the draft in the 1970s made the point moot.

The European history colloquium was essentially a survey of European intellectual history. The professor was Hisham Sharabi, a brilliant, erudite Lebanese who was passionately committed to the Palestinian cause. There were, as I recall, fourteen students in a course that ran fourteen weeks each semester and met for two hours once a week. We read all the books, but each week a student would lead off the discussion with a ten-minute presentation about the book of the week. You could do what you wanted with the ten minutes—summarize the book, talk about its central idea, or discuss an aspect of particular interest—but you had to do it in these ten minutes. Sharabi believed that if you couldn't, you didn't understand the book, and he strictly enforced the limit. He did make one exception, for a philosophy major, the first person I ever heard use the word "ontological"—for all I knew, it was a medical specialty. He ran on well past the ten-minute limit, and when he finally ran out of gas, Sharabi stared at him with his big, expressive eyes and said, "If I had a gun, I would shoot you." Ouch. I made my presentation on Joseph Schumpeter's *Capitalism, Socialism, and Democracy*. I'm not sure how good it was, but I used simple words and, believe it or not, finished in just over nine minutes.

I spent much of the fall of 1967 preparing for November's Conference on the Atlantic Community (CONTAC). As chairman of CONTAC's nine seminars, my job was to place the delegates, assign paper topics, and recruit experts for a total of eighty-one sessions. Georgetown brought students from Europe, Canada, and the United States together in a series of seminars and lectures to examine issues facing the community. I had participated in the conference two years earlier, where the most impressive student I met was a West Point cadet from Arkansas who was first in his class and a Rhodes scholar, Wes Clark. Our relations with some European countries were strained by European opposition to the Vietnam War, but the importance of NATO to European security in the Cold War made a serious rupture out of the question. The conference was a great success, thanks largely to the quality of the students.

Later in the fall, Daddy had gotten sick again. The cancer had spread, and it was clear that further treatment wouldn't help. He was in the hospital for a while, but he wanted to come home to die. He told Mother he didn't want me to miss too much school, so they didn't call me right away. One day he said, "It's time." Mother sent for me and I flew home. I knew it was coming, and I just hoped he would still know me when I got there, so that I could tell him I loved him.

By the time I arrived, Daddy had gone to bed for good, getting up only to go to the bathroom, and then only with help. He had lost a lot of weight and was weak. Every time he tried to get up, his knees buckled repeatedly; he was like a puppet whose strings were being pulled by jerking hands. He seemed to like it when Roger and I helped him. I guess taking him back and forth to the toilet was the last thing I ever did for him. He took it all in good humor, laughing and saying, wasn't it a hell of a mess and wasn't it good that it would be over soon. When he became so weak and unstrung he couldn't walk even with help, he had to give up the bathroom and use a bedpan, which he hated doing in front of the nurses—friends of Mother's who had come to help.

Though he was fast losing control of his body, his mind and voice were clear for about three days after I got home, and we had some good talks. He said we would be all right when he was gone and he was sure I would win a Rhodes scholarship when the interviews came in about a month. After a week, he was seldom more than half conscious, though he had surges of mental activity almost to the end. Twice he woke to tell Mother and me he was still there. Twice when he should have been too far gone or too drugged to think or speak (the cancer was way down in his chest cavity now, and there was no point in letting him suffer on aspirin, which is all he would take until then), he amazed us all by asking me if I was sure I could take all this time away from school, and if not, it wasn't really necessary for me to stay, since there wasn't much left to happen and we had had our last good talks. When he couldn't speak at all anymore, he would still wake and focus on someone and make sounds so that we could understand simple things like when he wanted to be turned over in the bed. I could only wonder at what else was passing through his mind.

After his final attempt to communicate, he lasted one and a half horrible days. It was awful, hearing the hard, sharp thrusts of his breathing and seeing his body bloat into disfigurement that did not look like anything I'd ever seen. Somewhere near the end, Mother came in and saw him, burst into tears, and told him she loved him. After all he had put her through, I hoped she meant it, more for her sake than for his.

Daddy's last days brought a classic country deathwatch into our house. Family and friends streamed in and out to offer their sympathy. Most of them brought food so we wouldn't have to cook, and so we could feed the other visitors. Since I hardly slept, and ate with everyone who came by, I gained ten pounds in the two weeks I was home. But it was comforting to have all that food and all those friends when there was nothing to do but wait for death to make its final claim.

It was raining on the day of the funeral. Often when I was a boy, Daddy would stare out the window into a storm and say, "Don't bury me in the rain." It was one of those old sayings without which you can't make conversation in the South, and I never paid all that much attention when he said it. Somehow, though, it registered with me that it was important to him, that he had some deep dread about being put to rest in the rain. Now that was going to happen, after all he had done through his long illness to deserve better.

We worried about the rain on the drive to the chapel and all through the funeral, as the preacher droned on, saying nice things about him that weren't true, that he would have scorned and laughed at had he heard them. Unlike me, Daddy never thought much of funerals in general and would not have liked his own very much, except for the hymns, which he had picked. When the funeral was over, we almost ran outside to see if it was still raining. It was, and on the slow drive to the cemetery we couldn't grieve for worrying about the weather.

Then, as we turned off the street into the narrow way of the cemetery, inching toward the freshly dug grave, Roger was the first to notice that the rain had stopped, and he almost shouted to us. We were unbelievably, irrationally overjoyed and relieved. But we kept the story to ourselves, allowing ourselves only small, knowing smiles, like the one we had seen so often on Daddy's face since he had come to terms with himself. On his last long journey to the end that awaits us all, he found a forgiving God. He was not buried in the rain.

A month after the funeral, I came home again for the Rhodes scholarship interview—I'd been interested since high school. Every year thirty-two American Rhodes scholars are chosen for two years of study at Oxford, paid for by the trust established in 1903 by Cecil Rhodes's will. Rhodes, who made a fortune in South Africa's diamond mines, provided for scholarships for young men from all the present and former British colonies who had demonstrated outstanding intellectual, athletic, and leadership qualities. He wanted to send people to Oxford who were interested and accomplished in more than academics, because he thought they would be more likely to "esteem the performance of public duties" over purely private pursuits. Over the years, selection committees had come to discount a lack of athletic prowess if a candidate had excelled in some other nonacademic field. In a few more years, the trust would be amended to allow women to compete. A student could apply in either the state where he lived or the one where he went to college. Every December, each state nominated two candidates, who then went to one of eight regional competitions in which scholars were chosen for the coming academic year. The selection process required the candidate to provide between five and eight letters of recommendation, write an essay on why he wanted to go to Oxford, and submit to interviews at the state and regional levels by panels composed of former Rhodes scholars, with a chairman who wasn't one. I asked Father Sebes, Dr. Giles, Dr. Davids, and my sophomore English professor, Mary Bond, to write letters, along with Dr. Bennett and Frank Holt from back home, and Seth Tillman, Senator Fulbright's speechwriter, who taught at the Johns Hopkins School of Advanced International Studies and had become a friend and mentor to me. At Lee Williams's suggestion, I also asked Senator Fulbright. I hadn't wanted to bother the senator because of his preoccupation with and deepening gloom over the war, but Lee said he wanted to do it, and he gave me a generous letter.

The Rhodes committee asked the recommenders to note my weaknesses along with my strengths. The Georgetown people said, charitably, that I wasn't much of an athlete. Seth said that, while I was highly qualified for the scholarship, "he is not particularly competent in the routine work which he does for the Committee; this work is below his intellectual capacity and he often seems to have other things on his mind." That was news to me; I thought I was doing a good job at the committee, but as he said, I had other things on my mind. Maybe that's why I had a hard time concentrating on my essay. Finally, I gave up trying to write it at home and checked in to a hotel on Capitol Hill about a block from the New Senate Office Building, to have complete quiet. It was harder than I thought it would be to explain my short life and why it made sense for them to send me to Oxford.

I began by saying that I had come to Washington "to prepare for the life of a practicing politician"; I asked the committee to send me to Oxford "to study in depth those subjects which I have only begun to investigate," in the hope that I could "mold an intellect that can stand the pressures of political life." I thought at the time that the essay was a pretty good effort. Now it seems a bit strained and overdone, as if I were trying to find the kind of voice in which a cultivated Rhodes scholar should speak. Maybe it was just the earnestness of youth and living in a time when so many things were overdone.

Applying in Arkansas was a big advantage. Because of the size of our state and its college population, there were fewer competitors; I probably wouldn't have made it to the regional level if I'd been from New York, California, or some other big state, competing against students from Ivy League schools that had well-honed systems to recruit and train their best students for the Rhodes competition. Of the thirty-two scholars elected in 1968, Yale and Harvard produced six each, Dartmouth three, Princeton and the Naval Academy two. The winners are more spread out today, as they should be in a country with hundreds of fine undergraduate schools, but the elite schools and the service academies still do very well.

The Arkansas committee was run by Bill Nash, a tall, spare man who was an active Mason and senior partner of the Rose Law Firm in Little Rock, the oldest west of the Mississippi, with its roots dating back to 1820. Mr. Nash was an old-fashioned, high-minded man who walked several miles to work every day, rain or shine. The committee included another Rose Law Firm partner, Gaston Williamson, who also served as the Arkansas member of the regional committee. Gaston was big, burly, and brilliant, with a deep, strong voice and a commanding manner. He had opposed what Faubus did at Central High and had done what he could to beat back the forces of reaction. He was extremely helpful to and supportive of me during the whole selection process and a source of wise advice later, when I became attorney general and governor. After Hillary went to work at Rose in 1977, he befriended and counseled her too. Gaston adored Hillary. He supported me politically and liked me well enough, but I think he always thought I wasn't quite good enough for her.

I got through the Arkansas interviews and was off to New Orleans for the finals. We stayed in the French Quarter at the Royal Orleans Hotel, where the interviews were held for the finalists from Arkansas, Oklahoma, Texas, Louisiana, Mississippi, and Alabama. The only preparation I did the night before was to reread my essay, read *Time*, *Newsweek*, and *U.S. News & World Report* cover to cover, and get a good night's sleep. I knew there would be unexpected questions and I wanted to be sharp. And I didn't want my emotions to get the better of me. New Orleans brought memories of previous trips: when I was a little boy watching Mother kneel by the railroad tracks and cry as Mammaw and I pulled away in the train; when we visited New Orleans and the Mississippi Gulf Coast on the only out-of-state vacation our whole family took together. And I couldn't get Daddy and his confident deathbed prediction that I would win out of my mind. I wanted to do it for him, too.

The chairman of the committee was Dean McGee of Oklahoma, head of the Kerr-McGee Oil Company and a powerful figure in Oklahoma business and political life. The member who impressed me most was Barney Monaghan, the chairman of Vulcan, a steel company in Birmingham, Alabama. He looked more like a college professor than a southern businessman, impeccably dressed in a three-piece suit.

The hardest question I got was about trade. I was asked whether I was for free trade, protectionism, or something in between. When I said I was pro–free trade, especially for advanced economies, my questioner shot back, "Then how do you justify Senator Fulbright's efforts to protect Arkansas chickens?" It was a good trick question, designed to make me feel I had to choose, on the spur of the moment, between being inconsistent on trade or disloyal to Fulbright. I confessed I didn't know anything about the chicken issue, but I didn't have to agree with the senator on everything to be proud to work for him. Gaston Williamson broke in and bailed me out, explaining that the issue wasn't as simple as the question implied; in fact, Fulbright had been trying to open foreign markets to our chickens. It had never occurred to me that I could blow the interview because I didn't know enough about chickens. It never happened again. When I was governor and President, people were amazed at how much I knew about how chickens are raised, processed, and marketed at home and abroad.

At the end of all twelve interviews, and a little time for deliberation, we were brought back into a reception room. The committee had selected one guy from New Orleans, two from Mississippi, and me. After we talked briefly to the press, I called Mother, who had been waiting anxiously by the phone, and asked her how she thought I'd look in English tweeds. Lord, I was happy—happy for Mother after all she'd lived through to get me to that day, happy that Daddy's last prediction came true, happy for the honor and the promise of the next two years. For a while the world just stopped. There was no Vietnam, no racial turmoil, no trouble at home, no anxieties about myself or my future. I had a few more hours in New Orleans, and I enjoyed the city they call "the Big Easy" like a native son.

When I got home, after a visit to Daddy's grave, we plunged into the holiday season. There was a nice write-up in the paper, even a laudatory editorial. I spoke to a local civic club, spent good time with my friends, and enjoyed a raft of congratulatory letters and phone calls. Christmas was nice but bittersweet; for the first time since my brother was born, there were only three of us.

After I returned to Georgetown there was one more piece of sad news. On January 17, my grandmother died. A few years earlier, after she had had a second stroke, she asked to go home to Hope to live in the nursing home downtown in what was the old Julia Chester Hospital. She requested and got the same room Mother was in when I was born. Her death, like Daddy's, must have set loose contradictory feelings in Mother. Mammaw had been hard on her. Perhaps because she was jealous that Papaw loved his only child so much, too often she made her daughter the target of her outbursts of rage. Her tantrums lessened after Papaw died, when she was hired as a nurse to a nice lady who took her on trips to Wisconsin and Arizona and fed some of her hunger to go beyond the circumstances of her confined, predictable life. And she had been wonderful to me in my first four years, when she taught me to read and count, clean my plate, and wash my hands. After we moved to Hot Springs, whenever I made straight A's in school she sent me five dollars. When I turned twenty-one, she still wanted to know if "her baby had his handkerchief." I wish she could have understood herself better and cared for herself and her family more. But she did love me, and she did her best to get me off to a good start in life.

I thought I had made a pretty good start, but nothing could have prepared me for what was about to happen. Nineteen sixty-eight was one of the most tumultuous and heartbreaking years in American history. Lyndon Johnson started the year expecting to hold his course in Vietnam, continue his Great Society assault on unemployment, poverty, and hunger, and pursue reelection. But his country was moving away from him. Though I was sympathetic to the zeitgeist, I didn't embrace the lifestyle or the radical rhetoric. My hair was short, I didn't even drink, and some of the music was too loud and harsh for my taste. I didn't hate LBJ; I just wanted to end the war, and I was afraid the culture clashes would undermine, not advance, the cause. In reaction to the youth protests and "countercultural" lifestyles, Republicans and many working-class Democrats moved to the right, flocking to hear conservatives like the resurgent Richard Nixon and the new governor of California, Ronald Reagan, a former FDR Democrat.

The Democrats were moving away from Johnson, too. On the right, Governor George Wallace announced that he would run for President as an independent. On the left, young activists like Allard Lowenstein were urging anti-war Democrats to challenge President Johnson in the Democratic primaries. Their first choice was Senator Robert Kennedy, who had been pressing for a negotiated settlement in Vietnam. He declined, fearing that if he ran, given his well-known dislike of the President, he would appear to be pursuing a vendetta rather than a principled crusade. Senator George McGovern of South Dakota, who was up for reelection in his conservative state, also declined. Senator Gene McCarthy of Minnesota did not. As the party's heir apparent to Adlai Stevenson's legacy of intellectual liberalism, McCarthy could be maddening, even disingenuous, in his efforts to appear almost saintly in his lack of ambition. But he had the guts to take on Johnson, and as the year dawned, he was the only horse the anti-warriors had to ride. In January, he announced that he would run in the first primary contest in New Hampshire.

In February, two events in Vietnam further hardened opposition to the war. The first was the impromptu execution of a person suspected of being a Vietcong by the chief of the South Vietnamese National Police, General Loan. Loan shot the man in the head in broad daylight on the street in Saigon. The killing was captured on film by the great photographer Eddie Adams, whose picture caused more Americans to question whether our allies were any better than our enemies, who were also undeniably ruthless.

The second, and far more significant, event was the Tet offensive, so named because it took place during the

Vietnamese holiday of Tet, which marked their new year. North Vietnamese and Vietcong forces launched a series of coordinated attacks on American positions all over South Vietnam, including strongholds like Saigon, where even the American embassy was under fire. The attacks were rebuffed and the North Vietnamese and Vietcong sustained heavy casualties, leading President Johnson and our military leaders to claim victory, but in fact, Tet was a huge psychological and political defeat for America, because Americans saw with their own eyes, in our first "television war," that our forces were vulnerable even in places they controlled. More and more Americans began to question whether we could win a war the South Vietnamese couldn't win for themselves, and whether it was worth sending even more soldiers into Vietnam when the answer to the first question seemed to be no.

On the home front, the Senate majority leader, Mike Mansfield, called for a bombing halt. President Johnson's secretary of defense, Robert McNamara, and his close advisor Clark Clifford, along with former secretary of state Dean Acheson, told the President it was time to "review" his policy of continuing escalation to achieve a military victory. Dean Rusk continued to support the policy, and the military had asked for 200,000 more troops to pursue it. Racial incidents, some of them violent, continued across the country. Richard Nixon and George Wallace formally declared their candidacies for President. In New Hampshire, McCarthy's campaign was gathering steam, with hundreds of anti-war students pouring into the state to knock on doors for him. Those who didn't want to cut their hair and shave worked in the back room of his campaign headquarters stuffing envelopes. Meanwhile, Bobby Kennedy continued to fret about whether he should get in the race too.

On March 12, McCarthy got 42 percent of the vote in New Hampshire to 49 percent for LBJ. Though Johnson was a write-in candidate who never came to New Hampshire to campaign, it was a big psychological victory for McCarthy and the anti-war movement. Four days later, Kennedy entered the race, announcing in the same Senate caucus room where his brother John had begun his campaign in 1960. He sought to defuse charges that he was driven by ruthless personal ambition by saying that McCarthy's campaign had already exposed the deep divisions within the Democratic Party, and he wanted to give the country a new direction. Of course, now he had a new "ruthlessness" problem: he was raining on McCarthy's parade, after McCarthy had challenged the President when Kennedy wouldn't.

I saw all this unfold from a peculiar perspective. My housemate Tommy Caplan was working in Kennedy's office, so I knew what was going on there. And I had begun dating a classmate who was volunteering at McCarthy's national headquarters in Washington. Ann Markusen was a brilliant economics student, captain of the Georgetown women's sailing team, a passionate anti-war liberal, and a Minnesota native. She admired McCarthy and, like many young people who worked for him, hated Kennedy for trying to take the nomination away from him. We had some ferocious arguments, because I was glad Kennedy was in. I had watched him perform as attorney general and senator and thought he cared more about domestic issues than McCarthy, and I was convinced he would be a much more effective President. McCarthy was a fascinating man, tall, gray-haired, and handsome, an Irish Catholic intellectual with a fine mind and a biting wit. But I had watched him on the Foreign Relations Committee, and he was too detached for my taste. Until he entered the New Hampshire primary, he seemed curiously passive about what was going on, content to vote the right way and say the right things.

By contrast, just before Bobby Kennedy announced for President, he was working hard to pass a resolution sponsored by Fulbright to give the Senate a say before LBJ could put 200,000 more troops in Vietnam. He had also been to Appalachia to expose the depth of rural poverty in America, and had made an amazing trip to South Africa, where he challenged young people to fight apartheid. McCarthy, though I liked him, gave me the impression he'd rather be home reading St. Thomas Aquinas than going into a tar-paper shack to see how poor people lived or flying halfway around the world to speak against racism. Every time I tried to make these arguments to Ann, she gave me hell, saying if Bobby Kennedy had been more principled and less political he would have done what McCarthy did. The underlying message, of course, was that I also was too political. I was really crazy about her then and hated to be on her bad side, but I wanted to win and I wanted to elect a good man who would also be a good President.

My interest grew more personal on March 20, four days after Kennedy announced for President, when President Johnson ended all draft deferments for graduate students, except for those in medical school, putting my future at Oxford in doubt. Johnson's decision triggered another shot of Vietnam guilt: like Johnson, I didn't believe graduate students should have draft deferments, but I didn't believe in our Vietnam policy either.

On Sunday night, March 31, President Johnson was scheduled to address the nation about Vietnam. There was speculation about whether he would escalate the war or cool it a little in the hope of starting negotiations, but nobody really saw what was coming. I was driving on Massachusetts Avenue, listening to the speech on my car radio. After speaking for some time, Johnson said he had decided to sharply restrict the bombing of North Vietnam, in the hope of finding a resolution to the conflict. Then, as I was passing by the Cosmos Club, just northwest of Dupont Circle, the President dropped his own bombshell: "With American sons in the fields far away, and our world's hopes for peace in the balance every day, I do not believe I should devote another hour or another day of my time to any personal partisan causes. . . . Accordingly, I shall not seek, and I will not accept, the nomination of my party for another term as your President." I pulled over to the curb in disbelief, feeling sad for Johnson, who had done so much for America at home, but happy for my country and for the prospect of a new beginning.

The feeling didn't last long. Four days later, on the night of April 4, Martin Luther King Jr. was killed on the balcony outside his room at the Lorraine Motel in Memphis, where he had gone to support striking sanitation workers. In the last couple of years of his life, he had broadened his civil rights agenda to include an assault on urban poverty and outspoken opposition to the war. It was politically necessary to fend off the challenge to his leadership from younger, more militant blacks, but it was clear to all of us who watched him that Dr. King meant it when he said he could not advance civil rights for blacks without also opposing poverty and the war in Vietnam.

The night before he was killed, Dr. King gave an eerily prophetic sermon to a packed house at Mason Temple Church. In an obvious reference to the many threats on his life, he said, "Like anybody I would like to live a long life. Longevity has its place. But I'm not concerned about that now. I just want to do God's will. And He's allowed me to go up to the mountain. And I've looked over, and I've seen the promised land. I may not get there with you, but I want you to know tonight that we as a people will get to the promised land. So I'm happy tonight. I'm not worried about anything. I'm not fearing any man. Mine eyes have seen the glory of the coming of the Lord!" The next evening, at 6 p.m., he was shot dead by James Earl Ray, a chronically disaffected, convicted armed robber who had escaped from prison about a year earlier.

Martin Luther King Jr.'s death shook the nation as no other event had since President Kennedy's assassination. Campaigning in Indiana that night, Robert Kennedy tried to calm the fears of America with perhaps the greatest speech of his life. He asked blacks not to be filled with hatred of whites and reminded them that his brother, too, had been killed by a white man. He quoted the great lines of Aeschylus about pain bringing wisdom, against our will, "through the awful grace of God." He told the crowd before him and the country listening to him that we would get through this time because the vast majority of blacks and whites "want to live together, want to improve the quality of our life, and want justice for all human beings who abide in our land." He ended with these words: "Let us dedicate ourselves to

what the Greeks wrote so many years ago: to tame the sav-
ageness of man and make gentle the life of this world. Let us
dedicate ourselves to that, and say a prayer for our country
and for our people."

Dr. King's death provoked more than prayer; some
feared, and others hoped, it marked the death of nonviolence, too. Stokely Carmichael said that white America had
declared war on black America and there was "no alternative to retribution." Rioting broke out in New York, Boston,
Chicago, Detroit, Memphis, and more than one hundred
other cities and towns. More than forty people were killed
and hundreds were injured. The violence was especially bad
in Washington, predominantly directed against black businesses all along Fourteenth and H streets. President Johnson
called out the National Guard to restore order, but the
atmosphere remained tense.

Georgetown was at a safe distance from the violence,
but we had a taste of it when a few hundred National
Guardsmen camped out in McDonough Gym, where our
basketball team played its games. Many black families were
burned out of their homes and took refuge in local
churches. I signed up with the Red Cross to help deliver
food, blankets, and other supplies to them. My 1963 white
Buick convertible, with Arkansas plates and the Red Cross
logo plastered on the doors, cut a strange figure in the
mostly empty streets, which were marked by still-smoking
buildings and storefronts with broken glass from looting. I
made the drive once at night, then again on Sunday morning, when I took Carolyn Yeldell, who had flown in for the
weekend, with me. In the daylight it felt safe, so we got out
and walked around a little, looking at the riot's wreckage. It
was the only time I've ever felt insecure in a black neighborhood. And I thought, not for the first or last time, that it was
sad and ironic that the primary victims of black rage were
blacks themselves.

Dr. King's death left a void in a nation desperately in
need of his allegiance to nonviolence and his belief in the
promise of America, and now in danger of losing both.
Congress responded by passing President Johnson's bill to

ban racial discrimination in the sale or rental of housing. Robert Kennedy tried to fill the void, too. He won the Indiana primary on May 7, preaching racial reconciliation while appealing to more conservative voters by talking tough on crime and the need to move people from welfare to work. Some liberals attacked his "law and order" message, but it was politically necessary. And he believed in it, just as he believed in ending all draft deferments.

In Indiana, Bobby Kennedy became the first New Democrat, before Jimmy Carter, before the Democratic Leadership Council, which I helped to start in 1985, and before my campaign in 1992. He believed in civil rights for all and special privileges for none, in giving poor people a hand up rather than a handout: work was better than welfare. He understood in a visceral way that progressive politics requires the advocacy of both new policies and fundamental values, both far-reaching change and social stability. If he had become President, America's journey through the rest of the twentieth century would have been very different.

On May 10, peace talks between the United States and North Vietnam began in Paris, bringing hope to Americans who were eager for the war to end, and relief to Vice President Hubert Humphrey, who had entered the race in late April and who needed some change in our fortunes to have any chance to win the nomination or the election. Meanwhile, social turmoil continued unabated. Columbia University in New York was shut down by protesters for the rest of the academic year. Two Catholic priests, brothers Daniel and Philip Berrigan, were arrested for stealing and burning draft records. And in Washington, barely a month after the riots, civil rights activists went on with Martin Luther King Jr.'s plans for a Poor People's Campaign, setting up a tent encampment on the Mall, called Resurrection City, to highlight the problems of poverty. It rained like crazy, turning the Mall to mud and making living conditions miserable. One day in June, Ann Markusen and I went down to see it and show support. Boards had been laid down between the tents so that you could walk without sinking into the mud, but after a couple of hours of wandering

around and talking to people, we were covered in it anyway.
It was a good metaphor for the confusion of the time.

May ended with the race for the Democratic nomination in
doubt. Humphrey began gaining delegates from party regulars in states without primary elections, and McCarthy
defeated Kennedy in the Oregon primary. Kennedy's hopes
for the nomination were riding on the California primary
on June 4. My last week in college was spent in high anticipation of the outcome, four days before our graduation.

On Tuesday night, Robert Kennedy won California,
thanks to a big showing among minority voters in Los
Angeles County. Tommy Caplan and I were thrilled. We
stayed up until Kennedy gave his victory speech, then went
to bed; it was nearly three in the morning in Washington. A
few hours later I was awakened by Tommy, who was shaking me and shouting, "Bobby's been shot! Bobby's been
shot!" A few minutes after we had turned off the television
and gone to bed, Senator Kennedy was walking through the
kitchen at the Ambassador Hotel when a young Arab,
Sirhan Sirhan, who was angry at Kennedy because of his
support for Israel, rained a hail of bullets down on him and
those surrounding him. Five others were wounded; they all
recovered. Bobby Kennedy was operated on for a severe
wound to the head. He died a day later, only forty-two, on
June 6, Mother's forty-fifth birthday, two months and two
days after Martin Luther King Jr. was killed.

On June 8, Caplan went to New York for the funeral at
St. Patrick's Cathedral. Senator Kennedy's admirers, both
the famous and the anonymous, had streamed past his cas-
ket all day and all night before the service. President Johnson, Vice President Humphrey, and Senator McCarthy were
there. So was Senator Fulbright. Ted Kennedy gave a magnificent eulogy for his brother, closing with words of power
and grace I will never forget: "My brother need not be idealized, or enlarged in death beyond what he was in life. He
should be remembered simply as a good and decent man,
who saw wrong and tried to right it, saw suffering and tried
to heal it, saw war and tried to stop it. Those of us who

loved him, and who take him to his rest today, pray that what he was to us and what he wished for others will some-day come to pass for all the world."

That is what I wanted, too, but it seemed further away than ever. We went through those last few college days in a numb fog. Tommy took the funeral train from New York to Washington, barely making it back for graduation. All the other graduation events had been canceled, but the com-mencement ceremony itself was set to go on as planned. Even that didn't work out, providing the first levity in days. Just as the commencement speaker, hometown mayor Wal-ter Washington, got up to speak, a tremendous storm cloud came out. He spoke for about thirty seconds, congratulating us, wishing us well, and saying that if we didn't get inside right then, we'd all drown. Then the rain came and we high-tailed it. Our class was ready to vote for Mayor Washington for President. That night, Tommy Caplan's parents took Tommy, Mother, Roger, me, and a few others out to dinner at an Italian restaurant. Tommy carried the conversation, at one point saying that understanding some subject or other required a "mature intellect." My eleven-year-old brother looked up and said, "Tom, am I a mature intellect?" It was good to end a roller-coaster day and a heartbreaking ten weeks with a laugh.

After a few days to pack up and say last good-byes, I drove back to Arkansas with my roommate Jim Moore to work on Senator Fulbright's reelection campaign. He seemed vul-nerable on two counts: first, his outspoken opposition to the Vietnam War in a conservative, pro-military state already upset with all the upheaval in America; and second, his refusal to adapt to the demands of modern congressional politics, which required senators and congressmen to come home on most weekends to see their constituents. Fulbright had gone to Congress in the 1940s, when expectations were very different. Back then members of Congress were expected to come home during vacations and the long sum-mer recess, to answer their mail and phone calls, and to see their constituents when they came to Washington. On the

weekends when Congress was in session, they were free to
stay in town, relax, and reflect, like most other working
Americans. When they did go back home on long breaks,
they were expected to keep office hours in the home office
and to take a few trips out to the heartland to see the folks.
Intensive interaction with voters was reserved for campaigns.

By the late sixties, the availability of easy air travel and
extensive local news coverage were rapidly changing the
rules for survival. More and more, senators and congressmen were coming home on most weekends, traveling to
more places when they got there, and making pronouncements for the local media whenever they could.

Fulbright's campaign encountered no little resistance
from people who disagreed with him on the war or thought
he was out of touch, or both. He thought the idea of flying
home every weekend was nuts and once said to me, in reference to his colleagues who did it, "When do they ever get
time to read and think?" Sadly, the pressures on members
of Congress to travel constantly have grown only more
intense. The rising costs of television, radio, and other
advertising and the insatiable appetite for news coverage
put many senators and congressmen on a plane every weekend and often out many weeknights for fund-raisers in the
Washington area. When I was President, I often remarked
to Hillary and my staff that I thought one reason congressional debate had grown so harshly negative was that too
many members of Congress were in a constant state of
exhaustion.

In the summer of '68, exhaustion wasn't Fulbright's
problem, though he was weary from fighting over Vietnam.
What he needed was not rest, but a way to reconnect with
voters who felt alienated from him. Luckily, he was blessed
with weak opponents. His main adversary in the primary
was none other than Justice Jim Johnson, who was back to
his old routine, traveling to county seats with a country
band, bashing Fulbright as soft on communism. Johnson's
wife, Virginia, was attempting to emulate George Wallace's
wife, Lurleen, who had succeeded her husband as governor.

The Republican Senate candidate was an unknown small-business man from east Arkansas, Charles Bernard, who said Fulbright was too liberal for our state.

Lee Williams had come down to run the campaign, with a lot of help from the young but seasoned politician who ran Senator Fulbright's Little Rock office, Jim McDougal (the Whitewater one), an old-fashioned populist who told great stories in colorful language and worked his heart out for Fulbright, whom he revered.

Jim and Lee decided to reintroduce the senator to Arkansas as "just plain Bill," a down-to-earth Arkansan in a red-checked sport shirt. All the campaign's printed materials and most of the TV ads showed him that way, though I don't think he liked it, and on most campaign days he still wore a suit. To hammer the down-home image into reality, the senator decided to make a grassroots campaign trip to small towns around the state, accompanied only by a driver and a black notebook filled with the names of his past supporters that had been compiled by Parker Westbrook, a staffer who seemed to know everyone in Arkansas who had the slightest interest in politics. Since Senator Fulbright campaigned only every six years, we just hoped all the folks listed in Parker's black notebook were still alive and kicking.

Lee Williams gave me the chance to drive the senator for a few days on a trip to southwest Arkansas, and I jumped at it. I was fascinated by Fulbright, grateful for the letter he had written for me to the Rhodes Scholarship Committee, and eager to learn more about what small-town Arkansans were thinking. They were a long way from urban violence and anti-war demonstrations, but a lot of them had kids in Vietnam.

One day Fulbright was being followed by a national television crew as we pulled in to a small town, parked, and went into a feed store where farmers bought grain for their animals. With cameras rolling, Fulbright shook hands with an old character in overalls and asked him for his vote. The man said he couldn't give it because Fulbright wouldn't stand up to the "Commies" and he'd let them "take over our country." Fulbright sat down on a pile of feed bags stacked on the floor and struck up a conversation. He told the man he'd stand up to the Communists at home if he could find them. "Well, they're all over," the man replied. Then Fulbright commented, "Really? Have you seen any around here? I've been looking all over and I haven't seen the first one." It was funny to watch Fulbright do his thing. The guy thought they were having a serious conversation. I'm sure the TV audience got a kick out of it, but what I saw bothered me. The wall had gone up in that man's eyes. It didn't matter that he couldn't find a Commie to save his soul. He had turned Fulbright off, and no amount of talking could bring the wall in his mind down again. I just hoped there were enough other voters in that town and the hundreds like it who were still reachable.

Notwithstanding the feed-store incident, Fulbright was convinced that small-town voters were mostly wise, practical, and fair-minded. He thought they had more time to reflect on things and were not all that easy for his right-wing critics to stampede. After a couple of days of visiting places where all the white voters seemed to be for George Wallace, I wasn't so sure. Then we came to Center Point, and one of the more memorable encounters of my life in politics. Center Point was a little place of fewer than two hundred people. The black notebook said the man to see was Bo Reece, a longtime supporter who lived in the best house in town. In the days before television ads, there was a Bo Reece in most little Arkansas towns. A couple of weeks before the election, people would ask, "Who's Bo for?" His choice would be made known and would get about two-thirds of the vote, sometimes more.

When we pulled up in front of the house, Bo was sitting on his porch. He shook hands with Fulbright and me, said he'd been expecting him, and invited us in for a visit. It was an old-fashioned house with a fireplace and comfortable chairs. As soon as we were settled, Reece said, "Senator, this country's got lots of troubles. A lot of things aren't right." Fulbright agreed, but he didn't know where Bo Reece was going, and neither did I—maybe straight to Wallace. Then

Bo told a story I'll remember as long as I live: "The other day I was talking to a planter friend of mine who grows cotton in east Arkansas. He has a bunch of sharecroppers working for him. [Sharecroppers were farmhands, usually black, who were literally paid with a small share of the crops. They often lived in run-down shacks on the farm and were invariably poor.] So I asked him, 'How are your sharecroppers doing?' And he said, 'Well, if we have a bad year, they break even.' Then he laughed and said, 'And if we have a good year, they break even.' " Then Bo said, "Senator, that ain't right and you know it. That's why we've got so much poverty and other troubles in this country, and if you get another term you've got to do something about it. The blacks deserve a better deal." After all the racist talk we'd been hearing, Fulbright nearly fell out of his chair. He assured Bo he'd try to do something about it when he was reelected, and Bo pledged to stick with him.

When we got back in the car, Fulbright said, "See, I told you, there's a lot of wisdom in these small towns. Bo sits on that porch and thinks things through." Bo Reece had a big impact on Fulbright. A few weeks later at a campaign rally in El Dorado, a south Arkansas oil town that was a hotbed of racism and pro-Wallace sentiment, Fulbright was asked what was the biggest problem facing America. Without hesitation he said, "Poverty." I was proud of him and grateful to Bo Reece.

When we were driving from town to town on those hot country roads, I would try to get Fulbright to talk. The conversations left me with great memories but sharply curtailed my career as his driver. One day we got into it over the Warren Court. I strongly favored most of its decisions, especially in civil rights. Fulbright disagreed. He said, "There is going to be a terrible backlash against this Supreme Court. You can't change society too much through the courts. Most of it has to come through the political system. Even if it takes longer, it's more likely to stick." I still think America came out way ahead under the Warren Court, but there's no doubt we've had a powerful reaction to it for more than thirty years now.

Four or five days into our trip, I started up one of those political discussions with Fulbright as we were driving out of yet another small town to our next stop. After about five minutes Fulbright asked me where I was going. When I told him, he said, "Then you better turn around. You're headed in exactly the opposite direction." As I sheepishly made the U-turn, he said, "You're going to give Rhodes scholars a bad name. You're acting like a damned egghead who doesn't know which way to drive."

I was embarrassed, of course, as I turned around and got the senator back on schedule. And I knew my days as a driver were over. But what the heck, I was just shy of my twenty-second birthday and had just had a few days of experiences and conversations that would last a lifetime. What Fulbright needed was a driver who could get him to the next place on time, and I was happy to go back to head-quarters work, to the rallies and picnics and the long dinners listening to Lee Williams, Jim McDougal, and the other old hands tell Arkansas political stories.

Not long before the primary, Tom Campbell came for a visit on his way to Texas for his Marine Corps officer training. Jim Johnson was having one of his courthouse-steps, country-band rallies that night in Batesville, about an hour and a half north of Little Rock, so I decided to show Tom a side of Arkansas he'd only heard about before. Johnson was in good form. After warming up the crowd, he held up a shoe and shouted, "You see this shoe? It was made in Communist Romania [he pronounced it "Rooo-*main*-yuh"]! Bill Fulbright voted to let these Communist shoes come into America and take jobs away from good Arkansas people working in our shoe factories." We had a lot of those folks back then and Johnson promised them and all the rest of us that when he got to the Senate there would be no more Commie shoes invading America. I had no idea whether we in fact were importing shoes from Romania, whether Fulbright had voted for a failed attempt to open our border to them, or whether Johnson made the whole thing up, but it made a good tale. After the speech Johnson stood on the steps and shook hands with the crowd. I patiently waited my turn. When he shook my hand, I told him he made me ashamed to be from Arkansas. I think my earnestness amused him. He just smiled, invited me to write him about my feelings, and moved on to the next handshake.

On July 30, Fulbright defeated Jim Johnson and two lesser-known candidates. Justice Jim's wife, Virginia, barely made it into the gubernatorial runoff, beating a young reformer named Ted Boswell by 409 votes out of more than 400,000 votes cast, despite the best efforts of the Fulbright folks to help him in the closing days of the campaign and in the six days following, when everybody was hustling to keep from getting counted out or to get some extra votes in the unreported precincts. Mrs. Johnson lost the runoff by 63 to 37 percent to Marion Crank, a state legislator from Foreman in southwest Arkansas, who had the courthouse crowd and the Faubus machine behind him. Arkansas had finally had enough of the Johnsons. We were not yet in the New South of the seventies, but we did have sense enough not to go backward.

In August, as I was winding down my involvement in the Fulbright campaign and getting ready to go to Oxford, I spent several summer nights at the home of Mother's friends Bill and Marge Mitchell on Lake Hamilton, where I was always welcome. That summer I met some interesting people at Marge and Bill's. Like Mother, they loved the races and over the years got to know a lot of the horse people, including two brothers from Illinois, W. Hal and "Donkey" Bishop, who owned and trained horses. W. Hal Bishop was more successful, but Donkey was one of the most memorable characters I've ever met. He was a frequent visitor in Marge and Bill's home. One night we were out at the lake talking about my generation's experiences with drugs and women, and Donkey mentioned that he used to drink a lot and had been married ten times. I was amazed. "Don't look at me like that," he said. "When I was your age, it wasn't like it is now. If you wanted to have sex, it wasn't even enough to say you loved 'em. You had to marry 'em!" I laughed and asked if he remembered all their names. "All but two," he replied. His shortest marriage? "One night. I woke up in a motel with a horrible hangover and a strange woman. I said, 'Who in the hell are you?' She said, 'I'm your wife, you SOB!' I got up, put my pants on, and got out of there." In the 1950s, Donkey met a woman who was different from all the rest. He told her the whole truth about his life and said if she'd marry him, he would never drink or carouse again. She took the unbelievable chance, and he kept his word for twenty-five years, until he died.

Marge Mitchell also introduced me to two young people who had just started teaching in Hot Springs, Danny Thomason and Jan Biggers. Danny came from Hampton, seat of Arkansas' smallest county, and he had a world of good country stories to prove it. When I was governor, we sang tenor side by side in the Immanuel Baptist Church choir every Sunday. His brother and sister-in-law, Harry and Linda, became two of Hillary's and my closest friends and played a big role in the '92 presidential campaign and our White House years.

Jan Biggers was a tall, pretty, talkative girl from Tuckerman, in northeast Arkansas. I liked her, but she had segregationist views from her upbringing, which I deplored. When I left for Oxford, I gave her a cardboard box full of paperback books on civil rights and urged her to read them. A few months later, she ran off with another teacher, John Paschal, the president of the local NAACP. They wound up in New Hampshire, where he became a builder, she kept teaching, and they had three children. When I ran for President, I was happily surprised to find that Jan was the Democratic chair in one of New Hampshire's ten counties.

Though I was preparing to go to Oxford, August was one of 1968's craziest months, and it was hard to look ahead. It began with the Republican convention in Miami Beach, where New York governor Nelson Rockefeller's bid to defeat a resurgent Richard Nixon showed just how weak the moderate wing of the party had become, and where Governor Ronald Reagan of California first emerged as a potential President with his appeal to "true" conservatives.

Nixon won on the first ballot, with 692 votes to 277 for Rockefeller and 182 for Reagan. Nixon's message was simple: he was for law and order at home, and peace with honor in Vietnam. Though the real political turmoil lay ahead when the Democrats met in Chicago, the Republicans had their share of turbulence, aggravated by Nixon's vice-presidential choice, Governor Spiro Agnew of Maryland, whose only national notoriety had come from his hard-line stance against civil disobedience. Baseball Hall of Famer Jackie Robinson, the first black to play in the major leagues, resigned his post as an aide to Rockefeller because he could not back a Republican ticket he saw as "racist." Martin Luther King Jr.'s successor, the Reverend Ralph Abernathy, moved the Poor People's Campaign from Washington to Miami Beach in hopes of influencing the Republican convention in a progressive way. They were disappointed by the platform, the floor speeches, and Nixon's appeals to the ultra-conservatives. After the Agnew nomination was announced, what had been a peaceful gathering against poverty turned into a riot. The National Guard was called out, and the by now predictable scenario unfolded: tear gas, beating, looting, fires. When it was over, three black men had been killed, a three-day curfew was imposed, and 250 people were arrested and later released to quiet charges of police brutality. But all the trouble only strengthened the law-and-order hand Nixon was playing to the so-called silent majority of Americans, who were appalled by what they saw as the breakdown of the fabric of American life.

The Miami strife was just a warm-up for what the Democrats faced when they met in Chicago later that month. At the beginning of the month, Al Lowenstein and others were still looking for an alternative to Humphrey. McCarthy was still hanging in there, with no real prospect of winning. On August 10, Senator George McGovern announced his own candidacy, clearly hoping to get the support of those who had been for Robert Kennedy. Meanwhile, Chicago was filling up with young people opposed to the war. A small number intended to make real trouble; the rest were there to stage various forms of peaceful protest, including the Yippies, who planned a "countercultural" "Festival of Life" with most of the celebrants high on marijuana, and the National Mobilization Committee, which had a more conventional protest in mind. But Mayor Richard Daley wasn't taking any chances: he put the entire police force on alert, asked the governor to send in the National Guard, and prepared for the worst.

On August 22, the convention claimed its first victim, a seventeen-year-old Native American shot by police who claimed he fired on them first near Lincoln Park, where the people gathered every day. Two days later, a thousand demonstrators refused to vacate the park at night as ordered. Hundreds of police waded into the crowd with nightsticks, as their targets threw rocks, shouted curses, or ran. It was all on television.

That was how I experienced Chicago. It was surreal. I had gone to Shreveport, Louisiana, with Jeff Dwire, the man my mother was involved with and was soon to marry. He was an unusual man: a World War II veteran of the Pacific theater who had permanently injured his abdominal muscles when he parachuted out of his damaged plane and landed on a coral reef; an accomplished carpenter; a slick Louisiana charmer; and the owner of the beauty salon where Mother got her hair done (he had worked his way through college as a hairdresser). He had also been a football player, a judo instructor, a home builder, a seller of oil-well equipment, and a securities salesman. He was married but separated from his wife, and he had three daughters. He had also served nine months in prison in 1962 for stock fraud. In 1956, he had raised $24,000 for a company that was going to make movies about colorful Oklahoma characters, including the gangster Pretty Boy Floyd. The U.S. attorney concluded the company spent the money as soon as it came in and never had any intention to make the movies. Jeff claimed he left the operation as soon as he knew it was a scam, but it was too late. I respected him for telling me about all this soon after we met. Whatever had really happened, Mother was serious about him and wanted us to spend some time together, so I agreed to go to

Louisiana with him for a few days while he pursued his involvement with a pre-fab housing company. Shreveport was a conservative city in northwest Louisiana, not far from the Arkansas border, with an ultra–right wing newspaper that gave me a hard spin every morning on what I had seen on television the night before. The circumstances were bizarre, but I sat glued to the TV for hours, taking time out to go to a few places and eat with Jeff. I felt so isolated. I didn't identify with the kids raising hell or with Chicago's mayor and his rough tactics, or with the people who were supporting him, which included most of the folks I had grown up among. And I was heartsick that my party and its progressive causes were disintegrating before my eyes.

Any hope that the convention might produce a unified party was dashed by President Johnson. In his first statement since his brother's funeral, Senator Edward Kennedy called for a unilateral bombing halt and a mutual withdrawal of U.S. and North Vietnamese forces from South Vietnam. His proposal was the basis of a compromise platform plank agreed to by the Humphrey, Kennedy, and McCarthy leaders. When General Creighton Abrams, the U.S. commander in Vietnam, told LBJ a bombing halt would endanger America's troops, the President demanded Humphrey abandon the Vietnam compromise plank in the platform, and Humphrey gave in. Later, in his autobiography, Humphrey said, "I should have stood my ground. . . . I should not have yielded." But he did, and the dam broke.

The convention opened on August 26. The keynoter was Senator Dan Inouye of Hawaii, a brave Japanese-American veteran of World War II, to whom I awarded the Congressional Medal of Honor in 2000, a belated recognition of the heroism that had cost him an arm, and very nearly his life, while his own people were being herded into detention camps back home. Inouye expressed sympathy for the protesters and their goals, but urged them not to abandon peaceful means. He spoke against "violence and anarchy," but also condemned apathy and prejudice "hiding behind the reach of law and order," a clear slap at Nixon and perhaps at the Chicago police tactics too. Inouye struck a good balance, but things were too far out of kilter to be righted by the power of his words.

More than Vietnam divided the convention. Some of the southern delegations were still resisting the party rule that the delegate-selection process be open to blacks. The credentials committee, including Arkansas congressman David Pryor, voted to accept the Mississippi challenge delegation led by civil rights activist Aaron Henry. The other southern delegations were seated, except for Georgia's, which was split, with half the seats given to a challenge slate headed by young state representative Julian Bond, now chairman of the NAACP; and Alabama's, which had sixteen of its delegates disqualified because they wouldn't pledge to support the party's nominee, presumably because Alabama's Governor Wallace was running as an independent.

Despite these disputes, the main point of contention was the war. McCarthy seemed miserable, back to his old diffident self, resigned to defeat, detached from the kids who were getting harassed or beaten every night in Lincoln Park or Grant Park when they refused to leave. In a last-minute effort to find a candidate most Democrats thought was electable and acceptable, people from Al Lowenstein to Mayor Daley sounded out Ted Kennedy. When he gave a firm no, Humphrey's nomination was secure. So was the Vietnam plank Johnson wanted. About 60 percent of the delegates voted for it.

The night the convention was to name its nominee, fifteen thousand people gathered in Grant Park to demonstrate against the war and Mayor Daley's tough tactics. After one of them started to lower the American flag, the police stormed into the crowd, beating and arresting people. When the demonstrators marched toward the Hilton, the police teargassed them and beat them again on Michigan Avenue. All the action was beamed into the convention hall by television. Both sides were inflamed. McCarthy finally addressed his supporters in Grant Park, telling them he would not abandon them and would not endorse Humphrey or Nixon. Senator Abe Ribicoff of Connecticut, in nominating McGovern, condemned the "Gestapo tactics in the streets of

Chicago." Daley leapt to his feet and, with the TV cameras on him, hurled an angry epithet at Ribicoff. When the speeches were over, the balloting began. Humphrey won handily, with the vote completed at about midnight. His choice for vice president, Senator Edmund Muskie of Maine, breezed through shortly afterward. Meanwhile, the protests continued outside the convention hall, led by Tom Hayden and black comedian Dick Gregory. The only uplifting thing to happen inside the hall, besides Inouye's keynote, was the final-day film tribute to Robert Kennedy, which brought the delegates to a frenzy of emotion. Wisely, President Johnson had ordered that it not be shown until after Humphrey was nominated.

In a final indignity, after the convention, the police stormed into the Hilton to beat and arrest McCarthy volunteers who were having a farewell party. They claimed the young people, while drowning their sorrows, had thrown objects down on them from the McCarthy staff's fifteenth-floor room. The next day, Humphrey stood foursquare behind Daley's handling of the "planned and premeditated" violence and denied that the mayor had done anything wrong.

The Democrats limped out of Chicago divided and discouraged, the latest casualties in a culture war that went beyond differences over Vietnam. It would reshape and realign American politics for the rest of the century and beyond, and frustrate most efforts to focus the electorate on the issues that most affect their lives and livelihoods, as opposed to their psyches. The kids and their supporters saw the mayor and the cops as authoritarian, ignorant, violent bigots. The mayor and his largely blue-collar ethnic police force saw the kids as foul-mouthed, immoral, unpatriotic, soft, upper-class kids who were too spoiled to respect authority, too selfish to appreciate what it takes to hold a society together, too cowardly to serve in Vietnam.

As I watched all this in my little hotel room in Shreveport, I understood how both sides felt. I was against the war and the police brutality, but growing up in Arkansas had given me an appreciation for the struggles of ordinary people who do their duty every day, and a deep skepticism about self-righteous sanctimony on the right or the left. The fleeting fanaticism of the left had not yet played itself out, but it had already unleashed a radical reaction on the right, one that would prove more durable, more well financed, more institutionalized, more resourceful, more addicted to power, and far more skilled at getting and keeping it.

Much of my public life was spent trying to bridge the cultural and psychological divide that had widened into a chasm in Chicago. I won a lot of elections and I think I did a lot of good, but the more I tried to bring people together, the madder it made the fanatics on the right. Unlike the kids in Chicago, they didn't want America to come back together. They had an enemy, and they meant to keep it.

FOURTEEN

I SPENT SEPTEMBER getting ready for Oxford, saying good-bye to friends, and watching the presidential campaign unfold. I was eligible for the draft so I checked in with the local board chairman, Bill Armstrong, about when I could expect to be called. Though graduate deferments had been abolished the previous spring, students were allowed to finish the term they were in. Oxford had three eight-week terms a year, divided by two five-week vacation periods. I was told that I wouldn't be in the October call, and that I might get to stay beyond one term, depending on how many people my local draft board had to supply. I wanted to go to Oxford badly, even if I got to stay only a couple of months. The Rhodes Trust would allow people to do their military service and come to Oxford afterward, but since I had decided to be in the draft, with no end in sight in Vietnam, it didn't seem prudent to think about afterward.

On the political front, though I thought we were deader than a doornail coming out of Chicago, and Humphrey was sticking with LBJ's Vietnam policy, I still wanted him to win. Civil rights alone was enough reason. Race still divided the South, and increasingly, with the spread of court-ordered busing of children out of their local schools to achieve racial balance across school districts, the rest of the country was dividing as well. Ironically, Wallace's candidacy gave Humphrey a chance, since most of his voters were law-and-order segregationists who would have voted for Nixon in a two-man race.

The country's cultural clashes continued to erupt. Antiwar demonstrators went after Humphrey more than Nixon or Wallace. The vice president was also bedeviled by continuing criticism of Mayor Daley's police tactics during the convention. While a Gallup poll said 56 percent of Americans approved of the police conduct toward the demonstrators,

most of them were not in the Democratic base, especially in
a three-way race including Wallace. As if all this were not
enough, the established order was further upset by two sets
of protesters at the Miss America pageant in Atlantic City. A
black group protested the absence of black contestants.
A women's liberation group protested the pageant itself
as degrading to women. For good measure, some of them
burned their bras, proof positive to many old-fashioned
Americans that something had gone terribly wrong.

In the presidential campaign, Nixon appeared to be
coasting to victory, attacking Humphrey as weak and inef-
fectual and saying as little as possible about what he would
do as President, except to pander to segregationists (and
court Wallace voters) by promising to reverse the policy of
withholding federal funds from school districts that refused
to comply with federal court orders to integrate their
schools. Nixon's running mate, Spiro Agnew, was the campaign's attack dog, aided by his speechwriter Pat Buchanan.
His harshness and verbal gaffes were becoming legendary.
Humphrey suffered loud demonstrators everywhere he
went. By the end of the month, Nixon was holding steady at
43 percent in the polls, while Humphrey had dropped
twelve points to 28 percent, just seven points ahead of Wallace at 21 percent. On the last day of September, in desperation, Humphrey publicly broke with President Johnson on
Vietnam, saying that he would stop the bombing of North
Vietnam as "an acceptable risk for peace." Finally, he had
become his own man, but there were only five weeks to go.

By the time Humphrey made his "free at last" speech, I
was in New York getting ready to set sail for Oxford.
Denise Hyland and I had a terrific lunch with Willie Morris,
then the young editor of *Harper's Magazine*. In my senior
year at Georgetown, I had read his wonderful memoir,
North Toward Home, and had become a lifetime fan. After
I won the Rhodes, I wrote Willie, asking if I could come to
see him when I was in New York. In the spring he received
me in his office on Park Avenue. I enjoyed the visit so much
I asked to see him again before I left, and for some reason,
maybe southern manners, he made the time.

On October 4, Denise went with me to Pier 86 on the Hudson River, where I would board the SS *United States* for England. I knew where the huge ocean liner was headed, but I had no idea where I was going.

The *United States* was then the fastest liner on the seas, but the trip still took nearly a week. It was a long-standing tradition for the Rhodes group to sail together so that they could get acquainted. The ship's leisurely pace and group dining did give us time to get to know one another (after the obligatory period of "sniffing each other out" like a pack of wary, well-bred hunting dogs), to meet some other passengers, and to decompress a little out of the hothouse American political environment. Most of us were so earnest we almost felt guilty about enjoying the trip; we were surprised to meet people who were far less obsessed with Vietnam and domestic politics than we were.

The most unusual encounter I had was with Bobby Baker, the notorious political protégé of Lyndon Johnson's who had been secretary of the Senate when the President was Senate majority leader. A year earlier, Baker had been convicted of tax evasion and various other federal offenses, but was still free while his case was on appeal. Baker seemed carefree, consumed with politics, and interested in spending time with the Rhodes scholars. The feeling wasn't generally reciprocated. Some of our group didn't know who he was; most of the rest saw him as the embodiment of the political establishment's corrupt cronyism. I didn't approve of what he apparently had done, but was fascinated by his stories and insights, which he was eager to share. It took only a question or two to get him started.

With the exception of Bobby Baker and his entourage, I mostly hung around with the other Rhodes scholars and the other young people on board. I especially liked Martha Saxton, a brilliant, lovely, aspiring writer. She was spending most of her time with another Rhodes scholar, but eventually I got my chance, and after our romance was over, we became lifelong friends. Recently, she gave me a copy of her latest book, *Being Good: Women's Moral Values in Early America.*

One day a man invited a few of us to his suite for cocktails. I had never had a drink before and had never wanted one. I hated what liquor had done to Roger Clinton and was afraid that it might have the same effect on me. But I decided the time had come to overcome my lifelong fear. When our host asked me what I wanted, I said Scotch and soda, a drink I had made for others when I worked as a bartender for a couple of private parties in Georgetown. I had no idea what it would taste like, and when I tried it I didn't like it very much. The next day I tried a bourbon and water, which I liked a little better. After I got to Oxford, I drank mostly beer, wine, and sherry, and when I came home, I enjoyed gin and tonic and beer in the summertime. A few times in my twenties and early thirties I had too much to drink. After I met Hillary we enjoyed champagne on special occasions, but fortunately, liquor never did much for me. Also, in the late seventies I developed an allergy to all alcoholic drinks except vodka. On balance, I'm glad I broke free of my fear of tasting liquor on the ship, and I'm relieved I never had a craving for it. I've had enough problems without that one.

By far the best part of the voyage was just what it was supposed to be: being with the other Rhodes scholars. I tried to spend some time with all of them, listening to their stories and learning from them. Many had far more impressive academic records than I did, and a few had been active in anti-war politics, on campuses or in the McCarthy and Kennedy campaigns. Several of those I liked most became lifetime friends, and an amazing number played an important part in my presidency: Tom Williamson, a black Harvard football player, who served as counsel to the Labor Department in my first term; Rick Stearns, a Stanford graduate, who got me into the national McGovern campaign and whom I appointed a federal judge in Boston; Strobe Talbott, editor of the *Yale Daily News*, who became my special advisor on Russia and deputy secretary of state after a distinguished career at *Time* magazine; Doug Eakeley, later my law school housemate, whom I appointed chair of the Legal Services Corporation; Alan Bersin, another Harvard football player from Brooklyn, whom I appointed U.S. attorney in San Diego, where he's now superintendent of schools; Willie Fletcher from Seattle, Washington, whom I appointed to the Ninth Circuit Court of Appeals; and Bob Reich, the already famous spark plug of our group, who served as secretary of labor in my first term. Dennis Blair, a Naval Academy grad, was an admiral in the Pentagon when I became President and later commander of our forces in the Pacific, but he got there without any help from me.

Over the next two years, we would all experience Oxford in different ways, but we shared in the uncertainties and anxieties of the times at home, loving Oxford, yet wondering what the devil we were doing there. Most of us threw ourselves into our new lives more than into our tutorials or lectures. Our conversations, personal reading, and trips seemed more important, especially to those of us who thought we were on borrowed time. After two years, a smaller percentage of the Americans would actually receive degrees than in any previous class of Rhodes scholars. In our own way, filled with youthful angst, we probably learned more at Oxford about ourselves, and about things that would matter for a lifetime, than most of our predecessors had.

After five days and a brief stop in Le Havre, we finally arrived at Southampton, where we caught our first glimpse of Oxford in the person of Sir Edgar "Bill" Williams, the warden of Rhodes House. He was waiting for us on the dock in a bowler hat, raincoat, and umbrella, looking more like an English dandy than like the man who, during World War II, had served as chief of intelligence to Field Marshal Montgomery.

Bill Williams herded us onto a bus for the ride to Oxford. It was dark and rainy so we didn't see much. When we got to Oxford, it was about 11 p.m. and the whole town was shut down tight as a drum, except for a little lighted truck selling hot dogs, bad coffee, and junk food on High Street, just outside University College, where I had been assigned. The bus let us off and we walked through the door into the main quadrangle, built in the seventeenth century, where we were met by Douglas Millin, the head porter, who controlled access to the college. Millin was a crusty old codger who took the college job after he retired from the navy. He was very smart, a fact he took pains to hide behind torrents of good-natured verbal abuse. He especially liked to work the Americans over. The first words I heard from him were directed at Bob Reich, who is less than five feet tall. He said he'd been told he was getting four Yanks, but they'd sent him only three and a half. He never stopped making fun of us, but behind it he was a wise man and a shrewd judge of people.

I spent a lot of time over the next two years talking to Douglas. In between the "bloody hells" and various other English epithets, he taught me how the college really worked, told me stories of the main professors and staff, and discussed current affairs, including the differences between Vietnam and World War II. Over the next twenty-five years, whenever I got back to England, I dropped in to see Douglas for a reality check. At the end of 1978, after I had been elected governor of Arkansas the first time, I took Hillary to England for a much-needed vacation. When we got to Oxford, I was feeling pretty proud of myself as we walked through the front door of the college. Then I saw Douglas. He didn't miss a beat. "Clinton," he said, "I hear you've just been elected king of some place with three men and a dog." I loved Douglas Millin.

My rooms were in the back of the college, behind the library, in Helen's Court, a quaint little space named after the wife of a previous master of the college. Two buildings faced each other across a small walled-in space. The older building on the left had two doors to two sets of student rooms on the ground floor and the second floor. I was assigned to the rooms on the left side of the second floor at the far entrance. I had a small bedroom and a small study that were really just one big room. The toilet was on the first floor, which often made for a cold walk down the stairs. The shower was on my floor. Sometimes it had warm water. The modern building on the right was for graduate students, who had two-story flats. In October 2001, I helped Chelsea unpack her things in the flat with a bedroom directly opposite the rooms I had occupied thirty-three years earlier. It was one of those priceless moments when the sunshine takes away all life's shadows.

I woke up on my first morning in Oxford to encounter one of the curiosities of Oxford life, my "scout" Archie, who took care of the rooms in Helen's Court. I was used to making my own bed and looking after myself, but gradually I gave in to letting Archie do the job he had been doing for almost fifty years by the time he got stuck with me. He was a quiet, kind man for whom I and the other boys developed real affection and respect. At Christmas and on other special occasions, the students were expected to give their scout a modest gift, and modest was all most of us could afford on the annual Rhodes stipend of $1,700. Archie let it be known that what he really wanted was a few bottles of Guinness stout, a dark Irish beer. I gave him a lot of it in my year in Helen's Court and occasionally shared a sip with him. Archie really loved that stuff, and thanks to him, I actually developed a taste for it too.

University life is organized around its twenty-nine colleges, then still divided by gender; there were far fewer women's colleges. The University's main role in students' lives is to provide lectures, which students may or may not attend, and to administer exams, which are given at the end of the entire course of study. Whether you get a degree and how distinguished it is depends entirely on your performance during examination week. Meanwhile, the primary means of covering the material is the weekly tutorial, which normally requires you to produce a short essay on the subject to be discussed. Each college has its own chapel, dining hall, and library. Most have remarkable architectural features; some have stunning gardens, even parks and lakes, or touch on the River Cherwell, which borders the old city on the east. Just below Oxford, the Cherwell runs into the Isis, part of the Thames, the massive river that shapes so much of London.

I spent most of the first two weeks walking around Oxford, an ancient and beautiful city. I explored its rivers, parks, tree-lined paths, churches, the covered market, and, of course, the colleges.

Though my college didn't have large grounds, and its oldest buildings date only to the seventeenth century, it suited me fine. In the fourteenth century, the fellows of the college forged documents to show that it was Oxford's oldest, with roots in the ninth-century rule of Alfred the Great. Indisputably, Univ, as everyone calls it, is one of the three oldest colleges, founded along with Merton and Balliol in the thirteenth century. In 1292, the governing statutes contained a set of strict rules, including a ban on singing ballads and speaking English. On a few rowdy nights, I almost wished my contemporaries were still confined to whispering in Latin.

University's most famous student, Percy Bysshe Shelley, enrolled in 1810 as a chemistry student. He lasted about a year, expelled not because he had used his knowledge to set up a small still in his room to make liquor, but because of his paper "The Necessity of Atheism." By 1894, Univ had reclaimed Shelley, in the form of a beautiful marble statue of the dead poet, who drowned off the coast of Italy in his late twenties. Visitors to the college who never read his poetry can tell, just by gazing on his graceful death pose, why he had such a hold on the young people of his time. In the twentieth century, Univ's undergraduates and fellows included three famous writers: Stephen Spender, C. S. Lewis, and V. S. Naipaul; the great physicist Stephen Hawking; two British prime ministers, Clement Attlee and Harold Wilson; Australian prime minister Bob Hawke, who still owns the college speed record in beer drinking; the actor Michael York; and the man who killed Rasputin, Prince Felix Yusupov.

While beginning to learn about Oxford and England, I was also trying to follow election developments from afar and was eagerly awaiting the absentee ballot with which I would cast my first vote for President. Although urban violence and student demonstrations continued, Humphrey was doing better. After his semi–declaration of independence from LBJ on Vietnam, he drew fewer protests and more support from young people. McCarthy finally endorsed him, in a typically halfhearted way, adding that he would not be a candidate for reelection to the Senate in 1970 or for

President in 1972. Meanwhile, Wallace committed a crippling error by naming former air force chief of staff Curtis LeMay as his vice-presidential partner. LeMay, who had urged President Kennedy to bomb Cuba during the missile crisis five years earlier, made his debut as a candidate by saying nuclear bombs were "just another weapon in the arsenal" and that "there are many times when it would be most efficient to use them." LeMay's remarks put Wallace on the defensive and he never recovered.

Meanwhile, Nixon kept at the strategy with which he was coasting to victory, refusing repeated invitations to debate Humphrey; he was bothered only by the universal unfavorable comparison of Spiro Agnew to Humphrey's running mate, Senator Muskie, and by the fear that Johnson would achieve an "October surprise" breakthrough in the Paris peace talks with a bombing halt. We now know that the Nixon campaign was being fed inside information about the talks by Henry Kissinger, who, as a consultant to Averell Harriman, was involved enough with the Paris talks to know what was going on. We also know that Nixon's campaign manager, John Mitchell, lobbied South Vietnam's president, Thieu, through Nixon's friend Anna Chennault, not to give in to LBJ's pressure to join the peace talks along with the government's South Vietnamese opposition, the National Liberation Front. Johnson knew about the Nixon team's efforts because of Justice Department–approved wiretaps on Anna Chennault and the South Vietnamese ambassador to Washington. Finally, on the last day of October, President Johnson announced a full bombing halt, Hanoi's agreement to South Vietnam's participation in the talks, and U.S. approval of a role for the National Liberation Front.

November opened with high hopes for Humphrey and his supporters. He was moving up fast in the polls and clearly thought the peace initiative would put him over the top. On November 2, the Saturday before the election, President Thieu announced that he wouldn't go to Paris because the NLF was included. He said that would force him into a coalition government with the Communists, and he would deal only with North Vietnam. The Nixon camp was quick to imply that LBJ had jumped the gun on his peace initiative, acting to help Humphrey without having all his diplomatic ducks in a row.

Johnson was furious, and gave Humphrey the information on Anna Chennault's efforts to sabotage the initiative on Nixon's behalf. There was no longer a need to keep it from the public to avoid undermining President Thieu, but amazingly, Humphrey refused to use it. Because the polls showed him in a virtual dead heat with Nixon, he thought he might win without it, and apparently he was afraid of a possible backlash because the facts didn't prove that Nixon himself knew what others, including John Mitchell, were doing on his behalf. Still, the implication was strong that Nixon had engaged in activity that was virtually treasonous. Johnson was furious at Humphrey. I believe LBJ would have leaked the bombshell if he had been running, and that if the roles had been reversed, Nixon would have used it in a heartbeat.

Humphrey paid for his scruples, or his squeamishness. He lost the election by 500,000 votes, 43.4 percent to 42.7 percent to 13.5 percent for Wallace. Nixon won 301 electoral votes, 31 over a majority, with close victories in Illinois and Ohio. Nixon got away with the Kissinger-Mitchell-Chennault gambit, but as Jules Witcover speculates in his book on 1968, *The Year the Dream Died*, it may have been a more costly escape than it appeared. Its success may have contributed to the Nixon crowd's belief that they could get away with anything, including all the shenanigans that surfaced in Watergate.

On November 1, I began to keep a diary in one of two leather-bound volumes Denise Hyland had given me when I left the United States. When Archie woke me with the good news about the bombing halt, I wrote: "I wish I could have seen Senator Fulbright today—one more instance of vindication for his tireless and tenacious battle." The next day I speculated that a cease-fire might lead to a troop reduction and my not being drafted, or at least "allow many of my friends already in the service to escape Vietnam. And maybe some now in those jungles can be saved from early death."

Little did I know that half our deaths were still to come. I closed my first two installments by "extolling the same virtue: hope, the fiber of my being, which stays with me even on nights like tonight when I have lost all power of analysis and articulation." Yes, I was young and melodramatic, but I already believed in what I was to term "a place called Hope" in my 1992 Democratic convention speech. It's kept me going through a lifetime.

On November 3, I forgot about the election for a while during a lunch with George Cawkwell, the dean of graduates at Univ. He was a big, imposing man who still looked every inch the rugby star he once had been, as a Rhodes scholar from New Zealand. At our first meeting, Professor Cawkwell had really dressed me down about my decision to change my course of studies. Soon after I arrived in Oxford, I had transferred out of the undergraduate program in politics, philosophy, and economics, called PPE, and into the B.Litt. in politics, which required a fifty thousand–word dissertation. I had covered virtually all the first year's work in PPE at Georgetown, and because of the draft, I didn't expect to have a second year at Oxford. Cawkwell thought I'd made a terrible mistake in passing up the weekly tutorials, in which essays are read, criticized, and defended. Largely because of Cawkwell's argument, I switched courses again, to the B.Phil. in politics, which does include tutorials, essays, exams, and a shorter thesis.

Election day, November 5, was also Guy Fawkes Day in England, the observance of his attempt to burn down Parliament in 1605. My diary says: "Everyone in England celebrates the occasion; some because Fawkes failed, some because he tried." That night we Americans had an election-watch party at Rhodes House. The largely pro-Humphrey crowd was cheering him on. We went to bed not knowing what happened, but we did know that Fulbright had won handily, a relief, since he had prevailed in the primary over Jim Johnson and two little-known contenders with only 52 percent of the vote. A great cheer went up at Rhodes House when his victory was announced.

On November 6, we learned that Nixon had won and

that, as I wrote, "Uncle Raymond and his cronies carried Arkansas for Wallace, our first deviation from the national (Democratic) ticket since achieving statehood in 1836. . . . I must send my ten dollars to Uncle Raymond, for I bet him last November that Arkansas, the most 'liberal' of the Southern states, would never go for Wallace, which just goes to show how wrong these pseudo-intellectuals can be!" ("Pseudo-intellectual" was a favorite Wallace epithet for anyone with a college degree who disagreed with him.) I noted that, unlike the South Vietnamese government, I was terribly disappointed that "after all that has occurred, after Humphrey's remarkable recovery, it has come to the end I sensed last January: Nixon in the White House."

Adding insult to injury, my absentee ballot never arrived and I missed my first chance to vote for President. The county clerk had mailed it by surface mail, not airmail. It was cheaper but it took three weeks, arriving long after the election.

The next day, I got back to my life. I called Mother, who had by then decided to marry Jeff Dwire and was so blissfully happy she made me feel good, too. And I mailed that ten-dollar check to Uncle Raymond, suggesting that the United States establish a national George Wallace Day, similar to Guy Fawkes Day. Everyone could celebrate: some because he ran for President, the rest of us because he ran so poorly.

The rest of the month was a blizzard of activity that pushed politics and Vietnam to the back of my brain for a while. One Friday, Rick Stearns and I hitchhiked and rode buses to Wales and back, while Rick read Dylan Thomas poems to me. It was the first time I had heard "Do Not Go Gentle into That Good Night." I loved it, and love it still when brave souls "rage against the dying of the light."

I also took several trips with Tom Williamson. Once we decided to do a role reversal on the bad stereotypes of sub-servient blacks and racist southern overlords. When the nice English driver stopped to pick us up, Tom said, "Boy, get in the backseat." "Yes suh," I replied. The English driver thought we were nuts.

Two weeks after the election I scored my first touchdown, called a "try," for Univ's rugby team. It was a big thing for a former band boy. Though I never really understood its subtleties, I liked rugby. I was bigger than most English boys and could normally make an acceptable contribution by running to the ball and getting in the opposition's way, or pushing hard in the second row of the "scrum," a strange formation in which the two sides push against each other for control of the ball, which is placed on the ground between them. Once, we went to Cambridge for a match. Though Cambridge is more serene than Oxford, which is larger and more industrialized, the opposing team played hard and rough. I got a blow on the head and probably sustained a minor concussion. When I told the coach I was dizzy, he reminded me that there were no substitutes and our side would be one man short if I came out: "Just get back on the field and get in someone's way." We lost anyway, but I was glad I hadn't quit the field. As long as you don't quit, you've always got a chance.

In late November, I wrote my first essay for my tutor, Dr. Zbigniew Pelczynski, a Polish émigré, on the role of terror in Soviet totalitarianism ("a sterile knife cutting into the collective body, removing hard growths of diversity and independence"), attended my first tutorial, and went to my first academic seminar. Apart from those meager efforts, I spent the rest of the month sort of wandering around. I went twice to Stratford-upon-Avon, Shakespeare's home, to see plays of his; to London twice, to see Ann Markusen's former Georgetown housemates Dru Bachman and Ellen McPeake, who were living and working there; to Birmingham to play basketball badly; and to Derby to speak to high school students and answer their questions about America on the fifth anniversary of President Kennedy's death.

As December began, I made plans for my surprise homecoming for Mother's wedding, filled with foreboding about my future and hers. A lot of Mother's friends were dead set against her marrying Jeff Dwire, because he had been to prison and because they thought he was still untrustworthy. To make things worse, he hadn't been able to finalize his divorce from his long-estranged wife.

Meanwhile, the uncertainty of my own life was reinforced when my friend Frank Aller, a Rhodes scholar at Queen's College, just across High Street from Univ, received his draft notice from his hometown selective-service board in Spokane, Washington. He told me he was going home to prepare his parents and girlfriend for his decision to refuse induction and to stay in England indefinitely to avoid going to jail. Frank was a China scholar who understood Vietnam well, and thought our policy was both wrong and immoral. He was also a good middle-class boy who loved his country. He was miserable on the horns of his dilemma. Strobe Talbott, who lived just down the street in Magdalen College, and I tried to console and support him. Frank was a good-hearted man who knew we were as opposed to the war as he was, and he tried to console us in return. He was particularly forceful with me, telling me that, unlike him, I had the desire and ability to make a difference in politics and it would be wrong to throw my opportunities away by resisting the draft. His generosity only made me feel more guilty, as the angst-ridden pages of my diary show. He was cutting me more slack than I could allow myself.

On December 19, I landed in a huge snowfall in Minneapolis for a reunion with Ann Markusen. She was home from her Ph.D. studies at Michigan State and as uncertain about her future, and ours, as I was. I loved her, but I was too uncertain of myself at that point in my life to make a commitment to anyone else.

On December 23, I flew home. The surprise came off. Mother cried and cried. She, Jeff, and Roger all seemed happy about the coming marriage, so happy that they didn't give me too much grief about my newly long hair. Christmas was merry in spite of last-ditch efforts by two of Mother's friends to get me to try to talk her out of marrying Jeff. I took four yellow roses to Daddy's grave and prayed that his family would support Mother and Roger in their new endeavor. I liked Jeff Dwire. He was smart, hardworking, good with Roger, and clearly in love with Mother. I was for the marriage, noting that "if all the skeptical well-wishers and the really pernicious ill-wishers are right about Jeff and

Mother, their union can hardly prove more of a failure than did its predecessors—his too," and for a while, I forgot all the tumult of 1968, the year that broke open the nation and shattered the Democratic Party; the year that conservative populism replaced progressive populism as the dominant political force in our nation; the year that law and order and strength became the province of Republicans, and Democrats became associated with chaos, weakness, and out-of-touch, self-indulgent elites; the year that led to Nixon, then Reagan, then Gingrich, then George W. Bush. The middle-class backlash would shape and distort American politics for the rest of the century. The new conservatism would be shaken by Watergate, but not destroyed. Its public support would be weakened, as right-wing ideologues promoted economic inequality, environmental destruction, and social divisions, but not destroyed. When threatened by its own excesses, the conservative movement would promise to be "kinder and gentler" or more "compassionate," all the while ripping the hide off Democrats for alleged weakness of values, character, and will. And it would be enough to provoke the painfully predictable, almost Pavlovian reaction among enough white middle-class voters to carry the day. Of course it was more complicated than that. Sometimes conservatives' criticisms of the Democrats had validity, and there were always moderate Republicans and conservatives of goodwill who worked with Democrats to make some positive changes.

Nevertheless, the deeply embedded nightmares of 1968 formed the arena in which I and all other progressive politicians had to struggle over our entire careers. Perhaps if Martin Luther King Jr. and Robert Kennedy had lived, things would have been different. Perhaps if Humphrey had used the information about Nixon's interference with the Paris peace talks, things would have been different. Perhaps not. Regardless, those of us who believed that the good in the 1960s outweighed the bad would fight on, still fired by the heroes and dreams of our youth.

FIFTEEN

NEW YEAR'S MORNING 1969—I opened the year on a happy note. Frank Holt had just been reelected to the supreme court, only two years after his defeat in the governor's race. I drove to Little Rock, to the judge's swearing-in ceremony. Predictably, he had urged us not to spend New Year's Day on this modest ritual, but more than fifty of us diehards showed up anyway. My diary says: "I told him I wasn't about to pull out just because he was winning!" Ironically, as a "new" justice, he was assigned to the old offices of Justice Jim Johnson.

On January 2, Joe Newman and I drove Mother home to Hope to tell what remained of her family that she was going to marry Jeff the next day. When we got home, Joe and I took the "The Roger Clintons" sign off the mailbox. With his sharp sense of irony, Joe laughed and said, "It's kinda sad that it comes off so easily." Despite the harbingers of doom, I thought the marriage would work. As I wrote in my diary, "If Jeff is nothing more than a con man, as some still insist, then color me conned."

The next night, the ceremony was short and simple. Our friend Reverend John Miles led them through their vows. Roger lit the candles. I was best man. There was a party afterward at which Carolyn Yeldell and I played and sang for the wedding guests. Some preachers would have refused church sanction to the wedding because Jeff was divorced, and so recently. Not John Miles. He was a pugnacious, tough, liberal Methodist who believed Jesus was sent by his Father God to give us all second chances.

On January 4, thanks to my friend Sharon Evans, who knew Governor Rockefeller, I was invited to lunch with the governor at his ranch on Petit Jean Mountain. I found Rockefeller friendly and articulate. We discussed Oxford and his son Winthrop Paul's desire to go there. The governor wanted me to keep in touch with Win Paul, who had spent a lot of his childhood in Europe, when he began his studies at Pembroke College in the fall.

After lunch, I had a good talk with Win Paul, after which we headed southwest for a rendezvous with Tom Campbell, who had driven to Arkansas from Mississippi, where he was in marine flight training. The three of us drove to the Governor's Mansion, which Win Paul had invited us to see. We were all impressed, and I left thinking I had just seen an important piece of Arkansas history, not the place that in a decade would become my home for twelve years.

On January 11, I flew back to England on the same plane with Tom Williamson, who was educating me about being black in America, and Frank Aller, who recounted his difficult holiday, in which his conservative father made getting a haircut, but not reporting for the draft, a precondition of Christmas at home. When I got back to Univ, I found in my stack of mail a remarkable letter from my old friend and baptismal partner, Marine Private Bert Jeffries. I recorded some excerpts of his stunning, sad message:

> . . . Bill, I've already seen many things and been through a lot no man of a right mind would want to see or go through. Over here, they play for keeps. And it's either win or lose. It's not a pretty sight to see a buddy you live with and become so close to, to have him die beside you and you know it was for no good reason. And you realize how easily it could have been you.
>
> I work for a Lieutenant Colonel. I am his body-guard. . . . On the 21st of November we came to a place called Winchester. Our helicopter let us off and the Colonel, myself, and two other men started looking over the area . . . there were two NVAs [North Vietnamese Army soldiers] in a bunker, they opened up on us. . . . The Colonel got hit and the two others were hit. Bill, that day I prayed. Fortunately I got the two of them before they got me. I killed my first man that day. And Bill, it's an awful

feeling, to know you took another man's life. It's a
sickening feeling. And then you realize how it
could have been you just as easily.

The next day, January 13, I went to London for my draft
exam. The doctor declared me, according to my fanciful
diary notes, "one of the healthiest specimens in the western
world, suitable for display at medical schools, exhibitions,
zoos, carnivals, and base training camps." On the fifteenth I
saw Edward Albee's *A Delicate Balance*, which was "my
second surrealistic experience in as many days." Albee's
characters forced the audience "to wonder if some day near
the end they won't wake up and find themselves hollow and
afraid." I was already wondering that.

President Nixon was inaugurated on January 20. His
speech was an attempt at reconciliation, but it "left me
pretty cold, the preaching of good old middle-class religion
and virtues. They will supposedly solve our problems with
the Asians, who do not come from the Judeo-Christian tradition; the Communists, who do not even believe in God;
the blacks, who have been shafted so often by God-fearing
white men that there is hardly any common ground left
between them; and the kids, who have heard those same
song-and-dance sermons sung false so many times they may
prefer dope to the audacious self-delusion of their elders."
Ironically, I believed in Christianity and middle-class
virtues, too; they just didn't lead me to the same place. I
thought living out our true religious and political principles
would require us to reach deeper and go further than Mr.
Nixon was prepared to go.

I decided to get back into my own life in England for
whatever time I had left. I went to my first Oxford Union
debate—Resolved: that man created God in his own image,
"a potentially fertile subject poorly ploughed." I went north
to Manchester, and marveled at the beauty of the English
countryside "quilted by those ancient rock walls without
mortar or mud or cement." There was a seminar on "Plural-
ism as a Concept of Democratic Theory," which I found

boring, just another attempt "to explain in more complex (therefore, more meaningful, of course) terms what is going on before our own eyes. . . . It is only so much dog-dripping to me because I am at root not intellectual, not conceptual about the actual, just damn well not smart enough, I reckon, to run in this fast crowd."

On January 27, the actual reared its ugly head again, as a few of us threw a party for Frank Aller on the day he officially became a draft resister, "walking along the only open road." Despite the vodka, the toasts, the attempts at humor, the party was a bust. Even Bob Reich, easily the wittiest of us, couldn't make it work. We simply could not lift the burden from Frank's shoulders "on this, the day when he put his money where his mouth was." The next day Strobe Talbott, whose draft status was already 1-Y because of an old football injury, became really unsuited for military service when his eyeglasses met up with John Isaacson's squash racket on the Univ court. The doctor spent two hours pulling glass out of his cornea. He recovered and went on to spend the next thirty-five years seeing things most of us miss.

For a long time, February has been a hard month for me, dominated by fighting the blues and waiting for spring to come. My first February in Oxford was a real zinger. I fought it by reading, something I did a lot of at Oxford, with no particular pattern except what my studies dictated. I read hundreds of books. That month I read John Steinbeck's *The Moon Is Down*, partly because he had just died and I wanted to remember him with something I hadn't read before. I reread Willie Morris's *North Toward Home*, because it helped me to understand my roots and my "better self." I read Eldridge Cleaver's *Soul on Ice* and pondered the meaning of soul. "Soul is a word I use often enough to be Black, but of course, and I occasionally think unfortunately, I am not. . . . The soul: I know what it is—it's where I feel things; it's what moves me; it's what makes me a man, and when I put it out of commission, I know soon enough I will die if I do not retrieve it." I was afraid then that I was losing it.

My struggles with the draft rekindled my long-standing doubts about whether I was, or could become, a really good person. Apparently, a lot of people who grow up in difficult circumstances subconsciously blame themselves and feel unworthy of a better fate. I think this problem arises from leading parallel lives, an external life that takes its natural course and an internal life where the secrets are hidden. When I was a child, my outside life was filled with friends and fun, learning and doing. My internal life was full of uncertainty, anger, and a dread of ever-looming violence. No one can live parallel lives with complete success; the two have to intersect. At Georgetown, as the threat of Daddy's violence dissipated, then disappeared, I had been more able to live one coherent life. Now the draft dilemma brought back my internal life with a vengeance. Beneath my new and exciting external life, the old demons of self-doubt and impending destruction reared their ugly heads again.

I would continue to struggle to merge the parallel lives, to live with my mind, body, and spirit in the same place. In the meantime, I have tried to make my external life as good as possible, and to survive the dangers and relieve the pain of my internal life. This probably explains my profound admiration for the personal courage of soldiers and others who put their lives at risk for honorable causes, and my visceral hatred of violence and abuse of power; my passion for public service and my deep sympathy for the problems of other people; the solace I have found in human companionship and the difficulty I've had in letting anyone into the deepest recesses of my internal life. It was dark down there.

I had been down on myself before, but never like this, for this long. As I said, I first became self-aware enough to know that those feelings rumbled around beneath my sunny disposition and optimistic outlook when I was a junior in high school, more than five years before I went to Oxford. It was when I wrote an autobiographical essay for Ms. Warneke's honors English class and talked about the "disgust" that "storms my brain."

The storms were really raging in February 1969, and I

tried to put them out by reading, traveling, and spending lots of time with interesting people. I would meet many of them at 9 Bolton Gardens in London, a spacious apartment that became my home away from Oxford on many weekends. Its full-time occupant was David Edwards, who had shown up at Helen's Court one night with Dru Bachman, Ann Markusen's Georgetown housemate, dressed in a zoot suit, a long coat with a lot of buttons and pockets, and flared pants. Before then, I'd seen zoot suits only in old movies. David's place in Bolton Gardens became an open house for a loose collection of young Americans, Britons, and others floating in and out of London. There were plenty of meals and parties, usually funded disproportionately by David, who had more money than the rest of us and was generous to a fault.

I also spent a lot of time alone at Oxford. I enjoyed the solitude of reading and was especially moved by a passage in Carl Sandburg's *The People, Yes*:

> Tell him to be alone often and get at himself
> and above all tell himself no lies about himself.
> . . .
> Tell him solitude is creative if he is strong
> and the final decisions are made in silent rooms.
> . . .
> He will be lonely enough
> to have time for the work
> he knows as his own.

Sandburg made me think something good could come of my wondering and worrying. I had always spent a lot of time alone, being an only child until I was ten, with both parents working. When I got into national politics, one of the more amusing myths propagated by people who didn't know me was that I hate to be by myself, probably because I relish the company of others, from huge crowds to small dinners and card games with friends. As President, I worked hard to schedule my time so that I'd have a couple of hours a day alone to think, reflect, plan, or do nothing. Often I slept less just to get the alone time. At Oxford, I was alone a lot, and I used the time to do the sorting out Sandburg said a good life requires.

In March, with spring coming, my spirits lifted along with the weather. During our five-week vacation break, I took my first trip to the Continent, taking a train to Dover to see the white cliffs, then going by ferry to Belgium, where I took a train to Cologne, Germany. At 9:30 p.m., I stepped out of the station into the shadow of the magnificent medieval cathedral just up the hill, and understood why Allied pilots in World War II risked their lives to avoid destroying it by flying too low in their efforts to bomb the nearby rail bridge over the Rhine River. I felt close to God in that cathedral, as I have every time I've returned to it. The next morning I met up with Rick Stearns, Ann Markusen, and my German friend Rudy Lowe, whom I'd met in 1967 at CONTAC in Washington, D.C., to tour Bavaria. In Bamberg, Rudy's thousand-year-old hometown, he took me to see the East German border nearby, where there was an East German soldier standing guard in a high outpost behind barbed wire on the edge of the Bavarian Forest.

While I was traveling, President Eisenhower died, "one of the final fragments that remained of the American Dream." So did my relationship with Ann Markusen, a casualty of the times and my incapacity for commitment. It would be a long time before we reestablished our friendship.

Back in Oxford, George Kennan came to speak. Kennan had grave reservations about our Vietnam policy, and my friends and I were eager to hear him. Unfortunately, he stayed away from foreign policy, and instead launched into a diatribe against student demonstrators and the whole anti-war "counterculture." After some of my cohorts, especially Tom Williamson, debated him for a while, the show was over. Our consensus reaction was neatly summed up in a droll comment by Alan Bersin: "The book was better than the movie."

A couple of days later, I had an amazing dinner and argument with Rick Stearns, probably the most politically mature and savvy of our group. My diary notes that Rick "tore into my opposition to the draft," saying that the end of it would ensure that the poor would bear an even larger burden of military service. Instead, "Stearns wants national service, with alternate means of fulfillment to the military, but with inducements of shorter service time and higher salaries to keep the military force to acceptable levels. He believes everyone, not just the poor, should give community service." Thus was planted a seed that more than twenty years later, in my first presidential campaign, would blossom into my proposal for a national community service program for young people.

In the spring of 1969, the only national service was military, and its dimensions were measured by the callous term "body count." By mid-April, the count included my boyhood friend Bert Jeffries. In the agony of the aftermath, his wife gave birth a month prematurely to their child, who, like me, would grow up with received memories of a father. When Bert died, he was serving in the marines with two of his closest friends from Hot Springs, Ira Stone and Duke Watts. His family got to select one person to bring his body home, a choice of some consequence since, under military regulations, that person didn't have to go back. They chose Ira, who had already been wounded three times, in part because Duke, who had had his own narrow escapes from death, had only a month left on his tour. I cried for my friend, and wondered again whether my decision to go to Oxford was not motivated more by the desire to go on living than by opposition to the war. I noted in my diary that "the privilege of living in suspension . . . is impossible to justify, but, perhaps unfortunately, only very hard to live with."

Back home, the war protests continued unabated. In 1969, 448 universities had strikes or were forced to close. On April 22, I was surprised to read in *The Guardian* that Ed Whitfield from Little Rock had led an armed group of blacks to occupy a building on the campuses of Cornell University in Ithaca, New York. Just the summer before, Ed had been criticized by young militant blacks in Little Rock when we worked together to help Fulbright get reelected.

A week later, on April 30, the war finally came directly home to me, with a strange twist that was a metaphor for those bizarre times. I received my draft notice: I was ordered to report for duty on April 21. It's clear the notice had been mailed on April 1, but like my absentee ballot a few months earlier, it had been sent by surface mail. I called home to make sure the draft board knew I hadn't been a draft resister for nine days and asked what I should do. They told me the surface mailing was their mistake, and besides, under the rules, I got to finish the term I was in, so I was instructed to come home for induction when I finished.

I decided to make the most of what seemed certain to be the end of my Oxford stay, savoring every moment of the long English spring days. I went to the little village of Stoke Poges to see the beautiful churchyard where Thomas Gray is buried and read his "Elegy Written in a Country Church- yard," then to London to a concert and a visit to Highgate Cemetery, where Karl Marx is buried beneath a large bust that is a powerful likeness of him. I spent as much time as I could with the other Rhodes scholars, especially Strobe Tal- bott and Rick Stearns, from whom I was still learning. Over breakfast at George's, an old-fashioned café on the second floor of Oxford's covered market, Paul Parish and I dis- cussed his application for conscientious-objector status, which I supported with a letter to his draft board.

In late May, along with Paul Parish and his lady friend, Sara Maitland, a witty, wonderful Scottish woman who later became a fine writer, I went to the Royal Albert Hall in London to hear the great gospel singer Mahalia Jackson. She was magnificent, with her booming voice and powerful, innocent faith. At the end of the concert, her young audi- ence crowded around the stage, cheering and begging for an encore. They still hungered to believe in something larger than themselves. So did I.

On the twenty-eighth, I gave a farewell party at Univ for my friends: fellows from the college I'd played rugby and shared meals with; Douglas and the other porters; my scout, Archie; the Warden and Mrs. Williams; George Cawkwell; and an assortment of American, Indian, Caribbean, and South African students I'd gotten to know. I just wanted to thank them for being a big part of my year. My friends gave me a number of going-away gifts: a walking stick, an English wool hat, and a paperback copy of Flaubert's *Madame Bovary*, which I still have.

I spent the first part of June seeing Paris. I didn't want to go home without having done so. I took a room in the Latin Quarter, finished reading George Orwell's *Down and Out in Paris and London*, and saw all the sights, including the amazing small memorial to the Holocaust just behind Notre Dame. It's easy to miss, but worth the effort. You walk downstairs at the end of the island into a small space, turn around, and find yourself peering into a gas chamber.

My guide and companion on the trip was Alice Chamberlin, whom I had met through mutual friends in London. We walked through the Tuileries, stopping at the ponds to watch the children and their sailboats; ate interesting and cheap Vietnamese, Algerian, Ethiopian, and West Indian food; scaled Montmartre; and visited the church called Sacré Coeur—where in reverence and humor I lit a candle for my friend Dr. Victor Bennett, who had died a few days before and who, for all his genius, was irrationally anti-Catholic. I was trying to cover all his bases. It was the least I could do after all he'd done for Mother, Daddy, and me.

By the time I got back to Oxford, it was light almost around the clock. In the wee hours of one morning, my English friends took me to the rooftop of one of Univ's buildings to watch the sun rise over the beautiful Oxford skyline. We were so pumped up we broke into the Univ kitchen, pinched some bread, sausages, tomatoes, and cheese, went back to my room for breakfast.

On June 24, I went to say good-bye to Bill Williams. He wished me well and said he expected me to become a "disgustingly enthusiastic, pompous old alumnus." That night I had my last Oxford meal at a pub with Tom Williamson and his friends. On the twenty-fifth, I said good-bye to

Oxford—permanently, I believed. I went to London to meet Frank, Mary, and Lyda Holt. After we attended a night session of Parliament, and Judge and Mrs. Holt went home, I took Lyda to meet some friends for my last dinner in England, grabbed a couple of hours' sleep at David Edwards's place, then got up early and headed for the airport with six friends who came along to see me off. We didn't know when, if ever, we'd see each other again. I hugged them and ran for the plane.

SIXTEEN

I ARRIVED IN NEW YORK at 9:45 p.m., nine hours late, thanks to delays on both ends. By the time I got to Manhattan, it was after midnight, so I decided to stay up all night to catch an early-morning flight. I woke up Martha Saxton, and we sat and talked for two hours on the front steps of her place on the Upper West Side, then went to an all-night diner, where I got my first good hamburger in months, talked to two cabdrivers, read E. H. Carr's *What Is History?*, and thought about the extraordinary year I'd lived through and what lay ahead. And I stared at my nicest going-away gift: two little memory cards with French sayings entitled "L'Amitié" and "Sympathie." They had been given to me by Anik Alexis, a beautiful black Caribbean woman who was living in Paris and going out with Tom Williamson. Nikki had saved those cards for eight years, since she was a schoolgirl. I treasured them because they reflected the gifts I had tried to give, share, and draw out of others. I framed them and have put them up in every place I've lived for the past thirty-five years.

I left the diner with less than twenty dollars to get home to Arkansas, yet I wrote in the last page of my diary that I felt like "a wealthy man indeed, full of good fortune, and friends, and hope and convictions a bit more specific and well thought out than the ones with which I started this book last November." In that crazy time, my mood went up and down like an elevator. For good or ill, Denise Hyland had sent me a second diary in the spring to chronicle whatever happened next.

When I got home at the end of June, I had about a month before reporting for induction, during which I was free to make other military arrangements. There were no available spots in the National Guard or reserves. I looked into the air force, but learned I couldn't become a jet pilot because I didn't have fusion vision. I had a weak left eye, which had often tilted outward when I was very young. It had largely corrected itself, but my vision still didn't come to a single point, and apparently the consequences in flight could be severe. I also took a physical for a naval officer program but failed it, too, this time because of poor hearing, a problem I hadn't noticed and wouldn't until a decade later when I entered politics and often couldn't hear or understand people talking to me in crowds. The best option left seemed to be enrolling in law school and joining the Army Reserve Officers' Training Corps at the University of Arkansas.

On July 17, I went to Fayetteville and in two hours was accepted by both. The officer in charge of the program, Colonel Eugene Holmes, told me he was taking me because I would be of greater service to the country as an officer than as a draftee. His second in command, Lieutenant Colonel Clint Jones, seemed more conservative and skeptical of me, but we had a pleasant talk about his daughter, whom I had known and liked in Washington. Joining ROTC meant that I would go on active duty after law school. Apparently, they couldn't formally enroll me until the next summer, because I had to go to summer camp before I could enter ROTC classes, but signing a letter of intent was enough for the draft board to waive my induction date and give me a 1-D Reservist classification. I had mixed feelings. I knew I had a chance to avoid Vietnam, "but somebody will be getting on that bus in ten days and it may be that I should be getting on it too."

But ten days later I was not on the bus. Instead, I was in my car driving to Texas for a reunion with my Georgetown roommates who were already in the military, Tom Campbell, Jim Moore, and Kit Ashby. On the way there and back, I was alert to things that would reorient me to America. Houston and Dallas were crowded with large new apartment complexes, sprawling in no apparent pattern. I imagined that they were the wave of the future and I wasn't sure I wanted to go there. I read some cultural significance into the bumper stickers and personalized license plates I saw.

My favorite bumper sticker said "Don't Blame Jesus If You Go to Hell." By far the best license tag was, unbelievably, attached to a hearse: "Pop Box." Apparently readers were supposed to fear hell but laugh at death.

I wasn't at the laughing stage yet, but I had always been aware of, and not all that uncomfortable with, my own mortality. Probably because my father had died before I was born, I started thinking about death at an early age. I've always been fascinated by cemeteries and enjoy spending time in them. On the way home from Texas I stopped in Hope to see Buddy and Ollie and visit the graves of my father and grandparents. As I picked the weeds from around their tombstones, I was struck again by how few years they'd had on earth: twenty-eight for my father, fifty-eight for Papaw, sixty-six for Mammaw (and back in Hot Springs, fifty-seven for my stepfather). I knew I might not have a long life and I wanted to make the most of it. My attitude toward death was captured by the punch line in an old joke about Sister Jones, the most devout woman in her church. One Sunday her normally boring minister preached the sermon of his life. At the end he shouted, "I want everyone who wants to go to heaven to stand up." The congregation leapt to their feet, everyone except Sister Jones. Her pastor was crestfallen. He said, "Sister Jones, don't you want to go to heaven when you die?" The good lady jumped right up and said, "Oh yes, preacher. I'm sorry. I thought you were trying to get up a load to go right now!"

The next six weeks in Hot Springs were more interesting than I could have imagined. I worked one week helping a sixty-seven-year-old man put up one of Jeff's pre-fab houses in the small settlement of Story, west of Hot Springs. The old guy worked me into the ground every day and shared a lot of his homespun wisdom and country skepticism with me. Just a month before, *Apollo 11* astronauts Buzz Aldrin and Neil Armstrong had left their colleague, Michael Collins, aboard spaceship *Columbia* and walked on the moon, beating by five months President Kennedy's goal of putting a man on the moon before the decade was out. The old carpenter asked me if I really believed it had happened. I said sure, I saw it on television. He disagreed; he said that he didn't believe it for a minute, that "them television fellers" could make things look real that weren't. Back then, I thought he was a crank. During my eight years in Washington, I saw some things on TV that made me wonder if he wasn't ahead of his time.

I spent most evenings and a lot of days with Betsey Reader, who had been a year ahead of me in school and was working in Hot Springs. She was a wonderful antidote to my unrelenting anxieties: wise, wistful, and kind. We were asked to go to the YMCA to be a semi-adult presence at some events for high schoolers and we sort of adopted three of them: Jeff Rosensweig, the son of my pediatrician, who was very knowledgeable about politics; Jan Dierks, a quiet, intelligent girl who was interested in civil rights; and Glenn Mahone, a hip, articulate black guy, who had a large Afro and liked to wear African dashikis, long, colorful shirts worn outside the pants. We went everywhere together and had a grand time.

Hot Springs had a couple of racial incidents that summer, and tensions were high. Glenn and I thought we could relieve them by forming an interracial rock band and hosting a free dance in the Kmart parking lot. He would sing and I'd play my sax. On the appointed night a big crowd showed up. We played up on a flatbed truck, and they danced and mingled on the pavement. Everything went well for about an hour. Then a handsome young black man asked a pretty blond girl to dance. They were good together—too good. It was too much for some of the rednecks to bear. A fight broke out, then another, and another. Before we knew it we had a full-fledged brawl on our hands and police cars in the parking lot. So ended my first initiative in racial reconciliation.

One day Mack McLarty, who had been elected to the legislature just out of college, came to Hot Springs for a Ford dealers' convention. He was already married and settled into serious business and politics. I wanted to see him and decided to play a little joke on him in front of his highly conventional colleagues. I made arrangements to meet him on the plaza outside our convention center. He didn't know I'd grown long hair and a beard. That was bad enough, but I took three people with me: two English girls who had stopped in Hot Springs on a cross-country bus trip and looked the way you look after two or three days on a bus; and Glenn Mahone with his Afro and dashiki. We looked like refugees from the Woodstock festival. When Mack walked out onto the plaza with two of his friends, we must have caused him heartburn. But he never broke a sweat; he just greeted me and introduced us around. Underneath his starched shirt and short hair were a heart and a brain that sympathized with the peace and civil rights movements. He's stuck with me through thick and thin for a lifetime, but I never put him to a sterner test.

As the summer wore on, I felt worse and worse about my decision to join the ROTC and go to Arkansas Law School. I had a hard time sleeping, and spent most nights in the den in the white reclining chair in which I'd watched Martin Luther King Jr.'s "I have a dream" speech six years earlier. I'd read until I could nod off for a few hours. Because I had joined the ROTC late, I couldn't go to the required summer camp until the following summer, so Colonel Holmes agreed to let me go back to Oxford for a second year, which meant that I wouldn't begin my post–law school military service for four years rather than three. I was still disturbed by my decision.

A conversation with Reverend John Miles's brother made me more uncertain. Warren Miles quit school at eighteen to join the marines and go to Korea, where he was wounded in action. He came home and went to Hendrix College, where he won a Rhodes scholarship. He encouraged me to bag the safety of my present course, join the marines, and go to Vietnam, where at least I'd really learn something. He dismissed my opposition to the war out of hand, saying there was not a thing I could do about the fact of the war, and as long as it was there, decent people ought to go, experience, learn, remember. It was a hell of an argument. But I already remembered. I remembered what I'd learned working on the Foreign Relations Committee, including the classified evidence that the American people were being misled about the war. And I remembered Bert Jeffries's letter telling me to stay away. I was really torn. As the son of a World War II veteran, and as someone who grew up on John Wayne movies, I had always admired people who served in the military. Now I searched my heart, trying to determine whether my aversion to going was rooted in conviction or cowardice. Given the way it played out, I'm not sure I ever answered the question for myself.

Near the end of September, while working my way back to Oxford, I flew to Martha's Vineyard for a reunion of anti-war activists who had worked for Gene McCarthy. Of course, I hadn't done so. Rick Stearns invited me, I think because he knew I wanted to come and they wanted another southerner. The only other one there was Taylor Branch, a recent graduate of the University of North Carolina, who had just been in Georgia registering blacks to vote. Taylor went on to a distinguished career in journalism, helped John Dean of Watergate fame and basketball great Bill Russell write their autobiographies, then wrote his magnificent Pulitzer Prize–winning book, *Parting the Waters*, the first volume of a planned trilogy on Martin Luther King Jr. and the civil rights movement. Taylor and I formed a friendship that would lead us into the Texas McGovern campaign together in 1972, and then, in 1993, into an almost monthly oral history of my presidency, without which many of my memories of those years would be lost.

Besides Rick and Taylor, there were four other men at the reunion whom I kept up with over the years: Sam Brown, one of the most prominent leaders of the student anti-war movement, later got involved in Colorado politics and, when I was President, served the United States with the Organization for Security and Cooperation in Europe; David Mixner, who had begun organizing fellow migrant workers at fourteen, visited me several times in England and later moved to California, where he became active in the struggle against AIDS and for gay rights, and supported me in 1992; Mike Driver became one of my most cherished friends over the next thirty years; and Eli Segal, whom I met in the McGovern campaign, became chief of staff of the Clinton-Gore campaign.

All of us who gathered that weekend have since led lives we couldn't have imagined as autumn dawned in 1969. We just wanted to help stop the war. The group was planning the next large protest, known as the Vietnam Moratorium, and I made what little contribution I could to their deliberations. But mostly I was thinking about the draft, and feeling more and more uncomfortable with the way I'd handled it. Just before I left Arkansas for Martha's Vineyard, I wrote a letter to Bill Armstrong, chairman of my local draft board, telling him I didn't really want to do the ROTC program and asking him to withdraw my 1-D deferment and put me back in the draft. Strobe Talbott came to Arkansas to visit and we discussed whether I should mail it. I didn't.

The day I flew out, our local paper carried the front-page news that Army Lieutenant Mike Thomas, who had defeated me for student council president in junior high school, had been killed in Vietnam. Mike's unit came under attack and took cover. He died when he went back into the line of fire to rescue one of his men who was trapped in their vehicle; a mortar shell killed them both. After his death, the army gave him a Silver Star, a Bronze Star, and a Purple Heart. Now almost 39,000 Americans had perished in Vietnam, with 19,000 casualties still to come.

On September 25 and 26, I wrote in my diary: "Reading *The Unfinished Odyssey of Robert Kennedy* [by David Halberstam], I was reminded again that I don't believe in deferments. . . . I cannot do this ROTC." Sometime in the next few days, I called Jeff Dwire, told him I wanted to be put back in the draft, and asked him to tell Bill Armstrong. On October 30, the draft board reclassified me 1-A. On October 1, President Nixon had ordered a change in Selective Service System policy to allow graduate students to finish the entire school year they were in, not just the term, so I wouldn't be called until July. I don't remember, and my diary doesn't indicate, whether I asked Jeff to talk to the

local board before or after I learned that graduate deferments had been extended to a full academic year. I do
remember feeling relieved both that I'd get to spend some
more time at Oxford and that the draft situation was
resolved: I was reconciled to the fact that I'd probably be
called up at the end of the Oxford year.

I also asked Jeff to talk to Colonel Holmes. I still felt an
obligation to him: he had helped keep me from induction on
July 28. Even though I was now 1-A again, if he held me to
my commitment to the ROTC program beginning with next
summer's camp, I thought I would have to do it. Jeff indicated that the colonel accepted my decision, but thought I
was making a mistake.

On December 1, pursuant to a bill signed by President
Nixon five days earlier, the United States instituted a draft
lottery, with a drawing in which all the days of the year were
pulled out of a bowl. The order in which your birthday
came up determined the order in which you could be
drafted. August 19 came up 311. Even with the high lottery
number, for months afterward, I thought I had a fair chance
of being drafted. On March 21, 1970, I got a letter from
Lee Williams saying that he had talked to Colonel Lefty
Hawkins, the head of the Arkansas Selective Service System,
who told him we would all be called.

When I got the high draft number, I called Jeff again and
asked him to tell Colonel Holmes that I hadn't gone back
into the draft knowing this would happen and that I understood that he could still call me on the ROTC obligation.
Then, on December 3, I sat down and wrote Colonel
Holmes. I thanked him for protecting me from the draft the
previous summer, told him how much I admired him, and
said I doubted that he would have admired me had he
known more about my political beliefs and activities: "At
least you might have thought me more fit for the draft than
for ROTC." I described my work for the Foreign Relations
Committee, "a time when not many people had more information about Vietnam at hand than I did." I told him that,
after I left Arkansas the previous summer, I did some work
for the Vietnam Moratorium in Washington and in En-

gland. I also told him I had studied the draft at Georgetown, and had concluded it was justified only when, as in World War II, the nation and our way of life were at stake. I expressed sympathy with conscientious objectors and draft resisters. I told him Frank Aller, whom I identified only as my roommate, was "one of the bravest, best men I know. His country needs men like him more than they know. That he is considered a criminal is an obscenity." Then I admitted I had considered being a resister myself, and accepted the draft "in spite of my beliefs for one reason: to maintain my political viability within the system." I also admitted that I had asked to be accepted in the ROTC program because it was the only way I could "possibly, but not positively, avoid both Vietnam and resistance." I confessed to the colonel that "after I signed the ROTC letter of intent I began to wonder whether the compromise I had made with myself was not more objectionable than the draft would have been, because I had no interest in the ROTC program in itself and all I seemed to have done was to protect myself from physical harm . . . after we had made our agreement and you had sent my 1-D deferment to my draft board, the anguish and loss of self-regard and self-confidence really set in." Then I told the colonel that I had written a letter to the draft board on September 12 asking to be put back into the draft but never mailed it. I didn't mention that I had asked Jeff Dwire to get me reclassified 1-A and that the local draft board had done so at the October meeting, because I knew Jeff had already told the colonel that. I said that I hoped that "my telling this one story will help you to understand more clearly how so many fine people have come to find themselves still loving their country but loathing the military, to which you and other good men have devoted years, lifetimes, of the best service you could give." It was how I felt at the time, as a young man deeply troubled and conflicted about the war. In any case, I still considered myself bound to the ROTC commitment if Colonel Holmes called me on it. Because he didn't reply to my letter, I didn't know for several months what he would do.

In March 1970, at about the same time I heard from Lee

Williams that he expected all the lottery numbers to be called, I received two tapes made by my family while David Edwards was visiting them in Hot Springs. The first tape contains a lot of good-natured bantering around our pool table, ending with Roger playing the saxophone for me while our German shepherd, King, howled. The second tape has personal messages from Mother and Jeff. Mother told me how much she loved me and urged me to get more rest. Jeff gave me an update on family matters, then spoke these words:

> I took the liberty of calling the Colonel a few days ago and visiting with him a little. He wishes you well and hopes you'll find time to drop by and say hello to him on your return. I would not be concerned at all regarding the ROTC program as far as he is concerned, because he apparently understands more about the general overall situation of our young people than people would give him credit for.

So by the second week of March 1970, I knew I was free of the ROTC obligation, but not the draft.

As it turned out, Lee Williams was wrong. The deescalation of the war reduced the need for new troops to the point that my number was never called. I always felt bad about escaping the risks that had taken the lives of so many of my generation whose claim to a future was as legitimate as mine. Over the years—as governor, when I was in charge of the Arkansas National Guard, and especially after I became President—the more I saw of America's military, the more I wished I'd been a part of it when I was young, though I never changed my feelings about Vietnam.

If I hadn't gone to Georgetown and worked on the Foreign Relations Committee, I might have made different decisions about military service. During the Vietnam era, 16 million men avoided military service through legal means; 8.7 million enlisted; 2.2 million were drafted; only 209,000 were alleged to have dodged the draft or resisted, of whom 8,750 were convicted.

Those of us who could have gone to Vietnam but didn't were nevertheless marked by it, especially if we had friends who were killed there. I was always interested to see how others who took a pass and later got into public life dealt with military issues and political dissent. Some of them turned out to be superhawks and hyperpatriots, claiming that personal considerations justified their failure to serve while still condemning those who opposed a war they themselves had avoided. By 2002, Vietnam apparently had receded so far into the shadows of the American psyche that in Georgia, Republican congressman Saxby Chambliss, who had a Vietnam-era deferment, was able to defeat Senator Max Cleland, who lost three limbs in Vietnam, by questioning his patriotism and commitment to America's security.

In stark contrast to the activities of the nonserving superhawks, America's efforts to reconcile and normalize relations with Vietnam were led by distinguished Vietnam veterans in Congress, like Chuck Robb, John McCain, John Kerry, Bob Kerrey, Chuck Hagel, and Pete Peterson, men who had more than paid their dues and had nothing to hide or prove.

When I returned to Oxford in early October for my surprise second year, the circumstances of my life were almost as complicated as they had been in Arkansas. I didn't have a place to stay, because until the end of summer I hadn't thought I was coming back, and we got guaranteed rooms in college only the first year. I lived with Rick Stearns for a couple of weeks, during which we worked on and participated in our own Vietnam Moratorium observance at the U.S. embassy in London on October 15, in support of the main event back in the United States. I also helped to organize a teach-in at the London School of Economics.

Eventually, I found a home for the rest of my stay at Oxford with Strobe Talbott and Frank Aller, at 46 Leckford Road. Someone else who had been slated to live with them left, and they needed me to share the rent. We paid about thirty-six pounds a month—$86.40 at the exchange rate of

$2.40 a pound. The place was pretty run-down but more than adequate for us. On the first floor there was a small sitting room and a bedroom for me, along with a kitchen and a bathroom, which was the first thing you saw when you entered the house. The bathroom door had a glass window covered with a portrait of a woman in pre-Raphaelite style on a thin sheet that made it look like stained glass from a distance. It was the most elegant part of the house. Strobe's and Frank's bedrooms and workspaces were on the second and third floors. We had a small, scraggly walled-in yard in the back.

Unlike me, Strobe and Frank were doing serious work. Frank was writing a thesis on the epic Long March in the Chinese civil war. He had been to Switzerland to see Edgar Snow, whose famous book *Red Star Over China* chronicles his unique experiences with Mao and his revolutionaries in Yenan. Snow had given Frank some of his unpublished notes to use, and it was clear that he was going to produce a scholarly work of real significance.

Strobe was working on an even bigger project, Nikita Khrushchev's memoirs. Khrushchev was known in the United States for his confrontations with Kennedy and Nixon, but as Cold War Soviets went, he was a reformer and a fascinating character. He had built the beautiful Moscow subway system and denounced Stalin's murderous excesses. After more orthodox conservative forces removed him from power and installed Brezhnev and Kosygin, Khrushchev secretly recorded his memoirs on tape, and arranged, I think through friends in the KGB, to get them to Jerry Schecter, then *Time* magazine's bureau chief in Moscow. Strobe was fluent in Russian and had worked for *Time* in Moscow the previous summer. He flew to Copenhagen to meet Schecter and get the tapes. When he got back to Oxford, he began the laborious process of typing Khrushchev's words out in Russian, then translating and editing them.

On many mornings, I would make breakfast for Frank and Strobe as they began their work. I was a pretty fair short-order cook. I'd take them the products of "Mother Clinton's Country Kitchen" and check on their work. I was especially fascinated to hear Strobe recount Khrushchev's tales of Kremlin intrigue. Strobe's seminal book, *Khrushchev Remembers*, made a major contribution in the West to the understanding of the inner workings and tensions of the Soviet Union, and raised the hope that someday internal reform might bring more freedom and openness.

On November 15, the second, larger Moratorium service was held, with more than five hundred people marching around Grosvenor Square in front of the U.S. Embassy. We were joined by Father Richard McSorley, a Jesuit on the Georgetown faculty who had long been active in the peace movement. As a chaplain in World War II, McSorley survived the Bataan death march, and he later became close to Robert Kennedy and his family. After the demonstration, we had a prayer service at St. Mark's Church near the embassy. Father McSorley recited the peace prayer of St. Francis of Assisi, and Rick Stearns read John Donne's famous lines that end "Never send to know for whom the bell tolls; it tolls for thee."

After Thanksgiving, Tom Williamson and I flew to Dublin to meet Hillary Hart and Martha Saxton, whom I had been seeing on and off for several months. More than thirty years later, Martha reminded me that on that trip I said she was too sad for me. Actually, back then, as anguished as I was about Vietnam, I was too sad for her, or anyone else. But even sad, I loved Ireland, and felt at home there. I hated to leave after just a weekend.

By Saturday, December 6, three days after I wrote the letter to Colonel Holmes, I was in London at David Edwards's flat for a big event, the Arkansas-Texas football game. Both teams were undefeated. Texas was ranked first and Arkansas second in the national polls. They were playing for the national championship in the last regular-season game of the one hundredth year of college football. I rented a shortwave radio, which wasn't too expensive but required a fifty-pound deposit, a lot of money for me. David whipped up a big pot of good chili. We had a few friends over who thought we had lost our minds as we whooped and hollered through a football game so exciting it was billed as the

Game of the Century. For a few hours, we were innocent again, totally caught up in the contest.

The game and its cultural and political contexts have been beautifully chronicled by Terry Frei in his book *Horns, Hogs, and Nixon Coming.* Frei subtitled his book *Texas v. Arkansas in Dixie's Last Stand*, because it was the last major sporting event involving two all-white teams.

A few days earlier, the White House had announced that President Nixon, a fanatic football fan, would attend the game and present the national championship trophy to the winner. Nine members of Congress would accompany him, including his Vietnam nemesis Senator Fulbright, who had played for the Razorbacks more than forty years earlier, and a young Texas congressman, George H. W. Bush. Also slated to come were White House aides Henry Kissinger and H. R. Haldeman, and Ron Ziegler, the press secretary.

Arkansas kicked off to Texas, forced a fumble on the first possession, and scored less than a minute and a half into the game. At halftime, with Arkansas still leading 7–0, President Nixon was interviewed. He said, "I expect to see both teams score in the second half. The question is whether Texas's superior manpower, and I mean probably a stronger bench, may win in the last quarter. That's the way I see it." On the first play of the fourth quarter, with Arkansas leading 14–0, the Texas quarterback, James Street, made an amazing forty-two-yard touchdown run on a busted play. Texas went for the two-point conversion, got it, and was behind only 14–8. On the next possession, Arkansas immediately took the ball down to the Texas seven. With the best field-goal kicker in the country, Arkansas could have kicked a field goal, making the score 17–8 and requiring Texas to score twice to win. But a pass play was called. The pass fell a little bit short and was intercepted. With just under five minutes left, Texas had a fourth down and three yards to go on its own forty-three-yard line. The quarterback completed a miraculous pass to a well-defended receiver at the Arkansas thirteen-yard line. Two plays later, Texas scored and took the lead, 15–14. On its last drive, Arkansas moved the ball down the field on short passes, mostly to its talented tailback, Bill Burnett, who was having a good day running the ball and who would soon become Colonel Eugene Holmes's son-in-law. After a thrilling game, Texas intercepted an Arkansas pass, ran the last minute and twenty-two seconds off the clock, and won 15–14.

It had been a magnificent game. Even several of the Texas players said neither team should have lost. The only really bad taste in my mouth came from President Nixon's prediction at halftime that Texas might well win the game in the fourth quarter. For years afterward, I think I held that against him almost as much as Watergate.

The fact that David Edwards and I went to the trouble of renting a shortwave radio to listen to a football game won't surprise anyone who grew up in America's sports-mad culture. Supporting the Razorback football team was central to the idea of being an Arkansan. Before our family got a television, I listened to all the games on my radio. In high school, I carried equipment for the Razorback band just to get into the games. At Georgetown, I watched all the Razorback games that were televised. When I moved back home, as a law professor, attorney general, and governor, I got to virtually every home game. When Eddie Sutton became the basketball coach and his wife, Patsy, took an active role in my 1980 campaign, I also began going to all the basketball games I could. When Coach Nolan Richardson's Arkansas team won the NCAA Championship over Duke in 1994, I was in the arena.

Of all the great football games I ever watched, only the Game of the Century had any impact on my political career. Though the anti-war demonstrators weren't shown on national television, they were there. One of them was perched up in a tree on the hill overlooking the stadium. The next day, his picture was in many of the daily and weekly papers in Arkansas. Five years later, in 1974, shortly before my first congressional election, my opponent's campaign workers called newspapers all over the congressional district asking if they had kept a copy of "that picture of Bill Clinton up in the tree demonstrating against Nixon at the Arkansas-Texas game." The rumor spread like wildfire and cost me a lot of votes. In 1978, when I ran for governor the first time, a state trooper in south Arkansas swore to several people that he was the very one who pulled me out of the tree that day. In 1979, my first year as governor, and ten years after the Game, when I was answering questions at a high school assembly in Berryville, about an hour's drive east of Fayetteville, a student asked me whether I had really been in the tree. When I asked who had heard the rumor, half the students and three-quarters of the teachers raised their hands. In 1983, fourteen years after the Game, I went to Tontitown, a small community north of Fayetteville, to crown the queen of the annual Grape Festival. After I did, the sixteen-year-old girl looked at me and said, "Did you really get up in that tree without any clothes on and demonstrate against President Nixon and the war?" When I said no, she replied, "Oh, shoot. That's one reason I've always been for you!" Even though I had even lost my clothes as the story ripened, the worm seemed to be turning on it. Alas, not long afterward, Fayetteville's irreverently liberal weekly paper, *The Grapevine*, finally put the loony old tale to rest with a story on the real protester, including the picture of him in the tree. The author of the article also said that when Governor Clinton was young, he was far too "preppy" to do anything as adventurous as that.

That long-ago football game was a chance for me to enjoy a sport I loved, and to feel closer to home. I had just started reading Thomas Wolfe's *You Can't Go Home Again* and was afraid it might turn out that way for me. And I was about to go farther away from home than I had ever been, in more ways than one.

At the end of the first week of December, during our long winter break, I began a forty-day trip that would take me from Amsterdam through the Scandinavian countries to Russia, then back to Oxford through Prague and Munich. It was, and remains, the longest trip of my life.

I went to Amsterdam with my artist friend Aimée Gautier. The streets were covered with Christmas lights and lined with charming shops. The famous red-light district featured perfectly legal prostitutes sitting on display in their windows. Aimée jokingly asked if I wanted to go into one of the places, but I declined.

We toured the main churches, saw the Van Goghs at the Municipal Museum and the Vermeers and Rembrandts at the Rijksmuseum. At closing time, we were asked to leave the wonderful old place. I went to the cloakroom to pick up our coats. There was only one other person left in line to pick up his. When he turned around, I found myself facing Rudolf Nureyev. We exchanged a few words and he asked me if I wanted to go get a cup of tea. I knew Aimée would love it, but just outside the front door, a handsome, frowning young man was anxiously pacing, obviously waiting for Nureyev, so I took a pass. Years later, when I was governor, I found myself in the same hotel with Nureyev in Taipei, Taiwan. We finally got our cup of tea late one night after we had fulfilled our respective obligations. Obviously he didn't recall our first meeting.

In Amsterdam, I said good-bye to Aimée, who was going home, and left on the train to Copenhagen, Oslo, and Stockholm. At the border between Norway and Sweden, I was almost put out in the middle of nowhere.

At a tiny railroad station, the guards searched the luggage of all the young people, looking for drugs. In my bag they found a lot of Contac pills, which I was taking to a friend in Moscow. Contac was relatively new and for some reason wasn't yet on the Swedish government's list of approved drugs. I tried to explain that the pills were just for colds, widely available in American drugstores and without any addictive qualities. The guard confiscated the Contac pills, but at least I wasn't thrown out into the snowy desolation for drug trafficking, where I might have become an interesting piece of ice sculpture, perfectly preserved until the spring thaw.

After a couple of days in Stockholm, I took an overnight ferry to Helsinki. Late in the night, as I was sitting by myself at a table in the dining area reading a book and drinking coffee, a fight broke out at the bar. Two very drunk men were fighting over the only girl there. Both men were too

inebriated to defend themselves but managed to land blows
on each other. Before long they were both gushing blood.
One of them was a member of the crew, with two or three of
his mates just standing there watching. Finally I couldn't
stand it anymore. I got up and walked over to stop the fight
before they did themselves serious damage. When I got
about ten feet from them, one of the other crewmen blocked
my way and said, "You can't stop the fight. If you try, they'll
both turn on you. And we'll help them." When I asked why,
he just smiled and replied, "We're Finns." I shrugged,
turned away, picked up my book, and went to bed, having
absorbed another lesson about different cultures. I bet neither one of them got the girl.

I checked in to a small hotel and began touring the city
with Georgetown classmate Richard Shullaw, whose father
was deputy chief of mission in the American embassy there.

On Christmas Day, the first I'd ever spent away from
home, I walked out onto Helsinki Bay. The ice was thick,
and there was enough snow on it to give some traction.
Amid all the natural beauty I saw a small wooden house a
few yards from the shore, and a small round hole in the ice
a few yards out. The house was a sauna, and soon a man
came out in a skimpy swimsuit. He marched straight out
onto the ice and lowered himself into the hole and its frigid
water. After a couple of minutes, he got out, went back into
the sauna, and repeated the ritual. I thought he was crazier
than the two guys in the bar. In time I came to enjoy the hot
steam of the sauna, but despite my growing love for Finland
during several trips since, I could never get into the ice
water.

On New Year's Eve, I boarded the train to Moscow with
an interim stop in Leningrad's Finland Station. It was the
same route Lenin had taken in 1917 when he returned to
Russia to take over the revolution. It was on my mind
because I had read Edmund Wilson's marvelous book *To
the Finland Station*. When we came to the Russian border,
another isolated outpost, I met my first real live Communist, a pudgy, cherubic-looking guard. When he eyed my
bags suspiciously, I expected him to check for drugs.

Instead, he asked in his heavily accented English, "Dirty books? Dirty books? Got any dirty books?" I laughed and opened my book bag, pouring out Penguin paperback novels by Tolstoy, Dostoevsky, and Turgenev. He was so disappointed. I guess he longed for contraband that would enliven those long, lonely nights on the frigid frontier.

The Soviet train was filled with spacious compartments. Each car had a giant samovar full of hot tea that was served along with black bread by an elderly woman. I shared my berth with an interesting man who had been the coach of the Estonian boxing team in the 1936 Olympics, three years before the Soviet Union absorbed the Baltic states. We both spoke enough German to communicate a little. He was a lively fellow who told me with absolute confidence that one day Estonia would be free again. In 2002, when I traveled to Tallinn, Estonia's beautiful old capital, I told this story to the audience I addressed. My friend, former president Lennart Meri, was at the speech and did some quick research for me. The man's name was Peter Matsov. He died in 1980. I think often of him and our New Year's Eve train ride. I wish he had lived another decade to see his dream come true.

It was nearly midnight and the dawn of a new decade when we pulled into Leningrad. I got out and walked for a few minutes, but all I saw were policemen dragging inebriated celebrants off the streets in a driving snowstorm. It would be nearly thirty years before I got to see the splendor of the city. By then the Communists were gone and its original name, St. Petersburg, had been restored.

On New Year's morning 1970, I began an amazing five days. I had prepared for the trip to Moscow by getting a guidebook and a good street map in English since I couldn't read the Russian Cyrillic script.

I checked in to the National Hotel, just off Red Square. It had a huge high-ceilinged lobby, comfortable rooms, and a nice restaurant and bar.

The only person I knew in Moscow was Nikki Alexis, who had given me the two friendship cards I loved when I went home from Oxford the previous summer. She was an amazing woman, born in Martinique in the West Indies, living in Paris because her father was a diplomat there. Nikki was studying at Lumumba University, named after the Congolese leader who was murdered in 1961, apparently with the complicity of the U.S. Central Intelligence Agency. Most of the students were poor people from poor countries. The Soviets obviously hoped that by educating them they'd be making converts when they went home.

One night I took a bus out to Lumumba University to have dinner with Nikki and some of her friends. One of them was a Haitian woman named Helene whose husband was studying in Paris. They had a daughter who was living with him. They had no money to travel and hadn't seen each other in almost two years. When I left Russia a few days later, Helene gave me one of those trademark Russian fur hats. It wasn't expensive but she had no money. I asked her if she was sure she wanted me to have it. She replied, "Yes. You were kind to me and you made me have hope." In 1994, when, as President, I made the decision to remove Haiti's military dictator, General Raoul Cedras, and return the democratically elected President Jean-Bertrand Aristide, I thought of that good woman for the first time in years, and wondered if she ever went back to Haiti.

Around midnight, I rode the bus to my hotel. There was only one other person on it. His name was Oleg Rakito and he spoke better English than I did. He asked me lots of questions and told me he worked for the government, virtually admitting he was assigned to keep an eye on me. He said he'd like to continue our conversation at breakfast the next morning. As we ate cold bacon and eggs he told me he read *Time* and *Newsweek* every week and loved the British pop star Tom Jones, whose songs he got on bootlegged tapes. If Oleg was pumping me for information because I had had a security clearance when I worked for Senator Fulbright, he came up dry. But I learned some things from him about the thirst of a young person behind the Iron Curtain for real information about the outside world. That stayed with me all the way to the White House.

Oleg wasn't the only friendly Russian I encountered.

President Nixon's policy of détente was having noticeable results. A few months earlier, Russian television had shown the Americans walking on the moon. People were still excited about it and seemed to be fascinated by all things American. They envied our freedom and assumed we were all rich. I guess, compared with most of them, we were. Whenever I took the subway, people would come up to me and say proudly, "I speak English! Welcome to Moscow." One night I shared dinner with a few hotel guests, a local cabdriver, and his sister. The girl had a bit too much to drink and decided she wanted to stay with me. Her brother had to drag her out of the hotel into the snow and shove her into his cab. I never knew whether he was afraid being with me would guarantee her a grilling by the KGB, or he just thought I was unworthy of his sister.

My most interesting Moscow adventure began with a chance encounter in the hotel elevator. When I got in, there were four other men in the car. One of them was wearing a Virginia Lions Club pin. He obviously thought I was a foreigner, with my long hair and beard, rawhide boots, and British navy pea jacket. He drawled, "Where you from?" When I smiled and said, "Arkansas," he replied, "Shoot, I thought you were from Denmark or someplace like that!" The man's name was Charlie Daniels. He was from Norton, Virginia, hometown of Francis Gary Powers, the U-2 pilot who had been shot down and captured in Russia in 1960. He was accompanied by Carl McAfee, a lawyer from Norton who had helped to arrange Powers's release, and a chicken farmer from Washington State, Henry Fors, whose son had been shot down in Vietnam. They had come all the way to Moscow to see if the North Vietnamese stationed there would tell the farmer whether his son was dead or alive. The fourth man was from Paris and, like the men from Virginia, a member of the Lions Club. He had joined them because the North Vietnamese spoke French. They all just came to Moscow without any assurances that the Russians would permit them to talk with the Vietnamese or that, if they did, any information would be forthcoming. None of them spoke Russian. They asked if I knew anyone who could help them. My old friend Nikki Alexis was studying English, French, and Russian at Patrice Lumumba University. I introduced her to them and they spent a couple of days together making the rounds, checking in with the American embassy, asking the Russians to help, finally seeing the North Vietnamese, who apparently were impressed that Mr. Fors and his friends would make such an effort to learn the fate of his son and several others who were missing in action. They said they would check into it and get back to them. A few weeks later, Henry Fors learned that his son had been killed when his plane was shot down. At least he had some peace of mind. I thought of Henry Fors when I worked to resolve POW/MIA cases as President and to help the Vietnamese find out what had happened to more than 300,000 of their people still unaccounted for.

On January 6, Nikki and her Haitian friend Helene put me on the train to Prague, one of the most beautiful old cities in Europe, still reeling from the Soviet repression of Alexander Dubček's Prague Spring reform movement in August 1968. I had been invited to stay with the parents of Jan Kopold, who played basketball with me at Oxford. The Kopolds were nice people whose personal history was closely entwined with that of modern Czechoslovakia. Mrs. Kopold's father had been editor in chief of the Communist newspaper *Rude Pravo*, died fighting the Nazis in World War II, and had a bridge in Prague named for him. Both Mr. and Mrs. Kopold were academics and had been big supporters of Dubček. Mrs. Kopold's mother also lived with them. She took me around town during the day when the Kopolds were working. They lived in a nice apartment in a modern high-rise with a beautiful view of the city. I stayed in Jan's room and was so excited I woke up three or four times a night just to stare at the skyline.

The Kopolds, like all the Czechs I met, held on to the belief that their chance at freedom would come again. They deserved it as much as anyone on earth. They were intelligent, proud, and determined. The young Czechs I met were especially pro-American. They supported our government in Vietnam because we were for freedom and the Soviets weren't. Mr. Kopold once said to me, "Even the Russians cannot defy forever the laws of historical development." Sure enough, they couldn't. In twenty years, Václav Havel's peaceful "Velvet Revolution" would reclaim the promise of Prague Spring.

Ten months after I left the Kopolds to go back to Oxford, I received the following notice from them, written on simple white paper with black borders: "With immense pain we want to inform his friends that on July 29 in the University Hospital in Smyrna, Turkey, died at the young age of 23 Jan Kopold. . . . For a long time it was his great desire to visit what remains of the Hellenic culture. It was not far from Troy that he fell from a height and succumbed from the injuries he sustained." I really liked Jan, with his ready smile and good mind. When I knew him, he was tortured by the conflict between his love of Czechoslovakia and his love of freedom. I wish he had lived to enjoy both.

After six days in Prague, I stopped in Munich to celebrate Faschingsfest with Rudy Lowe, then returned to England with renewed faith in America and democracy. For all its faults, I had discovered that my country was still a beacon of light to people chafing under communism. Ironically, when I ran for President in 1992, the Republicans tried to use the trip against me, claiming that I had consorted with Communists in Moscow.

With a new term, I got back into my tutorials in politics, including studies on the relevance of scientific theories to strategic planning; the problem of making a conscript army into a patriotic one, from Napoleon to Vietnam; and the problems China and Russia posed for U.S. policy. I read Herman Kahn on the probabilities of nuclear war, different destruction levels, and post-attack behavior. It was Strangelove-like and unconvincing. I noted in my diary that "what happens after the fireworks begin may not pursue the set course of any scientific systems and analysts' models."

While I was enduring another sunless English winter, letters and cards from home streamed in. My friends were getting jobs, getting married, getting on with their lives. Their normalcy looked pretty good after all the anguish I'd felt over Vietnam.

March and the coming of spring brightened things up a bit. I read Hemingway, tended to tutorials, and talked to my friends, including a fascinating new one. Mandy Merck had come to Oxford from Reed College in Oregon. She was hyperkinetic and highly intelligent, the only American woman I met at Oxford who was more than a match for her British counterparts in fast, free-flowing conversation. She was also the first openly lesbian woman I'd known. March was a big month for my awareness of homosexuality. Paul Parish came out to me, too, and was mortally afraid of being branded a social pariah. He suffered for a long time. Now he's in San Francisco, and, in his own words, "safe and legal." Mandy Merck stayed in England and became a journalist and gay-rights advocate. Back then, her brilliant banter brightened my spring.

Rick Stearns threw me for a loop one night when he told me I was unsuited for politics. He said Huey Long and I both had great southern political styles, but Long was a political genius who understood how to get and use power. He said my gifts were more literary, that I should be a writer because I wrote better than I spoke, and besides, I wasn't tough enough for politics. A lot of people have thought that over the years. Rick was close to right, though. I never loved power for power's sake, but whenever I got hit by my opponents, I usually mustered enough toughness to survive. Besides, I didn't think I could do anything else as well.

In early 1970, having received Jeff Dwire's tape recounting his conversation with Colonel Holmes and the high lottery number, I knew I was out of ROTC and wouldn't be drafted at least until late in the year. If I wasn't called, I was torn between coming back to Oxford for a third year, which the Rhodes scholarship would cover, or going to Yale Law School, if I was accepted.

I loved Oxford, maybe too much. I was afraid if I came back for a third year, I might drift into a comfortable but aimless academic life that would disappoint me in the end. Given my feelings about the war, I wasn't at all sure I'd ever make it in politics, but I was inclined to go back home to America and give it a chance.

In April, during the break between second and third terms, I took one last trip—to Spain, with Rick Stearns. I had been reading up on Spain and was totally mesmerized by it, thanks to André Malraux's *Man's Hope*, George Orwell's *Homage to Catalonia*, and Hugh Thomas's masterly *The Spanish Civil War*. Malraux explored the dilemma war presents to intellectuals, many of whom were drawn to the fight against Franco. He said the intellectual wants to make distinctions, to know precisely what he is fighting for and how he must fight, an attitude that is by definition anti-Manichean, but every warrior is by definition a Manichean. To kill and stay alive he must see things starkly as black and white, evil and good. I recognized the same thing in politics years later when the Far Right took over the Republican Party and the Congress. Politics to them was simply war by other means. They needed an enemy and I was the demon on the other side of the Manichean divide.

I never got over the romantic pull of Spain, the raw pulse of the land, the expansive, rugged spirit of the people, the haunting memories of the lost civil war, the Prado, the beauty of the Alhambra. When I was President, Hillary and I became friends with King Juan Carlos and Queen Sofía. On my last trip to Spain, President Juan Carlos had remembered my telling him of my nostalgia about Granada and took Hillary and me back there. After thirty years I walked through the Alhambra again, in a Spain now democratic and free of Francoism, thanks in no small part to him.

At the end of April when I got back to Oxford, Mother called to tell me that David Leopoulos's mother, Evelyn, had been murdered, stabbed four times in the heart in her antique store. The crime was never solved. I was reading Thomas Hobbes's *Leviathan* at the time and I remember thinking he might be right that life is "poor, nasty, brutish and short." David came to see me a few weeks later on his way back to army duty in Italy, and I tried to lift his spirits. His loss finally provoked me to finish a short story on

Daddy's last year and a half and his death. It got pretty good reviews from my friends, provoking me to write in my diary, "Perhaps I can write instead of be a doorman when my political career is in shambles." I had fantasized from time to time about being a doorman at New York's Plaza Hotel, at the south end of Central Park. Plaza doormen had nice uniforms and met interesting people from all over the world. I imagined garnering large tips from guests who thought that, despite my strange southern accent, I made good conversation.

In late May, I was accepted at Yale and decided to go. I finished up my tutorials on the concept of opposition, the British prime minister, and political theory, preferring Locke to Hobbes. On June 5, I gave one last speech to an American military high school graduation. I sat on a stage with generals and colonels, and in my speech told why I loved America, respected the military, and opposed the Vietnam War. The kids liked it, and I think the officers respected the way I said it.

On June 26, I took the plane to New York, after emotional good-byes, especially with Frank Aller, Paul Parish, and David Edwards, this time for real. Just like that, it was over, two of the most extraordinary years of my life. They began on the eve of Richard Nixon's election and ended as the Beatles announced they were breaking up and released their last movie to loving, mourning fans. I had traveled a lot and loved it. I had also ventured into the far reaches of my mind and heart, struggling with my draft situation, my ambivalence about my ambition, and my inability to have anything other than brief relationships with women. I had no degree, but I had learned a lot. My "long and winding road" was leading me home, and I hoped that, as the Beatles sang in "Hey Jude," I could at least "take a sad song and make it better."

SEVENTEEN

IN JULY, I went to work in Washington for Project Purse-strings, a citizens' lobby for the McGovern-Hatfield amendment, which called for a cutoff of funding for the Vietnam War by the end of 1971. We had no chance to pass it, but the campaign to do so provided a vehicle to mobilize and highlight growing bipartisan opposition to the war.

I got a room for the summer at the home of Dick and Helen Dudman, who lived in a great old two-story house with a big front porch in northwest Washington. Dick was a distinguished journalist. He and Helen both opposed the war and supported the young people who were trying to stop it. They were wonderful to me. One morning they invited me down to breakfast on the front porch with their friend and neighbor Senator Gene McCarthy. He was serving his last year in the Senate, having announced back in 1968 that he wouldn't run again. That morning he was in an open, expansive mood, offering a precise analysis of current events and expressing some nostalgia at leaving the Senate. I liked McCarthy more than I expected to, especially after he loaned me a pair of shoes to wear to the black-tie Women's Press Dinner, which I think the Dudmans got me invited to. President Nixon came and shook a lot of hands, though not mine. I was seated at a table with Clark Clifford, who had come to Washington from Missouri with President Truman and had served as a close advisor and then as defense secretary to President Johnson in his last year in office. On Vietnam, Clifford noted dryly, "It's really one of the most awful places in the world to be involved." The dinner was a heady experience for me, especially since I kept my feet on the ground in Gene McCarthy's shoes.

Shortly after I started at Pursestrings, I took a long weekend off and drove to Springfield, Massachusetts, for the wedding of my Georgetown roommate Marine Lieutenant Kit Ashby.

On the way back to Washington, I stopped in Cape Cod to visit Tommy Caplan and Jim Moore, who had also been at Kit's wedding. At night, we went to see Carolyn Yeldell, who was singing on the Cape with a group of young entertainers for the summer. We had a great time, but I stayed too long. When I got back on the road, I was dead tired. Before I even made it out of Massachusetts on the interstate highway, a car pulled out of a rest stop right in front of me. The driver didn't see me, and I didn't see him until it was too late. I swerved to miss him, but I hit the left rear of his car hard. The man and woman in the other car seemed to be dazed but unhurt. I wasn't hurt either, but the little Volkswagen Bug Jeff Dwire had given me to drive for the summer was badly mangled. When the police came, I had a big problem. I had misplaced my driver's license on the move home from England and couldn't prove I was a valid driver. There were no computerized records of such things back then, so I couldn't be validated until the morning. The officer said he'd have to put me in jail. By the time we got there it was about 5 a.m. They stripped me of my belongings and took my belt so that I couldn't strangle myself, gave me a cup of coffee, and put me in a cell with a hard metal bed, a blanket, a smelly stopped-up toilet, and a light that stayed on. After a couple of hours of semi-sleep, I called Tommy Caplan for help. He and Jim Moore went to court with me and posted my bond. The judge was friendly but reprimanded me about not having my license. It worked: after my night in jail, I was never without my license again.

Two weeks after my trip to Massachusetts, I was back in New England to spend a week in Connecticut working for Joe Duffey in the Democratic primary election for the U.S. Senate. Duffey was running as the peace candidate, aided primarily by the people who had made a good showing for Gene McCarthy two years earlier. The incumbent senator, Democrat Tom Dodd, was a longtime fixture in Connecticut politics. He had prosecuted Nazis at the Nuremberg War Crimes Tribunal and had a good progressive record, but he had two problems. First, he had been censured by the Senate for the personal use of funds that had been raised for him in his official capacity. Second, he had supported President Johnson on Vietnam, and Democratic primary voters were much more likely to be anti-war. Dodd was hurt and angered by the Senate censure and not ready to give up his seat without a fight. Rather than face a hostile electorate in the Democratic primary, he filed as an independent to run in the November general election. Joe Duffey was an ethics professor at Hartford Seminary Foundation and president of the liberal Americans for Democratic Action. Though he was a coal miner's son from West Virginia, his strongest supporters were prosperous, well-educated, anti-war liberals who lived in the suburbs, and young people drawn to his record on civil rights and peace. His campaign co-chairman was Paul Newman, who worked hard in the campaign. His finance committee included the photographer Margaret Bourke-White, artist Alexander Calder, *New Yorker* cartoonist Dana Fradon, and an extraordinary array of writers and historians, including Francine du Plessix Gray, John Hersey, Arthur Miller, Vance Packard, William Shirer, William Styron, Barbara Tuchman, and Thornton Wilder. Their names looked pretty impressive on the campaign stationery, but they weren't likely to impress many voters among blue-collar ethnics.

Between July 29 and August 5, I was asked to organize two towns in the Fifth Congressional District, Bethel and Trumbull. Both were full of old white wooden houses with big front porches and long histories that were chronicled in the local registers. In Bethel, we put in phones the first day and organized a telephone canvass, to be followed by personal deliveries of literature to all the undecided voters. The office was kept open long hours by dedicated volunteers, and I was pretty sure Duffey would get his maximum possible vote there. Trumbull didn't have a fully operational headquarters; the volunteers were phoning some voters and seeing others. I urged them to keep an office open from 10 a.m. to 7 p.m., Monday through Saturday, and to follow the Bethel canvassing procedure, which would guarantee two contacts with all persuadable voters. I also reviewed the operations in two other towns that were less well organized and urged the state headquarters to at least make sure they had complete voter lists and the capacity to do the phone canvass.

I liked the work and met a lot of people who would be important in my life, including John Podesta, who served superbly in the White House as staff secretary, deputy chief of staff, and chief of staff, and Susan Thomases, who, when I was in New York, let me sleep on the couch in the Park Avenue apartment where she still lives, and who became one of Hillary's and my closest friends and advisors.

When Joe Duffey won the primary, I was asked to coordinate the Third Congressional District for the general election. The biggest city in the district was New Haven, where I'd be going to law school, and the district included Milford, where I would be living. Doing the job meant that I'd miss a lot of classes until the election was over in early November, but I thought I could make it with borrowed notes and hard study at the end of term.

I loved New Haven with its cauldron of old-fashioned ethnic politics and student activists. East Haven, next door, was overwhelmingly Italian, while nearby Orange was mostly Irish. The towns farther away from New Haven tended to be wealthier, with the ethnic lines more blurred. The two towns at the eastern end of the district, Guilford and Madison, were especially old and beautiful. I spent a lot of time driving to the other towns in the district, making sure our people had a good campaign plan in place, and the support and materials they needed from the central headquarters. Since my Volkswagen had been ruined in the wreck in Massachusetts, I was driving a rust-colored Opel station wagon, which was better suited to delivering campaign materials anyway. I put a lot of miles on that old station wagon.

When my campaign work permitted, I attended classes in constitutional law, contracts, procedure, and torts. The most interesting class by far was Constitutional Law, taught by Robert Bork, who was later put on the Court of Appeals for the District of Columbia, and in 1987 was nominated for the Supreme Court by President Reagan. Bork was extremely conservative in his legal philosophy, aggressive in pushing his point of view, but fair to students who disagreed. In my one memorable exchange with him, I pointed out that his argument on the question at issue was circular. He replied, "Of course it is. All the best arguments are."

After the primary election, I did my best to bring the supporters of the other candidates into the Duffey campaign, but it was tough. I'd go into the heavily ethnic blue-collar areas and make my best pitch, but I could tell I was hitting a lot of stone walls. Too many white ethnic Democrats thought Joe Duffey, whom Vice President Agnew had called a "Marxist revisionist," was too radical, too identified with dope-smoking anti-war hippies. Many of the ethnic Democrats were turning against the war, too, but they still didn't feel comfortable in the company of those who had been against it before they were. The campaign to win them over was complicated by the fact that Senator Dodd was running as an independent, so the disgruntled Democrats had someplace else to go. Joe Duffey ran a fine campaign, pouring his heart and mind into it and inspiring young people all across the country, but he was defeated by the Republican candidate, Congressman Lowell Weicker, a maverick who later left the Republican Party and served as governor of Connecticut as an independent. Weicker got just under 42 percent of the vote, enough to beat Duffey handily. Duffey got less than 34 percent, with Senator Dodd garnering almost 25 percent. We got killed in ethnic towns like East Haven and West Haven.

I don't know if Duffey would have won if Dodd hadn't run, but I was sure the Democratic Party was headed for minority status unless we could get back the kind of folks who voted for Dodd. After the election I talked about it for hours with Anne Wexler, who had done a superb job as campaign manager. She was a great politician and related well to all kinds of people, but in 1970 most voters weren't buying the message or the messengers. Anne became a great friend and advisor to me over the years. After she and Joe

Duffey got married, I stayed in touch with them. When I was in the White House, I appointed him to run the United States Information Agency, which oversaw the Voice of America, where he took America's message to a world more receptive to him than the Connecticut electorate had been in 1970. I thought of it as Joe's last campaign, and he won it.

The brightest spot in November 1970 was the election of a young Democratic governor, Dale Bumpers, in Arkansas. He handily defeated former governor Faubus in the primary and won the general election over Governor Rockefeller in a landslide. Bumpers was an ex-marine and a great trial lawyer. He was funny as all get-out and could talk an owl out of a tree. And he was a genuine progressive who had led his small hometown of Charleston, in conservative western Arkansas, to peacefully integrate its schools, in stark contrast to the turmoil in Little Rock. Two years later he was reelected by a large margin, and two years after that he became one of our U.S. senators. Bumpers proved that the power of leadership to lift and unite people in a common cause could overcome the South's old politics of division. That's what I wanted to do. I didn't mind backing candidates who were almost certain to lose when we were fighting for civil rights or against the war. But sooner or later, you have to win if you want to change things. I went to Yale Law School to learn more about policy. And in case my political aspirations didn't work out, I wanted a profession from which I could never be forced to retire.

After the election, I settled into law school life, cramming for exams, getting to know some of the other students, and enjoying my house and my three housemates. Doug Eakeley, my fellow Rhodes scholar at Univ, found a great old house on Long Island Sound in Milford. It had four bedrooms, a good-sized kitchen, and a large screened-in porch that opened right onto the beach. The beach was perfect for cookouts, and when the tide was out, we had enough room for touch-football games. The only drawback to the place was that it was a summer house, with no insulation against the whipping winter winds. But we were young and got used to it. I still vividly remember spending one cold winter day after the election sitting on the porch with a blanket wrapped around me reading William Faulkner's *The Sound and the Fury*.

My other housemates at 889 East Broadway were Don Pogue and Bill Coleman. Don was more left wing than the rest of us, but he looked more blue collar. He was built like a concrete block and was strong as an ox. He drove a motorcycle to law school, where he engaged all comers in endless political debate. Luckily for us, he was also a good cook and was usually on good behavior, thanks to his equally intense but more nuanced English girlfriend, Susan Bucknell. Bill was one of the growing number of black students at Yale. His father was a liberal Republican lawyer— they still existed back then—who had clerked for Justice Felix Frankfurter on the Supreme Court and had served as secretary of transportation under President Ford. On the surface, Bill was the most laid-back of our group.

Besides my roommates, I knew only a few other students when I got back to Yale after the Duffey campaign, including my Boys Nation friend from Louisiana Fred Kammer, and Bob Reich. Because he was the secretary of our Rhodes class, Bob kept up with everyone and was a continuing source of information and humorous misinformation on what our old crowd was up to.

Bob was living in a house near campus with three other students, one of whom, Nancy Bekavac, became a special friend of mine. She was a passionate liberal whose anti-war convictions had been confirmed the previous summer when she worked in Vietnam as a journalist. She wrote beautiful poems, powerful letters, and great class notes, which she let me use when I showed up for class two months late.

Through Bill Coleman, I got to meet a number of the black students. I was interested in how they came to Yale, and what they planned to do with what, back then, was still an unusual opportunity for African-Americans. Besides Bill, I became friends with Eric Clay from Detroit, whom I later appointed to the U.S. court of appeals; Nancy Gist, a Wellesley classmate of Hillary's who served in the Justice Department when I was President; Lila Coleburn, who gave up law to become a psychotherapist; Rufus Cormier, a big, quiet man who'd starred at guard on the Southern Methodist University football team; and Lani Guinier, whom I tried to appoint assistant attorney general for civil rights, a sad story the details of which I'll relate later. Supreme Court Justice Clarence Thomas was a classmate too, but I never got to know him.

Near the end of the term, we heard that Frank Aller had decided to return to America. He moved back to the Boston area and went home to Spokane to face the draft music. He was arrested, arraigned, then released pending trial. Frank had decided that whatever impact he'd had by resisting had been achieved, and he didn't want to spend the rest of his life out of America, looking forward to a cold, bitter middle age in some Canadian or British university, forever defined by Vietnam. One night in December, Bob Reich said it seemed foolish for Frank to risk jail when there was so much he could do out of the country. My diary notes my reply: "A man is more than the sum of all the things he can do." Frank's decision was about who he was, not what he could do. I thought it was the right one. Not long after he got back, Frank had a psychiatric exam in which the doctor found him depressed and unfit for military service. He took his draft physical and, like Strobe, was declared 1-Y, draftable only in a national emergency.

On Christmas Day, I was back home in Hot Springs, a long way from Helsinki Bay, where I'd walked on the ice the previous Christmas. Instead, I walked the grounds of my old elementary school, counted my blessings, and marked the changes in my life. Several of my close friends were getting married. I wished them well and wondered whether I would ever do so.

I was thinking a lot about the past and my roots. On New Year's Day, I finished C. Vann Woodward's *The Burden of Southern History*, in which he noted southerners' "peculiar historical consciousness," what Eudora Welty called "the sense of place." Arkansas was my place. Unlike Thomas Wolfe, whose cascading prose I so admired, I knew

I could go home again. Indeed, I had to. But first, I had to finish law school.

I got to spend my second term at Yale as a proper law student with the heaviest class load of my stay there. My Business Law professor was John Baker, Yale Law's first black faculty member. He was very good to me, gave me some research work to supplement my meager income, and invited me to his house for dinner. John and his wife had gone to Fisk University, a black school in Nashville, Tennessee, in the early sixties, when the civil rights movement was in full flower. He told me fascinating stories about the fear they lived with and the joy he and his classmates found in the work of the movement.

I took Constitutional Law with Charles Reich, who was as liberal as Bob Bork was conservative, and the author of one of the seminal "countercultural" books about the 1960s, *The Greening of America.* My Criminal Law professor, Steve Duke, was a witty, acerbic man and a fine teacher with whom I later did a seminar on white-collar crime. I really enjoyed Political and Civil Rights, taught by Tom Emerson, a dapper little man who had been in FDR's administration and whose textbook we used. I also took Professor William Leon McBride's National Law and Philosophy, did some legal services work, and got a part-time job. For a few months, I drove to Hartford four times a week to help Dick Suisman, a Democratic businessman I'd met in the Duffey campaign, with his work on the city council. Dick knew I needed the work, and I think I was some help to him.

In late February, I flew to California for a few days to be with Frank Aller, Strobe Talbott, and Strobe's girlfriend, Brooke Shearer. We met in Los Angeles at the home of Brooke's extraordinarily welcoming and generous parents, Marva and Lloyd Shearer, who, for many years, wrote America's most widely read celebrity gossip column, Walter Scott's Personality Parade. Then in March I went up to Boston, where Frank was living and looking for work as a journalist, to see him and Strobe again. We walked in the woods behind Frank's house and along the New Hampshire coast nearby. Frank seemed glad to be home, but still sad. Even though he had escaped the draft and prison, he seemed caught in the throes of a depression, like that which Turgenev said "only the very young know and which has no apparent reason." I thought he'd get over it.

The spring lifted my spirits as it always did. The political news was a mixed bag. The Supreme Court unanimously upheld busing to achieve racial balance. The Chinese accepted an American invitation to reciprocate the visit of the American Ping-Pong team to China by sending their team to the United States. And the war protests continued. Senator McGovern came to New Haven on May 16, plainly with the intention of running for President in 1972. I liked him and thought he had a chance to win, because of his heroic record as a bomber pilot in World War II, his leadership of the Food for Peace program in the Kennedy administration, and the new rules for delegate selection for the next Democratic convention. McGovern was heading a commission to write them, for the purpose of ensuring a more diverse convention in terms of age, race, and gender. The new rules, plus the weight of anti-war liberals in the primaries, virtually assured that the old political bosses would have less influence and the party activists more in the 1972 nominating process. Rick Stearns had been working for the commission, and I was sure he'd be tough and smart enough to devise a system favorable to McGovern.

While law school and politics were going well, my personal life was a mess. I had broken up with a young woman who went home to marry her old boyfriend, then had a painful parting with a law student I liked very much but couldn't commit to. I was just about reconciled to being alone and was determined not to get involved with anyone for a while. Then one day, when I was sitting at the back of Professor Emerson's class in Political and Civil Rights, I spotted a woman I hadn't seen before. Apparently she attended even less frequently than I did. She had thick dark blond hair and wore eyeglasses and no makeup, but she conveyed a sense of strength and self-possession I had rarely seen in anyone, man or woman. After class I followed her out, intending to introduce myself. When I got a couple of feet from her, I reached out my hand to touch her shoulder, then immediately pulled it back. It was almost a physical reaction. Somehow I knew that this wasn't another tap on the shoulder, that I might be starting something I couldn't stop.

I saw the girl several times around school over the next few days, but didn't approach her. Then one night I was standing at one end of the long, narrow Yale Law Library talking to another student, Jeff Gleckel, about joining the *Yale Law Journal*. Jeff urged me to do it, saying it would assure me a good clerkship with a federal judge or a job with one of the blue-chip law firms. He made a good case, but I just wasn't interested; I was going home to Arkansas, and in the meantime preferred politics to the law review. After a while I suddenly stopped paying attention to his earnest entreaty because I saw the girl again, standing at the other end of the room. For once, she was staring back at me. After a while she closed her book, walked the length of the library, looked me in the eye, and said, "If you're going to keep staring at me and I'm going to keep staring back, we ought to at least know each other's names. Mine's Hillary Rodham. What's yours?" Hillary, of course, remembers all this, but in slightly different words. I was impressed and so stunned I couldn't say anything for a few seconds. Finally I blurted my name out. We exchanged a few words, and she left. I don't know what poor Jeff Gleckel thought was going on, but he never talked to me about the law review again.

A couple of days later, I was coming down the steps to the ground floor of the law school when I saw Hillary again. She was wearing a bright flowered skirt that nearly touched the floor. I was determined to spend some time with her. She said she was going to register for next term's classes, so I said I'd go, too. We stood in line and talked. I thought I was doing pretty well until we got to the front of the line. The registrar looked up at me and said, "Bill, what are you doing back here? You registered this morning." I turned beet red, and Hillary laughed that big laugh of hers. My

cover was blown, so I asked her to take a walk with me to
the Yale Art Gallery to see the Mark Rothko exhibit. I was
so eager and nervous that I forgot the university workforce
was on strike and the museum was closed. Luckily, there
was a guard on duty. I pleaded my case and offered to clean
up the branches and other litter in the museum's garden if
he'd let me in.

The guard took a look at us, figured it out, and let us in.
We had the whole exhibit to ourselves. It was wonderful,
and I've liked Rothko ever since. When we were done, we
went out to the garden, and I picked up the sticks. I suppose
I was being a scab for the first and only time in my life, but
the union didn't have a picket line outside the museum and,
besides, politics was the last thing on my mind. After I paid
my cleaning-up dues, Hillary and I stayed in the garden for
another hour or so. There was a large, beautiful Henry
Moore sculpture of a seated woman. Hillary sat in the
woman's lap, and I sat beside her talking. Before long, I
leaned over and put my head on her shoulder. It was our
first date.

We spent the next several days together, just hanging
around, talking about everything under the sun. The next
weekend Hillary went up to Vermont on a long-planned
visit to the man she had been dating. I was anxious about it.
I didn't want to lose her. When she got home late Sunday
night I called her. She was sick as a dog, so I brought her
some chicken soup and orange juice. From then on we were
inseparable. She spent a lot of time at our house on the
beach and quickly won over Doug, Don, and Bill.

She didn't do so well with my mother when she came to
visit a few weeks later, partly because she tried to cut her own
hair just before Mother arrived. It was a minor fiasco; she
looked more like a punk rocker than someone who had just
walked out of Jeff Dwire's beauty salon. With no makeup, a
work shirt and jeans, and bare feet coated with tar from
walking on the beach at Milford, she might as well have been
a space alien. The fact that I was obviously serious about her
gave Mother heartburn. In her book, Mother called Hillary a
"growth experience." It was a girl with "no makeup, Coke-

bottle glasses, and brown hair with no apparent style" versus a woman with hot-pink lipstick, painted-on eyebrows, and a silver stripe in her hair. I got a kick out of watching them try to figure each other out. Over time they did, as Mother came to care less about Hillary's appearance and Hillary came to care more about it. Underneath their different styles, they were both smart, tough, resilient, passionate women. When they got together, I didn't stand a chance.

By mid-May, I wanted to be with Hillary all the time. As a result, I met several of her friends, including Susan Graber, a Wellesley classmate of hers whom I later appointed to a federal judgeship in Oregon; Carolyn Ellis, a bright, funny Lebanese woman from Mississippi who could "out-southern" me and is now chancellor of the University of Mississippi; and Neil Steinman, the brightest man I met at Yale, who raised the first funds for me in Pennsylvania in 1992.

I learned about Hillary's childhood in Park Ridge, Illinois; her four years at Wellesley, where she switched her politics from Republican to Democrat because of civil rights and the war; her post-graduation trip to Alaska, where she slimed fish for a living; and her interest in legal services for poor people and in children's issues. I also heard about her famous commencement speech at Wellesley in which she articulated our generation's contradictory feelings of alienation from the political system and determination to make America better. The speech got a lot of national publicity and was her first brush with fame beyond the boundaries of her immediate environment. What I liked about her politics was that, like me, she was both idealistic and practical. She wanted to change things, and she knew that doing so required persistent effort. She was as tired as I was of our side getting beat and treating defeat as evidence of moral virtue and superiority. Hillary was a formidable presence in law school, a big fish in our small but highly competitive pond. I was more of a floating presence, drifting in and out.

A lot of the students we both knew talked about Hillary as if they were a little intimidated by her. Not me. I just wanted to be with her. But time was running out on us. Hillary had accepted a summer job at Treuhaft, Walker, and

Burnstein, a law firm in Oakland, California, and I had been asked to take a job as coordinator of the southern states for Senator McGovern. Until I met Hillary, I was really looking forward to it. I was going to be based in Miami, and the job required traveling throughout the South putting state campaigns together. I knew I'd be good at it, and though I didn't think McGovern could do very well in the general election in the South, I believed he could win a fair number of convention delegates during the primary season. Regardless, I'd have the political experience of a lifetime. It was a rare opportunity for a twenty-five-year-old, one I got from a combination of my friendship with Rick Stearns, who had an important post in the campaign, and affirmative action: they had to have at least one southerner in a responsible position!

The problem was, I no longer wanted to do it. I knew if I went to Florida, Hillary and I might be lost to each other. Though I found the prospect of the campaign exciting, I feared, as I wrote in my diary, that it would simply be "a way of formalizing my aloneness," letting me deal with people in a good cause but at arm's length. With Hillary there was no arm's length. She was in my face from the start, and, before I knew it, in my heart.

I screwed up my courage and asked Hillary if I could spend the summer with her in California. She was incredulous at first, because she knew how much I loved politics and how deeply I felt about the war. I told her I'd have the rest of my life for my work and my ambition, but I loved her and wanted to see if it could work out for us. She took a deep breath and agreed to let me take her to California. We had been together only about a month.

We stopped briefly in Park Ridge to meet her family. Her mother, Dorothy, was a lovely, attractive woman, whom I got along with from the start, but I was as alien to Hillary's father as Hillary was to Mother. Hugh Rodham was a gruff, tough-talking Republican who, to say the least, was suspicious of me. But the more we talked, the more I liked him. I resolved to keep at it until he came around. Soon we drove on to Berkeley, California, near her job in Oakland, where she would be staying in a small house owned by her mother's half sister, Adeline. After a day or two I drove back across the country to Washington, to tell Rick Stearns and Gary Hart, Senator McGovern's campaign manager, that I couldn't go to Florida after all. Gary thought I had lost my mind to pass up such an opportunity. I suppose Rich did, too. To them, I suppose I did look like a fool, but your life is shaped by the opportunities you turn down as well as by those you seize.

I did feel bad about leaving the campaign, and I offered to go to Connecticut for a couple of weeks to set up an organization there. As soon as I had signed up people in every congressional district, I headed back to California, this time by the southern route so that I could stop at home.

I enjoyed the drive west, including a visit in the Grand Canyon. I got there in the late afternoon and crawled out on a rock jutting over the canyon's edge to watch the sun go down. It was amazing the way the rocks, compressed into distinct layers over millions of years, changed colors as the canyon darkened from the bottom up.

After I left the canyon, I had a blistering drive across Death Valley, America's hottest spot, then turned north to my summer with Hillary. When I walked into her house in Berkeley, she greeted me with a peach pie—my favorite—that she'd baked herself. It was good, and it didn't last long. During the day, when she was at work, I walked all over the city, read books in the parks and coffee shops, and explored San Francisco. At night we'd go to movies or local restaurants or just stay in and talk. On July 24, we drove down to Stanford to hear Joan Baez sing in the open amphitheater. So that all her fans could see her, she charged only $2.50 for admission, a striking contrast to the high ticket prices of today's big concerts. Baez sang her old hits and, for one of the first times in public, "The Night They Drove Old Dixie Down."

When the summer ended, Hillary and I were nowhere near finished with our conversation, so we decided to live together back in New Haven, a move that doubtless caused both our families concern. We found an apartment on the ground floor of an old house at 21 Edgewood Avenue, near the law school.

The front door of our apartment opened into a tiny living room, behind which was a smaller dining-room area and an even smaller bedroom. Behind the bedroom were an old kitchen and a bathroom so small the toilet seat sometimes scraped against the bathtub. The house was so old that the floors sank from the walls to the middle at an angle so pronounced I had to put little wooden blocks under the inside legs of our small dining table. But the price was right for penurious law students: seventy-five dollars a month. The nicest thing about the place was the fireplace in the living room. I still remember sitting in front of the fire on a cold winter day as Hillary and I read Vincent Cronin's biography of Napoleon together.

We were too happy and too poor to be anything but proud of our new home. We enjoyed having friends over for meals. Among our favorite guests were Rufus and Yvonne Cormier. They were both children of African-American ministers in Beaumont, Texas, who grew up in the same neighborhood and had gone together for years before they married. While Rufus studied law, Yvonne was getting her Ph.D. in biochemistry. Eventually she became a doctor and he became the first black partner of the big Houston law firm Baker and Botts. One night at dinner, Rufus, who was one of the best students in our class, was bemoaning the long hours he spent studying. "You know," he said in his slow drawl, "life is organized backwards. You spend the best years studying, then working. When you retire at sixty-five, you're too old to enjoy it. People should retire between the ages of twenty-one and thirty-five, then work like hell till they die." Of course, it didn't work out that way. We're all closing in on sixty-five and still at it.

I really got into my third semester of law school, with courses in Corporate Finance, Criminal Procedure, Taxation, Estates, and a seminar in Corporate Social Responsibility. The seminar was taught by Burke Marshall, a legendary figure for his work as assistant attorney general for civil rights under Robert Kennedy, and Jan Deutsch, reputed to be the only person, up to that time, to make the Honors grade in all his classes at Yale Law. Marshall was small and wiry, with bright dancing eyes. He barely spoke above a whisper, but there was steel in his voice, and in his spine. Deutsch had an unusual, clipped, stream-of-consciousness speaking style, which moved rapidly from one unfinished sentence to another. This was apparently the result of a severe head injury incurred when he was hit by a car and flew a long distance in the air before coming down hard on concrete. He was unconscious for several weeks and woke up with a metal plate in his head. But he was brilliant. I figured out his speaking style and was able to translate him to classmates who couldn't unpack his words. Jan Deutsch was also the only man I'd ever met who ate all of an apple, including the core. He said all the good minerals were there. He was smarter than I was, so I tried it. Once in a while I still do, with fond memories of Professor Deutsch.

Marvin Chirelstein taught me both Corporate Finance and Taxation. I was lousy in Taxation. The tax code was riddled with too many artificial distinctions I couldn't care less about; they seemed to me to provide more opportunities for tax lawyers to reduce their clients' obligation to help pay America's way than to advance worthy social goals. Once, instead of paying attention to the class, I read Gabriel García Márquez's *One Hundred Years of Solitude*. At the end of the hour, Professor Chirelstein asked me what was so much more interesting than his lecture. I held up the book and told him it was the greatest novel written in any language since William Faulkner died. I still think so.

I redeemed myself in Corporate Finance when I aced the final exam. When Professor Chirelstein asked me how I could be so good at Corporate Finance and so bad at Taxation, I told him it was because corporate finance was like politics: within a given set of rules, it was a constant struggle for power, with all parties trying to avoid getting shafted but eager to shaft.

In addition to my classwork I had two jobs. Even with a scholarship and two different student loans, I needed the money. I worked a few hours a week for Ben Moss, a local lawyer, doing legal research and running errands. The research got old after a while, but the errands were interesting. One day I had to deliver some papers to an address in an inner-city high-rise. As I was climbing the stairs to the third or fourth floor, I passed a man in the stairwell with a glazed look in his eyes and a hypodermic needle and syringe hanging from his arm. He had just shot himself full of heroin. I delivered the papers and got out of there as quickly as I could.

My other job was less hazardous but more interesting. I taught criminal law to undergraduates in a law-enforcement program at the University of New Haven. My position was funded under the Federal Law Enforcement Assistance program, which had just started under Nixon. The classes were designed to produce more professional law officers who could make arrests, searches, and seizures in a constitutional manner. I often had to prepare my lectures late in the evening before the day I delivered them. To stay awake, I did a lot of my work at the Elm Street Diner, about a block away from our house. It was open all night, had great coffee and fruit pie, and was full of characters from New Haven's night life. Tony, a Greek immigrant whose uncle owned the place, ran the diner at night. He gave me endless free refills of coffee as I toiled away.

The street outside the diner was the border dividing the territory of two groups of streetwalking prostitutes. From time to time the police took them away, but they were always quickly back at work. The streetwalkers often came into the diner to get coffee and warm up. When they found out I was in law school, several would plop down in my booth in search of free legal advice. I did my best, but none took the best advice: get another job. One night, a tall black transvestite sat down across from me and said his social club wanted to raffle off a television to make money; he wanted to know if the raffle would run afoul of the law against gambling. I later learned what he was really worried about was that the television was stolen. It had been "donated" to the club by a friend who ran a fencing operation, buying stolen goods and reselling them at a discount. Anyway, I told him that other groups held raffles all the time and it was highly unlikely that the club would be prosecuted. In return for my wise counsel, he gave me the only fee I ever received for legal advice in the Elm Street Diner, a raffle ticket. I didn't win the television, but I felt well paid just at having the ticket with the name of the social club on it in bold print: The Black Uniques.

On September 14, as Hillary and I were walking into the Blue Bell Café, someone came up to me and said it was urgent that I call Strobe Talbott. He and Brooke were visiting his parents in Cleveland. My stomach was in knots as I fed change into the pay phone outside the café. Brooke answered the phone and told me Frank Aller had killed himself. He had just been offered a job to work in the Saigon bureau of the *Los Angeles Times*, had accepted it, and had gone home to Spokane, apparently in good spirits, to get his clothes together and prepare for the move to Vietnam. I think he wanted to see and write about the war he opposed. Perhaps he wanted to put himself in harm's way to prove he wasn't a coward. Just when things were working out on the surface of his life, whatever was going on inside compelled him to end it.

His friends were stunned, but we probably shouldn't have been. Six weeks earlier, I had noted in my diary that Frank was really in the dumps again, having to that point failed to find a newspaper job in Vietnam or China. I said he had "fallen finally, physically and emotionally, to the strains, contractions, pains of the last few years, which he has endured, mostly alone." Frank's close, rational friends assumed that getting his external life back on track would calm his inner turmoil. But as I learned on that awful day, depression crowds out rationality with a vengeance. It's a disease that, when far advanced, is beyond the reasoned reach of spouses, children, lovers, and friends. I don't think I ever really understood it until I read my friend Bill Styron's brave account of his own battle with depression and suicidal thoughts, *Darkness Visible: A Memoir of Madness*. When Frank killed himself, I felt both grief and anger—at him for doing it, and at myself for not seeing it coming and pushing him to get professional help. I wish I had known then what I know now, though maybe it wouldn't have made any difference.

After Frank's death, I lost my usual optimism and my interest in courses, politics, and people. I don't know what I would have done without Hillary. When we first got together, she had a brief bout with self-doubt, but she was always so strong in public I don't think even her closest friends knew it. The fact that she opened herself to me only strengthened and validated my feelings for her. Now I needed her. And she came through, reminding me that what I was learning, doing, and thinking mattered.

In the spring term, I was bored in all my classes but Evidence, taught by Geoffrey Hazard. The rules for what is and isn't admissible in a fair trial and the process of making an honest and reasoned argument on the facts available were fascinating to me and left a lasting impression. I always tried to argue the evidence in politics as well as law.

Evidence counted a lot in my major law school activity that term, the annual Barristers Union trial competition. On March 28, Hillary and I competed in the semifinals, from which four students plus two alternates would be chosen to participate in a full-blown trial to be written by a third-year student. We did well and both made the cut.

For the next month we prepared for the Prize Trial, *State* v. *Porter*. Porter was a policeman accused of beating a long-haired kid to death. On April 29, Hillary and I prosecuted Mr. Porter, with help from our alternate, Bob Alsdorf. The defense lawyers were Mike Conway and Tony Rood, with Doug Eakeley as their alternate. The judge was former Supreme Court Justice Abe Fortas. He took his role seriously and played it to the hilt, issuing ruling after ruling on both sides and objections, all the while evaluating the four of us to decide who would win the prize. If my performance in the semifinals was the best public speaking of my law school career, my effort in the Prize Trial was the worst. I had an off day and didn't deserve to win. Hillary, on the other hand, was very good. So was Mike Conway, who gave an effective, emotional closing argument. Fortas gave Conway the prize. At the time I thought Hillary didn't get it in part because the dour-faced Fortas disapproved of her highly unprosecutorial outfit. She wore a blue suede jacket, bright—and I mean bright—orange suede flared pants, and a blue, orange, and white blouse. Hillary became a fine trial lawyer, but she never wore those orange pants to court again.

Apart from the Prize Trial, I poured my competitive instincts into the McGovern campaign. Early in the year, I cleaned out my bank account to open a headquarters near the campus. I had enough money, about $200, to pay a month's rent and put in a telephone. In three weeks, we had eight hundred volunteers and enough small contributions to reimburse me and keep the place open.

The volunteers were important for the coming primary campaign, which I assumed we'd have to wage against the Democratic organization and its powerful boss, Arthur Barbieri. Four years earlier, in 1968, the McCarthy forces had done well in the primary in New Haven, partly because the Democratic regulars had taken Vice President Humphrey's victory for granted. I had no illusions that Barbieri would make that mistake again, so I decided to try to persuade him to endorse McGovern. To say it was a long shot is a gross understatement. When I walked into his office and introduced myself, Barbieri was cordial but businesslike. He sat back in his chair with his hands folded across his chest, displaying two huge diamond rings, one big circular one with lots of stones, the other with his initials, AB, completely filled with diamonds. He smiled and told me that 1972 would not be a replay of 1968, that he had already lined up his poll workers and a number of cars to take his people to the polls. He said he had dedicated $50,000 to the effort, a huge sum in those days for a town the size of New Haven. I replied that I didn't have much money, but I did have eight hundred volunteers who would knock on the doors of every house in his stronghold, telling all the Italian mothers that Arthur Barbieri wanted to keep sending their sons to fight and die in Vietnam. "You don't need that grief," I said.

"Why do you care who wins the nomination? Endorse McGovern. He was a war hero in World War II. He can make peace and you can keep control of New Haven." Barbieri listened and replied, "You know, kid, you ain't so dumb. I'll think about it. Come back and see me in ten days." When I returned, Barbieri said, "I've been thinking about it. I think Senator McGovern is a good man and we need to get out of Vietnam. I'm going to tell my guys what we're going to do, and I want you to be there to make the pitch."

A few days later, I took Hillary with me to the extraordinary encounter with Barbieri's party leaders at a local Italian club, the Melebus, in the basement of an old building downtown. The décor was all red and black. It was very dark, very ethnic, very un-McGovern. When Barbieri told his guys that they were going to support McGovern so that no more boys from New Haven would die in Vietnam, there were groans and gasps. "Arthur, he's almost a Commie," one man blurted out. Another said, "Arthur, he sounds like a fag," referring to the senator's High Plains nasal twang. Barbieri never flinched. He introduced me, told them about my eight hundred volunteers, and let me give my pitch, which was heavy on McGovern's war record and work in the Kennedy administration. By the time the evening was over, they came around.

I was ecstatic. In the entire primary process, Arthur Barbieri and Matty Troy of Queens in New York City were the only old-line Democratic bosses to endorse McGovern. Not all our troops were pleased. After the endorsement was announced, I got an angry late-night call from two of our stalwarts in Trumbull with whom I'd worked in the Duffey campaign. They couldn't believe I'd sold out the spirit of the campaign with such a nefarious compromise. "I'm sorry," I shouted into the phone, "I thought our objective was to win," and I hung up. Barbieri proved to be loyal and effective. At the Democratic convention, Senator McGovern got five of our congressional district's six votes on the first ballot. In the November vote, New Haven was the only Connecticut city that went for him. Barbieri was as good as his word. When I became President, I tracked him down. He was in ill health and had long since retired from politics. I invited him to the White House, and we had a good visit in the Oval Office not long before he died. Barbieri was what James Carville calls a "sticker." In politics, there's nothing better.

Apparently my work in Connecticut redeemed me in the eyes of the McGovern campaign. I was asked to join the national staff and work the Democratic National Convention in Miami Beach, concentrating on the South Carolina and Arkansas delegations.

Meanwhile, Hillary had gone to Washington to work for Marian Wright Edelman at the Washington Research Project, an advocacy group for children, which would soon be called the Children's Defense Fund. Her job was to investigate all-white southern academies that were established in response to court-ordered public school integration. In the North, white parents who didn't want their kids in inner-city schools could move to the suburbs. That wasn't an option in small southern towns—the suburbs were cow pastures and soybean fields. The problem was that the Nixon administration was not enforcing the law banning such schools from claiming tax-exempt status, a move that plainly encouraged southern whites to leave public schools.

I started my job for McGovern in Washington, first checking in with Lee Williams and my other friends on Senator Fulbright's staff, then going to see Congressman Wilbur Mills, the powerful chairman of the House Ways and Means Committee. Mills, who was a Washington legend for his detailed knowledge of the tax code and his skill in running his committee, had announced that he would be Arkansas' "favorite son" candidate at the Miami convention. Such candidacies were usually launched in the hope of preventing a state's delegation from voting for the front-runner, although back then a favorite son occasionally thought lightning might strike and he would at least wind up on the ticket as the vice-presidential nominee. In Mills's case, his candidacy served both purposes. The Arkansas

Democrats thought McGovern, who was far ahead in the delegate count, was sure to be trounced at home in the general election, and Mills doubtless thought he would be a better President. Our meeting was cordial. I told Chairman Mills that I expected the delegates to be loyal to him but that I would be working them to get their support on important procedural votes and on a second ballot if Senator McGovern needed one.

After the Mills meeting I flew to Columbia, South Carolina, to meet as many of the convention delegates there as possible. Many were sympathetic to McGovern, and I thought they would help us on crucial votes, despite the fact that their credentials were subject to challenge on the grounds that the delegation did not have as much racial, gender, and age diversity as the new rules written by the McGovern Commission required.

Before Miami, I also went to the Arkansas Democratic Convention in Hot Springs to court my home-state delegates. I knew that Governor Bumpers, who would chair the delegation in Miami, thought McGovern would hurt the Democrats in Arkansas, but as in South Carolina, a lot of the delegates were anti-war and pro-McGovern. I left for Miami feeling pretty good about both the delegations I was working.

At the convention in mid-July, the major candidates had their headquarters in hotels around Miami and Miami Beach, but their operations were run out of trailers outside the Convention Center. The McGovern trailer was overseen by Gary Hart as national campaign manager, with Frank Mankiewicz as national political director and public spokesman, and my friend Rick Stearns as the director of research and caucus state operations. Rick knew more about the rules than anyone else. Those of us who were working the delegations were on the floor, following instructions from the trailer. The McGovern campaign had come a long way, thanks to an array of committed volunteers, Hart's leadership, Mankiewicz's handling of the press, and Stearns's strategizing. With their help, McGovern had outfought and outpolled politicians who were more established, more charismatic, or both: Hubert Humphrey; Ed Muskie; Mayor John Lindsay of New York, who had switched parties to run; Senator Henry Jackson of Washington State; and George Wallace, who was paralyzed by a would-be assassin's bullet during the campaign. Congresswoman Shirley Chisholm of New York also ran, becoming the first African-American to do so.

We thought McGovern had enough votes to win on the first ballot if he could weather the challenge to the California delegation. The new McGovern rules required each state with a primary election to apportion its delegates as closely as possible to the percentage of votes they got. However, California still had a winner-take-all system and was asserting its right to keep it because the state legislature hadn't changed its election law by convention time. Ironically, McGovern favored the California system over his own rules because he had won the primary with 44 percent of the votes but had all of the state's 271 delegates pledged to him. The anti-McGovern forces argued that McGovern was a hypocrite and that the convention should seat only 44 percent, or 120 delegates, for him, with the other 151 being pledged to the other candidates in proportion to their share of the California primary vote. The Credentials Committee of the convention was anti-McGovern and voted to uphold the California challenge, seating only 120 of his delegates, and putting his first-ballot victory in doubt.

The Credentials Committee's decisions could be overturned by a majority of the convention delegates. The McGovern forces wanted to do that with California. So did the South Carolina delegation, which was in danger of losing its votes because it had also been found in violation of the rules; only 25 percent of the delegation were women, rather than the required half. McGovern was nominally against the South Carolina position because of that under-representation.

What happened next was complicated and not worth going into detail about. Essentially, Rick Stearns decided that we should lose the South Carolina vote, bind our opponents to a procedural rule that benefited our challenge; then we would win the California vote. It worked. The South Carolina delegation was seated, and our opponents smelled victory. But by the time they realized they had been tricked, it was too late; we picked up all 271 delegates and clinched the nomination. The California challenge was probably the greatest example of political jujitsu at a party convention since primary elections became the dominant mode of selecting delegates. As I've said, Rick Stearns was a genius on the rules. I was elated. Now McGovern was virtually guaranteed a first-ballot victory, and the folks from South Carolina, whom I had come to like a lot, could stay.

Alas, it was all downhill from there. McGovern entered the convention well behind but still within striking distance of President Nixon in the opinion polls, and we expected to pick up five or six points during the week, thanks to several days of intense media coverage. Getting that kind of bounce, however, requires the kind of disciplined control of events our forces had demonstrated with the delegate challenges. For some reason, it evaporated after that. First, a gay-rights group staged a sit-in at McGovern's hotel and refused to budge until he met with them. When he did, the media and the Republicans portrayed it as a cave-in that made him look both weak and too liberal. Then, on Thursday afternoon, after he picked Senator Tom Eagleton of Missouri to be his running mate, McGovern allowed other names to be put in nomination against him during the voting that night. Six more people got in the race, complete with nominating speeches, and a long roll-call vote. Though Eagleton's victory was a foregone conclusion, the other six got some votes. So did Roger Mudd of CBS News, the television character Archie Bunker, and Mao Tse-tung. It was a disaster. The useless exercise had taken all the prime-time television hours, when nearly eighteen million households were watching the convention. The intended media events—Senator Edward Kennedy's speech nominating McGovern and the nominee's own acceptance speech—were pushed back into the wee hours of the morning. Senator Kennedy was a champ and gave a rousing speech. McGovern's was good, too. He called on America to "come home . . . from deception in high

places . . . from the waste of idle hands . . . from prejudice. . . . Come home to the affirmation that we have a
dream . . . to the conviction that we can move our country
forward . . . to the belief that we can seek a newer world."
The problem was that McGovern began to talk at 2:48 a.m.,
or "prime time in Samoa," as the humorist Mark Russell
quipped. He had lost 80 percent of his television audience.

As if that weren't enough, it soon became public that
Eagleton had had treatment, including electric shock ther-
apy, for depression. Unfortunately, back then there was still
a great deal of ignorance about the nature and range of
mental-health problems, as well as the fact that previous
Presidents, including Lincoln and Wilson, had suffered from
periodic depression. The idea that Senator Eagleton would
be next in line to be President if McGovern were elected was
unsettling to many people, even more so because Eagleton
hadn't told McGovern about it. If McGovern had known
and picked him anyway, perhaps we could have made real
progress in the public's understanding of mental health, but
the way it came out raised questions not only about
McGovern's judgment but also about his competence as
well. Our vaunted campaign operation hadn't even vetted
Eagleton's selection with Missouri's Democratic governor,
Warren Hearnes, who knew about the mental-health issue.

Within a week after the Miami convention, we were in
even worse shape than when the Democrats had exited
Chicago four years earlier, looking both too liberal and too
inept. After the Eagleton story came out, McGovern first
said he stood by his running mate "1,000 percent." A few
days later, under withering, unrelenting pressure from his
own supporters, he dropped him. Then it took until the second week of August to get a replacement. Sargent Shriver,
President Kennedy's brother-in-law, said yes after Ted
Kennedy, Senator Abe Ribicoff of Connecticut, Governor
Reubin Askew of Florida, Hubert Humphrey, and Senator
Ed Muskie all declined to join the ticket. I was convinced
that most Americans would vote for a peace candidate who
was progressive but not too liberal, and before Miami I
thought we could sell McGovern. Now we were back to

square one. After the convention, I went to Washington to see Hillary, so exhausted I slept more than twenty-four hours straight.

A few days later, I packed up to go to Texas to help coordinate the general election campaign there. I knew it was going to be tough when I flew from Washington to Arkansas to pick up a car. I sat next to a young man from Jackson, Mississippi, who asked me what I was doing. When I told him, he almost shouted, "You're the only white person I've ever met for McGovern!" Later, when I was home watching John Dean testify about the misdeeds of the Nixon White House before Senator Sam Ervin's Watergate Committee, the phone rang. It was the young man whom I'd met on the airplane. He said, "I just called so you could say, 'I told you so.'" I never heard from him again, but I appreciated the call. It was amazing how far public opinion moved in just two years as Watergate unfolded.

In the summer of 1972, however, going to Texas was a fool's errand, although it was a fascinating one. Starting with John Kennedy in 1960, Democratic presidential campaigns often assigned out-of-staters to oversee important state campaigns on the theory that they could bring competing factions together and make sure all decisions put the candidate's interests, not parochial concerns, first. Whatever the theory, in practice, outsiders could inspire resentment on all sides, especially for a campaign as troubled as McGovern's, in an environment as fractured and contentious as Texas.

The campaign decided to send two of us to Texas, me and Taylor Branch, whom, as I've said, I'd first met on Martha's Vineyard in 1969. As an insurance policy, the campaign named a successful young Houston lawyer, Julius Glickman, to be the third member of our triumvirate. Since Taylor and I were both southerners and not averse to cooperating, I thought we might be able to make it work in Texas. We set up a headquarters on West Sixth Street in Austin, not far from the state Capitol, and shared an apartment on a hill just across the Colorado River. Taylor ran the headquarters operation and controlled the budget. We didn't have much money, so it was fortunate that he was tightfisted, and better than I was at saying no to people. I worked with the county organizations, and Julius lined up what support he could get from prominent Texans he knew, and we had a great staff of enthusiastic young people. Three of them became especially close friends of Hillary's and mine: Garry Mauro, who became Texas land commissioner and took a leading role in my presidential campaign; and Roy Spence and Judy Trabulsi, who founded an advertising agency that became the largest in America outside New York City. Garry, Roy, and Judy would support me and Hillary in all our campaigns.

The Texan who had by far the greatest impact on my career was Betsey Wright, a doctor's daughter from the small West Texas town of Alpine. She was just a couple years older than I was but much more experienced in grass-roots politics, having worked for the state Democratic Party and Common Cause. She was brilliant, intense, loyal, and conscientious almost to a fault. And she was the only person I had ever met who was more fascinated by and consumed with politics than I was. Unlike some of our more inexperienced colleagues, she knew we were getting the daylights beaten out of us, but she worked eighteen-hour days anyway. After I was defeated for governor in 1980, Hillary asked Betsey to come to Little Rock to help organize my files for a comeback. She did, and she stayed to run my successful campaign in 1982. Later, Betsey served as chief of staff in the governor's office. In 1992, she played a pivotal role in the presidential campaign, defending me and my record from the endless barrage of personal and political attacks with a skill and strength no one else could have mustered and maintained. Without Betsey Wright, I could not have become President.

After I had been in Texas a few weeks, Hillary joined me and the campaign, having been hired by Anne Wexler to do voter registration for the Democratic Party. She got on well with the rest of the staff, and brightened even my toughest days.

The Texas campaign got off to a rocky start, mostly because of the Eagleton disaster, but also because a lot of the local Democrats didn't want to be identified with McGovern. Senator Lloyd Bentsen, who had defeated the fiery liberal Senator Ralph Yarborough two years earlier, declined to be the campaign chairman. The gubernatorial nominee, Dolph Briscoe, a South Texas rancher who years later became a friend and supporter of mine, didn't even want to appear in public with our candidate. Former governor John Connally, who had been riding in the car with President Kennedy when he was killed nine years earlier and had been a close ally of President Johnson, was leading a group called Democrats for Nixon.

Still, Texas was too big to write off, and Humphrey had carried it four years earlier, though by only 38,000 votes. Finally, two elected state officials agreed to co-chair the campaign, Agriculture Commissioner John White and Land Commissioner Bob Armstrong. White, an old-fashioned Texas Democrat, knew we couldn't win but wanted the Democratic ticket to make the best showing possible in Texas. John later became chairman of the Democratic National Committee. Bob Armstrong was an ardent environmentalist who loved to play guitar and hang out with us at Scholtz's Beer Garden, the local bowling alley, or the Armadillo Music Hall, where he took Hillary and me to see Jerry Jeff Walker and Willie Nelson.

I thought things were looking up in late August when Senator McGovern and Sargent Shriver were slated to come to Texas to see President Johnson. Shriver was a likable man with a buoyant personality who brought energy and gravitas to the ticket. He had been a founder of the Legal Services Corporation, which provides legal assistance to the poor, President Kennedy's first director of the Peace Corps, and President Johnson's first director of the War on Poverty.

McGovern and Shriver's meeting with President Johnson went reasonably well but delivered few political benefits because Johnson insisted there be no press and because he already had issued a lukewarm endorsement of McGovern to a local newspaper a few days before they met. The main thing I got out of it was an autographed picture of the President, which he had signed when Taylor had gone out to the LBJ Ranch a few days before the meeting to finalize the arrangements. Probably because we were pro–civil rights southerners, Taylor and I liked Johnson more than most of our McGovern co-workers did.

After the meeting, McGovern went back to his hotel suite in Austin to meet with some of his main supporters and staff people. There were a lot of complaints about the disarray in the campaign. It certainly was disorganized. Taylor and I hadn't been there long enough to establish ourselves, much less a smooth organization, and our liberal base was dispirited after its candidate, Sissy Farenthold, lost a bruising primary battle for governor to Dolph Briscoe. For some reason, the highest-ranking state official who did support McGovern, Secretary of State Bob Bullock, wasn't even invited to meet him. McGovern wrote him an apology, but it was a telling oversight.

Not long after McGovern left Texas, the campaign decided we needed some adult supervision, so they sent down a crusty gray-haired Irishman from Sioux City, Iowa, Don O'Brien, who had been active in John Kennedy's campaign and had served as the U.S. attorney under Robert Kennedy. I liked Don O'Brien a lot, but he was an old-fashioned chauvinist who got on the nerves of a lot of our independent young women. Still, we made it work, and I was relieved because now I could spend even more time on the road. Those were my best days in Texas.

I went north to Waco, where I met the liberal insurance magnate, and a future supporter of mine, Bernard Rapoport; east to Dallas, where I met Jess Hay, a moderate but loyal Democratic businessman who also stayed my friend and supporter, and a black state senator, Eddie Bernice Johnson, who became one of my strongest allies in Congress when I was elected President; then to Houston, where I met and fell in love with the godmother of Texas liberals, Billie Carr, a big, raucous woman who reminded me a little of Mother. Billie took me under her wing and never let me go until the day she died, even when I disappointed her by being less liberal than she was.

I had my first extensive contacts with Mexican-Americans, commonly called Chicanos back then, and came to love their spirit, culture, and food. In San Antonio, I discovered Mario's and Mi Tierra, where I once ate three meals in eighteen hours.

I worked South Texas with Franklin Garcia, a tough labor organizer with a tender heart, and his friend Pat Robards. One night Franklin and Pat drove Hillary and me over the Rio Grande to Matamoros, Mexico. They took us to a dive with a mariachi band, a halfhearted stripper, and a menu that featured *cabrito*, barbequed goat head. I was so exhausted I fell asleep while the stripper was dancing and the goat head was looking up at me.

One day when I was driving alone in rural South Texas, I stopped at a filling station for gas and struck up a conversation with the young Mexican-American who was filling my tank and asked him to vote for McGovern. "I can't," he said. When I asked why, he replied, "Because of Eagleton. He should not have abandoned him. A lot of people have troubles. You have to stick with your friends." I never forgot his wise advice. When I was President, Hispanic-Americans knew I had tried to be their friend, and they stuck with me.

In the last week of the campaign, though all was lost, I had two memorable experiences. Congressman Henry B. Gonzales hosted the Bexar County Democratic Dinner in San Antonio at the Menger Hotel near the Alamo, where more than two hundred Texans under Jim Bowie and Davy Crockett died fighting for Texas's independence from Mexico. More than sixty years later, Teddy Roosevelt had stayed at the Menger while he was training the Rough Riders for their epic battle on San Juan Hill in Cuba. The Menger serves fantastic mango ice cream, to which I became addicted. On election eve 1992, when we stopped in San Antonio, my staff bought four hundred dollars' worth of it, and everyone on the campaign plane ate it all night long.

The speaker at the dinner was the House majority leader, Hale Boggs of Louisiana. He made an impassioned speech for McGovern and the Democrats. The next morning I got him up early to catch a plane to Alaska, where he was scheduled to campaign with Congressman Nick Begich. The following day, on a swing through the snowcapped mountains, their plane crashed and was never found. I admired Hale Boggs and wished we'd overslept that day. He left a remarkable family behind. His wife, Lindy, a lovely woman and a first-rate politician herself, took his New Orleans House seat and was one of my strongest supporters in Louisiana. I appointed her U.S. ambassador to the Vatican.

The other notable event occurred during Sargent Shriver's last visit to Texas. We had a great rally in McAllen, deep in South Texas, and rushed back to the airport, almost on time, to fly to Texarkana, where Congressman Wright Patman had raised a crowd of several thousand people on State Line Boulevard, the border between Arkansas and Texas. For some reason, our plane didn't take off. After a few minutes, we learned that a pilot flying a single-engine plane had become disoriented in the foggy night sky above McAllen and was circling the airport, waiting to be talked down. In Spanish. First they had to find an instrument-rated pilot who could speak Spanish, then they had to calm the guy down and bring him in. As the drama unfolded, I was sitting across from Shriver, briefing him on the Texarkana stop. If we had any doubt how low the campaign's fortunes had sunk, this removed it. Shriver took it all in stride and asked the flight attendants to serve dinner. Soon there were two planes full of staff and a large press corps eating steak on the tarmac in McAllen. When we finally got to Texarkana, more than three hours late, the rally had disbanded, but about two hundred diehards, including Congressman Patman, came to the airport to greet Shriver. He jumped off the plane and shook hands with every one of them as if it were the first day of a close election.

McGovern lost Texas 67 to 33 percent, a slightly better showing than he made in Arkansas, where only 31 percent of the voters supported him. After the election, Taylor and I stayed around a few days to thank people and wrap things up. Then Hillary and I went back to Yale, after a brief vacation in Zihuatanejo on Mexico's Pacific Coast. It's built up now, but then it was still a little Mexican hamlet with bumpy unpaved streets, open bars, and tropical birds in the trees.

We got through our finals in good shape, especially considering our long absence. I had to work hard to master the arcane rules of Admiralty Law, which I took only because I wanted to have a course taught by Charles Black, an eloquent, courtly Texan who was well liked and respected by the students and who was especially fond of Hillary. Much to my surprise, the jurisdiction of admiralty law extended to any waterway in the United States that had been navigable in its original condition. That included lakes built from damming once-navigable rivers around my hometown.

In the spring term of 1973, I took a full class load but was preoccupied with going home and with what was going to happen with Hillary. Both of us especially enjoyed staging that year's Barristers Union Prize Trial. We wrote a trial based on the characters in the movie *Casablanca*. Ingrid Bergman's husband was killed, and Humphrey Bogart was put on trial for it. Burke Marshall's friend and former colleague in the Justice Department, John Doar, came to New Haven with his young son to judge the trial. Hillary and I hosted him and were very impressed. It was easy to understand why he had been so effective in enforcing civil rights rulings in the South. He was quiet, direct, smart, and strong. He judged well, and Bogie was acquitted by the jury.

One day after my class in Corporate Tax, Professor Chirelstein asked me what I was going to do when I graduated. I told him I was going home to Arkansas and supposed I would just hang up a shingle on my own since I had no job offers. He said there was a sudden, unexpected vacancy on the faculty of the University of Arkansas Law School at Fayetteville. He suggested that I apply for the position and volunteered to recommend me. It had never occurred to me that I could or should get a teaching job, but I was intrigued by the idea. A few days later, in late March, I drove home for

Easter break. When I got to Little Rock, I pulled off the highway, went to a pay phone, called the law school dean, Wylie Davis, introduced myself, told him what I'd heard about the vacancy, and said I'd like to apply. He said I was too young and inexperienced. I laughed and told him I'd been hearing that for years, but if he was hard up, I'd be good for him, because I'd work hard and teach any courses he wanted. Besides, I wouldn't have tenure, so he could fire me at any time. He chuckled and invited me to Fayetteville for an interview; I flew there in the first week of May. I had strong letters of recommendation from Professor Chirelstein, Burke Marshall, Steve Duke, John Baker, and Caroline Dinegar, chair of the political science department at the University of New Haven, where I had taught Constitutional Law and Criminal Law to undergraduates. The interviews went well, and on May 12, I got a letter from Dean Davis offering me a position as an assistant professor at a salary of $14,706. Hillary was all for it, and ten days later I accepted.

It wasn't much money, but teaching would enable me to work off my National Defense Education loan rather than pay it off. My other law school loan was unique in that it required me and my classmates to pay our loans down with a small fixed percentage of our annual incomes until the aggregate debt of our class was retired. Obviously, those who made more paid more, but we all knew that when we borrowed the money. My experience with the Yale loan program was the stimulus for my desire to change the federal student-loan program when I became President, so that students would have the option of repaying their loans over a longer period of time as a fixed percentage of their income. That way, they would be less likely to drop out of school for fear of not being able to repay their loans, and less reluctant to take jobs with high social utility but low pay. When we gave students the option of income-contingent loans, a lot of them took it.

Though I hadn't been the most diligent student, I was pleased with my law school years. I had learned a lot from some brilliant and dedicated professors, and from my fellow students, more than twenty of whom I would later appoint to positions in the administration or the federal judiciary. I had come to a keener appreciation of the role the law plays in maintaining a sense of order and fairness in our society, and in providing a means to make social progress. Living in New Haven gave me a sense of the reality and ethnic diversity of urban America. And, of course, it was in New Haven that I met Hillary.

Thanks to the Duffey and McGovern campaigns, I had made some good friends who shared my passion for politics and learned more about the mechanics of electioneering. I had also learned again that winning elections as a progressive requires great care and discipline in crafting and presenting a message and a program that gives people the confidence to change course. Our society can absorb only so much change at a time, and when we move forward we must do it in a way that reaffirms our core convictions of opportunity and responsibility, work and family, strength and compassion—the values that have been the bedrock of America's success. Most people have their hands full raising their kids, doing their jobs, and paying the bills. They don't think about government policy as much as liberals do, nor are they as obsessed with power as the new right conservatives. They have a lot of common sense, and a desire to understand the larger forces shaping their lives, but can't be expected to abandon the values and social arrangements that at least enable them to survive and feel good about themselves. Since 1968, conservatives have been very good at convincing middle America that progressive candidates, ideas, and policies are alien to their values and threatening to their security. Joe Duffey was a coal miner's son who was morphed into a weak, ultra-liberal elitist. George McGovern was a genuine war hero, sent to the Senate by the conservatives of rural South Dakota, who was turned into a spineless, wild-eyed leftist who wouldn't stand up for America but would tax and spend it into oblivion. In both cases, the candidates and their campaigns made mistakes that reinforced the images their opponents were trying hard to create. I already knew enough about how difficult it was to push the rocks of civil rights, peace, and anti-poverty pro-

grams up the political hill to know we couldn't expect to
win all the time, but I was determined to stop helping our
opponents win without a fight. Later, both as governor and
as President, I made some of the same mistakes all over
again, but not as many as I would have had I not been given
the chance to work for those two good men, Joe Duffey and
George McGovern.

I was happy to be going home to the prospect of interesting work, but I still didn't know what to do about
Hillary, or what was best for her. I had always believed she
had as much (or more) potential to succeed in politics as I
did, and I wanted her to have her chance. Back then, I
wanted it for her more than she did, and I thought coming
to Arkansas with me would end the prospect of a political
career for her. I didn't want to do that, but I didn't want to
give her up, either. Hillary had already decided against
working for a big firm or clerking for a judge in favor of a
position with Marian Edelman's Children's Defense Fund in
its new office in Cambridge, Massachusetts, so we were
going to be a long way away from each other.

That was all we knew when we finished law school and
I took Hillary on her first overseas trip. I gave her a tour of
London and Oxford, then we went west to Wales, then back
into England to the Lake District, which I hadn't seen
before. It's beautiful and romantic there in the late spring.
One evening at sunset, on the shore of Lake Ennerdale, I
asked Hillary to marry me. I couldn't believe I'd done it.
Neither could she. She said she loved me but couldn't say
yes. I couldn't blame her, but I didn't want to lose her. So I
asked her to come home to Arkansas with me to see how
she liked it. And to take the Arkansas bar exam, just in case.

EIGHTEEN

IN JUNE, Hillary flew to Little Rock for a visit. I took her home the long way, to show her a part of the state I loved. We drove west up the Arkansas River for seventy miles to Russellville, then south down Highway 7 through the Ouachita Mountains and National Forest, stopping from time to time to look at the beautiful vistas. We spent a couple of days in Hot Springs with Mother, Jeff, and Roger, then went back to Little Rock for a prep course on the Arkansas bar exam, which proved helpful enough that both of us passed.

After the bar, Hillary went back to Massachusetts to start her job with the Children's Defense Fund, and I went to Fayetteville to begin my new life as a law professor. I found the perfect place to live, a beautiful little house designed by the famous Arkansas architect Fay Jones, whose stunning Thorncrown Chapel in nearby Eureka Springs won international awards and accolades. The house was on more than eighty acres of land about eight miles east of Fayetteville, on Highway 16. The land's eastern border was the middle fork of the White River. A few dozen cattle grazed the pasture. The house, built in the mid-1950s, was essentially a one-room structure, long and thin, divided down the middle, with the bathroom dropped like a block in the center. Both the front and back walls were a series of sliding glass doors, which, along with skylights in the bedroom and bathroom, guaranteed lots of light. Running in front of the whole length of the living room was a screened-in porch, which jutted out from the house as the land sloped down to the road. The house proved to be a godsend of peace and quiet, especially after I started my first campaign. I loved to sit on the porch and near the fireplace, and to walk in the field by the river with the cattle.

The house did have a couple of drawbacks. Mice visited every night. When I realized I couldn't get rid of them and they kept to themselves in the kitchen, I started leaving them bread crumbs. The outdoors was full of spiders, ticks, and other menaces. They didn't bother me much, but when a brown recluse spider bit Hillary, her leg swelled up enormously and took a long time to go back down. And the place was impossible to secure. We had a rash of burglaries across northwest Arkansas that summer. The culprit was hitting lots of rural houses up and down Highway 16. One evening when I came home, it looked as if someone had been there, but nothing was missing. Perhaps I'd scared him off. On impulse, I sat down and wrote a letter to the burglar, in case he came back:

> Dear Burglar:
>   Things in my house were so much the same, I could not tell whether or not you actually entered the house yesterday. If not, here is what you will find—a TV which cost $80 new one and a half years ago; a radio which cost $40 new three years ago; a tiny record player that cost $40 new three years ago; and a lot of keepsakes, little things, very few of which cost over $10. Almost all the clothes are over two or three years old. Hardly worth risking jail for.
>
>   William J. Clinton

I taped the letter to the fireplace. Unfortunately, the ploy didn't work. The next day when I was at work, the guy came back and took the TV, the radio, the record player, and one thing I purposely left off the list: a beautifully engraved German military sword from World War I. I was heartsick about losing it because Daddy had given it to me, and because, just a year earlier, the only other valuable thing I owned, the Selmer Mark VI tenor saxophone Mother and Daddy had given me in 1963, had been stolen out of my car in Washington. Eventually I replaced the sax with a 1935 Selmer "cigar cutter" model, but the sword proved irreplaceable.

I spent the last weeks of a very hot August preparing my classes and running around the university track in the hottest hours of the day, getting my weight down to 185 pounds for the first (and last) time since I was thirteen. In September, I began to teach my first classes: Antitrust, which I had studied at Yale and enjoyed very much, and Agency and Partnership, dealing with the nature of contractual relationships and the legal responsibilities that arise out of them. I had sixteen students in Antitrust and fifty-six in A and P. Antitrust law is rooted in the idea that the government should prevent the formation of monopolies as well as other noncompetitive practices in order to preserve a functioning, fair free-market economy. Since I knew that not all the students had a good grounding in economics, I tried hard to make the material clear and the principles understandable. Agency and Partnership, by contrast, seemed straightforward enough. I was afraid the students would get bored and also miss the importance and occasional difficulty of determining the exact nature of the relationships between parties in a common enterprise, so I tried to think of interesting and illuminating examples to keep the classroom discussion going. For example, the Watergate hearings and the White House response to the ongoing revelations had raised a lot of questions about the perpetrators of the break-in. Were they agents of the President, and if not, for whom and on whose authority were they acting? In all the classes I taught, I tried to get a lot of students involved in the discussions and to make myself easily available to them in my office and around the law school.

I enjoyed writing exams, which I hoped would be interesting, challenging, and fair. In the accounts I've read of my teaching years, my grading has been questioned, with the implication that I was too easy, either because I was too soft or too eager not to offend potential supporters when I ran for office. At Yale, the only grades were Honors, Pass, or Fail. It was usually pretty hard to get Honors and virtually impossible to fail. At many other law schools, especially those where the admissions standards were more lax, the grading tended to be tougher, with the expectation that 20 to 30 percent of a class should fail. I didn't agree with that. If a student got a bad grade, I always felt like a failure too, for not having engaged his or her interest or effort. Almost all the students were intellectually capable of learning enough to get a C. On the other hand, I thought a good grade should mean something. In my big classes, ranging from fifty to ninety students, I gave two or three A's and about the same number of D's. In one class of seventy-seven, I gave only one A, and only once did I flunk a student. Usually the students who were going to flunk would withdraw rather than risk an F. In two smaller classes, I gave more A's because the students worked harder, learned more, and deserved them.

Although the University of Arkansas Law School's first black students had entered twenty-five years earlier, it was not until the early seventies that a substantial number of them finally began to enter state law schools across the South. Many were not well prepared, especially those whose education had been confined to poor segregated schools. About twenty black students took my courses between 1973 and 1976, and I got to know the others. Almost all of them were working very hard. They wanted to succeed, and several of them lived under enormous emotional pressure because they were afraid they couldn't make it. Sometimes their fears were justified. I'll never forget reading one black student's exam paper with a mixture of disbelief and anger. I knew he had studied like a demon and understood the material, but his exam didn't show it. The right answers were in there, but finding them required digging through piles of misspelled words, bad grammar, and poor sentence construction. An A's worth of knowledge was hidden in the bushes of an F presentation, flawed by things he hadn't learned going all the way back to elementary school. I gave him a B−, corrected the grammar and spelling, and decided to set up tutoring sessions to help transform the black students' hard work and native intelligence into better results. I think they helped, both substantively and psychologically, though several of the students continued to struggle with their writing skills and with the emotional burden of having one foot through the door of opportunity and the other held back by the heavy weight of past segregation. When many of those students went on to distinguished careers as lawyers and judges, the clients they represented and the parties they judged probably had no idea how high a mountain they had had to climb to reach the bar or the bench. When the Supreme Court upheld the principle of affirmative action in 2003, I thought of my black students, of how hard they worked and all they had to overcome. They gave me all the evidence I'd ever need to support the Court's ruling.

Besides my interaction with the students, the best thing about being a law professor was being part of a faculty filled with people I liked and admired. My best friends on the faculty were two people my age, Elizabeth Osenbaugh and Dick Atkinson. Elizabeth was a brilliant Iowa farm girl, a good Democrat, and a devoted teacher who became good friends with Hillary, too. Eventually, she went back to Iowa to work in the attorney general's office. When I was elected President, I persuaded her to come to the Justice Department, but after a few years she again went back home, largely because she thought it would be better for her young daughter, Betsy. Sadly, Elizabeth died of cancer in 1998, and her daughter went to live with Elizabeth's brother. I have tried to keep in touch with Betsy over the years; her mother was one of the finest people I've ever known. Dick Atkinson was a friend from law school who had grown dissatisfied with private practice in Atlanta. I suggested he consider teaching and urged him to come to Fayetteville for an interview. He did, and was offered and accepted a position on our faculty. The students loved Dick, and he loved teaching. In 2003, he would become Dean of the Arkansas Law School. Our most famous and fascinating professor was Robert Leflar, the most eminent legal scholar our state ever produced, a recognized authority in torts, conflicts of law, and appellate judging. In 1973, he was already past the mandatory retirement age of seventy and was teaching a full load for a dollar a year. He had been on the faculty since he was twenty-six. For several years before I knew him, Bob had commuted weekly between Fayetteville and New York, where he taught a course in appellate judging to federal and

state judges at New York University Law School, a course
that more than half the Supreme Court justices had taken.
He was never late for class in either place.

Bob Leflar was a small, wiry man with huge, piercing
eyes, and he was still as strong as an ox. He couldn't have
weighed more than 150 pounds, but while working in his
yard he carried around big chunks of flagstone that I could
hardly lift. After every Razorback football homecoming
game, Bob and his wife, Helen, hosted a party in their
home. Sometimes guests would play touch football in the
front yard. I remember one game in particular, when Bob
and I and another young lawyer played against two big
young guys and a nine-year-old boy. The game was tied and
we all agreed that whoever scored next would win. Our side
had the ball. I asked Bob if he really wanted to win. He said,
"I sure do." He was as competitive as Michael Jordan. So I
told the third man on our team to center the ball, let the
rusher come after me, and go block the tall man defending
the backfield to the right. The nine-year-old was covering
Bob, on the assumption that I'd throw the ball to the taller,
younger man, or that if Bob got the ball the kid would be
able to touch him. I told Bob to block the kid to the right
too, then run hard left, and I'd throw the ball to him right
before the rusher got to me. When the ball was snapped,
Bob was so excited he knocked the boy to the ground and
ran left. He was wide open when our teammate completed
his blocking assignment. I lobbed the ball to Bob and he ran
across the goal line, the happiest seventy-five-year-old man
in America. Bob Leflar had a steel-trap mind, the heart of a
lion, a tough will, and a childlike love of life. He was sort of
a Democratic version of Strom Thurmond. If we had more
like him, we'd win more often. When Bob died at ninety-
three, I thought he was still too young to go.

Law school policies were set by the faculty at regular
meetings. On occasion I thought they ran too long and got
too mired in details best left to the dean and other administrators, but I learned a lot about academic governance and
politics in them. Generally, I deferred to my colleagues when
there was a consensus because I felt they knew more than I

did and had a longer-term commitment to the academic life. I did urge the faculty to undertake more pro bono activities and to relax the "publish or perish" imperative for professors in favor of greater emphasis on classroom teaching and spending more out-of-class time with students.

My own pro bono work included handling minor legal problems for students and a young assistant professor; trying—unsuccessfully—to persuade more doctors in Springdale, just north of Fayetteville, to accept poor patients on Medicaid; preparing a brief for the U.S. Supreme Court in an antitrust case at the request of Attorney General Jim Guy Tucker; and, in my first appearance as a lawyer in court, filing a brief to defend my friend State Representative Steve Smith in an election-law dispute in Madison County.

Huntsville, the county seat and Orval Faubus's hometown, had a little more than a thousand people. The Democrats held all the courthouse offices, from the judge and sheriff on down, but there were a lot of Republicans in the hills and hollows of north Arkansas, most of them descendants of people who had opposed secession in 1861. The Republicans had made a good showing in 1972, aided by the Nixon landslide, and they felt that if they could get enough absentee ballots thrown out, they might reverse the results of the local elections.

The case was tried in the old Madison County courthouse before Judge Bill Enfield, a Democrat who later became a friend and supporter of mine. The Democrats were represented by two real characters: Bill Murphy, a Fayetteville lawyer whose great passions were the American Legion, which he served as Arkansas commander, and the Democratic Party; and a local lawyer, W. Q. Hall, known as "Q," a one-armed wit with a sense of humor as sharp as the hook affixed to his left arm. The people hauled in to testify about why they voted absentee offered a vivid picture of the fierce loyalties, rough politics, and economic pressures that shaped the lives of Arkansas hill people. One man had to defend voting absentee at the last minute, without having applied in advance, as the law required. He explained that he worked for the state Game and Fish Commission, and he went down to vote on the day before the election because he had just been ordered to take the state's only bear trap over slow mountain roads to Stone County on election day. His vote was allowed. Another man was called back from his job in Tulsa, Oklahoma, to testify. He admitted that he had lived in Tulsa for more than ten years but still voted by absentee ballot in Madison County in every election, though he was no longer a legal resident there. When the Republican lawyer pressed him on it, he said with great emotion that Madison County was his home; that he had gone to Tulsa only because he couldn't make a living in the hills; that he didn't know or care anything about politics there; and that in another ten years or so, as soon as he could retire, he was coming home. I can't remember whether his vote was counted, but his attachment to his roots left a lasting impression on me.

Steve Smith testified about his role in gathering absentee ballots from residents in his father's nursing home. The law seemed to allow people associated with nursing homes to help residents fill out their ballots, but required the ballots to be mailed by a family member or someone with specific written authorization to do so. Steve had picked up all the ballots and dropped them in the nearest mailbox. I presented the judge with what I thought was a very persuasive brief, arguing that it was nonsensical to say Steve couldn't mail them; no one had suggested that he had tampered with them, or that the residents didn't want him to mail them. For all we knew, not all the elderly residents even had family members who could perform the chore. Judge Enfield ruled against me and Steve, but upheld enough of the absentee votes for County Judge Charles Whorton, Sheriff Ralph Baker, and their crew to stay in office.

I had lost my part of the case but gained invaluable insight into the lives of Arkansas hill people. And I had made friends with some of the most effective politicians I would ever know. If a new person moved into Madison County, they would know within a week if he or she was a Democrat or a Republican. The Republicans had to come to the courthouse to register to vote. The county clerk went to the Democrats' homes to register them. Two weeks before each election they called all the Democrats, asking for their votes. They were called again on election morning. If they hadn't voted by late afternoon, someone went to their homes and took them to the polls. On the day of my first general election, in 1974, I called Charles Whorton to see how we were doing. He said heavy rain had washed a bridge out in a remote part of the county and some of our folks couldn't get to the polls, but they were working hard and thought we would win by about 500 votes. I carried Madison County by 501 votes.

A couple of months after I moved to Fayetteville, I felt completely at home there. I loved teaching, going to Razorback football games, driving around in the mountains, and living in a university community of people who cared about the things I did. I made friends with Carl Whillock, a university vice president who had short gray hair and a very reserved manner. I first met him at lunch at Wyatt's Cafeteria in the big shopping mall on a hill between Fayetteville and Springdale. Everyone at our table was criticizing President Nixon except Carl, who didn't say a word. I had no idea what he thought, so I asked him. I'll never forget his monotone reply: "I agree with Harry Truman. He said Richard Nixon is the kind of man who would take wooden nickels off a dead man's eyes." In the old days, wooden nickels were the round wood objects morticians put on the eyes of corpses to keep them closed during the embalming process. Carl Whillock was a book you couldn't judge by its cover. Beneath his buttoned-down appearance was a tough mind and a brave heart.

I especially liked two women professors whose husbands were in the state legislature. Ann Henry taught at the Business School; her husband, Morriss, was an ophthalmologist and our state senator. Ann and Morriss became special friends to Hillary and me, and when we married, they hosted our wedding reception at their home. Diane Kincaid was a professor in the political science department, then married to State Representative Hugh Kincaid. Diane was beautiful, brilliant, and politically savvy. When Hillary moved to Fayetteville, Diane and Hillary became more than friends; they were soul mates, finding in each other's company the kind of understanding, stimulation, support, and love that come along all too rarely in life.

Though Fayetteville, like all of northwest Arkansas, was growing fast, it still had a quaint little town square with an old post office in the middle, which was later converted into a restaurant and bar. Retail stores, offices, and banks lined the four sides of the square, and every Saturday morning it was filled with a farmers' market offering fresh produce. My cousin Roy Clinton ran the Campbell-Bell Department Store on the northwest corner of the square. I traded with him and learned a lot about my new hometown. The courthouse was just a block off the square. The local lawyers who practiced there and had offices nearby included an impressive collection of wily older lawyers and bright young ones, many of whom would soon become strong supporters.

The local political hangout was Billie Schneider's Steakhouse on Highway 71, north of town. Billie was a hard-boiled, gravel-voiced, tough-talking woman who'd seen it all but never lost her consuming, idealistic passion for politics. All the local politicos hung out at her place, including Don Tyson, the chicken magnate whose operation would become the largest agricultural company in the world, and Don's lawyer, Jim Blair, a six-foot-five-inch idiosyncratic genius who would become one of my closest friends. A few months after I moved to Fayetteville, Billie closed the steakhouse and opened a bar and disco in the basement of a hotel across the street from the courthouse. All the same folks hung out there, but she also developed a big following among university students, whom she mobilized to work for her candidates in elections. Billie was a big part of my life until the day we buried her.

I left my mountain lair for a few days over Thanksgiving to visit Hillary in Cambridge. She and I didn't resolve our situation, but she did agree to come visit me over the Christmas holidays. I loved her and wanted to be with her, but I understood her reservations. I was passionate and driven, and nothing in my background indicated I knew what a stable marriage was all about. She knew that being married to me would be a high-wire operation in more ways than one. Also, Arkansas must still have seemed an alien place for her to settle, though she no longer felt it was the other side of the moon. And as I've said, I wasn't sure it was right for her. I still thought she should have her own political career. At that point in my life I thought that work was more important than having a personal life. I had met many of the ablest people of my generation, and I thought she was head and shoulders above them all in political potential. She had a big brain, a good heart, better organizational skills than I did, and political skills that were nearly as good as mine; I'd just had more experience. I loved her enough both to want her and to want the best for her. It was a high-class dilemma.

When I got back to Arkansas, political talk had begun in earnest. Like Democrats everywhere, our people were stirred up by Senator Sam Ervin's Watergate hearings and the continuation of the war. It appeared that we would have a chance to make some gains in the midterm congressional elections, especially after the price of oil shot up and gasoline began to be rationed. However, the local Democrats did not believe the prospects of unseating our congressman, John Paul Hammerschmidt, were very good. Hammerschmidt had a very conservative voting record and was a strong defender of President Nixon. But he also had a friendly, low-key manner, came home and traveled his district on most weekends, and had a fabulous casework operation, helping little towns get water and sewer grants and securing government benefits for constituents, often from programs he had voted to slash back in Washington. Hammerschmidt was in the lumber business, had good support from the small-business people in the district, and took care of the large timber, poultry, and trucking interests, which made up a significant portion of the economy.

I talked to several people that fall about whether they would be interested in running, including Hugh and Diane Kincaid, Morriss and Ann Henry, Steve Smith, and state representative Rudy Moore, who was Clark Whillock's brother-in-law. Everyone thought the race needed to be made, but no one wanted to make it; it seemed too unwinnable. Also, it seemed that Governor Bumpers, who was immensely popular, was likely to challenge Senator Fulbright in the Democratic primary. Fulbright was from Fayetteville, and most of my friends, though they liked Bumpers, felt obligated to help the senator in what was sure to be an all-uphill battle.

As it became clear that no one in our area who could run a strong race was willing to do it, I began to think about running myself. It seemed absurd on the face of it. I had been home only six months after nine years away. I was just three months into my new job. I had no contacts in most of the district. On the other hand, Fayetteville, with its students and liberal Democrats, was not a bad place to start. Hot Springs, where I grew up, was the biggest town in the south end of the district. And Yell County, where the Clintons were from, was part of it, too. All told, I had relatives in five of the district's twenty-one counties. I was young, single, and willing to work all hours of the day and night. And even if I didn't win, if I made a good showing, I didn't think it would hurt me in any future campaigns I might undertake. Of course, if I got waxed, my long-hoped-for political career could be over before it began.

I had a lot to think about when Hillary came to visit me shortly after Christmas. We were talking it over in my house one morning in early January when the phone rang. It was John Doar, with whom Hillary and I had spent some time the previous spring when he came to Yale to judge our *Casablanca* Prize Trial. He told me that he had just agreed to become the chief counsel for the House Judiciary Committee's inquiry into whether President Nixon should be impeached, and that Burke Marshall had recommended me to him. He wanted me to take a leave of absence from the law school, come to work, and help him recruit some other good young lawyers. I told him I was thinking about running for Congress, but I'd consider the offer and call him back the next day. I had to think fast, and as would so often happen in the years ahead, I turned to Hillary for judgment and advice. By the time I called John back, I had made up my mind. I thanked him for the offer but declined, saying that I had decided to make the long-shot race for Congress instead, because there were lots of gifted young lawyers who would give anything to work for him on the impeachment inquiry but no one else to take on the fight in Arkansas. I could tell John thought I was making a foolish mistake, and by every rational standard I was. But, as I've said before, a lot of your life is shaped by the opportunities you turn down as much as those you take up.

I suggested to John that he ought to sign up Hillary and our Yale classmates Mike Conway and Rufus Cormier. He laughed and said Burke Marshall had recommended them too. Eventually they all went to work for John and did an outstanding job. Doar wound up with an extraordinary array of talented young people, proving that, as I had expected, he didn't need me to have a great staff.

A couple of days before Hillary had to go back to Cambridge, I took her to Huntsville, about twenty-five miles east of my house, to see former governor Faubus. If I was going to run for Congress, I'd have to pay a courtesy call on him sooner or later. Besides, much as I disapproved of what he'd done at Little Rock, he was bright and had a brain full of Arkansas political lore, which I wanted to pick. Faubus lived in a beautiful big Fay Jones house his supporters had built for him when, after twelve years, he left the governor's office with no money. He was then living with his second wife, Elizabeth, an attractive Massachusetts woman who still wore a 1960s beehive hairdo and who, before her marriage, had had a brief career as a political commentator in Little Rock. She was extremely conservative, and was in stark contrast in both looks and outlook to the governor's first wife, Alta, who was a good hill-country populist and the editor of the local paper, the *Madison County Record*.

Hillary and I were ushered into the Faubus home and seated at a big round table in an all-glass alcove looking out on the Ozarks and the town below. For the next four or five hours, I asked questions and Orval talked, delivering a fascinating account of Arkansas history and politics: what life was like during the Depression and World War II, why he was still defending what he had done in Little Rock, and how he thought President Nixon's problems might or might not affect the congressional race. I didn't say much; I would just ask a new question when Faubus finished answering the previous one. Hillary didn't say anything. Surprisingly, for more than four hours Elizabeth Faubus didn't either. She just kept us supplied with coffee and cookies.

Finally, when it was obvious the interview was winding down, Elizabeth Faubus stared hard at me and said, "This is all very well, Mr. Clinton, but how do you feel about the international conspiracy to overthrow the United States?" I stared right back and replied, "Why, I'm against it, Mrs. Faubus. Aren't you?" Not long afterward, the Faubuses moved to Houston, where Orval was distraught after Elizabeth was brutally murdered in their apartment. When I was inaugurated governor in 1979, I invited all the former governors to attend, including Faubus. It was a controversial move among my progressive supporters, who felt I'd given the old rascal new life. The way it played out proved them right, a classic example of the old adage that no good deed goes unpunished. Still, I'd do it all over again just to have the Red-menace exchange with Elizabeth Faubus.

After Hillary left, I went to see Dean Davis, told him I wanted to run for Congress, and promised to keep up with all my class work and to make time for the students. I was assigned to teach Criminal Procedure and Admiralty in the spring term and had already done quite a bit of the preparation work. To my surprise, Wylie gave me his blessing, probably because it was too late to get anyone else to teach the courses.

Arkansas' Third District comprised twenty-one counties in the northwest quadrant of the state and was one of America's most rural congressional districts. It included the big counties of Washington and Benton in the extreme northwest; seven northern counties in the Ozarks; eight counties in the Arkansas River valley below; and four in the Ouachita Mountains in the southwest. Thanks to Wal-Mart, Tyson Foods and other poultry companies, and trucking companies like J. B. Hunt, Willis Shaw, and Harvey Jones, the towns in Benton and Washington counties were growing more prosperous, and more Republican. Eventually, the growth of evangelical Christian churches and the influx of retirees from the Midwest combined with the success of the big companies to make northwest Arkansas the most Republican and most conservative part of the state, with the exception of Fayetteville, where the university kept things in closer balance.

In 1974, Fort Smith, on the Oklahoma border, was both the district's biggest city, with a population of 72,286, and its most conservative. In the 1960s, the city fathers had turned down urban-renewal funds, which they believed were the first step to socialism, and when Watergate figure John Mitchell was indicted a few years later, his lawyers said Fort Smith was one of only three places in America where he could get a fair trial. What he would have gotten there was a hero's welcome. East of Fort Smith down the Arkansas River, and in the mountains to the north, the counties tended to be populist, socially conservative, and pretty evenly divided between Republicans and Democrats.

The mountain counties, especially Madison, Newton, and Searcy, were still fairly isolated. A few new people moved in, but many families had been on the same land for more than a hundred years. They spoke in a unique way, using vivid expressions I had never heard before. My favorite was a description of someone you really don't like: "I wouldn't piss in his ear if his brain was on fire." The rural counties in the southern part of the district tended to be more Democratic but still conservative, and the largest county, Garland, with Hot Springs as the county seat, usually voted Republican in presidential elections and had a lot of new Republican retirees from up north. The congressman was very popular there.

There were very few blacks, most of them concentrated in Fort Smith; Hot Springs, the district's second-largest city; and in the river valley towns of Russellville and Dardanelle in the southeast part of the district. Organized labor had a fairly strong presence in Fayetteville, Fort Smith, and Hot Springs, but not much elsewhere. Because of bad mountain roads and the predominance of old cars and pickups, the district had the highest gasoline usage per registered vehicle of any in the United States, a factor of no small importance given the rising price and shortage of gas. It also had the highest percentage of disabled veterans of any congressional district. Congressman Hammerschmidt was a World War II veteran who courted veterans heavily. In the previous election, the social and fiscal conservative forces had overwhelmed the hard-core Democrats and economic populists, as Nixon defeated McGovern 74 to 26 percent. Hammerschmidt got 77 percent. No wonder no one else wanted to make the race.

A few days after Hillary left, Carl Whillock took me on my first campaign trip, a swing across the district's northern counties. We stopped first in Carroll County. In Berryville, a town of about 1,300, I visited the store of Si Bigham, a prominent local Democrat, who had his four-year-old grandson with him. More than twenty years later, that little boy, Kris Engskov, would become my personal aide in the White House. I also met the local Methodist minister, Vic Nixon, and his wife, Freddie. They were liberal Democrats who opposed the Vietnam War, and they agreed to support me. They wound up doing far more. Freddie became my county coordinator, charmed the socks off the leaders in all the rural voting precincts, and later worked for me in the governor's office, where she never stopped trying to convince me that the death penalty was wrong. When Hillary and I got married, Vic performed the ceremony.

We drove on east to Boone County and then drove to Mountain Home, county seat of the district's northeastern-most county, Baxter. Carl wanted me to meet Hugh Hackler, a businessman who told us right off the bat that he was committed to another candidate in the primary. Still, we started talking. When he found out I was from Hot Springs, he told me Gabe Crawford was a good friend of his. When I replied that Gabe had been Daddy's best friend, Hugh got out of his commitment to the other guy and supported me. I also met Vada Sheid, who owned a furniture store and was the county treasurer. She noticed a loose button on my shirt and sewed it on while we visited. She became a supporter that day, too. She never sewed another button for me, but after I became governor and she went to the state Senate, her votes often bailed me out in other ways.

After we left Mountain Home, we drove south to Searcy County. We stopped in St. Joe, which had about 150 people, to see the county Democratic chairman, Will Goggins. Will was over eighty, but still sharp as a tack, physically strong, and passionate about his politics. When he said he'd be for me, I knew it meant a lot of votes, as you'll see. In the county seat of Marshall, I met George Daniel, who ran the local hardware store. George's younger brother, James, was a student at the law school who gave me one of my first thousand-dollar contributions; his older brother, Charles, was the county's doctor. I got a lot of laughs out of George's homespun humor and learned one searing lesson. A Vietnam veteran who'd been away from the county for several years came into his store one day and bought a pistol. He said he wanted to do some target practice. A day later he killed six people. It turned out he had just walked away from Fort Roots, the federal mental-health facility for veterans in North Little Rock, where he'd been for several years, apparently because of trauma from his war experiences. It took George Daniel a long time to get over that. And it was the best argument I ever encountered for the kind of background checks on gun buyers required by the Brady bill, which I finally signed into law in 1993, after nineteen more years of avoidable killings by known felons, stalkers, and people with mental disorders.

When Carl and I got back to Fayetteville, I was higher than a kite. I had always liked one-on-one "retail" politics when I was working for other candidates. Now I really loved going into the little towns, or stopping at country stores, cafés, and filling stations along the road. I was never very good at asking for money, but I liked going into people's homes and businesses and asking for their votes. Besides, you could never tell when you would meet a colorful character, hear an interesting story, learn something worth knowing, or make a new friend.

That first day on the campaign trail would be followed by scores of others just like it. I would set out in the morning from Fayetteville, work as many towns and counties as I could until late at night, then head back home if I had to teach the next day or, if I didn't, stay with a hospitable Democrat so that I could go on to the next county in the morning.

The next Sunday I went back east to finish up the mountain counties. I almost didn't make it. I had forgotten to fill the tank of my 1970 American Motors Gremlin before the weekend. Because of the gasoline shortage, federal law required filling stations to be closed on Sunday. But I had to get back to the hills. In desperation, I called the president of our local natural-gas company, Charles Scharlau, and asked him if he would let me have a tank of gas from the pump in his equipment yard. He told me to go on down there and he'd take care of it. To my astonishment he showed up and filled my gas tank himself. Charles Scharlau single-handedly kept my fledgling campaign going.

First I drove to Alpena to see the county Democratic chairman, Bo Forney, whom I had missed on my first stop there. I found his little house with no trouble. There was a pickup truck with a gun rack in the front yard, standard equipment for mountain men. Bo met me at the front door in jeans and a white T-shirt over his ample girth. He was watching TV and didn't say much as I made my pitch for his support. When I finished, he said that Hammerschmidt needed beating, and that although he would win his hometown of Harrison by a large margin, he thought we could do some good in the rural part of Boone County. Then he gave me the names of some people to see, told me I'd get more votes if I got a haircut, said he'd support me, and went back to his television. I wasn't sure what to make of Bo until I took a closer look at his pickup on my way back to the car. It had a bumper sticker that said "Don't Blame Me. I Voted for McGovern." Later, when I asked Bo about the bumper sticker, he said he didn't care what the critics said about McGovern, the Democrats were for the common people and the Republicans weren't, and that's all there was to it. When

I was President and Bo was in ill health, our mutual friend
and fellow yellow-dog Democrat Levi Phillips brought him
to spend the night with us in the White House. Bo had a
good time, but refused to sleep in the Lincoln Bedroom. He
couldn't forgive him for the Republican Party's excesses
during the Reconstruction Era after the Civil War, or for its
devotion to the wealthy and powerful throughout the twentieth century. Now that Bo and Mr. Lincoln are both in
heaven, I like to think they've gotten together and resolved
their differences.

After Alpena, I went to Flippin, a town of about a thousand in Marion County, which had more miles of unpaved
roads than any other in our state. I went to see two young
men I wanted to run my campaign there, Jim "Red" Milligan and Kearney Carlton. They put me between them in
Red's pickup and took off down one of those dirt roads to
Everton, a tiny place in the most remote part of the county,
to see Leon Swofford, who owned the only store and whose
support was worth a couple of hundred votes. About ten
miles out of town, Red stopped the truck in the middle of
nowhere. We were engulfed in dust. He took out a pack of
Red Man chewing tobacco, put a wad in his mouth, then
handed it to Kearney, who followed suit. Then Kearney
handed it to me and said, "We want to see what you're
made of. If you're man enough to chew this tobacco, we'll
be for you. If you're not, we'll kick you out and let you walk
back to town." I thought about it and said, "Open the
damn door." They glared at me for about five seconds, then
roared with laughter and took off down the road to Swofford's store. We got the votes there, and a lot more over the
years. If they had measured me by my taste for Red Man, I
might still be wandering the back roads of Marion County.

A few weeks later, I'd be tested like that again. I was in
Clarksville in the Arkansas River valley with my twenty-
two-year-old county leader, Ron Taylor, who was from a
prominent political family and politically wise well beyond
his years. He took me out to the county fair to see the county
sheriff, whose support Ron said we had to have to carry the
county. We found him at the rodeo grounds, holding the

reins of a horse. The rodeo was about to begin with a parade of horses marching around the arena. The sheriff handed me the reins and told me to join the parade and I'd be introduced to the crowd. He promised that the horse was well behaved. I was wearing a dark suit and tie and wing-tip shoes. I hadn't been on a horse since I was five, and then only to pose for a picture in a cowboy outfit. I had turned down the chewing tobacco, but I took the reins and mounted the horse. After a lifetime of watching cowboy movies, I thought, how hard could it be? When the opening ceremony started, I rode out into the arena just as if I knew what I was doing. About a quarter of the way around the arena, right after I'd been introduced, the horse stopped and reared up on its hind legs. Miraculously, I didn't fall off. The crowd clapped. I think they believed I'd done it on purpose. The sheriff knew better, but he supported me anyway.

I finished my round of the Ozarks in Newton County, one of the most beautiful places in America, home of the Buffalo River, which recently had been named the first river protected by Congress under the Wild and Scenic Rivers Act. I stopped first in Pruitt, a small settlement on the Buffalo, to see Hilary Jones. Though he lived in a modest home, he was a road builder and might have been the wealthiest man in the county. His family's Democratic heritage went all the way back to the Civil War and before, and he had the genealogical books to prove it. He was deeply rooted in his land along the river. His family had lost a lot of it in the Depression, and when he came home from World War II he worked for years to put it all back together again. The Buffalo's designation as a protected river was his worst nightmare. Most landowners along the river were given life tenancies; they couldn't sell the land to anyone but the government in their lifetimes, and when they died only the government could buy it. Because Hilary's homestead was on the main highway, the government was going to take it by eminent domain in the near future and make it part of the headquarters operation. He and his wife, Margaret, had eight children. They wanted the kids to have their land. There was an old cemetery on it where people born in the

1700s were buried. Whenever anyone died destitute and alone in the county, Hilary paid for the burial in his cemetery. I supported protecting the river, but I thought the government should have let the old homesteaders keep their land under a scenic easement, which would have precluded any development or environmental degradation but allowed families to pass the land on from generation to generation. When I became President, my experience with the folks on the Buffalo gave me a better understanding than most Democrats of the resentments a lot of western ranchers had when environmental considerations clashed with what they saw as their prerogatives.

Hilary Jones finally lost his fight with the government. It took a lot out of him, but it never killed his passion for politics; he moved into a new house and carried on. He spent a memorable night with Hillary and me in the White House. He almost cried when Hillary took him into the map room to show him the war map FDR was using when he died in Warm Springs, Georgia, in 1945. He worshipped FDR. Unlike Bo Forney, he spent the night in the Lincoln Bedroom. When he visited us in the White House, I kidded him about sleeping in Lincoln's bed, which Bo Forney had turned down. Hilary said at least he had "slept on the side of the bed that was under Andrew Jackson's picture."

From the day I met him until the day I flew home from the White House to speak at his funeral, Hilary Jones was my man in Newton County. He embodied the wild, beautiful spirit of a special place I had loved since I first saw it at sixteen.

The county seat, Jasper, was a town of fewer than four hundred people. There were two cafés, one frequented by Republicans, the other by Democrats. The man I wanted to see, Walter Brasel, lived beneath the Democratic café, which his wife ran. I got there on a Sunday morning and he was still in bed. As I sat in the little living room, he got up and began to put his pants on with the door from the living room to the bedroom open. He wasn't fully awake, slipped, and was rotund enough to literally roll over a couple of times until he was ten or fifteen feet out into the living room. I wanted his support, so I couldn't laugh. But he did. He said he'd once been young, thin, and fast, the starting guard on the Coal Hill High School basketball team, which he had led to the state championship over Little Rock Central High in the 1930s; he'd gained all his weight in the years when he was the county bootlegger, and never lost it. After a while, he said he'd be for me, maybe just so he could go back to bed.

Next, I drove out into the country to see Bill Fowler, who had a farm in Boxley. Bill had served as the Arkansas representative in the Agricultural Soil and Conservation Service in the Johnson administration. As we stood on a hillside with a spectacular view of the mountains, he said he would support me, but he didn't think Hammerschmidt would "have enough of Nixon's crap on him to stink by election day." He then offered this assessment of the President: "I hate to say this about a Republican, but Nixon could have been a wonderful President. He's brilliant and he's got a sackful of guts. But he's just sorry, and he can't help it." I thought about what he said all the way back to Fayetteville.

During the early weeks of the campaign, besides the retail politics, I tried to work through the mechanics. As I've mentioned, Uncle Raymond and Gabe Crawford co-signed a note for $10,000 to get me started, and I began to raise money, at first mostly in the Fayetteville area, then across the district and eventually throughout the state. Several of my friends from Georgetown, Oxford, and Yale and the McGovern and Duffey campaigns sent small checks. My largest contributor was my friend Anne Bartley, Governor Winthrop Rockefeller's stepdaughter, who later ran the Arkansas office in Washington, D.C., when I was governor. Eventually thousands of people gave, often one-, five-, or ten-dollar bills as we passed the bucket at rallies.

On February 25, I formally announced my candidacy with my family and a few friends at the Avanelle Motel, where Mother went for coffee most mornings before work.

Uncle Raymond gave me a little house in a good location for the Hot Springs headquarters. Mother, my Park

Avenue neighbor Rose Crane, and Bobby Hargraves, a young lawyer whose sister I had worked with in Washington, set up a first-class operation. Rose later moved to Little Rock and joined my administration when I became governor, but Mother kept building the organization and put it to work in future campaigns. The main headquarters was in Fayetteville, where my banker friend George Shelton agreed to be campaign chairman, and F. H. Martin, a young lawyer I played basketball with, signed on as treasurer. I rented an old house on College Avenue, which was kept open mostly by college students, and often on weekends by my cousin Roy's fifteen-year-old daughter, Marie Clinton, alone. We painted big CLINTON FOR CONGRESS signs and put them on both sides of the house. They're still there, having been painted over many times as new enterprises moved in. Today there's one word over the old signs: TATTOO. Eventually, my childhood friend Patty Howe opened a headquarters in Fort Smith, and others cropped up around the district as we got closer to the election.

By the time I went to Little Rock to file on March 22, I had three opponents: State Senator Gene Rainwater, a crew-cut conservative Democrat from Greenwood, just south of Fort Smith; David Stewart, a handsome young lawyer from Danville in Yell County; and Jim Scanlon, the tall, gregarious mayor of Greenland, a few miles south of Fayetteville. I was most worried about Stewart because he was attractive, articulate, and from the Clintons' home county, which I had hoped would go for me.

The first big political event of the campaign was on April 6: the River Valley Rally in Russellville, a college town in the east end of the district. It was an obligatory event, and all the candidates for federal, state, and local office were there, including Senator Fulbright and Governor Bumpers. Senator Robert Byrd of West Virginia was the featured speaker. He gave an old-time fire-and-brimstone speech and entertained the crowd by playing the fiddle. Then the candidates' speeches started, with the congressional candidates scheduled to speak last. By the time everyone else had taken three to five minutes, it was past ten o'clock. I knew the crowd would be tired and bored by the time we got up, but I took a gamble and chose to speak last. I figured it was my only chance to make an impression.

I had worked hard on the speech and had hammered it down to two minutes. It was a passionate call for a stronger Congress that would represent ordinary people against the concentration of power in the Republican administration and its allied economic interests. Though I had written the speech out, I gave it from memory and poured my heart into it. Somehow it struck a responsive chord with the audience, who, though tired after a long evening, found the energy to rise to their feet and cheer. As the crowd walked out, my volunteers gave them copies of the speech. I was off to a good start.

When the event was over, Governor Bumpers came up to me. After complimenting me on the speech, he said he knew I had worked for Senator Fulbright and thought he shouldn't be trying to unseat him. Then he stunned me by saying, "In twelve years or so, you may be facing the same decision regarding running against me. If you think it's the right thing to do, go on and run, and remember I told you to do it." Dale Bumpers was one smart cookie. He could have made a handsome living as a psychologist.

The next seven weeks were a blur of rallies, sale barns, pie suppers, money-raising, and retail politics. I got a big financial and organizational boost when the AFL-CIO, at its meeting in Hot Springs, endorsed me. The Arkansas Education Association also endorsed me because of my support for federal aid to education.

I spent a lot of time in the counties where I was less well known and that were less well organized than the Ozark Mountain counties: Benton County in the extreme north-west, the counties bordering both sides of the Arkansas River, and the southwest counties in the Ouachita Mountains. In Yell County my campaign was run by my cousin Mike Cornwell, the local funeral-home operator. Since he had buried all the kinfolk there, he knew everyone, and he had an upbeat personality that kept him going in the uphill battle against his neighbor in Danville, David Stewart.

There were an amazing number of people who took active roles in the campaign: idealistic young professional and business people, gifted local labor leaders, county and city officials, and die-hard Democrats, from high school students to seniors in their seventies and eighties.

By primary election day, we had outorganized and outworked the opposition. I got 44 percent of the vote, with Senator Rainwater barely edging out David Stewart for a spot in the runoff, 26 to 25 percent. Mayor Scanlon, who had no money but waged a game fight, got the rest.

I thought we would win handily in the June 11 runoff unless there was a very small turnout, in which case anything could happen. I didn't want my supporters to take the vote lightly and was alarmed when Will Goggins, the Democratic chairman of Searcy County, announced that all the voting there would be done in the courthouse on the square in Marshall. There was no way people living out in the country would drive thirty or forty miles over winding roads to vote in just one race. When I called and tried to talk him into opening more polling places, Will laughed and said, "Now, Bill, calm down. If you can't beat Rainwater without a big turnout here, you don't have a chance against Hammerschmidt. I can't afford to open rural polling places when only two or three people will vote. We'll need that money in November. You'll get whatever votes we cast."

On June 11, I won 69 to 31 percent, carrying the small turnout in Searcy County 177 to 10. After the November election, when I called Will to thank him for all his help, he said he wanted to put my mind at rest about something: "I know you think I rigged that runoff vote for you, but I didn't. Actually, you won 177 to 9. I gave Rainwater another vote because I couldn't stand to see anyone not in double figures."

The primary campaign was exhilarating for me. I had thrown myself into one unfamiliar circumstance after another and learned an enormous amount about people—the impact of government on their lives, and how their views of politics are shaped by both their interests and their values. I had also kept up with my teaching schedule. It was hard, but I enjoyed it and believed I did it pretty well except for one inexcusable mistake. After I gave exams in the spring, I had to grade them while the campaign was in full swing. I took my Admiralty exams in the car with me, grading them as we rode or at night when the campaign work was over. Somehow in the travel, I lost five of them. I was mortified. I offered the students the option of retaking the exam or getting full credit without a specific grade. They all took the credit, but one of them was particularly upset about it, because she was a good student who probably would have made an A, and because she was a good Republican who had worked for Congressman Hammerschmidt. I don't think she ever forgave me for losing the exam or for running against her old boss. I sure thought about it when, more than twenty years later, that former student, federal judge Susan Webber Wright, became the presiding judge in the Paula Jones case. Susan Webber Wright was plenty smart, and maybe I should have just given her an A. At any rate, for the general election, I took leave without pay from the law school.

During the summer I kept up the hectic pace, with breaks for my brother's high school graduation, my tenth high school reunion, and a trip to Washington to see Hillary and meet some of her co-workers on the impeachment inquiry staff. Hillary and all her colleagues were working themselves to a frazzle under John's stern demands to be thorough, fair, and absolutely closed-lipped. I was worried about how exhausted she was—she was thinner than I had ever seen her, so thin her lovely but large head seemed to be too big for her body.

Over the weekend I took her away for some rest and relaxation to the Outer Banks of North Carolina. We had a great time together and I was beginning to think Hillary might actually join me in Arkansas when the inquiry was finished. Earlier in the year on a trip to Fayetteville, she'd been invited by Dean Davis to interview for a position on the law faculty. She came back a few weeks later, impressed the committee, and was offered a job, so now she could both teach and practice law in Arkansas. The question was whether she would. At the moment I was more worried about how tired and skinny she was.

I went back home to the campaign and a far bigger health problem in my family. On July 4, I spoke at the Mount Nebo Chicken Fry for the first time since I represented Frank Holt there in 1966. Jeff, Mother, and Rose Crane drove up to hear me and help me work the crowd. I could tell Jeff wasn't feeling well and learned he hadn't been working much. He said it was too hard to stand all day. I suggested he come up to Fayetteville and spend a couple of weeks with me, where he could work the phones and give the headquarters some adult supervision. He took me up on the offer and seemed to enjoy it, but when I'd come home from the road at night, I could see he was ill. One night I was shocked to see him kneeling by the bed and stretched across it. He said he couldn't breathe lying down anymore and was trying to find a way to sleep. When he could no longer work a full day at headquarters, he went home. Mother told me his problem had to be a result of his diabetes or the medicine he had been taking for it for years. At the VA hospital in Little Rock, he was diagnosed with cardiomegaly, an enlargement and deterioration of the heart muscle. Apparently there was no cure for it. Jeff went home and tried to enjoy what was left of his life. A few days later when I was in Hot Springs campaigning, I met him briefly for coffee. He was on his way to the dog races in West Memphis, dapper as always, decked out in white shirt, pants, and shoes. It was the last time I ever saw him.

On August 8, President Nixon, his presidency doomed by the tapes he had kept of his conversations with aides, announced his intention of resigning the following day. I thought the President's decision was good for our country but bad for my campaign. Just a couple of days before the announcement, Congressman Hammerschmidt had defended Nixon and criticized the Watergate investigation in a front-page interview in the *Arkansas Gazette*. My campaign had been gaining momentum, but with the albatross of Nixon lifted from Hammerschmidt's shoulders, you could feel the air go out of it.

I got a second wind when Hillary called me a few days later to tell me she was coming to Arkansas. Her friend Sara Ehrman was driving her. Sara was more than twenty years older than Hillary and had seen in her the full promise of the new opportunities open to women. She thought Hillary was nuts to be coming to Arkansas after having done such good work and making so many friends in Washington, so she took her own good time getting Hillary to her destination, while trying to change her mind every few miles or so. When they finally got to Fayetteville it was Saturday night. I was at a rally in Bentonville, not far north, so they drove up to meet me. I tried to give a good speech, as much for Hillary and Sara as for the crowd. After I shook hands, we went back to Fayetteville and our future.

Two days later, Mother called to tell me Jeff had died in his sleep. He was only forty-eight years old. She was devastated, and so was Roger. Now she had lost three husbands and he had lost two fathers. I drove home and took care of the funeral arrangements. Jeff had wanted to be cremated, so we had to ship his body off to Texas because Arkansas didn't have a crematorium back then. When Jeff's ashes came back, in accordance with his instructions they were scattered over Lake Hamilton near his favorite fishing dock, while Mother and her friend Marge Mitchell watched.

I delivered the eulogy at his funeral. I tried to put into a few words the love he gave to Mother; the fathering guidance he gave to Roger; the friendship and wise counsel he gave to me; the kindness he showed to children and people down on their luck; the dignity with which he bore the pain of his past and his final illness. As Roger said so often in the days after he died, "He tried so hard." Whatever he was before he came into our lives, during his six short years with us he was a very good man. We all missed him for a long time.

Before Jeff got sick, I knew next to nothing about diabetes. It subsequently killed my 1974 campaign chairman,

George Shelton. It afflicts two children of my friend and former chief of staff Erskine Bowles, as well as millions of other Americans, with a disproportionate impact on our minority population. When I became President, I learned that diabetes and its complications account for a staggering 25 percent of all Medicaid costs. That's a big reason why, as President, I supported stem cell research and a diabetes self-care program that the American Diabetes Association called the most important advance in diabetes care since the development of insulin. I did it for Erskine's kids, for George Shelton, and for Jeff, who would have wanted more than anything to spare others his pain and premature end.

A few days after the funeral, Mother urged me, in her "get up and go on" way, to resume campaigning. Politics stops for death, but not for very long. So I went back to work, though I made sure to call and see Mother more often, especially after Roger left for Hendrix College in Conway in the fall. He was so concerned about her, he almost didn't go. Mother and I finally talked him into it.

As September arrived, I was still behind in the polls 59 to 23 percent after eight months of backbreaking work. Then I got lucky. On September 8, five days before the state Democratic convention in Hot Springs, President Ford granted Richard Nixon an unconditional pardon for all crimes he "committed or may have committed" while President. The country strongly disagreed. We were back in business.

At the state convention, all the attention was focused on my race. Governor Bumpers had defeated Senator Fulbright by a large margin in the primary, and there were no other serious contests on the ballot. I hated seeing Fulbright lose, but it was inevitable. The convention delegates were pumped up and we added fuel to the fire by packing the Hot Springs Convention Center with hometown friends and extra supporters from all over the district.

I gave a barn burner of a speech, articulating what I believed in a way that I hoped would unite the conservative and liberal populist elements in the district. I began by blasting President Ford's pardon of former President Nixon. One of my better lines was: "If President Ford wants to pardon anybody, he ought to pardon the administration's economic advisors."

Over the years, I changed my mind about the Nixon pardon. I came to see that the country needed to move on, and I believe President Ford did the right, though unpopular, thing, and I said so when we were together in 2000 to celebrate the two hundredth anniversary of the White House. But I haven't changed my mind about Republican economic policies. I still believe FDR was right when he said, "We have always known that heedless self-interest was bad morals. We now know that it is bad economics." That has even greater application today than it did in 1974.

We left Hot Springs on a roll. With seven weeks to go we had a chance, but a lot of work to do. Our headquarters operation was getting better and better. My best young volunteers were getting to be experienced pros.

They got some very good suggestions from the person the Democratic Party sent down to help us. His name was Jody Powell, and his boss, Governor Jimmy Carter of Georgia, had assumed a leading role in helping Democrats win in 1974. A couple of years later, when Jimmy Carter ran for President, a lot of us remembered and were grateful. When Hillary came down, she helped, too, as did her father and her younger brother, Tony, who put up signs all over north Arkansas and told the Republican retirees from the Midwest that the Rodhams were Midwest Republicans but that I was all right.

Several of my law students proved to be dependable drivers. When I needed them during my congressional campaign, there were a couple of airplanes I could borrow to fly around in. One of my pilots, sixty-seven-year-old Jay Smith, wore a patch over one eye and wasn't instrument-rated, but he had been flying in the Ozarks for forty years. Often when we hit bad weather, he swooped down below the clouds to follow a river valley through the mountains, all the while telling me stories or bragging on Senator Fulbright for knowing Vietnam was a mistake before anyone else did.

Steve Smith did a brilliant job of research on issues and Hammerschmidt's voting record. He came up with a series

of ingenious pamphlets comparing my positions on issues to
his votes on them, and we put out one a week for the last six
weeks of the campaign. They got good coverage in the local
papers, and Steve turned them into effective newspaper ads.
For example, the Arkansas River valley from Clarksville to
the Oklahoma border south of Fort Smith was full of coal
miners who had worked for decades in the open pit mines
that scarred the landscape until federal laws forced the land
to be restored. Many of the miners had debilitating black-
lung disease from all the years of breathing the coal dust
and were entitled to benefits from the federal government.
The congressman's casework operation helped them get the
benefits, but when the Nixon administration wanted to cut
back the program, he voted for the cutbacks. Folks in the
river valley didn't know that until Steve Smith and I told
them.

I also had a number of positive proposals, some of
which I advocated for twenty years, including a fairer tax
system, a national health-insurance program, public funding of presidential elections, a lean and more effective federal bureaucracy, more federal education funding and
creation of a federal Department of Education (it was then
still an office in the Department of Health, Education and
Welfare), and incentives to promote energy conservation
and solar power.

Thanks largely to financial support from the national
labor unions, which my friend and regional AFL-CIO leader
Dan Powell pushed hard for, we got enough money to do
some television ads. Old Dan Powell was talking about me
becoming President when I was still twenty-five points
behind for Congress. All I did was stand in front of a camera and talk. It forced me to think in twenty-eight-second
segments. After a while, I didn't need a stopwatch to tell me
whether I was a second or two long or short. Production
costs were low for the ads.

The TV ads may have been rudimentary, but our radio
ads were great. One memorable ad, produced in Nashville,
featured a country singer who sounded just like Arkansas-
born Johnny Cash. It opened, "If you're tired of eating

My father, William Jefferson Blythe, 1944

My father and my mother, Virginia Cassidy Blythe, at the Palmer House Hotel, Chicago, 1946

Mother and I

Here I am in 1949. *Above, far left:* at my father's gravesite on the afternoon Mother left for nurse's training in New Orleans; *above, center:* in our backyard; *above, right:* posing for a photo for Mother's Day

Above: My grandmother Edith Grisham Cassidy, 1949. She was a private duty nurse.

Below: My grandfather James Eldridge Cassidy (right) in his grocery store in Hope, Arkansas, 1946

Miss Marie Purkins' School for Little Folks in Hope. I'm at the far left, with Vince Foster next to me and Mack McLarty in the back row.

With my great-uncle Buddy Grisham, one of the lights of my life, during my first presidential campaign

My great-grandfather Lem Grisham came to visit me in the hospital when I broke my leg, March 1952.

Daddy (my stepfather, Roger Clinton)

Below: My brother, Roger, and I with Cora Walters, the wonderful woman who took care of us

Below, right: From my high school yearbook: the Three Blind Mice, better known as the 3 Kings—Randy Goodrum on piano, Joe Newman on drums

Mother and Daddy, 1965

Daddy and I at home in Hope, 1951

I'm in the front, right behind the photographer, as President John F. Kennedy addresses the Boys Nation delegates in the Rose Garden on July 24, 1963.

David Leopoulos and I as emcees of the Hot Springs High School Band Variety Show, 1964

Mother, Roger, our dog Susie, and I in the snow at our Park Avenue house, 1961

At a picnic with friends, including Carolyn Yeldell, David Leopoulos, Ronnie Cecil, and Mary Jo Nelson

Frank Holt meeting and greeting in his shirt-sleeves during his 1966 campaign for governor. (I'm in the light-colored suit.)

With my brother and my roommates at our graduation from Georgetown, 1968: (from left) Kit Ashby, Tommy Caplan, Jim Moore, and Tom Campbell

Above: My Oxford roommates: Strobe Talbott (left) and Frank Aller. I'm in my bearded phase.

Right: I surprised Mother by flying home for her wedding to Jeff Dwire, January 3, 1969. Reverend John Miles officiated, and I was best man. Roger's in the front.

With my mentor J. William Fulbright and his administrative assistant, Lee Williams, September 1989. During my Georgetown years, I was assistant clerk on Fulbright's Foreign Relations Committee.

Hillary and I with our Yale Law School Barristers Union classmates

Above: Campaigning for George McGovern in San Antonio, Texas, 1972

Right: Teaching at the University of Arkansas Law School, Fayetteville

Right: With George Shelton, my campaign chairman, and F. H. Martin, treasurer. While they passed away before my presidency, their sons both served in my administration.

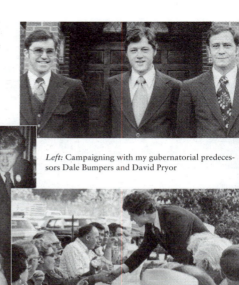

Left: Campaigning with my gubernatorial predecessors Dale Bumpers and David Pryor

Campaigning for Congress, 1974

Our wedding day, October 11, 1975

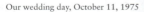

Celebrating my thirty-second birthday during the campaign. Hillary is in dark glasses.

Addressing the Arkansas legislature after I was sworn in as governor, January 9, 1979

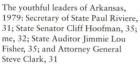

The youthful leaders of Arkansas, 1979: Secretary of State Paul Riviere, 31; State Senator Cliff Hoofman, 35; me, 32; State Auditor Jimmie Lou Fisher, 35; and Attorney General Steve Clark, 31

With Chelsea and Zeke

Hillary, Carolyn Huber, Emma Phillips, Chelsea, and Liza Ashley celebrate Liza's birthday in the Governor's Mansion in 1980.

Above: My announcement for governor in 1982. Hillary inscribed the picture "Chelsea's second birthday, Bill's second chance."

Left: With three of my strongest Arkansas supporters: Maurice Smith, Jim Pledger, and Bill Clark, 1998

Below, left: Visiting Arkansas Delta Project leaders, with whom I worked to bring economic development to their region

Below: Parents and students at the Governor's Mansion for High School Honors Day, celebrating the valedictorians and salutorians of Arkansas high schools

Above: At the Sanyo Electric plant in Japan

Left: My workday at the Tosco plant

Left to right: Henry Oliver; Gloria Cabe; Carol Rasco

At the Grand Ole Opry, Nashville, during the governors' conference, 1984. I'm standing next to Minnie Pearl; Hillary is at the far left.

Left: Chelsea's first day of school. *Middle:* Betsey Wright and I surprise Hillary for her birthday, 1983. *Right:* Chelsea is enjoying the sight of me holding "Boa Derek" for Proclamation Day.

Dancing with Chelsea and with Hillary at the Governor's Inaugural Ball, January 1991

With Dr. Billy Graham and my pastor, Dr. W. O. Vaught, fall 1989

With (clockwise, from left) Lottie Shackleford, Bobby Rush, Ernie Green, Carol Willis, Avis Lavelle, Bob Nash, and Rodney Slater at the National Democratic Convention, July 1992

Left: Tipper Gore took this picture on the road.

Below, left: in the "war room" James Carville and Paul Begala high five; *below:* campaigning in Stone Mountain, Georgia; *bottom:* Wall Street turns out for Hillary and me.

On the West Coast in 1992. *Top, left:* Cinco de Mayo; *top, right:* rally in Seattle; *right:* at a prayer meeting after the Los Angeles riots; *above:* greeting supporters in Los Angeles

Left: The Rodham family: (from left) Maria, Hugh, Dorothy, Hillary, and Tony. Hillary's father, Hugh, is seated.

The campaign team

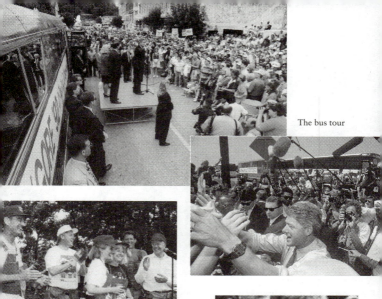

The bus tour

Hillary and I, Tipper and Al Gore, President Jimmy Carter, and (at left) Habitat for Humanity founder Millard Fuller celebrate Tipper's and my joint birthday.

President George H. W. Bush, Ross Perot, and I at the University of Richmond debate

The Arsenio Hall Show

Election night, November 3, 1992

My first day as President-elect. *Above, right:* with Mother; *below:* at Carolyn Yeldell Staley's house: (front row) Mother, Thea Leopoulos; (second row) Bob Aspell, me, Hillary, Glenda Cooper, Linda Leopoulos; (top row) Carolyn Staley, David Leopoulos, Mauria Aspell, Mary Jo Rodgers, Jim French, Tommy Caplan, Phil Jamison, Dick Kelley, Kit Ashby, Tom Campbell, Bob Dangremond, Patrick Campbell, Susan Jamison, Gail and Randy Goodrum, Thaddeus Leopoulos, Amy Ashby, Jim and Jane Moore, Tom and Jude Campbell, Will Staley

beans and greens and forgotten what pork and beefsteak means, there's a man you ought to be listening to." It went on to slam the Nixon administration for financing huge grain sales to the Soviet Union, which drove up the price of food and animal feed, hurting poultry and cattle operations. The song said, "It's time to push Earl Butz [Nixon's agriculture secretary] away from the trough." In between verses came this refrain: "Bill Clinton's ready, he's fed up too. He's a lot like me, he's a lot like you. Bill Clinton's gonna get things done, and we're gonna send him to Washington." I loved that spot. Don Tyson, whose costs of poultry production had soared with the grain sales and whose brother, Randal, was working hard for me, made sure I had enough money to run the song to death on rural radio.

As we moved closer to election day, the support got stronger and so did the opposition. I got the endorsement of the *Arkansas Gazette*, the state's largest newspaper, plus several papers in the district. I began to campaign hard in Fort Smith, where there was strong support from the black community, especially after I joined the local chapter of the NAACP. I found good support all over heavily Republican Benton County. Across the river from Fort Smith, four or five people practically worked themselves to death trying to turn Crawford County for me. I got a great reception in Scott County, south of Fort Smith, at the annual fox and wolf hunters' field trial. It was an all-night event out in the country, at which men who loved their dogs as much as their kids (and took just as good care of them) showed the dogs and then cut them loose to chase foxes and bay at the moon while the women kept mountains of food out on picnic tables all through the night. I was even getting some strong support from Harrison, the congressman's hometown, from a few brave souls who weren't afraid to take on the small-town establishment.

One of the most exciting rallies of the election occurred one fall afternoon on the White River, not far from the infamous Whitewater property I later invested in but never saw. The Democrats in the area were all stirred up because the Nixon Justice Department was trying to send the Democratic

sheriff of Searcy County, Billy Joe Holder, to jail for income
tax evasion. Under our 1876 constitution, the salaries of the
state and local officials have to be approved by a vote of the
people; they had last been raised in 1910. County officials
made just $5,000 a year. The governor made only $10,000,
but at least he had a mansion, and his transportation and
food costs were covered. A lot of the local officials were
forced to use their expense accounts, which as I recall were
about $7,000 a year, just to live. The Justice Department
wanted Sheriff Holder to go to jail for not paying income tax
on his personal expenditures from the account. I believe the
Holder case was the smallest income tax–evasion prosecution ever brought by the federal government, and the hill
people were convinced it was politically motivated. If so, it
backfired. After an hour and a half of deliberations, the jury
returned a verdict of not guilty. It turned out they voted to
acquit right away, then stayed in the jury room more than an
hour longer just to make it look right. Billy Joe walked out of
the courthouse and drove straight to our rally, where he was
greeted like a hero home from war.

On the way back to Fayetteville, I stopped in Harrison,
where the trial was held, to discuss it with Miss Ruth Wilson, a public accountant who did tax work for lots of hill
people. I told Miss Ruth that I understood she had helped
Holder's lawyer, my friend F. H. Martin, with the jury selection. She said she had. I asked her half jokingly if she had
packed it with Democrats. I'll never forget her reply: "No,
Bill, I didn't. Actually, there were a fair number of Republicans on that jury. You know, those young men who came
down from Washington to prosecute the sheriff were smart
fellows, and they looked real good in their expensive suits.
But they just didn't know our folks. It's the strangest thing.
Nine of those twelve jurors had been audited by the Internal
Revenue Service in the last two years." I was glad Ruth Wilson and her boys were on my side. After she worked over
those Washington lawyers, the Justice Department began to
ask prospective jurors in tax cases about their own experiences with the IRS.

With about two weeks to go, the congressman finally

got his campaign in gear. He had seen a poll that said if he didn't, my momentum might carry me to a narrow victory. His people pulled out all the stops. His business friends and the Republicans went to work. Someone began calling all the papers asking for the nonexistent photo of me demonstrating against President Nixon at the 1969 Arkansas-Texas game, giving birth to the infamous "tree story" I mentioned earlier. In Hot Springs, the chamber of commerce had a big dinner to thank him for all he'd done. Several hundred people showed up, and it received extensive coverage in the local paper. Across the district, Republicans scared businesspeople by charging that I had so much support from unions, I would be a puppet for organized labor in Congress. In Fort Smith, six thousand postcards we sent to political supporters identified in our phone canvass were never delivered. Apparently my labor support didn't extend to the postal workers there. The cards were found a few days after the election in the trash outside the main post office. The state branch of the American Medical Association came out strongly for Hammerschmidt, hitting me for my efforts to get doctors in the Springdale area to treat poor people on Medicaid. Hammerschmidt even got federal revenue-sharing funds to pave the streets of Gilbert, a small town in Searcy County, a few days before the election. He carried it 38–34, but it was the only township in the county he won.

I got an inkling of just how effective his work had been the weekend before the election when I went to a closing rally at the Hot Springs Convention Center. We didn't have as many people there as had attended his dinner a few days before. Our people had worked their hearts out, but they were tired.

Still, on election day, I thought we might win. As we gathered in my headquarters to watch the returns, we were nervous but hopeful. We led in the vote count until nearly midnight, because the largest and most Republican county, Sebastian, reported late. I carried twelve of the fifteen counties with fewer than eight thousand total votes, including every voting box along the Buffalo River in Newton and Searcy counties. But I lost five of the six biggest counties, suffering narrow defeats of fewer than five hundred votes each in Garland County, where I grew up, and Washington County, where I lived, losing Crawford County by eleven hundred votes and getting killed in Benton and Sebastian counties, where my combined losses were twice the total margin of victory. We each won one county by about two to one. He won Sebastian County, the biggest, and I won Perry County, the smallest. It seems ironic now, when rural Americans vote overwhelmingly Republican in national elections, that I began my political career with a profoundly rural base, born of intense personal contact and responsiveness to both their resentments and their real problems. I was on their side, and they knew it. The final total vote was 89,324 to 83,030, about 52 to 48 percent.

The Democrats had a good night nationally, picking up forty-nine House seats and four seats in the Senate, but we just couldn't overcome Hammerschmidt's enormous popularity and his last-minute push. When the campaign began, his approval rating was 85 percent. I had whittled it down to 69 percent, while mine had gone from zero to 66 percent, very good but not good enough. Everybody said I made a good showing and had a bright future. That was nice to hear, but I'd wanted to win. I was proud of our campaign and I felt that somehow I had let the steam go out of it in the last few days, and in so doing let down all the people who worked so hard for me and the changes we wanted to make. Maybe if I'd had the money and the sense to run effective television ads on the congressman's voting record, it would have made a difference. Probably not. Nevertheless, in 1974, I saw firsthand, in thousands of encounters, that middle-class voters would support government activism to solve their problems, and those of the poor, but only if the effort was made with due care for their tax dollars, and if efforts to increase opportunity were coupled with an insistence on responsibility.

After I spent a few days traveling and calling around to thank people, I went into a funk. I spent most of the next six weeks at Hillary's house, a nice place near campus. Mostly I just lay on the floor, nursing my regrets and trying to figure

out how I was going to pay off my campaign debt of over
$40,000. My new salary of $16,450 was more than enough
to live on and pay off my law school debts, but nowhere
near enough to cover the debt from the campaign. Sometime in December, there was a big band dance at the university, which Hillary coaxed me into taking her to. After we
danced a few hours, I began to feel better. Still, it would be
a good while before I realized the congressman had done me
a favor by beating me. If I had won and gone to Washington, I'm sure I never would have been elected President. And
I would have missed the eighteen great Arkansas years that
lay ahead.

NINETEEN

IN JANUARY 1975, I went back to my teaching, the only full year I did it uninterrupted by politics. In the spring term, I taught Antitrust and held a seminar in White-Collar Crime; in summer school, Admiralty and Federal Jurisdiction; in the fall, White-Collar Crime again and Constitutional Law. In Constitutional Law, I spent two full weeks on *Roe* v. *Wade*, the Supreme Court decision that gave women a constitutional privacy right to an abortion in the first two trimesters of pregnancy, the approximate amount of time it takes a fetus to become "viable"—that is, able to live outside the mother's womb. After viability, the Court ruled, the state could protect a child's interest in being born against the mother's decision not to have it, unless her life or health would be threatened by continued pregnancy or childbirth. Some of my students who saw Constitutional Law as just another course in which they had to memorize the rule of law in each case couldn't understand why I spent so much time on *Roe*. It was easy to remember the three-trimester rule and the reasoning behind it.

I made them delve deeper, because I thought then, and still believe, that *Roe* v. *Wade* is the most difficult of all judicial decisions. Whatever they decided, the Court had to play God. Everyone knows life begins biologically at conception. No one knows when biology turns into humanity or, for the religious, when the soul enters the body. Most abortions that don't involve the life or health of the mother are chosen by scared young women and girls who don't know what else to do. Most people who are pro-choice understand that abortions terminate potential life and believe that they should be legal, safe, and rare and that we should support young mothers who decide to complete their pregnancies, as most of them do. Most ardent pro-lifers are all for prosecuting doctors but grow less certain when their argument that an abortion is a crime is carried to its logical conclusion: prosecuting the mother for murder. Even the fanatics who bomb abortion clinics don't target the women who keep them in business. Also, as we've learned first with Prohibition and later with our drug laws, which have more support than a total ban on abortion does, it's hard to apply the criminal law to acts that a substantial portion of the citizenry doesn't believe should be labeled crimes.

I thought then and still believe that the Court reached the right conclusion, though, as so often happens in American politics, its action sparked a powerful reaction, the growth of an active, effective national anti-abortion movement, which over time drastically reduced the practical availability of abortions in many places and drove large numbers of voters into the new right wing of the Republican Party. Regardless of what opinion polls show about voters' positions on abortion, our national ambivalence about it means that its impact on elections depends on which side feels more threatened. For most of the last thirty years, for example, during which a woman's right to choose has been secure, pro-choice voters have felt free to vote for or against candidates on other issues, while for anti-abortion voters, the other issues often didn't matter. Nineteen ninety-two was an exception. The highly publicized court of appeals decision in the *Webster* case, narrowing the right to choose, combined with the prospect of Supreme Court vacancies in the near future, threatened and galvanized the pro-choice voters, so I and other pro-choice candidates weren't hurt by our position that year. After I was elected, with the right to choose secure again, pro-choice suburbanites again felt free to vote for anti-abortion Republicans for other reasons, while pro-life Democrats and independents, who approved of my record on economic and other social issues, nevertheless often felt compelled to support pro-life candidates who were almost always conservative Republicans.

In 1975, I didn't know or care much about the politics of abortion. I was interested in the Supreme Court's herculean effort to reconcile conflicting convictions about law, morality, and life. In my opinion they did about the best they could do, lacking access to the mind of God. Whether my students agreed with me or not, I wanted them to think hard about it.

In the fall, I got a new teaching assignment: I was asked to come down to the university's Little Rock campus once a week to teach a night seminar in Law and Society to students who worked during the day in law enforcement. I was eager to do it and enjoyed my interaction with people who seemed genuinely interested in how their work in police departments and sheriffs' offices fit into the fabric of both the Constitution and citizens' daily lives.

Besides teaching, I kept my hand in politics and did some interesting legal work. I was appointed to head a state Democratic Party committee on affirmative action. It was designed to assure increased participation by women and minorities in party affairs without falling into the trap of the McGovern rules, which gave us delegates to the national convention who were representative of every demographic group but often hadn't ever really worked for the party and couldn't get any votes. The assignment gave me a chance to travel the state meeting Democrats, both black and white, who cared about the issue.

The other thing that kept me politically active was the necessity to pay off my campaign debt. I finally did it in much the way we financed the campaign, with lots of small-dollar events and with the help of some generous larger givers. I got my first $250 from Jack Yates, a fine lawyer in Ozark who, along with his partner, Lonnie Turner, had worked hard for me in the election. Jack gave me the check within two weeks after the election. At the time, I wasn't sure where my next dollar was coming from and I never forgot it. Sadly, a couple of months after he helped me, Jack Yates died of a heart attack. After the funeral, Lonnie Turner asked me if I would take over Jack's black-lung cases. The Nixon administration had promulgated new rules making it harder to get benefits and requiring the cases of people already receiving them to be reviewed. In many cases, the benefits were being revoked. I began to drive down to the Ozarks once or twice a week to review the files and interview the old miners, with the understanding that any pay I got would come from fees from the cases I won.

Lonnie knew I cared a lot about the issue and was familiar with how the program worked. It's true that when the black-lung program was first implemented the evaluations were too lax and some people did get benefits who didn't need them, but as so often happens with government programs, the attempt to correct the problem went too far in the other direction.

Even before I took over Jack Yates's cases, I had agreed to try to help another man in his fight for black-lung benefits. Jack Burns Sr., from a small town south of Fort Smith, was the father of the administrator of Ouachita Hospital in Hot Springs, where Mother worked. He was about five feet four inches tall and couldn't have weighed much more than one hundred pounds. Jack was an old-fashioned man of quiet dignity, who was severely damaged by black lung. He was entitled to the benefits, and he and his wife badly needed them to help pay their bills. In the months we worked together, I came to respect both his patience and his determination. When we won his case, I was almost as happy as he was.

I think there were more than one hundred cases like Jack Burns's in the stack of files Lonnie Turner gave me. I enjoyed going down to Ozark from Fayetteville over the winding road known as the "Pig Trail" to work on them. The cases were heard first by an administrative law judge, Jerry Thomasson, who was a fair-minded Republican. They could then be appealed to the federal judge in Fort Smith, Paul X. Williams, who was a sympathetic Democrat. So was his longtime clerk, Elsijane Trimble Roy, who was a great help to me. I was elated when President Carter appointed her Arkansas' first female federal judge.

While I continued my teaching, politics, and law work, Hillary was settling into life in Fayetteville. I could tell she really liked being there, maybe even enough to stay. She taught Criminal Law and Trial Advocacy, and oversaw both the legal-aid clinic and the students who did work for prison inmates. Some of the crusty old lawyers and judges and a few of the students didn't know what to make of her at first, but eventually she won them over. Because there is a constitutional right to a lawyer in a criminal case, our judges assigned local lawyers to represent poor defendants, and since poor criminal defendants almost never paid, the bar wanted Hillary's clinic to handle their cases. In its first year, it served more than three hundred clients and became an established institution at the law school. In the process, Hillary earned the respect of our legal community, helped a lot of folks who needed it, and established the record that, a few years later, led President Carter to appoint her to the board of directors of the national Legal Services Corporation.

Jimmy Carter was our featured speaker on Law Day, near the end of the spring term. It was clear that he was running for President. Hillary and I spoke with him briefly, and he invited us to continue the conversation down in Little Rock, where he had another engagement. Our talk confirmed my sense that he had a good chance to be elected. After Watergate and all the country's economic problems, a successful southern governor who wasn't involved in Washington's politics and could appeal to people the Democrats had lost in 1968 and 1972 seemed like a breath of fresh air. Six months earlier, I had gone to Dale Bumpers and urged him to run, saying, "In 1976, someone like you is going to be elected. It might as well be you." He seemed interested but said it was out of the question; he had just been elected to the Senate, and Arkansas voters wouldn't support him if he immediately started running for President. He was probably right, but he would have been a terrific candidate and a very good President.

Besides our work and normal social life with friends, Hillary and I had a few adventures in and around Fayetteville. One night we drove south down Highway 71 to Alma to hear Dolly Parton sing. I was a big Dolly Parton fan, and she was, you might say, in particularly good form that night. But the most enduring impact of the evening was that it was my first exposure to the people who brought her to Alma, Tony and Susan Alamo. At the time, the Alamos sold fancy performance outfits in Nashville to many of the biggest country music stars. That's not all they did. Tony, who looked like Roy Orbison on speed, had been a promoter of rock-and-roll concerts back in California, when he met Susan, who had grown up near Alma but had moved out west and become a television evangelist. They teamed up, and he promoted her as he had his rock and rollers. Susan had white-blond hair and often wore floor-length white dresses to preach on TV. She was pretty good at it, and he was great at marketing her. They built a small empire, including a large farming operation manned by devoted young followers as transfixed by them as the young acolytes of the Reverend Sun Myung Moon were by their leader. When Susan got cancer, she wanted to come home to Arkansas. They bought a big house in Dyer, her hometown, opened the place in Alma, where Dolly Parton sang, as well as a smaller version of their Nashville country outfit store just across the road, and had a big truckload of food from their California farm delivered each week to feed them and their Arkansas contingent of young laborers. Susan got on TV at home, and enjoyed some success until she finally succumbed to her illness. When she died, Tony announced that God had told him he was going to raise her from the dead someday, and he put her body in a glass box in their home to await the blessed day. He tried to keep their empire going with the promise of Susan's return, but a promoter is lost without his product. Things went downhill. When I was governor, he got into a big fight with the government over taxes and staged a brief, nonviolent standoff of sorts around his house. A couple of years later, he got involved with a younger woman. Lo and behold, God spoke to him again and told him Susan wasn't coming back after all, so he took her out of the glass box and buried her.

In the summer, I taught both semesters of summer school to earn some extra money and had a good time hanging around Fayetteville with Hillary and our friends. One day, I drove her to the airport for a trip back east. As we were driving down California Drive, we passed a beautiful little jagged brick house set back on a rise with a stone wall bracing up the

front yard. There was a FOR SALE sign in the yard. She
remarked on how pretty the place was. After I dropped her
off, I checked the house out. It was a one-story structure of
about eleven hundred square feet, with a bedroom, a bathroom, a kitchen with breakfast room attached, a small dining
room, and a gorgeous living room that had a beamed ceiling
half again as high as the others in the house, a good-looking
offset fireplace, and a big bay window. There was also a large
screened-in porch that could double as a guest bedroom most
of the year. The house had no air-conditioning, but the big
attic fan did a good job. The price was $20,500. I bought the
house with a $3,000 down payment, big enough to get the
monthly mortgage payments down to $174.

I moved what little furniture I had into my new house
and bought enough other things so that the place wasn't
totally bare. When Hillary came back from her trip, I said,
"Remember that little house you liked so much? I bought it.
You have to marry me now, because I can't live there
alone." I took her to see the house. It still needed a lot of
work, but my rash move did the trick. Although she had
never even told me she was prepared to stay in Arkansas,
she finally said yes.

On October 11, 1975, we were married in the big living
room of the little house at 930 California Drive, which had
been replastered under the watchful eye of Marynm Bassett,
a fine decorator who knew our budget was limited. For
example, she helped us pick out bright yellow wallpaper for
the breakfast room, but we put it on ourselves, an experience that reaffirmed my limitations as a manual laborer.
Hillary wore an old-fashioned Victorian lace dress that I
loved, and the Reverend Vic Nixon married us in the presence of Hillary's parents and brothers, Mother, Roger (who
served as best man), and a few close friends: Hillary's closest
friend from Park Ridge, Betsy Johnson Ebeling, and her
husband, Tom; her Wellesley classmate Johanna Branson;
my young cousin Marie Clinton; my campaign treasurer,
F. H. Martin, and his wife, Myrna; our best friends on the
law faculty, Dick Atkinson and Elizabeth Osenbaugh; and
my childhood friend and tireless campaign worker Patty

Howe. Hugh Rodham never thought he'd be giving his mid-western Methodist daughter to a Southern Baptist in the Arkansas Ozarks, but he did it. By then I had been working on him and the rest of the Rodhams for four years. I hoped I had won them over. They certainly had captured me.

After the ceremony, a couple hundred of our friends gathered at Morriss and Ann Henry's house for a reception, and that evening we danced the night away at Billie Schneider's place in the Downtown Motor Inn. At about 4 a.m., after Hillary and I had gone to bed, I got a call from my younger brother-in-law, Tony, who was at the Washington County jail. While he was driving one of the guests home after the party, he was pulled over by a state trooper, not because he was speeding or weaving on the road, but because his tipsy rider was dangling her feet out of the car's back window. After he stopped Tony, the deputy could see he had been drinking, so he hauled him in. When I got down to the jail to bail him out, Tony was shivering. The jailer told me that our sheriff, Herb Marshall, a Republican whom I liked, kept the jail real cold at night to keep the drunks from throwing up. As we were leaving, Tony asked me if I would get another man released who was in town making a movie with Peter Fonda. I did. He was shaking worse than Tony, so badly that when he got in his car to drive away, he rammed right into Hillary's little yellow Fiat. Even though I bailed him out, the guy never paid me for the costs of the car repair. On the other hand, at least he didn't leave his dinner on the floor of the county jail. So ended my first night as a married man.

For the longest time I'd never thought I'd get married. Now that I was, it felt right, but I wasn't sure where it would lead us.

Probably more has been written or said about our marriage than about any other in America. I've always been amazed at the people who felt free to analyze, criticize, and pontificate about it. After being married for nearly thirty years and observing my friends' experiences with separations, reconciliations, and divorces, I've learned that marriage, with all its magic and misery, its contentments and disappointments, remains a mystery, not easy for those in it to understand and largely inaccessible to outsiders. On October 11, 1975, I didn't know any of that. All I knew then was that I loved Hillary, the life, work, and friends we now had in common, and the promise of what we could do together. I was proud of her, too, and thrilled to be in a relationship that might not ever be perfect, but would certainly never be boring.

After our sleepless wedding night, we went back to work. We were in the middle of a school term, and I had black-lung hearings to attend. Two months later, we finally had a honeymoon in Acapulco, an unusual one, with Hillary's whole family and the girlfriend of one of her brothers along. We all spent a week together in a beautiful penthouse suite, walking on the beach, enjoying the restaurants. I know it was different, but we had a great time. I adored Hillary's mother, Dorothy, and enjoyed spending time with her father and brothers, playing pinochle and swapping stories. Like me, they were storytellers, and all of them could spin a good yarn.

I read one book in Acapulco, Ernest Becker's *The Denial of Death*—heavy reading for a honeymoon, but I was only a year older than my father was when he died, and I had just taken a big step. It seemed like a good time to keep exploring the meaning of life.

According to Becker, as we grow up, at some point we become aware of death, then the fact that people we know and love die, then the fact that someday we, too, will die. Most of us do what we can to avoid it. Meanwhile, in ways we understand only dimly if at all, we embrace identities and the illusion of self-sufficiency. We pursue activities, both positive and negative, that we hope will lift us beyond the chains of ordinary existence and perhaps endure after we are gone. All this we do in a desperate push against the certainty that death is our ultimate destiny. Some of us seek power and wealth, others romantic love, sex, or some other indulgence. Some want to be great, others to do good and be good. Whether we succeed or fail, we are still going to die. The only solace, of course, is to believe that since we were created, there must be a Creator, one to whom we matter and will in some way return.

Where does Becker's analysis leave us? He concludes: "Who knows what form the forward momentum of life will take in the time ahead. . . . The most that any one of us can seem to do is to fashion something—an object or ourselves—and drop it into the confusion, make an offering of it, so to speak, to the life force." Ernest Becker died shortly before *The Denial of Death* was published, but he seemed to have met Immanuel Kant's test of life: "How to occupy properly that place in creation that is assigned to man, and how to learn from it what one must be in order to be a man." I've spent a lifetime trying to do that. Becker's book helped convince me it was an effort worth making.

In December, I had another political decision to make. Many of my supporters wanted me to run for Congress again. The debt was paid off, and they wanted a rematch. I thought Congressman Hammerschmidt would be harder to beat this time, even if Jimmy Carter won the party's nomination. More important, I had lost my desire to go to Washington; I wanted to stay in Arkansas. And I was getting more interested in state government, thanks in part to the opportunity Attorney General Jim Guy Tucker had given me to write a brief to the U.S. Supreme Court on behalf of our state in an antitrust case involving the setting of interest rates on credit cards. Jim Guy was running for Congress, for the seat vacated by the retirement of Wilbur Mills, so the attorney general's job would be open and it had a lot of appeal for me.

While I was mulling it over, my friend David Edwards, who was working for Citibank, called and asked us to go to Haiti with him. He said he had enough frequent-flier miles built up to pay for our tickets, and he wanted to give us the trip as a wedding present. Barely a week after we returned from Mexico, we were off again.

By late 1975, Papa Doc Duvalier had passed from the scene, succeeded by his son, a portly young man whom everybody called Baby Doc. We saw him one day when he

drove across the big square from his official residence in
Port-au-Prince to lay a wreath at the monument to Haitian
independence, a statue of a powerful freed slave blowing
on a conch. His security force, the infamous Tontons
Macoutes, were everywhere, and intimidating with their
sunglasses and machine guns.

The Duvaliers had managed to dominate, pillage, and
mismanage Haiti until it was the poorest country in our
hemisphere. Port-au-Prince was still beautiful in places but
had the feel of faded glory. I remember especially the frayed
carpeting and broken pews in the National Cathedral.
Despite the politics and poverty, I found the Haitians fascinating. They seemed lively and intelligent, and they produced beautiful folk art and captivating music. I marveled
at the way so many of them seemed not only to survive but
to enjoy life.

I was particularly intrigued by the voodoo religion and
culture to which I had had some limited exposure in New
Orleans, and that existed alongside Catholicism in Haiti.

The name of the traditional Haitian religion comes from
the Fon language of Benin in West Africa, where voodoo
originated. It means "God" or "spirit," without the conno-
tations of black magic and witchcraft attached to it in so
many movies. Voodoo's central ritual is a dance during
which spirits possess believers. On the most interesting day
of the trip, I got the chance to observe voodoo in practice.
David's Citibank contact in Port-au-Prince offered to take
him, Hillary, and me to a nearby village to meet an unusual
voodoo priest. Max Beauvoir had spent fifteen years outside
Haiti, studying at the Sorbonne in Paris and working in
New York. He had a beautiful blond French wife and two
bright young daughters. He had been a practicing chemical
engineer until his voodoo-priest grandfather, on his deathbed, chose Max to succeed him. Max was a believer, and he
did it, though it must have proved a challenge for his French
wife and westernized kids.

We arrived in the late afternoon, an hour or so before
the dance ceremony, which Max opened to paying tourists

as a way of covering some of the costs of his operation. He explained that in voodoo, God is manifest to humans through spirits that represent forces of light and darkness, good and evil, which are more or less in balance. After Hillary, David, and I finished our brief course in voodoo theology, we were escorted back to an open area and seated with other guests who had come to witness the ceremony, in which spirits are called forth and enter into the bodies of dancing believers. After several minutes of rhythmic dancing to pounding drums, the spirits arrived, seizing a woman and a man. The man proceeded to rub a burning torch all over his body and walk on hot coals without being burned. The woman, in a frenzy, screamed repeatedly, then grabbed a live chicken and bit its head off. Then the spirits left and those who had been possessed fell to the ground.

A few years after I witnessed this extraordinary event, a Harvard University scientist named Wade Davis, in Haiti searching for an explanation for the phenomenon of zombies, or walking dead, also went to see Max Beauvoir. According to his book *The Serpent and the Rainbow*, with the help of Max and his daughter, Davis managed to unravel the mystery of zombies, those who apparently die and rise to life again. They are administered a dose of poison by secret societies as punishment for some offense. The poison, tetrodotoxin, is extracted from puffer fish. In proper doses, it can paralyze the body and reduce respiration to such low levels that even the attending doctor believes the person is dead. When the poison wears off, the person wakes up. Similar cases had been reported in Japan, where puffer fish is a delicacy if properly prepared, and deadly if not.

I describe my brief foray into the world of voodoo because I've always been fascinated by the way different cultures try to make sense of life, nature, and the virtually universal belief that there is a nonphysical spirit force at work in the world that existed before humanity and will be here when we all are long gone. Haitians' understanding of how God is manifest in our lives is very different from that of most Christians, Jews, or Muslims, but their documented

experiences certainly prove the old adage that the Lord
works in mysterious ways.

By the time we got back from Haiti, I had determined to run
for attorney general. I took another leave from teaching at
the law school and got to work. I had two opponents in the
Democratic primary: George Jernigan, the secretary of
state; and Clarence Cash, who was head of the consumer
protection division in Jim Guy Tucker's office. Both were
articulate and not much older than I. Jernigan seemed to be
the more formidable of the two, with a lot of friends in Governor Pryor's organization, at several county courthouses,
and among conservatives across the state. Strangely, no
Republicans filed, making it the only time I ever ran without
opposition in the general election.

    I knew I'd have to run the campaign out of Little Rock.
Besides being the capital city, it is in the center of the state
and has both the biggest vote and the largest fund-raising
potential. I set up headquarters in an old house a couple of
blocks from the Capitol building. Wally DeRoeck, a young
banker from Jonesboro, agreed to be my campaign chairman. Steve Smith, who had done such good work in the
Congress race, signed on as campaign manager. The office
was run by Linda McGee, who did a terrific job on a shoestring budget: We ran the whole campaign on less than
$100,000. Somehow Linda kept the place open long hours,
paid the bills, and managed the volunteers. I was offered a
place to stay by Paul Berry, whom I had met and liked when
he ran Senator McClellan's Arkansas office and who was
then a vice president at Union Bank. Apart from everything
else, he insisted on my sleeping in his apartment's only bed,
even if I got in from the road at two or three in the morning. Night after night I'd drag in to find him asleep on the
couch in the living room, with a light on in the kitchen,
where he'd left out my favorite snack, peanut butter and
carrots.

    Longtime friends like Mack McLarty and Vince Foster
helped me break into the Little Rock business and profes-

sional communities. I still had good support from labor leaders, though some of it fell off when I refused to sign a petition supporting labor's effort to repeal Arkansas' right-to-work law by putting the question on the November ballot. Right-to-work laws enable people to work in plants with unionized workforces without paying union dues. Back then, the law appealed to my libertarian side. I later learned that Senator McClellan was so impressed by my position that he asked Paul Berry to call his main supporters and tell them he was for me. A few years later, I changed my mind about right to work. It's wrong, I think, for someone to reap the superior salaries, health care, and retirement plans normally found in union plants without making a contribution to the union that secures those benefits.

My base in the Third District seemed secure. All the folks who had worked for me in 1974 were willing to go again. I got some extra help from Hillary's brothers, both of whom had moved to Fayetteville and enrolled at the university. They also added a lot of fun to our lives. One night, Hillary and I went over to their place for dinner and spent the whole evening listening to Hugh regale us with tales of his adventures in Colombia with the Peace Corps—stories that sounded as if they came straight out of *One Hundred Years of Solitude* but that he swore were all true. He also made us piña coladas that tasted like fruit juice but packed quite a punch. After two or three I was so sleepy that I went outside and climbed into the back of my Chevy El Camino pickup truck, which I had inherited from Jeff Dwire. The back was covered in Astroturf, so I slept like a lamb. Hillary drove me home, and the next day I went back to work. I loved that old truck and drove it until it completely wore out.

Out in the state, I found strong support in and around Hope, where I was born, and in the five or six counties outside the Third District where I had relatives. I got off to a good start among blacks in central, south, and east Arkansas, thanks to former students who were practicing law in those areas. And I had support from Democratic activists who had cheered my race against Hammerschmidt

from the sidelines or been involved in the work of my affirmative action committee. Despite all that, there were still
gaping holes in the organization. Most of the campaign was
an attempt to fill them.

As I traveled the state, I had to contend with the rise of a
new political force, the Moral Majority, founded by the
Reverend Jerry Falwell, a conservative Baptist minister from
Virginia who had won a large television following and was
using it to build a national organization committed to
Christian fundamentalism and right-wing politics. In any
part of the state, I might find myself shaking hands with
someone who would ask if I was a Christian. When I said
yes, I would be asked if I was a born-again Christian. When
I said yes, there would be several more questions, apparently supplied by Falwell's organization. Once when I was
campaigning in Conway, about thirty miles east of Little
Rock, I was in the county clerk's office, where absentee ballots are cast. One of the women who worked there started
in on me with the questions. Apparently, I gave the wrong
answer to one of them, and before I left the courthouse she
had cost me four votes. I didn't know what to do. I wasn't
about to answer a question about religion falsely, but I
didn't want to keep losing votes. I called Senator Bumpers, a
good liberal Methodist, for advice. "Oh, I get that all the
time," he said. "But I never let them get past the first question. When they ask me if I'm a Christian, I say, 'I sure hope
so, and I've always tried to be. But I really think that's a
question only God can judge.' That usually shuts them up."
After Bumpers finished, I laughed and told him now I knew
why he was a senator and I was just a candidate for attorney
general. And for the rest of the campaign, I used his answer.

The funniest thing that happened in the race occurred in
Mississippi County, in far northeast Arkansas. The county
had two cities, Blytheville and Osceola, and a host of towns
dominated by planters who farmed huge plots of land. Typically, their farmworkers and the small merchants whose
incomes they made possible voted for the planters' choice,
normally the most conservative person running—in this
case, Secretary of State Jernigan. The county also had a

strong local organization, headed by the county judge, "Shug" Banks, who was also for Jernigan. It looked hopeless, but the county was too big to ignore, so I devoted one Saturday to working Blytheville and Osceola. I was by myself and, to put it mildly, it was a discouraging day. In both towns, though I found some support, thanks to my former law students, most people I met either were against me or didn't know who I was and didn't care to learn. Still, I shook every available hand, finishing in Osceola about eleven at night. I finally gave up when I realized I still had a three-hour drive back to Little Rock and didn't want to fall asleep at the wheel.

As I was driving south through a string of little settlements, I remembered that I hadn't eaten all day and was hungry. When I came to a place called Joiner, I saw a light on in a beer joint. In the hope that it also served food, I pulled over and went in. The only people there were the man at the bar and four guys playing dominoes. After ordering a hamburger, I went outside to call Hillary from the pay phone. When I walked back in, I decided to introduce myself to the domino players. The first three, like so many people I'd met that day, didn't know who I was and didn't care. The fourth man looked up and smiled. I'll never forget his first words: "Kid, we're going to kill you up here. You know that, don't you?" I replied that I'd gotten that impression after a day of campaigning, but I was sorry to hear it confirmed. "Well, we are," he continued. "You're a long-haired hippie professor from the university. For all we know, you're a Communist. But I'll tell you something. Anybody who would campaign at a beer joint in Joiner at midnight on Saturday night deserves to carry one box. So you hide and watch. You'll win here. But it'll be the only damn place you win in this county."

The man's name was R. L. Cox, and he was as good as his word. On election night, I was crushed in the other voting precincts controlled by the big farmers, but I got 76 votes in Joiner and my two opponents got 49. It was the only place in Mississippi County I carried, except for two black precincts in Blytheville that were turned the weekend before the election by a black funeral-home operator, LaVester McDonald, and the local newspaper editor, Hank Haines.

Luckily, I did better almost everywhere else, winning more than 55 percent of the total vote and carrying sixty-nine of the seventy-five counties, thanks to a big vote in south Arkansas, where I had lots of relatives and good friends, and a whopping 74 percent in the Third Congressional District. All the people who had worked so hard for me in 1974 were finally rewarded with a victory.

The summer after the election was a happy time for Hillary and me. We spent the first two months just having fun in Fayetteville with our friends. Then, in mid-July, we took a trip to Europe, stopping in New York to attend one night of the Democratic convention, after which we flew to Paris to meet up with David Edwards, who was working there. After a couple of days, we set out for Spain. Just after we crossed the Pyrenees, I got a message asking me to call the Carter campaign. When I returned the call from the village of Castro Urdiales, I was asked to chair the campaign in Arkansas, and I accepted immediately. I strongly supported Jimmy Carter, and though I was scheduled to teach in the fall at Fayetteville, I knew I could do the job. Carter was immensely popular in Arkansas because of his progressive record, his farming experience, his genuine commitment to his Southern Baptist faith, and his personal contacts, which included four prominent Arkansans who had been in his class at the Naval Academy. The issue in Arkansas was not whether the state would vote for him but by how much. After all the lost elections, the prospect of winning two in one year was too tempting to pass up.

We finished our vacation in Spain with a stop in Guernica, the town memorialized in Picasso's remarkable painting of its bombing in the Spanish civil war. When we got there, a Basque festival was in progress. We liked the music and dancing but had a hard time with one of the native delicacies, cold fish in milk. We explored the nearby caves with their prehistoric drawings and spent a glorious day in the shadow of the snowcapped Pyrenees on a hot beach that had a little restaurant with good, inexpensive food and beer at a nickel a glass. At the border on the way back into France—by this time it was early August, the vacation month in Europe—cars were stretched out before us as far as we could see, testament to the good sense of Europeans that life is more than work. For me, that adage would get harder and harder to live by.

When we got back home, I went to Little Rock to set up a campaign operation with Craig Campbell, a former executive of the state Democratic Party, who worked for Stephens, Inc., in Little Rock, then the largest investment bank in America outside Wall Street. It was owned by Witt and Jack Stephens. Witt Stephens was a longtime power in state politics. Jack, who was ten years younger, had gone to the Naval Academy with Jimmy Carter. Craig was a big, good-looking, fun-loving guy who was deceptively sensitive in personal and political ways that made him very effective.

I traveled the state to make sure we had a functioning organization in every county. One Sunday night, I went to a little black church just outside Little Rock. The pastor was Cato Brooks. When we got there, the place was already rocking to the music of a great gospel choir. During the second or third song, the door flew open and a young woman who looked like Diana Ross, in black knee-high boots and a tight knit dress, strode down the aisle, waved to the choir, and sat down at the organ. I had never heard organ music like that before. It was so powerful I wouldn't have been surprised if the instrument had levitated and left the church under its own power. When Cato got up to preach, four or five of the men of the church gathered around him, sitting on folding chairs. He chanted and sang virtually his entire sermon in rhythmic cadences punctuated by the sound of the spoons that the men were beating on their knees. After the sermon, the Reverend Brooks introduced me to speak for Carter. I was fired up, but I was nowhere near as good as Cato. When I sat down, he told me the church would be for Carter and suggested I leave because they were going to be there for another hour or so. A few steps outside the church, a voice behind me said, "Hey, white boy, you want some help with your campaign?" It was the organist, Paula Cotton. She became one of our best volunteers. Cato Brooks moved to Chicago not long after the campaign. He was too good to keep down on the farm.

While I was working in Arkansas, Hillary joined the Carter campaign, too, taking on a much tougher assignment. She became the field coordinator in Indiana, a state that traditionally votes Republican in presidential elections but that the Carter staff hoped his farm roots would give him a chance to win. She worked hard and had some interesting adventures, which she eagerly recounted to me in daily phone conversations and during my one trip to Indianapolis.

The fall campaign was a roller coaster. Carter came out of the convention in New York with a thirty-point lead over President Ford, but the country was more evenly divided than that. President Ford made an impressive effort to catch up, mostly by questioning whether a southern governor, whose main promise was to give us a government as honest as the American people, had the experience to be President. In the end, Carter defeated Ford by about 2 percent of the popular vote and by 297 electoral votes to 240. The election was too close for our side to prevail in Indiana, but we carried Arkansas with 65 percent, just two points less than President Carter's 67 percent margin in his native Georgia and seven points better than the next largest victory margin, in West Virginia.

After the campaign, Hillary and I settled back into our home for a few months as I completed my final teaching assignments, in Admiralty and Constitutional Law. In three years and three months I had taught eight courses in five semesters and a summer session, taught two courses to law-enforcement officers in Little Rock, run for office twice, and managed the Carter campaign. And I had loved every minute of it, regretting only the time it took me away from our life and friends in Fayetteville, and that little house at 930 California Drive that brought Hillary and me so much joy.

TWENTY

FOR THE LAST couple of months of 1976, I commuted to Little Rock to prepare for my new job. Paul Berry got me some office space on the eighteenth floor of the Union Bank building, where he worked, so I could interview prospective staff members.

A lot of idealistic and able people applied for jobs. I persuaded Steve Smith to become my chief of staff, to make sure we came up with some good policy initiatives while handling the work that came in the door. There were only twenty lawyers on the staff. Some very good ones wanted to stay on with me. I hired some new lawyers, among them young women and black attorneys—enough to make our legal staff 25 percent female and 20 percent black, both numbers unheard of in those days.

Sometime in December, Hillary and I found a house at 5419 L Street in the Hillcrest section of Little Rock, a nice old neighborhood close to downtown. At 980 square feet, it was even smaller than our home in Fayetteville and cost a lot more, $34,000, but we could afford it, because in the previous election the voters had approved an increase in the salaries of state and local officials for the first time since 1910, raising the attorney general's salary to $26,500 a year. And Hillary found a good job at the Rose Law Firm, which was full of experienced, highly regarded lawyers and bright younger ones, including my friend Vince Foster and Webb Hubbell, a huge former football star for the Razorbacks who would become one of Hillary's and my closest friends. From then on, she earned much more than I did every year until the year I became President and she gave up her practice.

In addition to issuing opinions on questions of state law, the attorney general's office prosecuted and defended civil suits on behalf of the state; represented the state in criminal appeals to the state supreme court and in criminal cases in federal court; provided legal advice to state boards and commissions; and protected consumer interests through lawsuits, lobbying the legislature, and appearing in utility-rate cases before the state Public Service Commission (PSC). The workload was large, varied, and interesting.

The year got off to a fast start. The legislature went into session in early January and there was a PSC hearing on a request for a large rate increase for Arkansas Power and Light Company, based on the cost of AP&L's participation in a large nuclear power plant at Grand Gulf, Mississippi, that was being built by its parent company, Middle South Utilities (now Entergy). Since Middle South didn't serve customers directly, the costs of the Grand Gulf plant had to be allocated among its subsidiaries serving Arkansas, Louisiana, Mississippi, and the city of New Orleans. The Grand Gulf case would consume a lot of my time and attention over the next few years. I had two problems with it: first, because the parent company was building the plant, advance approval by our state PSC was not required, even though our ratepayers were required to pay for 35 percent of it; and second, I thought we could meet the increased demand for electricity much less expensively through energy conservation and more efficient use of existing plants.

In preparing for the hearing, Wally Nixon, a lawyer on my staff, came across the work of Amory Lovins, which demonstrated the enormous potential and economic benefits of energy conservation and solar power. I thought what he said made sense and I got in touch with him. At the time, the conventional wisdom among business and political leaders was that economic growth required constantly increasing electricity production. No matter how strong the evidence supporting it, conservation was viewed as a harebrained fantasy of fuzzy-headed intellectuals. Unfortunately, too many people still look at it that way.

For more than twenty years, as attorney general, governor, and President, I tried to push an alternative-energy policy, using the work of Amory Lovins and others to support my argument. Though I made some modest progress in all three jobs, the opposition remained fierce, especially after the conservatives took over Congress in 1995. Al Gore and I tried for years without success to get them to adopt a 25 percent tax credit for the production or purchase of clean energy and energy conservation technology, with mountains of evidence to support our position. The Republicans blocked it every time. I used to joke that one of the most significant achievements of my second term was that I had finally found a tax cut Newt Gingrich and Tom DeLay wouldn't support.

Working with the state legislature was fascinating, not only because the issues were interesting and unpredictable, but also because the House and Senate were full of colorful people, and because sooner or later half the state seemed to show up to lobby for or against some measure. One day early in the legislative session, I appeared at a committee hearing to speak against a measure. The room was packed with people representing interests who were for it, including Vince Foster. And Hillary. He had brought her along for the experience, not knowing I would be appearing for the other side. We just smiled at each other and did our jobs. Luckily, the Rose firm had gotten an opinion from the American Bar Association saying it could hire the wife of the attorney general and setting out the steps necessary to avoid conflicts of interest. Hillary followed them to the letter. After I became governor, and she was a full partner at the Rose firm, she gave up her portion of the annual profits made from state bond business, legal work the firm had been doing since the 1940s.

When I took office, there was a serious backlog of opinions and other work. We often worked until midnight to catch up, and in the process we developed a great rapport and had a terrific time. On Fridays, when the legislature wasn't in session, I allowed casual dress and encouraged everyone to go for a long lunch at a nearby haunt that had first-rate hamburgers, pinball machines, and a shuffleboard game. The old unpainted shack also had a big canoe on the roof and an ominous name, the Whitewater Tavern.

The growing strength of the Moral Majority and like-minded groups gave rise to some legislation that many moderate and progressive legislators didn't want to pass but didn't want to be on record as voting against. The obvious tactic was to get the attorney general to say the bill was unconstitutional. This was an example of another of Clinton's laws of politics: If someone can shift the heat from himself to you, he'll do it every time.

The funniest bills were offered by Representative Arlo Tyer of Pocahontas, in northeast Arkansas. Arlo was a decent man who wanted to stay one step ahead of the Moral Majority. He introduced a bill to make it illegal to show X-rated movies anywhere in Arkansas, even to adults. I was asked whether the bill was an unconstitutional restriction on the freedom of speech. I could just see the headlines: "Attorney General Comes Out for Dirty Movies!" I called Bob Dudley, a district judge from Arlo's hometown, to find out why he'd introduced the bill. "Do you have a lot of X-rated movies up there?" I asked. Dudley, who was a real wit, said, "No. We don't have any movie theaters at all. He's just jealous of the rest of you seeing all that stuff."

As soon as the movie bill died, Arlo came up with another gem: a $1,500-a-year tax on every couple in Arkansas who lived together without benefit of wedlock. The headline alarm bell went off in my brain again: "Clinton Comes Out for Living in Sin!" I went to see Representative Tyer on this one. "Arlo," I asked, "how long do a man and a woman have to cohabit to pay this tax? A year, a month, a week? Or is a one-night stand enough?" "You know, I hadn't thought about that," he replied. "And what about enforcement?" I went on. "Are you and I going to get baseball bats and knock down doors to see who's doing what with whom?" Arlo shrugged and said, "I hadn't thought about that either. Maybe I better pull that bill down." I walked back to my office relieved to have dodged another bullet. To my surprise, some of my staff seemed disappointed. A couple of them had decided they wanted the bill to pass and our office to enforce it. They had even imagined their new uniforms: T-shirts emblazoned with the acronym SNIF, for Sex No-no Investigation Force.

We had a tougher time when it came to gay rights. Two years earlier, Attorney General Jim Guy Tucker had spearheaded a new criminal code through the legislature. It simplified and clarified the definitions of more than one hundred years of complicated and overlapping crimes. It also eliminated so-called status offenses, which had been condemned by the Supreme Court. A crime requires committing a forbidden act, intentionally or recklessly; just being something society deems undesirable isn't enough. For example, being a drunk wasn't a crime. Neither was being a homosexual, though it had been before the new code was adopted.

Representative Bill Stancil took a lot of heat from the conservative pastors in his hometown of Fort Smith for his vote in favor of the revised criminal code. They said he had voted to legalize homosexuality. Stancil was a good man who had been one of Arkansas' best high school football coaches. He was a muscular, square-jawed, broken-nosed guy, and subtlety wasn't his strong point. He couldn't believe he had voted for homosexuality and was determined to rectify his error before the religious right could punish him for it, so he introduced a bill to make homosexual acts a crime. For good measure, he criminalized bestiality too, causing one of his wittier colleagues to remark that he obviously didn't have many farmers in his district. Stancil's bill described in excruciating detail every conceivable variation of both kinds of forbidden intercourse. A pervert could read it and escape the urge to buy pornographic material for a whole week.

There was no way to beat the bill on a direct vote. Moreover, the Supreme Court was a long way from its 2003 decision declaring that consensual homosexual relations are protected by the right to privacy, so getting an opinion from me saying the bill was unconstitutional wasn't an option. The only possible strategy was to delay the bill to death. In the House, three young liberals who were great allies of mine—Kent Rubens, Jody Mahoney, and Richard Mays—decided to offer an interesting amendment. Word got out that something was afoot, and I joined a packed gallery above the House chamber to watch the fireworks go off. One of the guys rose and praised Stancil's bill, saying it was about time someone stood up for morality in Arkansas. The only problem, he said, was that the bill was too weak, and he wanted to offer a "little amendment" to strengthen it. Then, with a straight face, he proposed the addition, making it a Class D felony for any member of the legislature to commit adultery in Little Rock while the legislature was in session.

The entire gallery was engulfed in peals of laughter. On the floor, however, the silence was deafening. For many legislators from small towns, coming to Little Rock for the session was the only fun they had—the equivalent of two months in Paris. They were not amused, and several of them told the three wise guys they'd never pass another bill unless the amendment was withdrawn. It was. The bill sailed through and was sent to the Senate.

We had a better chance to kill it there, because it was assigned to a committee chaired by Nick Wilson, a young senator from Pocahontas who was one of the brightest and most progressive members of the legislature. I thought he might be persuaded to keep the bill bottled up until the legislature adjourned.

On the last day of the session, the bill was still in Nick's committee and I was counting the hours until adjournment. I called him about it several times and hung around until I was almost an hour late in leaving for a speech in Hot Springs. When I could finally wait no longer, I called him one last time. He said they would adjourn in half an hour and the bill was dead, so I left. Fifteen minutes later, a powerful senator who favored the bill offered Nick Wilson a new building for the vocational technical school in his district if he'd let the bill go through. As Speaker Tip O'Neill used to say, all politics is local. Nick let the bill go, and it passed easily. I was sick. A few years later, the present congressman from Little Rock, Vic Snyder, tried to repeal the bill when he was in the state Senate. He failed too. As far as I know, the law was never enforced, but we had to wait for the 2003 Supreme Court decision to invalidate the law.

Another really interesting problem I faced as attorney general was literally a matter of life and death. One day I got a call from the Arkansas Children's Hospital. It had just recruited a gifted young surgeon who was being asked to operate on Siamese twins who were joined at the chest, using the same systems to breathe and pump blood. The systems couldn't support them both much longer, and without surgery to separate them, they both would die. The problem was that the surgery would certainly kill one of them. The hospital wanted an opinion saying that the doctor couldn't be prosecuted for manslaughter for killing the twin who wouldn't survive the surgery. Strictly speaking, I couldn't guarantee him that, because an attorney general's opinion protects the person receiving it from civil suits but not from criminal prosecution. Nevertheless, the opinion would be a powerful deterrent to an overzealous prosecutor. I gave him an official letter stating my opinion that the certain death of one of the twins to save the life of the other would not be a crime. The doctor performed the operation. One twin died. But the other one lived.

Most of the work we did was far more conventional than the examples I've cited. For two years, we worked hard to issue truly well-written opinions, do a good job for the state agencies and with the criminal cases, improve the quality of nursing-home care, and hold down utility rates, including a vigorous effort to keep the cost of a pay-phone call down to a dime, when nearly every other state was raising it to twenty-five cents.

Apart from my work, I got around the state as much as I could to broaden my contacts and strengthen my organization for the next election. In January 1977, I gave my first speech as an elected official at a Rotary Club banquet in Pine Bluff, the largest city in southeast Arkansas. I had gotten 45 percent of the vote there in 1976, but I needed to do better in future races. The five hundred people at the dinner provided a good opportunity to improve. It was a long evening, with a lot of speeches and an interminable number of introductions. Often the people who run such events are afraid that everyone who isn't introduced will go home mad. If so, there weren't many unhappy people after that dinner. It was nearly 10 p.m. when my host got up to introduce me. He was more nervous than I was. The first words out of his mouth were "You know, we could stop here and have had a very nice evening." I know he meant to suggest the best was yet to come, but that's not how it came out. Thank goodness, the crowd laughed, and I got a good reception to my speech, mostly because it was short.

I also attended several events in the black community. One day I was invited by the Reverend Robert Jenkins to his inauguration as the new pastor of Morning Star Baptist Church. It was a little white wooden church in North Little Rock with enough pews to seat 150 people comfortably. On a very hot Sunday afternoon, there were about three hundred people there, including ministers and choirs from several other churches, and one other white person, our county judge, Roger Mears. Every choir sang and every preacher offered congratulations. When Robert got up to preach, the congregation had been there a good while. But he was young, handsome, a powerful speaker, and he held their attention. He began slowly, saying he wanted to be an accessible pastor but not a misunderstood one. "I want to say a special word to the ladies of the church," he said. "If you need a pastor, you can call on me anytime of the day or night. But if you need a man, call on the Lord. He'll get you one." Such candor would have been unthinkable in a mainline white church, but his crowd appreciated it. He got a loud chorus of amens.

As Robert got into his sermon, the temperature seemed to rise. All of a sudden an older lady sitting near me stood up, shaking and shouting, seized by the spirit of the Lord. A moment later a man got up in an even louder and more uncontrolled state. When he couldn't calm down, a couple of the churchmen escorted him to a little room in the back of the church that held the choir robes and closed the door. He continued to shout something unintelligible and bang against the walls. I turned around just in time to see him literally tear the door off its hinges, throw it down, and run out into the churchyard screaming. It reminded me of the scene at Max Beauvoir's in Haiti, except these people believed they had been moved by Jesus.

Not long afterward, I saw white Christians have similar

experiences, when my finance officer in the attorney general's office, Dianne Evans, invited me to the annual summer camp meeting of the Pentecostals in Redfield, about thirty miles south of Little Rock. Dianne was the daughter of Pentecostal ministers, and like other devout women of her faith, she wore modest clothes and no makeup and didn't cut her hair, which she rolled up into a bun. Back then, the strict Pentecostals didn't go to movies or sporting events. Many wouldn't even listen to nonreligious music on the car radio. I was interested in their faith and practices, especially after I got to know Dianne, who was smart, extremely competent at her job, and had a good sense of humor. When I kidded her about all the things Pentecostals couldn't do, she said they had all their fun in church. I was soon to discover how right she was.

When I got to Redfield, I was introduced to the state leader of the Pentecostals, Reverend James Lumpkin, and other prominent ministers. Then we went out into the sanctuary, which held about three thousand people. I sat up on the stage with the preachers. After my introduction and other preliminaries, the service got going with music as powerful and rhythmic as anything I had heard in black churches. After a couple of hymns, a beautiful young woman got up from one of the pews, sat down at the organ, and began to sing a gospel song I had never heard before, "In the Presence of Jehovah." It was breathtaking. Before I knew it, I was so moved I was crying. The woman was Mickey Mangun, the daughter of Brother Lumpkin and wife of the Reverend Anthony Mangun, who, along with Mickey and his parents, pastored a large church in Alexandria, Louisiana. After a rousing sermon by the pastor, which included speaking "in tongues"—uttering whatever syllables the Holy Spirit brings out—the congregation was invited to come to the front and pray at a row of knee-high altars. Many came, raising their hands, praising God, and also speaking in tongues. It was a night I would never forget.

I made that camp meeting every summer but one between 1977 and 1992, often taking friends with me. After a couple of years, when they learned I was in my church choir, I was invited to sing with a quartet of balding ministers known as the Bald Knobbers. I loved it and fit right in, except for the hair issue.

Every year I witnessed some amazing new manifestation of the Pentecostals' faith. One year the featured pastor was an uneducated man who told us God had given him the power to memorize the Bible. He quoted more than 230 verses in his sermon. I had my Bible with me and checked his memory. I stopped after the first twenty-eight verses; he never missed a word. Once I saw a severely handicapped young man who came every year to answer the altar call in his automated wheelchair. He was near the back of the church, which sloped down to the front. He rolled his wheelchair on full speed and barreled down the aisle. When he got about ten feet from the altar, he slammed on the brakes, throwing himself out of the wheelchair into the air and landing perfectly on his knees just at the altar, where he proceeded to lean over and praise God just like everybody else.

Far more important than what I saw the Pentecostals do were the friendships I made among them. I liked and admired them because they lived their faith. They are strictly anti-abortion, but unlike some others, they will make sure that any unwanted baby, regardless of race or disability, has a loving home. They disagreed with me on abortion and gay rights, but they still followed Christ's admonition to love their neighbors. In 1980, when I was defeated for reelection as governor, one of the first calls I got was from one of the Bald Knobbers. He said three of the ministers wanted to come see me. They arrived at the Governor's Mansion, prayed with me, told me they loved me just as much now as they had when I was a winner, and left.

Besides being true to their faith, the Pentecostals I knew were good citizens. They thought it was a sin not to vote. Most of the preachers I knew liked politics and politicians, and they could be good practical politicians themselves. In the mid-eighties, all over America, fundamentalist churches were protesting state laws requiring that their child-care centers meet state standards and be licensed. It had become a very hot issue in some places, with at least one minister in a midwestern state choosing to go to jail rather than comply with the child-care standards. The issue had the potential to explode in Arkansas, where we had had some problems with a religious child-care center and where new state standards for child care were pending. I called in a couple of my Pentecostal pastor friends and asked what the real problem was. They replied that they had no problem meeting the state health and safety standards; their problem was in the demand that they get a state license and display it on the wall. They considered child care to be a critical part of their ministry, which they thought should be free from state interference under the First Amendment's guarantee of freedom of religion. I gave them a copy of the new state standards and asked them to read them and tell me what they thought. When they came back the next day, they said the standards were fair. I then proposed a compromise: religious child-care centers wouldn't have to be certified by the state if the churches agreed to remain in substantial compliance with them and to allow regular inspections. They took the deal, the crisis passed, the standards were implemented, and as far as I know, the church-run centers never had any problems.

One Easter in the eighties, Hillary and I took Chelsea to see the Easter Messiah service at the Manguns' church in Alexandria. The sound and light systems were first-rate, the scenery was realistic, including live animals, and all the performers were members of the church. Most of the songs were original and beautifully performed. When I was President and happened to be in Fort Polk, near Alexandria, at Eastertime, I went back to the Messiah service and talked the traveling press corps into coming with me, along with Louisiana's two black congressmen, Cleo Fields and Bill Jefferson. In the middle of the service, the lights went out. A woman began to sing a well-known hymn in a powerful deep voice. The reverend leaned over to Congressman Jefferson and asked, "Bill, you think this church member is white or black?" Bill said, "She's a sister. No doubt about it." After a couple of minutes, the lights came back up, revealing a small white woman in a long black dress with her hair piled up on her head. Jefferson just shook his head, but another black man sitting a couple of rows ahead of us couldn't contain himself. He blurted out, "My God, it's a white librarian!" By the end of the show, I saw several of my normally cynical press-corps people with tears in their eyes as the power of the music pierced the walls of their skepticism.

Mickey Mangun and another Pentecostal friend, Janice Sjostrand, sang at the dedicatory church service at my first inauguration and brought the house down. As he was leaving the church, Colin Powell, the chairman of the Joint Chiefs of Staff, leaned over to me and asked, "Where did you find white women who could sing like that? I didn't know there were any." I smiled and told him knowing people like them was one reason I got elected President.

During my second term, when the Republicans were trying to run me out of town and a lot of the pundits were saying I was dead meat, Anthony Mangun called me and asked if he and Mickey could come see me for twenty minutes. I said, "Twenty minutes? You're going to fly all the way up here for twenty minutes?" He replied, "You're busy. That's all it'll take." I told him to come on up. A few days later, Anthony and Mickey sat alone with me in the Oval Office. He said, "You did a bad thing but you're not a bad man. We raised our children together. I know your heart. Don't give up on yourself. And if you're going down, and the rats start to leave the sinking ship, call me. I rode up with you, and I want to go down with you." Then we prayed together and Mickey gave me a tape of a beautiful song she had written to shore me up. It was entitled "Redeemed." After twenty minutes, they got up and flew home.

Knowing the Pentecostals has enriched and changed my life. Whatever your religious views, or lack of them, seeing people live their faith in a spirit of love toward all people, not just their own, is beautiful to behold. If you ever get a chance to go to a Pentecostal service, don't miss it.

Toward the end of 1977, the political talk started again. Senator McClellan had announced his retirement after almost thirty-five years in the Senate, setting the stage for an epic battle to be his successor. Governor Pryor, who had come close to defeating McClellan six years earlier, was going to run. So were Jim Guy Tucker and the congressman from the Fourth District in south Arkansas, Ray Thornton, who had achieved prominence as a member of the House Judiciary Committee during the Nixon impeachment proceedings. He was also the nephew of Witt and Jack Stephens, so he had guaranteed financing for his campaign.

I had to decide whether to get into the Senate race too. A recent poll had me in second place, about ten points behind the governor and a little ahead of the two congressmen. I had been an elected official less than a year, but unlike the congressmen, I represented the entire state, was home all the time, and had the good fortune to have a job that, when well done, naturally engenders public approval. Not many people are against consumer protection, better care of the elderly, lower utility rates, and law and order.

But I decided to run for governor instead. I liked state government and wanted to stay home. Before I could get into the race, I had one last big case to handle as attorney general. I did it long distance. After Christmas, Hillary and I went to Florida to see Arkansas play Oklahoma in the Orange Bowl. Coach Lou Holtz, in his first year at Arkansas, had led the Razorbacks to a 10–1 season and a sixth-place national ranking; their only loss was at the hands of top-ranked Texas. Oklahoma was ranked second nationally, having also lost to Texas, but more narrowly.

No sooner had we arrived than a firestorm broke out in Arkansas involving the football team. Coach Holtz suspended three players from the team, which prevented them from playing in the bowl game, for their involvement in an incident in the players' dorm involving a young woman. They weren't just any three players. They were the starting tailback, who was the leading rusher in the Southwest Conference; the starting fullback; and the starting flanker, who had blinding speed and was a genuine pro prospect. The three of them accounted for most of the team's offense. Although no criminal charges were filed, Holtz said that he was suspending the players because they had violated the "do right" rule, and that he was coaching his charges to be good men as well as good football players.

The three players filed a lawsuit seeking reinstatement, claiming the suspension was arbitrary and may have been based on racial considerations, since the three players were black and the woman was white. They also lined up support on the team. Nine other players said they wouldn't play in the Orange Bowl either unless the three were reinstated.

My job was to defend Holtz's decision. After talking with Frank Broyles, who had become athletic director, I decided to stay in Florida, where I could consult closely with him and Holtz. I asked Ellen Brantley on my staff to handle things in the federal court in Little Rock. Ellen had gone to Wellesley with Hillary and was a brilliant attorney; I thought it wouldn't do any harm to have a woman arguing our side of the case. Meanwhile, the support for Holtz and playing the game began to build among the players.

For a few hectic days, I spent eight or more hours a day on the phone, talking to Ellen back in Little Rock and to Broyles and Holtz in Miami. The pressure and criticism were getting to Holtz, especially the charge that he was a racist. The only evidence against him was the fact that when he had coached at North Carolina State, he had endorsed ultra-conservative Senator Jesse Helms for reelection. After spending hours talking to Holtz, I could tell he wasn't a racist, nor was he political. Helms had been decent to him and he had returned the favor.

On December 30, three days before the game, the players dropped their suit and released their nine allies from their commitment not to play. It still wasn't over. Holtz was so upset he told me that he was going to call Frank Broyles and resign. I immediately called Frank and told him not to answer the phone in his room that night no matter what. I was convinced Lou would wake up in the morning wanting to win the game.

For the next two days the team worked like crazy. They had been eighteen-point underdogs to start, and after the three stars were out, the game was taken off the odds chart. But the players whipped one another up into a frenzy.

On the night of January 2, Hillary and I sat in the Orange Bowl watching Oklahoma go through warm-ups. The day before, top-ranked Texas had lost to Notre Dame in the Cotton Bowl. All Oklahoma had to do was beat crippled Arkansas to win the national championship. Along with everybody else, they thought it was going to be a cakewalk.

Then the Razorbacks took the field. They trotted out in a straight line and slapped the goalpost before they started their drills. Hillary watched them, grabbed my arm, and said, "Just look at them, Bill. They're going to win." With smothering defense and a record-setting 205 yards rushing from reserve back Roland Sales, the Razorbacks routed Oklahoma 31–6, perhaps the biggest and certainly the most unlikely victory in the storied history of Arkansas football. Lou Holtz is a high-strung, skinny little fellow who paced the sidelines in a way that reminded Hillary of Woody Allen. I was grateful that this bizarre episode gave me the chance to know him well. He's brilliant and gutsy, perhaps the best on-the-field coach in America. He's had other great seasons at Arkansas, Minnesota, Notre Dame, and South Carolina, but he'll never have another night quite like that one.

With the Orange Bowl case behind me, I went home to make my next move. After Senator McClellan publicly announced his retirement, I went to see him to thank him for his service and ask his advice. He strongly urged me to run for his seat; he didn't want David Pryor to win it and had no particular ties to Tucker and Thornton. He said that the worst I could do was lose, as he had done on his first try, and that if I lost, I was young and could try again, as he had. When I told him I was thinking of running for governor, he said that was a bad idea, that all you did in the governor's office was make people mad. In the Senate you could do big things for the state and the nation. The governor's office, he said, was a short trip to the political graveyard. Historically, McClellan's analysis was right. While Dale Bumpers had ridden the wave of New South prosperity and progressivism from the governor's office to the Senate, he was the exception to the rule. Times were tough in Pryor's tenure and he was facing a stiff challenge whether I ran or not. And it was hard to serve as governor longer than four years. Since Arkansas adopted a two-year term in 1876, only two governors, Jeff Davis before World War I and Orval Faubus, had served more than four years. And Faubus had to do wrong at Central High to hang on.

McClellan, at age eighty-two, was still sharp as a tack, and I respected his advice. I was also surprised by his encouragement. I was much more liberal than he was, but the same could be said for all his potential successors. For some reason, we got along, in part because I had been away at law school when Governor Pryor ran against him and therefore couldn't have helped Pryor, which I would have done had I been home. I also respected the serious work McClellan had done to crack organized-crime networks. They were a threat to all Americans, regardless of their political views or economic circumstances. Not long after our meeting, Senator McClellan died before he could finish his term.

Despite his advice and the assurances of support for the Senate race that I'd received from around the state, I decided to run for governor. I was excited by the prospect of what I could accomplish, and I thought I could win. Though my age, thirty-one, was more likely to be an issue against me in a race for governor than one for the Senate, because of the heavy management and decision-making responsibilities, the competition wasn't as stiff as it was in the Senate race.

Four other candidates ran in the Democratic primary: Joe Woodward, a lawyer from Magnolia in south Arkansas who had been active in Dale Bumpers's campaigns; Frank Lady, a lawyer from northeast Arkansas, who was a conservative evangelical Christian, the favored candidate of the Moral Majority voters, and the first, but not the last, of my opponents to publicly criticize Hillary, explicitly for practicing law and implicitly for retaining her maiden name when we married; Randall Mathis, the articulate county judge of Clark County, just south of Hot Springs; and Monroe Schwarzlose, a genial old turkey farmer from southeast Arkansas. Woodward promised to be the strongest candidate. He was intelligent and articulate and had contacts all over the state because of his work with Bumpers. Still, I started with a big lead. All I had to do was keep it. Because all the real interest was in the Senate race, I just had to run hard, avoid mistakes, and go on doing a good job as attorney general.

Despite its relative lack of drama, the campaign had its interesting moments. The "tree story" surfaced again when a state policeman who was supporting Joe Woodward swore he had taken me out of that infamous tree back in 1969. In Dover, north of Russellville, I answered another challenge to my manhood by participating in a tug-of-war with a bunch of very large log haulers. I was the smallest man on either team and they put me in front. We pulled the rope back and forth across a hole full of water and mud. My side lost, and I wound up caked in mud, with my hands torn and bleeding from pulling the rope so hard. Fortunately, a friend who had urged me to compete gave me a new pair of khakis so that I could return to the campaign trail. In St. Paul, a town of about 150 near Huntsville, I was shaking hands with all the marchers in the Pioneer Day parade, but I chickened out when I saw a man walking right toward me with his pet on a leash. It was a full-grown bear. I don't know who was reassured by the leash, but I sure wasn't.

Believe it or not, tomatoes played a role in the 1978 campaign. Arkansas grows a lot of them in Bradley County, most of them picked by migrant laborers who travel from South Texas through Arkansas up the Mississippi River all the way to Michigan, following the warming weather and ripening crops. As attorney general, I had gone to Hermitage, in the southern part of the county, to a community meeting on the problems the small farmers were having in implementing new federal standards for their workers' housing. They simply couldn't afford it. I got them some help from the Carter administration so that they could build the required facilities and stay in business. The people were very grateful, and after I announced for governor they scheduled a Bill Clinton Appreciation Day, which included the high school band leading a parade down the main street. I was excited about it and glad a reporter from the *Arkansas Gazette* was driving down with me to cover the story. On the way, she asked me a lot of questions about the campaign and the issues. I said something that called into question my support for the death penalty, and that became the day's story. The whole town of Hermitage turned out, but the event, and the work that gave rise to it, remained a secret to the rest of the state. I complained about it for days until finally my staff decided the only way to shut me up was to make fun of me. They had T-shirts printed up with the words "You Should Have Seen the Crowd at Hermitage!" At least I got about all the votes down there and I learned to be more careful in dealing with reporters.

A few weeks later, I was back in Bradley County to work the tomato vote again at Warren's annual Pink Tomato Festival, and I entered the tomato-eating contest. Three of the seven or eight competitors were young men much bigger than I was. We each got a paper sack full of tomatoes, which had been carefully weighed. When the bell sounded, we ate as many as we could in the allotted time, which I think was five minutes, a long time for a crowd to watch grown men behave like pigs at the trough. Any part of the tomato that was not consumed had to be put back in the sack, so that the exact weight of tomatoes consumed could be determined. Like a fool, I tried to win. I always did. I finished third or fourth and felt pretty sick for a couple of days. It wasn't all for nothing, though; I got most of the votes in Warren, too. But I never entered the contest again.

The U.S. Congress had passed the equal-rights amendment to the Constitution and referred it to the states for ratification, but the requisite three-quarters of the state legislatures had not ratified it and never would. Even so, it was still a hot-button issue among Arkansas' social conservatives, for several reasons. Senator Kaneaster Hodges, whom David Pryor had appointed to finish Senator McClellan's term, had given an eloquent speech on the Senate floor in support of the ERA. Our friend Diane Kincaid had bested Phyllis Schlafly, the nation's leading opponent of the amendment, in a highly publicized debate before the Arkansas legislature. And Hillary and I were on record supporting it. The opponents of the ERA predicted an end to civilization as we knew it if the amendment passed: women in combat, unisex bathrooms, broken families where uppity women no longer were subject to their husbands.

Because of the ERA, I had a minor run-in with Frank Lady's supporters at a rally of about five hundred people in Jonesboro, in northeast Arkansas. I was giving my campaign speech outlining my proposals for education and economic development when an older woman in a Lady T-shirt started screaming at me, "Talk about the ERA! Talk about the ERA!" Finally I said, "Okay. I'll talk about it. I'm for it. You're against it. But it won't do as much harm as you think it will or as much good as those of us who support it wish it would. Now let's get back to schools and jobs." She wouldn't let it go. She screamed, "You're just promoting homosexuality!" I looked at her, smiled, and said, "Ma'am, in my short life in politics, I've been accused of everything under the sun. But you're the first person who ever accused me of promoting homosexuality." The crowd roared. Even some of the Lady supporters laughed. And then I got to finish my talk.

On primary election day, I got 60 percent of the vote and carried seventy-one of the seventy-five counties. The vote in the Senate race was split almost evenly among Pryor, Tucker, and Thornton. The governor got 34 percent, and Jim Guy Tucker got a few more votes than Ray Thornton, so there would be a runoff. The conventional wisdom was that Pryor was in trouble because, as an incumbent governor, he should have polled well over 40 percent. Because I liked him and had enjoyed working with him in state government, I urged him to seek advice from my new pollster, Dick Morris, a young political consultant who had been active in New York City politics. Morris was a brilliant, abrasive character, brimming with ideas about politics and policy. He believed in aggressive, creative campaigns, and was so cocksure about everything that a lot of people, especially in a down-home place like Arkansas, found him hard to take. But I was stimulated by him. And he did me a lot of good, partly because I refused to be put off by his manner and partly because I had good instincts about when he was right and when he wasn't. One thing I really liked about him was that he would tell me things I didn't want to hear.

In the fall campaign, my opponent was a cattleman and the chairman of the state Republican Party, Lynn Lowe. The race was uneventful except for the press conference on the steps of the Capitol in which his campaign accused me of being a draft dodger. I referred them to Colonel Holmes. I won the election with 63 percent of the vote, carrying sixty-nine of the seventy-five counties.

At thirty-two, I was the governor-elect of Arkansas, with two months to assemble a staff, put together a legislative program, and wrap up my work as attorney general. I had really enjoyed the job, and thanks to the hard work and dedication of a fine staff, we had accomplished a lot. We cleaned out the backlog of requests for legal opinions, issuing a record number of them; recovered more than $400,000 in consumer claims, more than in the previous five years of the division's existence combined; told the state boards that regulate professions that they could no longer ban price advertising by the professional groups they regulated, a common practice in those days all across America; pushed for better nursing-home care and an end to age discrimination against the elderly; intervened in more utility-rate hearings than the office had ever done before, saving the ratepayers millions of dollars; drafted and passed legislation to compensate victims of violent crime; and protected the privacy rights of citizens with regard to personal information held by state agencies. One other thing I accomplished was especially important to me. I convinced the required three-quarters of both legislative chambers to amend the state's voting rights law to restore the right to vote to convicted felons upon completion of their sentences. I argued that once the offender had paid in full, he should be restored to full citizenship. I did it for Jeff Dwire, a hardworking, tax-paying citizen, who never got a pardon and who died a thousand deaths every election day. Sadly, more than twenty-five years later the federal government and most states still haven't followed suit.

TWENTY-ONE

WE STARTED PLANNING for my first term after the primary election in May and really got going after November, converting the headquarters into a transition office. Rudy Moore and Steve Smith, who had both served in the legislature, helped me as we prepared budgets, drafted bills to enact my policy priorities, analyzed the major management challenges, and began to hire a staff and cabinet.

In December, the Democratic Party held its midterm convention in Memphis. I was asked to travel across the Mississippi River to moderate a health-care panel featuring Joe Califano, President Carter's secretary of health, education, and welfare, and Senator Edward Kennedy, the Senate's chief advocate for universal health coverage. Califano was articulate in his defense of the President's more incremental approach to health-care reform, but Kennedy won the crowd with an emotional plea for ordinary Americans to have the same coverage that his wealth provided for his son, Teddy, when he got cancer. I enjoyed the experience and the national exposure, but was convinced that the convention only highlighted our intra-party differences, when it was supposed to unite and reinvigorate Democrats in nonpresidential election years. The midterm meetings were later abandoned.

Not long before Christmas, Hillary and I took a much-needed vacation to England. We spent Christmas Day with my friend from Oxford Sara Maitland and her husband, Donald Lee, an American who had become a priest in the Church of England. It was Donald's first Christmas church service. He had to be a little nervous, but he began the service with a surefire winner, a children's sermon. He sat down on the steps in front of a lovely nativity scene and asked all the children to come and sit with him. When they settled down, he said, "Children, this is a very special day." They nodded. "Do you know what day this is?" "Yes," they said. Donald beamed and asked, "What day is it?" In unison, they all shouted, "Monday!" I don't know how he carried on. Perhaps he was consoled by the fact that in his church, kids told the literal truth.

In a month, it was time to move into the Governor's Mansion and get ready for the inauguration. The mansion was a big colonial-style house of about ten thousand square feet in the beautiful old Quapaw Quarter of Little Rock, not far from the Capitol. The main house was flanked by two smaller ones, with the one on the left serving as a guesthouse and the one on the right providing a headquarters for the state troopers who watched the place and answered the phone twenty-four hours a day. The mansion had three large, handsome public rooms, a big kitchen, and a little breakfast room on the first floor; a spacious basement, which we converted into a rec room complete with pinball machine; and living quarters on the second floor. Despite its overall size, the mansion's living area occupied just five small rooms and two modest bathrooms. Still, it was such a step up from our little house on L Street that we didn't have enough furniture to fill the five rooms.

The hardest thing about the transition was getting used to the security. I had always prided myself on my self-sufficiency and prized my private time. I had been self-supporting since I was twenty, and over the years had gotten used to cleaning house, running errands, and cooking. When Hillary and I got together, we shared the household duties. Now other people cooked the meals, cleaned the house, and ran the errands. Since I was sixteen, I had enjoyed driving alone in my own car, listening to music and thinking. I couldn't do that anymore. I liked to jog every day, usually before or after work. Now, I was being followed by a trooper in an unmarked car. It really bothered me at first—it made me want to run up one-way streets the wrong way. In time I got used to it and came to appreciate the work the folks at the mansion and the troopers did; they gave me more time for the job. Because the troopers drove me, I got a lot of paperwork done in transit. Eventually we agreed that I'd drive myself to church on Sundays. It wasn't much of a concession, since my church and the Methodist church Hillary attended were both within a mile of the mansion, but I really looked forward to my Sunday freedom ride. One of the troopers ran with me when he was on duty, and I liked that a lot better than being followed. After I had been in office several years and there was clearly no imminent threat, I often ran alone in the mornings, but along a predictable downtown route with lots of people around. Frequently I ended those runs at the McDonald's or the local bakery, both about a half mile from the mansion, where I'd get a cup of water, then walk back home.

The troopers did have real security work to do on occasion. In my first term, an escapee from one of our mental institutions called the mansion and said he was going to kill me. Since he had decapitated his mother a few years earlier, they took it seriously. He was caught and returned to confinement, which might have been his subconscious desire when he called. One day, a massive man carrying a railroad spike walked into the governor's office and said he needed to meet with me all alone. He was not admitted. In 1982, when I was trying to regain the governor's office, a man called and said he'd had a message from God telling him my opponent was the instrument of the Lord and I was the instrument of the devil and he was going to do God's will and eliminate me. He turned out to be an escapee from a Tennessee mental institution. He had an odd-caliber revolver and went from gun store to gun store trying to buy ammunition for it, and because he couldn't produce any identification, he didn't succeed. Still, I had to wear an uncomfortable bulletproof jacket for several days near the end of the campaign. Once, when the front door was accidentally left unlocked, a deranged but harmless woman got halfway up the stairs to our living quarters before the troopers caught her as she was calling out to me. Another time, a small, wiry man in combat boots and shorts was apprehended trying to break down the front door. He was high on some kind of drug mixture that made him so strong it took two troopers bigger than I am to subdue him, and then only after he'd thrown one of them off and put his head through a window in the troopers' quarters. He was carried away in a straitjacket strapped to a stretcher. Later, when he sobered up, the man apologized to the troopers and thanked them for keeping him from doing anyone harm.

The troopers who served me became an issue in my first term as President when two of them who were disgruntled and had financial problems spread stories about me for a modest amount of money and fame and the hope of a bigger payoff. But most of those who served on the security detail were fine people who did their jobs well, and several of them became good friends. In January 1979, I wasn't sure I'd ever get used to twenty-four-hour security coverage, but I was so excited about my job I didn't have much time to think about it.

In addition to the traditional inaugural ball, we hosted a night of Arkansas entertainment called "Diamonds and Denim." All the performers were Arkansans, including the great soul singer Al Green, who later turned to gospel music and the ministry, and Randy Goodrum, the pianist in our high school trio, the 3 Kings. At thirty-one, he had already won a Grammy award for his songwriting. I joined him on sax for "Summertime," the first time we'd played together since 1964.

The inauguration was a big event. Hundreds of people from all over the state came, as did friends Hillary and I had made over the years, including my old roommate Tommy Caplan; Dave Matter, who managed my losing campaign at Georgetown; Betsey Wright; my pro–civil rights Boys Nation buddies from Louisiana, Fred Kammer and Alston Johnson; and three friends from Yale, Carolyn Ellis, Greg Craig, and Steve Cohen. Carolyn Yeldell Staley also came home from Indiana to sing.

I worked hard on my inaugural address. I wanted both to capture the historical moment and to tell my fellow Arkansans more about the values and ideals I was bringing to the governor's office. The night before, Steve Cohen had given me an idea I added to the speech when he'd said he was feeling two things he hadn't in a long time, "pride and hope." I said some things in that speech that I believe as strongly today as I did then, words that capture what I've tried to do in all my public work, including the presidency:

> For as long as I can remember, I have believed passionately in the cause of equal opportunity, and I will do what I can to advance it.
>
> For as long as I can remember, I have deplored the arbitrary and abusive exercise of power by those in authority, and I will do what I can to prevent it.
>
> For as long as I can remember, I have rued the waste and lack of order and discipline that are too often in evidence in governmental affairs, and I will do what I can to diminish them.
>
> For as long as I can remember, I have loved the land, air, and water of Arkansas, and I will do what I can to protect them.
>
> For as long as I can remember, I have wished to ease the burdens of life for those who, through no fault of their own, are old or weak or needy, and I will try to help them.
>
> For as long as I can remember, I have been saddened by the sight of so many of our independent, industrious people working too hard for too little because of inadequate economic opportunities, and I will do what I can to enhance them. . . .

The next day I went to work for what would prove to be two of the most exhilarating and exhausting, rewarding and frustrating years of my life. I was always in a hurry to get things done, and this time my reach often exceeded my grasp. I think a fair summary of my first gubernatorial term is that it was a policy success and a political disaster.

In the legislative session I had two major spending priorities, education and highways, and a host of other substantive reforms in health, energy, and economic development. In 1978, Arkansas ranked last among all states in per capita education spending. A study of our schools conducted by Dr. Kern Alexander, a nationally recognized expert in education policy from the University of Florida, concluded that our system was dismal: "From an educational standpoint, the average child in Arkansas would be much better off attending the public schools of almost any other state in the country." We had 369 school districts, many too small to offer needed courses in math and science. There were no state standards or evaluation systems. And teacher pay was pitifully low in most places.

The legislature passed almost all my education proposals, prodded by the Arkansas Education Association, which represented most of the teachers; the associations representing the administrators and school board members; and pro-education legislators, including Clarence Bell, the powerful chairman of the Senate Education Committee. They approved a 40 percent increase in funding over the next two years, including a $1,200 teacher pay raise in each year; a 67 percent increase for special education; increases for textbook costs, transportation, and other operations; and, for the first time, aid to school districts for programs for gifted and talented children and for transporting kindergarten students, a big step toward universal kindergarten.

The money was tied to efforts to raise standards and improve quality, something I always tried to do. We passed the first state programs mandating testing to measure pupil performance and indicate areas that needed improvement, a requirement that all teachers take the National Teacher Examination before they could be certified, and a bill prohibiting the firing of teachers for "arbitrary, capricious, or discriminatory" reasons. We also established the Arkansas Governor's School for gifted and talented students, which met for the first time at Hendrix College in the summer of 1980. Hillary and I spoke to the first class. It was one of my proudest achievements, and it's still going strong.

In two other areas I was less successful. The Alexander report recommended reducing the number of school districts to two hundred, which would have saved a lot of money on administrative costs. But I couldn't even pass a bill to create a commission to study it, because so many small towns believed that if they didn't have their own districts, "city folks" would close their schools and destroy their communities.

The other area in which I met resistance involved the formula by which school aid was distributed. Several school districts had filed a suit contending that our system was unfair, and that, when coupled with differences in local property-tax revenues, the inequalities in spending per child across the state were so great they were unconstitutional. The formula didn't take adequate account of differences in property values or student population shifts, and it gave more money per student to the very small districts, where the overhead costs per student were much higher. This system was hard to change, because giving more to some districts meant giving less to others. Both groups were well represented in the legislature, and when the losers saw the printouts showing what the changes would do to their districts, they fought hard to stop them. We adjusted the formula, but not by much. It would take a 1983 state supreme court decision invalidating the school formulas before we could really change things.

The highway program I proposed was designed to deal with the deterioration of our state highways, county roads, and city streets, and the need for new construction. Arkansas hadn't had a good road program in more than a decade, and potholes and slow travel were costing people time and money. There was a lot of support for a road program, but there were big disagreements about how to fund it. I proposed a hefty tax package featuring large increases for heavy trucks, which did most of the damage, and substantial ones for cars. At the time, car tags, like truck licenses, were priced according to vehicle weight. I thought this was unfair, since the weight differences for cars, unlike trucks, were not significant in terms of road damage, and the heavier cars were older and usually belonged to people with lower incomes. Instead, I proposed to set fees for car tags based on the value of the car, with the owners of the most expensive new ones paying $50 and of the oldest, least valuable paying $20. Under my proposal, the owners of old, heavy cars would not have had to pay more.

Some of the seasoned legislators said we shouldn't raise the license fees at all, and instead should finance the road program with an increase in fuel taxes. Organized labor was against that because ordinary drivers would have to pay substantially more over the course of a year, though they wouldn't feel it since the tax would be buried in the price of fuel purchases. I agreed with labor on the merits, but a gas-tax increase would have been far less politically damaging than what I did.

None of the organized groups except the highway contractors supported my proposal. The trucking, poultry, and timber interests said they couldn't afford the increases on their big trucks, and they got them reduced. The new-car dealers said I wanted to charge their customers too much, and licensing based on value would be an administrative nightmare. I thought their arguments were particularly weak, but the legislature bought them. The highway lobby was represented in the Senate by Knox Nelson, a wily legislator and road contractor himself, who wanted the money but didn't really care how it was raised. In the end, the legislature approved a large increase in revenue from car tags but within the old weight structure, nearly doubling the price for heavy cars from $19 to $36. I had a decision to make. I could sign the bill into law and have a good road program paid for in an unfair way, or veto it and have no road program at all. I signed the bill. It was the single dumbest mistake I ever made in politics until 1994, when I agreed to ask for a special prosecutor in the Whitewater case when there was not a shred of evidence to justify one.

In Arkansas, people's car license fees come due every year on their birthdays, when they have to go to the revenue offices in their local counties to renew them. After the increase went into effect on July 1, every single day, for a whole year, a new group of people would come into their revenue offices to find their birthday present from me: the price of their car tags had doubled. Many of them were country people who had driven more than twenty miles to the county seat to buy their new tags. Often they had no checkbooks and had brought only enough cash to pay the previous cost of the tags, so they had to drive all the way back home, get more cash out of the family stash, and come back. When they got back and had to wait in line, as they often did, the only thing they had to look at in the spartan revenue offices was a picture of the governor smiling down on them.

In late 1978, when I was first elected governor, Hilary Jones had made a prophetic comment to me. He said the hill people had carried me through three elections, but I would have to get my votes in the cities now. When I asked him why, he replied that I was going to work on schools and economic development, which the state needed, but that anything I did to raise school standards would threaten the rural schools; that I'd never be able to get many new jobs into poor rural areas; and that the recent U.S. Supreme Court ruling that government employees who weren't in policy-making positions could no longer be replaced for political reasons meant that I couldn't even fire the current state employees in the rural counties and bring our people in. "I'll still do all I can for you," Hilary said, "but it'll never be like it was up here again." As he was about so many things, Hilary was right on target. Over the course of my winning campaigns for governor, I got more and more support from independent and Republican voters in the cities and suburbs, but I never recovered the depth of support I had enjoyed among white rural voters in the Third District and much of the rest of the state. Now, on top of all the things I couldn't help, I had shot myself in the foot with the car-tag increase, blowing five years of hard work among rural Arkansans—and a lot of blue-collar city people, too— with the stroke of a pen.

The pattern of good policy and bad politics wasn't confined to legislative matters. I organized the governor's office without a chief of staff, giving different areas of responsibility to Rudy Moore, Steve Smith, and John Danner, a policy analyst from California whose wife, Nancy Pietrafesa, was an old friend of Hillary's. Nancy was working in the administration, too, on education. President Kennedy had organized his White House in a similar way, but his guys all had short hair, boring suits, white shirts, and dark, narrow ties. Rudy, Steve, and John all had beards and were less constrained in their dress code. My conservative critics in the legislature had a field day with them. Eventually, several inter-office conflicts broke out. I decided to make Rudy chief of staff, have Steve oversee a lot of the policy initiatives, and release John Danner and his wife, Nancy, from their responsibilities. With an inexcusable loss of nerve, I asked Rudy to tell them. He did it and they quit. Although I tried to talk to them about it later, our relationship never recovered. I doubt that they ever forgave me for not handling it myself, and I don't blame them. They were good people who worked hard and had good ideas; through inexperience, I had put them in an impossible situation. It was my mistake.

I also got into hot water for bringing in a lot of people from out of state to run the Department of Health, the Department of Human Services and its divisions of Social Services and Mental Health, the Department of Education, and the new Department of Energy. They were able and well intentioned, but they needed more contacts and experience dealing with their constituencies to make the big changes we were seeking.

These problems were aggravated by my own lack of experience and my youth. I looked even younger than my thirty-two years. When I became attorney general, George Fisher, the talented cartoonist for the *Arkansas Gazette*, drew me in a baby carriage. When I became governor he promoted me to a tricycle. It wasn't until I became President that he took me off the tricycle and put me in a pickup truck. And he was a supporter. It should have set off an alarm bell, but it didn't.

After a nationwide search, Dr. Robert Young, who had run a successful rural health clinic in West Virginia, was appointed director of the Department of Health. I wanted him to deal with the serious problems of health-care access and quality in Arkansas' rural areas. Dr. Young and Orson Berry, director of the Rural Health Office, came up with an innovative plan to establish clinics that required a doctor to be in attendance at least once every two weeks, with nurse practitioners and physician's assistants manning them full-time and providing the diagnostic services and treatment for which they were trained. Despite the insufficient number of doctors willing to practice in rural areas, studies showed that most patients preferred a nurse practitioner or physician's assistant because they spent more time with patients; and a nurse-midwife program in Mississippi County had cut the infant mortality rate there in half.

Arkansas doctors strongly opposed the plan. Dr. Jim Webber, representing the family physicians, said, "We don't believe a little bit of care is better than nothing." Notwithstanding the doctors' opposition, the Carter administration approved a grant funding our plan. We opened four rural clinics, started building three others, and expanded the Mississippi County Nurse Midwife Program with nurse practitioners. And the work we did won praise across the nation.

We tried to work with the physicians whenever we could. I supported appropriations to build an intensive-care nursery at the Arkansas Children's Hospital to care for extremely premature and other endangered newborns, and to establish a radiation-therapy institute at the University Medical Center to provide better treatment to cancer patients. I appointed Hillary to chair a Rural Health Advisory Committee, to recommend further improvements and help prioritize the large number of requests for help from rural communities. We worked harder to recruit doctors to rural areas, set up a loan fund to provide up to $150,000 of state money to any doctor who would set up a clinic in a town with six thousand or fewer people, and allowed family practitioners in small towns to apply for $6,000 a year in income supplements. The doctors strongly supported all these initiatives, which were especially remarkable because the economic downturn in 1980 forced severe cutbacks in the Department of Health's budget. Still, the doctors never forgave Dr. Young, or me, for not consulting them more and not going more slowly on the rural health clinics. By August 1980, the Arkansas Medical Society was asking for his resignation. When I left office in 1981, some of my initiatives were cut back, illustrating the point that you can have good policy without good politics, but you can't give people good government without both.

Energy was a huge issue because of OPEC's steep increases in the price of oil, which raised prices for everything else, too. In this area, we had good policy and better politics, though I still made some powerful enemies. I got the legislature to upgrade the Arkansas Energy Office to a cabinet-level department and attempted to build a broad coalition of ratepayers, utilities, businesses, and government to save ratepayers money; give utilities, businesses, and homeowners incentives to promote conservation; and help develop new sources of clean energy. I thought we could become more self-sufficient and a national leader in both conservation and alternative fuels. We passed legislation allowing tax deductions for energy conservation and renewable energy expenditures for residential, commercial, and industrial use, and exempted mixed fuels that were at least 10 percent alcohol from the state gas tax. We provided energy audits to industrial and commercial businesses and gave 50 percent matching grants to schools, hospitals, and other public institutions for the purchase and installation of energy conservation programs. The federal government provided funds for such initiatives, and we were the first state in the country to get them. When I took office, according to federal government statistics our energy conservation program was the worst in the country. After a year, we ranked ninth overall and third in industrial conservation.

Our efforts at utility regulation were mostly successful but much more controversial. I wanted the Energy Department to be able to intervene in the Public Service Commission's rate hearings and to be able to get information on, and inspect, nuclear power facilities. The legislature, prodded by its senior member, Max Howell, who was liberal on education and taxes but close to the utilities, watered down my first request and refused to fund the second. When I persuaded Arkansas Power and Light to offer interest-free conservation loans to its customers and charge the cost of making them to the ratepayers, everyone who understood the issue applauded, knowing it was a far cheaper way of increasing energy availability than building new power plants. Unfortunately, a number of legislators, who thought conservation amounted to subversion of the free-enterprise system, raised so much hell that AP&L felt compelled to shelve the program. The utility did continue to support our extensive efforts to weatherize the homes of low-income people, which made them cooler in the summer and warmer in the winter, and cut their utility bills considerably.

Alas, even our conservation efforts didn't escape controversy. An investigative reporter discovered that one of the projects we funded was a boondoggle. It was designed to train low-income people to chop wood and distribute it to other poor people to burn in their stoves. The Special Alternative Wood Energy Resources project had a descriptive acronym, SAWER, but a lousy record. It had spent $62,000 to train six woodchoppers and cut three cords of wood. I fired the director and got someone else who fixed the program, but it was the waste that stuck in the public's mind. To most Arkansans, $62,000 was a lot of money.

On the regulatory front, we were outgunned on two big issues. First, we did our best to stop what was called "pancaking" by utilities. If they asked for a 10 percent rate increase and got only 5 percent, they could collect the 10 percent while they appealed the decision in court. Meanwhile, they could file for another rate increase and do it all over again, thus pancaking unapproved rates on top of one another. Even if the utilities lost their appeals, which they usually did, the effect of the pancaking was to force ratepayers, including many poor people, to give them massive low-interest loans. It was wrong, but once again the utilities had more swat with the legislature than I did, killing the anti-pancaking bill in committee.

Second, I continued to fight with AP&L and its parent, Middle South Utilities, over the plan to make Arkansas ratepayers foot the bill for 35 percent of the Grand Gulf nuclear plants in Mississippi, while AP&L proposed to build six coal-fired plants in Arkansas, and demand for electricity in our state was declining so much that AP&L was planning to sell electricity from one of its existing plants to out-of-state users. Under the law, utilities were entitled to a profit, euphemistically called a "rate of return," on all their expenses. And under the Grand Gulf plan, Arkansas ratepayers would have to pay for more than a third of the construction costs, plus the rate of return, even if they never used any of the power. AP&L had no ownership in the plant; it belonged to an independent subsidiary with no ratepayers, and its construction and financing plan had to be approved only by the federal government, which subjected the project to far less than adequate scrutiny. When these facts were published in the *Arkansas Gazette* they caused a firestorm of protest. AP&L was urged to pull out of Grand Gulf by the chairman of the Public Service Commission. We organized a massive postcard campaign to the Federal Energy Regulatory Commission, urging it to reverse the Grand Gulf decision and give Arkansas relief. All to no avail.

The Grand Gulf arrangement was eventually upheld by the District of Columbia Court of Appeals, which had jurisdiction over cases involving federal regulatory agencies. The opinion was written by Judge Robert Bork, my old Constitutional Law professor. Just as he had been at Yale, he was all for states' rights when it came to restrictions on individual liberty. On the other hand, when big business was involved, he thought the federal government should have the final say and protect business from meddlesome state efforts to look out for ordinary citizens. In 1987, in testimony I researched and wrote myself for the Senate Judiciary Committee, Bork's decision in the Grand Gulf case was one of the grounds I cited for opposing his nomination to the U.S. Supreme Court.

I worked hard on an energy plan against stiff opposition, but I had made a powerful adversary in AP&L, which had offices in most counties. And I wasn't through making enemies. I was upset by what I thought were excessive clear-cutting practices by some of our timber companies and appointed Steve Smith to head a task force to look into it. Steve was still in his firebrand phase. He scared the timber folks and made them mad. All I wanted the clear-cutters to do was to reduce the size of their big cuts and leave adequate buffers along roads and streams to reduce soil erosion. My loudest critics claimed I wanted to put every log hauler and mill worker out of business. We got nowhere, and Steve got disgusted and went home to the hills not long afterward.

I even made some people mad in my economic development work. That's hard to do. I was determined to broaden the state's efforts beyond the traditional function of recruiting new industries, to include the expansion of existing industries and aid to small and minority businesses and farmers in marketing their products at home and abroad. We dramatically increased the activity of our state's European office in Brussels and I took the first Arkansas trade mission to the Far East—to Taiwan, Japan, and Hong Kong. We became the first state in America to have our own program for handling hazardous waste products approved by the federal government. We were also successful in the traditional work of recruiting new industries, with increased investments over previous years of 75 percent in 1979 and 64 percent in 1980. How could I make anybody mad with that record? Because I changed the name of the department, from the Arkansas Industrial Development Commission to the Department of Economic Development, to reflect its new, broader scope of activity. The AIDC, it turned out, was a sacred brand name to many influential businesspeople who had served on the commission and to local chamber of commerce directors all over the state who had worked with the agency. They were not satisfied by my appointment of Jim Dyke, a successful Little Rock businessman, to lead the new department. If I hadn't changed its name, I could have done all the same things without the adverse fallout. In 1979 and 1980, I seemed to have an affinity for adverse fallout.

I made a similar mistake in education. I appointed Dr. Don Roberts, superintendent of schools in Newport News, Virginia, to be director of education. Don had been an administrator in the Little Rock system a few years earlier, so he knew a lot of the players, and he had a friendly, low-key manner and got along well with most of them. He implemented the reforms I passed in the legislature, plus one of his own, a teacher-training program called PET, Program for Effective Teaching. The problem was that to get Don in, I had to ask for the resignation of the department's longtime director, Arch Ford. Arch was a fine gentleman who had devoted decades of dedicated service to Arkansas' schoolchildren. It was time for him to retire, though, and this time, I didn't make the mistake of letting someone else ask him to go. But I could have handled it better, giving him a big send-off and taking pains to make it look like his idea. I just blew it.

In the human services area, we got generally good reviews. We took the sales tax off prescription drugs, a measure especially helpful to seniors, and increased the homestead-property tax exemption for them by two-thirds. All told, more than twenty-five bills directly benefiting the elderly were passed, including tougher standards for nursing homes and an expansion of home health care.

Nineteen seventy-nine was the International Year of the Child. Hillary, who was serving as chair of the Arkansas Advocates for Children and Families, an organization she had helped to found, took the lead in pushing some meaningful changes, including passing a Uniform Child Custody Act to eliminate custody problems for families moving in and out of our state; reducing the average daily population of our youth-service detention centers by 25 percent; developing better inpatient and community-based treatment for severely disturbed children; and placing 35 percent more children with special needs in adoptive homes.

Finally, I got involved in welfare reform for the first time. The Carter administration named Arkansas one of a handful of states to participate in a "workfare" experiment, in which able-bodied food-stamp recipients were required to register for work in order to keep getting the stamps. The experience sparked my abiding interest in moving toward a more empowering, work-oriented approach to helping poor people, one that I carried with me all the way to the White House and the signing of the welfare reform bill of 1996.

As 1980 dawned, I felt good about the governorship

and my life. I had made some powerful interests angry, and gripes about the car tags were growing, but I had a long list of progressive legislative and administrative initiatives of which I was very proud.

In September, our friends Diane Kincaid and Jim Blair were married in Morriss and Ann Henry's backyard, where Hillary and I had had our wedding reception four years earlier. I performed the ceremony, as the Arkansas Constitution allows governors to do, and Hillary served as both bridesmaid and best man. The politically correct Blairs referred to her as "best person." I couldn't argue with that.

Besides being the best, Hillary was pregnant—very pregnant. We badly wanted to have a child and had been trying for some time without success. In the summer of 1979, we decided to make an appointment with a fertility expert in San Francisco as soon as we got back from a short vacation in Bermuda, but we had a wonderful time, so wonderful we never made it to San Francisco. Soon after we got home, Hillary found out she was pregnant. She kept working for several months, and we attended Lamaze classes in anticipation of my participating in a natural childbirth. I really enjoyed those classes and the time we spent with the other expectant parents, who were mostly middle-class working people just as excited as we were. A few weeks before her delivery date, Hillary was having a few problems. Her doctor told her she absolutely couldn't travel. We had complete confidence in him and understood that she had to observe his travel ban. Unfortunately, that meant she couldn't go with me to the annual Washington meeting of the National Governors Association, including dinner at the White House with President and Mrs. Carter. I went to the conference; took Carolyn Huber, who had left the Rose Law Firm to run the Governor's Mansion for us, to the White House dinner, called home every few hours, and returned as soon as I could on the night of February 27.

Fifteen minutes after I walked into the Governor's Mansion, Hillary's water broke, three weeks early. I was nervous as a cat, carrying around my list of Lamaze materials to take to Arkansas Baptist Hospital. The state troopers who worked at the mansion were nervous, too. I asked them to get the bag of ice cubes for Hillary to suck on while I gathered the other stuff. They did—a nine-pound bag, enough to last her through a week of labor. With the trunk loaded with Hillary's ice, the troopers got us to the hospital in no time. Soon after we arrived, we learned Hillary would have to give birth by cesarean section because the baby was "in breech," upside down in the womb. I was told that hospital policy did not permit fathers in the delivery room when an operation was necessary. I pleaded with the hospital administrator to let me go in, saying that I had been to surgeries with Mother and that they could cut Hillary open from head to toe and I wouldn't get sick or faint, whereas Hillary was on edge, because she had never been a hospital patient in her entire life and she needed me there. They relented. At 11:24 p.m., I held Hillary's hand and looked over the screen blocking her view of the cutting and bleeding to see the doctor lift our baby out of her body. It was the happiest moment of my life, one my own father never knew.

Our little girl was a healthy six pounds, one and three-quarters ounces, and she cried on cue. While Hillary was in the recovery room, I carried Chelsea out to Mother and anyone else who was available to see the world's most wonderful baby. I talked to her and sang to her. I never wanted that night to end. At last I was a father. Despite my love for politics and government and my growing ambitions, I knew then that being a father was the most important job I'd ever have. Thanks to Hillary and Chelsea, it also turned out to be the most rewarding.

When we got home from the hospital, Chelsea had a ready-made extended family in the Governor's Mansion staff, including Carolyn Huber and Eliza Ashley, who had cooked there forever. Liza thought I looked too young to be governor in part because I was thin; she said if I were "more stout" I'd look the part, and she was determined to make it happen. She's a great cook, and unfortunately she succeeded.

The Rose firm gave Hillary four months of parental leave to get Chelsea off to a good start. Because I was the boss, I could control when I went to the office, so I arranged my work to be home a lot in those first few months. Hillary and I talked often about how fortunate we were to have had that critical time to bond with Chelsea. Hillary told me that most other advanced countries provided paid parental leave to all citizens, and we believed that other parents should have the same priceless opportunity we'd had. I thought about those first months with Chelsea in February 1993, when I signed my first bill into law as President, the Family and Medical Leave Act, which allows most American workers three months off when a baby is born or a family member is ill. By the time I left office, more than thirty-five million Americans had taken advantage of the law. People still come up to me, tell me their stories, and thank me for it.

After we got Chelsea settled in, I went back to work in a year that would be dominated by politics and disasters. Often the two were indistinguishable.

One of the things candidates don't discuss much and voters don't consider carefully in races for governor or President is crisis management. How will the Chief Executive handle natural or man-made disasters? I had more than my fair share in my first term as governor. The state was deluged in winter ice storms when I took office. I called out the National Guard to get generators to people without electricity, clear rural roads, and pull vehicles out of ditches. In the spring of 1979, we had a string of tornadoes, which required me to ask President Carter to officially declare Arkansas a disaster area, making us eligible for federal funds. We opened disaster-assistance centers to help people who'd lost their homes, businesses, and farm crops. We had to do it all over again when the spring of 1980 brought more tornadoes.

In the summer of 1980, we had a terrible heat wave that killed more than one hundred people and brought the worst drought in fifty years. Senior citizens were most at risk. We kept the senior centers open longer and provided state and federal money to buy electric fans, rent air conditioners, and help pay electric bills. We also got strong support from the

Carter administration in the form of low-interest loans for poultry producers who'd lost millions of chickens, and farmers whose fields had burned up. The roads were collapsing under the heat, and we had a record number of fires, nearly eight hundred, forcing me to ban outdoor burning. Rural Arkansas was not in a positive frame of mind heading toward the November election.

Besides the natural disasters, we had some crises brought on by human accident or design. The damage they caused was more psychological than physical or financial, but it was profound. In the spring of 1979, the Ku Klux Klan and its national director, David Duke, decided to hold a meeting in Little Rock. I was determined to avoid the violence that had erupted between Klansmen and protesters recently during a similar rally in Decatur, Alabama. My public safety director, Tommy Robinson, studied the Decatur situation and put in place stringent security measures to avoid a repeat. We had a lot of state troopers and local police on the ground, with instructions to arrest people at the first sign of disorder. Eventually, six people were arrested, but no one was hurt, thanks largely to the deterrent effect of the large police presence. I felt good about how we handled the Klan situation, and it increased my confidence that we could deal properly with anything that might happen in the future. A year later, something much bigger came up.

In the spring of 1980, Fidel Castro deported 120,000 political prisoners and other "undesirables," many of them with criminal records or mental problems, to the United States. They sailed to Florida, seeking asylum and creating a massive problem for the Carter administration. I knew immediately that the White House might want to send some of the Cubans to Fort Chaffee, a large installation near Fort Smith, because it had been used as a relocation center in the mid-seventies for Vietnamese refugees. That relocation was largely successful, and many Vietnamese families were still living in western Arkansas and doing well.

When I discussed the issue with Gene Eidenberg, the White House official handling the Cuban issue for the President, I told him the Vietnamese effort had worked well in part because of preliminary screenings in the Philippines and Thailand to weed out those who shouldn't be admitted to the United States in the first place. I suggested he put an aircraft carrier or other large vessel off the coast of Florida and do the same kind of screening. I knew that most of the refugees weren't criminals or crazy, but they were being portrayed that way in the press, and the screening process would build public support for those who did come in. Gene said screening would be pointless because there was no place to send the rejects. "Sure there is," I said. "We still have a base at Guantánamo, don't we? And there must be a gate in the fence that divides it from Cuba. Take them to Guantánamo, open the door, and march them back into Cuba." Castro was making America look foolish and the President look powerless. Jimmy Carter already had his hands full with inflation and the Iranian hostage crisis; he didn't need this. My proposal seemed to me to be a good way for the President to look strong, turn lemons into lemonade, and pave the way for public acceptance of the refugees who were allowed to stay. When the White House dismissed my suggestion out of hand, I should have known we were in for a long, rough ride.

On May 7, the White House notified me that Fort Chaffee would be used to resettle some of the Cubans. I urged the White House to take strong security precautions and made a statement to the press saying the Cubans were fleeing "a Communist dictatorship" and pledging to "do all I can to fulfill whatever responsibilities the President imposes upon Arkansans" to facilitate their resettlement. By May 20, there were nearly twenty thousand Cubans at Fort Chaffee. Almost as soon as they arrived, disturbances by young, restless Cubans, tired of being fenced in and uncertain about their future, became a staple of daily life inside the fort. As I have said, Fort Smith was a very conservative community, and most people were none too happy in the first place about the Cubans coming. When reports of the disturbances were publicized, people in Fort Smith and nearby towns became frightened and angry, especially those who lived in the little town of Barling, which borders the fort. As Sheriff Bill Cauthron, who was strong and sensible throughout the crisis, said in an interview: "To say that they [local residents] are scared is an understatement. They are arming themselves to the teeth, and that only makes the situation more volatile."

On Monday night, May 26, a couple hundred refugees charged the barricades and ran out of the fort through an unguarded gate. At dawn the next morning, primary election day, I called sixty-five National Guardsmen to Fort Chaffee, flew to Fayetteville with Hillary to vote, then went to the fort, where I spent the day talking to people on the ground and at the White House. The commanding officer, Brigadier General James "Bulldog" Drummond, was an impressive man with a sterling combat record. When I complained that his troops had let the Cubans off base, he told me he couldn't stop them; he had been told by his immediate superior that a federal statute, the *posse comitatus* law, prohibits the military from exercising law-enforcement authority over civilians. Apparently, the army had concluded that the law covered the Cubans, though their legal status was uncertain. They weren't citizens or legal immigrants, but they weren't illegal aliens either. Since they had broken no law, Drummond was told he couldn't keep them at the fort against their will just because the local population detested and feared them. The general said his sole mission was to keep order on the base. I called the President, explained the situation, and demanded that someone be given authority to keep the Cubans on the base. I was afraid people in the area were going to start shooting them. There had been a run on handguns and rifles in every gun store within fifty miles of Chaffee.

The next day I again spoke to the President, who said that he was sending more troops and that they would maintain order and keep the Cubans inside the base. Gene Eidenberg told me that the Justice Department was sending the Pentagon a letter saying the military had the legal authority to do so. By the end of the day, I was able to relax a little and to ponder the primary election, in which my only opponent, the old turkey farmer Monroe Schwarzlose, got 31 percent of the vote, thirty times the vote he had received in

the 1978 primary. The rural folks were sending me a message about the car tags. I hoped they had gotten it out of
their system, but they hadn't.

On the night of June 1, all hell broke loose. One thousand Cubans ran out of the fort, right past federal troops,
and onto Highway 22, where they began walking toward
Barling. Once again, the troops didn't lift a finger to stop
them. So I did. The only barrier between the Cubans and
several hundred angry and armed Arkansans was composed
of state troopers under the command of Captain Deloin
Causey, a dedicated and coolheaded leader; the National
Guardsmen; and Sheriff Bill Cauthron's deputies. I had
given Causey and the National Guard strict instructions not
to let the Cubans pass. I knew what would happen if they
did: a bloodbath that would make the Little Rock Central
High crisis look like a Sunday afternoon picnic. The Cubans
kept coming at our people and began throwing rocks.
Finally, Causey told the state police to fire shots over their
heads. Only then did they turn around and go back to the
fort. When the smoke cleared, sixty-two people had been
injured, five of them from the shotgun blasts, and three of
Fort Chaffee's buildings had been destroyed. But no one
was killed or hurt too badly.

I flew up to Chaffee as soon as I could to meet with General Drummond. We had a real shouting match. I was out-
raged that his troops hadn't stopped the Cubans after the
White House had assured me the Pentagon had received
Justice Department approval to do so. The general didn't
flinch. He told me he took his orders from a two-star general in San Antonio, Texas, and no matter what the White
House had said to me, his orders hadn't changed. Drummond was a real straight shooter; he was obviously telling
the truth. I called Gene Eidenberg, told him what Drummond had said, and demanded an explanation. Instead I got
a lecture. Eidenberg said he'd been told I was overreacting
and grandstanding after my disappointing primary showing. It was obvious that Gene, whom I considered a friend,
didn't understand the situation, or me, as well as I had
thought he did.

I was fit to be tied. I told him that since he obviously didn't have confidence in my judgment, he could make the next decision: "You can either come down here and fix this right now, tonight, or I'm going to shut the fort down. I'll put National Guardsmen at every entrance and no one will go in or out without my approval."

He was incredulous. "You can't do that," he said. "It's a federal facility."

"That may be," I shot back, "but it's on a state road and I control it. It's your decision."

Eidenberg flew to Fort Smith on an air force plane that night. I picked him up, and before we went to the fort I took him on a tour of Barling. It was well after midnight, but down every street we drove, at every house, armed residents were on alert, sitting on their lawns, on their porches, and, in one case, on the roof. I'll never forget one lady, who looked to be in her seventies, sitting stoically in her lawn chair with her shotgun across her lap. Eidenberg was shocked by what he saw. After we finished the tour he looked at me and said, "I had no idea."

After the tour, we met with General Drummond and other federal, state, and local officials for an hour or so. Then we talked to the horde of press people who had gathered. Eidenberg promised that the security problem would be fixed. Later that day, June 2, the White House said the Pentagon had received clear instructions to maintain order and keep the Cubans on the base. President Carter also acknowledged that the people of Arkansas had suffered needless anxiety and promised that no more Cubans would be sent to Fort Chaffee.

Delays with the screening process seemed to be the root cause of the turmoil, and the people doing the screening made an effort to speed it up. When I went to visit the fort not long afterward, the situation was calmer and everyone seemed to be in a better frame of mind.

While things seemed to be settling down, I was still troubled by what had happened, or hadn't, between May 28, when Eidenberg told me the army had been ordered to keep the Cubans from leaving Chaffee, and June 1, when they let one thousand of them escape. Either the White House hadn't told me the truth, or the Justice Department was slow in getting its legal opinion to the Pentagon, or someone in the Pentagon had defied a lawful order of the Commander in Chief. If that's what happened, it amounted to a serious breach of the Constitution. I'm not sure the whole truth ever came out. As I learned when I got to Washington, after things go wrong, the willingness to take responsibility often vanishes.

In August, Hillary and I went to Denver for the summer meeting of the National Governors Association. All the talk was of presidential politics. President Carter seemed to have survived a vigorous challenge to his renomination from Senator Edward Kennedy, but Kennedy had not withdrawn. We had breakfast with the famous criminal lawyer Edward Bennett Williams, whom Hillary had known for years and who had wanted her to come to work for him after law school. Williams was strongly for Kennedy, and believed he'd have a better chance to defeat Ronald Reagan in the fall campaign because the President was bedeviled by a bad economy and the ten-month-long captivity of our hostages in Iran.

I disagreed with him on the politics and the merits. Carter had done a lot of good things as President, wasn't responsible for the OPEC price increases that had fueled the inflation, and had few good options for dealing with the hostage crisis. Besides, despite the problems with the Cubans, the Carter White House had been good to Arkansas, giving financial aid and support for our reform efforts in education, energy, health, and economic development. I had also been given remarkable access to the White House, for both business and pleasure. In the latter category, the best visit was when I took Mother to hear Willie Nelson sing on the South Lawn of the White House at a picnic the President hosted for NASCAR. After the event, Mother and I accompanied Nelson and the President's son Chip to the Hay-Adams Hotel, across Lafayette Square from the White House, where Willie sat at the piano and sang for us until two in the morning.

For all those reasons, I was feeling good about my relationship with the White House as the National Governors Association meeting began. The Democratic governors and their Republican counterparts held separate meetings. I had been elected vice chairman of the Democratic governors at the winter meeting, thanks to my nomination by Governor Jim Hunt of North Carolina, who would become one of my closest friends among the governors and an ally in the fight for education reform all the way through the White House years. Bob Strauss, the chairman of the Democratic National Committee, asked me to get the Democratic Governors Association to endorse President Carter over Senator Kennedy. After a quick canvass of the governors present, I told Strauss the vote would be twenty to four for Carter. We had a civilized debate, with Strauss speaking for the President and Governor Hugh Carey of New York arguing for Kennedy. After the 20–4 vote, Strauss and I spoke briefly to the press, touting the endorsement as a show of confidence in and political boost for President Carter at a time when he needed it.

About fifteen minutes later, I was told the White House was trying to reach me on the phone. Apparently the President wanted to thank me for helping line up the governors' support. Appearances can be deceiving. What the President wanted to tell me was that the weather was about to turn cold in Pennsylvania and Wisconsin, where the rest of the Cubans were being housed. Because those forts weren't insulated from the winter weather, he said it would be necessary to move the refugees. Then came the kicker. Now that the security problems were solved at Fort Chaffee, they would be moved there. I responded, "Mr. President, you promised that no more refugees would be sent to Arkansas. Send them to a fort in some warm place out west you're not going to win in November anyway." The President replied that he'd considered that but couldn't do it because it would cost $10 million to outfit a facility out west. I said, "Mr. President, your word to the people of Arkansas is worth $10 million." He disagreed, and we ended the conversation.

Now that I've been President, I have some idea of the

pressures Jimmy Carter was under. He was dealing with both rampant inflation and a stagnant economy. The American hostages in Iran had been held by the Ayatollah Khomeini for almost a year. The Cubans weren't rioting anymore, so they were the least of his problems. Pennsylvania and Wisconsin had both voted for him in 1976, and they had more electoral votes than Arkansas, which he had won with almost two-thirds of the vote. I was still more than twenty points ahead of my opponent, Frank White, in the polls, so how could I be hurt?

At the time I saw it differently. I knew the President would be hurt badly by breaking his commitment to Arkansas. Whether or not the forts in Wisconsin and Pennsylvania had to be closed for weather or for political reasons, sending the remaining Cubans to the one place he had promised not to, in order to save $10 million, was nuts. I called Rudy Moore and my campaign chairman, Dick Herget, to see what they thought I should do. Dick said I should fly directly to Washington to see the President. If I couldn't change his mind, I should talk to the press outside the White House and withdraw my support for his reelection. But I couldn't do that, for two reasons. First, I didn't want to look like a modern version of Orval Faubus and other southern governors who resisted federal authority in the civil rights years. Second, I didn't want to do anything to help Ronald Reagan beat Carter. Reagan was running a great campaign, with a big head of steam, fueled by the hostages, the bad economy, and the intense support of right-wing groups outraged about everything from abortion to Carter's turning the Panama Canal over to Panama.

Gene Eidenberg asked me not to announce the relocation until he could come to Arkansas and put the best face on it. The story leaked anyway, and Gene's visit to Arkansas did little to help. He made a convincing case that there would be no further security problems, but he couldn't deny that the President was breaking a clear commitment to the state that had been more supportive of him than any other outside his native Georgia. I won a larger role in controlling the security arrangements and made some improvements,

but I was still the President's man in Arkansas who had
failed to hold him to his word.

I returned home from Denver to a very volatile political
situation. My opponent in the general election, Frank White,
was gaining ground. White was a big man with a booming
voice and a bombastic style that belied his background as a
graduate of the Naval Academy, savings-and-loan executive,
and former director of the Arkansas Industrial Development
Commission under Governor Pryor. He had strong support
from all the interest groups I'd taken on, including utility,
poultry, trucking, and timber companies, and the medical
associations. He was a born-again Christian with the strong
backing of the state chapter of the Moral Majority and other
conservative activists. And he had the pulse of the country
people and blue-collar workers upset about the car tags. He
also had the advantage of a generally disgruntled mood, due
to the economy and the drought. When the bad economy led
state revenues to decline below projections, I was forced
to lower state spending to balance the budget, including education cuts that reduced the second year's $1,200 pay raise
for teachers to about $900. Many teachers didn't care about
the state's budget problems; they had been promised $1,200
for two years and they wanted the second installment. When
it didn't come, the intensity of their support for me faded
considerably.

Back in April, Hillary and I had seen Frank White at an
event and I told her that no matter what the polls said, he
was starting with 45 percent of the vote. I had made that
many people mad. After the announcement that all the
refugees would be housed at Fort Chaffee, White had his
mantra for the election: Cubans and Car Tags. That's all he
talked about for the rest of the campaign. I campaigned
hard in August but without much success. At factory gates,
workers changing shifts said they wouldn't vote for me
because I had made their economic woes worse and
betrayed them by raising the car tags. Once while campaigning in Fort Smith, near the bridge to Oklahoma, when I
asked a man for his support, he gave a more graphic version
of the answer I'd heard hundreds of times: "You raised my

car tags. I wouldn't vote for you if you were the only SOB on the ballot!" He was angry and red in the face. In exasperation, I pointed over the bridge to Oklahoma and said, "Look over there. If you lived in Oklahoma your car tags would be more than twice as expensive as they are now!" Suddenly all the red drained out of his face. He smiled, put his hand on my shoulder, and said, "See, kid, you just don't get it. That's one reason I live on this side of the border."

At the end of August, I went to the Democratic National Convention with the Arkansas delegation. Senator Kennedy was still in the race, though he was clearly going to lose. I had some good friends working for Kennedy who wanted me to encourage him to withdraw before the balloting and make a generous speech supporting Carter. I liked Kennedy and thought it was best for him to be gracious, so that he wouldn't be blamed if Carter lost. The blood between the two candidates was bad, but my friends thought I might be able to persuade him. I went to the senator's hotel suite and gave it my best shot. Kennedy ultimately did withdraw and endorse the President, though when they appeared on the platform together he didn't do a very good job of faking an enthusiasm he clearly didn't feel.

By convention time, I was the chairman of the Democratic Governors Association and was invited to give a five-minute address. National conventions are noisy and chaotic. The delegates normally listen only to the keynote address and the presidential and vice-presidential acceptance speeches. If you're not giving one of those three, your only chance of being heard over the constant din of floor talk is to be compelling and quick. I tried to explain the painful, profoundly different economic situation we were experiencing, and to argue that the Democratic Party had to change to meet the challenge. Ever since World War II, Democrats had taken America's prosperity for granted; their priorities were extending its benefits to more and more people and fighting for social justice. Now we had to deal with inflation and unemployment, big government deficits, and the loss of our competitive edge. Our failure to do so had driven more people to support Republicans or to join the growing cadre of alienated nonvoters. It was a good speech that took less than the allotted five minutes, but nobody paid much attention to it.

President Carter left the convention with all the problems he had when it started, and without the boost a genuinely enthusiastic, united party usually gives its nominee. I returned to Arkansas determined to try to salvage my own campaign. It kept getting worse.

On September 19, I was home in Hot Springs after a long day of politics when the commander of the Strategic Air Command called me to say that there had been an explosion in a Titan II missile silo near Damascus, Arkansas, about forty miles northwest of Little Rock. The story was unbelievable. An air force mechanic was repairing the missile when he dropped his three-pound wrench. It fell seventy feet to the bottom of the silo, bounced up, and punctured the tank full of rocket fuel. When the highly toxic fuel mixed with the air, it caused a fire, then a huge explosion that blew the 740-ton concrete top off the silo, killed the mechanic, and injured twenty other air force personnel who were near the opening. The explosion also destroyed the missile and catapulted its nuclear warhead into the cow pasture where the silo was located. I was assured that the warhead wouldn't detonate, that no radioactive material would be released, and that the military would remove it safely. At least my state wasn't going to be incinerated by Arkansas' latest brush with bad luck. I was beginning to feel snakebit, but tried to make the best of the situation. I instructed my new director of public safety, Sam Tatom, to work out an emergency evacuation plan with federal officials in case something went wrong with one of the seventeen remaining Titan II missiles.

After all the other things we'd been through, now Arkansas had the world's only cow pasture with its very own nuclear warhead. A few days after the incident, Vice President Mondale came to our state Democratic convention in Hot Springs. When I asked him to make sure the military cooperated with us on a new emergency plan for the missiles, he picked up the phone and called Harold Brown, the secretary of defense. His first words were "Damn it, Harold, I know I asked you to do something to get the Cuban problem off Arkansas' mind, but this is a little extreme." Contrary to his restrained public demeanor, Mondale had a great sense of humor. He knew we were both tanking, and he still made it funny.

The last few weeks of the campaign were dominated by a new phenomenon in Arkansas politics: completely negative television ads. There was a tough one on the car tags. But White's most effective campaign ad showed rioting Cubans, with a strong voice-over telling viewers that the governors of Pennsylvania and Wisconsin cared about their people and they got rid of the Cubans, but I cared more about Jimmy Carter than the people of Arkansas, "and now we've got them all." When Hillary and I first saw it, we thought it was so outrageous that no one would believe it. A poll taken right before the ad started running had shown that 60 percent of the people thought I'd done a good job at Fort Chaffee, while 3 percent thought I'd been too tough and 20 percent, the hard-core right, too weak. I could have satisfied them only by shooting every refugee who left the fort.

We were wrong about the ads. They were working. In Fort Smith, local officials, including Sheriff Bill Cauthron and Prosecuting Attorney Ron Fields, strongly defended me, saying I had done a good job and had taken risks to protect the people around the fort. As we all know now, a press conference will not counter the effect of a powerful negative ad. I was sinking in the quicksand of Cubans and car tags.

Several days before the election, Hillary called Dick Morris, whom I had replaced with Peter Hart because my people hated dealing with Dick's abrasive personality. She asked him to do a poll to see if there was anything we could do to pull it out. To his credit, Dick did the poll, and with characteristic bluntness said that I would probably lose. He made a couple of suggestions for ads, which we followed, but as he predicted, it was too little, too late.

On election day, November 4, Jimmy Carter and I got 48 percent of Arkansas' vote, down from his 65 percent in 1976 and my 63 percent in 1978. However, we lost in very

different ways. The President carried fifty of the seventy-five
counties, holding on to the Democratic strongholds where
the Cuban issue cut into but didn't eliminate his margin of
victory, and getting annihilated in the more conservative
Republican areas in western Arkansas, where there was a
high turnout, fueled by voters' anger over his broken pledge
on the Cubans, and by Reagan's alliance with Christian fundamentalists and their opposition to abortion and the
Panama Canal treaties. Arkansas still hadn't gone over to
the Republicans. Carter's 48 percent was seven points better
than his national percentage. If it hadn't been for the broken
pledge, he would have carried the state.

By contrast, I carried only twenty-four counties, including those with heavy black populations and a few where
there was more support for or less opposition to the highway program. I lost all eleven counties in Democratic northeast Arkansas, almost all the rural counties in the Third
District, and several in south Arkansas. I had been killed by
the car tags. The main effect of the Cuban ad was to take
away voters who had been supporting me despite their
reservations. Public approval of my performance on the
Cuban issue kept my poll ratings higher than they would
have been in the face of the car tags, the interest groups'
opposition, and the dour economic situation. What happened to me in 1980 was strikingly similar to what happened to President George H. W. Bush in 1992. The Gulf
War kept his poll numbers high, but underneath there was a
lot of discontent. When people decided they weren't going
to vote for him on the war issue, I moved ahead. Frank
White used the Cuban ad to do the same thing to me.

In 1980, I ran better than President Carter in the Republican areas in western Arkansas, where there was more
direct knowledge of how I had handled the Cuban situation.
In Fort Smith and Sebastian County, I actually led the
Democratic ticket, because of Fort Chaffee. Carter got 28
percent. Senator Bumpers, who had practiced law there for
more than twenty years but who had committed the unpar-
donable sin of voting to "give away" the Panama Canal, got
30 percent. I got 33 percent. That's how bad it was.

On election night I was in such bad shape I didn't think I could bear to face the press. Hillary went down to the headquarters, thanked the workers, and invited them to the Governor's Mansion the next day. After a fitful night's sleep, Hillary, Chelsea, and I met with a couple hundred of our die-hard supporters on the back lawn of the mansion. I gave them the best speech I could, thanking them for all they'd done, telling them to be proud of all we'd accomplished, and offering my cooperation to Frank White. It was a pretty upbeat talk considering the circumstances. Inside, I was full of self-pity and anger, mostly at myself. And I was filled with regret that I would no longer be able to do the work I loved so much. I expressed the regret but kept the whining and anger to myself.

At that moment, there didn't seem to be much future for me in politics. I was the first Arkansas governor in a quarter of a century denied a second two-year term, and probably the youngest ex-governor in American history. John McClellan's warning about the governor's office being a graveyard seemed prophetic. But since I had dug my own grave, the only sensible thing to do seemed to be to start climbing out.

On Thursday, Hillary and I found a new home. It was a pretty wooden house, built in 1911, on Midland Avenue in the Hillcrest area of Little Rock, not too far from where we'd lived before moving into the Governor's Mansion. I called Betsey Wright and asked her if she'd come help me get my files organized before I left office. To my joy, she agreed. She moved into the Governor's Mansion and worked every day with my friend State Representative Gloria Cabe, who had also been defeated for reelection after supporting all my programs.

My remaining two months in office were tough on my staff. They needed to find jobs. The usual route out of politics is through one of the big companies that do a lot of business with state government, but we had angered all of them. Rudy Moore did a good job trying to help everyone and make sure we cleared up all outstanding public business before we turned the office over to Frank White. He and my scheduler, Randy White, also reminded me, in my periods of self-absorption, that I needed to show more concern for my staff and their future welfare. Most of them had no savings to sustain a long job hunt. Several had young children. And many had worked only for the state, including a number of people who had been with me in the attorney general's office. Though I really liked the people who had worked for me and felt grateful to them, I'm afraid I didn't demonstrate that as clearly as I should have on many of the days after I lost.

Hillary was especially good to me in that awful period, balancing love and sympathy with an uncanny knack for keeping me focused on the present and the future. The fact that Chelsea didn't have a clue that anything bad had happened helped me realize that it was not the end of the world. I got great calls of encouragement from Ted Kennedy, who said I'd be back, and Walter Mondale, who showed extraordinary good humor in the face of his own disappointing defeat. I even went to the White House to say good-bye to President Carter and thank him for all the good things his administration had done to help Arkansans. I was still upset about his broken pledge and how it contributed to my defeat and led to his loss in Arkansas, but I felt history would be kinder to him because of his energy and environmental policies, especially the establishment of the massive Arctic National Wildlife Refuge in Alaska, and his accomplishments in foreign policy—the Camp David agreement between Israel and Egypt, the Panama Canal treaties, and the elevation of the human rights issue.

Like the rest of the employees of the governor's office, I had to find a job, too. I got several interesting offers or inquiries from out of state. My friend John Y. Brown, governor of Kentucky, who had made a fortune with Kentucky Fried Chicken, asked if I'd be interested in applying for the presidency of the University of Louisville. In typical John Y. short-speak, he made the pitch: "Good school, nice house, great basketball team." California governor Jerry Brown told me his chief of staff, Gray Davis, himself a future governor, was leaving and asked me to replace him. He said that he couldn't believe I'd been thrown out over car tags, that

California was a place full of people who had moved there from other states and I'd fit right in, and that he'd guarantee my ability to influence policy in areas I cared about. I was approached about taking over the World Wildlife Fund, a Washington-based conservation group, which did work I admired. Norman Lear, producer of some of the most successful television shows in history, including *All in the Family*, asked me to become head of the People for the American Way, a liberal group established to counter conservative assaults on First Amendment freedoms. And several people asked me to run for chairman of the Democratic National Committee against Charles Manatt, a successful Los Angeles lawyer with Iowa roots. The only job offer I got in Arkansas was from Wright, Lindsey & Jennings, a fine law firm, which asked me to become "of counsel" for $60,000 a year, almost twice what I'd made as governor.

I took a hard look at the Democratic committee job, because I loved politics and thought I understood what needed to be done. In the end, I decided it wasn't right for me. Besides, Chuck Manatt wanted it badly and probably already had the votes to win before I got interested. I discussed it with Mickey Kantor, a partner of Manatt's whom I had gotten to know when he served with Hillary on the board of the Legal Services Corporation. I liked Mickey a lot and trusted his judgment. He said if I wanted another chance at elected office, I shouldn't try for the party job. He also advised against becoming Jerry Brown's chief of staff. The other out-of-state jobs had some appeal to me, especially the one at the World Wildlife Fund, but I knew they didn't make sense. I wasn't ready to give up on Arkansas or myself, so I accepted the offer from Wright, Lindsey & Jennings.

Almost immediately after I lost, and for months afterward, I asked everybody I knew why they thought it had happened. Some of the answers, beyond Cubans, car tags, and making all the interest groups angry at the same time, surprised me. Jimmy "Red" Jones, whom I had appointed adjutant general of the Arkansas National Guard after he'd had a long career as state auditor, said I had alienated the voters with too many young beards and out-of-staters in important positions. He also thought Hillary's decision to keep her maiden name had hurt; it might be all right for a lawyer, but not for a first lady. Wally DeRoeck, who had been my chairman in 1976 and 1978, said I got so caught up in being governor that I stopped thinking about everything else. He told me that after I became governor, I never asked him about his children again. In harsher language, my friend George Daniel, who owned the hardware store in Marshall up in the hills, said the same thing: "Bill, the people thought you were an asshole!" Rudy Moore told me I had complained a lot about how much trouble I was in but never seemed to really focus on my political problems hard and long enough to figure out what to do about them. Mack McLarty, my oldest friend, who knew me like the back of his hand, said he thought I was preoccupied all year by the arrival of Chelsea. He said I had always been saddened by the fact that I never knew my own father, that I really wanted to focus on being Chelsea's father, except when something like the Cuban crisis tore me away, and that I just didn't have my heart in the campaign.

After I was out of office a few months, it became clear to me that all these explanations had some validity. By that time, more than a hundred people had come up to me and said they'd voted against me to send a message but wouldn't have done it if they'd known I was going to lose. I thought of so many things I could have done if I'd had my head on straight. And it was painfully clear that thousands of people thought I'd gotten too big for my britches, too obsessed with what I wanted to do and oblivious to what they wanted me to do. The protest vote was there, all right, but it didn't make the difference. The post-election polls showed that 12 percent of the voters said they'd supported me in 1978 but voted the other way in 1980 because of the car tags. Six percent of my former supporters said it was because of the Cubans. With all my other problems and mistakes, if I had been free of either of these two issues, I would have won. But if I hadn't been defeated, I probably never would have become President. It was a near-death experience, but an invaluable one, forcing me to be more sensitive to the political problems inherent in progressive politics: the system can absorb only so much change at once; no one can beat all the entrenched interests at the same time; and if people think you've stopped listening, you're sunk.

On my last day in the governor's office, after taking a picture of ten-month-old Chelsea sitting in my chair holding the telephone, I went up to the legislature to give my farewell address. I recounted the progress we'd made, thanked the legislators for their support, and pointed out that we still had America's second-lowest tax burden and that, sooner or later, we would have to find a politically acceptable way to broaden our revenue base to make the most of our potential. Then I walked out of the Capitol and into private life, a fish out of water.

TWENTY-TWO

WRIGHT, LINDSEY & JENNINGS WAS, by Arkansas standards, a large firm with a fine reputation and a varied practice. The support staff were able and friendly and went out of their way to help settle me in and make me feel at home. The firm also allowed me to bring my secretary, Barbara Kerns, who had been with me for four years by then and knew all my family, friends, and supporters. It even provided Betsey Wright office space so that she could keep working on my files and, as it turned out, plan the next campaign. I did some legal work and brought in a couple of modest clients, but I'm sure the lifeline the firm threw me didn't make it any money. All the firm really got out of it was my everlasting gratitude and some legal business defending me when I became President.

Though I missed being governor and the excitement of politics, I enjoyed the more normal pace of my life, coming home at a reasonable hour, being with Hillary as we watched Chelsea grow into her life, going out to dinner with friends, and getting to know our neighbors, especially the older couple who lived directly across the street, Sarge and Louise Lozano. They adored Chelsea and were always there to help out.

I resolved to stay away from public speaking for several months, with one exception. In February, I drove to Brinkley, about an hour east of Little Rock on the interstate, to speak at the Lions Club banquet. The area had voted for me in 1980, and my strongest supporters there all urged me to come. They said it would lift my spirits to be with folks who were still supporters, and it did. After the dinner, I went to a reception at the home of my county leaders, Don and Betty Fuller, where I was gratified and a little surprised to meet people who actually wanted me to be governor again. Back in Little Rock, most people were still trying to get on good terms with the new governor. One man whom I'd appointed to a position in state government and who wanted to stay on under Governor White actually crossed the street in downtown Little Rock one day when he saw me walking toward him. He was afraid to be seen shaking hands with me in broad daylight.

While I was grateful for the kindness of my friends in Brinkley, I didn't go out speaking again in Arkansas for several months. Frank White was beginning to make mistakes and lose some legislative battles, and I didn't want to get in his way. He kept his campaign pledge to pass bills changing the name of the Economic Development Department back to the Arkansas Industrial Development Commission and abolishing the Department of Energy. But when he tried to abolish the rural health clinics Hillary and I had established, large numbers of people who depended on them showed up to protest. His bill was defeated, and he had to be content with stopping the building of more clinics that would have served others who really needed them.

When the governor introduced a bill to roll back the cartag increase, the director of the Highway Department, Henry Gray, the highway commissioners, and the road builders put up strong resistance. They were building and repairing roads and making money. A lot of legislators listened to them, because their constituents liked the roadwork even if they had resisted paying for it. In the end, White got a modest rollback in the fees, but most of the money stayed in the program.

The governor's biggest legislative problem arose, ironically, out of a bill he passed. The so-called creation science bill required that every Arkansas school that taught the theory of evolution had to spend an equal amount of time teaching a theory of creation consistent with the Bible: that humans did not evolve out of other species around one hundred thousand years ago, but instead were created by God as a separate species a few thousand years ago.

For much of the twentieth century, fundamentalists had opposed evolution as being inconsistent with a literal reading of the biblical account of human creation, and in the early 1900s, several states, including Arkansas, outlawed the teaching of evolution. Even after the Supreme Court struck down such bans, most science texts didn't discuss evolution until the 1960s. By the late sixties, a new generation of fundamentalists were at it again, this time arguing that there was scientific evidence to support the Bible's creation story, and evidence that cast doubt on the theory of evolution. Eventually, they came up with the idea of requiring that schools that taught evolution had to give comparable attention to "creation science."

Because of intense lobbying efforts by fundamentalist groups like FLAG (Family, Life, America under God) and the governor's support, Arkansas was the first state to legally embrace the creation science notion. The bill passed without much difficulty: we didn't have many scientists in the legislature, and many politicians were afraid to offend the conservative Christian groups, who were riding high after electing a President and a governor. After Governor White signed the bill, there was a storm of protest from educators who didn't want to be forced to teach religion as science, from religious leaders who wanted to preserve the constitutional separation of church and state, and from ordinary citizens who didn't want Arkansas to become the laughingstock of the nation.

Frank White became an object of ridicule for the opponents of the creation science law. George Fisher, the *Arkansas Gazette* cartoonist who drew me on a tricycle, began presenting the governor with a half-peeled banana in his hand, implying that he hadn't fully evolved and was perhaps the proverbial "missing link" between humans and chimpanzees. When he started feeling the heat, Governor White protested that he hadn't read the bill before he signed it, digging himself into a deeper hole. Eventually, the creation science bill was declared unconstitutional by Judge Bill Overton, who did a masterly job at the trial and wrote a clear, compelling opinion saying the bill required the teaching of religion, not science, and therefore breached the Constitution's wall between church and state. Attorney General Steve Clark declined to appeal the decision.

Frank White had problems that went beyond the legislative session. His worst move was sending prospective appointees for the Public Service Commission to be interviewed by the Arkansas Power and Light Company, which had been seeking substantial increases in utility rates for the last few years. When the story came out, the press pounded the governor over it. People's electric rates were going up far more steeply than the car tags had. Now they had a governor who wanted to give AP&L prior approval of the people who would decide whether or not the company got to raise its rates even higher.

Then there were the verbal gaffes. When the governor announced a trade mission to Taiwan and Japan, he told the press how glad he was to be going to the Middle East. The incident gave George Fisher the inspiration for one of his funniest cartoons: the governor and his party getting off an airplane in the middle of a desert, complete with palm trees, pyramids, robed Arabs, and a camel. With banana in hand, he looks around and says, "Splendid! Whistle us up a rickshaw!"

While all this was going on, I made a few political trips out of state. Before I lost, I had been invited by Governor John Evans to speak at the Idaho Jefferson-Jackson Day dinner. After I got beat he asked me to come on anyway.

I went to Des Moines, Iowa, for the first time, to speak to a Democratic Party workshop for state and local officials. My friend Sandy Berger asked me to come to Washington to have lunch with Pamela Harriman, wife of the famous Democratic statesman Averell Harriman, who had been FDR's envoy to Churchill and Stalin, governor of New York, and our negotiator at the Paris peace talks with North Vietnam. Harriman met Pamela during World War II when she was married to Churchill's son and living at 10 Downing Street. They married thirty years later, after his second wife died. Pamela was in her early sixties and still a beautiful woman. She wanted me to join the board of Democrats for the 80's, a new political action committee she had formed to raise money and promote ideas to help Democrats come back into power. After the lunch, I accompanied

Pam to her first television interview. She was nervous and wanted my advice. I told her to relax and speak in the same conversational tone she'd used during our lunch. I joined her board and over the next few years spent a number of great evenings at the Harrimans' Georgetown house, with its political memorabilia and impressionist art treasures. When I became President, I named Pamela Harriman ambassador to France, where she had gone to live after World War II and the breakup of her first marriage. She was wildly popular and immensely effective with the French, and very happy there until she died, on the job, in 1997.

By the spring, the governor looked vulnerable in the next election and I began to think of a rematch. One day, I drove from Little Rock to Hot Springs to see Mother. About halfway there, I pulled into the parking lot of the gas station and store at Lonsdale. The man who owned it was active in local politics, and I wanted to see what he thought about my chances. He was friendly but noncommittal. As I walked back to my car, I ran into an elderly man in overalls. He said, "Aren't you Bill Clinton?" When I said I was and shook his hand, he couldn't wait to tell me he had voted against me. "I'm one of those who helped beat you. I cost you eleven votes—me, my wife, my two boys and their wives, and five of my friends. We just leveled you." I asked him why and got the predictable reply: "I had to. You raised my car tags." I pointed to a spot on the highway not far from where we were standing and said, "Remember that ice storm we had when I took office? That piece of road over there buckled and cars were stuck in the ditch. I had to get the National Guard to pull them out. There were pictures of it in all the papers. Those roads had to be fixed." He replied, "I don't care. I still didn't want to pay it." For some reason, after all he'd said, I blurted out, "Let me ask you something. If I ran for governor again, would you consider voting for me?" He smiled and said, "Sure I would. We're even now." I went right to the pay phone, called Hillary, told her the story, and said I thought we could win.

I spent most of the rest of 1981 traveling and calling around the state. The Democrats wanted to beat Frank

White, and most of my old supporters said they'd be with me if I ran. Two men with a deep love for our state and a passion for politics took a particular interest in helping me. Maurice Smith owned a 12,000-acre farm and the bank in his little hometown of Birdeye. He was about sixty years old, short and thin, with a craggy face and a deep, gravelly voice he used sparingly but to great effect. Maurice was smart as a whip and good as gold. He had been active in Arkansas politics a long time—and was a genuine progressive Democrat, a virtue his whole family shared. He didn't have a racist or an elitist bone in his body, and he had supported both my highway program and my education program. He wanted me to run again, and he was prepared to take the lead role in raising the funds necessary to win and in getting support from well-respected people who hadn't been involved before. His biggest coup was George Kell, who had made the Hall of Fame playing baseball for the Detroit Tigers and was still the radio announcer for the Tiger games. Throughout his stellar baseball career, Kell had kept his home in Swifton, the small northeast Arkansas town where he grew up. He was a legend there and had lots of admirers all over the state. After we got acquainted, he agreed to serve as the campaign treasurer.

Maurice's support gave my campaign instant credibility, which was important because no Arkansas governor had ever been elected, defeated, and elected again, though others had tried. But he gave me much more. He became my friend, confidant, and advisor. I trusted him completely. He was somewhere between a second father and an older brother to me. For the rest of my time in Arkansas, he was involved in all my campaigns and the work of the governor's office. Because Maurice loved the give-and-take of politics, he was especially effective in pushing my programs in the legislature. He knew when to fight and when to deal. He kept me out of a lot of the trouble I'd had in the first term. By the time I became President, Maurice was in ill health. We spent one happy evening on the third floor of the White House reminiscing about our times together.

I never met a single person who didn't like and respect

Maurice Smith. A few weeks before he died, Hillary was back in Arkansas and went to the hospital to see him. When she returned to the White House, she looked at me and said, "I just love that man." In the last week of his life, we talked twice on the telephone. He told me he didn't think he'd get out of the hospital this time and just wanted me to know "I'm proud of everything we did together and I love you." It was the only time he ever said that.

When Maurice died in late 1998, I went home to speak at his funeral, something I had to do too much of as President. On the way down to Arkansas, I thought of all he had done for me. He was finance chairman of all my campaigns, master of ceremonies at every inauguration, my chief of staff, a member of the university board of trustees, director of the Highway Department, chief lobbyist for legislation for the disabled—the favorite cause of his wife, Jane. But most of all, I thought of the day after I lost the 1980 election, when Hillary, Chelsea, and I were standing on the lawn of the Governor's Mansion. As I slumped under the weight of my defeat, a small man put his hand on my shoulder, looked me in the eye, and said in that wonderful raspy voice, "That's all right. We'll be back." I still miss Maurice Smith.

The other man in that category was L. W. "Bill" Clark, a man I barely knew before he sought me out in 1981 to discuss what I'd have to do to regain the governor's office. Bill was a strongly built man who loved a good political fight and had a keen understanding of human nature. He was from Fordyce in southeast Arkansas and owned a mill that shaped white oak lumber into staves for the casks that hold sherry and whiskey. He sold a lot of them in Spain. He also owned a couple of Burger King restaurants. One day in the early spring, he invited me to go to the races with him at Oaklawn Park in Hot Springs. I had been out of office only a couple of months, and Bill was surprised that so few people came up to our box to say hello. Instead of discouraging him, the cool treatment I got fired his competitive instincts. He decided he was going to get me back to the governor's office come hell or high water. I went to his Hot Springs lake house several times in 1981 to talk politics and meet friends he was trying to recruit to help us. At those small dinners and parties, I met several people who agreed to take leading roles in the campaign in south Arkansas. Some of them had never supported me before, but Bill Clark brought them over. I owe Bill Clark a lot for all he did for me over the next eleven years, to help me win elections and pass my legislative program. But mostly I owe him for believing in me at a time when I wasn't always able to believe in myself.

While I was out on the hustings, Betsey Wright was working hard to get the mechanics in place. In the last several months of 1981, she, Hillary, and I talked to Dick Morris about how to launch my campaign, flying to New York at Dick's suggestion to meet with Tony Schwartz, a famous expert in political media, who rarely left his Manhattan apartment. I found Schwartz and his ideas about how to influence both the thoughts and feelings of voters fascinating. It was clear that if I wanted to win in 1982, just two years after being thrown out of office, I had to walk a fine line with Arkansans. I couldn't tell the voters they'd made a mistake in defeating me. On the other hand, if I wore the hair shirt too much, I would have a hard time convincing voters to give me another chance to serve. It was a problem we all thought hard about, as Betsey and I labored over the lists and devised strategies for the primary and general elections.

Meanwhile, as 1981 drew to a close, I took two very different trips that prepared me for the battle ahead. At the invitation of Governor Bob Graham, I went to Florida to address the state Democratic convention, which met in the Miami area every two years in December. I gave an impassioned plea for the Democrats to fight back in the face of Republican attack ads. I said it was all well and good to let them strike the first blow, but if they hit us hard below the belt, we should "take a meat ax and cut their hands off." It was a bit melodramatic, but the right wing had taken over the Republican Party and changed the rules of political combat, while their hero, President Reagan, smiled and appeared to stay above it all. The Republicans thought they could win election wars indefinitely with their verbal assault weapons. Perhaps they could, but I for one was determined never to practice unilateral disarmament again.

The other trip I took was a pilgrimage with Hillary to the Holy Land, led by the pastor of Immanuel Baptist Church, W. O. Vaught. In 1980, at Hillary's urging, I had joined Immanuel and begun to sing in the choir. I hadn't been a regular churchgoer since I left home for Georgetown in 1964, and I'd stopped singing in the church choir a few years before then. Hillary knew that I missed going to church, and that I admired W. O. Vaught because he had forsaken the hellfire-and-brimstone preaching of his early ministry in favor of carefully teaching the Bible to his congregation. He believed that the Bible was the inerrant word of God but that few people understood its true meaning. He immersed himself in the study of the earliest available versions of the scriptures, and would give a series of sermons on one book of the Bible or an important scriptural subject before going on to something else. I looked forward to my Sundays in the choir loft of the church, looking at the back of Dr. Vaught's bald head and following along in my Bible, as he taught us through the Old and New Testaments.

Dr. Vaught had been going to the Holy Land since 1938, ten years before the state of Israel came into being. Hillary's parents came down from Park Ridge to stay with Chelsea so that we could join the group he led in December 1981. We spent much of our time in Jerusalem, retracing the steps Jesus walked and meeting local Christians. We saw the spot where Christians believe Jesus was crucified and the small cave where Christ is believed to have been buried and from which He arose. We also went to the Western Wall, holy to Jews, and to the Muslim holy sites, the Al-Aqsa Mosque and the Dome of the Rock, the point from which Muslims believe Mohammed rose to heaven and his rendezvous with Allah. We went to the Church of the Holy Sepulcher; to the Sea of Galilee, where Jesus walked on water; to Jericho, possibly the world's oldest city; and to Masada, where a band of Jewish warriors, the Zealots, withstood a long, furious Roman assault until they were finally overcome and entered the pantheon of martyrs. Atop Masada, as we looked down on the valley below, Dr. Vaught reminded us that history's greatest armies, including those of Alexander the Great and Napoleon, had marched through it, and that the book of Revelation says that at the end of time, the valley will flow with blood.

That trip left a lasting mark on me. I returned home with a deeper appreciation of my own faith, a profound admiration for Israel, and for the first time, some understanding of Palestinian aspirations and grievances. It was the beginning of an obsession to see all the children of Abraham reconciled on the holy ground in which our three faiths came to life.

Not long after I got home, Mother got married to Dick Kelley, a food broker she had known for years and had been seeing for a while. She had been single for more than seven years, and I was happy for her. Dick was a big, attractive guy who loved the races as much as she did. He also loved to travel and did a lot of it. He would take Mother all over the world. Thanks to Dick, she went to Las Vegas often but also got to Africa before I did. The Reverend John Miles married them in a sweet ceremony at Marge and Bill Mitchell's place on Lake Hamilton, which ended with Roger singing Billy Joel's "Just the Way You Are." I would come to love Dick Kelley and grow ever more grateful for the happiness he brought Mother, and me. He would become one of my favorite golf companions. Well into his eighties, when he played his handicap and I played mine, he beat me more than half the time.

In January 1982, golf was the last thing on my mind; it was time to start the campaign. Betsey had taken to Arkansas like a duck to water and had done a great job putting together an organization of my old supporters and new people who were disenchanted with Governor White. Our first big decision was how to begin. Dick Morris suggested that before I made a formal announcement I should go on television to acknowledge the mistakes that led to my defeat and ask for another chance. It was a risky idea, but the whole idea of running just two years after I had lost was risky. If I lost again, there would be no more comebacks, at least not for a long time.

We cut the ad in New York at Tony Schwartz's studio. I thought the only way it would work was if it contained both an honest acknowledgment of my past mistakes and the promise of the kind of positive leadership that had attracted popular support the first time I ran. The ad aired without prior notice on February 8. My face filled the screen as I told the voters that since my defeat I had traveled the state talking with thousands of Arkansans; that they had told me I'd done some good things but made big mistakes, including raising the car-tag fees; and that our roads needed the money but I was wrong to raise it in a way that hurt so many people. I then said that when I was growing up, "my daddy never had to whip me twice for the same thing"; that the state needed leadership in education and economic development, areas in which I had done a good job; and that if they'd give me another chance, I'd be a governor who had learned from defeat that "you can't lead without listening."

The ad generated a lot of conversation and seemed at least to have opened the minds of enough voters to give me a chance. On February 27, Chelsea's birthday, I made my official announcement. Hillary gave me a picture of the three of us at the event, with the inscription "Chelsea's second birthday, Bill's second chance."

I promised to focus on the three issues I thought were most important to the state's future: improving education, bringing in more jobs, and holding down utility rates. These were also the issues on which Governor White was most vulnerable. He had cut the car-tag fees $16 million, while his Public Service Commission had approved $227 million in rate increases for Arkansas Power and Light, hurting both consumers and businesses. The down economy had cost us a lot of jobs, and state revenue was too meager to allow anything to be done for education.

The message was well received, but the big news on that day was Hillary's declaration that she was taking my name. From now on, she would be known as Hillary Rodham Clinton. We had been discussing it for weeks. Hillary had been convinced to do it by the large number of our friends who said that, though the issue never showed up as a negative in our polls, it bothered a lot of people. Even Vernon Jordan had mentioned it to her when he came to Little Rock to visit us a few months earlier. Over the years Vernon had become a close friend of ours. He was one of the nation's foremost civil rights leaders, and he was a person on whom his friends could always rely. He was a southerner and older than we were by enough years to understand why the name issue mattered. Ironically, the only person outside our inner circle to mention it to me was a young progressive lawyer from Pine Bluff who was a big supporter of mine. He asked me if Hillary's keeping her maiden name bothered me. I told him that it didn't, and that I had never thought about it until someone brought it up. He stared at me in disbelief and said, "Come on, I know you. You're a real man. It's got to bother you!" I was amazed. It was neither the first nor the last time that something other people cared about didn't mean a thing to me.

I made it clear to Hillary that the decision was hers alone and that I didn't think the election would turn on her name. Not long after we started seeing each other, she had told me that keeping her maiden name was a decision she had made as a young girl, long before it became a symbol of women's equality. She was proud of her family heritage and wanted to hang on to it. Since I wanted to hang on to her, that was fine by me. Actually, it was one of the many things I liked about her.

In the end, Hillary decided, with her typical practicality, that keeping her maiden name wasn't worth offending the people who cared about it. When she told me, my only advice was to tell the public the truth about why she was doing it. My TV ad carried a genuine apology for real mistakes. This wasn't the same thing, and I thought we'd both look phony if we presented her new name as a change of heart. In her statement, she was very matter-of-fact about it, essentially telling the voters she'd done it for them.

We opened the primary campaign leading in the polls but facing formidable opposition. At the outset, the strongest candidate was Jim Guy Tucker, who had lost the Senate race four years earlier to David Pryor. Since then he had made a good deal of money in cable television. He appealed to the same progressive base I did, and the scars of his defeat had had two more years than mine to heal. I had a better organi- zation in the rural counties than he did, but more rural vot- ers were still mad at me. They had a third alternative in Joe Purcell, a decent, low-key man who had been attorney gen- eral and lieutenant governor and done a good job with both positions. Unlike Jim Guy and me, he had never made any- body mad. Joe had wanted to be governor for a long time, and though he was no longer in the best of health, he thought he could win by portraying himself as everybody's friend and less ambitious than his younger competitors. Two other candidates also filed: state senator Kim Hendren, a conservative from northwest Arkansas, and my old nemesis, Monroe Schwarzlose. Running for governor was keeping him alive.

My campaign would have collapsed in the first month if I hadn't learned the lessons of 1980 about the impact of negative television ads. Right off the bat, Jim Guy Tucker put up an ad criticizing me for commuting the sentences of first-degree murderers in my first term. He highlighted the case of a man who got out and killed a friend just a few weeks after his release. Since the voters hadn't been aware of that issue, my apology ad didn't immunize me from it, and I dropped behind Tucker in the polls.

The Board of Pardons and Paroles had recommended the commutations in question for two reasons. First, the board and the people running the prison system felt it would be much harder to maintain order and minimize vio- lence if the "lifers" knew they could never get out no matter how well they behaved. Second, a lot of the older inmates had extensive health problems that cost the state a lot of money. If they were released, their health costs would be covered by the Medicaid program, which was funded mostly by the federal government.

The case featured in the ad was truly bizarre. The man whom I made eligible for parole was seventy-two years old and had served more than sixteen years for murder. In all that time, he had been a model prisoner with only one disciplinary mark against him. He was suffering from arteriosclerosis, and the prison doctors said he had about a year to live and probably would be completely incapacitated within six months, costing the prison budget a small fortune. He also had a sister in southeast Arkansas who was willing to take him in. About six weeks after he was paroled, he was drinking beer with a friend in the other man's pickup truck, with a gun rack in the back. They got into a fight and he grabbed the gun, shot the man dead, and took his Social Security check. Between the time of his arrest and his trial for that offense, the judge released the helpless-looking old man into his sister's custody. A few days after that, he got on the back of a motorcycle driven by a thirty-year-old man and rode north, all the way up to Pottsville, a little town near Russellville, where they tried to rob the local bank by driving the motorcycle right through the front door. The old boy was sick all right, but not in the way the prison doctors thought.

Not long afterward, I was in Pine Bluff in the county clerk's office. I shook hands with a woman who told me the man who'd been killed in his pickup was her uncle. She was kind enough to say, "I don't hold you responsible. There's no way in the wide world you could have known he'd do that." Most voters weren't as forgiving. I promised not to commute the sentences of any more first-degree murderers and said I'd require greater participation by victims in the decisions of the Board of Pardons and Paroles.

And I hit back at Tucker, following my own admonition to take the first hit, then counterpunch as hard as I could. With the help of David Watkins, a local advertising executive who was also from Hope, I ran an ad criticizing Jim Guy's voting record in Congress. It was poor because he had started running for the Senate not long after he began his term in the House of Representatives, so he wasn't there to vote much. One of the attendance ads featured two people sitting around a kitchen table, talking about how they wouldn't get paid if they showed up for work only half the time. We traded blows like that for the rest of the campaign. Meanwhile, Joe Purcell traveled around the state in a van, shaking hands and staying out of the TV-ad war.

Besides the air war, we waged a vigorous ground campaign. Betsey Wright ran it to perfection. She drove people hard, and lost her temper from time to time, but everybody knew she was brilliant, committed, and the hardest-working person in our campaign. We were so much on the same wavelength that she often knew what I was thinking, and vice versa, before we ever said a word. It saved a lot of time.

I started the campaign by traveling around the state with Hillary and Chelsea in a car driven by my friend and campaign chairman, Jimmy "Red" Jones, who had been state auditor for more than twenty years and who still had a good following among small-town leaders. Our strategy was to win Pulaski and the other big counties, carry the south Arkansas counties where I had a leg up, hold a large majority of the black vote, and turn the eleven counties in northeast Arkansas, which had all switched their support from me to Frank White in 1980. I went after those eleven counties with the same zeal I'd brought to winning the rural counties of the Third District in 1974. I made sure I campaigned in every little town in the region, often spending the night with new supporters. This strategy also got votes in the larger cities, where people were impressed when the pictures of me shaking hands in places candidates never visited appeared in their newspapers.

Betsey and I also signed up three young black leaders who proved invaluable. Rodney Slater left Attorney General Steve Clark's staff to help. Even back then, he was a powerful speaker, drawing on his deep knowledge of the scriptures to fashion powerful arguments for our cause. I had known Carol Willis when he was a student at the law school in Fayetteville. He was a great old-fashioned politician who knew all the players in the rural areas like the back of his hand. Bob Nash, who was working on economic development for the Rockefeller Foundation, helped on nights and weekends.

Rodney Slater, Carol Willis, and Bob Nash stayed with me for the next nineteen years. They worked for me the whole time I was governor. When I was President, Rodney served as federal highway administrator and secretary of transportation. Carol kept our fences mended with black America at the Democratic National Committee. Bob started as undersecretary of agriculture, then came to the White House as director of personnel and appointments. I don't know what I would have done without them.

Perhaps the defining moment of the primary campaign came at a meeting of about eighty black leaders from the Delta who came to hear from Jim Guy Tucker and me so that they could decide which one of us to support. Tucker had already won the endorsement of the Arkansas Education Association by promising teachers a big pay raise without a tax increase. I had countered with the endorsement of several teachers and administrators who knew the state's bad economy wouldn't permit Tucker's promise to be kept and who remembered what I had done for education in my first term. I could still win with a split among educators, but not with a split among blacks in the Delta. I had to have nearly all of them.

The meeting was held in Jack Crumbly's barbeque place in Forrest City, about ninety miles east of Little Rock. Jim Guy had come and gone by the time I got there, leaving a good impression. It was late and I was tired, but I made the best case I could, emphasizing the black appointments I'd made and my efforts to help long-ignored rural black communities get money for water and sewer systems.

After I finished, a young black lawyer from Lakeview, Jimmy Wilson, got up to speak. He was Tucker's main supporter in the Delta. Jimmy said I was a good man and had been a good governor, but that no Arkansas governor who had lost for reelection had ever been elected again. He said Frank White was terrible for blacks and had to be defeated. He reminded them that Jim Guy had a good civil rights record in Congress and had hired several young black people to work for him. He said Jim Guy would be as good for blacks as I would, and he could win. "I like

Governor Clinton," he said, "but he's a loser. And we can't afford to lose." It was a persuasive argument, all the more so because he had the guts to do it with me sitting there. I could feel the crowd slipping away.

After a few seconds of silence, a man stood up in the back and said he'd like to be heard. John Lee Wilson was the mayor of Haynes, a small town of about 150 people. He was a heavy man of medium height, dressed in jeans and a white T-shirt, which bulged with the bulk of his huge arms, neck, and gut. I didn't know him very well and had no idea what he would say, but I'll never forget his words.

"Lawyer Wilson made a good speech," he began, "and he may be right. The governor may be a loser. All I know is, when Bill Clinton became governor, the crap was running open in the streets of my town, and my babies was sick because we didn't have no sewer system. Nobody paid any attention to us. When he left office, we had a sewer system and my babies wasn't sick anymore. He did that for a lot of us. Let me ask you something. If we don't stick with folks who stick with us, who will ever respect us again? He may be a loser, but if he loses, I'm going down with him. And so should you." As the old saying goes, it was all over but the shouting, one of those rare moments when one man's words actually changed minds, and hearts.

Unfortunately, John Lee Wilson died before I was elected President. Near the end of my second term, I made a nostalgic trip back to east Arkansas to speak at Earle High School. The school principal was Jack Crumbly, the host of that fateful meeting almost two decades earlier. In my remarks, I told the story of John Lee Wilson's speech for the first time in public. It was televised across east Arkansas. One person who watched it, sitting in her little house in Haynes, was John Lee Wilson's widow. She wrote me a very moving letter saying how proud John would have been to have the President praising him. Of course I praised him. If it hadn't been for John Lee, I might be writing wills and divorce settlements instead of this book.

As we got close to election day, my support went up and down among voters who couldn't decide whether to give me another chance. I was worried about it until I met a man in a café one afternoon in Newark, in northeast Arkansas. When I asked for his vote, he said, "I voted against you last time, but I'm going to vote for you this time." Although I knew the answer, I still asked him why he voted against me. "Because you raised my car tags." When I asked him why he was voting for me, he said, "Because you raised my car tags." I told him I needed every vote I could get, and I didn't want to make him mad, but it didn't make any sense for him to vote for me for the same reason he'd voted against me before. He smiled and said, "Oh, it makes all the sense in the world. You may be a lot of things, Bill, but you ain't dumb. You're the very least likely one to ever raise those car tags again, so I'm for you." I added his impeccable logic to my stump speech for the rest of the campaign.

On May 25, I won the primary election with 42 percent of the vote. Under the counterassault of my ads and the strength of our organization, Jim Guy Tucker fell to 23 percent. Joe Purcell had parlayed his issue- and controversy-free campaign into 29 percent of the vote and a spot in the runoff, two weeks away. It was a dangerous situation. Tucker and I had driven each other's negative ratings up with the attack ads, and Purcell appealed to the Democrats who hadn't gotten over the car-tag increase. There was a good chance he could win just by being the un-Clinton. I tried for ten days to smoke him out, but he was shrewd enough to stay in his van and shake a few hands. On the Thursday night before the election, I did a poll that said the race was dead even. That meant I'd probably lose, since the undecided vote usually broke against the incumbent, which I effectively was. I had just put up an ad highlighting our differences on whether the Public Service Commission, which sets electric rates, should be elected rather than appointed, a change I favored and Joe opposed. I hoped it would make a difference, but I wasn't sure.

The very next day, I was handed the election in the guise of a crippling body blow. Frank White badly wanted Purcell to win the runoff. The governor's negative ratings were even higher than mine, and I had the issues and an organized campaign on my side. By contrast, White felt certain that Joe Purcell's poor health would become a decisive factor in the general election campaign, guaranteeing White a second term. On Friday night, when it was too late for me to counter on television, Frank White began running a TV ad attacking me for raising the car-tag fee and telling people not to forget it. He got the time to run it heavily all weekend by persuading his business supporters to pull their commercials so that he could put the attack ad up. I saw the ad and knew it would turn a close race. I couldn't get a response to it on television until Monday, and by then it would be too late. This was an unfair advantage that was later disallowed by a federal regulation requiring stations to place ads that respond to last-minute attacks over the weekend, but that was no help to me.

Betsey and I called David Watkins and asked him to open his studio so that I could cut a radio ad. We worked on the script and met David about an hour before midnight. By that time Betsey had lined up some young volunteers to drive the ad to radio stations all over the state in time for them to be run early Saturday morning. In my radio response, I asked people if they'd seen White's ad attacking me and asked them to think about why he was interfering with a Democratic primary. There was only one answer: he wanted to run against Joe Purcell, not me, because I would beat him and Joe couldn't. I knew most Democratic primary voters intensely opposed the governor and would hate the thought of being manipulated by him. David Watkins worked all night long making enough copies of our ad to saturate the state. The kids started driving them to the radio stations at about four in the morning, along with checks from the campaign to purchase a heavy buy. The radio spot was so effective that by Saturday night, White's own television ad was working for me. On Monday we put our response up on television too, but we had already won the battle by then. The next day, June 8, I won the runoff 54 to 46 percent. It was a near-run thing. I had won most of the big counties and those with a substantial number of black voters, but was still struggling in the rural Democratic counties where the car-tag issue wouldn't die. It would take another two years to repair the damage completely.

The fall campaign against Frank White was rough but fun. This time the economy was hurting him, not me, and he had a record I could run against. I hit him on his utility ties and lost jobs, and ran positive ads on my issues. He had a great attack ad featuring a man trying to scrape the spots off a leopard; it said that, just like a leopard, I couldn't change my spots. Dick Morris did a devastating ad taking White to task for letting utilities have big rate increases while cutting back from four to three the number of monthly prescriptions the elderly could get under Medicaid. The tagline was: "Frank White—Soft on utilities. Tough on the elderly." Our funniest radio ad came in response to a barrage of false charges. Our announcer asked if it wouldn't be nice to have a guard dog that would bark every time a politician said something that wasn't true. Then a dog barked, "Woof, woof!" The announcer repeated each charge, and the dog barked again just before he answered it. There were, as I recall, four "woof, woof's" in all. By the time it had run a few days, workers were good-naturedly barking "Woof, woof!" at me when I shook hands at plant gates during shift changes. White further solidified the black vote by saying blacks would vote for a duck if it ran as a Democrat. Shortly after that, Bishop L. T. Walker of the Church of God in Christ told his people they had to get "Old Hoghead" out of office.

There comes a time in every campaign when you know in your bones whether you're going to win or lose. In 1982, it happened to me in Melbourne, the county seat of Izard County in north Arkansas. I had lost the county in 1980 over the car tags despite the fact that the local legislator, John Miller, had voted to raise them. John was one of the most senior members of the legislature and probably knew more about all aspects of state government than anyone else in Arkansas. He was working hard for me and arranged for me to tour the local McDonnell Douglas plant, which made component parts for airplanes.

Even though the workers belonged to the United Auto Workers union, I was nervous, because most of them had voted against me just two years before. I was met at the front door by Una Sitton, a good Democrat who worked in the front office. Una shook my hand and said, "Bill, I think you're going to enjoy this." When I opened the door to the plant, I was almost knocked over by the loud sound of Willie Nelson singing one of my favorite songs, Steve Goodman's "City of New Orleans." I walked in to the opening line of the chorus: "Good morning, America, how are you? Don't you know me, I'm your native son." The workers cheered. All of them but one were wearing my campaign buttons. I made my way down each aisle, shaking hands to the music and fighting back the tears. I knew the election was over. My people were bringing their native son home.

Near the end of almost all my campaigns, I turned up at the morning shift at the Campbell's Soup factory in Fayetteville, where the workers prepared turkeys and chickens for soups. At 5 a.m., it was the earliest shift change in Arkansas. In 1982, it was cold and rainy when I began shaking hands in the dark. One man joked that he had intended to vote for me, but was having second thoughts about voting for someone with no better sense than to campaign in the dark in a cold rain.

I learned a lot on those dark mornings. I'll never forget seeing one man drop his wife off. When the door to their pickup opened, there were three young children sitting between them. The man told me they had to get the kids up at a quarter to four every morning. After he took his wife to work, he dropped the kids off with a babysitter who took them to school, because he had to be at work by seven.

It's easy for a politician in this mass-media culture to reduce electioneering to fund-raisers, rallies, advertisements, and a debate or two. All that may be enough for the voters to make an intelligent decision, but the candidates miss out on a lot, including the struggles of people who have their hands full just getting through the day and doing the best they can for their kids. I had made up my mind that if those folks gave me another chance, I'd never forget them.

On November 2, they gave me that chance. I won 55 percent of the vote, carrying fifty-six of the seventy-five counties, losing eighteen counties in Republican western Arkansas and one in south Arkansas. Most of the white rural counties came back, though the margins in several were close. The margin wasn't close in the largest county, Pulaski. I swept the eleven counties in northeast Arkansas where we had worked especially hard. And the black vote was staggering.

One black leader I particularly liked, Emily Bowens, was mayor of the small community of Mitchellville in southeast Arkansas. I had helped her in my first term, and she repaid the debt in full: I won Mitchellville 196–8 in the primary runoff with Purcell. When I called her to thank her for getting me 96 percent of the vote, she apologized for the eight votes we lost. "Governor, I'll find those eight people and straighten them out by November," she promised. On November 2, I carried Mitchellville 256–0. Emily had turned the eight and registered fifty-two more.

After the election, I heard from people all over the country. Ted Kennedy and Walter Mondale called just as they had in 1980. And I received some wonderful letters. One came from an unlikely source: General James Drummond, who had commanded the troops during the Cuban crisis at Fort Chaffee two years earlier. He said he was glad I won, because "while it may have seemed that we marched to different drums at Fort Chaffee . . . I appreciated and admired your leadership, your principles, and your willingness to stand up and be counted for the people of Arkansas." I admired Drummond too, and his letter meant more to me than he could have known.

The Democrats did well all over the country and especially in the South, winning a majority of the thirty-six governorships, picking up seats in the House of Representatives, up for grabs largely because of America's troubled economy. Among the new governors were two old ones besides me: George Wallace of Alabama, who had apologized to black voters for his racist past from his wheelchair; and Michael Dukakis of Massachusetts, who, like me, had been defeated after his first term and had just defeated the man who beat him.

My supporters were ecstatic. After a long, history-making campaign, they had every right to their raucous celebration. By contrast, I was feeling strangely subdued. I was happy but didn't feel like gloating over my victory. I didn't blame Frank White for beating me last time or for wanting to be governor again. Losing had been my fault. What I mostly felt on election night, and for days afterward, was a deep, quiet gratitude that the people of the state I loved so much were willing to give me another chance. I was determined to vindicate their judgment.

TWENTY-THREE

ON JANUARY 11, 1983, I took the oath of office for the second time, before the largest crowd ever to attend an inauguration in our state. The celebrants had brought me back from the political grave, and their support would keep me in the governor's office for ten more years, the longest period I ever stayed in one job.

The challenge I faced was to keep my promise to be more responsive to the people while maintaining my commitment to move our state forward. The task was complicated, and made more important, by the dismal state of the economy. The state's unemployment rate was 10.6 percent. In December, as governor-elect, I had gone to Trumann, in northeast Arkansas, to shake hands with six hundred workers at the Singer Plant, which had made wooden cabinets for sewing machines for decades, as they walked out of the plant for the last time. The plant closing, one of many we had endured over the last two years, dealt a body blow to the economy of Poinsett County and had a discouraging impact on the whole state. I can still see the look of despair on so many of the Singer workers' faces. They knew that they had worked hard, and that their livelihoods were being swept away by forces beyond their control.

Another consequence of the poor economy was a falloff in state revenues, leaving too little money for education and other essential services. It was clear to me that, if we were going to get out of this fix, I had to focus the state's attention, and mine, on education and employment. For the next decade, that's what I did. Even when my administration took important initiatives in health care, the environment, prison reform, and other areas, or in appointing more minorities and women to important positions, I tried never to let the spotlight stray too far from schools and jobs. They were the keys to opportunity and empowerment for our people, and to maintaining the political support I needed to keep pursuing positive changes. I had learned in my first term that if you give equal time to all the things you do, you run the risk of having everything become a blur in the public's mind, leaving no clear impression that anything important was being done. My longtime friend George Frazier from Hope once told an interviewer, "If he has a flaw, and we all do, I think Bill's flaw is that he sees so much that needs to be done." I never cured that flaw, and I kept trying to do a lot, but for the next decade I focused most of my energy, and my public statements, on schools and jobs.

Betsey Wright had done such a good job with the campaign that I was convinced she could manage the governor's office. In the beginning I also asked Maurice Smith to serve as executive secretary, to add some maturity to the mix and to ensure cordial relations with the senior legislators, lobbyists, and power brokers. I had a strong education team with Paul Root, my former world history teacher, and Don Ernst. My legal counsel, Sam Bratton, who had been with me in the attorney general's office, was also an expert in education law.

Carol Rasco became my aide for health and human services. Her qualifications were rooted in experience: Her older child, Hamp, was born with cerebral palsy. She fought for his educational and other rights, and in the process acquired a detailed knowledge of state and federal programs for the disabled.

I persuaded Dorothy Moore, from Arkansas City in deep southeast Arkansas, to greet people and answer phones in the reception area. Miss Dorothy was already in her seventies when she started, and she stayed until I left the governor's office. Finally, I got a new secretary. Barbara Kerns had had enough of politics and stayed behind at the Wright firm. In early 1983, I hired Lynda Dixon, who took care of me for a decade and continued to work in my Arkansas office when I became President.

My most notable appointment was Mahlon Martin as director of finance and administration, arguably the most important job in state government after the governorship. Before I appointed him, Mahlon was city manager of Little

Rock, and a very good one. He was black, and an Arkansan through and through—he always wanted to take the first day of deer season off from work. In tough times, he could be creative in finding solutions to budget problems, but he was always fiscally responsible. In one of our two-year budget cycles in the 1980s, he had to cut spending six times to balance the books.

Shortly after I became President, Mahlon began a long, losing battle against cancer. In June 1995, I went back to Little Rock to dedicate the Mahlon Martin Apartments for low-income working people. Mahlon died two months after the dedication. I never worked with a more gifted public servant.

Betsey saw to it that my time was scheduled differently than it had been in my first term. I had been perceived as being inaccessible then, in part because I accepted so many daytime speaking engagements out in the state. Now I spent more time in the office and more personal time with legislators when they were in session, including after-hours card games I really enjoyed. When I did attend out-of-town events, it was usually at the request of one of my supporters. Doing those events rewarded people who had helped me, reinforced their positions in their communities, and helped to keep our organization together.

No matter how far away the event was or how long it lasted, I always came home at night so that I could be there when Chelsea woke up. That way I could have breakfast with her and Hillary and, when Chelsea got old enough, take her to school. I did that every day until I started running for President. I also put a little desk in the governor's office where Chelsea could sit and read or draw. I loved it when we were both at our desks working away. If Hillary's law practice took her away at night or overnight, I tried to be at home. When Chelsea was in kindergarten, she and her classmates were asked what their parents did for a living. She reported that her mother was a lawyer and her father "talks on the telephone, drinks coffee, and makes 'peeches." At bedtime, Hillary, Chelsea, and I would say a little prayer or two by Chelsea's bed, then Hillary or I would read

Chelsea a book. When I was so tired I fell asleep reading, as I often did, she would kiss me awake. I liked that so much I often pretended to be asleep when I wasn't.

A week into my new term, I gave my State of the State address to the legislators, recommending ways to deal with the severe budget crisis and asking them to do four things I thought would help the economy: expand the Arkansas Housing Development Agency's authority to issue revenue bonds to increase housing and create jobs; establish enterprise zones in high-unemployment areas in order to provide greater incentives to invest in them; give a jobs tax credit to employers who created new jobs; and create an Arkansas Science and Technology Authority, patterned in part on the Port Authority of New York and New Jersey, to develop the scientific and technological potential of the state. These measures, all of which were enacted into law, were forerunners of similar initiatives that passed when I became President in another time of economic trouble.

I argued hard for my utility reforms, including the popular election of Public Service Commission members, but I knew I couldn't pass most of them, because Arkansas Power and Light Company and the other utilities had so much influence in the legislature. Instead, I had to be content to appoint commissioners I thought would protect the people and the state's economy without bankrupting the utilities.

I proposed and passed some modest educational improvements, including a requirement that all districts offer kindergarten, and a law allowing students to take up to half their courses in a nearby school district if the home district didn't offer them. That was important because so many of the smaller districts didn't offer chemistry, physics, advanced math, or foreign languages. I also asked the legislature to raise cigarette, beer, and liquor taxes and to allocate more than half of our projected new revenues to the schools. That was all we could do, given our financial condition and the fact that we were awaiting a state supreme court decision on a case claiming that, because our school financing system was so unequal in its distribution of funds, it was unconstitutional. If the court ruled for the plaintiffs, as I hoped it would, I would have to call a special session of the legislature to deal with it. As it was, the legislature was required to meet only sixty days every two years. Though the legislators usually stayed a few days longer, something often came up after they had gone home that required me to call them back. The supreme court decision would do that. Such a session would be difficult, but it might give us the chance to do something really big for education, because the legislature, the public, and the press could focus on it in a way that was impossible in a regular session, when so many other things were going on.

In April, the National Commission on Excellence in Education, appointed by U.S. Secretary of Education Terrel Bell, issued a stunning report entitled *A Nation at Risk*. The report noted that on nineteen different international tests, American students were never first or second and were last seven times; 23 million American adults, 13 percent of all seventeen-year-olds, and up to 40 percent of minority students were functionally illiterate; high school students' average performance on standardized tests was lower than it had been twenty-six years earlier, when *Sputnik* was launched; scores on the principal college entrance exam, the Scholastic Aptitude Test, had been declining since 1962; one-quarter of all college math courses were remedial—that is, teaching what should have been learned in high school or earlier; business and military leaders reported having to spend increasing amounts of money on remedial education; and finally, these declines in education were occurring at a time when the demand for highly skilled workers was increasing sharply.

Just five years earlier, Dr. Kern Alexander had said children would be better off in the schools of almost any state other than Arkansas. If our whole nation was at risk, we had to be on life support. In 1983, 265 of our high schools offered no advanced biology, 217 no physics, 177 no foreign language, 164 no advanced math, 126 no chemistry. In the 1983 regular session, I asked the legislature to authorize a fifteen-member Education Standards Committee to make specific recommendations on new curriculum standards. I put together an able and fully representative committee and asked Hillary to chair it. She had done an excellent job chairing the Rural Health Committee and the board of the national Legal Services Corporation in my first term. She was very good at running committees, she cared about children, and by naming her I was sending a strong signal about how important education was to me. My reasoning was sound, but it was still a risky move, because every significant change we proposed was sure to rattle some interest group.

In May, the state supreme court declared our school financing system unconstitutional. We had to write a new aid formula, then fund it. There were only two alternatives: take money away from the wealthiest and smallest districts and give it to the poorest and fastest-growing ones, or raise enough new revenues so that we could equalize funding without hurting the presently overfunded districts. Since no district wanted its schools to lose money, the court decision gave us the best opportunity we'd ever have to raise taxes for education. Hillary's committee held hearings in every county in the state in July, getting recommendations from educators and the public. She gave me their report in September, and I announced that I would call the legislature into session on October 4 to deal with education.

On September 19, I delivered a televised address to explain what was in the education program, to advocate a one-cent increase in the sales tax and a hike in the severance tax on natural gas to pay for it, and to ask the people to endorse it. Despite the support we had built for the program, there was still a strong anti-tax feeling in the state, aggravated by the poor economy. In the previous election, one man in Nashville, Arkansas, asked me to do just one thing if I won: spend his tax dollars as if I lived like him, on $150 a week. Another man helping to build Little Rock's new Excelsior Hotel asked me to remember that while the state needed more taxes, he was in his last day on the job and didn't have another one waiting. I had to win those people to the cause.

In my speech, I argued that we couldn't create more jobs

without improving education, citing examples from my own efforts to recruit high-technology companies. Then I said we couldn't make real advances as long as "we are last in spending per child, teacher salaries, and total state and local taxes per person." What we needed to do was to both raise the sales tax and approve standards recommended by Hillary's committee, "standards which, when implemented, will be among the nation's best."

The standards included required kindergarten; a maximum class size of twenty through third grade; counselors in all elementary schools; uniform testing of all students in third, sixth, and eighth grades, with mandatory retention of those who failed the eighth-grade test; a requirement that any school in which more than 15 percent of students failed had to develop a plan to improve performance and, if its students didn't improve within two years, be subject to management changes; more math, science, and foreign language courses; a required high school curriculum of four years of English and three years of math, science, and history or social studies; more time on academic work during the school day and an increase in the school year from 175 to 180 days; special opportunities for gifted children; and a requirement that students stay in school until the age of sixteen. Until then, students could leave after the eighth grade, and a lot of them did. Our dropout rate was more than 30 percent.

The most controversial proposal I made was to require all teachers and administrators to take and pass the National Teacher Examination in 1984, "by the standards now applied to new college graduates who take the test." I recommended that teachers who failed be given free tuition to take regular courses and be able to take the test as many times as possible until 1987, when the school standards would be fully effective.

I also proposed improvements in vocational and higher education, and a tripling of the adult education program to help dropouts who wanted to get a high school diploma.

At the end of the speech, I asked the people to join Hillary and me in wearing blue ribbons to demonstrate support for the program and our conviction that Arkansas could be a "blue ribbon" state, in the front ranks of educational excellence. We ran television and radio ads asking for support, distributed thousands of postcards for people to send their legislators, and passed out tens of thousands of those blue ribbons. Many people wore them every day until the legislative session was over. The public was beginning to believe we could do something special.

It was an ambitious program: Only a handful of states then required as strong a core curriculum as the one I proposed. None required students to pass an eighth-grade test before going to high school. A few required them to pass tests in the eleventh or twelfth grade to get a diploma, but to me, that was like closing the barn door after the cow is out. I wanted the students to have time to catch up. No state required elementary school counselors, though more and more young children were coming to school from troubled homes with emotional problems that inhibited their learning. And no state allowed its education department to force management changes in nonperforming schools. Our proposals went well beyond those of the *Nation at Risk* report.

The biggest firestorm by far was generated by the teacher-testing program. The Arkansas Education Association (AEA) went ballistic, accusing me of degrading teachers and using them as scapegoats. For the first time in my life, I was charged with racism, on the assumption that a higher percentage of black teachers would fail the test. Cynics accused Hillary and me of grandstanding to increase our popularity among people who would otherwise oppose any tax increase. While it was true that the teacher test was a strong symbol of accountability to many people, the case for the test came out of the hearings the Standards Committee had held across the state. Many people complained about particular teachers who didn't know the subjects they were teaching or who lacked basic literacy skills. One woman handed me a note the teacher had sent home with her child. Of the twenty-two words in it, three were misspelled. I had no doubt that most teachers were able and dedicated, and I knew that most of those with problems had probably had inferior educations themselves; they would have the chance to improve their skills and take the test again. But if we were going to raise taxes to increase teacher pay, and if the standards were going to work for the kids, the teachers had to be able to teach them.

The legislature met for thirty-eight days to consider the fifty-two bills in my agenda and related items offered by the lawmakers themselves. Hillary made a brilliant presentation before the House and Senate, prompting Representative Lloyd George of Yell County to say, "It looks like we might have elected the wrong Clinton!" We had opposition from three quarters: the anti-tax crowd; rural school districts that feared they would be consolidated because they couldn't meet the standards; and the AEA, which threatened to defeat every legislator who voted for teacher testing.

We countered the argument that the test was degrading to teachers with a statement from several teachers at Little Rock Central High, widely recognized as the best in the state. They said they were glad to take the test, in order to reinforce public confidence. To beat back the argument that the test was racist, I persuaded a group of prominent black ministers to support my position. They argued that black children were most in need of good teachers, and those who failed the test would be given other chances to pass. I also got invaluable support from Dr. Lloyd Hackley, the African-American chancellor of the University of Arkansas at Pine Bluff, a predominantly black institution. Hackley had done an amazing job at UAPB and was a member of Hillary's Education Standards Committee. In 1980, when college graduates first had to take a test to be certified to teach, 42 percent of the UAPB students failed. By 1986, the pass rate had increased dramatically. Dr. Hackley's nursing graduates improved the most in the same period. He argued that black students had been held back more by low standards and low expectations than by discrimination. The results he got proved him right. He believed in his students and got a lot out of them. All our children need educators like him.

Near the end of the legislative session, it looked as if the AEA might be able to beat the testing bill. I went back and forth to the Senate and House repeatedly to twist arms and make deals for votes. Finally, I had to threaten not to allow my own sales-tax bill to pass if the testing wasn't passed along with it.

It was a risky gambit: I could have lost both the tax and the testing law. Organized labor opposed the sales-tax raise, saying it was unfair to working families because I had failed to secure an income tax rebate as an offset for the sales tax on food. Labor's opposition brought some liberal votes to the anti-tax side, but they couldn't get a majority. There was a lot of support for the program from the outset, and by the time the tax vote came up, we had passed a new formula and the standards were approved. Without a sales-tax increase, many districts would lose state aid under the new formula, and most of them would have to enact large local property-tax increases to meet the standards. By the last day of the session, we had it all: the standards, the teacher-testing law, and an increase in the sales tax.

I was elated, and totally exhausted, as I piled into the car to drive sixty miles north to appear at the annual governor's night in Fairfield Bay, a retirement village full of middle-class folks who'd come to Arkansas from up north because it was warmer but still had four seasons and low taxes. Most of them, including the retired educators, supported the education program. One amateur carpenter made me a little red schoolhouse with a plaque on it commemorating my efforts.

As the smoke cleared from the session, Arkansas began to get a lot of positive national coverage for our education reforms, including praise from Secretary of Education Bell. However, the AEA didn't give up; it filed a lawsuit against the testing law. Peggy Nabors, the AEA president, and I had a heated debate on the *Phil Donahue Show*, one of several arguments we had in the national media. The company that owned the National Teacher Examination refused to let us use it for existing teachers, saying it was a good measure of whether someone should be allowed to teach in the first place but not of whether a teacher who couldn't pass it should be able to keep teaching. So we had to develop a whole new test. When the test was first given to teachers and administrators in 1984, 10 percent failed. About the same percentage failed in subsequent attempts. In the end, 1,215 teachers, about 3.5 percent of our total, had to leave the classroom because they couldn't pass the test. Another 1,600 lost their certification because they never took it. In the 1984 election, the AEA refused to endorse me and many of education's best friends in the legislature because of the testing law. Their efforts managed to defeat only one legislator, my old friend Senator Vada Sheid from Mountain Home, who had sewn a button on my shirt when I first met her in 1974. The teachers went door-to-door for her opponent, Steve Luelf, a Republican lawyer who had moved to Arkansas from California. They didn't talk about the teacher test. Unfortunately, neither did Vada. She made a mistake common to candidates who take a position supported by a disorganized majority but opposed by an organized and animated minority. The only way to survive the onslaught is to make the issue matter as much in the voting booth to those who agree with you as it does to those who disagree. Vada just wanted the whole thing to go away. I always felt bad about the price she paid for helping our children.

Over the next two years, teacher pay went up $4,400, the fastest growth rate in the nation. Although we still ranked forty-sixth, we were finally above the national average in teacher pay as a percentage of state per capita income, and almost at the national average in per-pupil expenditures as a percentage of income. By 1987, the number of our school districts had dropped to 329, and 85 percent of the districts had increased their property-tax rates, which can be done only by a popular vote, to meet the standards.

Student test scores rose steadily across the board. In 1986, the Southern Regional Education Board gave a test to eleventh graders in five southern states. Arkansas was the only state to score above the national average. When the same group was tested five years earlier, in 1981, our students scored below the national average. We were on our way.

I continued to push for educational improvements for the rest of my time as governor, but the new standards, funding, and accountability measures laid the foundation for all the later progress. Eventually I reconciled with the AEA and its leaders, as we worked together year after year to improve our schools and our children's future. When I look back on my career in politics, the 1983 legislative session on education is one of the things I'm proudest of.

In the summer of 1983, the governors met in Portland, Maine. Hillary, Chelsea, and I had a great time, getting together with my old friend Bob Reich and his family, and going with the other governors to a cookout at Vice President Bush's house in the beautiful oceanside town of Kennebunkport. Three-year-old Chelsea marched up to the vice president and said she needed to go to the bathroom. He took her by the hand and led her there. Chelsea appreciated it, and Hillary and I were impressed by George Bush's kindness. It wouldn't be the last time.

Nevertheless, I was upset with the Reagan administration, and had come to Maine determined to do something about it. It had just dramatically tightened the eligibility rules for federal disability benefits. Just as with the black-lung program ten years earlier, there had been abuses of the disability program, but the Reagan cure was worse than the problem. The regulations were so strict they were ridiculous. In Arkansas, a truck driver with a ninth-grade education had lost his arm in an accident. He was denied disability benefits on the theory that he could get a desk job doing clerical work.

Several Democrats in the House, including Arkansas congressman Beryl Anthony, were trying to overturn the rules. Beryl asked me to get the governors to call for their reversal. The governors were interested in the issue, because a lot of our disabled constituents were being denied benefits, and because we were being held partly responsible. Although the program was funded by the federal government, it was administered by the states.

Since the matter wasn't on our agenda, I had to get the

relevant committee to vote to overturn the rules by two-thirds, then get 75 percent of the governors present to support the committee action. It was important enough to the White House that the administration sent two assistant secretaries from the Department of Health and Human Services to work against my efforts. The Republican governors were in a bind. Most of them agreed that the rules needed to be changed and certainly didn't want to defend them in public, but they wanted to stick with their President. The Republican strategy was to kill our proposal in committee. My head count indicated we would win in the committee by a single vote, but only if all our votes showed up. One of those votes was Governor George Wallace. Ever since he had been confined to a wheelchair by a would-be assassin's bullet, it took him a couple of hours every morning to get ready to face the day. On this morning, George Wallace had to get up two hours earlier than usual to go through his painful preparations. He came to the meeting and cast a loud "aye" vote for our resolution, after telling the committee how many Alabama working people, black and white, had been hurt by the new disability rules. The resolution passed out of the committee, and the National Governors Association adopted it. Subsequently, Congress overturned the regulations, and a lot of deserving people got the help they needed to survive. It might not have happened if George Wallace hadn't returned to the populist roots of his youth on an early Maine morning when he stood tall in his wheelchair.

At the end of the year, our family accepted an invitation from Phil and Linda Lader to attend their New Year's weekend gathering in Hilton Head, South Carolina, called Renaissance Weekend. The event was then only a couple of years old. Fewer than one hundred families gathered to spend three days talking about everything under the sun, from politics and economics to religion and our personal lives. The attendees were of different ages, religions, races, and backgrounds, all bound together by a simple preference for spending the weekend in serious talk and family fun rather than all-night parties and football games. It was

an extraordinary bonding experience. We revealed things
about ourselves and learned things about other people that
would never have come out under normal circumstances.
And all three of us made a lot of new friends, many of
whom helped in 1992 and served in my administration. We
went to Renaissance Weekend virtually every year after
that until the millennium weekend, 1999–2000, when the
national celebration at the Lincoln Memorial required our
presence in Washington. After I became President, the event
had swelled to more than 1,500 people and had lost some of
its earlier intimacy, but I still enjoyed going.

In early 1984, it was time to run for reelection again.
Even though President Reagan was far more popular in
Arkansas, and across the country, than he had been in 1980,
I felt confident. The whole state was excited about implementing the school standards, and the economy was getting
a little better. My main primary opponent was Lonnie
Turner, the Ozark lawyer I'd worked with on black-lung
cases back in 1975, after his partner, Jack Yates, died. Lonnie thought the school standards were going to close rural
schools, and he was mad about it. It made me sad because
of our long friendship and because I thought he should have
known better. In May, I won the primary easily, and after a
few years we made up.

In July, Colonel Tommy Goodwin, the director of the
state police, asked to see me. I sat with Betsey Wright in
stunned silence as he told me that my brother had been
videotaped selling cocaine to an undercover state police officer, one who ironically had been hired in an expansion of
state anti-drug efforts I had asked the legislature to fund.
Tommy asked me what I wanted him to do. I asked him
what the state police would normally do in a case like this.
He said Roger wasn't a big-time dealer but a cocaine addict
who was selling the stuff to support his habit. Typically,
with someone like him, they'd set him up a few more times
on videotape to make sure they had him dead to rights, then
squeeze him with the threat of a long prison term to make
him give up his supplier. I told Tommy to treat Roger's case
just like any other. Then I asked Betsey to find Hillary. She

was at a restaurant downtown. I went by to pick her up and told her what had happened.

For the next six miserable weeks, no one outside the state police knew, except Betsey, Hillary, and, I believe, my completely trustworthy press secretary, Joan Roberts. And me. Every time I saw or talked to Mother I was heartsick. Every time I looked in the mirror I was disgusted. I had been so caught up in my life and work that I'd missed all the signs. Shortly after Roger went to college in 1974, he formed a rock band that was good enough to make a living from playing clubs in Hot Springs and Little Rock. I went to hear him several times and thought that with Roger's distinctive voice and the band's musical ability, they had real promise. He clearly loved doing it, and though he went back to Hendrix College a couple of times, he would soon drop out again to return to the band. When he was working, he stayed up all night and slept late. During the racing season, he played the horses heavily. He also bet on football games. I never knew how much he won or lost, but I never asked. When our family gathered for holiday meals, he invariably came late, seemed on edge, and got up a time or two during dinner to make phone calls. The warning signs were all there. I was just too preoccupied to see them.

When Roger was finally arrested, it was big news in Arkansas. I made a brief statement to the press, saying that I loved my brother but expected the law to take its course, and asking for prayers and privacy for my family. Then I told my brother and Mother the truth about how long I'd known. Mother was in shock, and I'm not sure the reality registered on her. Roger was angry, though he got over it later when he came to terms with his addiction. We all went to counseling. I learned that Roger's cocaine habit, about four grams a day, was so bad it might have killed him if he hadn't had the constitution of an ox, and that his addiction was rooted, in part, in the scars of his childhood and perhaps a genetic predisposition to addiction he shared with his father.

From the time he was arrested until almost the date of his court appearance, Roger couldn't admit that he was an addict. Finally one day, as we were sitting at the breakfast table, I told him that if he wasn't an addict, I wanted him to go to jail for a very long time, because he had been selling poison to other people for money. Somehow, that got through to him. After he admitted his problem, he began the long road back.

The case had been taken over by the U.S. attorney, Asa Hutchinson. Roger gave up his supplier, an immigrant even younger than he was, who got cocaine from family or friends in his home country. Roger pleaded guilty to two federal offenses before Judge Oren Harris, who had been chairman of the Commerce Committee in the House of Representatives before going to the bench. Judge Harris was in his early eighties but still sharp and very wise. He sentenced Roger to three years on one charge and two years on the other, and suspended the three-year sentence because of his cooperation. Roger served fourteen months, most of it in a federal facility for nonviolent offenders, which was hard on him but probably saved his life.

Hillary and I were in court with Mother when he was sentenced. I was impressed by the way the whole thing was handled by Judge Harris, and by the U.S. attorney. Asa Hutchinson was professional, fair, and sensitive to the agony my family was experiencing. I wasn't at all surprised when later he was elected to Congress from the Third District.

In the summer, I led the Arkansas delegation to the Democratic convention in San Francisco to see Walter Mondale and Geraldine Ferraro nominated and to give a five-minute tribute to Harry Truman. We were in trouble to start with, and it was all over when Mondale said he would propose a hefty tax increase to reduce the budget deficit. It was a remarkable act of candor, but he might as well have proposed a federal car-tag fee. Still, the city put on a great convention. San Francisco had lots of pleasant small hotels within walking distance of the convention center, and well-organized traffic, so we avoided the crushing traffic jams that characterize many conventions. The Arkansas host, Dr. Richard Sanchez, was heavily invested in the efforts to treat and prevent the relatively new disease of AIDS, which was sweeping the city. I asked Richard about the problem and what could be done about it. That was my first real exposure to a battle that would claim a lot of my attention in the White House and afterward.

I had to leave San Francisco early to return to Arkansas to recruit a high-tech industry for our state. In the end it didn't pan out, but I couldn't have done any good staying in California anyway. We were headed for defeat. The economy was rebounding and the President told us it was "morning again in America," while his surrogates sneered at those of us on the other side as "San Francisco Democrats," a not-so-veiled allusion to our ties to the city's large gay population. Even Vice President Bush fell into the macho mode, saying he was going to "kick a little ass."

In the November election, Reagan defeated Mondale 59 to 41 percent. The President won 62 percent of the vote in Arkansas. I received 63 percent in my race against Woody Freeman, an appealing young businessman from Jonesboro.

After our family enjoyed Chelsea's fifth Christmas and our second Renaissance Weekend, it was time for a new legislative session, this one devoted to modernizing our economy.

Even though the overall economy was improving, unemployment was still high in states like Arkansas that were dependent on agriculture and traditional industries. Most of America's job growth of the eighties came in the high-technology and service sectors, and was concentrated in and around urban areas, primarily in states on or near the East and West coasts. The industrial and agricultural heartland was still in bad shape. The pattern was so pronounced that people began to refer to America as having a "bicoastal" economy.

It was obvious that in order to accelerate job and income growth, we had to restructure our economy. The development package I presented to the legislature had some financial components that were new to Arkansas but already in place in other states. I proposed to broaden the state's housing agency into a Development and Finance

Authority that would be able to issue bonds to finance industrial, agricultural, and small-business projects. I recommended that the state's public pension funds set targets of investing at least 5 percent of their assets in Arkansas. We were a capital-poor state; we didn't need to export public funds when there were good investment options at home. I recommended allowing state-chartered banks to hold assets they foreclosed on for longer periods of time, primarily to avoid dumping farmland in an already depressed market, which would make it even harder for farmers to hold on. I also asked the legislature to allow state-chartered banks not only to lend money, but also to make modest equity investments in farms and businesses that couldn't borrow any more money, with the provision that the farmer or small-business person had a right to buy the bank out within three years. Other farm-state governors were especially interested in this bill, and one of them, Bill Janklow of South Dakota, passed a version of it through his legislature.

The economic proposals were innovative but too complex to be well understood or widely supported. However, after I made appearances at several committee hearings to answer questions and did a lot of one-on-one lobbying, the legislature passed them all.

More than a decade after the U.S. Supreme Court decision in *Roe* v. *Wade* authorized it, our legislature banned abortions performed in the third trimester of pregnancy. The bill was sponsored by Senator Lu Hardin of Russellville, a Christian whom I liked very much, and Senator Bill Henley, a Catholic who was Susan McDougal's brother. The bill passed easily, and I signed it into law. A decade later, when congressional Republicans were pushing a bill to ban so-called partial-birth abortions with no exemption for the health of the mother, I urged them instead to adopt a federal statute banning late-term abortions unless the life or health of the mother was at stake. Because several states still hadn't passed laws like the one I signed in 1985, the bill I proposed would have outlawed more abortions than the bill banning the partial-birth procedure, which normally is used to minimize damage to the mother's body. The GOP leadership turned me down.

Besides the economic package and the abortion bill, the legislature adopted my proposals to set up a fund to compensate victims of violent crime; strengthen our efforts to reduce and deal with child abuse; establish a fund to provide health care for indigents, mostly poor pregnant women, not covered by the federal Medicaid program; make Martin Luther King Jr.'s birthday a state holiday; and create a program to provide better training for school principals. I had become convinced that school performance depended more on the quality of a principal's leadership than on any other single factor. The years ahead only strengthened that conviction.

The only real fireworks in a session otherwise devoted to good government and harmless legislative sideshows came from the herculean effort of the AEA to repeal the teacher-testing law just weeks before the test was scheduled to be given for the first time. In a clever move, the teachers got Representative Ode Maddox to sponsor the repeal. Ode was a highly respected former superintendent in his little town of Oden. He was a good Democrat who kept a large old photograph of FDR up in the school auditorium into the 1980s. He was also a friend of mine. Despite the best efforts of my supporters, the repeal passed the House. I immediately put an ad on the radio telling the people what had happened and asking them to call the Senate in protest. The switchboard was flooded with calls and the bill was killed. Instead, the legislature passed a bill that I supported requiring all certified educators, not just those working in 1985, to take and pass the test by 1987 to keep their certification.

The AEA said teachers would boycott the test. The week before it was given, 4,000 teachers demonstrated outside the Capitol and heard a representative of the National Education Association accuse me of "assassinating the dignity of the public schools and its children." A week later, more than 90 percent of our 27,600 teachers showed up for the test.

Before the legislature went home, we had one last bit of

fireworks. The Highway Department had gone all over the state pushing a new road program, to be financed by an increase in gasoline and diesel taxes. The department sold it to the local business and farm leaders, and it passed rather handily, creating a problem for me. I liked the program and thought it would be good for the economy, but in the election I had pledged not to support a major tax increase. So I vetoed the bill and told its sponsors I wouldn't fight their efforts to override it. The override passed easily, the only time in twelve years one of my vetoes was overturned.

I also engaged in some national political activity in 1985. In February, I narrated the Democrats' response to President Reagan's State of the Union address. The State of the Union was a great forum for Reagan's speaking skills, and whoever gave our brief response had a hard time making any impression. Our party took a different tack that year, featuring the new ideas and economic achievements of several of our governors and mayors. I also got involved in the newly formed Democratic Leadership Council, a group dedicated to forging a winning message for the Democrats based on fiscal responsibility, creative new ideas on social policy, and a commitment to a strong national defense.

The summer governors' conference, held in Idaho, was marked by an unusual partisan fight over a fund-raising letter for the Republican governors signed by President Reagan. The letter took some hard shots at their Democratic colleagues for being too liberal with tax-and-spend policies, a violation of our unwritten commitment to keep the governors' meetings bipartisan. The Democrats were so angry we threatened to block the election of Republican governor Lamar Alexander of Tennessee to the chairmanship of the National Governors Association, normally a routine action since he was the vice chair and the chairmanship rotated by party every year. I liked Lamar and doubted he had his heart in the attack on his Democratic colleagues; after all, he, too, had raised taxes to fund higher school standards. I helped to broker a resolution to the conflict, in which the Republicans apologized for the letter and said they wouldn't do it again, and we voted for Lamar for chairman. I was elected vice chairman. We did a lot of good work in the governors' conferences in the seventies and eighties. In the 1990s, when the Republican governors gained the majority and got more in line with their national party, the old cooperative spirit diminished. That might have been good politics, but it impaired the search for good policy.

On our way to Idaho, Hillary, Chelsea, and I stopped for a few happy days in Montana, thanks largely to Governor Ted Schwinden. After we spent the night with him, Ted got us up at dawn to take a helicopter up the Missouri River and watch the wildlife waking up to the day. Then we took a four-wheel-drive vehicle equipped with rail connectors along the Burlington Northern rail line for a couple hundred miles, a trip that included a dramatic crossing of a three-hundred-foot-deep gorge. And we drove a rented car up the "highway to the sun," where we watched marmots scramble around above the snow line, then spent a few days at Kootenai Lodge on Swan Lake. After all my travels, I still think western Montana is one of the most beautiful places I've ever seen.

The political trips I took were a minor diversion from my main mission after the legislature went home in 1985, and for the rest of the decade: building the Arkansas economy. I enjoyed the challenge, and I got pretty good at it. First, I had to stop bad things from happening. When International Paper announced plans to close a mill in Camden that had been operating since the 1920s, I flew to New York to see the company president, John Georges, and asked him what it would take to keep the mill open. He gave me a list of five or six things he wanted. I delivered on all but one, and he kept the plant open. When my friend Turner Whitson called to tell me the shoe plant in Clarksville was closing, I turned for help to Don Munro, who had managed to keep six shoe-making facilities open in Arkansas during the worst of the eighties recession. I offered him $1 million in assistance and he took over the plant. The workers found out about their jobs being saved at a meeting to help them file for unemployment and retraining benefits.

When the Sanyo company told me it was planning to close its television-assembly plant in Forrest City, Dave Harrington and I flew to Osaka, Japan, to see Satoshi Iue, the president of Sanyo, a vast company with more than 100,000 employees worldwide. I had become friends with Mr. Iue over the years. After I was defeated for governor in 1980, he sent me a beautiful piece of Japanese calligraphy that said "Though the river may force you to change course, hold fast to what you believe." I had it framed, and when I was reelected in 1982, it hung at the entrance to our bedroom so that I would see it every day. I told Mr. Iue that we couldn't handle the loss of Sanyo's jobs in eastern Arkansas, where the Delta counties all had unemployment rates higher than 10 percent. I asked him if he would keep the plant open if Wal-Mart would sell Sanyo's televisions. After he agreed, I flew back to Arkansas and asked Wal-Mart to help. In September 2003, Satoshi Iue came to Chappaqua for lunch. By then, Wal-Mart had bought more than twenty million of those television sets.

It wasn't all rescue missions. We also made some new things happen, financing new high-tech ventures, involving the universities in helping start new businesses, taking successful trade and investment missions to Europe and Asia, and supporting the expansion of successful plants like the ones run by the Daiwa Steel Tube Industries in Pine Bluff and the Dana Company in Jonesboro, which made transmissions with the help of skilled workers and amazing robots.

Our biggest coup was getting NUCOR Steel Company to come to northeast Arkansas. NUCOR was a highly profitable company that made steel by melting already-forged metal rather than creating it from scratch. NUCOR paid workers a modest weekly wage and a bonus based on profits—a bonus that usually accounted for more than half the workers' income. By 1992, the Arkansas NUCOR workers' average income was about $50,000. Moreover, NUCOR gave every employee an extra $1,500 a year for every child he or she had in college. One of its employees educated eleven children with the company's help. NUCOR had no corporate jet and operated with a tiny headquarters staff out of rented space in North Carolina. The founder, Ken Iverson, inspired great loyalty the old-fashioned way: he earned it. In the only year NUCOR's earnings were down in the 1980s, Iverson sent a letter to his employees apologizing for the cut in their pay, which was applied across the board because NUCOR had a strict no-layoff policy. The benefits and burdens were shared equally, except for the boss. Iverson said it wasn't the workers' fault that market conditions were poor, but he should have figured out a way to deal with them. He told his workers he was taking a 60-percent pay cut, three times theirs, a dramatic departure from the common practice for the last two decades of raising executive pay at a far greater rate than that of other employees, whether the company is doing well or not. Needless to say, no one at NUCOR wanted to quit.

When the Van Heusen shirt company announced it was closing its Brinkley plant, Farris and Marilyn Burroughs, who had been involved with the workers and community for years, decided to buy it and keep it open, but they needed more customers for their shirts. I asked David Glass, the president of Wal-Mart, if he would stock them. Again, Wal-Mart came to the rescue. Shortly afterward, I hosted a lunch for Wal-Mart executives and our economic development people to encourage the company to buy more products made in America and to advertise this practice as a way to increase sales. Wal-Mart's "Buy America" campaign was a great success and helped to reduce resentment against the giant discounter for putting small-town merchants out of business. Hillary loved the program and supported it strongly when she went on the Wal-Mart board a couple of years later. At its high-water mark, Wal-Mart's merchandise was about 55 percent American made, about 10 percent more than that of its nearest competitor. Unfortunately, after a few years Wal-Mart abandoned the policy in its marketing drive to be the lowest-cost retailer, but we made the most of it in Arkansas while it lasted.

The work I did in education and economic development convinced me that Arkansas, and America, had to make some big changes if we wanted to preserve our economic and political leadership in the global economy. We simply weren't well educated or productive enough. We had been losing ground in average incomes since 1973, and by the 1980s, four in ten workers were experiencing declining incomes. The situation was intolerable, and I was determined to do what I could to change it.

My efforts helped to broaden my political base, garnering support from Republicans and conservative independents who had never voted for me before. Even though Arkansas had been in the top ten states in new-job growth as a percentage of total employment in two of the last three years, I couldn't convert everybody. When the oil refinery in El Dorado was about to close, costing us more than three hundred good union jobs, I helped convince some businesspeople from Mississippi to buy and operate it. I knew how much it meant to those workers' families and to the local economy, and I looked forward to shaking hands at the plant gate at the next election. It was a home run, until I met a man who angrily said he wouldn't vote for me under any circumstances. When I responded, "Don't you know I saved your job?" he replied, "Yeah, I know you did, but you don't care a thing about me. You only did it so you'd have one more poor sucker to tax. That's why you want me to have a job, so you can tax me. I wouldn't vote for you for all the money in the world." You can't win 'em all.

In early 1986, I launched my campaign for reelection, this one for a four-year term. In 1984, the voters had passed an amendment to change executive terms from two to four years for the first time since our Reconstruction Era Constitution was adopted in 1874. If I won, I would become the second-longest-serving Arkansas governor after Orval Faubus. He won his longevity because of Little Rock Central High. I wanted to win mine on schools and jobs.

Ironically, my main opponent in the primary was Faubus himself. He was still angry at me because, in my first term, I refused to have the state buy his beautiful Fay Jones house in Huntsville and put it into the state park system to be used as a retreat. I knew he was strapped for cash, but so was the state, and I couldn't justify the expense. Faubus was going to rail against the new education standards, saying they had brought consolidation and high taxes to rural areas, which hadn't gotten any of the new jobs I was always bragging about.

And once I got by Faubus, Frank White was waiting. He was trying to win the best two out of three. Between the two of them, I knew a lot of charges would fly. I felt confident that Betsey Wright, Dick Morris, David Watkins, and I could deal with whatever came up, but I was concerned about how Chelsea would react to people saying bad things about her father. She was six and had begun to watch the news and even to read the paper. Hillary and I tried to prepare her for what White and Faubus might say about me and how I would respond. Then, for several days, we would take turns playing one of the candidates. One day Hillary was Frank White, I was Faubus, and Chelsea was me. I accused her of ruining the small schools with misguided education ideas. She shot back, "Well, at least I didn't use the state police to spy on my political enemies the way you did!" Faubus had actually done that in the aftermath of the Central High crisis. Not bad for a six-year-old.

I won the primary with more than 60 percent of the vote, but Faubus pulled a third of it. Even at seventy-six, he still had some juice in rural areas. Frank White took up where Faubus left off. Although he had called teachers "greedy" when they pushed for higher pay during his tenure, he got the endorsement of the Arkansas Education Association in the Republican primary when he changed his position from support of the teacher test to opposition. Then he started in on Hillary and me.

White began by saying the new education standards were too burdensome and needed to be changed. I hit that one out of the park, saying if he were elected, he would "delay them to death." Then he went after Hillary, alleging she had a conflict of interest because the Rose firm was representing the state in its fight against the Grand Gulf nuclear plants. We had a good response to that charge, too. First, the Rose firm was working to save Arkansans money by lifting the burden of the Grand Gulf plants, while White, as a board member of one of the Middle South Utilities companies, had voted three times to go forward with construction of the plants. Second, the Public Service Commission hired the Rose firm because all the other big firms were representing utilities or other parties in the case. Both the legislature and the attorney general approved the hiring. Third, the money the state paid to the Rose firm was subtracted from the firm's income before Hillary's partnership profits were calculated, so she made no money from it. White seemed more interested in defending the utility's effort to soak Arkansas ratepayers than protecting them from a conflict of interest. I asked him if his attacks on Hillary meant he wanted to run for first lady instead of governor. Our campaign even made bumper stickers and buttons that said, "Frank for First Lady."

White's final charges did him in. He had been working for Stephens, Inc., then the largest bond house outside Wall Street. Jack Stephens had supported me when I first ran for governor, but then he drifted to the right, heading Democrats for Reagan in 1984, and by 1986 he had become a Republican. His older brother, Witt, was still a Democrat and supporting me, but Jack ran the bond house. And Frank White was his guy. For many years, Stephens had controlled the state's bond business. When I dramatically expanded the volume of bond issues, I insisted that we open all of them to competitive bidding by national firms, and that we let more Arkansas firms have the opportunity to sell the bonds. The Stephens firm still got its fair share, but it didn't control all the issues as it had in the past and would again if White won the election. One of the Arkansas firms that got some business was headed by Dan Lasater, who built a successful bond firm in Little Rock before he lost it all to a cocaine habit. Lasater had been a supporter of mine and a friend of my brother's, with whom he had partied hard when they were both chained to cocaine, as too many young people were in the 1980s.

When Betsey Wright and I were preparing for our television debate with White, we learned that he was going to challenge me to take a drug test with him. The ostensible reason was to set a good example, but I knew White was hoping I wouldn't do it. The blizzard of rumors spawned by Lasater's downfall included one that I had been part of Dan's party circle. It wasn't true. Betsey and I decided to take a drug test before the debate. When White hit me on television with his challenge, I smiled and said Betsey and I had already taken a test and he and his campaign manager, Darrell Glascock, should follow suit. Glascock had been subjected to his share of rumors too. Their clever trick had backfired.

White turned up the heat with the nastiest TV ad I'd ever seen. He showed Lasater's office, followed by a tray of cocaine, with an announcer saying I'd taken campaign contributions from a cocaine-using felon, then given him state bond business. The clear implication was that I'd given Lasater preferred treatment and at the least I had known about his cocaine habit when I did. I invited the *Arkansas Gazette* to review the records of the Development Finance Authority, and the paper ran a front-page story showing how many more bond houses had done business with the state since I'd taken over from Governor White. The number had gone from four to fifteen, and Stephens still had handled over $700 million of bond business, more than twice as much as any other Arkansas firm. I also hit back with a TV ad that began by asking people if they'd seen White's ad and actually showing a few seconds of it. Then my ad cut to a picture of Stephens, Inc., with the announcer saying White worked there and the reason he was attacking me was that neither Stephens nor anyone else controlled the state's business any longer, but they would if White became governor again. It was one of the most effective commercials I ever ran, because it was a strong response to a low blow, and because the facts spoke for themselves.

I was also glad that Roger and Mother hadn't let themselves get too hurt by White's bringing up Roger's drug problem. After he got out of prison, Roger served six months in a halfway house in Texas, and then moved to north Arkansas, where he worked for a friend of ours in a quick-stop service station. He was about to move to Nashville, Tennessee, and was healthy enough not to let the old story drag him down. Mother was happy with Dick Kelley, and by now knew that politics was a rough game in which the only answer to a low blow is winning.

In November, I won with 64 percent, including a staggering 75 percent in Little Rock. I was gratified that the victory gave me the opportunity to smash the suggestion that I had abused the governor's office and the implication that drugs had something to do with it. Despite the tough campaign, I wasn't very good at holding a grudge. Over the years, I came to like Frank White and his wife, Gay, and to enjoy being on programs with him. He had a great sense of humor, he loved Arkansas, and I was sad when he died in 2003. Thankfully, I also reconciled with Jack Stephens.

As far as I was concerned, the campaign against Faubus and White was a battle against Arkansas' past and against the emerging politics of personal destruction. I wanted to focus the people on the issues and on the future, by defending our education reforms and promoting our economic initiatives. The *Memphis Commercial Appeal* reported that "Clinton's stump speeches in the area sound as much like seminars on the economy as pleas for votes and most political analysts agree that the strategy is working."

I often told the story of my visit to the Arkansas Eastman chemical plant in rural Independence County. During the tour, my host kept saying that all the anti-pollution equipment was run by computers and he wanted me to meet the guy who was running them. He built him up so much that by the time I got to the computer control room, I expected to meet someone who was a cross between Albert Einstein and the Wizard of Oz. Instead, the man running the computers was wearing cowboy boots, jeans with a belt adorned with a big silver rodeo buckle, and a baseball cap. He was listening to country music and chewing tobacco. The first thing he said to me was "My wife and I are going to vote for you, because we need more jobs like this." This guy raised cattle and horses—he was pure Arkansas—but he knew his prosperity depended more on what he knew than on how much he could do with his hands and back. He had seen the future and he wanted to go there.

In August, when the National Governors Association met in Hilton Head, South Carolina, I became the chairman and celebrated my fortieth birthday. I had already agreed to serve as chairman of the Education Commission of the States, a group dedicated to gathering the best education ideas and practices and spreading them across the nation. Lamar Alexander had also appointed me to be the Democratic co-chairman of the governors' task force on welfare reform, to work with the White House and Congress to develop a bipartisan proposal to improve the welfare system so that it would promote work, strengthen families, and meet children's basic needs. Though I had secured an increase in Arkansas' meager monthly welfare benefits in 1985, I wanted welfare to be a way station on the road to independence.

I was excited with these new responsibilities. I was both a political animal and a policy wonk, always eager to meet new people and explore new ideas. I thought the work would enable me to be a better governor, strengthen my network of national contacts, and gain a better understanding of the emerging global economy and how America should deal with its challenges.

As 1986 drew to a close, I took a quick trip to Taiwan to address the Tenth Annual Conference of Taiwanese and American Leaders about our future relations. The Taiwanese were good customers for Arkansas soybeans and a wide variety of our manufactured products, from electric motors to parking meters. But America's trade deficit was large and growing, and four in ten American workers had suffered declining incomes in the previous five years. Speaking for all the governors, I acknowledged America's responsibility to cut our deficit to bring down interest rates and increase domestic demand, to restructure and reduce the debt of our Latin American neighbors, to relax export controls on high-technology products, and to improve the education and productivity of our workforce. Then I challenged the Taiwanese to reduce trade barriers and invest more of their huge cash reserves in America. It was my first speech on global economics to a foreign audience. Making it forced me to sort out exactly what I thought should be done and who should do it.

By the end of 1986, I had formed some basic convictions about the nature of the modern world, which later developed into the so-called New Democrat philosophy that was the backbone of my 1992 campaign for President. I outlined them in a speech to the year-end management meeting of Gannett, the newspaper chain that had just bought the *Arkansas Gazette.*

> . . . these are the new rules that I believe should provide the framework within which we make policy today:
>
> (1) Change may be the only constant in today's American economy. I was at an old country church celebration in Arkansas about three months ago to celebrate its 150th anniversary. There were about seventy-five people there, all packed in this small wooden church. After the service, we went out under the pine trees to have a potluck lunch, and I found myself talking to an old man who was obviously quite bright. Finally, I asked him, "Mister, how old are you?" He said, "I'm eighty-two." "When did you join this church?" "Nineteen sixteen," he said. "If you had to say in one sentence, what is the difference between our state now and in 1916?" He was quiet for a moment, then said, "Governor, that's pretty easy. In 1916 when I got up in the morning I knew what was going to happen, but when I get up in the morning now, I don't have any idea." That is about as good a one-sentence explanation about what has happened to America as Lester Thurow could give. . . .
>
> (2) Human capital is probably more important than physical capital now. . . .
>
> (3) A more constructive partnership between business and government is far more important than the dominance of either.

(4) As we try to solve problems which arise out of the internationalization of American life and the changes in our own population, cooperation in every area is far more important than conflict. . . . We have to share responsibilities and opportunities—we're going up or down together.

(5) Waste is going to be punished . . . it appears to me that we are spending billions of dollars of investment capital increasing the debt of corporations without increasing their productivity. More debt should mean increased productivity, growth, and profitability. Now it means, too often, less employment, less investment for research and development, and forced restructuring to service nonproductive debt. . . .

(6) A strong America requires a resurgent sense of community, a strong sense of mutual obligations, and a conviction that we cannot pursue our individual interests independent of the needs of our fellow citizens. . . .

If we want to keep the American dream alive for our own people and preserve America's role in the world, we must accept the new rules of successful economic, political, and social life. And we must act on them.

Over the next five years, I would refine my analysis of globalization and interdependence and propose more initiatives to respond to them, juggling as best I could my desire to be a good governor and to have a positive impact on national policy.

In 1987, my agenda for the legislative session, "Good Beginnings, Good Schools, Good Jobs," was consistent with the work I was doing with the National Governors Association under the theme "Making America Work." In addition to recommendations that built on our previous efforts in education and economic development, I asked the legislature to help me get the growing number of poor children off to a good start in life by increasing health-care coverage for poor mothers and children, starting with prenatal care in order to lower the infant-mortality rate and reduce avoidable damage to newborns; to increase parenting education for mothers of at-risk children; to provide more special education in early childhood to kids with learning problems; to increase the availability of affordable child care; and to strengthen child-support enforcement.

From Hillary, I had learned most of what I knew about early-childhood development and its importance to later life. She had been interested in it as long as I'd known her, and had taken a fourth year at Yale Law School to work on children's issues at the Yale Child Study Center and Yale–New Haven Hospital. She had worked hard to import to Arkansas an innovative preschool program from Israel called HIPPY, which stands for Home Instruction Programs for Preschool Youngsters, a program that helps to develop both parenting skills and children's ability to learn. Hillary set up HIPPY programs all across the state. We both loved going to the graduation exercises, watching the children show their stuff and seeing the parents' pride in their kids and themselves. Thanks to Hillary, Arkansas had the largest program in the country, serving 2,400 mothers, and their children showed remarkable progress.

The main focus of my economic development efforts was to increase investment and opportunity for poor people and distressed areas, most of them in rural Arkansas. The most important proposal was to provide more capital to people who had the potential to operate profitable small businesses but couldn't borrow the money to get started. The South Shore Development Bank in Chicago had been instrumental in helping unemployed carpenters and electricians set themselves up in business on the city's South Side to renovate abandoned buildings that otherwise would have been condemned. As a result, the whole area recovered.

I knew about the bank because one of its employees, Jan Piercy, had been one of Hillary's best friends at Wellesley. Jan told us South Shore got the idea to fund artisans who were skilled but not creditworthy by conventional standards from the work of the Grameen Bank of Bangladesh,

founded by Muhammad Yunus, who had studied economics at Vanderbilt University before going home to help his
people. I arranged to meet him for breakfast in Washington
one morning, and he explained how his "micro-credit" program worked. Village women who had skills and a reputation for honesty but no assets were organized in teams.
When the first borrower repaid her small loan, the next one
in line got hers, and so on. When I first met Yunus, the
Grameen Bank already had made hundreds of thousands of
loans, with a repayment rate higher than that for commercial lenders in Bangladesh. By 2002, Grameen had made
them to more than 2.4 million people, 95 percent of them
poor women.

If the idea worked in Chicago, I thought it would work
in economically distressed areas in rural Arkansas. As
Yunus said in an interview, "Anywhere anybody is rejected
by the banking system, you have room for a Grameen-type
program." We set up the Southern Development Bank Corporation in Arkadelphia. The Development Finance Authority put up some of the initial money, but most of it came
from corporations that Hillary and I asked to invest in it.

When I became President, I secured congressional
approval for a national loan program modeled on the
Grameen Bank, and featured some of our success stories at
a White House event. The U.S. Agency for International
Development also funded two million micro-credit loans a
year in poor villages in Africa, Latin America, and East
Asia. In 1999, when I went to South Asia, I visited Muhammad Yunus and some of the people he'd set up in business,
including women who'd used the loans to buy cell phones,
which they charged villagers to use to call their relatives and
friends in America and Europe. Muhammad Yunus should
have been awarded the Nobel Prize in Economics years ago.

My other major interest was welfare reform. I asked the
legislature to require recipients with children three years old
or over to sign a contract committing themselves to a course
of independence, through literacy, job training, and work. In
February, I went to Washington with several other governors
to testify before the House Ways and Means Committee on

welfare prevention and reforms. We asked Congress to give
us the tools to "promote work, not welfare; independence,
not dependence." We argued that more should be done to
keep people off welfare in the first place, by reducing adult
illiteracy, teen pregnancy, the school dropout rate, and alcohol and drug abuse. On welfare reform, we advocated a
binding contract between the recipient and the government,
setting out the rights and responsibilities of both parties.
Recipients would commit to strive for independence in
return for the benefits, and the government would commit to
help them, with education and training, medical care, child
care, and job placement. We also asked that all welfare
recipients with children age three or older be required to
participate in a work program designed by the states, that
each welfare recipient have a caseworker committed to a
successful transition to self-sufficiency, that efforts to collect
child-support payments be intensified, and that a new formula for cash assistance be established consistent with each
state's cost of living. Federal law allowed states to set
monthly benefits wherever they chose as long as they weren't
lower than they had been in the early seventies, and they
were all over the place.

I had spent enough time talking to welfare recipients
and caseworkers in Arkansas to know that the vast majority
of them wanted to work and support their families. But they
faced formidable barriers, beyond the obvious ones of low
skills, lack of work experience, and inability to pay for child
care. Many of the people I met had no cars or access to public transportation. If they took a low-wage job, they would
lose food stamps and medical coverage under Medicaid.
Finally, many of them just didn't believe they could make it
in the world of work and had no idea where to begin.

At one of our governors' meetings in Washington, along
with my welfare reform co-chair, Governor Mike Castle of
Delaware, I organized a meeting for other governors on
welfare reform. I brought two women from Arkansas who
had left welfare for work to testify. One young woman from
Pine Bluff had never been on an airplane or an escalator
before the trip. She was restrained but convincing about the

potential of poor people to support themselves and their children. The other witness was in her mid to late thirties. Her name was Lillie Hardin, and she had recently found work as a cook. I asked her if she thought able-bodied people on welfare should be forced to take jobs if they were available. "I sure do," she answered. "Otherwise we'll just lay around watching the soaps all day." Then I asked Lillie what was the best thing about being off welfare. Without hesitation, she replied, "When my boy goes to school and they ask him, 'What does your mama do for a living?' he can give an answer." It was the best argument I've ever heard for welfare reform. After the hearing, the governors treated her like a rock star.

When I tackled welfare reform as President, I was always somewhat amused to hear some members of the press characterize it as a Republican issue, as if valuing work was something only conservatives did. By 1996, when Congress passed a bill I could sign, I had been working on welfare reform for more than fifteen years. But I didn't consider it a Democratic issue. Or even a governors' issue. Welfare reform was about Lillie Hardin and her boy.

TWENTY-FOUR

THANKS TO THE four-year term, the dedication and ability of my staff and cabinet, a good working relationship with the legislature, and the strength of my political organization, I also had the space to move into the national political arena.

Because of the visibility I got from my work on education, economics, and welfare reform, and my chairmanships of the National Governors Association and the Education Commission of the States, I received a lot of invitations to speak out of state in 1987. I accepted more than two dozen of them, in fifteen states. While only four were Democratic Party events, they all served to broaden my contacts and to heighten speculation that I might enter the presidential race.

Although I was only forty in the spring of 1987, I was interested in making the race, for three reasons. First, by historical standards the Democrats had an excellent chance to recapture the White House. It seemed clear that Vice President Bush would be the nominee of the Republican Party, and up until then the only vice president to win the presidency directly from that office had been Martin Van Buren, in 1836, who succeeded Andrew Jackson in the last election in which there was no effective opposition to the Democratic Party. Second, I felt very strongly that the country had to change direction. Our growth was fueled primarily by big increases in defense spending and large tax cuts that disproportionately benefited the wealthiest Americans and drove up the deficit. The big deficits led to high interest rates, as the government competed with private borrowers for money, and that in turn drove up the value of the dollar, making imports cheaper and American exports more expensive. At a time when Americans were beginning to improve their productivity and competitive position, we were still losing manufacturing jobs and farms. Moreover, because of the budget deficit, we weren't investing enough in the education, training, and research required to maintain high wages and low unemployment in the global economy. That's why 40 percent of the American people had suffered a decline in real income since the mid-1970s.

The third reason I was seriously considering entering the race is that I thought I understood what was happening and could explain it to the American people. Also, because I had a strong record on crime, welfare reform, accountability in education, and fiscal responsibility, I didn't think the Republicans could paint me as an ultra-liberal Democrat who didn't embrace mainstream values and who thought there was a government program for every problem. I was convinced that if we could escape the "alien" box the Republicans had put us in since 1968, except for President Carter's success in 1976, we could win the White House again.

It was a tall order, because it's not easy to get people to change their political frame of reference, but I thought I might be able to do it. So did several of my fellow governors. When I went to the Indianapolis 500 race in the spring, I ran into Governor Bob Kerrey of Nebraska. I liked Bob a lot and thought he, too, would be a good presidential candidate. He had won the Medal of Honor in Vietnam and, like me, was a fiscal conservative and social progressive who had been elected in a state far more Republican than Arkansas. To my surprise, Bob encouraged me to run and said he'd be my chairman in the midwestern states if I did.

There was one obstacle at home to my running for President: Dale Bumpers was seriously considering it. I had been encouraging him to run since late 1974. He almost did in 1984, and he had an excellent chance to win this time. He had served in the marines in World War II, had been a great governor, and was the best speaker in the Senate. I knew that Dale would be a good President and that he would have a better chance to win than I would. I would have been happy to support him. I wanted our side to win and change the direction of the country.

On March 20, as I was jogging down Main Street in

Little Rock, a local reporter chased me down to say that Senator Bumpers had just issued a statement saying he wouldn't run for President. He just didn't want to do it. A few weeks earlier, Governor Mario Cuomo of New York had made the same decision. I told Hillary and Betsey I wanted to take a serious look at the race.

We raised a little money for the exploratory effort, and Betsey sent people to do spadework in Iowa, New Hampshire, and some of the southern states that would vote in a bloc the next year on "Super Tuesday" shortly after the New Hampshire primary. On May 7, the primary looked even more winnable when Senator Gary Hart, who had almost upset Vice President Mondale in 1984, withdrew from the race after his relationship with Donna Rice was exposed. I thought Gary had made an error by challenging the press to tail him to see if they could find any dirt, but I felt bad for him, too. He was a brilliant, innovative politician who was always thinking about America's big challenges and what to do about them. After the Hart affair, those of us who had not led perfect lives had no way of knowing what the press's standards of disclosure were. Finally I concluded that anyone who believed he had something to offer should just run, deal with whatever charges arose, and trust the American people. Without a high pain threshold, you can't be a successful President anyway.

I set July 14 as a deadline for making a decision. Several of my old friends from past political battles came down to Little Rock, including Mickey Kantor, Carl Wagner, Steve Cohen, John Holum, Kevin O'Keefe, Jim Lyons, Mike Driver, and Sandy Berger. They all thought I should run; it seemed too good a chance to pass up. Still, I was holding back. I knew I was ready to be a good candidate, but I wasn't sure I had lived long enough to acquire the wisdom and judgment necessary to be a good President. If elected, I would be forty-two, about the same age Theodore Roosevelt was when he was sworn in after President McKinley's assassination, and a year younger than John Kennedy when he was elected. But they had both come from wealthy, politically prominent families, and had grown up in a way that made them comfortable in the circles of power. My two favorite Presidents, Lincoln and FDR, were fifty-one when they took office, fully mature and in command of themselves and their responsibilities. On my fifty-first birthday, Al Gore gave me an account of the Cherokee Indian Nation's view of the aging process. The Cherokees believe a man does not reach full maturity until he is fifty-one.

The second thing that bothered me was the difficulties a campaign would pose for my governorship. Nineteen eighty-seven was the deadline for implementing the school standards. I had already called one special session to raise money for schools and overcrowded prisons. It had been a knockdown fight that had strained my relations with several legislators, and it very nearly ended in failure before we scraped together enough votes at the last minute to do what had to be done. I knew that, in all probability, I'd have to call another special session in early 1988. I was determined to fully implement the school standards and build on them; it was the only chance most poor kids in my state had for a better future. Chelsea's elementary school was about 60 percent black, and more than half the kids were from low-income families. I remember how one little boy she invited to her birthday party at the mansion almost didn't come because he couldn't afford to buy her a present. I was determined to give that little boy a better chance than his parents had had.

The *Arkansas Gazette*, which had supported me in every campaign, ran an editorial arguing that I shouldn't run for both of the reasons that concerned me. While acknowledging my strong potential for national leadership, the *Gazette* said, "Bill Clinton is not ready to be President" and "Governor Clinton is needed in Arkansas."

Ambition is a powerful force, and the ambition to be President has led many a candidate to ignore both his own limitations and the responsibilities of the office he currently holds. I always thought I could rise to any occasion, stand the most withering fire, and do two or three jobs at once. In 1987, I might have made a decision rooted in self-confidence and driven by ambition, but I didn't. What finally decided the question for me was the one part of my life politics couldn't reach: Chelsea. Carl Wagner, who was also the father of an only daughter, told me I'd have to reconcile myself to being away from Chelsea for most of the next sixteen months. Mickey Kantor was talking me through it when Chelsea asked me where we were going for summer vacation. When I said I might not be able to take one if I ran for President, Chelsea replied, "Then Mom and I will go without you." That did it.

I went into the dining room of the Governor's Mansion, where my friends were eating lunch, told them I wasn't running, and apologized for bringing them all down. Then I went to the Excelsior to make my announcement to a few hundred supporters. I did my best to explain how I had come so close, yet backed away:

> I need some family time; I need some personal time. Politicians are people too. I think sometimes we forget it, but they really are. The only thing I or any other candidate has to offer in running for President is what's inside. That's what sets people on fire and gets their confidence and their votes, whether they live in Wisconsin or Montana or New York. That part of my life needs renewal. The other, even more important reason for my decision is the certain impact that this campaign would have had on our daughter. The only way I could have won, getting in this late, after others had been working up to two years, would be to go on the road full-time from now until the end, and to have Hillary do the same. . . . I've seen a lot of kids grow up under these pressures and a long, long time ago I made a promise to myself that if I was ever lucky enough to have a child, she would never grow up wondering who her father was.

Though she had said she would support me whichever way I went, Hillary was relieved. She thought I should finish the work I had started in Arkansas and keep building a national base of support. And she knew it was not a good time for me to be away from our families. Mother was having problems in her anesthesia work, Roger had been out of prison only a couple of years, and Hillary's parents were moving to Little Rock. In January 1983, during my swearing-in speech to the legislature, Hugh Rodham had slumped in his chair. He had suffered a massive heart attack and was rushed to the University Medical Center for quadruple-bypass surgery. I was with him when he woke up. After I realized he was lucid, I said, "Hugh, the speech wasn't good enough to give anyone a heart attack!" In 1987, he had a minor stroke. Hugh and Dorothy didn't need to stay up in Park Ridge alone. We wanted them nearby, and they were looking forward to the move, mostly to be near their only grandchild. Still, it would be a big adjustment for them.

Finally, Hillary was happy I didn't run because she disagreed with the conventional wisdom that the Democrats were likely to win in 1988. She didn't think the Reagan Revolution had run its course and believed that, despite the Iran-Contra affair, George Bush would win as a more moderate version of Reagan. Four years later, when prospects for victory looked much darker, with President Bush's approval ratings over 70 percent, Hillary encouraged me to run. As usual, she was right both times.

After the decision was announced, I felt as though the weight of the world had been lifted from my shoulders. I was free to be a father, husband, and governor, and to work and speak on national issues unencumbered by immediate ambitions.

In July, Hillary, Chelsea, and I went to the summer governors' conference in Traverse City, Michigan, to wrap up my year as chairman. I was succeeded by New Hampshire governor John Sununu, who promised to continue our work for welfare reform, and with whom I had a good relationship. After we adjourned, the Democratic governors went to Mackinaw Island, where Governor Jim Blanchard brought us together to meet with all our presidential candidates, including Senator Al Gore, Senator Paul Simon, Senator Joe Biden, Congressman Dick Gephardt, the Reverend Jesse

Jackson, former governor Bruce Babbitt of Arizona, and Governor Mike Dukakis. I thought we had a good field, but I favored Dukakis. In Massachusetts he had presided over a successful high-tech economy, had balanced budgets, and had advanced both education and welfare reform. He was governing as a "New Democrat," and he knew what it was like to lose an election to negative attacks and make a successful comeback. Even though most Americans thought of Massachusetts as a liberal state, I believed we could sell him because he was a successful governor and would avoid the errors that had sunk us in previous elections. Besides, we were friends. Mike was relieved when I didn't enter the race and gave me an early birthday present, a T-shirt inscribed with the words "Happy 41st. Clinton in '96. You'll only be 49!"

At the end of the meeting, Jim Blanchard put on a terrific rock-and-roll concert featuring Motown artists from the sixties, including the Four Tops, Martha Reeves and the Vandellas, and Jr. Walker, a legendary tenor sax player who could make the horn play an octave higher than most of us mere mortals could. Near the end of the show, a young woman came up to me and invited me to play the sax with all the groups on the Motown standard "Dancin' in the Street." I hadn't played a note in three years. "Is there any sheet music?" I asked. "No," she said. "What key is it in?" She answered, "I don't have a clue." "Can I have a couple of minutes to warm up the horn?" Again, "No." I gave the only possible answer: "Okay, I'll do it." I went up to the stage. They gave me a horn, promptly attached a mike to the bell, and the music started. I played as softly as I could until I tuned the horn and figured out the key. Then I joined in and did pretty well. I still keep a picture of Jr. Walker and me doing a riff together.

September was a busy month. With the new school year starting, I appeared on NBC's *Meet the Press* along with Bill Bennett, who had succeeded Terrel Bell as President Reagan's secretary of education. I got along well with Bennett, who appreciated my support for accountability and teaching kids basic values in school, and he didn't disagree when

I said the states needed more federal help to pay for early-childhood programs. When Bennett criticized the National Education Association as an obstacle to accountability, I said I thought the NEA was doing better on that score and reminded him that Al Shanker, leader of the other big teachers union, the American Federation of Teachers, supported both accountability and values education.

Unfortunately, my relationship with Bill Bennett didn't fare well after I became President and he began promoting virtue for a living. Although he had once inscribed a book to me with the words "To Bill Clinton, the Democrat who makes sense," he apparently came to believe that either he had been wrong or I had lost whatever sense I had when I wrote those words.

Around the time of the *Meet the Press* interview, Senator Joe Biden, the chairman of the Judiciary Committee, asked me to testify against Judge Robert Bork, who had been nominated to the U.S. Supreme Court by President Reagan. I knew Joe wanted me because I was a white southern governor; the fact that I had been Bork's student in Constitutional Law was an added bonus. Before I agreed, I read most of Bork's articles, important judicial opinions, and published reports of his speeches. I concluded that Judge Bork should not go on the Supreme Court. In an eight-page statement, I said I liked and respected Bork as a teacher and thought President Reagan should have considerable latitude in his appointments, but I still believed the nomination should be rejected by the Senate. I argued that Bork's own words demonstrated that he was a reactionary, not a mainstream conservative. He had criticized almost every major Supreme Court decision expanding civil rights except *Brown* v. *Board of Education.* In fact, Bork had been one of two lawyers, along with William Rehnquist, to advise Barry Goldwater to vote against the Civil Rights Act of 1964. As a southerner, I knew how important it was not to reopen the wounds of race by disturbing those decisions. Bork had the most restrictive view on what the Supreme Court can do to protect individual rights of anyone who had been nominated to the Supreme Court in decades. He thought "dozens" of court decisions needed to be reversed. For example, he said a married couple's right to use contraceptives was no more deserving of privacy protection from government action than a utility's right to pollute the air. In fact, as his ruling against Arkansas in the Grand Gulf case showed, he thought utilities and other business interests were entitled to *more* protection than individual citizens from government actions he disagreed with. However, when it came to protecting business interests, he threw judicial restraint out the window in favor of activism. He even said federal courts shouldn't enforce antitrust laws because they were based on a flawed economic theory. I asked the Senate not to take the risk that Judge Bork would act on his long-held convictions rather than on the more moderate assurances he was then giving in the confirmation process.

I had to file the testimony rather than give it in person, because the hearings were delayed and I had to leave for a trade mission to Europe. In late October, the Senate rejected the Bork nomination, 58–42. I doubt that my testimony influenced a single vote. Previously President Reagan had nominated Judge Antonin Scalia, who was as conservative as Bork but hadn't said and written as much to prove it. He sailed through. In December 2000, in the case of *Bush* v. *Gore*, he wrote the Saturday opinion of the Supreme Court granting an unprecedented injunction to stop counting votes in Florida. Three days later, by a 5–4 vote, the Supreme Court gave the election to George W. Bush, partly on the ground that the outstanding disputed ballots couldn't be counted by midnight of that day as Florida law required. Of course not: the Supreme Court had stopped the counting of legal votes three days before. It was an act of judicial activism that might have made even Bob Bork blush.

After the trade mission, Hillary and I joined John Sununu and Governor Ed DiPrete of Rhode Island for a meeting with our Italian counterparts in Florence. It was the first trip to Italy for Hillary and me, and we fell in love with Florence, Siena, Pisa, San Gimignano, and Venice. I was also fascinated by the economic success of northern Italy, which had a higher per capita income than Germany. One of the reasons for the region's prosperity seemed to be the extraordinary cooperation of small-business people in sharing facilities and administrative and marketing costs, as northern Italian artisans had been doing for centuries, since the development of medieval guilds. Once more I had found an idea I thought might work in Arkansas. When I got home, we helped a group of unemployed sheet-metal workers set up businesses and cooperate in cost-sharing and marketing as I had observed Italian leatherworkers and furniture makers doing.

In October, America's economy took a big jolt when the stock market fell more than 500 points in one day, the biggest one-day drop since 1929. By coincidence, the richest man in America, Sam Walton, was sitting in my office when the market closed. Sam was the leader of the Arkansas Business Council, a group of prominent businesspeople euphemistically known as "the Good Suit Club." They were committed to improving education and the economy in Arkansas. Sam excused himself to see what had happened to Wal-Mart stock. All his wealth was tied up in the company. He'd lived in the same house for decades and drove an old pickup truck. When Sam came back, I asked him how much he'd lost. "About a billion dollars," he said. In 1987, that was still a lot of money, even to Sam Walton. When I asked him if he was worried, he said, "Tomorrow I'm going to fly to Tennessee to see the newest Wal-Mart. If there are plenty of cars in the parking lot I won't be worried. I'm only in the stock market to raise money to open more stores and to give our employees a stake in the company." Almost all of the people who worked for Wal-Mart owned some of its stock. Walton was a stark contrast to the new breed of corporate executives who insisted on big pay increases even when their companies and workers weren't doing well, and on golden parachutes when their companies failed. When the collapse of many stocks in the first years of the new century exposed a new wave of corporate greed and corruption, I thought back to that day in 1987 when Sam Walton lost a billion dollars of his wealth. Sam was a Republican. I doubt he ever

voted for me. I didn't agree with everything Wal-Mart did
back then and I don't agree with some of the company's
practices that have become more common since he died. As
I said, Wal-Mart doesn't "buy American" as much as it used
to. It's been accused of using large numbers of illegal immigrants. And, of course, the company is anti-union. But
America would be better off if all our companies were run
by people dedicated enough to see their own fortunes rise
and fall with those of their employees and stockholders.

I ended 1987 with my third speech of the decade at the
Florida Democratic convention, saying as I always did that
we had to face the facts and get the American people to see
them as we did. President Reagan had promised to cut
taxes, raise defense spending, and balance the budget. He
did the first two but couldn't do the third because supply-
side economics defies arithmetic. As a result, we had
exploded the national debt, failed to invest in our future,
and allowed wages to decline for 40 percent of our people. I
knew the Republicans were proud of their record, but I
looked at it with the perspective of the two old dogs watching young kids break-dancing. One old dog says to the
other, "You know, if we did that, they'd worm us."

I told the Florida Democrats, "We have to do nothing
less than create a new world economic order and secure the
place of the American people within it." The central arguments I made were "We've got to pay the price today to
secure tomorrow" and "We're all in it together."

In retrospect, my speeches in the late eighties seem interesting to me because of their similarity to what I would say
in 1992 and what I tried to do as President.

In 1988, I traveled to thirteen states and the District of
Columbia to speak on topics about evenly divided between
politics and policy. The policy speeches mostly concerned
education and the need for welfare-reform legislation, which
we were hoping would pass the Congress by the end of the
year. But the most important political speech for my future
was one called "Democratic Capitalism," which I delivered
to the Democratic Leadership Council in Williamsburg, Vir-

ginia, on February 29. From then on, I got more active in
the DLC, because I thought it was the only group committed to developing the new ideas Democrats needed both to
win elections and do right by the country. In Williamsburg,
I spoke about the need to make access to the global economy "democratic"—that is, available to all citizens and
communities. I had become a convert to William Julius Wilson's argument, articulated in his book *The Truly Disadvantaged*, that there were no race-specific solutions to hard-core
unemployment and poverty. The only answers were schools,
adult education and training, and jobs. Meanwhile, at
home, I continued to wrestle with budget problems facing
schools and prisons, to promote my agenda for "good
beginnings, good schools, and good jobs," and to push for
tax-reform and lobbying-reform legislation. Eventually,
because the legislature wouldn't pass them, both these items
were put on the ballot for the next election. The interest
groups advertised heavily against them. Lobbying reform
passed, and tax reform failed.

Governor Dukakis was moving to secure the Democratic
nomination for President. A couple of weeks before our
convention opened in Atlanta, Mike asked me to nominate
him. He and his campaign leaders told me that, though he
was leading in the polls against Vice President Bush, the
American people didn't know him very well. They had concluded that the nominating speech was an opportunity to
introduce him as a leader whose personal qualities, record
in office, and new ideas made him the right person for the
presidency. Because I was his colleague, his friend, and a
southerner, they wanted me to do it and to take the entire
allotted time, about twenty-five minutes. This was a departure from the usual practice, which was to have three people
representing different groups within our party give five-
minute nominating speeches. No one paid much attention
to them, but they made the speakers and their constituents
happy.

I was flattered by the invitation, but wary. As I've said,

conventions are loud meet-and-greet affairs where the words coming from the platform are usually just background music, except for the keynote address and the presidential and vice-presidential acceptance speeches. I had been to enough conventions to know that another long speech would bomb unless the delegates and media were prepared for it and the conditions in the hall remained conducive to it. I explained to the Dukakis people that the speech would work only if I spoke with the lights down and the Dukakis floor operation worked to keep the delegates quiet. Also, they couldn't clap too much or it would substantially increase the length of the speech. I told them I knew that was going to be a lot of trouble, and if they didn't want to do it, I'd give him a rousing five-minute endorsement instead.

On the day of the speech, July 20, I brought a copy of my remarks to Mike's suite and showed it to him and his people. I told them that, as written, it would take about twenty-two minutes to deliver, and if there wasn't too much applause we could stay within the twenty-five-minute window. I described how I could cut 25 percent of the speech, or 50 percent, or 75 percent, if they thought that would be better. A couple of hours later I called back to see what they wanted me to do. I was told to give it all. Mike wanted America to know him as I did.

That night, I was introduced and walked out to strong music. As I began to speak, the lights were dimmed. It was all downhill after that. I wasn't through three sentences before the lights came up again. Then every time I mentioned Mike's name, the crowd roared. I knew right then I should scrap the speech in favor of the five-minute option, but I didn't. The real audience was watching on television. If I could ignore the distractions in the hall, I could still tell the folks at home what Mike wanted them to hear:

> I want to talk about Mike Dukakis. He's come so far, so fast that everybody wants to know what kind of person he is, what kind of governor he's been, and what kind of President he'll be.
>
> He's been my friend a long time. I want you to

know my answer to those questions, and why I believe we should make Mike Dukakis the first American President born of immigrant parents since Andrew Jackson.

As I proceeded to answer the questions, the convention got back to talking, except to cheer when Mike's name was mentioned. I felt as if the speech was a two hundred–pound rock I was pushing up a hill. I later joked that I knew I was in trouble when, at the ten-minute mark, the American Samoan delegation started roasting a pig.

A few minutes later, the ABC and NBC networks started roasting me, showing the distracted convention hall and asking when I was going to finish. Only CBS and the radio networks ran the entire speech without critical commentary. The convention press people obviously hadn't been told how long I was expected to speak, or what I was trying to do. Also, the way I wrote the speech was all wrong. In an attempt to tell Mike's story without too much interruption by applause, I made it both too conversational and too "teachy." It was a big mistake to think I could speak only to people watching on TV without regard to how I would go over with the delegates.

I had some good lines, but, alas, the biggest applause I got was near the painful end, when I said, "In closing. . . ." It was thirty-two minutes of total disaster. I kidded Hillary afterward that I wasn't sure just how badly I'd bombed until we were walking out of the arena and she started going up to total strangers and introducing me as her first husband.

Fortunately, Mike Dukakis wasn't hurt by my misadventure. He got good reviews for naming Lloyd Bentsen as his running mate; they both gave good speeches; and the ticket left Atlanta with a hefty lead in the polls. On the other hand, I was a dead man walking.

On July 21, Tom Shales wrote a devastating piece in the *Washington Post* that summed up the press reaction to my speech: "As Jesse Jackson had electrified the hall on Tuesday, Governor Bill Clinton of Arkansas calcified it Wednesday night." He called it "Windy Clinty's classic clinker," and described in agonizing detail what the networks did to fill time until I finished.

When we woke up the next morning, Hillary and I knew I had jumped into another pit I'd have to dig myself out of. I had no idea how to begin, except to laugh at myself. My first public response was: "It wasn't my finest hour. It wasn't even my finest hour and a half." I kept my game face on, but I promised myself I would never again abandon my own instincts about a speech. And except for a brief moment in my speech to Congress on health care in 1994, I didn't.

I was never so glad to get back home in my life. Arkansans were mostly supportive. My paranoid supporters thought I'd been set up by somebody. Most people just thought I'd sacrificed my normal spark and spontaneity to the shackles of a written speech. Robert "Say" McIntosh, a volatile black restaurateur with whom I'd had an on-again, off-again relationship, rose to my defense, slamming the media coverage and hosting a free lunch at the state Capitol for anyone who turned in a postcard or letter hitting back at one of my national media critics. More than five hundred people showed up. I got about seven hundred letters on the speech, 90 percent of them positive. Apparently the people who wrote them had all heard the speech on radio or watched it on CBS, where Dan Rather at least waited until it was over to get his digs in.

A day or so after I returned, I got a call from my friend Harry Thomason, producer of the successful TV show *Designing Women*, which his wife, Linda Bloodworth, wrote. Harry was the brother of Danny Thomason, who sang next to me in the church choir. Hillary and I had gotten to know him and Linda in my first term when he came back to Arkansas to film a Civil War television movie, *The Blue and the Gray*. Harry told me I could make silk out of this sow's ear, but I had to move fast. He suggested I go on the Johnny Carson show and poke fun at myself. I was still shell-shocked and told him I needed a day to think about it. Carson had been having a field day with the speech in his monologues. One of his more memorable lines was "The speech went over about as well as a Velcro condom." But there really wasn't much to consider—I couldn't end up any worse off than I already was. The next day I called Harry and asked him to try to set up the Carson appearance. Carson normally didn't invite politicians on the show, but apparently he made an exception because I was too good a punching bag to pass up, and because I agreed to play the sax, which he could use as an excuse to keep his ban at least on nonmusical politicians. The sax argument was Harry's idea, not the last clever one he would think up for me.

A couple of days later, I was on a plane to California, with Bruce Lindsey and my press secretary, Mike Gauldin. Before the show, Johnny Carson came by the room where I was waiting and said hello, something he almost never did. I guess he knew I had to be hurting and wanted to put me at ease. I was slated to come onstage shortly after the show started, and Carson began by telling the audience not to worry about my appearance because "we've got plenty of coffee and extra cots in the lobby." Then he introduced me. And introduced me. And introduced me. He dragged it out forever by telling everything his researchers could find out about Arkansas. I thought he was going to take longer than I did in Atlanta. When I finally came out and sat down, Carson took out a huge hourglass and put it down next to me so that the whole world could see the sand running down. This performance would be time limited. It was hilarious. It was even funnier to me because I'd brought my own hourglass, which the studio people said I absolutely could not take out. Carson asked me what had happened in Atlanta. I told him I wanted to make Mike Dukakis, who wasn't known for his oratorical skills, look good, and "I succeeded beyond my wildest imagination." I told him Dukakis liked the speech so much, he wanted me to go to the Republican convention to nominate Vice President Bush, too. Then I claimed I'd blown the speech on purpose, because "I always wanted to be on this show in the worst way, and now I am." Johnny then asked if I thought I had a political future. I deadpanned an answer: "It depends on how I do on this show tonight." After we traded one-liners for a few minutes and got good laughs from the studio audience, Johnny invited me to play the sax with Doc Severinsen's band. We did an upbeat version of "Summertime," which went over at least as well as the jokes. Then I settled in to enjoy the next guest, the famous English rocker Joe Cocker, as he sang his latest hit, "Unchain My Heart."

After it was over, I was relieved and thought it had gone about as well as possible. Harry and Linda threw a party for me with some of their friends, including two other Arkansans, Oscar-winning actress Mary Steenburgen, and Gil Gerard, whose first claim to fame was his starring role in *Buck Rogers in the 25th Century*.

I took a red-eye flight home. The next day, I learned that the Carson show had earned good ratings nationwide and astronomical ones in Arkansas. Normally, not enough Arkansans stayed up late enough to earn those ratings, but the honor of the state was at stake. When I walked into the state Capitol, a hometown crowd was there to clap, cheer, and hug me for my performance. At least in Arkansas, the Carson show had put the Atlanta debacle behind me.

Things seemed to be looking up for me, and the rest of America, too. CNN named me the political winner of the week, after dubbing me its big loser just the week before. Tom Shales said that I had "recovered miraculously" and that "people who watch television love this kind of come-back story." But it wasn't quite over. In August, Hillary, Chelsea, and I went to Long Island, New York, to spend a few days on the beach with our friend Liz Robbins. I was asked to umpire at the annual charity softball game between artists and writers who spend summers there. I still have a picture of myself calling balls and strikes on the pitching of Mort Zuckerman, now publisher of the New York *Daily News* and *U.S. News & World Report*. When I was introduced on the field, the announcer joked that he hoped I didn't take as long to make the calls as I did to finish the speech in Atlanta. I laughed, but I was groaning inside. I didn't know what the crowd thought until the inning was over. A tall man stood up in the stands, walked out on the field, and came up to me. He said, "Don't pay any attention to the criticism. I actually listened to the speech and I liked it a lot." It was Chevy Chase. I had always liked his movies. Now he had a fan for life.

Neither my bad speech nor the good Carson show had much to do with the real work I did as governor, but the ordeal had taught me all over again that how people perceive politicians has a big impact on what they can accomplish. It had also given me a healthy dose of humility. I knew that for the rest of my life I would be more sensitive to people who found themselves in embarrassing or humiliating situations. I had to admit to Pam Strickland, an *Arkansas Democrat* reporter I really respected, "I'm not so sure it's bad for politicians to get knocked on their rear every now and then."

Unfortunately, while things were looking up for me, they weren't going so well for Mike Dukakis. George Bush had given a marvelous acceptance speech at his convention, offering a "kinder, gentler" Reaganism and telling us to "Read my lips: no new taxes." Moreover, the vice president's kinder, gentler approach didn't extend to Mike Dukakis. Lee Atwater and company went after him like a pack of rabid dogs, saying Mike didn't believe in pledging allegiance to the flag or being tough on criminals. An "independent" group with no overt ties to the Bush campaign ran an ad featuring a convicted killer named Willie Horton, who had been released on a Massachusetts prison-furlough program. Not coincidentally, Horton was black. His opponents were performing reverse plastic surgery on Dukakis, who didn't help himself by not responding quickly and vigorously to the attacks and by allowing himself to be photographed in a tank wearing a helmet that made him look more like *MAD Magazine*'s Alfred E. Neuman than a potential Commander in Chief of the armed forces.

In the fall, I flew up to Boston to see what I could do to help. By then Dukakis had fallen well behind in the polls. I pleaded with the people in the campaign to hit back; to at least tell the voters that the federal government, of which Bush was a part, furloughed prisoners too. But they never did it enough to suit me. I met Susan Estrich, the campaign manager, whom I liked and who I thought was shouldering too much of the blame for Mike's problems, and Madeleine Albright, a professor at Georgetown who had worked in the Carter White House. She was the foreign policy advisor. I was very impressed with her intellectual clarity and toughness, and resolved to keep in touch with her.

Dukakis found his voice in the last three weeks of the campaign, but he never recovered the New Democrat image that the negative ads and his insufficiently aggressive debate performances had destroyed. In November, Vice President Bush defeated him 54 to 46 percent. We didn't carry Arkansas either, though I tried. Dukakis was a good man and a fine governor. He and Lloyd Bentsen would have served our country well in the White House. But the Republicans had defined him right out of the race. I couldn't blame them for sticking with a strategy that worked, but I didn't think it was good for America.

In October, while the campaign for President was in the homestretch, I was involved in two exciting policy developments. I began a new initiative with the governors of our neighbor states, Ray Mabus of Mississippi and Buddy Roemer of Louisiana, to revive our economies. Both were young, articulate, Harvard-educated progressives. To highlight our commitment, we signed a compact on a barge in the middle of the Mississippi River at Rosedale. Not long afterward, we took a trade mission to Japan together. And we supported the successful effort of Senator Bumpers and Congressman Mike Espy of Mississippi to establish a Lower Mississippi Delta Development Commission to study and make recommendations to improve the economies of poor counties on both sides of the river, from southern Illinois to New Orleans, where the Mississippi flows into the Gulf of Mexico. The all-white counties in the northern part of the Delta region were in about as bad shape as the heavily black counties in the south. All three governors served on the Delta commission. For a year, we had hearings up and down the river in small towns time had passed by, and we came up with a report that led to the establishment of a full-time office and an ongoing effort to improve the economy and quality of life in the poorest part of America outside the Native American tribal lands.

On October 13, I was invited to the White House for President Reagan's signing of the long-awaited welfare reform bill. It was a true bipartisan accomplishment, the work of Democratic and Republican governors; Democratic congressman Harold Ford of Tennessee and Republican congressman Carroll Campbell of South Carolina; House Ways and Means Committee chairman Dan Rostenkowski and Senate Finance Committee chairman Pat Moynihan, who knew more about the history of welfare than anyone else; and the White House staff. I was impressed by, and appreciative of, the way the Congress and the White House had worked with the governors. Harold Ford even invited Republican governor Mike Castle of Delaware and me to participate in his subcommittee's meeting to "mark up" the bill into the final version to be presented for a vote. I hoped and believed the legislation would help move more people from welfare to work, while providing more support to their children.

I was also glad to see President Reagan go out of office on a positive note. He had been badly battered by the illegal Iran-Contra affair, which the White House had approved, and which might have led to his impeachment had the Democrats been half as ruthless as Newt Gingrich. Despite my many disagreements with Reagan, I liked him personally, and I enjoyed listening to his stories when I sat at his table at the White House dinner for the governors and when a few of the governors had lunch with him after his last address to us in 1988. Reagan was something of a mystery to me, at once friendly and distant. I was never sure how much he knew about the human consequences of his harshest policies, or whether he was using the hard-core right or was being used by them; the books about him don't give a definitive answer, and because he developed Alzheimer's disease, we'll probably never know. Regardless, his own life is both more interesting and more mysterious than the movies he made.

I spent the last three months of 1988 getting ready for the next legislative session. In late October, I released a seventy-page booklet, *Moving Arkansas Forward into the 21st Century*, outlining the program I would present to the legislature in January. It reflected the work and recommendations of more than 350 citizens and public officials who had served on boards and commissions dealing with our most critical challenges. The booklet was filled with specific innovative ideas, including school health clinics to fight teen pregnancy; health coverage through schools for uninsured children; parents' and students' right to choose to attend a public school other than the one in their geographical area; expansion of the HIPPY preschool program to all seventy-five counties; a report card on every school, every year, comparing students' performance with the previous year and with other schools in the state; a provision for state takeover of failing school districts; and a big expansion of the adult literacy program, designed to make Arkansas the first state to "obliterate adult illiteracy among working-age citizens."

I was particularly excited about the literacy initiative, and the prospect of turning illiteracy from a stigma into a challenge. The previous fall, when Hillary and I went to a PTA meeting at Chelsea's school, a man had come up to me and said he'd seen me on television talking about literacy. He told me he had a good job but had never learned to read. Then he asked if I could get him into a literacy program without his employer knowing about it. I happened to know the employer and was sure he'd be proud of the man, but he was afraid, so my office got him into a reading program without his employer's knowledge. After that incident, I began to say illiteracy was nothing to be ashamed of, but doing nothing about it would be.

For all its sweep and new specifics, the program's central theme was the same one I had been hammering away on for the last six years: "Either we invest more in human capital and develop our people's capacity to cooperate or we are headed for long-term decline." Our old strategy of selling Arkansas as a beautiful state with hardworking people, low wages, and low taxes had lost its relevance a decade earlier, due to the new realities of the global economy. We had to keep working to change it.

After stumping the state for the rest of the year, I presented the program to the legislature on January 9, 1989. During the speech, I introduced Arkansans who supported it and the increased taxes necessary to pay for it: a school board president who had never voted for me but had been converted to the cause of education reform; a welfare mother who had enrolled in our work program and finished high school, started college, and gotten a job; a World War II veteran who had just learned to read; and the manager of the new $500 million Nekoosa Paper mill in Ashdown, who told the legislators he had to have a better-educated workforce because "our productivity plan requires our workers to know statistics, and a lot of them don't understand that."

I argued that we could afford to raise taxes. Our unemployment rate was still above the national average, down to 6.8 percent from 10.6 percent six years earlier. We ranked forty-sixth in per capita income, but were still forty-third in per capita state and local taxes.

At the end of my address, I noted that, a few days earlier, Representative John Paul Capps, a friend and strong supporter of my program, was quoted in the press as saying that the people "were getting sick and tired of Bill Clinton giving the same old speech." I told the legislature that I was sure many people were tired of hearing me say the same things, but that "the essence of political responsibility is being able to concentrate on what is really important for a long period of time until the problem is solved." I said I would talk about something else "when the unemployment rate is below the national average and income above the national average in our state . . . when no company passes us by because they think we can't carry the load in the new world economy . . . when no young person in this state ever has to leave home to find a good job." Until then, "we've got to do our duty."

I got some inspiration for giving the same old speech when Tina Turner came to Little Rock for a concert. After working through her new repertoire, Tina closed the show with her first top-ten hit, "Proud Mary." As soon as the band started playing it, the crowd went wild. Tina walked up to the mike, smiled, and said, "You know, I've been singing this song for twenty-five years. But it gets better every time I do it!"

I was hoping my old song was still effective, too, but there was evidence to support John Paul Capps's assertion that Arkansans, including the legislators, were growing tired of my constant urgings. The legislature passed most of my specific reform proposals, but wouldn't raise the taxes necessary to fund the more expensive initiatives in health care and education, including another large increase in teacher salaries and the expansion of early-childhood education to three- and four-year-olds. An early January poll showed that a majority of voters supported greater spending on education and that I was ahead of other prospective candidates for governor in 1990, but the poll also indicated that half the respondents wanted a new governor.

Meanwhile, some of my own first-rate people were getting tired too, and wanted to go on to other challenges, including the exuberant state chairman of the Democratic Party, Lib Carlisle, a businessman I'd talked into taking the position when it would only take, I told him, a half day a week. He later joked that I must have been referring to the time he'd have left for his own business.

Fortunately, talented new people were still willing to come serve. One of the best, and most controversial, appointments I made was Dr. Joycelyn Elders to be director of the Department of Health. I told Dr. Elders I wanted to do something about teen pregnancy, which was a huge problem in Arkansas. When she advocated the establishment of school-based health clinics that, if the local school boards approved, would provide sex education and promote both abstinence and safe sex, I supported her. There were already a couple of clinics in operation, and they seemed to be popular and successful in reducing out-of-wedlock births.

Our efforts generated a firestorm of opposition from fundamentalists, who favored a "just say no" policy. It was bad enough in their eyes that Dr. Elders was pro-choice. Now they claimed that our efforts to set up school-based clinics would lead to sexual encounters by hordes of young people who would never even have considered doing such a thing if Joycelyn hadn't promoted the clinics. I doubted that Dr. Elders and her ideas even occurred to overheated teenagers in the backseats of their cars. It was a fight worth making.

When I became President, I appointed Joycelyn Elders surgeon general, and she was very popular with the public-health community for her continued willingness to stick her neck out for sound, if controversial, health policies. In December 1994, after we had suffered staggering losses in the midterm congressional elections to the Republican right, Dr. Elders made headlines again for suggesting that teaching children to masturbate might be a good way to reduce the likelihood of teen pregnancy. At the time, I had all I could handle to maintain the support of skittish congressional Democrats, and I was determined to fight the Republicans on their radical proposals to cut education, health care, and environmental protection. Now I faced the prospect that Gingrich and company could divert the attention of the press and the public away from their budget cuts by pillorying us. At any other time, we probably could have faced the heat, but I had already loaded the Democrats down with my controversial budget, NAFTA, the failed health-care effort, and the Brady bill and the assault weapons ban, which the National Rifle Association had used to beat about a dozen of our House members. I decided I had to ask for her resignation. I hated to, because she was honest, able, and brave, but we had already shown enough political tone-deafness to last through several presidential terms. I hope someday she'll forgive me. She did a lot of good with the two appointments I gave her.

The biggest staff loss I sustained in 1989 was Betsey Wright. In early August she announced that she was taking a leave of absence for several weeks. I asked Jim Pledger to do double duty at Finance and Administration and as her temporary replacement. Betsey's announcement caused a lot of gossip and speculation, because everyone knew she ran a tight ship in the governor's office and kept a close eye on everything that was going on in state government. John Brummett, the acerbic columnist for the *Arkansas Gazette*, wrote a column wondering whether our trial separation might end in divorce. He thought not, because we were too important to each other. That we were, but Betsey needed to get away. She had been working herself to death since my defeat in 1980, and it was taking its toll. We were both worka-holics who got more irritable when we were exhausted. In 1989, we were trying to do a lot in a difficult climate, and we too often took our frustrations out on each other. At the end of the year, Betsey formally resigned as chief of staff after a decade of selfless service. In early 1990, I named Henry Oliver, a retired FBI agent and former chief of police in Fort Smith, as Betsey's successor. Henry didn't really want to do it, but he was my friend and believed in what we were trying to do, so he gave me a good year.

Betsey came back in the '92 campaign to help defend me against attacks on my record and my personal life. Then, after a stint in Washington with Anne Wexler's lobbying firm early in my presidency, she went home to Arkansas to live in the Ozarks. Most Arkansans will never know the large role she played in giving them better schools, more jobs, and an honest, effective state government, but they should. I couldn't have accomplished much of what I did as governor without her. And without her, I never would have survived the Arkansas political wars to become President.

At the beginning of August, President Bush announced that he was inviting the nation's governors to an education sum-mit the following month. We met September 27 and 28 at the University of Virginia in Charlottesville. Many of the Democrats were skeptical of the meeting, because the Presi-dent and his secretary of education, Lauro Cavazos, made it clear the meeting was not a prelude to a large increase in federal support for education. I shared their concern, but I was excited by the prospect that the summit could produce a road map for the next steps in education reform, just as the *Nation at Risk* report had done in 1983. I believed the President's interest in education reform was genuine, and agreed with him that there were important things we could do without new federal money. For example, the administration supported giving parents and students the right to choose a public school other than the one to which they were assigned. Arkansas had just become the second state after Minnesota to adopt the proposal, and I wanted the other forty-eight states to follow suit. I also believed that, if the summit produced the right kind of report, governors could use it to build public support for more investment in education. If people knew what they would get for their money, their aversion to new taxes might lessen. As the co-chairman of the Governors' Task Force on Education, along with Governor Carroll Campbell of South Carolina, I wanted to build a consensus among the Democrats, then to work with the Republicans on a statement reflecting the outcome of the summit.

President Bush opened the meeting with a brief but eloquent speech. Afterward, we all took a stroll around the central lawn to give the photographers something for the evening news and morning papers, then went to work. The President and Mrs. Bush hosted a dinner that night. Hillary sat at the President's table and got into a debate with him about how bad America's infant-mortality rate was. The President couldn't believe it when she said eighteen countries did a better job than we did in keeping babies alive until the age of two. When she offered to get him the evidence, he said he would find it himself. He did, and the next day he gave me a note for Hillary saying she was right. It was a gracious gesture that reminded me of the day in Kennebunkport six years earlier when he had personally escorted three-year-old Chelsea to the bathroom.

When Carroll Campbell was called home to deal with an emergency, I was left to work out the details of a summit

statement with the NGA chairman, Republican governor
Terry Branstad of Iowa; the association's education staffer,
Mike Cohen; and my aide, Representative Gloria Cabe.
Laboring until well after midnight, several of us hammered
out a statement committing the governors and the White
House to development of a set of specific education goals to
be achieved by the year 2000. Unlike the standards movement of the last decade, these goals would be focused on
outputs, not inputs, obligating all of us to achieve certain
results. I argued that we would look foolish unless we came
out of Charlottesville with a bold commitment that would
put new energy into education reform.

From the start, most of the governors were behind the
cause and supported the idea of making the summit the start
of something big. Some of the President's people weren't so
sure. They were afraid of committing him to a big idea that
could get him into trouble by raising expectations of new
federal funding. Because of the deficit and the President's
"no new taxes" pledge, that wasn't in the cards. In the end,
the White House came around, thanks to John Sununu,
who was then the White House chief of staff. Sununu convinced his White House colleagues that the governors
couldn't go home empty-handed, and I promised to minimize public pressure from the governors for more federal
money. The final summit declaration said, "The time has
come, for the first time in U.S. history, to establish clear
national performance goals, goals that will make us interna-
tionally competitive."

At the end of the summit, President Bush handwrote me
a very cordial note, thanking me for working with his staff
on the summit and saying he wanted to keep education
reform "out there above the fray" as we headed into the
1990 midterm election. I wanted that, too. The governors'
education committee immediately began a process to develop
the goals, working with the White House domestic-policy
advisor, Roger Porter, who had gone to Oxford as a Rhodes
scholar a year after I did. We worked furiously over the next
four months to reach agreement with the White House in
time for the President's State of the Union address.

By the end of January 1990, we had agreed on six goals for the year 2000:

- By the year 2000, all children in America will start school ready to learn.
- By the year 2000, the high school graduation rate will increase to at least 90 percent.
- By the year 2000, American students will leave grades four, eight, and twelve having demonstrated competency in challenging subject matter including English, mathematics, science, history, and geography; and every school in America will ensure that all students learn to use their minds well, so they may be prepared for responsible citizenship, further learning, and productive employment in our modern economy.
- By the year 2000, U.S. students will be first in the world in science and mathematics achievement.
- By the year 2000, every adult in America will be literate and will possess the knowledge and skills necessary to compete in a global economy and exercise the rights and responsibilities of citizenship.
- By the year 2000, every school in America will be free of drugs and violence and will offer a disciplined environment conducive to learning.

On January 31, I sat in the gallery of the House of Representatives as President Bush announced these goals, said they were developed jointly by the White House and the Governors' Task Force on Education, and reported that they would be part of a more comprehensive goals-and-objectives statement that we would present to all the governors at their winter meeting the next month.

The document the governors adopted in late February was a worthy successor to the 1983 *Nation at Risk* report. I was proud to have been a part of it, impressed by the knowledge and commitment of my fellow governors, and grateful to the President, John Sununu, and Roger Porter. For the next eleven years, as governor and President, I worked hard to reach the national education goals. We had set the bar high. When you set a high bar and reach for it, even if you fall short, you wind up well ahead of where you started.

I spent the last months of 1989 trying to decide what to do with the rest of my life. There were good arguments against running for a fifth term. I was discouraged by my inability to raise the funds necessary to keep moving forward in education, early-childhood development, and health care. I could stop after ten years, look back on a decade of real accomplishments under difficult circumstances, and leave open the option of running for President in 1992. Finally, if I ran again, I might not win. I had already served longer than anyone but Orval Faubus. And the polls indicated that a lot of people wanted a new governor.

On the other hand, I loved both politics and policy. And I didn't want to leave office with the bad taste of 1989's money failures in my mouth. I still had an able, energetic, and extremely honest team. The whole time I was governor, only twice had I been offered money to make a decision a particular way. A company that wanted to win the bid to provide medical services in the prison system offered me a substantial amount through a third party. I had the company taken off the bid list. A county judge asked me to see an elderly man who wanted a pardon for his nephew. The old fellow had had no contact with state government in decades and obviously thought he was doing what he had to do when he offered me $10,000 for the pardon. I told the man it was lucky for him I was hard of hearing, because he might have just committed a crime. I suggested that he go home and give the money to his church or a charity, and said I'd look into his nephew's case.

On most days, I still looked forward to going to work, and I had no idea what I'd do if I gave it up. At the end of October, I went out to the state fair, as I did every year. That year, I sat at a booth for several hours and talked to anyone who wanted to see me. Along toward the end of the day, a man in overalls who looked to be about sixty-five dropped by to visit. It was an enlightening experience. "Bill, are you gonna run again?" he asked. "I don't know," I replied. "If I do, will you vote for me?" "I guess so. I always have," he answered. "Aren't you sick of me after all these years?" I inquired. He smiled and said, "No, I'm not, but everybody else I know is." I chuckled and answered, "Don't they think I've done a good job?" He shot back, "Sure they do, but you got a paycheck every two weeks, didn't you?" It was a classic example of another of Clinton's laws of politics: All elections are about the future. I was supposed to do a good job, just like everyone else who worked for a living. A good record is helpful mostly as evidence that you'll do what you say if reelected.

In November, the Berlin Wall, symbol of the Cold War divide, fell. Like all Americans, I cheered at the sight of young Germans tearing it down and taking chunks of it for souvenirs. Our long standoff against Communist expansion in Europe was ending with the victory of freedom, thanks to the united front presented by NATO and the constancy of American leaders from Harry Truman to George Bush. I thought back to my own trip to Moscow almost twenty years earlier, the eagerness of young Russians for information and music from the West, and the hunger for freedom that it represented. Not long afterward, I received two pieces of the Berlin Wall from my longtime friend David Ifshin, who had been in Berlin on that fateful night of November 9 and joined in with the Germans in chipping away at the wall. David had been an intense and visible opponent of the Vietnam War. His joy at the fall of the wall symbolized the promise that all Americans saw in the post–Cold War era.

In December, my old pastor and mentor, W. O. Vaught, lost his battle with cancer. He had retired from Immanuel a few years earlier and was replaced by Dr. Brian Harbour, a fine young pastor who represented the dwindling ranks of progressive Southern Baptists with whom I identified. Dr. Vaught had remained active in retirement until his illness made him too weak to travel and speak. A couple of years earlier, he had come to visit me in the Governor's Mansion. He said he wanted to tell me three things. First, he said he knew I was concerned about the morality of capital punishment, though I had always supported it. He told me that the biblical commandment "Thou shall not kill" did not forbid lawful executions, because the root Greek word did not cover all killing. He said the literal meaning of the commandment was "Thou shall not commit murder." Second, he said he was concerned about fundamentalist attacks on me for my pro-choice position on abortion. He wanted me to know that, while he believed abortion was usually wrong, the Bible did not condemn it, nor did it say life begins at conception, but when life has been "breathed into" a baby, when it is slapped on the behind after being taken out of the mother's body. I asked him about the biblical statement that God knows us even when we are in our mother's womb. He replied that the verse simply refers to God being omniscient, and that it might as well have said God knew us even before we were in our mother's womb, even before anyone in our direct line was born.

The final thing Dr. Vaught said took me aback. He said, "Bill, I think you're going to be President someday. I think you'll do a good job, but there's one thing above all you must remember: God will never forgive you if you don't stand by Israel." He believed God intended the Jews to be at home in the Holy Land. While he didn't disagree that the Palestinians had been mistreated, he said the answer to their problem had to include peace and security for Israel.

In mid-December, I went to see Dr. Vaught. He was wasting away, too weak to leave his bedroom. He asked me to move his Christmas tree into his bedroom so that he could enjoy it in his last days. Fittingly, Dr. Vaught died on Christmas Day. Jesus never had a more faithful follower. And I never had a more faithful pastor and counselor. Now I would have to navigate the path he had predicted, and the perils of my own soul, without him.

TWENTY-FIVE

WHILE I WAS TRYING to decide whether to run again, the governor's race was shaping up to be a real donnybrook, whether I ran or not. Years of pent-up ambitions were being unleashed. On the Democratic side, Jim Guy Tucker, Attorney General Steve Clark, and Rockefeller Foundation president Tom McRae, whose grandfather had been governor, all announced they would run. They were all friends of mine, and had good ideas and progressive records. On the Republican side, the contest was even more interesting. It involved two formidable former Democrats: Congressman Tommy Robinson, who didn't like Washington, and Sheffield Nelson, former president of Arkansas-Louisiana Gas Company, who said he had switched parties because the Democratic Party had moved too far to the left. It was the standard explanation white southerners gave, but more interesting coming from him because he had supported Senator Ted Kennedy against President Carter in 1980.

Robinson and Nelson, and their backers, all onetime friends, went after one another with a vengeance, in a race full of name-calling and mudslinging, which included Robinson's charge that Nelson and Jerry Jones, a longtime friend of both men who owned some of the gas fields that supplied Arkla, were rapacious businessmen who soaked Arkla's ratepayers for personal gain, and Nelson's charge that Robinson was unstable and unfit to be governor. About all they agreed on was that I had raised taxes too much and had too little to show for it in terms of educational improvement and economic development.

On the Democratic side, Steve Clark withdrew from the race, leaving Jim Guy Tucker and Tom McRae, who took a different approach, more clever than that of the Republicans, to discourage me from running. They said I'd done a lot of good, but I was out of new ideas and out of time. Ten

years as governor was long enough. I couldn't get anything
done in the legislature anymore, and four more years would
give me too much control over all aspects of state government. McRae had met with "focus groups" of representative voters who said they wanted to continue the direction
I'd set in economic development, but were open to new
ideas from a new leader. I thought there was something to
their argument, but I didn't believe they could get more out
of our conservative anti-tax legislators than I could.

Finally, still uncertain of what to do, I set a March 1
deadline to announce my decision. Hillary and I hashed it
over dozens of times. There was some press speculation that
she would run if I didn't. When asked about it, I said she'd
be a great governor but I didn't know if she would run.
When I discussed it with her, Hillary said she'd cross that
bridge if I decided not to run, but what she might do should
be no part of my decision. She knew, before I did, that I
wasn't ready to hang it up.

In the end I couldn't bear the thought of walking away
from a decade of hard work, with my last year marked by
repeated failures to fund further improvements in education. I never was one for quitting, and whenever I was
tempted, something always happened to give me heart. In
the mid-eighties, when our economy was in the tank, I was
about to land a new industry for a county where one in four
people was unemployed. At the last minute, Nebraska
offered the company an extra million dollars and I lost the
deal. I was crushed and felt I had failed the whole county.
When Lynda Dixon, my secretary, saw me slumped in my
chair with my head in my hands, she tore off the daily scrip-
ture reading from the devotional calendar she kept on her
desk. The verse was Galatians 6:9: "Let us not grow weary
while doing good, for in due season we shall reap if we do
not lose heart." I went back to work.

On February 11, I witnessed the ultimate testimonial to
the power of perseverance. Early that Sunday morning,
Hillary and I got Chelsea up and took her down to the kitchen
of the Governor's Mansion to see what we told her would be
one of the most important events she'd ever witness. Then we

turned on the television and watched Nelson Mandela take the last steps in his long walk to freedom. Through twenty-seven years of imprisonment and abuse, Mandela had endured, and triumphed, to end apartheid, liberate his own mind and heart from hatred, and inspire the world.

At the March 1 press conference, I said I would run for a fifth term, "although the fire of an election no longer burns in me," because I wanted another chance to finish the job of improving education and modernizing the economy, and because I thought I could do a better job of it than the other candidates. I also promised to keep bringing new people into state government and to bend over backward to avoid abuse of power.

Looking back on it, I can see how the statement looked ambivalent and a touch arrogant, but it was an honest expression of how I felt, as I began the first campaign since 1982 that I could have lost. I got a break soon afterward, when Jim Guy Tucker decided to withdraw from the race and run for lieutenant governor instead, saying a divisive primary would only increase the chances of a Republican victory in the fall, no matter who won. Jim Guy had made a judgment that he could win the lieutenant governor's race easily, then become governor in four years. He was almost certainly right, and I was relieved.

Still, I couldn't take the primary for granted. McRae was waging a vigorous campaign and had a lot of friends and admirers around the state from his years of good work at the Rockefeller Foundation. When he made his formal announcement, he had a broom in his hand and said he wanted to make a clean sweep of state government, clearing out old ideas and career politicians. The broom tactic had worked for my neighbor David Boren when he ran for governor of Oklahoma in 1974. I was determined that it wouldn't work this time. Gloria Cabe agreed to manage the campaign, and she put together an effective organization. Maurice Smith raised the money. And I followed a simple strategy: to outwork my opponents, do my job, and continue to preach new ideas, including college scholarships for all high school students with a B average or better; and a "plant the future" initiative to plant ten million more trees a year for a decade to do our part to reduce greenhouse gases and global warming.

McRae was forced to become more critical of me, which I think made him somewhat uncomfortable, but which had some impact. All the candidates hit me for my involvement in national politics. In late March, I went to New Orleans to accept the chairmanship of the Democratic Leadership Council. I was convinced the group's ideas on welfare reform, criminal justice, education, and economic growth were crucial to the future of the Democratic Party and the nation. The DLC's positions were popular in Arkansas, but my high profile was a potential liability in the race, so I got back home as soon as I could.

In April, the AFL-CIO refused for the first time to endorse me. Bill Becker, their president, had never really liked me. He thought the sales-tax increase was unfair to working people, opposed the tax incentives I'd supported to lure new jobs to Arkansas, and blamed me for the failure of the tax-reform referendum in 1988. He was also furious that I had supported a $300,000 loan guarantee to a business involved in a labor dispute. I spoke to the labor convention, defending the tax increase for education and expressing amazement that Becker would blame me for the failure of tax reform, which I had supported but the people voted against. I also stood by the loan guarantee because it saved 410 jobs: the company sold its products to Ford Motor Company, and the loan enabled it to build a two-month inventory, without which Ford would have canceled the firm's contract and put it out of business. Within two weeks, eighteen local unions defied Becker and endorsed me anyway. They didn't fall into the classic liberal trap of making the perfect the enemy of the good. If the people who voted for Ralph Nader in 2000 hadn't made the same mistake, Al Gore would have been elected President.

The only dramatic moment of the primary came when I was out of state again. While I was in Washington presenting the report of the Delta Development Commission to

Congress, McRae called a press conference at the state Capitol to criticize my record. He thought he would have the Arkansas press all to himself. Hillary thought otherwise. When I called her the night before, she said she thought she might show up at the conference. McRae had a cardboard likeness of me by his side. He attacked me for being absent from the state, implied that I had refused to debate him, and began to criticize my record by posing questions for me and supplying the answers himself.

In the middle of McRae's routine, Hillary stepped out of the crowd and interrupted him. She said Tom knew I was in Washington promoting the Delta commission's recommendations, which would help Arkansas. She then produced a prepared summary of several years of Rockefeller Foundation reports praising my work as governor. She said that he had been right in the reports, and that Arkansas should be proud: "We've made more progress than any other state except South Carolina, and we're right up there with them."

It was unheard of for a candidate's wife, much less the first lady, to confront an opponent like that. Some people criticized Hillary for it, but most people knew she had earned the right to defend the work we had done together for years, and it broke McRae's momentum. When I got home, I lit into him for his attacks and went after his economic development strategy, saying he wanted to build a wall around Arkansas. I won the election with 55 percent of the vote over McRae and several other challengers, but Tom had run a smart campaign on a shoestring budget, and had done well enough to encourage the Republicans about their prospects in the fall.

Sheffield Nelson beat Tommy Robinson in the Republican primary and promised to run against me on my "tax and spend" record. The strategy was flawed. Nelson should have run as a moderate Republican, praised my work in education and economic development, and said ten years was long enough—I should be given a gold watch and a respectable retirement. By switching from his original position in support of the school standards and the sales-tax increase to pay for them, Nelson allowed me to escape the straitjacket of tired incumbency and run as the only candidate of positive change.

The fact that Nelson was running against the education program and taxes had the added benefit that, if I won, I could argue to the legislators that the people had voted for more progress. As we moved toward election day, the AFL-CIO finally endorsed me. The Arkansas Education Association "recommended" me because of my commitment to raising teacher salaries, Nelson's promise not to raise taxes for four years, and AEA president Sid Johnson's desire to bury the hatchet and get on with business.

Nelson, meanwhile, moved farther to the right, advocating a reduction in welfare benefits for illegitimate children and hitting me for vetoing a bill the National Rifle Association had pushed through the legislature. The bill would have prohibited local governments from enacting any restrictions on firearms or ammunition. It was a smart move by the NRA, because state legislators were invariably more rural and pro-gun than city councils, but I thought the bill was bad policy. If the Little Rock City Council wanted to ban cop-killer bullets in the face of increasing gang activity, I thought they should have the right to do so.

The work of the governor's office didn't stop for the campaign. In June, I approved the first executions in Arkansas since 1964. John Swindler was convicted of murdering an Arkansas policeman and two South Carolina teenagers. Ronald Gene Simmons killed his wife, three sons, four daughters, a son-in-law, a daughter-in-law, four grandchildren, and two people he had grudges against. Simmons wanted to die. Swindler didn't. They were both executed in June. I didn't have qualms about either of them, but I knew there were tougher cases awaiting us.

I had also begun to commute the sentences of a few murderers with life sentences, so that they could be eligible for parole. As I explained to the voters, I had not commuted a sentence for years, after the bad experience during my first term, but both the Prison Board and the Paroles and Pardons

Board pleaded with me to resume commuting some lifers. Most states made lifers eligible for parole after serving several years. In Arkansas the governor had to commute their sentences. The decisions weren't easy or popular, but were necessary to keep peace and order in a prison system where 10 percent of the inmates were serving life terms. It's fortunate that many lifers are unlikely to repeat their crimes and can return to society without risk to others. This time, we made extensive efforts to contact the victims' families for comments. Surprisingly, many did not object. Also, most of those whose sentences were commuted were old or had committed their crimes when they were very young.

In mid-September, a disgruntled former employee of the Development Finance Authority first raised the "sex question" against me. Larry Nichols had made more than 120 phone calls from his office to conservative supporters of the Nicaraguan Contras, a cause the national Republicans strongly supported. Nichols's defense was that he was calling the Contra supporters to get them to lobby congressional Republicans to support legislation beneficial to his agency. His excuse didn't fly, and he was fired when the calls were discovered. Nichols called a press conference on the steps of the Capitol and accused me of using the finance agency's funds to carry on affairs with five women. I drove into my parking place in front of the Capitol not long after Nichols had made his charges and was hit cold with the story by Bill Simmons of the Associated Press, the senior member of the political press and a good reporter. When Simmons asked me about the charges, I just suggested he call the women. He did, they all denied it, and the story basically died. None of the television stations or newspapers ran it. Only one conservative radio announcer who supported Nelson talked about it, actually naming one of the women, Gennifer Flowers. She threatened to sue him if he didn't stop. The Nelson campaign tried to stoke the rumors, but without corroboration or evidence.

At the end of the campaign, Nelson put on a television ad that was misleading but effective. The announcer raised a series of issues and asked what I would do about them. To

each question, my own voice answered, "Raise and spend."
Nelson's campaign had lifted those three words from a section in my State of the State address, in which I compared
Arkansas' budget with that of the federal government.
While Washington could engage in deficit spending, if we
didn't have money, we had to "raise and spend, or not
spend at all." I put out a response ad comparing Nelson's
claim to what I had really said and told the voters that if
they couldn't trust Nelson not to mislead them in the campaign, they couldn't trust him to be governor. A couple of
days later, I was reelected, 57 to 43 percent.

The victory was sweet in many ways. The people had
decided to let me serve fourteen years, longer than any other
Arkansas governor in history. And for the first time, I had
carried Sebastian County, which was then still the most
hard-core Republican big county in the state. In a campaign
appearance in Fort Smith, I had promised that if I did win
there, Hillary and I would dance down Garrison Avenue,
the town's main street. A couple of nights after the election,
along with a few hundred supporters, we kept our commitment. It was cold and raining, but we danced away and
enjoyed every minute of it. We had waited sixteen years for
a general-election win there.

The only really dark moment of the general election was
purely personal. In August, Mother's doctor discovered a
lump in her right breast. Forty-eight hours later, while Dick,
Roger, and I waited in the hospital, Mother had the lump
removed. After the procedure, she was her usual chipper self
and was back at work on the campaign in no time, though
she faced months of chemotherapy. The cancer had aleady
spread to twenty-seven nodes in her arm, but she didn't tell
anyone this—including me. In fact, she never told us how
bad it was until 1993.

In December, I resumed my work for the Democratic Leadership Council, launching the Texas DLC chapter in Austin. In
my speech, I argued that, contrary to our liberal critics, we
were good Democrats. We believed in keeping the American

dream alive for all people. We believed in government, though not in the status quo. And we believed government was spending too much on yesterday and today—interest on debt, defense, more money for the same health care—and too little on tomorrow: education, the environment, research and development, the infrastructure. I said the DLC stood for a modern, mainstream agenda: the expansion of opportunity, not bureaucracy; choice in public schools and child care; responsibility and empowerment for poor people; and reinventing government, away from the top-down bureaucracy of the industrial era, to a leaner, more flexible, more innovative model appropriate for the modern global economy.

I was trying to develop a national message for the Democrats, and the effort fueled speculation that I might enter the presidential race in 1992. During the recent campaign, I had said on more than one occasion that I would serve out my term if elected. That's what I thought I would do. I was excited about the coming legislative session. Though I strongly disagreed with many of his decisions, like killing the Brady bill and vetoing the Family and Medical Leave Act, I liked President Bush and had a good relationship with the White House. Also, a campaign to defeat him looked hopeless. Saddam Hussein had invaded Kuwait, and the United States was beginning its buildup for the Gulf War, which in two months would drive the President's approval ratings into the stratosphere.

On the morning of January 15, 1991, with ten-year-old Chelsea holding the Bible for me, I took the oath of office in Little Rock for the last time. Following the custom, I delivered my informal address in the crowded chamber of the House of Representatives, then, at noon, made a more formal address at the public ceremony, which was held in the Capitol rotunda because of inclement weather. The new legislature had more women and blacks than ever. The Speaker of the House, John Lipton, and the president pro tempore of the Senate, Jerry Bookout, were progressives and strong supporters of mine. Jim Guy Tucker was lieutenant governor, probably the ablest person ever to hold the job, and we were working together, rather than at cross-purposes, for the first time in years.

I dedicated my inaugural address to the men and women from Arkansas serving in the Persian Gulf, and noted that it was appropriate that we were making a new beginning on Martin Luther King Jr.'s birthday, because "we must go forward into the future together or we will all be limited in what we achieve." Then I outlined the most ambitious program I had ever proposed, in education, health care, highways, and the environment.

In education, I proposed a big increase in adult literacy and training programs; apprenticeships for non-college-bound youths; college scholarships for all middle-class and low-income kids who took the required courses, made a B average, and stayed off drugs; preschool programs for poor kids; a new residential high school for math and science students; conversion of fourteen vo-tech schools into two-year colleges; and a $4,000 raise for teachers over two years. I asked the legislature to raise the sales tax half a cent and the corporate income tax half a percent to pay for them.

There were also several reform measures in my package, including health insurance for pregnant women and for children; the removal of more than 250,000 taxpayers, more than 25 percent of the total, from the state income tax rolls; and an income tax credit to offset the sales-tax increase for up to 75 percent of the taxpayers.

And for the next sixty-eight days, I worked to pass the program, bringing legislators to my office; going to their committee hearings to argue personally for bills; cornering them in the halls, at nighttime events, or early in the morning at the Capitol cafeteria; hanging around with them outside the chambers or in the cloakrooms; calling them late at night; and bringing opposing legislators and their allied lobbyists together to hammer out compromises. By the end of the session, virtually my entire program had passed. The tax proposals received between 76 and 100 percent of the vote in both houses, including the votes of a majority of Republican lawmakers.

Ernest Dumas, one of the state's most distinguished and

astute columnists, said, "For education, it was one of the best legislative sessions in the state's history, arguably the best." Dumas noted that we also passed the largest highway program ever; greatly expanded health care for poor families; improved the environment by passing proposals for solid-waste recycling and reduction and for "weakening the hand of polluting industries at the state's pollution control agency"; and "spurned a few religious zealots" by providing school health clinics in poor communities.

The legislature had its biggest fight over the school health clinics. I favored allowing the clinics to distribute condoms if the local school board approved. So did the Senate. The more conservative House was devoutly anti-condom. Finally the legislature adopted a compromise offered by Representative Mark Pryor, who in 2002 became Arkansas' junior U.S. senator: no state money could be used to buy condoms, but if bought with other funds, they could be distributed. Bob Lancaster, a witty columnist for the *Arkansas Gazette*, wrote a hilarious article chronicling the struggle of the "condom Congress." He called it, with apologies to Homer, the "Trojans War."

The legislature also passed the National Rifle Association's bill to prohibit cities and counties from adopting local gun-control ordinances, the same measure I had vetoed in 1989. No southern legislature could say no to the NRA. Even in the more liberal Senate, this bill passed 26–7. At least I got the Senate to pass it late, so I could veto it after they went home and they couldn't override it. After the bill was sent to me, I had an extraordinary encounter with the young NRA lobbyist who came down from Washington to push the bill. He was very tall and well dressed and spoke with a clipped New England accent. One day he stopped me as I was crossing the rotunda from the House to the Senate side of the Capitol. "Governuh, Governuh, why don't you just let this bill become law without your signature?" I explained for the umpteenth time why I didn't support the bill. Then he burst out, "Look, Governuh, you're going to run for President next year, and when you do, we're going to beat your brains out in Texas if you veto this bill." I knew I was getting older and more seasoned when I didn't slug him. Instead, I smiled and said, "You don't get it. I don't like this bill. You know gun control will never be a problem in Arkansas. You've just got a chart on the wall in your fancy office in Washington with this bill at the top and all the states listed below. You don't give a damn about the merits of this bill. You just want to put a check by Arkansas on that chart. So you get your gun and I'll get mine. We'll saddle up and meet in Texas." As soon as the legislature went home, I vetoed the bill. Soon afterward, the NRA began running television ads attacking me. It wasn't until I began writing this account that I realized that in my confrontation with the NRA lobbyist, I had acknowledged that I was considering running for President. At the time, I didn't think there was a chance I'd do it. I just didn't like to be threatened.

After the session, Henry Oliver told me he wanted to leave. I hated to lose him, but after decades of proud service in the marines, the FBI, and local and state government, he had earned the right to go home. For the time being, Gloria Cabe and Carol Rasco took over his responsibilities.

I spent the next few months making sure our massive legislative program was well implemented and traveling the country for the Democratic Leadership Council. Because I was out there making the case for how we could regain "mainstream, middle-class" voters who "have left the party in droves for twenty years," the press continued to speculate that I might run in 1992. In an interview in April, I joked about it, saying, "As long as nobody runs, everybody can be on the list, and it's kind of nice. It makes my mother happy to read my name in the paper."

While I still didn't believe I could or should run, and President Bush's approval ratings were still above 70 percent in the afterglow of the Gulf War, I was beginning to think a DLC Democrat who could relate both to the party's traditional base and to swing voters might have a chance, because the country had serious problems that weren't being addressed in Washington. The President and his team seemed determined to coast to victory on the wings of the

Gulf War. I had seen enough in Arkansas and in my travels around the country to know America couldn't coast through four more years. As 1991 unfolded, more and more people came to share that view.

In April, I went to Los Angeles to speak to a luncheon for Education First, a citizens' group dedicated to improving public education. After Sidney Poitier introduced me, I recounted three recent experiences with education in California that reflected both promise and peril for America's future. The promise I had seen more than a year earlier when I spoke at California State University in Los Angeles to students with roots in 122 other nations. Their diversity was a good omen for our ability to compete with and relate to the rest of the global community. The perils were evident when Hillary and I visited with sixth-graders in East Los Angeles. They were great kids who had big dreams and a deep desire for normal lives. They told us their number one fear was of being shot going to and from school. They also said they did practice drills crouching under their desks in the event of a drive-by shooting. The children's number two fear was that, when they turned thirteen, they would have to join a gang and smoke crack cocaine or face severe beatings from their contemporaries. My experience with those kids had a profound impact on me. They deserved better.

On another California trip, this time to discuss education with the Business Roundtable, a telephone company executive told me that 70 percent of his job applicants flunked the company's entrance examination, even though virtually all of them were high school graduates. I asked the audience if the United States, fresh from victory in the Gulf War, could hope to lead the post–Cold War world if childhood was dangerous and our schools were inadequate.

Of course, it was one thing to say the country had problems and quite another to say what the federal government should do about them, and to say it in a way that could be heard by citizens conditioned by the Reagan-Bush years to believe the federal government was the source of our problems, not the solution. Making that case was the mission of the Democratic Leadership Council.

In early May, I went to Cleveland to preside over the DLC convention. A year earlier, in New Orleans, we had issued a statement of principles intended to move beyond the tired partisan debate in Washington by creating a dynamic but centrist progressive movement of new ideas rooted in traditional American values. While the DLC had been criticized for being too conservative by some of our party's leading liberals, like Governor Mario Cuomo and the Reverend Jesse Jackson (who said DLC stood for "Democratic Leisure Class"), the convention attracted an impressive array of creative thinkers, innovative state and local officials, and businesspeople concerned about our economic and social problems. Many prominent national Democrats, including several prospective presidential candidates, were also there. Among the speakers were Senators Sam Nunn, John Glenn, Chuck Robb, Joe Lieberman, John Breaux, Jay Rockefeller, and Al Gore. Besides me, the governors there were Lawton Chiles of Florida and Jerry Baliles of Virginia. The House members there mostly represented conservative constituencies, like Dave McCurdy of Oklahoma, or had an interest in national security and foreign policy, like Steve Solarz of New York. Former senator Paul Tsongas and former governor Doug Wilder of Virginia, both of whom would soon be running for President, were there. A number of talented black leaders participated, including Governor Wilder; Mayor Mike White of Cleveland; Vince Lane, the creative chairman of the Chicago Housing Authority; Congressman Bill Gray of Pennsylvania; and Congressman Mike Espy of Mississippi.

I opened the convention with a keynote address designed to make the case that America needed to change course and that the DLC could and should lead the way. I began with a litany of America's problems and challenges and a rebuke of the years of Republican neglect, then noted that the Democrats had not been able to win elections, despite Republican failures, "because too many of the people that used to vote for us, the very burdened middle class we are talking about, have not trusted us in national elections to defend our national interests abroad, to put their values into our social policy at home, or to take their tax money and spend it with discipline."

I applauded the leadership of the Democratic Party under Ron Brown, our first black chairman, whom I had supported. Brown had made a real effort to broaden the party's base, but we needed a message with specific proposals to offer the American people:

> The Republican burden is their record of denial, evasion, and neglect. But our burden is to give the people a new choice, rooted in old values, a new choice that is simple, that offers opportunity, demands responsibility, gives citizens more say, provides them responsive government—all because we recognize that we are a community. We are all in this together, and we are going up or down together.

The opportunity agenda meant economic growth through free and fair trade, as well as more investment in new technologies and in world-class education and skills. The responsibility agenda required something of all citizens: national service for young people in return for college aid; welfare reforms that required able-bodied parents to work but provided more support for their children; tougher child-support enforcement; more efforts by parents to keep their kids in school; a "reinvented" government, with less bureaucracy and more choices in child care, public schools, job training, elderly care, neighborhood policing, and the management of public housing. The community agenda required us to invest more in our millions of poor children, and to reach across the racial divide, to build a politics based on lifting up all Americans, not dividing them against one another.

I tried hard to break through all the either/or debates that dominated national public discourse. In the conventional Washington wisdom, you had to be for excellence or equity in education; for quality or universal access in health care; for a cleaner environment or more economic growth; for work or child-rearing in welfare policy; for labor or business in the workplace; for crime prevention or punishing criminals; for family values or more spending for poor families. In his remarkable book *Why Americans Hate Politics*, the journalist E. J. Dionne labels these as "false choices," saying in each instance that Americans thought we should not choose "either/or" but "both." I agreed, and tried to illustrate my beliefs with lines like "Family values will not feed a hungry child, but you cannot raise that hungry child very well without them. We need both."

I wound up the speech by citing the lesson I had learned in Professor Carroll Quigley's Western Civilization class more than twenty-five years earlier, that the future can be better than the past, and that each of us has a personal, moral responsibility to make it so: "That is what the new choice is all about, that is what we are here in Cleveland to do. We are not here to save the Democratic Party. We are here to save the United States of America."

That speech was one of the most effective and important I ever made. It captured the essence of what I had learned in seventeen years in politics and what millions of Americans were thinking. It became the blueprint for my campaign message, helping to change the public focus from President Bush's victory in the Gulf War to what we had to do to build a better future. By embracing ideas and values that were both liberal and conservative, it made voters who had not supported Democratic presidential candidates in years listen to our message. And by the rousing reception it received, the speech established me as perhaps the leading spokesman for the course I passionately believed America should embrace. Several people at the convention urged me to run for President, and I left Cleveland convinced that I had a good chance to capture the Democratic nomination if I did run, and that I had to consider entering the race.

In June, my friend Vernon Jordan asked me to go with him to Baden-Baden, Germany, to the annual Bilderberg Conference, which brings together prominent business and political leaders from the United States and Europe to discuss current issues and the state of our transatlantic relationship.

I always enjoyed being with Vernon and was stimulated by my conversations with the Europeans, including Gordon Brown, a brilliant Scottish Labour Party member who would become chancellor of the exchequer when Tony Blair was elected prime minister. I found the Europeans generally supportive of President Bush's foreign policies but very concerned by the continued drift and weakness of our economy, which hurt them as well as us.

At Bilderberg, I ran into Esther Coopersmith, a Democratic activist who had served as part of our UN delegation during the Carter years. Esther was on her way to Moscow with her daughter Connie, and she invited me to join them to observe firsthand the changes that were unfolding in the last days of the Soviet Union. Boris Yeltsin was about to be elected president of the Russian Republic with an even more explicit repudiation of Soviet economics and politics than Gorbachev had espoused. It was a brief but interesting trip.

When I got back to Arkansas, I was convinced that a lot of America's challenges in foreign relations would involve economic and political issues that I understood and could handle if I were to run and actually become the President. Still, as July dawned, I was genuinely torn about what to do. I had told Arkansans in the 1990 election that I would finish my term. The success of the 1991 legislative session had given me a new burst of enthusiasm for my job. Our family life was great. Chelsea was happy in a new school, with good teachers, good friends, and her passion for ballet. Hillary was doing well in her law practice and enjoyed great popularity and respect in her own right. After years of high-tension political struggles, we were settled and happy. Moreover, President Bush still looked unbeatable. An early June poll in Arkansas showed that only 39 percent of the people wanted me to run, and that I would lose my own state to the President 57 to 32 percent, with the rest undecided. Moreover, I wouldn't be stepping into an empty primary field. Several other good Democrats seemed likely to run, so the nomination fight was sure to be hard. And history was against me. Only one governor of a small state had ever been elected President, Franklin Pierce of New Hampshire in 1852.

Beyond the political considerations, I genuinely liked President Bush and appreciated the way he and his White House had worked with me on education. Though I strongly disagreed with his economic and social policies, I thought he was a good man and nowhere near as ruthless or right-wing as most of the Reaganites. I didn't know what to do. In June, on a trip to California, I was picked up at the airport and driven to my speech by a young man named Sean Landres. He encouraged me to run for President and said he had found the perfect theme for the campaign. He then put on a tape of Fleetwood Mac's hit "Don't Stop Thinkin' About Tomorrow." It struck him, and me, as exactly what I was trying to say.

When I was in Los Angeles, I discussed the pros and cons of running with Hillary's friend Mickey Kantor, who by then had become a close friend and trusted advisor of mine as well. When we started, Mickey said I should hire him for a dollar, so our conversations would be privileged. A few days later, I sent him a check for a dollar, with a note that said I had always wanted a high-priced lawyer and was sending the check "in firm belief that you get what you pay for." I got a lot of good advice for that dollar, but I still didn't know what to do. Then came the phone call that changed things.

One July day, Lynda Dixon told me that Roger Porter was on the phone from the White House. As I've said, I had worked with Roger on the education goals project and had a high regard for his ability to be loyal to the President and still work with the governors. Roger asked me if I was going to run for President in 1992. I told him that I hadn't decided, that I was happier being governor than I'd been in years, that my family life was good and I was reluctant to disrupt it, but that I thought the White House was being too passive in dealing with the country's economic and social problems. I said I thought the President should use the enormous political capital he had as a result of the Gulf War to tackle the country's big issues. After five or ten minutes of what I thought was a serious conversation, Roger cut it off and got to the point. I'll never forget the first words of the message he had been designated to deliver: "Cut the crap, Governor." He said "they" had reviewed all the potential candidates against the President. Governor Cuomo was the most powerful speaker, but they could paint him as too liberal. All the senators could be defeated by attacks on their voting records. But I was different. With a strong record in economic development, education, and crime, and a strong DLC message, I actually had a chance to win. So if I ran, they would have to destroy me personally. "Here's how Washington works," he said. "The press has to have somebody in every election, and we're going to give them you." He went on to say the press were elitists who would believe any tales they were told about backwater Arkansas. "We'll spend whatever we have to spend to get whoever we have to get to say whatever they have to say to take you out. And we'll do it early."

I tried to stay calm, but I was mad. I told Roger that what he had just said showed what was wrong with the administration. They had been in power so long they thought they were entitled to it. I said, "You think those parking spaces off the West Wing are yours, but they belong to the American people, and you have to earn the right to use them." I told Roger that what he had said made me more likely to run. Roger said that was a nice sentiment, but he was calling as my friend to give me fair warning. If I waited until 1996, I could win the presidency. If I ran in 1992, they would destroy me, and my political career would be over.

After the conversation ended, I called Hillary and told her about it. Then I told Mack McLarty. I never heard from or saw Roger Porter again until he attended a reception for the White House Fellows when I was President. I wonder if he ever thinks about that phone call and whether it influenced my decision.

Ever since I was a little boy I have hated to be threatened. As a kid, I got shot by a BB gun and slugged by a much bigger boy because I wouldn't walk away from threats. In the campaign and for eight years afterward, the Republicans would make good on theirs, and as Roger

Porter had predicted, they got lots of help from some members of the press. Like the childhood BB shot in my leg and the roundhouse blow to my jaw, their attacks hurt. The lies hurt, and the occasional truth hurt more. I just tried to keep focused on the job at hand and the impact of my work on ordinary people. When I could do that, it was easier to stand up against those who craved power for its own sake.

The next three months rushed by in a blur. At July 4 picnics in northeast Arkansas, I saw the first "Clinton for President" signs, but was encouraged by some to wait until 1996 to run and by others, who were angry at me for raising taxes again, not to run at all. When I went to Memphis for the dedication of the National Civil Rights Museum on the site of the Lorraine Motel, where Martin Luther King Jr. was slain, several citizens urged me to run, but Jesse Jackson was still upset about the DLC, which he saw as conservative and divisive. I hated to be at cross-purposes with Jesse, whom I admired, especially for his efforts to persuade black youngsters to stay in school and off drugs. Back in 1977, we had marked the twentieth anniversary of the integration of Little Rock Central High with a joint appearance at the school, in which he told the students to "open your brains and not your veins."

Drugs and youth violence were still big issues in 1991. On July 12, I traveled to Chicago, to visit the public-housing projects and see what they were doing to protect kids. In late July, I went to a Little Rock hospital to visit the black comedian Dick Gregory, who had been arrested for staging a sit-in in a store that sold drug paraphernalia, along with four members of a local anti-drug group, DIGNITY (Doing In God's Name Incredible Things Yourself). The group was led by black ministers and the local leader of the Black Muslims. It represented the kind of adult responsibility for solving our social problems that Jackson also espoused, the DLC advocated, and I thought was essential if we were going to turn things around.

In August, the campaign began to take shape. I gave speeches in a number of places and formed an exploratory committee, with Bruce Lindsey as treasurer. The committee allowed me to raise money to pay travel and other expenses without becoming a candidate. Two weeks later, Bob Farmer of Boston, who had been Dukakis's chief fund-raiser, resigned as treasurer of the Democratic National Committee to help me raise money. I began to get help from Frank Greer, an Alabama native who in 1990 had produced television commercials for me that had both intellectual and emotional appeal, and Stan Greenberg, a pollster who had done focus groups for the 1990 campaign and had conducted extensive research on the so-called Reagan Democrats and what it would take to bring them home. I wanted Greenberg to be my pollster. I hated to give up Dick Morris, but by then he had become so involved with Republican candidates and officeholders that he was compromised in the eyes of virtually all Democrats.

After we set up the exploratory committee, Hillary, Chelsea, and I went to the summer meeting of the National Governors Association in Seattle. My colleagues had just voted me the most effective governor in the country in the annual survey conducted by *Newsweek* magazine, and several of them urged me to run. When the NGA meeting concluded, our family took a boat from Seattle to Canada for a short vacation in Victoria and Vancouver.

As soon as I got home, I started touring the state, including a lot of unannounced stops, to ask my constituents if I should run and whether they would release me from my pledge to serve my full term if I did. Most people said I should run if I thought it was the right thing to do, though few thought I had a chance to win. Senator Bumpers, Senator Pryor, and our two Democratic congressmen, Ray Thornton and Beryl Anthony, all made supportive statements. Lieutenant Governor Jim Guy Tucker, House Speaker John Lipton, and Senate President Jerry Bookout assured me they would take care of the state in my absence.

Hillary thought I should run, Mother was strongly in favor of it, and even Chelsea wasn't against it this time. I told her I'd be there for the important things, like her ballet performance in *The Nutcracker* at Christmastime, her school events, the trip to Renaissance Weekend, and her birthday party. But I knew, too, that I'd miss some things: playing another duet with her on my sax at her piano recital; making Halloween stops, with Chelsea in her always unique costume; reading to her at night; and helping with her homework. Being her father was the best job I ever had; I just hoped I could do it well enough in the long campaign ahead. When I wasn't around, I missed it as much as she did. But the telephone helped, and the fax machine did too—we sent a lot of math problems back and forth. Hillary would be gone less than I would, but when we were both away, Chelsea had a good support system in her grandparents, Carolyn Huber, the Governor's Mansion's staff, and her friends and their parents.

On August 21, I got a big break when Senator Al Gore announced that he wouldn't run. He had run in 1988, and if he had run again in 1992 we would have split the vote in the southern states on Super Tuesday, March 10, making it much harder for me to win. Al's only son, Albert, had been badly injured when he was hit by a car. Al decided he had to be there for his family during his son's long, hard recovery, a decision I understood and admired.

In September, I visited Illinois again and spoke to the leading Democrats of Iowa, South Dakota, and Nebraska in Sioux City, Iowa, and to the Democratic National Committee in Los Angeles. The Illinois stop was particularly important because of the primary calendar. The nomination fight began with the Iowa caucuses, which I could pass up because Senator Tom Harkin of Iowa was running and was sure to win his home state. Then came New Hampshire, then South Carolina, then Maryland, Georgia, and Colorado. Then the eleven Super Tuesday southern states. Then Illinois and Michigan on March 17, St. Patrick's Day.

Senator Gore's campaign had been derailed four years earlier when he didn't follow his impressive showing in the southern states with other victories. I thought I could win in Illinois, for three reasons: Hillary was from there, I had worked in southern Illinois with the Delta Commission, and a number of prominent black leaders in Chicago had Arkansas roots. In Chicago, I met with two young political activists, David Wilhelm and David Axelrod, who would become involved in the campaign. They were idealistic, tempered by the fire of Chicago election battles, and in tune with my politics. Meanwhile, Kevin O'Keefe was driving all over the state, building the organization necessary to win.

Michigan voted on the same day as Illinois, and I hoped to do well there, too, thanks to former governor Jim Blanchard, Wayne County executive Ed McNamara, and a lot of people, black and white, who had come to Michigan from Arkansas to work in the automobile plants. After Michigan and Illinois, the next big state to vote was New York, where my friend Harold Ickes was busy lining up support, and Paul Carey, son of former governor Hugh Carey, was raising money.

On September 6, I finished organizing the governor's office for the campaign when Bill Bowen agreed to become my executive secretary. Bill was the president of Commercial National Bank, one of the state's most respected business leaders, and the prime organizer behind the so-called Good Suit Club, the business leaders who had supported the successful education program in the 1991 legislature. Bowen's appointment reassured people that the state's business would be well taken care of while I was away.

In the weeks leading up to my announcement, I began to get a taste of the difference between running for President and a campaign for state office. First, abortion was a big issue, because it was assumed that if President Bush were reelected, he would have enough Supreme Court vacancies to fill to secure a majority for reversing *Roe* v. *Wade*. I had always supported *Roe* but opposed public funding of abortions for poor women, so my position didn't really please either side. It wasn't fair to poor women, but I had a hard time justifying funding abortions with the money of taxpayers who believed it was the equivalent of murder. Also, the question was really moot, since even the Democratic Congress had repeatedly failed to provide abortion funding.

Besides abortion, there were the personal questions. When asked if I had ever smoked marijuana, I said I had never broken the drug laws in America. It was a tacit but awkward admission that I had tried it in England. There were also a lot of rumors about my personal life. On September 16, at Mickey Kantor's and Frank Greer's urging, Hillary and I appeared at the Sperling Breakfast, a regular meeting of Washington journalists, to answer press questions. I didn't know if it was the right thing to do, but Mickey was persuasive. He argued that I had said before that I hadn't been perfect, people knew it, and "You might as well tell them and try to take the sting out of what may or may not happen later in the campaign."

When a reporter asked the question, I said that, like a lot of couples, we'd had problems, but we were committed to each other and our marriage was strong. Hillary backed me up. As far as I know, I was the only candidate who had ever said as much. It satisfied some of the reporters and columnists; for others, my candor simply confirmed that I was a good target.

I'm still not sure I did the right thing in going to the breakfast, or in getting onto the slippery slope of answering personal questions. Character is important in a President, but as the contrasting examples of FDR and Richard Nixon show, marital perfection is not necessarily a good measure of presidential character. Moreover, that wasn't really the standard. In 1992, if you had violated your marriage vows, gotten divorced, and remarried, the infidelity wasn't considered disqualifying or even newsworthy, while couples who stayed married were fair game, as if divorce was always the more authentic choice. Given the complexity of people's lives and the importance of both parents in raising children, that's probably not the right standard.

Notwithstanding the personal questions, I got more than my fair share of favorable press coverage in the early days from thoughtful journalists who were interested in my ideas and policies and in what I had done as governor. I also knew I could start the campaign with a core of enthusiastic supporters across the country thanks to the friends Hillary and I had made over the years, and lots of Arkansans who were willing to travel to other states to campaign for me. They were undeterred by the fact that I was virtually unknown to the American people and far behind in the polls. So was I. Unlike 1987, this time I was ready.

TWENTY-SIX

OCTOBER 3 WAS a beautiful autumn morning in Arkansas, crisp and clear. I started the day that would change my life in the usual way, with an early-morning jog. I went out the back gate of the Governor's Mansion, through the old Quapaw Quarter, then downtown to the Old State House. The grand old place, where I had held my first reception when I was sworn in as attorney general in 1977, was already decked out in American flags. After I ran past it, turned, and headed for home, I saw a newspaper vending machine. Through the glass, I could read the headline: "Hour Arrives for Clinton." On the way home, several passersby wished me well. Back at the mansion I took a last look at my announcement speech. I had worked on it until well past midnight; it was full of what I felt was good rhetoric and specific policy proposals, but still too long, so I cut a few lines.

At noon, I was introduced on the stage by our state treasurer, Jimmie Lou Fisher, who had been with me since 1978. I started out a little awkwardly, probably because of the conflicting feelings flooding through me. I was at once reluctant to abandon the life I knew and eager for the challenge, a little afraid but sure I was doing the right thing. I spoke for more than half an hour, thanking my family, friends, and supporters for giving me the strength "to step beyond a life and job I love, to make a commitment to a larger cause: preserving the American dream, restoring the hopes of the forgotten middle class, reclaiming the future for our children." I closed with a pledge to "give new life to the American dream" by forming a "new covenant" with the people: "more opportunity for all, more responsibility from everyone, and a greater sense of common purpose."

When it was over, I felt elated and excited, but maybe relieved more than anything else, especially after Chelsea wisecracked, "Nice speech, Governor." Hillary and I spent the rest of the day receiving well-wishers, and Mother, Dick, and Roger all seemed happy about it, as did Hillary's family. Mother acted as if she knew I would win. As well as I knew her, I couldn't be sure if it was truly how she felt or just another example of her "game face." That night we gathered around the piano with old friends. Carolyn Staley played, just as she had done since we were fifteen. We sang "Amazing Grace" and other hymns, and lots of songs from the sixties, including "Abraham, Martin, and John," a tribute to the fallen heroes of our generation. I went to bed believing we could cut through the cynicism and despair and rekindle the fire those men had lit in my heart.

Governor Mario Cuomo once said we campaign in poetry but we govern in prose. The statement is basically accurate, but a lot of campaigning is prose, too: putting together the nuts and bolts, going through the required rituals, and responding to the press. Day two of the campaign was more prose than poetry: a series of interviews designed to get me on television nationally and in major local markets, and to answer the threshold question of why I had gone back on my commitment to finish my term and whether that meant I was untrustworthy. I answered the questions as best I could and moved on to the campaign message. It was all prosaic, but it got us to day three.

The rest of the year was full of the frantic activity of a late-starting campaign: getting organized, raising money, reaching out to specific constituencies, and working New Hampshire.

Our first headquarters was in an old paint store on Seventh Street near the Capitol. I had decided to base the campaign out of Little Rock instead of Washington. It made travel arrangements a little more complicated, but I wanted to stick close to my roots and to get home often enough to be with my family and handle official business that required my presence. But staying in Arkansas also had another big benefit: it helped our young staff keep focused on the work at hand. They weren't distracted by the pervasive Washington rumor mill and they didn't get too carried away by the surprisingly favorable press coverage I received early in the campaign, or too depressed by the torrent of negative press soon to come.

After a few weeks, we had outgrown the paint store and moved nearby to the old office of the Department of Higher Education, which we used until we outgrew it, too, just before the Democratic convention. Then we moved again, downtown to the *Arkansas Gazette* building, which had become vacant a few months earlier upon the purchase and subsequent dismantling of the *Gazette* by the owner of the *Arkansas Democrat*, Walter Hussman. The *Gazette* building would be our home for the rest of the campaign, which, from my point of view, was the only good result of the loss of the oldest independent newspaper in America west of the Mississippi.

The *Gazette* had stood for civil rights in the fifties and sixties, and had staunchly supported Dale Bumpers, David Pryor, and me in our efforts to modernize education, social services, and the economy. In its glory days, it was one of the best papers in the country, bringing well-written and wide-ranging national and international stories to readers in the far corners of our state. In the 1980s, the *Gazette* began to face competition from Hussman's *Arkansas Democrat*, which until then had been a much smaller afternoon paper. The newspaper war that followed had a foreordained outcome, because Hussman owned other profitable media properties, which allowed him to absorb tremendous operating losses at the *Democrat* in order to take advertising and subscribers away from the *Gazette*. Not long before I announced for President, Hussman acquired the *Gazette* and consolidated its operations into his paper, renaming it the *Arkansas Democrat-Gazette*. Over the years, the *Democrat-Gazette* would help to make Arkansas a more Republican state. The overall tone of its editorial page was conservative and highly critical of me, often in very personal terms. In this the paper faithfully reflected the views of its publisher. Though I was sad to see the *Gazette* fall, I was glad to have the building. Perhaps I was hoping that the ghosts of its progressive past would keep us fighting for tomorrow.

We started out with an all-Arkansas staff, with Bruce Lindsey as campaign director and Craig Smith, who had handled my appointments to boards and commissions, as finance director. Rodney Slater and Carol Willis were already hard at work contacting black political, religious, and business leaders across the country. My old friend Eli Segal agreed to help me build a national staff.

I had already met with one person I was sure I wanted on the team, a talented young staffer for Congressman Dick Gephardt, the Democratic majority leader. George Stephanopoulos, the son of a Greek Orthodox priest, was a Rhodes scholar who had previously worked for my friend Father Tim Healy when he ran the New York Public Library. I liked George immediately, and knew he could serve as a bridge to the national press and the congressional Democrats, as well as make a contribution to thinking through the intellectual challenges of the campaign.

Eli met with him, confirmed my judgment, and George came to work as deputy campaign manager in charge of communications. Eli also saw David Wilhelm, the young Chicago political operative whom I wanted on the team. We offered him the job of campaign manager, and he quickly accepted. David was, in political language, a "two-fer": besides managing the overall campaign, he would be a special help in Illinois. I was convinced that, with David as campaign manager, along with Kevin O'Keefe as a state organizer, we could now win a clear victory in Illinois to follow up on the anticipated sweep of the southern states on Super Tuesday. Soon afterward, we also persuaded another young Chicagoan, Rahm Emanuel, to join our campaign. Rahm had worked with Wilhelm in the successful campaigns of Mayor Richard Daley and Senator Paul Simon. He was a slight, intense man who had studied ballet and, though an American citizen, had served in the Israeli army. Rahm was so aggressive he made me look laid-back. We made him finance director, a job in which an underfunded campaign needs an aggressor. Craig Smith went to work on our state campaign organizations, a job better suited to his considerable political skills. Soon Bruce Reed left the Democratic

Leadership Council to become our policy director. Eli also interviewed two women who would play important roles in the campaign. Dee Dee Myers from California became the press secretary, a job that would require her to handle more incoming fire than she possibly could have anticipated. Though she was very young, she rose to the challenge. Stephanie Solien, from Washington State, became our political director. She was married to Frank Greer, but that's not why I hired her. Stephanie was smart, politically astute, and less hard-edged than most of the boys. She provided both the good work and the good chemistry every high-tension effort needs. As the campaign progressed, young people from all over America just showed up to pick up the extra load.

On the financial front, we made do in the beginning with generous early help from Arkansans, Bob Farmer's efforts in Massachusetts and with regular Democratic donors who would give just because he asked them, and donations from friends around the country that helped me qualify for matching funds from the federal government. To do that, a candidate must raise $5,000 in each of twenty states, in amounts not exceeding $250 per contribution. In some states, my governor friends took care of it. In Texas, my longtime supporter Truman Arnold raised a much-needed $30,000. Unlike many wealthy people, Truman seemed to become an even more committed Democrat as he got richer.

Somewhat surprisingly, a lot of people in the Washington, D.C., area wanted to help, in particular Democratic lawyer and fund-raiser Vic Raiser and my friend from Renaissance Weekend Tom Schnieder. In New York, I got invaluable early help not only from our friends Harold Ickes and Susan Thomases but also from Ken Brody, a Goldman Sachs executive who decided he wanted to get heavily involved in Democratic politics for the first time. Ken told me he had been a Republican because he thought the Democrats had a heart but their head was in the wrong place. Then, he said, he had gotten close enough to the national Republicans to see that they had a head but no heart, and decided to join the Democrats because he thought it was easier to change minds than hearts, and luckily for me, he figured I was the best place to start. Ken took me to a dinner with high-powered New York businesspeople, including Bob Rubin, whose tightly reasoned arguments for a new economic policy made a lasting impression on me. In every successful political campaign, people like Ken Brody somehow appear, bringing energy, ideas, and converts.

In addition to money-raising and organizing, I had to reach out to constituencies that were predominantly Democratic. In October, I spoke to a Jewish group in Texas, saying that Israel should trade land for peace; to blacks and Hispanics in Chicago; and to Democratic Party groups in Tennessee, Maine, New Jersey, and California, all of which were considered swing states, meaning they could go either way in the general election. In November, I spoke in Memphis to the convention of the Church of God in Christ, America's fastest-growing black denomination. I worked the South: Florida, South Carolina, Louisiana, and Georgia. Florida was important, because its December 15 straw poll at the Democratic convention would be the first contested vote. President Bush was beginning to slip in the polls and didn't help himself by saying that the economy was in good shape. I spoke to the National Education Association and the annual meeting of the American Israel Public Affairs Committee in Washington. I went south again to North Carolina, Texas, and Georgia. In the West, I made stops in Colorado and South Dakota; in Wyoming, where Governor Mike Sullivan endorsed me; and in the Republican stronghold of Orange County, California, where I picked up the support of Republican telecommunications executive Roger Johnson and others who were disillusioned with President Bush's economic policy.

While all this was going on, however, the main focus of the campaign was New Hampshire. If I ran poorly there, I might not do well enough in the states that followed to last until Super Tuesday. Though I was running dead last in the polls in mid-November, I liked my chances. New Hampshire is a small state, less than half the size of Arkansas, with very well-informed primary voters who take seriously their responsibility to carefully evaluate the candidates and their positions. To compete effectively, a good organization and persuasive television ads are necessary, but nowhere near sufficient. You must also do well in an endless stream of small house parties, town meetings, rallies, and unscheduled handshaking. A lot of New Hampshire citizens won't vote for anyone who hasn't personally asked for their support. After all my years in Arkansas politics, that kind of campaigning was second nature to me.

Even more than the political culture, the economic distress and the inevitable emotional trauma it spawned made me feel at home in New Hampshire. It was like Arkansas ten years earlier. After prospering throughout the 1980s, New Hampshire had the nation's fastest-growing welfare and food-stamp rolls, and the highest rate of bankruptcies. Factories were closing and banks were in trouble. Lots of people were unemployed and genuinely afraid—afraid of losing their homes and their health insurance. They didn't know if they would be able to send their kids to college. They doubted Social Security would be solvent when they reached their retirement years. I knew how they felt. I had known many Arkansans in similar situations. And I thought I knew what needed to be done to turn things around.

The campaign organization began with two gifted young people, Mitchell Schwartz and Wendy Smith, who moved to Manchester and opened the state headquarters. They were soon joined by Michael Whouley, a Boston Irishman and world-class organizer, and my friend of forty years Patty Howe Criner, who moved up from Little Rock to explain and defend me and my record. Before long we had a big steering committee co-chaired by two lawyers I'd met through the DLC, John Broderick and Terry Shumaker, whose office, fortuitously, was in the same building that more than a century earlier had housed the law office of President Franklin Pierce.

The competition was stiff. All the announced candidates were running hard in New Hampshire. Senator Bob Kerrey, the Medal of Honor winner and former Nebraska governor, attracted a lot of interest because he was a political maverick:

a fiscal conservative and a social liberal. The centerpiece of his campaign was a sweeping proposal to provide health coverage for all Americans, a big issue in a state where the number of people losing their health insurance was rising daily after a decade in which the cost of health insurance nationally had risen at three times the overall rate of inflation. Kerrey also had a powerful argument that his military record and his popularity in conservative Republican Nebraska made him the most electable Democrat against President Bush.

Senator Tom Harkin of Iowa was the Senate's leading advocate for the rights of the disabled; an authority on science and technology issues, which were important to the growing number of New Hampshire suburban voters; and a longtime ally of the labor movement. He argued that it would take an authentic populist campaign to win in November, not a DLC message, which he said had no appeal to "real" Democrats.

Former senator Paul Tsongas of Lowell, Massachusetts, had retired at a young age from a successful career in the Senate to battle cancer. He had become a fitness fanatic who swam vigorously, and publicly, to demonstrate that he was cured and able to be President. Tsongas argued that his premature brush with mortality had liberated him from conventional political constraints, making him more willing than the rest of us to tell voters hard truths they didn't necessarily want to hear. He had some interesting ideas, which he put forward in a widely distributed campaign booklet.

Governor Doug Wilder had made history by becoming Virginia's first African-American governor. He argued that his ability to win in a conservative southern state and his record on education, crime, and balanced budgets proved his electability.

Soon after I entered the race, former governor Jerry Brown of California also announced. Jerry said he wouldn't take contributions in amounts over $100 and tried to position himself as the only genuine reformer in the race. The focus of his campaign became a proposal to scrap the complex tax code in favor of a uniform "flat" tax of 13 percent on all Americans. In 1976, as a young governor, Jerry entered the late primaries and won several of them in a last-minute effort to stop Jimmy Carter. In 1979, I served with him in the National Governors Association, where I came to appreciate his quick mind and often unusual analysis of current events. The only quality his unique political persona lacked was a sense of humor. I liked Jerry, but he took every conversation awfully seriously.

For more than two months after I announced, the campaign was shadowed by the specter that there might be yet another candidate, Governor Mario Cuomo of New York. Cuomo was a huge figure in Democratic politics, our finest orator and a passionate defender of Democratic values during the Reagan-Bush years. Many people thought the nomination was his for the asking, and for a good while I thought he would ask. He took some hard shots at the DLC, at me, and at my ideas on welfare reform and national service. I was magnanimous in public, but I fumed in private and said some things about Mario I regret. I think I was so stung by his criticism because I had always admired him. In mid-December he finally announced that he wouldn't run. When some of my hard comments about him became public during the New Hampshire primary, all I could do was apologize. Thank goodness, he was big enough to accept it. In the years ahead, Mario Cuomo would become a valued advisor and one of my strongest defenders. I wanted to put him on the Supreme Court, but he didn't want that job, either. I think he loved his life in New York too much to give it up, a fact the voters didn't fully appreciate when they denied him a fourth term in 1994.

At the outset of the campaign, I thought my strongest competitor in New Hampshire would be Harkin or Kerrey. Before long, it was clear that I had been mistaken: Tsongas was the man to beat. His hometown was practically on the New Hampshire state line; he had a compelling life story; he demonstrated the toughness and determination to win; and, most important, he was the only other candidate who was competing with me on the essential battleground of ideas, message, and specific, comprehensive proposals.

Successful presidential campaigns require three basic things. First, people have to be able to look at you and imagine you as President. Then you have to have enough money and support to become known. After that, it's a battle of ideas, message, and issues. Tsongas met the first two criteria and was out to win the ideas battle. I was determined not to let him do it.

I scheduled three speeches at Georgetown to flesh out my New Covenant theme with specific proposals. They were delivered to students, faculty, supporters, and good press coverage in beautiful, old, wood-paneled Gaston Hall, in the Healy Building. On October 23, the topic was responsibility and community; on November 20, economic opportunity; on December 12, national security.

Together, these speeches allowed me to articulate the ideas and proposals I had developed over the previous decade as governor and with the Democratic Leadership Council. I had helped to write, and deeply believed in, the DLC's five core beliefs: Andrew Jackson's credo of opportunity for all and special privileges for none; the basic American values of work and family, freedom and responsibility, faith, tolerance, and inclusion; John Kennedy's ethic of mutual responsibility, asking citizens to give something back to their country; the advancement of democratic and humanitarian values around the world, and prosperity and upward mobility at home; and Franklin Roosevelt's commitment to innovation, to modernizing government for the information age and encouraging people by giving them the tools to make the most of their own lives.

I was amazed by some of the criticisms of the DLC from the Democratic left, who accused us of being closet Republicans, and from some members of the political press, who had comfortable little boxes marked "Democrat" and "Republican." When we didn't fit neatly in their ossified Democratic box, they said we didn't believe in anything. The proof was that we wanted to win national elections, something Democrats apparently weren't supposed to do.

I believed the DLC was furthering the best values and principles of the Democratic Party with new ideas. Of course, some liberals honestly disagreed with us on welfare reform, trade, fiscal responsibility, and national defense. But our differences with the Republicans were clear. We were against their unfair tax cuts and big deficits; their opposition to the Family and Medical Leave bill and the Brady bill; their failure to adequately fund education or push proven reforms, instead of vouchers; their divisive tactics on racial and gay issues; their unwillingness to protect the environment; their anti-choice stance; and much more. We also had good ideas, like putting 100,000 community police on the streets; doubling the Earned Income Tax Credit to make work more attractive and life better for families with modest incomes; and offering young people a chance to do community service in return for assistance to pay for college.

The principles and proposals I advocated could hardly be called Republican-lite or lacking in conviction. Instead, they helped to modernize the Democratic Party and later would be adopted by resurgent center-left parties all over the world, in what would be called the "Third Way." Most important, the new ideas, when implemented, would prove to be good for America. The 1991 Georgetown speeches gave me the invaluable opportunity to demonstrate that I had a comprehensive agenda for change and was serious about implementing it.

Meanwhile, back in New Hampshire, I put out a campaign booklet of my own, outlining all the specific proposals made in the Georgetown speeches. And I scheduled as many town meetings as possible. One of the early ones was held in Keene, a beautiful college town in the southern part of the state. Our campaign workers had put up flyers around town, but we didn't know how many people would show up. The room we rented held about two hundred. On the way to the meeting, I asked a veteran campaigner how many people we needed to avoid embarrassment. She said, "Fifty." And how many to be judged a success? "A hundred and fifty." When we arrived, there were four hundred people. The fire marshal made us put half of them in another room, and I had to do two meetings. It was the first time I knew we could do well in New Hampshire.

Usually I talked for fifteen minutes or so and spent an hour or more answering questions. At first I worried about being too detailed and "policy wonky" in the answers, but I soon realized that people were looking for substance over style. They were really hurting and wanted to understand what was happening to them and how they could get out of the fix they were in. I learned a lot just listening to the questions I got from people at those town meetings and other campaign stops.

An elderly couple, Edward and Annie Davis, told me they often had to choose between buying their prescription drugs and buying food. A high school student said her unemployed father was so ashamed he couldn't look at his family over dinner; he just hung his head. I met veterans in American Legion halls and found they were more concerned with the deterioration of health care at Veterans Administration hospitals than with my opposition to the Vietnam War. I was especially moved by the story of Ron Machos, whose son Ronnie was born with a heart problem. He had lost his job in the recession and couldn't find another one with health insurance to cover the large medical costs he knew were coming. When the New Hampshire Democrats held a convention to hear from all the candidates, a group of students carrying a CLINTON FOR PRESIDENT banner, who had been recruited by their teacher, my old friend from Arkansas Jan Paschal, led me to the podium. One of them made a particular impression on me. Michael Morrison was in a wheelchair, but it didn't slow him down. He was supporting me because he was being raised by a single mother on a modest income, and he thought I was committed to giving all kids a chance to go to college and get a good job.

By December, the campaign was on a roll. On December 2, James Carville and his partner, Paul Begala, joined us. They were colorful characters and a hot political property, having recently helped elect Governor Bob Casey and Senator Harris Wofford in Pennsylvania, and Governor Zell Miller in Georgia. Zell first got Carville on the phone for me so that I could set up a meeting with him and Begala. Like Frank Greer and me, they were part of an endangered but hardy political species, white southern Democrats. Carville was a Louisiana Cajun and ex-marine who had a great strategic sense and a deep commitment to progressive politics. He and I had a lot in common, including strong-willed, down-to-earth mothers whom we adored. Begala was a witty dynamo from Sugar Land, Texas, who blended aggressive populism with his Catholic social conscience. I wasn't the only candidate who wanted to hire them, and when they signed on, they brought energy, focus, and credibility to our efforts.

On December 10, I spoke to the Conference of Presidents of Major American Jewish Organizations, and two days later I delivered the third and final Georgetown speech, on national security. I got a lot of help with the speeches from my longtime friend Sandy Berger, who had been deputy director of policy planning in the State Department during the Carter years. Sandy recruited three other Carter-era foreign policy experts to help—Tony Lake, Dick Holbrooke, and Madeleine Albright—along with a bright, Australian-born expert on the Middle East, Martin Indyck. All would play important roles in the years ahead. In mid-December, it was enough that they helped me cross the threshold of understanding and competence in foreign affairs.

On December 15, I won the nonbinding Florida straw poll at the state Democratic convention with 54 percent of the delegates. I knew many of them from my three visits to the convention in the 1980s, and I had by far the strongest campaign organization, headed by Lieutenant Governor Buddy McKay. Hillary and I also worked the delegates hard, as did her brothers, Hugh and Tony, who lived in Miami, and Hugh's wife, Maria, a Cuban-American lawyer.

Two days after the Florida win, an Arkansas fund-raiser netted $800,000 for the campaign, far more than had ever before been raised at a single event there. On December 19, the *Nashville Banner* became the first newspaper to endorse me. On December 20, Governor Cuomo said he wouldn't run. Then Senator Sam Nunn and Governor Zell Miller of Georgia gave the campaign a huge boost when they endorsed me. Georgia's primary came just before Super Tuesday, along with Maryland's and Colorado's.

Meanwhile, President Bush's troubles mounted, as Pat Buchanan announced his intention to enter the GOP primaries with a George Wallace–like attack on the President from the right. Conservative Republicans were upset with the President for signing a $492 billion deficit-reduction package passed by the Democratic Congress because, in addition to spending cuts, it contained a five-cent gas-tax increase. Bush had brought the Republican convention to its feet in 1988 with his famous line "Read my lips: no new taxes." He did the responsible thing in signing the deficit-reduction package, but in doing so he broke his most visible campaign commitment and violated the anti-tax theology of his party's right-wing base.

The conservatives didn't direct all their fire at the President; I got my fair share, too, from a group called ARIAS, which stood for Alliance for the Rebirth of an Independent American Spirit. ARIAS was led in part by Cliff Jackson, an Arkansan whom I'd known and liked at Oxford, but who was now a conservative Republican with a deep personal animosity toward me. When ARIAS ran TV, radio, and newspaper ads attacking my record, we responded quickly and aggressively. The attacks might have done the campaign more good than harm, because answering them highlighted my accomplishments as governor, and because the source of the attacks made them suspect among New Hampshire Democrats. Two days before Christmas, a New Hampshire poll placed me second to Paul Tsongas and closing fast. The year ended on a good note.

On January 8, Governor Wilder withdrew from the race, reducing the competition for African-American voters, especially in the South. At about the same time, Frank Greer produced a great television ad, highlighting New Hampshire's economic problems and my plan to remedy them, and we moved ahead of Tsongas in public polls. By the second week of January, our campaign had raised $3.3 million in less than three months, half of it from Arkansas. It seems a paltry sum today, but it was good enough to lead the field in early 1992.

The campaign seemed to be on track until January 23, when the Little Rock media received advance notice of a story in the February 4 issue of the tabloid newspaper *Star*, in which Gennifer Flowers said she had carried on a twelve-year affair with me. Her name had been on the list of five women Larry Nichols alleged I had affairs with during the 1990 governor's race. At the time, she had strongly denied it. At first we didn't know how seriously the press would take her about-face, so we stuck with the schedule. I took a long drive to Claremont, in southwestern New Hampshire, to tour a brush factory. The people who ran it wanted to sell their products to Wal-Mart, and I wanted to help them. At some point, Dee Dee Myers went into the plant's small office and called headquarters. Flowers was claiming that she had tapes of ten phone conversations with me that supposedly proved the truth of her allegations.

A year earlier, Flowers's lawyer had written a letter to a Little Rock radio station threatening a libel suit because one of its talk-show hosts had repeated some of the allegations in a Larry Nichols press release, saying the station had "wrongfully and untruthfully" accused her of having an affair. We didn't know what was on whatever tapes Flowers might have, but I remembered the conversations clearly, and I didn't think there could be anything damaging on them. Flowers, whom I'd known since 1977 and had recently helped get a state job, had called me to complain that the media were harassing her even at the place she was singing at night, and that she felt her job was threatened. I commiserated with her, but I hadn't thought it was a big deal. After Dee Dee went to work trying to discover more about what the *Star* was planning to publish, I called Hillary and told her what was going on. Fortunately, she was staying at the Georgia Governor's Mansion on a campaign trip, and Zell and Shirley Miller were wonderful to her.

The Flowers story hit with explosive force, and it proved irresistible to the media, though some of the stories cast doubt on her accusations. The press reported that Flowers had been paid for the story, and that she had vigorously denied an affair a year earlier. The media, to their credit, exposed Flowers's false claims about her education and work history. These reports, however, were dwarfed by the allegations. I was dropping in the New Hampshire polls, and Hillary and I decided we should accept an invitation from the CBS program *60 Minutes* to answer questions about the charges and the state of our marriage. It was not an easy call. We wanted to defend against the scandal coverage and to get back to the real issues without demeaning ourselves and adding fuel to the fire of personal-destruction politics, which I had deplored even before it burned me. I had already said I hadn't lived a perfect life. If that was the standard, someone else would have to be elected President.

We taped the program at the Ritz-Carlton in Boston on Sunday morning, January 26, for showing later that night, after the Super Bowl. We talked to the interviewer, Steve Kroft, for over an hour. He began by asking if Flowers's story was true. When I said it wasn't, he asked if I had had any affairs. Perhaps I should have used Rosalynn Carter's brilliant response to a similar question in 1976: "If I had, I wouldn't tell you." Since I wasn't as blameless as Mrs. Carter, I decided not to be cute. Instead, I said that I had already acknowledged causing pain in my marriage, that I had already said more about the subject than any other politician ever had and would say no more, and that the American people understood what I meant.

Kroft, unbelievably, asked me again. His only goal in the interview was to get a specific admission. Finally, after a series of questions about Gennifer Flowers, he got around to Hillary and me, referring to our marriage as an "arrangement." I wanted to slug him. Instead, I said, "Wait a minute. You're looking at two people who love each other. This is not an arrangement or an understanding. This is a marriage." Hillary then said she was sitting in the interview with me "because I love him and I respect him and I honor what he's been through and what we've been through together. And you know, if that's not enough for people, then heck, don't vote for him." After the early mud wrestling, Kroft grew more civil, and there were some good exchanges about Hillary's and my life together. They were all cut out when the long interview was edited, down to about ten minutes, apparently because the Super Bowl shortened the program.

At some point during the session, the very bright, very hot overhead light above the couch Hillary and I were sitting on came loose from its tape on the ceiling and fell. It was directly above Hillary's head, and if it had hit her, she could have been burned badly. Somehow I saw it out of the corner of my eye and jerked her over onto my lap a split second before it crashed on the spot where she had been sitting. She was scared, and rightly so. I just stroked her hair and told her that it was all right and that I loved her. After the ordeal, we flew home to watch the show with Chelsea. When it was over, I asked Chelsea what she thought. She said, "I think I'm glad you're my parents."

The next morning I flew to Jackson, Mississippi, for a breakfast organized by former governor Bill Winter and Mike Espy, both of whom had endorsed me early. I was uncertain whether anyone would come and what the reception would be. To my immense relief, they had to get extra chairs for a larger-than-expected crowd that seemed genuinely glad to see me. So I went back to work.

It wasn't over, however. Gennifer Flowers gave a press conference to a packed house in New York's Waldorf-Astoria Hotel. She repeated her story and said she was sick of lying about it. She also acknowledged that she had been approached by a "local Republican candidate" who asked her to go public, but she declined to name him. Some of her tapes were played at the press conference, but except for proving that I had talked to her on the telephone, a fact I hadn't denied, the content of the tapes was anticlimactic, given all the hoopla about them.

Despite some later coverage, the Flowers media circus was ending. I think the chief reason was that we had managed to put it in the right perspective on *60 Minutes*. The public understood that I hadn't been perfect and wasn't pretending to be, but people also knew that there were many more important issues confronting the country. And a lot of people were repelled at the "cash for trash" aspects of the coverage. At about this time, Larry Nichols decided to drop his lawsuit, and he issued a public apology for, in his words, trying to "destroy" me: "The media has made a circus out of this thing and now it's gone way too far. When that *Star* article first came out, several women called asking if I was willing to pay them to say that they had had an affair with Bill Clinton. This is crazy." Questions were raised about the tapes that were played at Flowers's press conference. The *Star* declined to release the original tapes. A Los Angeles television station retained an expert who stated that while he didn't know that the tape was, in his words, "doctored," it definitely had been "selectively edited." CNN also ran some critical coverage, based on the analysis of its own expert.

As I've said, I first met Gennifer Flowers in 1977 when I was attorney general and she was a television reporter for a local station who often interviewed me. Soon afterward, she left Arkansas to pursue an entertainment career, I believe as a backup singer for country music star Roy Clark. At some point, she moved to Dallas. In the late eighties, she moved back to Little Rock to be near her mother and called to ask me to help her find a state job to supplement her income from singing. I referred her to Judy Gaddy on my staff, who was responsible for referring the many job seekers who asked for help with state employment to various agencies. After nine months, Flowers finally got a position paying less than $20,000 a year.

Gennifer Flowers struck me as a tough survivor who'd had a less-than-ideal childhood and disappointments in her career but kept going. She was later quoted in the press as saying that she might vote for me and, on another occasion, that she didn't believe Paula Jones's allegations of sexual harassment. Ironically, almost exactly six years after my January 1992 appearance on *60 Minutes*, I had to give a deposition in the Paula Jones case, and I was asked questions about Gennifer Flowers. I acknowledged that, back in the 1970s, I had had a relationship with her that I should not have had. Of course, the whole line of questioning had nothing to do with Jones's spurious sexual-harassment claim; it was just a part of the long, well-financed attempt to damage and embarrass me personally and politically. But I was under oath, and of course, if I hadn't done anything wrong, I couldn't have been embarrassed. My critics leapt on it. Ironically, even though they were sure the rest of the deposition was untruthful, this one answer they accepted as fact. The fact is, there was no twelve-year affair. Gennifer Flowers still has a suit against James Carville and Hillary for allegedly slandering her. I don't wish her ill, but now that I'm not President anymore, I do wish she'd let them be.

A few days after the firestorm broke, I called Eli Segal and pleaded with him to come down to Little Rock to be a mature, settling presence in the headquarters. When he asked how I could want the help of someone like him, who had worked only in losing presidential campaigns, I cracked, "I'm desperate." Eli laughed and came, becoming the campaign's chief of staff in charge of the central office, finances, and the campaign plane. Early in the month, Ned McWherter, Brereton Jones, and Booth Gardner, respectively the governors of Tennessee, Kentucky, and Washington, endorsed me. Those who had already done so, including Dick Riley of South Carolina, Mike Sullivan of Wyoming, Bruce King of New Mexico, George Sinner of North Dakota, and Zell Miller of Georgia, reaffirmed their support. So did Senator Sam Nunn, with the caveat that he wanted to "wait and see" what further stories came out.

A national poll said that 70 percent of the American people thought the press shouldn't report on the private lives of public figures. In another, 80 percent of the Democrats said their votes wouldn't be affected even if the Flowers story was true. That sounds good, but 20 percent is a lot to give up right off the bat. Nevertheless, the campaign picked up steam again, and it seemed that at least we could finish a strong second to Tsongas, which I thought would be good enough to get me to the southern primaries.

Then, just as the campaign seemed to be recovering, there was another big shock when the draft story broke. On February 6, the *Wall Street Journal* ran a story on my draft experience and on my relationship with the ROTC program at the University of Arkansas in 1969. When the campaign began, I was unprepared for the draft questions, and I mistakenly said I had never had a draft deferment during my Oxford years; in fact, I did have one from August 7 through October 20, 1969. Even worse, Colonel Eugene Holmes, who had agreed to let me join the program, now claimed that I had misled him to get out of the draft. In 1978, when reporters asked him about the charge, he said he had dealt with hundreds of cases and didn't recall anything specific about mine. Coupled with my own misstatement that I had never had a deferment, the story made it seem that I was misleading people about why I wasn't drafted. That wasn't true, but at the time I couldn't prove it. I didn't remember and didn't find Jeff Dwire's tape relaying his friendly conversation with Holmes in March 1970, after I was out of the ROTC program and back in the draft. Jeff was dead, as was Bill Armstrong, the head of my local draft board. And all draft records from that period had been destroyed.

Holmes's attack surprised me, because it contradicted his earlier statements. It's been suggested that Holmes may have had some help with his memory from his daughter Linda Burnett, a Republican activist who was working for President Bush's reelection.

Closer to the election, on September 16, Holmes would issue a more detailed denunciation questioning my "patriotism and integrity" and saying again that I had deceived him. Apparently, the statement was drafted by his daughter, with "guidance" from the office of my old opponent, Congressman John Paul Hammerschmidt, and had been revised by several Bush campaign officials.

A few days after the story broke, and just a week from election day in New Hampshire, Ted Koppel, anchor of ABC's *Nightline*, called David Wilhelm and said that he had a copy of my now famous draft letter to Colonel Holmes, and that ABC would be doing a story about it. I had forgotten all

about the letter, and ABC agreed to send us a copy, which
they graciously did. When I read it, I could see why the Bush
campaign was sure that the letter and Colonel Holmes's
revised account of the ROTC episode would sink me in New
Hampshire.

That night Mickey Kantor, Bruce Lindsey, James
Carville, Paul Begala, George Stephanopoulos, Hillary, and I
met in one of our rooms at the Days Inn Motel in Manchester. We were getting killed in the press. Now there was a
double-barreled attack on my character. All the television
pundits said I was dead as a doornail. George was curled up
on the floor, practically in tears. He asked if it wasn't time to
think about withdrawing. Carville paced the floor, waving
the letter around and shouting, "Georgie! Georgie! That's
crazy. This letter is our friend. Anyone who actually reads it
will think he's got character!" Though I loved his "never say
die" attitude, I was calmer than he was. I knew that George's
only political experience had been in Washington, and that,
unlike us, he might actually believe the press should decide
who was worthy and who wasn't. I asked, "George, do you
still think I'd be a good President?" "Yes," he said. "Then
get up and go back to work. If the voters want to withdraw
me, they'll do it on election day. I'm going to let them
decide."

The words were brave, but I was dropping in the polls
like a rock in a well. I was already in third place, and it
looked as if I might fall into single digits. On Carville's and
Mickey Kantor's advice, we took out an ad in the *Manchester Union Leader* containing the full text of the letter, and
bought two thirty-minute segments on television to let voters call in and ask me about the charges and whatever else
was on their minds. One hundred fifty Arkansans dropped
what they were doing and came to New Hampshire to
go door-to-door. One of them, Representative David
Matthews, had been a law student of mine and one of the
strongest supporters of my legislative programs and my
campaigns at home. David was an eloquent and persuasive
speaker who soon became my chief surrogate after Hillary.
After he warmed up the crowd for me at several rallies, I

think some people thought he should have been the candidate. Six hundred more Arkansans listed their names and home phone numbers in a full-page ad in the *Union Leader*, urging New Hampshire Democrats to call them if they wanted to know the truth about their governor. Hundreds of calls were made.

Of all the Arkansans who came to help, no one made a bigger difference than my closest childhood friend, David Leopoulos. After the Flowers story broke, David heard TV commentators say I was finished. He was so upset, he got in his car and drove three days to New Hampshire. He couldn't afford a plane ticket. When he reached our headquarters, Simon Rosenberg, my young press aide, scheduled him for an interview on a Boston radio station with a large New Hampshire audience. He hit it out of the park, just by talking about our forty-year friendship and making me seem more human. Then he spoke to a gathering of our discouraged volunteers from across the state. When he finished, he had them in tears and full of resolve for the final push. David worked the state for a whole week, doing radio interviews and passing out homemade flyers with pictures of our childhood friends as proof that I was a real person. At the end of his journey, I saw him at a rally in Nashua, where he hooked up with fifty other Arkansans, including Carolyn Staley, my old jazz partner Randy Goodrum, and my grade-school friend Mauria Aspell. The "Friends of Bill" probably saved the campaign in New Hampshire.

A few days before the election, I went down to New York for a long-planned fund-raiser. I wondered if anyone would come, even if only to see a dead man walking. As I made my way through the Sheraton Hotel kitchen to the ballroom, I shook hands with the waiters and kitchen workers, as I always did. One of the waiters, Dimitrios Theofanis, engaged me in a brief conversation that made him a friend for life. "My nine-year-old boy studies the election in school and he says I should vote for you. If I do, I want you to make my boy free. In Greece, we were poor but we were free. Here, my boy can't play in the park across the street alone or walk down the street to school by himself because it is too dangerous. He's not free. So if I vote for you, will you make my boy free?" I almost cried. Here was a man who actually cared about what I could do for his son's safety. I told him that community police officers, who would walk the blocks and know the residents, could help a lot, and that I was committed to funding 100,000 of them.

I was already feeling better, but when I walked into the ballroom, my spirits soared: seven hundred people were there, including my Georgetown friend Denise Hyland Dangremond and her husband, Bob, who had come from Rhode Island to show moral support. I went back to New Hampshire thinking I might survive.

In the last few days of the campaign, Tsongas and I had a heated disagreement over economic policy. I had proposed a four-point plan to create jobs, help businesses get started, and reduce poverty and income inequality: cut the deficit in half in four years, with spending reductions and tax increases on the wealthiest Americans; increase investment in education, training, and new technologies; expand trade; and cut taxes modestly for the middle class and a lot more for the working poor. We had done our best to cost out each proposal, using figures from the Congressional Budget Office. In contrast to my plan, Tsongas said that we should just focus on cutting the deficit, and that the country couldn't afford the middle-class tax cut, though he was for a cut in the capital gains tax, which would benefit wealthy Americans most. He called me a "pander bear" for proposing the tax cuts. He said he'd be the best friend Wall Street ever had. I shot back that we needed a New Democrat economic plan that helped both Wall Street and Main Street, business and working families. A lot of people agreed with Tsongas's contention that the deficit was too big for my tax cuts, but I thought we had to do something about the two-decade growth in income inequality and the shift of the tax burden to the middle class in the 1980s.

While I was glad to debate the relative merits of our competing economic plans, I was under no illusion that the questions about my character had gone away. As the campaign drew to a close, I told an enthusiastic crowd in Dover what I really believed about the "character issue":

> It has been absolutely fascinating to me to go through the last few weeks and see these so-called character issues raised, conveniently, after I zoomed to the top by talking about your problems and your future and your lives.
>
> Well, character is an important issue in a presidential election, and the American people have been making character judgments about their politicians for more than two hundred years now. And most of the time they've been right, or none of us would be here today. I'll tell you what I think the character issue is: Who really cares about you? Who's really trying to say what he would do specifically if he were elected President? Who has a demonstrated record of doing what they're talking about? And who is determined to change your life rather than to just get or keep power? . . .
>
> I'll tell you what I think the character issue in this election is: How can you have the power of the presidency and never use it to help people improve their lives 'til your life needs saving in an election? That's a character issue. . . .
>
> I'll tell you something. I'm going to give you this election back, and if you'll give it to me, I won't be like George Bush. I'll never forget who gave me a second chance, and I'll be there for you 'til the last dog dies.

"'Til the last dog dies" became the rallying cry for our troops in the last days of the New Hampshire campaign. Hundreds of volunteers worked furiously. Hillary and I shook every hand we could find. The polls were still discouraging, but the pulse felt better.

On election morning, February 18, it was cold and icy. Young Michael Morrison, Jan Paschal's wheelchair-bound student, woke in anticipation of working a polling place for me. Unfortunately, his mother's car wouldn't start. Michael was disappointed but not deterred. He rode his motorized wheelchair out into the cold morning and onto the shoulder of the slick road, then wheeled himself into the winter wind for two miles to reach his duty station. Some people thought the election was about the draft and Gennifer Flowers. I thought it was about Michael Morrison; and Ronnie Machos, the little boy with a hole in his heart and no health insurance; and the young girl whose unemployed father hung his head in shame over the dinner table; and Edward and Annie Davis, who didn't have enough money to buy food and the medicine they needed; and the son of an immigrant waiter in New York who couldn't play in the park across the street from where he lived. We were about to find out who was right.

That night, Paul Tsongas won with 35 percent, but I finished a strong second with 26 percent, well ahead of Kerrey with 12 percent, Harkin with 10 percent, and Brown with 9 percent. The rest of the votes went to write-ins. At the urging of Joe Grandmaison, a New Hampshire supporter I'd known since the Duffey campaign, I spoke to the media early, and at Paul Begala's suggestion said New Hampshire had made me "the Comeback Kid." Tsongas had annihilated me in the precincts closest to the Massachusetts state line. From ten miles north into New Hampshire, I had actually won. I was elated and profoundly grateful. The voters had decided that my campaign should go on.

I had come to love New Hampshire, to appreciate its idiosyncrasies, and to respect the seriousness of its voters, even those who chose someone else. The state had put me through the paces and made me a better candidate. So many people had befriended Hillary and me and lifted us up. A surprising number of them worked in my administration, and I kept in touch with several more over the next eight years, including hosting a New Hampshire Day at the White House.

New Hampshire demonstrated just how deeply the American people wanted their country to change. On the Republican side, Pat Buchanan's upstart campaign had won

37 percent of the vote, and the President's national approval ratings had dropped below 50 percent for the first time since the Gulf War. Although he still led both Paul Tsongas and me in the polls, the Democratic nomination was clearly worth having.

After New Hampshire, the rest of the primaries and caucuses came on at such a pace that the kind of "retail" politics New Hampshire demands became impossible to replicate. On February 23, Tsongas and Brown were the victors in the Maine caucuses, with Tsongas receiving 30 percent and Brown 29 percent. I was a distant third at 15 percent. With the exception of Iowa, the states with a caucus system drew far fewer people into the delegate-selection process than primaries did. Thus, the caucuses favored candidates with a hard core of intense supporters. They usually, but not always, were more left-leaning than the Democrats as a whole, and well to the left of the general election voters. On February 25, voters in the South Dakota primary gave more support to their neighbors Bob Kerrey and Tom Harkin than to me, though I made a respectable showing on just one trip to a rally at a horse ranch.

March was a big month. It opened with primaries in Colorado, Maryland, and Georgia. I had a lot of friends in Colorado, like Jim Lyons and Mike Driver, and former governor Dick Lamm was my Rocky Mountain coordinator, but the best I could do was a three-way split with Brown and Tsongas. Brown got 29 percent, I received 27 percent, with Tsongas right behind at 26 percent. In Maryland, I started out with a strong organization, but some supporters shifted to Tsongas when I dipped in the New Hampshire polls. He defeated me there.

Georgia was the big test. I hadn't won a primary yet, and I had to win there, and win convincingly. It was the largest state to vote on March 3 and the first in the South. Zell Miller had moved the primary date up a week, to separate Georgia from the southern Super Tuesday states. Georgia was an interesting state. Atlanta is a diverse, cosmopolitan city, with one of the highest concentrations of corporate headquarters of any other city in America. Outside Atlanta, the state is culturally conservative. For example, despite his great popularity, Zell had tried and failed to get the state legislature to take the Confederate cross off the state flag, and when his successor, Governor Roy Barnes, did it, he was defeated for reelection. The state also has a large military presence, long protected by its congressional leaders. It was no accident that Sam Nunn was chairman of the Senate Armed Services Committee. When the draft story broke, Bob Kerrey said that when I got to Georgia, the voters would split me open like a "soft peanut," a clever hit, because Georgia grows more peanuts than any other state. A couple of days after the New Hampshire vote, I flew to Atlanta. When my plane landed, I was met by Mayor Maynard Jackson, an old friend, and Jim Butler, a prosecuting attorney and Vietnam veteran who smiled and said he was one soldier who didn't want to split me open like a soft peanut.

The three of us rode downtown for a rally in a shopping mall. I got onto the stage with a large crowd of prominent Democrats who were supporting me. Before long, the stage built for the occasion couldn't support all of us; it just collapsed, throwing bodies everywhere. I wasn't hurt, but one of my co-chairs, Calvin Smyre, an African-American state representative, wasn't so lucky. He fell and broke his hip. Later, Craig Smith joked to Calvin that he was the only one of my supporters who literally "busted his ass" for me. He sure did. But so did Zell Miller, Congressman John Lewis, and a lot of other Georgians. And so did a number of Arkansans who had organized themselves into the "Arkansas Travelers." The Travelers campaigned in almost every state with a presidential primary. They always made a difference, but they were particularly effective in Georgia. The political press said that to go forward I had to win decisively there, with at least 40 percent of the vote. Thanks to my friends and my message, I won 57 percent.

The following Saturday, in South Carolina, I picked up my second win, with 63 percent of the vote. I had a lot of help from Democratic officials, plus former governor Dick

Riley, and friends from Renaissance Weekend. Tom Harkin made a last-ditch effort to derail me, and Jesse Jackson, a South Carolina native, went around the state with him criticizing me. Despite the attacks, and the crass response to them I carelessly made at a radio station in a room with a live microphone, other black leaders stayed hitched. I received a large majority of the black vote, as I had in Georgia. I think it surprised my opponents, all of whom had strong convictions and good records on civil rights. But I was the only southerner, and both I and the Arkansas blacks supporting me brought years of personal connections to black political, educational, business, and religious leaders all across the South and beyond.

As in Georgia, I also got good support from white primary voters. By 1992, most of the whites who wouldn't support a candidate with close ties to the black community had already become Republicans. I got the votes of those who wanted a President to reach across racial lines to attack the problems that plagued all Americans. The Republicans tried to keep this group's numbers small by turning every election into a culture war, and turning every Democrat into an alien in the eyes of white voters. They knew just what psychological buttons to push to get white voters to stop thinking, and when they got away with it, they won. Besides trying to win the primary, I was trying to keep enough white voters thinking to be competitive in the South in the general election.

After Georgia, Bob Kerrey withdrew from the race. After South Carolina, Tom Harkin did, too. Only Tsongas, Brown, and I headed into Super Tuesday, with its eight primaries and three caucuses. Tsongas defeated me badly in the primaries in his home state of Massachusetts and neighboring Rhode Island, and won the caucuses in Delaware. But the southern and border states made the day a rout for our campaign. In all the southern primaries—in Texas, Florida, Louisiana, Mississippi, Oklahoma, and Tennessee—I won a majority of the vote. In Texas, with the help of friends I'd made in the 1972 McGovern campaign and a big majority among Mexican-Americans, I won with 66 percent. In all the other primary states I did better than that, except for Florida, which, after a hotly contested race, went 51 percent Clinton, 34 percent Tsongas, 12 percent Brown. I also won the caucuses in Hawaii, thanks to Governor John Waihee, and in Missouri, where Lieutenant Governor Mel Carnahan endorsed me, despite having his own primary campaign for governor. He won anyway.

After Super Tuesday, I had just a week to cement my strategy of building an insurmountable lead in Illinois and Michigan. Only a month earlier, I had been in free fall, with all the media "experts" predicting my demise. Now I was in the lead. However, Tsongas was still very much alive. On the day after Super Tuesday, he quipped that, because of my strong showing in the southern primaries, he would consider me as his vice-presidential running mate. The next day he, too, was in the Midwest, questioning my character, my record as governor, and my electability. For him the character issue was the middle-class tax cut. A new poll showed that around 40 percent of the American people also doubted my honesty, but I doubted that they were thinking about the tax issue.

There was nothing to do but stick to my strategy and press on. In Michigan, I visited the small town of Burton, near Flint, where a large majority of the residents had come from Arkansas, looking for jobs in the auto industry. On March 12, I spoke in Macomb County, near Detroit, the prototypical home of the Reagan Democrats, voters who had been lured away from our party by Reagan's anti-government, strong-defense, tough-on-crime message. In fact, these suburban voters had begun voting Republican in the 1960s, because they thought the Democrats no longer shared their values of work and family, and were too concerned with social programs, which they tended to see as taking their tax money and giving it to blacks and wasteful bureaucrats.

I told a full house at Macomb County Community College that I would give them a new Democratic Party, with economic and social policies based on opportunity for and responsibility from all citizens. That included corporate

executives earning huge salaries without regard to their performance, working people who refused to upgrade their
skills, and poor people on welfare who could work. Then I
told them we couldn't succeed unless they were willing to
reach across racial lines to work with all people who shared
those values. They had to stop voting along the racial
divide, because "the problems are not racial in nature. This
is an issue of economics, of values."

The next day, I gave the same message to a few hundred
black ministers and other activists at the Reverend Odell
Jones's Pleasant Grove Baptist Church in inner-city Detroit.
I told the black audience, many of whom had Arkansas
roots, that I had challenged the white voters in Macomb
County to reach across the racial divide, and now I was
challenging them to do the same, by accepting the responsibility part of my agenda, including welfare reform, tough
child-support enforcement, and anti-crime efforts that
would promote the values of work, family, and safety in
their neighborhoods. The twin speeches got quite a bit of
attention, because it was unusual for a politician to challenge Macomb County whites on race or inner-city blacks
on welfare and crime. When both groups responded
strongly to the same message, I wasn't surprised. In their
heart of hearts, most Americans know that the best social
program is a job, that the strongest social institution is the
family, and that the politics of racial division are self-
defeating.

In Illinois, I visited a cheesecake factory with black,
Hispanic, and Eastern European immigrant employees to
highlight the company's commitment to giving all employees who hadn't finished high school access to a GED program. I met a new citizen from Romania who said he would
cast his first vote for me. I worked in the black and Hispanic communities with two young activists, Bobby Rush
and Luis Gutierrez, both of whom would later be elected to
Congress. I toured an energy-efficient housing project with
a young Hispanic community leader, Danny Solis, whose
sister Patti went to work for Hillary in the campaign and
has been with her ever since. And I marched in Chicago's

St. Patrick's Day parade, to the cheers of supporters and jeers of opponents, both enhanced by the beer that was in ample supply at bars along the parade route.

Two days before the election, I debated Paul Tsongas and Jerry Brown on television in Chicago. They knew it was make-or-break time, and they went after me. Brown grabbed the spotlight with a harsh attack on Hillary, saying that I had steered state business to the Rose firm to increase her income and that a poultry company her firm represented got special treatment from the Department of Pollution Control and Ecology because of her. The charges were ridiculous and the vehemence with which Jerry made them angered me. I explained the facts, as I had done when Frank White attacked Hillary's law practice in the 1986 governor's race. The Rose firm had represented the State of Arkansas in the bond business since 1948. It represented the state against the utilities that wanted Arkansas to pay for the Grand Gulf nuclear plant. Hillary had all legal fees paid by the state deleted from the firm's income before her partnership share was calculated, so she didn't receive any benefit from them, as even rudimentary research would have shown. Moreover, there was no evidence that the Rose firm's clients secured special favors from any state agency. I shouldn't have lost my temper, but the charges were plainly baseless. Subconsciously, I suppose I also felt guilty that Hillary had been forced to defend me so much, and I was glad to be able to rise to her defense.

Everyone who knew her knew she was scrupulously honest, but not everyone knew her, and the attacks hurt. On the morning after the debate, we were shaking hands at the Busy Bee Coffee Shop in Chicago when a reporter asked her what she thought of Brown's charges. She gave a good answer about trying to have both a career and a family life. The reporter then asked if she could have avoided the appearance of a conflict. Of course, that's exactly what she did and what she should have said. But she was tired and stressed. Instead, she said, "I suppose I could have stayed home and baked cookies and had teas, but what I decided to do was fulfill my profession, which I entered before my husband was in public life. And I've worked very, very hard to be as careful as possible, and that's all I can tell you."

The press picked up the "tea and cookies" remark and played it as a slam on stay-at-home mothers. The Republican culture warriors had a field day, portraying Hillary as a "militant feminist lawyer" who would be the ideological leader of a "Clinton-Clinton administration" that would push a "radical feminist" agenda. I hurt for her. Over the years, I don't know how many times I'd heard her champion the importance of ensuring choices for women, including the choice to stay home with their children, a decision most mothers, single and married, simply couldn't afford anymore. Also, I knew she liked to bake cookies and have her women friends for tea. With one off-the-cuff remark, she had given our opponents another weapon to do what they did best—divide and distract the voters.

It was all forgotten the next day when we won in Illinois, Hillary's home state, with 52 percent to 25 percent for Tsongas and 15 percent for Brown, and in Michigan, with 49 percent to 27 percent for Brown and 18 percent for Tsongas. If Brown's attack on Hillary had any effect, it probably hurt him in Illinois. Meanwhile, President Bush handily defeated Pat Buchanan in both states, effectively ending his challenge. Although the division in the Republican ranks was good for me, I was glad to see Buchanan defeated. He had played to the dark side of middle-class insecurity. For example, in one southern state he visited a Confederate cemetery but wouldn't even walk across the street to visit the black cemetery.

After a great celebration in Chicago's Palmer House Hotel, complete with Irish green confetti in honor of the holiday, we got back to business. On the surface, the campaign was in great shape. Underneath, things weren't so clear. One new poll showed me running even with President Bush. Another, however, showed me well behind, even though the President's job approval had dropped to 39 percent. A survey of Illinois voters as they left their polling places said half the Democrats were unhappy with their choice of presidential candidates. Jerry Brown was unhappy, too. He said he might not support me if I won the nomination.

On March 19, Tsongas withdrew from the campaign, citing financial problems. That left Jerry Brown as my only opponent as we headed toward the Connecticut primary on March 24. It was assumed I would win in Connecticut, because most of the Democratic leaders had endorsed me, and I had friends there going back to my law school days. Though I campaigned hard, I was worried. It just didn't feel good. The Tsongas supporters were mad at me for driving him from the race; they were going to vote for him anyway or switch to Brown. By contrast, my supporters had a hard time getting stirred up, because they thought I had the nomination in the bag. I was worried that a low turnout could cost me the election. That's exactly what happened. The turnout was around 20 percent of the registered Democrats, and Brown beat me, 37 to 36 percent. Twenty percent of the voters were die-hard Tsongas supporters who stood by their man.

The next big test was in New York on April 7. Now that I had lost in Connecticut, if I didn't win in New York, the nomination would be in danger again. With its tough, insatiable twenty-four-hour news cycle and its rough-and-tumble interest group politics, New York seemed to be the ideal place to derail my campaign.

TWENTY-SEVEN

IN POLITICS, there's nothing quite like a New York election. First, there are three geographically and psychologically distinct regions of the state: New York City with its five very different boroughs; Long Island and the other suburban counties; and upstate. There are large black and Hispanic populations, the nation's largest population of Jewish Americans, plus well-organized groups of Indians, Pakistanis, Albanians, and just about any other ethnic group you can imagine. There is also a lot of diversity within New York's black and Hispanic populations—New York's Hispanics include people from Puerto Rico and all the Caribbean nations, including more than 500,000 from the Dominican Republic alone.

My outreach to the ethnic communities was organized by Chris Hyland, a Georgetown classmate who lived in lower Manhattan, one of the most ethnically diverse neighborhoods in America. When Hillary and I visited a group of elementary school students displaced by the attack on the World Trade Center in September 2001, we found children from eighty different national and ethnic groups. Chris started by buying about thirty ethnic newspapers and locating the leaders mentioned in them. After the primaries, he organized a fund-raiser in New York with 950 ethnic leaders, then moved to Little Rock to organize ethnic groups across the country, making an important contribution to victory in the general election, and laying the foundation for our continuing unprecedented contact with ethnic communities once we got to the White House.

The unions, especially the public employee groups, have a huge presence and are politically astute and effective. In New York City, the politics of the primary were further complicated by the fact that both party regulars and liberal reformers were active and often saw themselves at odds with each other. Gay-rights groups were organized and vocal about the need to do more about AIDS, which in 1992 still claimed more victims in America than any other country. The press was an ever-present cacophony of traditional newspapers, led by the *New York Times*, the tabloids, vigorous local TV stations, and talk radio—all in hot competition for the latest story.

While the New York campaign didn't really begin until after the Connecticut primary, I had been working the state for months with the invaluable help and expert advice of Harold Ickes, the namesake and son of FDR's famous secretary of the interior. By 1992, we had been friends for more than twenty years. Harold is a thin, intense, brilliant, passionate, and occasionally profane man, a unique blend of liberal idealism and practical political skills. As a young man, he'd worked as a cowboy out west and had been badly beaten working for civil rights in the South. In campaigns, he was a loyal friend and a ferocious opponent who believed in the power of politics to change lives. He knew the personalities, issues, and power struggles of New York like the back of his hand. If I was about to go through hell, I was at least making the trip with a man who stood a chance of getting me out alive.

In December 1991, Harold, who had already helped line up important support in Manhattan, Brooklyn, and the Bronx, arranged for me to speak to the Queens Democratic Committee. He suggested we ride the subway from Manhattan to the meeting. My being a country boy on the subway got more press coverage than my speech, but the appearance was important. Shortly afterward, the Queens Democratic chairman, Congressman Tom Manton, endorsed me. So did Queens congressman Floyd Flake, who was also the minister of Allen African Methodist Episcopal Church.

In January, I visited a high school in Brooklyn to observe Martin Luther King Jr.'s birthday with African-American congressman Ed Towns and the Brooklyn Democratic chair, Clarence Norman. The kids talked a lot about the problem of guns and knives in their school. They wanted a President who would make their lives safer. I went to a debate in the

Bronx, moderated by the borough president, Fernando Ferrer, who would become a supporter. I took the ferry to Staten Island and campaigned there. In Manhattan, the borough president, Ruth Messinger, worked hard for me, as did her young aide, Marty Rouse, who helped me make inroads into the gay community. Victor and Sara Kovner convinced a number of the liberal reformers to support me and became good friends. Guillermo Linares, who was one of the first Dominicans elected to the city council, became one of the first prominent Latinos to endorse me. I campaigned on Long Island and in Westchester County, where I now live.

The unions made a bigger difference in New York than in any previous primary. Among the largest and most active were the New York affiliates of AFSCME, the American Federation of State, County, and Municipal Employees. After I appeared before its executive board, AFSCME was the first big union to endorse me. I had worked closely with AFSCME as governor, and had become a dues-paying member. But the real reason for the endorsement was that the union's president, Gerald McEntee, decided that he liked me and that I could win. McEntee was a good man to have on your side. He was effective, fiercely loyal, and didn't mind a tough fight. I also had the support of the United Transportation Union and, by the end of March, the Communications Workers of America and the International Ladies' Garment Workers Union. The teachers were helpful, even though I had not yet received a formal endorsement. In addition to the unions, I also had a strong group of business supporters, mobilized by Alan Patricof and Stan Shuman.

The most important and enduring encounter I had with an ethnic group was with the Irish. Late one night, I met with the Irish Issues Forum organized by Bronx assemblyman John Dearie. Harold Ickes and New York City tax commissioner Carol O'Cleireacain had helped me prepare. The legendary Paul O'Dwyer, who was about eighty-five, and his son Brian were there, as were Niall O'Dowd, editor of the *Irish Voice*, journalist Jimmy Breslin, Queens comptroller Peter King, a Republican, and about a hundred other Irish activists. They wanted me to promise to appoint a special representative to push for an end to the violence in Northern Ireland on terms that were fair to the Catholic minority. I had also been encouraged to do this by Boston mayor Ray Flynn, an ardent Irish Catholic and a strong supporter of mine. I had been interested in the Irish issue since "the Troubles" began in 1968, when I was at Oxford. After a lengthy discussion, I said I would do it and that I would push for an end to discrimination against Northern Ireland's Catholics in economics and other areas. Though I knew it would infuriate the British and strain our most important transatlantic alliance, I had become convinced that the United States, with its huge Irish diaspora, including people who funneled money to the Irish Republican Army, might be able to facilitate a breakthrough.

Soon I put out a strong statement reaffirming my commitment, drafted by my foreign policy aide Nancy Soderberg. My law school classmate, former congressman Bruce Morrison, of Connecticut, organized Irish-Americans for Clinton. The group would play a major role in the campaign and in the work we would do afterward. As Chelsea noted in her Stanford senior thesis on the Irish peace process, I first got involved in the Irish issue because of the politics of New York, but it became one of the great passions of my presidency.

In an ordinary Democratic primary, a campaign with this kind of support would be assured an easy victory. But this was not an ordinary primary. First, there was the opposition. Jerry Brown was working like a demon, determined to rally the liberal voters in this last, best chance to stop my campaign. Paul Tsongas, encouraged by his showing in Connecticut, let it be known that he wouldn't mind his supporters voting for him one more time. The presidential candidate of the New Alliance Party, an articulate, angry woman named Lenora Fulani, did what she could to help them, bringing her supporters to a health-care event I held in a Harlem hospital and shouting down my speech.

Jesse Jackson practically moved to New York to help Brown. His most important contribution was to persuade Dennis Rivera, head of one of the city's largest and most active unions, Service Employees International Union Local 1199, not to endorse me and to help Jerry instead. Brown returned the favor by saying that, if nominated, he would name Jesse as his running mate. I thought Brown's announcement would help him among New York's black voters, but it also galvanized a lot of new support for me in the Jewish community. Jackson was believed to be too close to Black Muslim leader Louis Farrakhan, who was known for anti-Semitic remarks. Still, Jesse's support was a net plus for Brown in New York.

Then there was the media. The big papers had been camping out in Arkansas for weeks, looking for whatever they could find on my record and my personal life. The *New York Times* had started the ball rolling in early March with the first of its Whitewater stories. In 1978, Hillary and I, along with Jim and Susan McDougal, took out bank loans of more than $200,000 to invest in land along the White River in northwest Arkansas. Jim was a land developer whom I had met when he ran Senator Fulbright's office in Little Rock. We hoped to subdivide the property and sell it at a profit to retirees who had begun moving to the Ozarks in large numbers in the sixties and seventies. McDougal had been successful in all his previous land ventures, including one in which I had invested a few thousand dollars and earned a modest profit. Unfortunately, in the late seventies, interest rates went through the roof, the economy slowed, land sales dropped, and we lost money on the venture.

By the time I became governor again in 1983, McDougal had bought a small savings-and-loan and named it Madison Guaranty Savings and Loan. A few years later, he retained the Rose Law Firm to represent it. When the savings-and-loan crisis hit America, Madison was facing insolvency and sought to inject new cash into the operation by selling preferred stock and forming a subsidiary to provide brokerage services. To do this, McDougal had to get permission from the state securities commissioner, Beverly Bassett Schaffer, whom I had appointed. Beverly was a first-class lawyer, the sister of my friend Woody Bassett, and the wife of Archie Schaffer, Senator Dale Bumpers's nephew.

The *Times* article was one of a series of articles on White-water. The reporter questioned whether there was a conflict in Hillary's representing an entity regulated by the state. She had personally signed one letter to Commissioner Schaffer explaining the preferred stock proposal. The reporter also implied that Madison had received special treatment in getting its "novel" financing proposals approved and that Schaffer had not exercised appropriate oversight over the institution when it was failing.

The facts did not support the accusations and innuendos. First, the financing proposals the commissioner approved were normal for the time, not novel. Second, as soon as an independent audit showed Madison to be insolvent, in 1987, Schaffer pushed federal regulators to shut it down, well before they were willing to do so. Third, Hillary had billed Madison for a grand total of twenty-one hours of legal work at the Rose Law Firm over a two-year period. Fourth, we never borrowed any money from Madison, but we did lose money on the Whitewater investment. That's the essential Whitewater picture. The *New York Times* reporter clearly was talking to Sheffield Nelson and other adversaries of mine in Arkansas who would have been happy to create "character problems" in other areas besides the draft and Flowers. In this case, doing so required ignoring inconvenient facts and misrepresenting the record of a dedicated public servant like Schaffer.

The *Washington Post* weighed in with an article designed to show I'd been too close to the poultry industry and had failed to stop it from spreading the waste from its chicken and hog operations onto farmland. A little animal waste made good fertilizer, but when the volume of waste was too great for the land to absorb, rain washed it into streams, polluting them so that they were unsafe for fishing and swimming. In 1990 the state Department of Pollution Control and Ecology found that more than 90 percent of the streams in northwest Arkansas, where the poultry industry was concentrated, were polluted. We spent several million dollars trying to correct the problem, and two years later, the Pollution Control people said over 50 percent of the streams met the standard for recreational use. I got the industry to agree to a set of "best management practices" to clean up the rest. I was criticized for not mandating an industry cleanup—something easier said than done. The Democratic Congress could not do it; the agricultural interests had enough influence to get themselves completely exempted from federal regulations when Congress passed the Clean Water Act. Poultry was Arkansas' biggest business and number one employer and very influential in the state legislature. Under the circumstances, I thought we had done a pretty good job, though it was the weakest spot in an otherwise solid environmental record. Both the *Washington Post* and the *New York Times* wound up doing articles on the subject, with the *Post* suggesting by late March that the Rose Law Firm had somehow gotten the state to go easy on the poultry industry.

I tried to keep things in perspective. The press had an obligation to examine the record of someone who might be President. Most reporters knew nothing about Arkansas or me when they started. Some of them had negative preconceptions about a poor, rural state and the people who lived there. I had also been identified as 1992's "character problem" candidate; that made the media vulnerable to whatever dirt they were handed to support the preconception.

Intellectually, I understood all this, and I remembered and appreciated the positive coverage I had received earlier in the campaign. Nevertheless, it felt more and more as if the investigative stories were being prepared on the basis of "shoot first, ask questions later." Reading them felt like an out-of-body experience. The press seemed determined to prove that everyone who thought I was fit to be President was a fool: the Arkansas voters who had elected me five times; my fellow governors, who had voted me the most effective governor in the country; the education experts who had praised our reforms and progress; lifelong friends who were campaigning for me all over the country. In Arkansas, even my honest adversaries knew I worked hard and wouldn't take a nickel to see the cow jump over the moon. Now it seemed I had snookered all these people from the

age of six on. At one point, when things got really bad in
New York, Craig Smith told me he didn't read the papers
anymore, "because I don't recognize the person they're talking about."

Near the end of March, Betsey Wright, who was at Harvard doing a stint at the Kennedy School, came to my rescue. She had worked hard for years to build our progressive
record and to run a tight ethical operation. She had a prodigious memory, knew the records, and was more than willing
to fight with reporters to set the record straight. When she
moved into the headquarters as director of damage control,
I felt much better. Betsey stopped a lot of factually incorrect
stories, but she couldn't stop them all.

On March 26, the smoke seemed to clear a little when
Senator Tom Harkin, the Communications Workers of
America, and the International Ladies' Garment Workers
Union endorsed me. I was also helped when Governor
Cuomo and New York senator Pat Moynihan criticized
Jerry Brown's 13 percent flat-tax proposal and said it would
hurt New York. It was a rare day in the campaign; the news
was dominated by people concerned with issues and their
impact on people's lives.

On March 29, I was back in the soup again, with a
problem of my own making. Jerry Brown and I were in a
televised candidates' forum on WCBS in New York when
a reporter asked me if I had ever tried marijuana at Oxford.
This was the first time I had ever been asked that specific
question directly. In Arkansas, when asked generally if I had
ever used marijuana, I had given an evasive answer, saying I
had never broken the drug laws of the United States. This
time, I gave a more direct and answer: "When I was in England, I experimented with marijuana a time or two and I
didn't like it. I didn't inhale and I never tried it again."

Even Jerry Brown said the press should lay off because
the issue wasn't relevant.

But the press had found another character issue. As for
the "didn't inhale" remark, I was stating a fact, not trying
to minimize what I had done, as I tried to explain until I was
blue in the face. What I should have said was that I couldn't

inhale. I had never smoked cigarettes, didn't inhale with the pipe I occasionally smoked at Oxford, and tried but failed to inhale the marijuana smoke. I don't know why I even mentioned it; maybe I thought I was being funny, or perhaps it was just a nervous reaction to a subject I didn't want to discuss. My account was corroborated by the respected English journalist Martin Walker, who later wrote an interesting and not altogether flattering book on my presidency, *Clinton: The President They Deserve*. Martin said publicly that he'd been at Oxford with me and had seen me try but fail to inhale at a party. By then it was too late. My unfortunate account of my marijuana misadventures was cited by pundits and Republicans throughout 1992 as evidence of my character problem. And I had given late-night TV hosts fodder for years of jokes.

As the old country song goes, I didn't know whether to "kill myself or go bowling." New York was suffering from severe economic and social problems. The Bush policies were making things worse. Yet every day seemed to be punctuated by television and print reporters shouting "character" questions at me. Radio talk-show host Don Imus called me a "redneck bozo." When I went on Phil Donahue's television show, all he did for twenty minutes was ask me questions about marital infidelity. After I gave my standard answer, he kept on asking. I rebuffed him and the audience cheered. He kept right on.

Whether I had a character problem or not, I sure had a reputation problem, one I had been promised by the White House more than six months earlier. Because the President is both the head of state and the Chief Executive of the government, he is in a sense the embodiment of people's idea of America, so reputation is important. Presidents going back to George Washington and Thomas Jefferson have guarded their reputations jealously: Washington, from criticism of his expense accounts during the Revolutionary War; Jefferson, from stories about his weakness for women. Before he became President, Abraham Lincoln suffered from debilitating episodes of depression. Once he was unable to leave his house for a whole month. If he had had to run under modern conditions, we might have been deprived of our greatest President.

Jefferson even wrote about the obligation of a President's associates to protect his reputation at all costs: "When the accident of situation is to give us a place in history, for which nature had not prepared us by corresponding endowments, it is the duty of those about us carefully to veil from the public eye the weaknesses, and still more, the vices of our character." The veil had been ripped from my weaknesses and vices, both real and imagined. The public knew more about them than about my record, message, or whatever virtues I might have. If my reputation was in tatters, I might not be able to be elected no matter how much people agreed with what I wanted to do, or how well they thought I might do it.

In the face of all the character attacks, I responded as I always did when my back was against the wall—I plowed on. In the last week of the campaign, the clouds began to lift. On April 1, during a meeting with President Bush at the White House, President Carter made a widely reported comment that he supported me. It couldn't have come at a better time. No one had ever questioned Carter's character, and his reputation had continued to grow after he left the presidency, because of his good works at home and around the world. In one comment, he more than made up for the problems he had caused me during the Cuban refugee crisis in 1980.

On April 2, Jerry Brown was booed in a speech to the Jewish Community Relations Council in New York for suggesting Jesse Jackson as his running mate. Meanwhile, Hillary and I spoke to a large crowd at a midday rally on Wall Street. I got some boos, too, for referring to the eighties as a decade of greed and opposing a cut in the capital gains tax. After the speech, I worked the crowd, shaking hands with supporters and trying to convince the dissenters.

Meanwhile, we poured the whole campaign operation into the state. Besides Harold Ickes and Susan Thomases, Mickey Kantor was camped out in a hotel suite, joined by Carville, Stephanopoulos, Stan Greenberg, and Frank Greer and his partner, Mandy Grunwald. As always, Bruce Lindsey was with me. His wife, Bev, came up, too, to make sure all the public events were well planned and executed. Carol Willis organized a busload of black Arkansans to come to New York City to talk about what I had done as governor for and with blacks. Black ministers from home called counterparts in New York to ask for pulpit time for our people on the Sunday before the election. Lottie Shackleford, a Little Rock city director and vice chair of the National Democratic Committee, spoke in five churches that Sunday. Those who knew me were putting a dent in the Reverend Jackson's efforts to bring a big majority of New York's black voters to Brown.

Some people in the press were coming around. Maybe the tide was turning; I even got a cordial reception on Don Imus's radio show. *Newsday* columnist Jimmy Breslin, who cared a lot about the Irish issue, wrote, "Say what you want, but do not say that he quits." Pete Hamill, the New York *Daily News* columnist whose books I'd read and enjoyed, said, "I've come to respect Bill Clinton. It's the late rounds and he's still there." The *New York Times* and the *Daily News* endorsed me. Amazingly, so did the *New York Post*, which had been more relentless in its attacks than any other paper. Its editorial said: "It speaks strongly to his strength of character that he has already survived a battering by the press on personal questions unprecedented in the history of American politics. . . . He has continued to campaign with remarkable tenacity. . . . In our view, he has manifested extraordinary grace under pressure."

On April 5, we got good news from Puerto Rico, where 96 percent of the voters supported me. Then, on April 7, with a low turnout of about a million voters, I carried New York with 41 percent. Tsongas finished second with 29 percent, just ahead of Brown at 26 percent. A majority of African-Americans cast their ballots for me. That night I was battered and bloodied but elated. My one-sentence take on the campaign was a line from a gospel song I'd heard in Anthony Mangun's church: "The darker the night, the sweeter the victory."

When I was doing research for this book, I read the account of the New York primary in *The Comeback Kid* by Charles Allen and Jonathan Portis. In it, the authors refer to something Levon Helm, the drummer for the Band and an Arkansas native, said in the great rock documentary *The Last Waltz* about what it's like for a southern boy to come to New York hoping to make it into the big time: "You just go in the first time and you get your ass kicked and you take off. Soon as it heals up, you come back and you try it again. Eventually, you fall right in love with it."

I didn't have the luxury of taking time off to heal, but I knew just how he felt. Like New Hampshire, New York had tested and taught me. And like Levon Helm, I had come to love it. After our rocky start, New York became one of my strongest states for the next eight years.

On April 7, we also won in Kansas, Minnesota, and Wisconsin. On April 9, Paul Tsongas announced that he would not reenter the race. The fight for the nomination was effectively over. I had more than half the 2,145 delegates I needed to be nominated, and had only Jerry Brown to compete with the rest of the way in. But I was under no illusions about how badly damaged I had been, or how little I could do about it before the Democratic convention in July. I was also exhausted. I had lost my voice and put on a lot of weight, about thirty pounds. I had gained the weight in New Hampshire, most of it in the last month of the campaign, when I suffered from a flu bug that filled my chest with fluid at night so I couldn't sleep for more than an hour without waking to cough. I kept alert on adrenaline and Dunkin' Donuts, and I had a bulging waistline to prove it. Harry Thomason bought me some new suits, so that I didn't look like a balloon about to burst.

After New York, I went home for a week to rest my voice, start getting back in shape, and think about how to get out of the hole I was in. While I was in Little Rock, I won the Virginia caucuses and received the endorsement of the leaders of the AFL-CIO. On April 24, the United Auto Workers endorsed me, and on April 28, I won a large majority in the

Pennsylvania primary. Pennsylvania could have been tough. Governor Bob Casey, whom I admired for his tenacity in running three times before he won, had been very critical of me. He was strongly anti-abortion. As he struggled with his own life-threatening health problems, the issue became more and more important to him, and he had a hard time supporting pro-choice candidates. So did a lot of other pro-life Democrats in the state. Still, I always felt good about Pennsylvania. The western part of the state reminded me of north Arkansas. I related well to the people in Pittsburgh and in the smaller cities in the middle of the state. And I loved Philadelphia. I carried the state with 57 percent. More important, exit polls showed that more than 60 percent of the Democrats who voted thought I had the integrity to serve as President, up from 49 percent in the New York exit polls. The integrity number improved because I had had three weeks to run a positive issue-oriented campaign in a state that badly wanted to hear it.

The Pennsylvania victory was welcome, but overshadowed by the prospect of a formidable new challenger, H. Ross Perot. Perot was a Texas billionaire who had made his fortune with EDS, Electronic Data Systems, a company that did a lot of government work, including some for Arkansas. He had become nationally known when he financed and engineered the rescue of EDS employees from Iran after the fall of the Shah. He had a blunt but effective speaking style, and he was convincing a lot of Americans that, with his business acumen, financial independence, and penchant for bold action, he could do a better job of running the country than either President Bush or I.

By the end of April, several published polls had him running ahead of the President, with me in third place. I found Perot to be an interesting man and was fascinated by his phenomenal early popularity. If he entered the race, I thought his boom would play itself out, but I couldn't be sure. So I stuck to my knitting, picking up the endorsement of "super delegates"—current and former elected officials who had a guaranteed vote at the convention. One of the first super delegates to come out for me was Senator Jay

Rockefeller of West Virginia. Jay had been my friend since we sat together at governors' meetings. And since New Hampshire, he had been giving me advice on health care, which he knew more about than I did.

On April 29, the day after the Pennsylvania vote, Los Angeles erupted in riots, after an all-white jury in neighboring Ventura County acquitted four white Los Angeles police officers of charges involving the beating of Rodney King, a black man, in March 1991. A bystander had videotaped the beating, and the tape had been released and shown on televisions across America. It looked as if King had offered no resistance when stopped, but was beaten brutally anyway.

The verdict inflamed the black community, which had long felt that the Los Angeles Police Department was riddled with racism. After a three-day rampage in South Central Los Angeles, more than 50 people were dead, more than 2,300 were injured, thousands of people had been arrested, and damages from looting and burning were estimated to be higher than $700 million.

On Sunday, May 3, I was in Los Angeles to speak to the Reverend Cecil "Chip" Murray's First AME Church about the need to heal our racial and economic rifts. And I toured the damaged areas with Maxine Waters, who represented South Central Los Angeles in Congress. Maxine was a smart, tough politician who had endorsed me early, despite her long friendship with Jesse Jackson. The streets looked like a war zone, full of burned and looted buildings. As we walked, I noticed a grocery store that appeared to be intact. When I asked Maxine about it, she said the store had been "protected" by people from the neighborhood, including gang members, because its owner, a white businessman named Ron Burkle, had been good to the community. He hired local people, all the employees were union members with health insurance, and the food was of the same quality as that in Beverly Hills groceries and sold at the same prices. At the time, that was unusual: because inner-city residents are less mobile, their stores often had inferior food at higher prices. I had met Burkle for the first time just a few hours earlier, and I resolved to get to know him better. He became one of my best friends and strongest supporters.

At a meeting in Maxine's house, I listened as South Central residents related stories about their problems with the police, the tension between Korean-American merchants and their black customers, and the need for more jobs. I pledged to support initiatives to empower inner-city residents, by initiating enterprise zones to encourage private investment and community development banks to make loans to low- and moderate-income people. I learned a lot on the trip, and it got good press coverage. It also made an impression in the city that I cared enough to come before President Bush did. The lesson was not lost on perhaps the best politician in the talented Bush family: in 2002, President George W. Bush came to Los Angeles for the tenth anniversary of the riots.

During the rest of May, a series of primary victories added to my delegate total, including a 68 percent win in Arkansas on the twenty-sixth, rivaling the best I'd ever done in a contested primary at home. Meanwhile, I campaigned in California, hoping to complete my fight for the nomination in Jerry Brown's home state. I called for federal aid to make our schools safer and for an all-out effort to turn back the tide of AIDS in America. And I began the search for a vice-presidential nominee. I entrusted the vetting process to Warren Christopher, a Los Angeles lawyer who had been President Carter's deputy secretary of state, and who had a well-deserved reputation for competence and discretion. In 1980, Chris had negotiated the release of our hostages in Iran. Sadly, their release was delayed until the day of President Reagan's inauguration, proof that all leaders play politics, even in a theocracy.

Meanwhile, Ross Perot's still-undeclared candidacy continued to gather steam. He resigned as chairman of his company and continued to rise in the polls. Just as I was about to wrap up the nomination, the papers were filled with headlines like "Clinton Set to Clinch Nomination, but All Eyes Are on Perot," "U.S. Primary Season Near End, Perot

Man to Watch," and "New Poll Shows Perot Leading Bush and Clinton." Perot was unburdened by President Bush's record or my primary battle scars. For the Republicans, he must have seemed a Frankenstein's monster of their own making: a businessman who had slipped into the space created by their assault on me. For Democrats, he was also a bad dream, proof that the President could be defeated, but perhaps not by their wounded nominee.

On June 2, I won the primaries in Ohio, New Jersey, New Mexico, Alabama, Montana, and California, where I defeated Brown 48 to 40 percent. Finally, I had clinched the nomination. Of all the primary votes cast in 1992, I had received more than 10.3 million, or 52 percent. Brown got nearly 4 million votes, 20 percent; Tsongas received about 3.6 million, 18 percent; the rest were cast for the other candidates and those who voted for uncommitted delegates.

But the big story that night was the willingness of so many voters in both parties, according to exit polls, to desert their parties' nominees to vote for Perot. It put a big damper on our celebration at the Los Angeles Biltmore. As Hillary and I watched the returns in my suite, even I was having trouble maintaining my congenital optimism. Not long before we were scheduled to go down to the ballroom to give a victory speech, Hillary and I had a visitor—Chevy Chase. Just as he had done on Long Island four years earlier, he showed up at a low moment to lift my spirits. This time, we were joined by his movie partner Goldie Hawn. By the time they finished making jokes about the absurd situation we were in, I was feeling better and ready to roll on.

Once again, press pundits said I was dead. Now Perot was the man to beat. A Reuters news service story captured the situation in one line: "Bill Clinton, who struggled for months to avoid publicity about his personal life, Friday faced an even worse political curse—being ignored." President Nixon predicted that Bush would beat Perot in a close race, with me a distant third.

Our campaign had to regain momentum. We decided to reach out to specific constituencies and the general public directly, and to keep pushing the issues. I went on Arsenio

Hall's late-night TV show, which was especially popular with younger viewers. I wore sunglasses and played "Heartbreak Hotel" and "God Bless the Child" on my sax. I answered viewers' questions on *Larry King Live*. On June 11 and 12, the Democratic platform committee produced a draft that reflected my philosophy and campaign commitments, and avoided the polarizing language that had hurt us in the past.

On June 13, I appeared before the Reverend Jesse Jackson's Rainbow Coalition. At the outset, both Jesse and I saw it as an opportunity to bridge our differences and build a united front for the campaign. It didn't work out that way. The night before I spoke, the popular rap artist Sister Souljah addressed the coalition. She was a bright woman who could have an impact on young people. A month earlier, in an interview in the *Washington Post* after the Los Angeles riots, she had made some astounding comments: "If black people kill black people every day, why not have a week and kill white people? . . . So if you're a gang member and you would normally be killing somebody, why not kill a white person?"

I suppose Sister Souljah thought she was simply expressing the anger and alienation of young blacks and telling them to stop killing one another. But that's not what she said. My staff, especially Paul Begala, argued that I had to say something about her remarks. Two of my most important core concerns were combating youth violence and healing the racial divide. After challenging white voters all across America to abandon racism, if I kept silent on Sister Souljah I might look weak or phony. Near the end of my talk, I said of her remarks, "If you took the words 'white' and 'black' and reversed them, you might think David Duke was giving that speech. . . . We have an obligation, all of us, to call attention to prejudice whenever we see it."

The political press reported my comments as a calculated attempt to appeal to moderate and conservative swing voters by standing up to a Democratic core constituency. That's how Jesse Jackson saw it, too. He thought I had abused his hospitality to make a demagogic pitch to white

voters. He said Sister Souljah was a fine person who had
done community service work and I owed her an apology.
And he threatened not to support me, even suggesting he
might back Ross Perot. Actually, I had considered condemning Sister Souljah's remarks as soon as she made them, when
I was in Los Angeles for a meeting of the Show Coalition, an
entertainment group. In the end I didn't do it, because the
Show Coalition event was for charity and I didn't want to
politicize it. When the Rainbow Coalition brought us on virtually back to back, I decided I had to speak up.

At the time, I didn't really understand the rap culture.
Over the years, Chelsea often told me it was full of highly
intelligent but profoundly alienated young people and urged
me to learn more about it. Finally, in 2001, she gave me six
rap and hip-hop CDs and made me promise to listen to
them. I did. While I still preferred jazz and rock, I enjoyed a
lot of the music, and I saw that she was right about the intelligence, and the alienation. But I think I was right to speak
out against Sister Souljah's apparent advocacy of race-based
violence, and I believe most African-Americans agreed with
what I said. Still, after Jesse criticized me, I resolved to try
harder to reach out to inner-city young people who felt left
out and left behind.

On June 18, I had my first meeting with Boris Yeltsin,
who was in Washington to see President Bush. When foreign leaders visit another country, it is customary for them
to meet with the leader of the political opposition. Yeltsin
was polite and friendly, but slightly patronizing. I had been
a big admirer of his since he stood up on a tank to oppose
an attempted coup ten months earlier. On the other hand,
he plainly preferred Bush and thought the President was
going to be reelected. At the end of our talk, Yeltsin said I
had a good future even if I didn't get elected this time. I
thought he was the right man to lead post-Soviet Russia,
and I left the meeting convinced I could work with him if I
succeeded in disappointing him about the outcome of the
election.

I added a needed bit of levity to the campaign that week.
Vice President Dan Quayle said he intended to be the "pit

bull terrier" of the election campaign. When asked about it, I said Quayle's claim would strike terror into the heart of every fire hydrant in America.

On June 23, I turned serious again, reissuing my economic plan with minor revisions based on the latest government report that the deficit would be larger than previously estimated. It was risky, because in order to keep my pledge to cut the deficit in half in four years, I had to trim the middle-class tax-cut proposal. The Republicans on Wall Street didn't like the plan either, because I proposed to raise income taxes on the wealthiest Americans and corporations; both were paying a much smaller percentage of the total tax load after twelve years of Reagan and Bush. We couldn't cut the deficit in half with spending cuts only, and I felt that those who had benefited most in the 1980s should pay half the cost. And I was determined not to fall into the "rosy scenarios" trap the Republicans had followed for twelve years, in which they constantly overestimated revenues and underestimated outlays in order to avoid hard choices. The revised economic plan was put together under the supervision of my new economic policy aide, Gene Sperling, who had left the staff of Governor Mario Cuomo in May to join the campaign. He was brilliant, rarely slept, and worked like a demon.

By the end of June, the vigorous public outreach and policy efforts were beginning to show results. A June 20 poll had the race a three-way dead heat. It wasn't all my doing. Perot and President Bush were engaged in a bitter, highly personal argument. There was plainly no love lost between the two Texans, and there were some bizarre elements to their spat, including Perot's strange claim that Bush had conspired to disrupt his daughter's wedding.

While Perot was fighting with Bush over his daughter, I took a day away from the campaign to pick Chelsea up at the end of her annual trip to northern Minnesota for a German-language summer camp. Chelsea started pushing to go to camp when she was only five, saying she wanted to "see the world and have adventures." The Concordia Language Camps in Minnesota's lake country featured several villages that were replicas of those in the countries whose languages were being taught. When the young people checked in, they got new names and some foreign currency, then spent the next two or four weeks speaking the language of the village. Concordia had villages speaking the Western European and Scandinavian languages, as well as Chinese and Japanese. Chelsea chose the German camp and went every summer for several years. It was a wonderful experience and an important part of her childhood.

I spent the first weeks of July picking a running mate. After exhaustive research, Warren Christopher recommended I consider Senator Bob Kerrey; Senator Harris Wofford of Pennsylvania, who had worked with Martin Luther King Jr. and in President Kennedy's White House; Congressman Lee Hamilton of Indiana, the highly respected chairman of the House Foreign Affairs Committee; Senator Bob Graham of Florida, with whom I'd become friends when we served as governors together; and Senator Al Gore of Tennessee. I liked them all. Kerrey and I had worked together as governors, and I didn't hold the tough things he had said in the campaign against him. He was a figure who could attract Republican and independent voters. Wofford was a deeply moral advocate of health-care reform and civil rights. He also had a good relationship with Governor Bob Casey, which could ensure my winning Pennsylvania. Hamilton was impressive for his knowledge of foreign affairs and his strength in a conservative district in southeastern Indiana. Graham was one of the three or four best governors of the 150 or so I served with over twelve years, and he would almost certainly bring Florida into the Democratic column for the first time since 1976.

In the end, I decided to ask Al Gore. At first, I didn't think I would. On our previous encounters, the chemistry between us had been correct but not warm. His selection defied the conventional wisdom that the vice-presidential candidate should provide political and geographic balance: We were from neighboring states. He was even younger than I was. And he, too, was identified with the New Democrat wing of the party. I believed his selection would work precisely because it didn't have the traditional kind of balance. It would present America with a new generation of leadership and prove I was serious about taking the party and the country in a different direction. I also thought his selection would be good politics in Tennessee, the South, and other swing states.

Moreover, Al would provide balance in a far more important way: He knew things I didn't. I knew a lot about economics, agriculture, crime, welfare, education, and health care, and had a good grasp of the major foreign policy issues. Al was an expert on national security, arms control, information technology, energy, and the environment. He was one of ten Senate Democrats to support President Bush in the first Gulf War. He had attended the global biodiversity conference in Rio de Janeiro, and strongly disagreed with President Bush's decision not to support the treaty that came out of it. He had recently written a bestselling book, *Earth in the Balance*, arguing that problems like global warming, the depletion of the ozone layer, and the destruction of rain forests required a radical reorientation of our relationship to the environment. He had given me an autographed copy of the book the previous April. I read it, learned a lot, and agreed with his argument. Besides knowing more about subjects that we'd have to deal with if elected, Al understood Congress and the Washington culture far better than I did. Most important, I thought he would be a good President if something happened to me, and I thought he'd have an excellent chance to be elected after I finished.

I set up shop in a Washington hotel to meet with a few people I was considering. Al came over late one night, at eleven, to minimize the chance of being seen by the press. The hour was more comfortable for me than for him, but he was alert and in good spirits. We talked for two hours about the country, the campaign, and our families. He was obviously devoted to and proud of Tipper and his four children. Tipper was an interesting person, an accomplished woman who had become famous for her campaign against violent and vulgar lyrics in contemporary music, and who had a passionate and well-informed interest in improving mental-health care.

After our talk, I liked him and was convinced that he, and Tipper, would be a big addition to our campaign.

On July 8, I called Al and asked him to be my running mate. The next day, he and his family flew to Little Rock for the announcement. The picture of all of us standing together on the back porch of the Governor's Mansion was big news across the nation. Even more than the words we spoke, it conveyed the energy and enthusiasm of young leaders committed to positive change. The next day, after Al and I went for a jog in Little Rock, we flew to his hometown, Carthage, Tennessee, for a rally and a visit with his parents, both of whom had a large influence on him. Al Gore Sr. had been a three-term U.S. senator, a supporter of civil rights, and an opponent of the Vietnam War, positions that helped to defeat him in 1970 but that also ensured him an honored place in American history. Al's mother, Pauline, was equally impressive. When it was rare for women to do so, she had graduated from law school and then briefly practiced law in southwest Arkansas.

On July 11, Hillary, Chelsea, and I flew to New York for the Democratic convention. We had had a good five weeks, while Bush and Perot fought with each other. For the first time, some polls showed me in the lead. With four nights of television coverage, the convention would either strengthen our position or undermine it. In 1972 and 1980, Democrats had been crippled by showing the American people a divided, dispirited, undisciplined party. I was determined not to let that happen again. So was DNC chairman Ron Brown. Harold Ickes and Alexis Herman, Ron's deputy and the CEO of the convention, took charge of our operation to make sure we showcased unity, new ideas, and new leaders. It didn't hurt that rank-and-file Democrats were desperate to win after twelve years of Republican control of the White House. Still, we had plenty to do to pull the party together and project a more positive image. For example, our research showed that most Americans didn't know that Hillary and I had a child, and thought I had grown up in wealth and privilege.

Conventions are heady affairs for the nominee. This one

was especially so. After months of being told I was lower than a snake's belly, I was now being held up as a paragon of all things good and true. In New Hampshire and afterward, with all the character attacks, I had to fight to keep my temper in check and minimize my tendency to whine when exhausted. Now I had to rein in my ego and remember not to get carried away by all the praise and positive press.

As the convention opened, we were making good progress on party unity. Tom Harkin had endorsed me earlier. Now Bob Kerrey, Paul Tsongas, and Doug Wilder made supportive comments. So did Jesse Jackson. Only Jerry Brown held out. Harkin, who had become one of my favorite politicians, said Jerry was on an ego trip. There was also a minor flap when Ron Brown refused to let Governor Bob Casey speak to the convention, not because he wanted to speak against abortion but because he wouldn't agree to endorse me. I was inclined to let Casey talk, because I liked him, respected the convictions of pro-life Democrats, and thought we could get a lot of them to vote for us on other issues and on my pledge to make abortion "safe, legal, and rare." But Ron was adamant. We could disagree on the issues, he said, but no one should get the microphone who wasn't committed to victory in November. I respected the discipline with which he had rebuilt our party, and I deferred to his judgment.

The opening night of the convention featured seven of our women candidates for the U.S. Senate. Hillary and Tipper also made brief appearances. Then came the keynote speeches by Senator Bill Bradley, Congresswoman Barbara Jordan, and Governor Zell Miller. Bradley and Jordan were more famous and gave good talks, but Miller brought the audience to tears with this story:

> My father, who was a teacher, died when I was two weeks old, leaving a young widow with two small children. But with my mother's faith in God—and Mr. Roosevelt's voice on the radio—we kept going.

After my father's death, my mother with her own hands cleared a small piece of rugged land. Every day she waded into a neighbor's cold mountain creek, carrying out thousands of smooth stones to build a house. I grew up watching my mother complete that house from the rocks she'd lifted from the creek and cement she mixed in a wheelbarrow—cement that today still bears her handprints. Her son bears her handprints, too. She pressed her pride and her hopes and her dreams deep into my soul. So, you see, I know what Dan Quayle means when he says it's best for children to have two parents. You bet it is. And it would be good if they could all have trust funds, too. We can't all be born rich, handsome, and lucky. And that's why we have a Democratic Party.

He then extolled the contributions of every Democratic President from FDR through Carter, and said we believed government could improve education, human rights, civil rights, economic and social opportunity, and the environment. He attacked Republicans for policies favoring the wealthy and special-interest groups, and supported my plans on the economy, education, health care, crime, and welfare reform. It was a strong New Democrat message, exactly what I wanted the country to hear. When Zell Miller was elected to the Senate in 2000, Georgia had become more conservative and so had he. He became one of President Bush's strongest supporters, voting for huge tax cuts that exploded the deficits and disproportionately benefited the wealthiest Americans, and budgets that threw poor children out of after-school programs, unemployed workers out of job training, and uniformed police off the streets. I don't know what caused Zell to change his views on what was best for America, but I will always remember what he did for me, the Democrats, and America in 1992.

The second day featured a presentation of the platform, and strong speeches by President Carter, Tom Harkin, and Jesse Jackson. When Jesse decided to support me, he went all the way, with a barn burner that brought the house down. However, the most emotional part of the evening was devoted to health care. Senator Jay Rockefeller talked about the need for health insurance for all Americans. His point was illustrated by my New Hampshire friends Ron and Rhonda Machos, who were by then expecting their second child and were saddled with $100,000 in medical bills from little Ronnie's open-heart surgery. They said they felt like second-class citizens, but they knew me and I was their "best hope for the future."

Two of the featured health-care speakers were people with AIDS: Bob Hattoy and Elizabeth Glaser. I wanted them to bring the reality of a problem too long ignored by politicians into America's living rooms. Bob was a gay man who worked for me. He said, "I don't want to die. But I don't want to live in an America where the President sees me as the enemy. I can face dying because of a disease, but not because of politics." Elizabeth Glaser was a beautiful, intelligent woman, the wife of Paul Michael Glaser, who had starred in the successful TV series *Starsky and Hutch*. She had been infected when she hemorrhaged during the birth of her first child and received a transfusion contaminated with the virus. She passed it on to her daughter through her breast milk and to her next child, a son, in utero. By the time she spoke to the convention, Elizabeth had founded the Pediatric AIDS Foundation, lobbied hard for more money for research and care, and lost her daughter, Ariel, to AIDS. She wanted a President who would do more about it. Not long after I was elected, Elizabeth, too, lost her fight with AIDS. It was heartbreaking to Hillary, me, and countless others who loved her and followed her lead. I am thankful that her son, Jake, survives, and that his father and Elizabeth's friends have carried on her work.

By the third day of the convention, a national poll showed me in first place, with a double-digit lead over President Bush. I started the morning with a jog in Central Park. Then Hillary, Chelsea, and I had a real treat when Nelson Mandela came to our suite for a visit. He was the convention guest of Mayor David Dinkins. Properly, he said he

wasn't taking sides in the election, but he expressed appreciation for the Democrats' long opposition to apartheid.
Mandela wanted the United Nations to send a special envoy
to investigate an outbreak of violence in South Africa, and I
said I would support his request. His visit was the beginning
of a great friendship for all of us. Mandela plainly liked
Hillary, and I was really struck by the attention he paid to
Chelsea. In the eight years I was in the White House, he
never talked to me without asking about her. Once, during a
phone conversation, he asked to speak to her, too. I've seen
him show the same sensitivity to children, black and white,
who crossed his path in South Africa. It speaks to his fundamental greatness.

Wednesday was a big night at the convention, with rousing speeches by Bob Kerrey and Ted Kennedy. There was a
moving film tribute to Robert Kennedy, introduced by his
son, Congressman Joe Kennedy of Massachusetts. Then
Jerry Brown and Paul Tsongas spoke. Jerry bashed President Bush. So did Paul Tsongas, but he spoke up for Al Gore
and me, too. After all he'd been through, it was a brave and
classy thing to do.

Then came the big moment: Mario Cuomo's nominating
speech. He was still our party's best orator, and he didn't
disappoint. With lofty rhetoric, stinging rebukes, and well-
reasoned arguments, Cuomo made the case that it was time
for "someone smart enough to know; strong enough to do;
sure enough to lead: the Comeback Kid, a new voice for a
new America." After Congresswoman Maxine Waters and
Congressman Dave McCurdy of Oklahoma, my other nominators, spoke, the roll was called.

Alabama passed to Arkansas so that my home state
could cast the first votes. Our Democratic chair, George
Jernigan, who had run against me for attorney general sixteen years earlier, gave the honor to another Clinton delegate. Then my mother simply said, "Arkansas proudly casts
our forty-eight votes for our favorite son and my son, Bill
Clinton." I wondered what Mother was thinking and feeling, beyond her bursting pride; whether her mind wandered
back forty-six years, to the twenty-three-year-old widow

who gave me life, or back over all the troubles she had borne with a bright smile to give me and my brother as normal a life as possible. I loved watching her and was grateful that someone had thought to let her start the tide rolling.

As the roll call continued, Hillary, Chelsea, and I were making our way to Madison Square Garden from our hotel and stopped inside Macy's department store, where we gathered to watch the voting on television. When Ohio cast 144 votes for me, I crossed the majority threshold of 2,145 and was finally the official Democratic nominee. During the demonstration that followed, the three of us walked onto the stage. I was the first candidate to come to the convention before the night of my acceptance speech since John Kennedy did it in 1960. In brief remarks, I said, "Thirty-two years ago another young candidate who wanted to get the country moving again came to the convention to say a simple thank you." I wanted to identify with the spirit of John Kennedy's campaign, to thank my nominators and the delegates, and "to tell you that tomorrow night I will be the Comeback Kid."

Thursday, July 16, was the final day of the convention. So far, we had had three great days, in the hall and on television. We had showcased not only our national leaders but also our rising stars, as well as ordinary citizens. We had hammered home our new ideas. But it would all count for nothing unless Al Gore and I were effective in our acceptance speeches. The day began with a surprise, as had so many days in this wild campaign season: Ross Perot withdrew from the race. I called him, congratulated him on his campaign, and said I agreed with him on the need for fundamental political reform. He declined to endorse either President Bush or me, and I went into the convention's last night unsure whether his withdrawal would help or hurt.

After Al Gore was nominated by acclamation, he gave a rip-roaring speech, which he began by saying he'd dreamed as a boy growing up in Tennessee that he would, one day, be the warm-up act for Elvis, the nickname the staff gave me during the campaign. Al then launched into a litany of the Bush administration's failings, saying after each one, "It's time for them to go." After he did it a couple of times, the delegates took over for him, sending sparks throughout the hall. Then he extolled my record, outlined the challenges we faced, and talked about his family and our obligation to leave a stronger, more united nation to the next generation. Al had given a really good speech. He had done his part. Now it was my turn.

Paul Begala wrote the first draft of the speech. We were trying to do a lot with it—biography, campaign rhetoric, and policy. And we were trying to appeal to three different groups—hard-core Democrats, independents and Republicans dissatisfied with the President but unsure of me, and people who didn't vote at all because they didn't think it made a difference. Paul, as always, had some great lines. And George Stephanopoulos had kept notes of the ones that had worked best on the stump during the primary campaign. Bruce Reed and Al From helped sharpen the policy section. To bring me on, my friends Harry and Linda Bloodworth Thomason produced a short film entitled "The Man from Hope." It pumped the crowd up, and I walked onto the platform to tremendous applause.

The speech started slowly, with a bow to Al Gore, thanks to Mario Cuomo, and a salute to my primary opponents. Then came the message: "In the name of all those who do the work and pay the taxes, raise the kids and play by the rules, in the name of the hardworking Americans who make up our forgotten middle class, I proudly accept your nomination for President of the United States. I am a product of that middle class, and when I am President, you will be forgotten no more."

Next, I told the story of the people who had had the greatest impact on me, beginning with my mother, from her travails as a young widow with a baby to support to her current struggle with breast cancer, saying, "Always, always, always she taught me to fight." I talked about my grandfather and how he taught me "to look up to people other folks looked down on." And I paid tribute to Hillary for teaching me that "all children can learn and that each of us has a duty to help them do it." I wanted America to know that my fighting spirit started with my mother, my commitment to racial equality started with my grandfather, and my concern for the future of all our children started with my wife.

And I wanted people to know that everybody could be part of our American family: "I want to say something to every child in America tonight who is out there trying to grow up without a mother or father: I know how you feel. You are special too. You matter to America. And don't ever let anybody tell you you can't become whatever you want to be."

For the next several minutes, I laid out my critique of the Bush record and my plan to do better. "We have gone from first to thirteenth in the world in wages since Reagan and Bush took office." . . . "Four years ago he promised 15 million new jobs by this time, and he's over 14 million short." . . . "The incumbent President says unemployment always goes up a little before a recovery begins, but unemployment only has to go up one more person before a real recovery can begin. And Mr. President, you are that man." I said my New Covenant of opportunity, responsibility, and community would give us "an America in which the doors of college are thrown open again to the sons and daughters of stenographers and steelworkers," "an America in which middle-class incomes, not middle-class taxes, are going up," "an America in which the rich are not soaked, but the middle class is not drowned either," "an America where we end welfare as we know it."

Then I made an appeal for national unity. To me, it was the most important part of the speech, something I had believed in since I was a little boy:

> Tonight every one of you knows deep in your heart that we are too divided. It is time to heal America.
>
> And so we must say to every American: Look beyond the stereotypes that blind us. We need each other. All of us, we need each other. We don't have a person to waste. And yet for too long politicians have told most of us that are doing all right that

what's really wrong with America is the rest of us. Them.

Them, the minorities. Them, the liberals. Them, the poor, them, the homeless, them, the people with disabilities. Them, the gays.

We've gotten to where we've nearly them'ed ourselves to death. Them and them and them.

But this is America. There is no them; there is only us. One nation, under God, indivisible, with liberty and justice for all.

That is our Pledge of Allegiance and that's what the New Covenant is all about. . . .

As a teenager I heard John Kennedy's summons to citizenship. And then, as a student at Georgetown, I heard that call clarified by a professor named Carroll Quigley, who said to us that America was the greatest nation in history because our people had always believed in two great ideas: that tomorrow can be better than today, and that every one of us has a personal, moral responsibility to make it so.

That kind of future entered my life the night our daughter, Chelsea, was born. As I stood in that delivery room, I was overcome with the thought that God had given me a blessing my own father never knew: the chance to hold my child in my arms.

Somewhere at this very moment, a child is being born in America. Let it be our cause to give that child a happy home, a healthy family, and a hopeful future. Let it be our cause to see that that child has a chance to live to the fullest of her God-given capacities. . . . Let it be our cause that we give this child a country that is coming together, not coming apart—a country of boundless hopes and endless dreams; a country that once again lifts its people and inspires the world.

Let that be our cause, our commitment, and our New Covenant.

My fellow Americans, I end tonight where it all began for me: I still believe in a place called Hope. God bless you and God bless America.

When my speech was over and the applause had died down, the convention ended with a song written for the occasion by Arthur Hamilton and my old friend and fellow high-school musician Randy Goodrum, "Circle of Friends." It was sung by the Broadway star Jennifer Holiday, backed by the Philander Smith College Choir from Little Rock; ten-year-old Reggie Jackson, who had wowed the convention Monday night singing "America the Beautiful"; and my brother, Roger. Before long they had us all singing "Let's join a circle of friends, one that begins and never ends."

It was a perfect end to the most important speech I'd ever delivered. And it worked. We were widening the circle. Three different polls showed my message had strongly res-onated with the voters, and we had a big lead, of twenty or more points. But I knew we couldn't hold that margin. For one thing, the Republican cultural base of white voters with a deep reluctance to vote for any Democratic presidential candidate was about 45 percent of the electorate. Also, the Republicans had not held their convention yet. It was sure to give President Bush a boost. Finally, I'd just had six weeks of good press coverage and a week of direct, completely positive access to America. It was more than enough to push all the doubts about me into the recesses of public con-sciousness, but, as I well knew, not enough to erase them.

TWENTY-EIGHT

THE NEXT MORNING, July 17, Al, Tipper, Hillary, and I drove over to New Jersey to begin the first of several bus tours across America. They were designed to bring us into small towns and rural areas never visited in modern presidential campaigns, which had become dominated by rallies in major media markets. We hoped the bus tour, the brainchild of Susan Thomases and David Wilhelm, would keep the excitement and momentum of the convention going.

The trip was a 1,000-mile jaunt through New Jersey, Pennsylvania, West Virginia, Ohio, Kentucky, Indiana, and Illinois. It was filled with stump speeches and handshaking at scheduled and unscheduled stops. On the first day, we worked our way through eastern and central Pennsylvania, reaching our last stop, York, at 2 a.m. Thousands of people had waited up for us. Al gave his best 2 a.m. version of the stump speech. I did the same, and then we shook supporters' hands for the better part of an hour before the four of us collapsed for a few hours' sleep. We spent the next day riding across Pennsylvania, bonding with each other as well as the crowds, growing more and more relaxed and excited, buoyed by the enthusiasm of people who came out to see us at the rallies or just along the highway. At a truck stop in Carlisle, Al and I climbed up into the big trucks to shake hands with drivers. At a Pennsylvania Turnpike rest stop, we tossed a football in the parking lot. Somewhere on the trip we even fit in a round of miniature golf. On the third day, we worked our way out of western Pennsylvania and into West Virginia, where we toured Weirton Steel, a large integrated producer that the employees had bought from its former owner and kept running. That night we went to Gene Branstool's farm near Utica, Ohio, for a cookout with a couple hundred farmers and their families, then stopped in a nearby field, where ten thousand people were waiting. I was stunned by two things: the size of the crowd and the size of the corn crop. It was the tallest and thickest I had ever seen, a good omen. The next day we visited Columbus, Ohio's capital city, then made our way into Kentucky. As we crossed the state line, I was convinced we could win Ohio, as Jimmy Carter had done in 1976. It was important. Since the Civil War, no Republican had won the presidency without capturing Ohio.

On the fifth and final day, after a big rally in Louisville, we drove through southern Indiana and into southern Illinois. All along the way, people were standing in fields and along the road waving our signs. We passed a big combine all decked out in an American flag and a Clinton-Gore poster. By the time we got to Illinois, we were late, as we were every day, because of all the unscheduled stops. We didn't need any more of them, but a small group was standing at a crossroads holding a big sign that said "Give us eight minutes and we'll give you eight years!" We stopped. The last rally of the evening was one of the most remarkable of the campaign. When we pulled into Vandalia, thousands of people holding candles had filled the square around the old state Capitol Building where Abraham Lincoln had served a term in the legislature before the seat of government was moved to Springfield. It was very late when we finally pulled into St. Louis for another short night.

The bus tour was a smashing success. It took us, and the national media, to places in the American heartland too often overlooked. America saw us reaching out to the people we had promised to represent in Washington, which made it harder for the Republicans to paint us as cultural and political radicals. And Al, Tipper, Hillary, and I had gotten to know one another in a way that would have been impossible without those long hours on the bus.

The next month we did four more bus tours, this time shorter ones of one or two days. The second tour took us up the Mississippi River, from St. Louis to Hannibal, Missouri, Mark Twain's hometown, to Davenport, Iowa, up through

Wisconsin, and all the way to Minneapolis, where Walter Mondale held a crowd of ten thousand for two hours by giving them regular updates on our progress.

The most memorable moment of the second bus tour came in Cedar Rapids, Iowa, where, after a meeting on biotechnology and a tour of the Quaker Oats packaging plant, we held a rally in the parking lot. The crowd was large and enthusiastic, except for a loud group of opponents holding pro-life signs and jeering at me from the back. After the speeches, I got off the stage and began working the crowd. I was surprised to see a white woman wearing a pro-choice button and holding a black baby in her arms. When I asked her whose child it was, she beamed and said, "She's my baby. Her name is Jamiya." The woman told me that the child was born HIV-positive in Florida, and she had adopted her, even though she was a divorcée struggling to raise two children on her own. I'll never forget that woman holding Jamiya and proudly proclaiming, "She's my baby." She, too, was pro-life, just the kind of person I was trying to give a better shot at the American dream.

Later in the month, we did a one-day tour of California's San Joaquin Valley, and two-day trips through Texas and what we'd missed of Ohio and Pennsylvania, ending up in western New York. In September we bused through south Georgia. In October we did two days in Michigan and, in one hectic day, made ten towns in North Carolina.

I had never seen anything like the sustained enthusiasm the bus trips engendered. Of course, part of it was that people in small towns weren't accustomed to seeing presidential candidates up close—places like Coatesville, Pennsylvania; Centralia, Illinois; Prairie du Chien, Wisconsin; Walnut Grove, California; Tyler, Texas; Valdosta, Georgia; and Elon, North Carolina. But mostly it was the connection our bus made between the people and the campaign. It represented both the common touch and forward progress. In 1992, Americans were worried but still hopeful. We spoke to their fears and validated their enduring optimism. Al and I developed a good routine. At each stop, he would list all of America's problems and say, "Everything that should be down is up, and everything that should be up is down." Then he would introduce me and I'd tell people what we intended to do to fix it. I loved those bus tours. We motored through sixteen states and in November won thirteen of them.

After the first bus tour, one national poll showed me with a two-to-one lead over President Bush, but I didn't take it too seriously because he hadn't really started to campaign. He began in the last week of July, with a series of attacks. He said that my plan to trim defense increases would cost a million jobs; that my health-care plan would be a government-run program "with the compassion of the KGB"; that I wanted "the largest tax increase in history"; and that he would set a better "moral tone" as President than I would. His aide Mary Matalin edged out Dan Quayle in the race for the campaign's pit bull, calling me a "sniveling hypocrite." Later in the campaign, with Bush sinking, a lot of his careerist appointees started leaking to the press that it was anybody's fault but theirs. Some of them were even critical of the President. Not Mary. She stood by her man to the end. Ironically, Mary Matalin and James Carville were engaged and soon would be married. Although they were from opposite ends of the political spectrum, they were equally aggressive true believers whose love added spice to their lives, and whose politics enlivened both the Bush campaign and mine.

In the second week of August, President Bush persuaded James Baker to resign as secretary of state and return to the White House to oversee his campaign. I thought Baker had done a good job at State, except on Bosnia, where I felt the administration should have opposed the ethnic cleansing more vigorously. And I knew he was a good politician who would make the Bush campaign more effective.

Our campaign needed to be more effective, too. We had won the nomination by organizing around the primary schedule. Now that the convention was behind us, we needed much better coordination among all the forces, with a single strategic center. James Carville took it on. He needed an assistant. Because Paul Begala's wife, Diane, was expecting their first child, he couldn't come to Little Rock full-time, so reluctantly, I gave up George Stephanopoulos from the campaign plane. George had demonstrated a keen understanding of how the twenty-four-hour news cycle worked, and now knew we could fight bad press as well as enjoy the good stories. He was the best choice.

James put all the elements of the campaign—politics, press, and research—into a big open space in the old newsroom of the *Arkansas Gazette* building. It broke down barriers and built a sense of camaraderie. Hillary said it was like a "war room," and the name stuck. Carville put a sign on the wall as a constant reminder of what the campaign was about. It had just three lines:

> Change vs. More of the Same
> The Economy, stupid
> Don't forget health care

Carville also captured his main battle tactic in a slogan he had printed on a T-shirt: "Speed Kills . . . Bush." The War Room held meetings every day at 7 a.m. and 7 p.m. to assess Stan Greenberg's overnight polls, Mandy Grunwald's latest ads, the news, and the attacks from Bush, and to formulate responses to the attacks and unfolding events. Meanwhile, young volunteers worked around the clock, pulling in whatever information they could get from our satellite dish, tracking the news and the opposition on their computers. It's all routine stuff now, but then it was new, and our use of technology was essential to the campaign's ability to meet Carville's goal of being focused and fast.

Once we knew what we wanted to say, we got the message out, not only to the media but to our "rapid-response" teams in every state, whose job it was to transmit it to our supporters and local news outlets. We sent pins with "Rapid-Response Team" on them to those who agreed to do daily duty. By the end of the campaign, thousands of people were wearing them.

By the time I got my morning briefing from Carville, Stephanopoulos, and whoever else needed to be on call that day, they could lay out exactly where we were and what we needed to do. If I disagreed, we argued. If there was a close policy or strategic call, I made it. But mostly I just listened in amazement. Sometimes I complained about what wasn't going well, like speeches I thought were long on rhetoric and short on argument and substance, or the backbreaking schedule that was more my fault than theirs. Because of allergies and exhaustion, I griped too much in the mornings. Luckily, Carville and I were on the same wavelength, and he always knew when I was serious and when I was just blowing off steam. I think the others on call came to understand it too.

The Republicans held their convention in Houston in the third week of August. Normally, the opposition goes underground during the other party's convention. Though I would follow the usual practice and keep a low profile, our rapid-response operation would be out in force. It had to be. The Republicans had no choice but to throw the kitchen sink at me. They were way behind, and their slash-and-burn approach had worked in every election since 1968, except for President Carter's two-point victory in the aftermath of Watergate. We were determined to use the rapid-response team to turn the Republican attacks back on them.

On August 17, as their convention opened, I still had a twenty-point lead, and we rained on their parade a little when eighteen corporate chief executives endorsed me. It was a good story, but it didn't divert the Republicans from their game plan. They started off by calling me a "skirt chaser" and a "draft dodger," and accused Hillary of wanting to destroy the American family by allowing children to sue their parents whenever they disagreed with parental disciplinary decisions. Marilyn Quayle, the vice president's wife, was particularly critical of Hillary's alleged assault on "family values." The criticisms were based on a wildly distorted reading of an article Hillary had written when she was in law school, arguing that, in circumstances of abuse or severe neglect, minor children had legal rights independent of their parents. Almost all Americans would agree with a fair reading of her words, but, of course, since so few people had seen her article, hardly anyone who heard the charges knew whether they were true or not.

The main attraction on the Republicans' opening night was Pat Buchanan, who sent the delegates into a frenzy with his attacks on me. My favorite lines included his assertion that, while President Bush had presided over the liberation of Eastern Europe, my foreign policy experience was "pretty much confined to having had breakfast once at the International House of Pancakes" and his characterization of the Democratic convention as "radicals and liberals . . . dressed up as moderates and centrists in the greatest single exhibition of cross-dressing in American political history." The polls showed Buchanan hadn't helped Bush, but I disagreed. His job was to stop the hemorrhaging on the right by telling conservatives who wanted change that they couldn't vote for me, and he did it well.

The Clinton-bashing continued throughout the convention, with our rapid-response operation firing back. The Reverend Pat Robertson referred to me as "Slick Willie" and said I had a radical plan to destroy the American family. Since I had been for welfare reform before Robertson figured out that God was a right-wing Republican, the charge was laughable. Our rapid-response team beat it back. They were also especially good at defending Hillary from the anti-family attacks, comparing the Republicans' treatment of her to their Willie Horton tactics against Dukakis four years earlier.

To reinforce our claim that the Republicans were attacking me because all they cared about was holding on to power, while we wanted power to attack America's problems, Al, Tipper, Hillary, and I had dinner with President and Mrs. Carter on August 18. Then we all spent the next day—both Tipper's and my birthday—building a house with members of Habitat for Humanity. Jimmy and Rosalynn Carter had supported Habitat for years. The brainchild of Millard Fuller, a friend of ours from Renaissance Weekend, Habitat uses volunteers to build houses for and with poor people, who then pay for the cost of the materials. The organization had already become one of America's largest home builders and was expanding into other countries. Our work presented a perfect contrast to the shrill attacks of the Republicans.

President Bush made a surprise visit to the convention on the night he was nominated, as I had, bringing his entire all-American-looking family. The next night, he gave an effective speech, wrapping himself in God, country, and family, and asserting that, unfortunately, I didn't embrace those values. He also said that he had made a mistake in signing the deficit-reduction bill with its gas-tax hike and that, if reelected, he'd cut taxes again. I thought his best line was saying I would use "Elvis economics" to take America to "Heartbreak Hotel." He contrasted his service in World War II with my opposition to Vietnam by saying, "While I bit the bullet, he bit his nails."

Now the Republicans had had their free shot at America, and though the conventional wisdom was that they had been too negative and extreme, the polls showed they had cut into my lead. One poll had the race down to ten points, another to five. I thought that was about right, and that if I didn't blow the debates or make some other error, the final margin would be somewhere between what the two surveys showed.

President Bush left Houston in a feisty mood, comparing his campaign to Harry Truman's miraculous comeback victory in 1948. He also went around the country doing what only incumbents can do: spending federal money to get votes. He pledged aid to wheat farmers and the victims of Hurricane Andrew, which had devastated much of south Florida, and he offered to sell 150 F-16 fighter planes to Taiwan and 72 F-15s to Saudi Arabia, securing jobs in defense plants located in critical states.

In late August, we both appeared before the American Legion Convention in Chicago. President Bush got a better reception than I did from his fellow veterans, but I did better than expected by confronting the draft issue and my opposition to the Vietnam War head-on. I said I still believed the Vietnam War was a mistake, but "if you choose to vote against me because of what happened twenty-three years ago, that's your right as an American citizen, and I respect that. But it is my hope that you will cast your vote while looking toward the future." I also got a good round of applause by promising new leadership at the Department of Veterans Affairs, whose director was unpopular with the veterans' groups.

After the American Legion meeting, I got back to my message of changing America's direction in economic and social policy, bolstered by a new study showing that the rich were getting richer while poor Americans were getting poorer. In early September, I was endorsed by two important environmental groups, the Sierra Club and the League of Conservation Voters. And I went to Florida a few days after President Bush did to observe the damage from Hurricane Andrew. I had dealt with a lot of natural disasters as governor, including floods, droughts, and tornadoes, but I had never seen anything like this. As I walked down streets littered with the wet ruins of houses, I was surprised to hear complaints from both local officials and residents about how the Federal Emergency Management Agency was handling the aftermath of the hurricane. Traditionally, the job of FEMA director was given to a political supporter of the President who wanted some plum position but who had had no experience with emergencies. I made a mental note to avoid that mistake if I won. Voters don't choose a President based on how he'll handle disasters, but if they're faced with one, it quickly becomes the most important issue in their lives.

On Labor Day, the traditional opening of the general election campaign, I went to Harry Truman's hometown of Independence, Missouri, to rally working people to our cause. Truman's outspoken daughter, Margaret, helped by saying at the rally that I, not George Bush, was the rightful heir to her father's legacy.

On September 11, I went to South Bend, Indiana, to deliver an address to the students and faculty at Notre Dame, America's most famous Catholic university. On the same day, President Bush was in Virginia to address the conservative Christian Coalition. I knew Catholics across the country would take notice of both events. The church hierarchy agreed with Bush's opposition to abortion, but I was far closer to the Catholic positions on economic and social justice. The Notre Dame appearance bore a striking resemblance, with roles reversed, to John Kennedy's 1960 speech to the Southern Baptist ministers. Paul Begala, a devout Catholic, helped prepare my remarks, and Boston mayor Ray Flynn and Senator Harris Wofford came along to lend moral support. I was nearly halfway through the speech before I could tell how it was going. When I said, "All of us must respect the reflection of God's image in every man and woman, and so we must value their freedom, not just their political freedom, but their freedom of conscience in matters of family and philosophy and faith," there was a standing ovation.

After Notre Dame, I went out west. In Salt Lake City, I made my case to the National Guard Convention, where I was well received, because my reputation for leading the Arkansas National Guard was good, and because I was introduced by Congressman Les Aspin, the respected chairman of the House Armed Services Committee. In Portland, Oregon, we had an amazing rally. More than ten thousand people filled the downtown streets, with many more leaning out of their office windows. During the speeches, supporters threw hundreds of roses onto the stage, a nice gesture in Oregon's City of Roses. For more than an hour after the event, I went up and down the streets, shaking hands with what seemed like thousands of people.

On September 15, the western swing got its biggest boost when thirty high-tech leaders in traditionally Republican Silicon Valley endorsed me. I had been working on Silicon Valley since the previous December, with the help of Dave Barram, vice president of Apple Computer. Dave had been recruited to the campaign by Ira Magaziner, my friend from Oxford, who had worked with high-tech executives and knew that Barram was a Democrat. Many of Barram's Republican cohorts shared his disillusionment with the economic policies of the Bush administration and its failure to appreciate the explosive potential of Silicon Valley's entrepreneurs. A few days before my first trip, according to the *San Jose Mercury News*, President Bush's trade representative, Carla Hills, had endorsed the view that "it makes no difference whether the United States exports potato chips or silicon chips." The high-tech executives disagreed, and so did I.

Among those who came out for me were prominent Republicans like John Young, president of Hewlett-Packard; John Sculley, chairman of Apple Computer; investment banker Sandy Robertson; and one of Silicon Valley's few open Democrats at the time, Regis McKenna. At our meeting in the Technology Center of Silicon Valley at San Jose, I also issued a national technology policy, which Dave Barram had worked for months to help me prepare. In calling for greater investment in scientific and technological research and development, including specific projects important to Silicon Valley, I staked out a position at odds with the Bush administration's aversion to government-industry partnerships. At the time, Japan and Germany were outperforming America economically, in part because government policy in those countries was targeted to support potential areas of growth. By contrast, American policy was to subsidize politically powerful, established interests like oil and agriculture, which were important but which had much less potential than technology to generate new jobs and new entrepreneurs. The high-tech leaders' announcement provided an enormous boost to the campaign, giving credibility to my claim to be pro-business as well as pro-labor, and linking me to the economic forces that most represented positive change and growth.

While I was garnering support for rebuilding the economy and reforming health care, the Republicans were working hard to tear me down. President Bush, in his convention speech, had accused me of raising taxes 128 times in Arkansas and enjoying it every time. In early September, the Bush campaign repeated the charge again and again, though the *New York Times* said it was "false," the *Washington Post* called it highly "exaggerated" and "silly," and even the

Wall Street Journal said it was "misleading." The Bush list included a requirement that used-car dealers post a $25,000 bond, modest fees for beauty pageants, and a one-dollar court cost imposed on convicted criminals. Conservative columnist George Will said that, by the President's criteria, "Bush has raised taxes more often in four years than Clinton has in ten."

The Bush campaign devoted most of the rest of September to attacking me on the draft. President Bush said over and over that I should "just tell the truth" about it. Even Dan Quayle felt free to go after me on it, despite the fact that his family connections had gotten him into the National Guard and away from Vietnam. The vice president's main point seemed to be that the media weren't giving my case the same critical scrutiny he had received four years earlier. Apparently he hadn't followed the news out of New Hampshire and New York.

I got some good help in countering the draft attack. In early September, Senator Bob Kerrey, my Medal of Honor–winning primary opponent, said it shouldn't be an issue. Then on the eighteenth, on the back lawn of the Arkansas Governor's Mansion, I received the endorsement of Admiral Bill Crowe, who had been chairman of the Joint Chiefs of Staff under President Reagan and briefly under Bush. I was very impressed by Crowe's straightforward, down-home manner and deeply grateful that he would stick his neck out for someone he barely knew but had come to believe in.

The political impact of what Bush and I were doing was uncertain. Some of his convention edge had worn off, but throughout September the polls bounced back and forth between a lead of 9 and 20 percent for me. The basic dynamic of the campaign had been set: Bush claimed to represent family values and trustworthiness, while I was for economic and social change. He said I was untrustworthy and anti-family, while I said he was dividing America and holding us back. On any given day, a substantial number of voters were torn between which one of us was better.

Besides the issues dispute, we spent September arguing

about the debates. The bipartisan national commission recommended three of them, with different formats. I accepted
immediately, but President Bush didn't like the commission's debate formats. I claimed his objections were a fig leaf
to cover his reluctance to defend his record. The disagreement continued for most of the month, which forced all
three of the scheduled debates to be canceled. As they were,
I went to each of the proposed debate sites to campaign,
making sure the disappointed citizens knew who had cost
their cities their moment in the national spotlight.

The worst thing to happen to us in September was far
more personal than political. Paul Tully, the veteran Irish
organizer Ron Brown had sent to Little Rock to coordinate
the Democratic Party's efforts with ours, dropped dead in
his hotel room. Tully was only forty-eight, an old-school
political pro and a fine man we had all come to adore and
depend on. Just as we were entering the homestretch,
another of our leaders was gone.

The month ended with some surprising developments.
Earvin "Magic" Johnson, the HIV-positive former All-Star
guard of the Los Angeles Lakers, abruptly resigned from the
National Commission on HIV/AIDS and endorsed me, disgusted with the administration's lack of attention to, and
action on, the AIDS problem. President Bush changed his
mind about the debates and challenged me to four of them.
And, most surprising, Ross Perot said he was thinking of
reentering the presidential race, because he didn't think the
President or I had a serious plan to reduce the deficit. He
criticized Bush for his no-tax pledge and said I wanted to
spend too much money. Perot invited both campaigns to
send delegations to meet him and discuss the matter.

Because neither of us knew which of us would be hurt
more if Perot got back in, and we both wanted his support if
he didn't, each campaign sent a high-level team to meet with
him. Our side was uneasy about it, because we thought he
had already decided to run and this was just high theater to
increase his prestige, but in the end I agreed that we ought
to keep reaching out to him. Senator Lloyd Bentsen, Mickey
Kantor, and Vernon Jordan went on my behalf. They got a

cordial reception, as did the Bush people. Perot announced that he had learned a lot from both groups. Then a couple of days later, on October 1, Perot announced that he felt compelled to get back into the race as a "servant" of his volunteers. He had been helped by quitting the race back in July. In the ten weeks he was out of it, the memory of his nutty fight with Bush the previous spring had faded, while the President and I had kept each other's problems fresh in the public mind. Now the voters and the press took him even more seriously because the two of us had courted him so visibly.

As Perot was getting back in, we finally reached an agreement with the Bush people on debates. There would be three of them, plus a vice-presidential debate, all crammed into nine days, between October 11 and 19. In the first and third, we would be questioned by members of the press. The second would be a town hall meeting in which citizens would ask the questions. At first, the Bush people didn't want Perot in the debates, because they thought he would be attacking the President, and any extra votes he garnered would come from potential Bush supporters rather than those who might go for me. I said I had no objection to Perot's inclusion, not because I agreed that Perot would hurt Bush more—I wasn't convinced of that—but because I felt that, in the end, he would have to be included and I didn't want to look like a chicken. By October 4, both campaigns agreed to invite Perot to participate.

In the week leading up to the first debate, I finally endorsed the controversial North American Free Trade Agreement, which the Bush administration had negotiated with Canada and Mexico, with the caveat that I wanted to negotiate side agreements ensuring basic labor and environmental standards that would be binding on Mexico. My labor supporters were worried about the loss of low-wage manufacturing jobs to our southern neighbor and strongly disagreed with my position, but I felt compelled to take it, for both economic and political reasons. I was a free-trader at heart, and I thought America had to support Mexico's economic growth to ensure long-term stability in our hemisphere. A couple of days later, more than 550 economists, including nine Nobel Prize winners, endorsed my economic program, saying it was more likely than the President's proposals to restore economic growth.

Just as I was determined to focus on economics in the run-up to the debates, the Bush camp was equally determined to keep undermining my character and reputation for honesty. They were facilitating a search request with the National Records Center in Suitland, Maryland, for all the information in my passport files on my forty-day trip to northern Europe, the Soviet Union, and Czechoslovakia back in 1969–70. Apparently, they were chasing down bogus rumors that I had gone to Moscow to pursue anti-war activities or had tried to apply for citizenship in another country to avoid the draft. On October 5, there were news reports that the files had been tampered with. The passport story dragged out all month. Though the FBI said the files had not been tampered with, what had occurred put the Bush campaign in a bad light. A senior State Department political appointee pushed the National Records Center, which had more than 100 million files, to put the search of mine ahead of two thousand other requests that had been filed earlier, and that normally took months to process. A Bush appointee also ordered the U.S. embassies in London and Oslo to conduct an "extremely thorough" search of their files for information on my draft status and citizenship. At some point, it was revealed that even my mother's passport files were searched. It was hard to imagine that even the most paranoid right-wingers could think that a country girl from Arkansas who loved the races was subversive.

Later, it came out that the Bush people had also asked John Major's government to look into my activities in England. According to news reports, the Tories complied, although they claimed their "comprehensive" but fruitless search of their immigration and naturalization documents was in response to press inquiries. I know they did some further work on it, because a friend of David Edwards's told David that British officials had questioned him about what David and I did in those long-ago days. Two Tory campaign strategists came to Washington to advise the Bush campaign on how they might destroy me the way the Conservative Party had undone Labour Party leader Neil Kinnock six months earlier. After the election, the British press fretted that the special relationship between our two countries had been damaged by this unusual British involvement in American politics. I was determined that there would be no damage, but I wanted the Tories to worry about it for a while.

The press had a field day with the passport escapade, and Al Gore called it a "McCarthyite abuse of power." Undeterred, the President kept asking me to explain the trip to Moscow and continued to question my patriotism. In an interview on CNN with Larry King, I said I loved my country and had never considered giving up my American citizenship. I don't think the public paid much attention to the passport flap one way or the other, and I was kind of amused by the whole thing. Of course it was an abuse of power, but a pathetically small one compared with Iran-Contra. It just showed how desperate the Bush people were to hang on to power, and how little they had to offer for America's future. If they wanted to spend the last month of the campaign barking up the wrong tree, that was fine with me.

In the days leading up to the first debate, I worked hard to be well prepared. I studied the briefing book diligently and participated in several mock-debate sessions. President Bush was played by Washington lawyer Bob Barnett, who had performed the same role four years earlier for Dukakis. Perot's stand-in was Congressman Mike Synar of Oklahoma, who had Ross's sayings and accent down pat. Bob and Mike wore me out in tough encounters before each debate. After each of our sessions, I was just glad I didn't have to debate them; the election might have turned out differently.

The first debate was finally held on Sunday, October 11, Hillary's and my seventeenth wedding anniversary, at Washington University in St. Louis. I went into it encouraged by the endorsements in that morning's editions of the *Washington Post* and the *Louisville Courier-Journal*. The *Post* editorial said, "This country is drifting and worn down; it badly needs to be reenergized and given new direction. Bill Clinton is the only candidate with a chance of doing that." That was exactly the argument I wanted to make in the debate. Yet despite my lead in the polls and the *Post* endorsement, I was on edge, because I knew I had the most to lose. In a new Gallup poll, 44 percent of the respondents said they expected me to win the debate, and 30 percent said they could be swayed by it. President Bush and his advisors had decided the only way to sway that 30 percent was to beat people over the head with my alleged character problems until the message sank in. Now, in addition to the draft, the Moscow trip, and the citizenship rumor, the President was attacking me for participating in anti-war demonstrations in London "against the United States of America, when our kids are dying halfway around the world."

Perot got the first question from one of three journalists, who rotated in a process moderated by Jim Lehrer of *The MacNeil/Lehrer NewsHour*. He was given two minutes to say what separated him from the other two candidates. Ross said he was supported by the people, not parties or special interests. Bush and I got one minute to respond. I said I represented change. The President said he had experience. We then discussed experience. Then President Bush was given his moment: "Are there important issues of character separating you from these two men?" He hit me on the draft. Perot responded that Bush had made his mistakes as a mature man in the White House, not as a young student. I said that Bush's father, as a U.S. senator from Connecticut, was right to criticize Senator Joe McCarthy for attacking the patriotism of loyal Americans, and the President was wrong to attack my patriotism, and that what America needed was a President who would bring our country together, not divide it.

We went on like that for an hour and a half, discussing taxes, defense, the deficit, jobs and the changing economy, foreign policy, crime, Bosnia, the definition of family, the legalization of marijuana, racial divisions, AIDS, Medicare, and health-care reform.

All of us did reasonably well. After the debate the press

was hustled by each candidate's "spinners" saying why their man had won. I had three good ones in Mario Cuomo, James Carville, and Senator Bill Bradley. One of President Bush's boosters, Charlie Black, invited the press to watch a new TV ad attacking me on the draft. The spinners could have some effect on the news stories about the debate, but those who had watched it had already formed their opinions.

I thought that, on balance, I gave the best answers in terms of specifics and arguments, but that Perot did better in presenting himself as folksy and relaxed. When Bush said Perot didn't have government experience, Perot said the President "had a point. I don't have any experience in running up a $4 trillion debt." Perot had big jug ears, which were accentuated by his short crew cut. On the deficit he said, "We've got to collect taxes" to eliminate it, but if anyone had a better idea, "I'm all ears." By contrast, I was a bit tight and at times seemed almost overprepared.

The good news was that the President gained no ground. The bad news was that Perot looked credible again. In the beginning, if he rose in the polls, his support would come from genuinely undecided voters or from those leaning toward both the President and me. But I well knew that if Ross rose much above 10 percent, most of his new voters would be those who wanted change but still weren't quite comfortable with me. The post-debate polls showed that among those who watched, a significant number now had more confidence in my ability to be President. They also showed that more than 60 percent of those who watched viewed Perot more favorably than they had before the debate. With three weeks to go, he was keeping the race unpredictable.

Two nights later, on October 13, in the vice-presidential debate in Atlanta, Al Gore clearly got the better of Dan Quayle. Perot's running mate, retired admiral James Stockdale, was likable but a nonfactor, and his performance took a little steam out of the momentum Perot had gained after the St. Louis debate. Quayle was effective in staying on message: Clinton wanted to raise taxes and Bush wouldn't; Clinton had no character and Bush did. He repeated what, in retrospect, was one of my worst public statements. In early 1991, after the Congress authorized President Bush to attack Iraq, I was asked how I would have voted. I was for the resolution, but I answered, "I guess I would have voted with the majority if it was a close vote. But I agree with the arguments the minority made." At the time, I hadn't thought I would be running for President in 1992. Both Arkansas senators had voted against authorizing the war. They were my friends, and I just didn't want to embarrass them publicly. When I entered the race, the comment looked wishy-washy and slick. Al's strategy was to hit back briefly on Quayle's attacks and keep talking about our positive plans for America. His best line was in response to Quayle's support for congressional term limits, a pet cause for conservatives: "We're fixin' to limit one."

Two nights later, on October 15, we had the second debate, in Richmond, Virginia. This was the one I wanted, a town hall meeting where we would be questioned by a representative group of local undecided voters.

My big worry this time was my voice. It was so bad right before the first debate that I could hardly speak above a whisper. When I had lost it during the primary, I saw a specialist in New York and got a voice coach, who taught me a set of exercises to open my throat and push the sound up through my sinus cavities. They involved humming; singing pairs of vowels, back to back, always beginning with *e*, like *e-i, e-o, e-a*; and repeating certain phrases to get the feel of pushing the sound up through the damaged cords. My favorite phrase was "Abraham Lincoln was a great orator." Whenever I said it, I thought about Lincoln's high, almost squeaky voice, and the fact that at least he was smart enough not to lose it. When my voice was off, a lot of the young staffers good-naturedly poked fun at me by repeating the humming exercises. It was funny, but losing my voice wasn't. A politician without a voice isn't worth much. When you lose yours repeatedly, it's frightening, because there's always the lurking fear that it won't come back. When it first happened, I thought my allergies had caused it. Then I learned that the problem was acid reflux, a relatively common condition in which stomach acid comes back up the esophagus and scalds the vocal cords, usually during sleep. Later, when I began to take medication and sleep on a wedge to elevate my head and shoulders, it got better. On the eve of the second debate, I was still struggling.

Carole Simpson of ABC News moderated the debate with questions from the audience. The first question, about how to guarantee fairness in trade, went to Ross Perot. He gave an anti-trade answer. The President gave a pro-trade response. I said I was for free and fair trade and we needed to do three things: make sure our trading partners' markets were as open as ours; change the tax code to favor modernizing plants at home rather than moving them abroad; and stop giving low-interest loans and job-training funds to companies that move to other countries when we didn't provide the same assistance to needy companies at home.

After trade we went to the deficit, then to negative campaigning. Bush hit me again for demonstrating against the Vietnam War in England. I replied, "I'm not interested in his character. I want to change the character of the presidency. And I'm interested in what we can trust him to do and what you can trust me to do and what you can trust Mr. Perot to do for the next four years."

After that, we discussed a series of issues—the cities, highways, gun control, term limits, and health-care costs. Then came the question that turned the debate. A woman asked, "How has the national debt personally affected each of your lives? And if it hasn't, how can you honestly find a cure for the economic problems of the common people if you have no experience in what's ailing them?" Perot went first, saying the debt caused him to "disrupt my private life and my business to get involved in this activity." He said he wanted to lift the debt burden from his children and grandchildren. Bush had a hard time saying how he had been affected personally. The questioner kept pushing him, saying she'd had friends who had been laid off, who couldn't make their mortgage and car payments. Then, strangely, Bush said he'd been to a black church and read in the bulletin about teen pregnancies. Finally, he said it's not fair to say you can't know what a problem is like unless you have it. When my turn came, I said I'd been governor of a small state for twelve years. I knew people by name who had lost their jobs and businesses. I'd met a lot more in the last year all over the country. I had run a state government and seen the human consequences of cuts in federal services. Then I told the questioner that the debt was a big problem, but not the only reason we had no growth: "We're in the grip of a failed economic theory." At one point during these exchanges, President Bush made a bad moment worse for himself by nervously looking at his watch. It made him seem even more out of touch. Though we moved on to other matters, like Social Security, pensions, Medicare, America's responsibilities as a superpower, education, and the possibility of an African-American or a woman being elected President, the debate was essentially over after our answers to the woman's question about the personal impact of the debt on us.

President Bush was effective in his closing statement by asking the audience to think about who they wanted to be President if our country faced a major crisis. Perot spoke well about education, the deficit, and the fact that he'd paid more than a billion dollars in taxes, "and for a guy that started out with everything he owned in the trunk of his car, that ain't bad." I began by saying that I had tried to answer the questions "specifically and pointedly." I highlighted Arkansas' programs in education and jobs and the support I had from twenty-four retired generals and admirals and several Republican businesspeople. I then said, "You have to decide whether you want change or not." I urged them to help me replace "trickle-down" economics with "invest-and-grow" economics.

I loved the second debate. Whatever questions they had about me, real voters most wanted to know about things that affected their lives. A CBS News post-debate poll of 1,145 voters said 53 percent of them thought I had won, compared with 25 percent for Bush and 21 percent for Perot. Five debate coaches interviewed by the Associated Press said that I had won, based on style, specifics, and my obvious comfort level with a format I'd been working with throughout the campaign, and long before that in Arkansas. I liked direct contact with citizens, and I trusted their unfiltered judgment.

As we headed into the third debate, a CNN/*USA Today* poll had my lead back to fifteen points, 47 percent to 32 percent for Bush to 15 percent for Perot.

Hillary and I went into Ypsilanti with our crew a day early to prepare for the last debate on the campus of the Michigan State University in East Lansing. As they had for the two previous debates, Bob Barnett and Mike Synar put me through my paces. I knew this would be the roughest ride for me. President Bush was a tough, proud man who was finally fighting hard to hold on to his job. And I was sure that, sooner or later, Perot, too, would turn his fire on me.

More than 90 million people watched the last debate on October 19, the largest audience we had drawn. We were questioned half the time by Jim Lehrer, half the time by a panel of journalists. It was President Bush's best performance. He accused me of being a tax-and-spend liberal, a Jimmy Carter clone, and a waffler who couldn't make up his mind. On the waffling issue I had a pretty good retort: "I can't believe he's accused me of taking two sides of an issue. He said 'trickle-down economics is voodoo economics' and now he's its biggest practitioner." When he hit the Arkansas economy, I got to reply that Arkansas had always been a poor state, but in the last year we were first in job creation, fourth in the percentage increase in manufacturing jobs, fourth in the percentage increase in personal income, and fourth in the decline in poverty, with the second-lowest state and local tax burden in the country: "The difference between Arkansas and the United States is that we're going in the right direction and this country's going in the wrong direction." I said that, instead of apologizing for signing the deficit-reduction plan with its gas-tax increase, the President should have acknowledged that his error was in saying "Read my lips" in the first place. Perot took us both on, saying he had grown up five blocks from Arkansas and my experience as governor of such a small state was "irrelevant" to presidential decision making, and accusing Bush of telling Saddam Hussein that the United States would not respond if he invaded northern Kuwait. We both whacked him back.

The second half of the debate featured questions by the panel of journalists. On the whole, it was more structured and less feisty, a bit like the first debate. However, there were some made-for-TV moments. Helen Thomas of United Press International, the senior White House correspondent, asked me: "If you had it to do over again, would you put on the nation's uniform?" I said I might answer the draft questions better, but I still thought Vietnam was a mistake. I then noted that we'd had some pretty good non-veteran Presidents, including FDR, Wilson, and Lincoln, who opposed the Mexican War. When I said Bush had made news in the first debate by saying he would put James Baker in charge of economic policy, but I would make news by putting myself in charge of economic policy, Bush got off a good line: "That's what worries me." The three of us brought the debates to an end with effective closing statements. I thanked the people for watching and caring about the country, and said again that I wasn't interested in attacking anyone personally. I complimented Ross Perot on his campaign and raising the profile of the deficit. And I said of President Bush, "I honor his service to our country, I appreciate his efforts, and I wish him well. I just believe it's time to change. . . . I know we can do better."

It's hard to say who won the third debate. I did a good job defending Arkansas and my record, and in discussing the issues, but I may have qualified too many of my answers. I had seen enough Presidents who had to change course to want my hands tied later by blanket statements in the debates. With his back against the wall, President Bush did well on everything except his attack on my record in Arkansas; that would work only in an unanswered paid ad, where the voters couldn't hear the facts. He was better at questioning what kind of President I would be, playing into the perception of Democrats as being weak on foreign policy and tax-happy, and reminding people that the last southern Democratic governor to be elected President presided over a period of high interest rates and inflation. Perot was witty and comfortable in his own skin, which I thought would reassure his supporters and perhaps sway some of the undecided voters. Three of the post-debate polls showed me winning the debate, but the CNN/*USA Today* poll, the only one to show Perot the victor, said 12 percent had changed their preference after the debate, more than half of them going to Perot.

Still, on balance, the debates were good for me. More Americans thought I had the ability to be a good President, and the give-and-take on the issues allowed me a chance to push my positive proposals. I wish we could have done them for two more weeks. Instead, we headed for the home-stretch, a frenzied rush to as many states as possible, with the airwaves full of negative ads from my opponents, and a shot against Bush from me featuring his most famous statement: "Read my lips." Frank Greer and Mandy Grunwald did a good job with our ads, and our rapid-response team answered theirs effectively, but it wasn't the same as having all the candidates in one room. Now they were coming after me, and I had to hang on.

On October 21, the campaign got a little comic relief when Burke's Peerage, England's leading genealogical authority, said that President Bush and I were both descendants of thirteenth-century English royalty and were distant cousins, at least twenty times removed. Our common ancestor was King John. Bush was descended through John's son King Henry III, making him Queen Elizabeth's thirteenth cousin. Appropriately, my royal connections were both less impressive and offset by equally strong democratic ties. My Blythe kinfolk were descendants of both Henry III's sister Eleanor and her husband, Simon de Montfort, Earl of Leicester, who defeated the king in battle and forced him to accept the most representative parliament up to that time. Alas, in 1265 the king broke his oath to honor the Parliament, a breach that led to the battle of Evesham, in which poor Simon was killed. The spokesman for Burke's Peerage said that Simon's body "was hacked into a multitude of pieces, bits being sent out around the country—a finger, perhaps, to a village, a foot to a town—to show what happened to democrats." Now that I knew that the roots of my differences with the President went back seven hundred years, I suppose I couldn't blame his campaign for being faithful to the tactics of his ancestors. Burke's Peerage also traced the Blythes back to the village of Gotham, which, according to English legend, was a haunt of madmen. I knew I had to be a little crazy to run for President, but I hated to think it was genetic.

On October 23, our campaign got another boost from the high-tech sector when the leaders of more than thirty computer-software companies, including Microsoft executive vice president Steve Ballmer, endorsed me. But it wasn't over. A week after the last debate, a CNN/*USA Today* poll had my lead over President Bush down to seven points, 39 to 32 percent, with Perot at 20 percent. Just as I had feared, Perot's advertising, coupled with President Bush's attacks on me, were moving votes to Perot at my expense. On October 26, while campaigning in North Carolina, Al Gore and I tried to keep the lead by hitting the Bush administration over "Iraqgate," the channeling of U.S. government–backed credits to Iraq through the Atlanta branch of a bank owned by the Italian government. Ostensibly for agricultural purposes, the credits had been siphoned off by Saddam Hussein to rebuild his military and weapons program after the Iran-Iraq war. Two billion dollars of the credits were never repaid, leaving U.S. taxpayers with the bill. The banker in Atlanta who was indicted for his role in the fraud negotiated a sweetheart plea bargain with the U.S. attorney's office, which, unbelievably, was headed by a Bush appointee who had represented Iraqi interests in the credit flap shortly before his appointment, although he said he had recused himself from this investigation. By the time Al and I mentioned it, the FBI, the CIA, and the Justice Department were all investigating each other for what they had or hadn't done in the affair. It was a real mess, but probably too complicated to affect any voters this late in the campaign.

Perot was still the wild card. On October 29, a Reuters news article began: "If President George Bush wins reelection, he will owe a major debt of gratitude to a tough-talking Texas billionaire who dislikes him." The article went on to say that the debates had altered Perot's image, allowing him to double his support, mostly at my expense, and taking away the monopoly I had had on the "change" issue. That day's CNN/*USA Today* poll had my lead down to two points, though five other polls and Stan Greenberg's poll for our campaign had the margin holding at seven to ten points. Whatever the number, the race was still volatile.

During the last week, I campaigned as hard as I could. So did President Bush. On Thursday, at a campaign rally in suburban Michigan, he referred to Al Gore and me as "bozos," a comparison to the clown Bozo, who probably found the reference more unflattering than we did. On the Friday before the election, Iran-Contra special prosecutor Lawrence Walsh, a Republican from Oklahoma, indicted President Reagan's defense secretary, Caspar Weinberger, and five others, with a note in the indictment suggesting that President Bush had played a greater role in and knew more about the illegal sales of arms to Iran authorized by the Reagan White House than he had previously admitted. Whether it would hurt him or not, I didn't know; I was too busy to think about it. The timing was ironic, though, considering the strenuous efforts the administration had made to dig into my passport files and the pressure they had been applying, which we didn't know about at the time, to get the U.S. attorney in Arkansas, a Bush appointee, to implicate me in the investigation of the failure of Madison Guaranty Savings and Loan.

Over the last weekend, Bush directed all his paid media fire at me. And Perot, believing 30 percent of my support was "soft" and could shift to him at the last minute, finally joined in, big-time. He spent a reported $3 million on thirty-minute television "infomercials," trashing Arkansas. He said if I was elected, "we'll all be plucking chickens for a living." The program listed twenty-three areas where Arkansas ranked near the bottom of all states. Apparently, he no longer thought Arkansas was irrelevant. Our team had a big argument about whether to respond. Hillary wanted to go after Perot. I thought we at least had to defend Arkansas. We had done well by never letting any charge go unanswered. Everyone else thought the attacks were too little, too late, and we should just stick with the game plan. Reluctantly, I agreed. My team had been right about the big questions so far, and I was too tired and keyed up to trust my judgment over theirs.

I began the weekend with a morning rally that filled a high school football stadium in Decatur, Georgia, outside Atlanta. Governor Zell Miller, Senator Sam Nunn, Congressman John Lewis, and other Democrats who had stuck with me all the way were there. But the big draw was Hank Aaron, the baseball star who had broken Babe Ruth's home-run record in 1974. Aaron was a genuine local hero, not only for his baseball exploits but also for his work on behalf of poor children after he laid down his bat. There were 25,000 people at the Georgia rally. Three days later, I would carry Georgia by just 13,000 votes. From then on, Hank Aaron loved to kid me that he had personally delivered Georgia's electoral votes with his Saturday-morning plug. He may have been right.

After Georgia, I campaigned in Davenport, Iowa, then flew to Milwaukee, where I did my last televised town hall meeting and cut my last television spot, urging people to vote, and vote for change. On Sunday night, after campaign stops in Cincinnati and Scranton, the Rodhams' hometown, we flew to New Jersey for a big rally at the Meadowlands, a musical extravaganza featuring rock, jazz, and country musicians and movie stars who were supporting me. Then I played sax and danced with Hillary before 15,000 people at the Garden State Park racetrack in Cherry Hill, New Jersey, where a horse named Bubba Clinton, the name my brother had called me by since he was a toddler, had recently won a race at 17-to-1 odds. My odds were better now, but they had once been far longer. One man who bet 100 pounds on me in April with a London bookmaker when the odds were 33 to 1 made about $5,000. There's no telling what he could have made if he'd placed the bet in early February when I was being battered in New Hampshire.

Hillary and I woke up Monday morning in Philadelphia, the birthplace of our democracy, and the first leg of a four thousand–mile, eight-state, round-the-clock campaign swing. While Al and Tipper Gore campaigned in other battleground states, three Boeing 727s, decorated in red, white, and blue, took Hillary, me, our staff, and a horde of media on the twenty-nine-hour jaunt. At Philadelphia's Mayfair Diner, the first stop, when a man asked me what would be the first thing I would do if elected, I replied, "I'm going to thank God." On to Cleveland. With my voice failing again, I said, "Teddy Roosevelt once said we should speak softly and carry a big stick. Tomorrow, I want to talk softly and carry Ohio." At an airport rally outside Detroit, flanked by several of Michigan's elected officials and union leaders who had worked so hard for me, I croaked, "If you will be my voice tomorrow, I will be your voice for four years." After stops in St. Louis and Paducah, Kentucky, we flew to Texas for two visits. The first was in McAllen, deep in South Texas near the Mexican border where I had been stranded with Sargent Shriver twenty years earlier. It was after midnight when we got to Fort Worth, where the crowd was kept awake by the famous country-rocker Jerry Jeff Walker. When I got back to the plane, I learned that my staff had bought four hundred dollars' worth of mango ice cream from the Menger Hotel in San Antonio, just across the street from the Alamo. They had all heard me say how much I loved that ice cream, which I had discovered when working in the McGovern campaign in 1972. There was enough of it to feed the three planeloads of weary travelers all night.

Meanwhile, back at headquarters in Little Rock, James Carville had gathered our people, more than a hundred of them, for a last meeting. After George Stephanopoulos introduced him, James gave an emotional speech, saying that love and work were the two most precious gifts a person could give, and thanking all our people, most of them very young, for those gifts.

We flew from Texas to Albuquerque, New Mexico, for a very early-morning rally with my old friend Governor Bruce King. Afterward, at about 4 a.m., I devoured a breakfast of

Mexican food, then headed for Denver, the last stop. We had a big, enthusiastic early-morning crowd. After Mayor Wellington Webb, Senator Tim Wirth, and my partner in education reform Governor Roy Roemer fired them up, Hillary gave the speech and I forced my last campaign words of gratitude and hope through swollen vocal cords. Then it was home to Little Rock.

Hillary and I were greeted at the airport by Chelsea, other family members, friends, and our headquarters staff. I thanked them for all they'd done, then left with my family for the drive to our polling place, the Dunbar Community Center, which is in a mostly African-American neighborhood less than a mile from the Governor's Mansion. We spoke to the folks gathered around the center and signed in with the election officials there. Then, just as she had done since she was six, Chelsea went into the voting booth with me. After I closed the curtain, Chelsea pulled down the lever by my name, then hugged me tight. After thirteen months of backbreaking effort, it was all that was left for us to do. When Hillary finished voting, the three of us embraced, went outside, answered a few press questions, shook a few hands, and went home.

For me, election days have always embodied the great mystery of democracy. No matter how hard pollsters and pundits try to demystify it, the mystery remains. It's the one day when the ordinary citizen has as much power as the millionaire and the President. Some people use it and some don't. Those who do choose candidates for all kinds of reasons, some rational, some intuitive, some with certainty, others skeptically. Somehow, they usually pick the right leader for the times; that's why America is still around and doing well after more than 228 years.

I had entered the race largely because I thought I was right for these times of dramatic change in how Americans live, work, raise children, and relate to the rest of the world. I had worked for years to understand how political leaders' decisions play out in people's lives. I believed I understood what needed to be done and how to do it. But I also knew I was asking the American people to take a big gamble. First, they weren't used to Democratic Presidents. Then there were the questions about me: I was very young; was the governor of a state most Americans knew little about; had opposed the Vietnam War and avoided military service; held liberal views on race and rights for women and gays; often seemed slick when I spoke of achieving ambitious goals that, at least on the surface, seemed mutually exclusive; and had lived a far from perfect life. I had worked my heart out to convince the American people that I was a risk worth taking, but the constantly shifting polls and the resurgence of Perot showed that many of them wanted to believe in me but still harbored doubts. On the stump, Al Gore asked voters to think about what headline they wanted to read the day after the election: "Four More Years," or "Change Is on the Way." I thought I knew what their answer would be, but on that long November day, like everyone else, I had to wait to find out.

When we got home, the three of us watched an old John Wayne movie until we dozed off for a couple of hours. In the afternoon, I went jogging with Chelsea downtown and stopped at McDonald's for a cup of water, as I had countless times before. After I got back to the Governor's Mansion, I didn't have to wait much longer. The returns started to come in early, at about 6:30 p.m. I was still in my jogging clothes when I was projected the winner in several states in the East. A little over three hours later, the networks projected me the overall winner, when Ohio went our way by 90,000 votes out of almost 5 million cast, a victory margin of less than 2 percent. It seemed fitting, because Ohio had been one of the states to guarantee me the nomination in the June 2 primaries, and the state whose votes had officially put me over the top at our convention in New York. The turnout was huge, the highest since the early 1960s, with more than 100 million people voting.

When all 104,600,366 votes were counted, the final margin of victory was about 5.5 percent. I finished with 43 percent of the vote, to 37.4 percent for President Bush and 19 percent for Ross Perot, the best showing for a third-party candidate since Teddy Roosevelt garnered 27 percent with his Bull Moose Party in 1912. Our baby-boom ticket did best among voters over sixty-five and those under thirty. Our own generation apparently had more doubts about whether we were ready to lead the country. The late Bush-Perot tag-team attack on Arkansas had shaved two or three points off our high-water mark a few days before the election. It had hurt, but not badly enough.

The victory margin in the electoral college was larger. President Bush won eighteen states with 168 electoral votes. I received 370 electoral votes from thirty-two states and the District of Columbia, including every state that borders the Mississippi River from north to south except Mississippi, and all the New England and mid-Atlantic states. I also won in some unlikely places, like Georgia, Montana, Nevada, and Colorado. Eleven states were decided by 3 percent or less: Arizona, Florida, Virginia, and North Carolina went for the President; besides Ohio, Georgia, Montana, Nevada, New Hampshire, Rhode Island, and New Jersey voted narrowly for me. I received 53 percent of the vote in Arkansas, my highest total, and won twelve other states by 10 percent or more, including some large ones: California, Illinois, Massachusetts, and New York. While Perot kept me from getting a majority of the popular vote, his presence on the ballot almost certainly added to my margin in the electoral college.

How did Americans come to choose their first baby-boom President, the third youngest in history, only the second governor of a small state, carrying more baggage than an ocean liner? Surveys of voters leaving the polls indicated that the economy was by far the biggest issue for them, followed by the deficit and health care, with the character issue trailing. In the end, I had won the debate over what the election was about. In a presidential campaign, that is more important than whether the voters agree with a candidate on specific issues. But the economy alone didn't do it. I was also helped by James Carville and a brilliant campaign team who kept me and everyone else focused and on message through all the ups and downs; by Stan Greenberg's insightful polling and the campaign's effective paid media; by able people who led the campaign at the grass roots; by a Democratic Party united by Ron Brown's skill and the desire to win after a dozen years in the wilderness; by extraordinarily high levels of support from minorities and women, who also elected a Congress with six female senators and forty-seven female members of the House, up from twenty-eight; by the initial disunity and overconfidence among the Republicans; by surprisingly positive press coverage in the general election, in stark contrast to the going-over I got in the primaries; by the extraordinary performance of Al and Tipper Gore in the campaign, and the generational change we all represented; and by the New Democrat philosophy and ideas I had developed in Arkansas and with the DLC. Finally, I was able to win because Hillary and my friends stayed with me through the fire, and because I didn't give up when I got beat up.

Early on election night, President Bush called to congratulate me. He was gracious and pledged a smooth transition, as did Dan Quayle. After a last look at my victory speech, Hillary and I said a prayer thanking God for our blessings and asking for divine guidance in the work ahead. Then we got Chelsea and drove down to the Old State House for the big event.

The Old State House was my favorite building in Arkansas, full of my state's history and my own. It was the place where I had received well-wishers when I was sworn in as attorney general sixteen years earlier, and where I had announced for President thirteen months ago. We walked onto the stage to greet Al and Tipper and the thousands of people who had filled the downtown streets. I was overwhelmed when I looked out into the faces of all those people, so full of happiness and hope. And I was filled with gratitude. I loved seeing my mother's tears of joy, and I hoped that my father was looking down on me with pride.

When I started this remarkable odyssey, I could never have anticipated how hard it would be, or how wonderful.

The people in the crowd and millions like them had done their part. Now I had to prove them right. I began by saying, "On this day, with high hopes and brave hearts, in massive numbers, the American people have voted to make a new beginning." I asked those who had voted for President Bush and Ross Perot to join me in creating a "re-United States," then closed with these words:

> This victory was more than a victory of party; it was a victory for those who work hard and play by the rules, a victory for people who felt left out and left behind and want to do better. . . . I accept tonight the responsibility that you have given me to be the leader of this, the greatest country in human history. I accept it with a full heart and a joyous spirit. But I ask you to be Americans again, too, to be interested not just in getting but in giving, not just in placing blame but in assuming responsibility, not just in looking out for yourselves but in looking out for others, too. . . . Together, we can make the country that we love everything it was meant to be.

TWENTY-NINE

ON THE DAY AFTER the election, awash in congratulatory calls and messages, I went to work on what is called the transition. Is it ever! There was no time to celebrate, and we didn't take much time to rest, which was probably a mistake. In just eleven weeks, my family and I had to make the transition from our life in Arkansas into the White House. There was so much to do: select the cabinet, important sub-cabinet officials, and the White House staff; work with the Bush people on the mechanics of the move; begin briefings on national security and talk to foreign leaders; reach out to congressional leaders; finalize the economic proposals I would present to Congress; develop a plan to implement my other campaign commitments; deal with a large number of requests for meetings and the desire of many of our campaign workers and major supporters to know as soon as possible whether they would be part of the new administration; and respond to unfolding events. There would be a lot of them in the next seventy days, especially overseas: in Iraq, where Saddam Hussein was seeking relief from UN sanctions; Somalia, where President Bush had dispatched U.S. troops on a humanitarian mission to avert mass starvation; and Russia, where the economy was in shambles, President Yeltsin faced growing opposition from ultra-nationalists and unconverted Communists, and the withdrawal of Russian troops from the Baltic nations had been delayed. The "to do" list was growing.

Several weeks earlier, we had quietly established a transition-planning operation in Little Rock, under a board that included Vernon Jordan, Warren Christopher, Mickey Kantor, former San Antonio mayor Henry Cisneros, Doris Matsui, and former Vermont governor Madeleine Kunin. The staff director was Gerald Stern, who was on leave from his job as executive vice president of Occidental Petroleum.

Obviously, we didn't want to look as if we'd taken the outcome of the election for granted, so the operation was kept
low-key, with an unlisted telephone number and no sign on
the door of the offices on the thirteenth floor of the Worthen
Bank building.

When George Stephanopoulos came over to the mansion
on Wednesday, Hillary and I asked him to continue being
our communications director in the White House. I would
have been happy to have James Carville there too, to help
develop strategy and keep us on message, but he didn't
think he was suited to government and two days earlier he
had cracked to reporters, "I wouldn't live in a country
whose government would hire me."

On Wednesday afternoon, I met with the transition
board and received my first briefing papers. At 2:30 p.m., I
held a short press conference on the back lawn of the Governor's Mansion. Because President Bush was in another
tense situation with Iraq, I emphasized that America "has
only one President at a time" and that "America's foreign
policy remains solely in his hands."

On my second day as President-elect, I spoke with a few
foreign leaders, and went to the office to take care of some
state business and thank the governor's staff for the fine job
they had done while I was away. That night we had a party
for the campaign staff. I was still so hoarse I could barely
squeak out "Thank you." I spent most of the time shaking
hands and walking around with signs on my shirt that said
"Sorry, I can't talk" and "You did a good job."

On Friday, I named Vernon Jordan as chairman and
Warren Christopher as director of my transition board. The
announcement of their appointments was well received in
Washington and in Little Rock, where both were respected
by the campaign staff, many of whom were beginning to
show predictable and understandable signs of exhaustion,
irritability, and anxiety about the future, as the euphoria of
our victory wore off.

In the second week of the transition, the pace picked up.
I spoke about Middle East peace with Israeli prime minister
Yitzhak Rabin, Egyptian president Hosni Mubarak, and

Saudi Arabia's King Fahd. Vernon and Chris filled out most of the senior transition staff with Alexis Herman, deputy chair of the Democratic Party, and Mark Gearan, who had managed Al Gore's campaign, as deputy directors; DLC president Al From in domestic policy; Sandy Berger, along with my campaign aide Nancy Soderberg in foreign policy; and Gene Sperling and my old Rhodes classmate Bob Reich, then a Harvard professor and author of several thought-provoking books on the global economy, in economic policy. The vetting of all candidates for important positions would be overseen by Tom Donilon, a sharp Washington lawyer and longtime Democratic activist. Donilon's job was important; defeating a President's appointments because of financial or personal problems in their backgrounds or previously unexamined opinions had become a regular part of Washington political life. Our vetters were supposed to make sure that anyone who was willing to serve could survive the scrutiny.

A few days later, former South Carolina governor Dick Riley joined the transition team to oversee the sub-cabinet appointments. Riley had a backbreaking job. At one point, he was getting more than three thousand résumés, as well as a couple of hundred phone calls, a day. Many of the calls were from members of Congress and governors who expected him to return the calls personally. So many people who had contributed to our victory wanted to serve that I was worried about able, deserving people falling through the cracks, and some of them did.

The third week of the transition was devoted to reaching out to Washington. I invited House Speaker Tom Foley, House majority leader Dick Gephardt, and Senate majority leader George Mitchell to Little Rock for dinner and a morning meeting. It was important for me to get off on the right foot with the Democratic leaders. I knew I had to have their support to succeed, and they knew the American people would hold us all accountable for breaking the partisan gridlock in Washington. It would require some compromise on my part and theirs, but after our meetings I was confident we could work together.

On Wednesday, I went to Washington for two days to meet with President Bush, other congressional Democrats, and the Republican leaders in Congress. My meeting with the President, scheduled to last an hour, went almost twice that long and was both cordial and helpful. We talked about a wide variety of issues, and I found the President's review of our foreign policy challenges particularly insightful.

From the White House, I drove two miles into north Washington, to a neighborhood beset by poverty, unemployment, drugs, and crime. On Georgia Avenue, I got out of the car and walked for a block, shaking hands and talking to merchants and other citizens about their problems and what I could do to help. Eight people had been killed the previous year within a mile of where I stopped. I got food from a Chinese takeout where the workers operated behind bulletproof glass for safety. Parents of school-aged children said they were frightened because so many of their kids' classmates brought guns to school. The people who lived in Washington's inner city were often forgotten by Congress and the White House, despite the fact that the federal government still retained substantial control over the city's affairs. I wanted the city's residents to know I cared about their problems and wanted to be a good neighbor.

On Thursday, I went for a morning jog, running out the door of the Hay-Adams Hotel, just across Lafayette Square from the White House, down a street filled with homeless people who had spent the night there, over to the Washington Monument and the Lincoln Memorial, then back to the McDonald's near the hotel. I got a cup of coffee and met a fifty-nine-year-old man who told me he'd lost his job and everything he had in the recession. I walked back to the hotel thinking about that man, and how I could manage to keep in touch with the problems of people like him from behind the wall that surrounds every President.

Later, after breakfast with fourteen Democratic congressional leaders, I had a private visit with the Senate minority leader, Bob Dole. I had always respected Dole, because of his courageous recovery from his World War II wounds and because he had worked with Democrats on issues like food stamps and disability rights. On the other hand, he was a partisan, and had wasted no time on election night in saying that because I didn't "even win by a majority . . . there's not a clear mandate there." Therefore, Dole said, his responsibility was "to bring our party together, to reach out to try to attract independent and Perot supporters to put up our own agenda." Dole and I had a good talk, but I left the meeting unsure of what our relationship, or his agenda, would be. After all, Dole wanted to be President too.

I also had a cordial meeting with the House minority leader, Bob Michel, an old-fashioned conservative from Illinois, but I regretted that the Republican whip, Newt Gingrich of Georgia, was away on vacation. Gingrich was the political and intellectual leader of the conservative Republicans in the House, and he believed a permanent Republican majority could be forged by uniting the cultural and religious conservatives with voters who were anti–big government and anti-tax. He had skewered President Bush for signing the Democrats' deficit-reduction package in 1990 because it contained a gas-tax increase. I could only imagine what he intended to do to me.

Back at the hotel, I met with General Colin Powell, chairman of the Joint Chiefs of Staff. Having risen to the highest ranks with the support of Presidents Reagan and Bush, Powell would serve his last nine months as chairman under a very different Commander in Chief. He was opposed to my proposal to allow gays to serve in the military, even though during the Gulf War, which made him a popular hero, the Pentagon had knowingly allowed more than one hundred gays to serve, dismissing them only after the conflict, when they were no longer needed. Despite our differences, General Powell made it clear that he would serve as best he could, including giving me his honest advice, which is exactly what I wanted.

Hillary and I ended our Washington stay with a dinner party given by Pamela Harriman. The previous night, Vernon and Ann Jordan had also invited some people to have dinner with us. These parties, along with a later one given by Katharine Graham, were designed to introduce Hillary and me to important people in Washington's political, press, and business circles. To most of them, we were still strangers.

After spending a last Thanksgiving in the Governor's Mansion with my family, including our annual visit to a shelter that a friend of ours ran for women and children who had fled from domestic abuse, Hillary and I flew with Chelsea and her friend Elizabeth Flammang to Southern California for a little rest with our friends the Thomasons and for a courtesy call on President Reagan. Reagan had set up shop in a very nice building located on property once used by Twentieth Century Fox to produce movies. I really enjoyed the visit. Reagan was a great storyteller, and after eight years in the White House he had some good ones I wanted to hear. At the close of the meeting, he gave me a jar of his trademark jelly beans, colored red, white, and blue. I would keep it in my office for eight years.

In December, I got down to the business that people hire Presidents to do: making decisions. Since I had promised to focus on the economy "like a laser beam," I began with that. On December 3, I had a one-on-one meeting at the Governor's Mansion with Alan Greenspan, chairman of the Federal Reserve Board. The Fed chairman has enormous influence over the economy, largely through the Fed's setting of short-term interest rates, which in turn affect long-term rates on business and consumer loans, including home mortgages. Because Greenspan was a brilliant student of all aspects of the economy and a seasoned Washington power player, his pronouncements in speeches and congressional testimony carried great weight. I knew Greenspan was a conservative Republican who was probably disappointed by my election, but I thought we could work together for three reasons: I believed in the independence of the Federal Reserve; like Greenspan, I thought it was essential to cut the deficit; and he, too, had once been a tenor saxophone player, who, like me, had decided he'd be better off doing something else for a living.

A week later, I began my cabinet announcements with my economic team, starting with Lloyd Bentsen, the chairman of the Senate Finance Committee, as secretary of the Treasury. Bentsen was a pro-business Democrat who still had concern for ordinary people. Tall and lean with a patrician bearing, he came from a wealthy South Texas family, and after service as a bomber pilot in Italy during World War II he was elected to the U.S. House of Representatives. After three terms there, he left the House to go into business, then, in 1970, was elected to the Senate, defeating Congressman George H. W. Bush. I liked Bentsen and thought he would be perfect for the Treasury job: he was respected on Wall Street, effective with Congress, and committed to my goals of restoring growth and reducing poverty. Bentsen's deputy secretary would be Roger Altman, vice chairman of the Blackstone Group investment firm and a lifelong Democrat and financial whiz who would strengthen our team and our ties to Wall Street. The other Treasury appointee, Larry Summers, who would become undersecretary for international affairs, was the youngest tenured professor at Harvard at the age of twenty-eight. He was even brighter than his reputation had led me to believe.

I chose Leon Panetta, the California congressman who chaired the House Budget Committee, to be the director of the Office of Management and Budget (OMB), always a critical position but especially important for me, because I was committed to crafting a budget that both reduced the deficit and increased spending in areas vital to our long-term prosperity, like education and technology. I didn't know Leon before I interviewed him, but I was very impressed with his knowledge, energy, and down-to-earth manner. I named the other finalist for the OMB job, Alice Rivlin, as Leon's deputy. Like him, she was a deficit "hawk," and sensitive to people who needed federal help.

I asked Bob Rubin to take on a new job: coordinating economic policy in the White House as chair of a National Economic Council, which would operate in much the same way the National Security Council did, bringing all the relevant agencies together to formulate and implement policy. I had become convinced that the federal government's economic policy making was neither as organized nor as effective as it could be. I wanted to bring together not only the tax and budget functions of Treasury and the OMB, but also the work of the Commerce Department, the Office of the U.S. Trade Representative, the Council of Economic Advisers, the Export-Import Bank, the Labor Department, and the Small Business Administration. We had to utilize every possible resource to implement the kind of comprehensive, sophisticated economic program necessary to benefit every income group and every region. Rubin was just the man to do it. Somehow he managed to be understated and intense at the same time. He had been co-chairman of Goldman Sachs, the big New York investment firm, and if he could balance all of its egos and interests, he had a good chance to succeed with the job I had given him. The National Economic Council represented the biggest change in White House operations in years, and thanks to Rubin, it would serve America well.

I announced that Laura Tyson, a respected economics professor at the University of California at Berkeley, would be chair of the Council of Economic Advisers. Laura impressed me with her knowledge of technology, manufacturing, and trade, the microeconomic issues I felt had been too long ignored in the making of national economic policy.

I also named Bob Reich labor secretary. The Labor post had languished under Reagan and Bush, but I saw it as a big part of our economic team. Bob had written some good books on the need for greater labor-management cooperation and the importance of both flexibility and security in the modern workplace. I believed he could both defend labor's interests in the health, safety, and welfare of working men and women and secure key labor support for our new economic policy.

I asked Ron Brown to be the commerce secretary, fulfilling a campaign commitment to elevate the importance of a department that had been considered a "second tier" agency for too long. With his unique mixture of brains and bravado, Ron had brought the DNC back from the dead, uniting its liberal and labor bases with those who embraced the new approach of the Democratic Leadership Council. If anyone could enliven the Commerce bureaucracy to advance America's commercial interests, he could. Ron would become the first African-American secretary of commerce and one of the most effective leaders the department ever had.

On the day I announced Ron Brown's appointment, I also resigned as governor of Arkansas. I could no longer devote any time to the job, and Lieutenant Governor Jim Guy Tucker was more than ready and able to take over. One disappointing thing about leaving office in December was that I fell twenty-four days short of breaking Orval Faubus's record as my state's longest-serving governor.

On December 14 and 15, with the major economic positions filled, I hosted an economic summit in Little Rock. We had been working on it for six weeks, under the leadership of Mickey Kantor; John Emerson, a friend of Hillary's who had supported me in California; and Erskine Bowles, a successful North Carolina businessman who had supported me for President because of my New Democrat philosophy and my support for fetal-tissue research. Diabetes ran in Erskine's family, and he believed, as I did, that the research was essential to unlocking the mysteries of diabetes and other presently incurable medical conditions.

When the conference was announced, everybody in America seemed to want to attend, and we had a hard time keeping the crowd small enough to fit into the hall at the Little Rock Convention Center while leaving adequate space for the enormous number of press people from all over the world who wanted to cover it. Finally, they pared the list of delegates down to 329, ranging from heads of Fortune 500 companies to Silicon Valley executives to shop owners, and including labor leaders, academics, an Alaskan homesteader, and the chief of the Cherokee Indian Nation, whose imposing name was Wilma Mankiller.

When the conference opened, the atmosphere was electric, almost as if it were a rock concert for policy makers. The media called it a "wonkfest." The panels produced some keen insights and new ideas, and clarified the choices I faced. There was an overwhelming consensus that my number one priority should be to reduce the deficit, even if it meant less of a middle-class tax cut, or giving up on one altogether. "Mickey's Retreat," as we called the conference, was a smashing success, and not just in the eyes of the policy wonks. A poll released after the conference indicated that 77 percent of the American people approved of my preparations for taking over the presidency.

The economic conference sent a loud and clear message that, as I had promised, America was moving forward, away from trickle-down to invest-and-grow economics, away from neglect of those who were losing ground in the changing global economy to an America that once again offered opportunity to every responsible citizen. Eventually I would name Mickey Kantor to be U.S. trade representative, Erskine Bowles to head the Small Business Administration, and John Emerson to the White House staff. If anyone had earned a place on the team, they had.

Just before the economic conference, I announced that Mack McLarty would be White House chief of staff. It was an unusual choice because while Mack had served on two federal commissions under President Bush, he was hardly a Washington insider, a fact that concerned him. He told me he would prefer another job more suited to his business background. Nevertheless, I pressed Mack to accept the position, because I was convinced he could organize the White House staff to function smoothly and create the kind of team atmosphere in which I wanted to work. He was disciplined and intelligent; he had great negotiating skills and the ability to keep up with and follow through on many things at once. He was also a loyal friend of more than forty years, and I knew I could count on him not to shield me from diverse points of view and sources of information. In the first months of our tenure, both he and I would suffer from some of our tone deafness about Washington's political and press culture, but thanks to Mack, we also would accomplish a lot and create a spirit of cooperation that many previous White House staffs lacked.

Between December 11 and 18, I moved closer to my goal of naming the most diverse administration in history. On the eleventh, I named University of Wisconsin chancellor Donna Shalala as secretary of health and human services and Carol Browner, the state of Florida's environmental director, to head the Environmental Protection Agency. Hillary and I had known Shalala, a four-foot eleven-inch dynamo of Lebanese ancestry, for years. I didn't know Browner before I interviewed her, but was impressed with her; my friend Governor Lawton Chiles thought highly of her; and Al Gore wanted her to have the job. Both women would serve my entire eight years, building long lists of important achievements. On the fifteenth, the story broke that I would ask Dr. Joycelyn Elders, the Arkansas Health Department director, the second black woman to graduate from the University of Arkansas Medical School, and a national authority on pediatric diabetes, to be U.S. surgeon general, America's top public-health official.

On the seventeenth, I announced the selection of Henry Cisneros to be secretary of housing and urban development. With his unusual combination of great political gifts and a caring heart, Henry had become the most popular Hispanic politician in America. He was well qualified for the job, with a brilliant record as mayor in revitalizing San Antonio. I also named Jesse Brown, an African-American ex-marine and Vietnam veteran, who was the executive director of the Disabled American Veterans, to be secretary of the Department of Veterans Affairs.

On December 21, I named Hazel O'Leary, an African-American utility executive from Northern States Power Company in Minnesota, to be secretary of energy, and Dick Riley to be secretary of education. Hazel was an expert on natural gas, and I wanted to support its development because it was cleaner than oil and coal, and in ample supply. Dick and I had been friends for years. His modest manner was deceptive. He had long endured an agonizing spinal condition, despite which he had built a successful legal and political career and a fine family. And he had been a great education governor. In the campaign, I had often cited an article saying Arkansas had made more progress in education in the last ten years than any other state except South Carolina.

On Tuesday, December 22, I announced my entire national security team: Warren Christopher as secretary of state, Les Aspin as secretary of defense, Madeleine Albright as ambassador to the United Nations, Tony Lake as national security advisor, Jim Woolsey as director of the Central Intelligence Agency, and Admiral Bill Crowe as head of the President's Foreign Intelligence Advisory Board.

Christopher had been President Carter's deputy secretary of state and had played a major role in negotiating the release of American hostages from Iran. He had served me well in the vice-presidential and cabinet selection processes and shared my basic foreign policy objectives. Some people thought his personality was too restrained for him to be effective, but I knew he could get things done.

I asked Les Aspin to be secretary of defense after it became clear that Sam Nunn wouldn't accept the appointment. As chairman of the House Armed Services Committee, Aspin probably knew more about defense than anyone else in the House of Representatives, understood the security challenges of the post–Cold War world, and was committed to modernizing our military to meet them.

I had been impressed with Madeleine Albright, a popular professor at Georgetown University, since I first met her during the Dukakis campaign. A native of Czechoslovakia and friend of Václav Havel, she was a passionate and articulate advocate of democracy and freedom. I thought she would be an ideal spokesperson for us at the United Nations in the post–Cold War era. Because I also wanted her counsel on national security matters, I elevated the UN ambassador's job to cabinet rank.

The national security advisor decision was difficult for me, because both Tony Lake and Sandy Berger had done a great job educating and advising me on foreign policy throughout the campaign. Tony was a little older and Sandy had worked for him in the Carter State Department, but I had known Sandy longer and better. In the end, the matter was resolved when Sandy came to me and suggested that I appoint Tony national security advisor and make him the deputy.

The CIA job was filled last. I wanted to appoint Congressman Dave McCurdy of Oklahoma, chairman of the House Intelligence Committee, but much to my disappointment, he declined. I had met Jim Woolsey, a longtime figure in the Washington foreign policy establishment, in late 1991 at a national security discussion Sandy Berger organized with a diverse group of Democrats and independents with more robust views on national security and defense than our party typically projected. Woolsey was clearly intelligent and interested in the job. After one interview, I offered it to him.

After the national security announcements, I was close to meeting my self-imposed deadline of appointing the cabinet by Christmas. On Christmas Eve day we made it: in addition to officially announcing Mickey Kantor's appointment, I nominated Congressman Mike Espy of Mississippi to be secretary of agriculture; Federico Peña, the former mayor of Denver, as secretary of transportation; former Arizona governor Bruce Babbitt as secretary of the interior; and Zoë Baird, the general counsel for Aetna Life and Casualty, to be the first female attorney general.

Espy was active in the DLC, understood agricultural issues, and, along with Congressmen Bill Jefferson of New Orleans and John Lewis of Atlanta, was one of the first prominent black leaders outside Arkansas to endorse me. I didn't know Peña well, but he had been a fine mayor and had spearheaded the building of Denver's massive new airport. The airline industry was in trouble and needed a transportation secretary who understood its problems. Bruce Babbitt had been one of my favorite fellow governors. Brilliant, iconoclastic, and witty, he had won election in traditionally Republican Arizona and had succeeded as an activist, progressive governor. I hoped he could pursue our environmental agenda with less fallout in the western states than President Carter had suffered.

Originally, I had hoped to make Vernon Jordan attorney

general. He had been a distinguished civil rights lawyer and was well thought of in corporate America. But Vernon, like James Carville, was determined not to come into government. When he bowed out in early December, during a talk on the back porch of the Governor's Mansion, I considered several people before ultimately choosing Zoë Baird.

I didn't know Zoë until I interviewed her. In addition to her work as Aetna's counsel, she had served in the Carter White House, had been an advocate for the poor, and, though she was only forty, seemed to have an unusually mature understanding of the attorney general's role and the challenges she would face.

Though I would later elevate some other positions to cabinet level, including those of drug czar, director of the Small Business Administration, and director of the Federal Emergency Management Agency, I had made the Christmas deadline with a cabinet of unquestionable competence and unprecedented diversity.

It was a good story, but not the main one of the day. President Bush gave a big Christmas present to some former associates, and potentially to himself, when he pardoned Caspar Weinberger and five others who had been indicted in the Iran-Contra scandal by Independent Counsel Lawrence Walsh. Weinberger's trial was about to get under way, and President Bush was likely to be called as a witness. Walsh angrily denounced the pardons as completing a six-year cover-up, saying it "undermines the principle that no man is above the law. It demonstrates that powerful people with powerful allies can commit serious crimes in high office—deliberately abusing the public trust—without consequence." Since now none of the defendants could be called to testify in court under oath, if there were any more facts to come out, they probably never would. Just two weeks earlier, Walsh had learned that the President and his lawyer, Boyden Gray, had failed for more than a year to hand over Bush's own contemporaneous notes relating to Iran-Contra, despite repeated requests to do so.

I disagreed with the pardons and could have made more

of them but didn't, for three reasons. First, the President's pardon power is absolute under our Constitution. Second, I wanted the country to be more united, not more divided, even if the split would be to my political advantage. Finally, President Bush had given decades of service to our country, and I thought we should allow him to retire in peace, leaving the matter between him and his conscience.

On the day after Christmas, I got a pleasant surprise when it was announced that *Time* magazine would name me "Man of the Year," saying that I had been given the opportunity "to preside over one of the periodic reinventions of the country—those moments when Americans dig out of their deepest problems by reimagining themselves." When asked about the honor, I said I was flattered by it but worried about the troubled world, about getting bogged down because there was so much to do, and about whether the move to Washington would be good for Chelsea. Chelsea would do just fine, but my other concerns proved to be well founded.

Hillary, Chelsea, and I spent New Year's in Hilton Head at Renaissance Weekend, as we had been doing every year for nearly a decade. I loved being with old friends, playing touch football on the beach with kids and a few rounds of golf with a new set of clubs Hillary had given me. I enjoyed attending the discussion panels, where I always learned things from people who talked about everything from science to politics to love. That year, I especially liked one entitled "What I'd Tell the President over a Brown Bag Lunch."

Meanwhile, President Bush was going out in full stride. He visited our troops in Somalia, then called me to say he was headed to Russia to sign a strategic arms limitation treaty, START II, with Boris Yeltsin. I supported the treaty and said I was prepared to push its ratification in the Senate. Bush was also being helpful to me, telling other world leaders he wanted me to "succeed as President" and that they would find me "a good man to work with" on important problems.

On January 5, Hillary and I announced that we would

enroll Chelsea in a private school, Sidwell Friends. Until that time, she had always been in public schools, and there were some good ones in the District of Columbia. After discussing it with Chelsea, we decided on Sidwell primarily because it guaranteed her privacy. She was about to turn thirteen, and Hillary and I wanted to give her the chance to live out her teenage years as normally as possible. She wanted that, too.

On January 6, with only two weeks to go before the inauguration, and the day before my first meeting with my economic team, the Bush administration's OMB director, Richard Darman, announced that the coming year's budget deficit would be even higher than previously estimated. (My staff was convinced Darman had known about the larger deficit earlier and had delayed his bad-news announcement until after the election.) Regardless, now it was going to be much more difficult to juggle the competing priorities: to cut the deficit in half without weakening the fragile economic recovery in the short run; to find the right combination of spending cuts and tax increases necessary to reduce the deficit and increase spending in areas vital to our long-term economic prosperity; and to ensure more tax fairness for middle- and lower-income working people.

The next day, the economic team gathered around the dining-room table in the Governor's Mansion to discuss our dilemma and explore which policy choices would produce the most growth. According to traditional Keynesian economic theory, governments should run deficits in bad economic times and balanced budgets or surpluses in good times. Therefore, the combination of tough spending cuts and tax increases necessary to halve the deficit seemed to be the wrong medicine for the present moment. That's why FDR, after being elected on a promise to balance the budget, abandoned deficit reduction in favor of big spending to put people back to work and stimulate the private economy.

The problem with applying the traditional analysis to current conditions was that under Reagan and Bush, we had built in a large structural deficit that persisted in good times and bad. When President Reagan took office, the national debt was $1 trillion. It tripled during his eight years, thanks to the big tax cuts in 1981 and increases in spending. Under President Bush, the debt continued to increase again, by one-third, in just four years. Now it totaled $4 trillion. Annual interest payments on the debt were the third-largest item in the federal budget after defense and Social Security.

The deficit was the inevitable result of so-called supply-side economics, the theory that the more you cut taxes, the more the economy will grow, with the growth producing more tax revenue at lower rates than previously had been collected at higher ones. Of course it didn't work, and the deficits exploded throughout the recovery of the 1980s. Though supply-side theory was bad arithmetic and lousy economics, the Republicans stayed with it because of their ideological aversion to taxes, and because, in the short run, supply-side was good politics. "Spend more, tax less" sounded good and felt good, but it had put our country in a deep hole and left a cloud over our children's future.

Coupled with our large trade deficit, the budget deficit required us to import tremendous amounts of capital every year to finance our overspending. To attract that kind of money and avoid a precipitous drop in the value of the dollar, we had to keep interest rates far higher than they should have been during the economic downturn that preceded my election. Those high interest rates inhibited economic growth and amounted to a huge indirect tax on middle-class Americans who paid more for home mortgages, car payments, and all other purchases financed through borrowing.

After we sat down to work, Bob Rubin, who was running the meeting, called on Leon Panetta first. Leon said the deficit had gotten worse because tax revenues were down in the sluggish economy, while spending was up, as more people qualified for government assistance and health-care costs soared. Laura Tyson said that if current conditions continued, the economy would probably grow at a rate of 2.5 to 3 percent over the next years, not enough to lower unemployment much or to ensure a sustained recovery. Then we got down to the meat of the coconut, as Alan Blinder, another of my economic advisors, was asked to

analyze whether a strong deficit-reduction package would
spur growth and new jobs by bringing down interest rates,
since the government wouldn't provide as much competition with the private sector in borrowing money. Blinder
said that would happen, but that the positive effects would
be offset for a couple of years by the negative economic
impact of less government spending or higher taxes, unless
the Federal Reserve and the bond market responded to our
plan by lowering interest rates substantially. Blinder
thought that after so many false promises on deficit reduction over the last few years, a strong positive response by
the bond market was unlikely. Larry Summers disagreed,
saying that a good plan would convince the market to lower
rates because there was no threat of inflation as the economy recovered. He cited the experience of some Asian countries to support his view.

This was the first of many exchanges we would have
about the power over the lives of ordinary Americans exercised by thirty-year-old bond traders. Often my loud complaints about this, and Bob Rubin's retorts to them, were
funny, but the issue was dead serious. With national unemployment stuck at above 7 percent, we had to do something.
Tyson and Blinder seemed to be saying that, for the long-
term health of the economy, we had to cut the deficit, but
that doing so would slow down growth in the short term.
Bentsen, Altman, Summers, and Panetta bought the bond-
market argument and believed deficit reduction would
accelerate economic growth. Rubin was just running the
meeting, but I knew he agreed with them. So did Al Gore.

Bob Reich missed the meeting but sent me a memo the
next day, arguing that while the debt was a higher percentage of the gross domestic product than it should be, investment in education, training, and non-defense research and
development were all at a much lower percentage of GDP
than in the pre-Reagan years, and underinvestment was
hurting the economy as much as the big deficits. He said the
goal should not be to cut the deficit in half but to return it,
and investments, to the percentage of GDP they had been
before the Reagan-Bush years. He argued that the invest-

ments would increase productivity, growth, and employment, enabling us to reduce the deficit, but if we went for deficit reduction only, a stagnant economy with anemic revenues couldn't cut it in half anyway. I think Gene Sperling pretty much agreed with Reich.

While I was mulling it all over, we moved on to a discussion about how to achieve the deficit reduction we needed. In my campaign plan, *Putting People First*, I had proposed more than $140 billion in budget cuts. With the deficit numbers higher, we would have to cut more to reach my goal of halving the deficit in four years. That led to the first of many discussions of what should be cut. For example, you could save a lot by reducing the cost-of-living allowances, called COLAs, on Social Security, but as Hillary pointed out, almost half of all Americans over sixty-five relied on Social Security to live above the poverty line; the COLA cut would hurt them. We didn't have to make final decisions, and couldn't without discussing it with congressional leaders, but it was obvious that, whatever we ultimately decided, it wouldn't be easy.

In the campaign, in addition to the budget cuts, I had also proposed raising a comparable amount in new revenues, all from wealthy individuals and corporations. Now, to cut the deficit in half we would have to raise more revenues, too. And we would almost certainly have to scrap the broad-based middle-class tax cut, though I was still determined to cut taxes for working families earning about $30,000 a year or less by doubling the Earned Income Tax Credit. Those people's incomes had been losing ground for twenty years, and they needed the help; moreover, we had to make lower-income jobs more attractive than public assistance if we were to be successful in moving people from welfare to work. Lloyd Bentsen went over the list of possible tax increases, saying that any tax would be hard to pass and the most important thing was to prevail. If our plan failed in Congress, it could endanger my presidency. Bentsen said we should present a number of options to Congress, so that if I failed to pass one or two, I could still claim success and avoid being crippled politically.

After the tax presentation, Roger Altman and Larry Summers argued for a short-term stimulus package to go with the deficit-reduction plan. They recommended about $20 billion of spending and business-tax reductions that at best would give the economy a boost, and at the least would prevent it from sliding back into a recession, which they thought was about a 20 percent possibility. Then Gene Sperling made a presentation of options for new investments, arguing for the most expensive one, about $90 billion, which would meet all my campaign commitments immediately.

After the presentations, I decided the deficit hawks were right. If we didn't get the deficit down substantially, interest rates would remain high, preventing a sustained, strong economic recovery. Al Gore strongly agreed. But, as we discussed how much deficit reduction we needed, I was concerned about the short-term drag that Laura Tyson and Alan Blinder predicted—and Roger Altman and Gene Sperling feared—might occur. After nearly six hours, we were headed in the deficit-reduction direction. Clearly, economic policy making, at least in this environment, was not science, and if it was art, it had to be beautiful in the eyes of the beholders in the bond market.

A week later, we held a second meeting in which I abandoned the middle-class tax cuts; agreed to look at savings in Social Security, Medicare, and Medicaid; and supported Al Gore's suggestion of a broad-based energy tax, called a BTU tax, on the heat content of energy at the wholesale level. Al said that while the BTU tax would be controversial in states that produced coal, oil, and natural gas, it would fall on all sectors of the economy, lessening the burden on ordinary consumers, and would promote energy conservation, something we badly needed more of.

For several hours more, we again debated how much deficit reduction we had to try for, beginning five years out and working back to the present. Gore took a hard line, saying if we went for the biggest possible reduction, we'd get credit for courage and create a new reality, making it possible to do previously unthinkable things, like requiring Social Security beneficiaries above a certain income level to pay income tax on their benefits. Rivlin agreed with him. Blinder said it might work if the Fed and the bond market believed us. Tyson and Altman were skeptical about avoiding short-term economic contractions. Sperling and Reich, who was present at this meeting, held out for more investments.

So did Stan Greenberg, Mandy Grunwald, and Paul Begala, who weren't part of the meetings and were afraid I was sacrificing everything I believed in under the influence of people who weren't part of our campaign and didn't care about the ordinary Americans who had elected me. In late November, Stan had sent me a memo saying my honeymoon with voters would be short-lived unless I moved quickly to address the problem of jobs and declining incomes. Sixty percent of those who said their finances had worsened in 1992, about a third of the electorate, had voted for me. He thought I could lose them with this plan. George Stephanopoulos, who sat in on the meetings, had to try to explain to Stan and his allies that the deficit was killing the economy, and that if we didn't fix it, there would be no economic recovery and no tax revenues to spend on education, middle-class tax cuts, or anything else. Bentsen and Panetta wanted as much deficit reduction as we could pass in Congress, an amount less than Gore and Rivlin advocated, but still a lot. Rubin, as moderator, was again keeping his own counsel, but I sensed he was with Bentsen and Panetta. After hearing everyone out, so was I.

At some point, I asked Bentsen how much we'd have to reduce the deficit to rally the bond market. He said about $140 billion in the fifth year, with a five-year total of $500 billion. I decided to go with the $500 billion figure, but even with new spending cuts and revenue increases, we still might not be able to meet the target of cutting the deficit in half by the end of my first term. It all depended on the rate of growth.

Because of the possibility that our strategy would produce a short-term slowdown, we searched for ways to promote more growth. I met with executives of the Big Three automakers and Owen Bieber, president of the United Auto Workers, who said that while Japanese cars had almost 30 percent of the American market, Japan was still largely closed to American cars and auto-parts suppliers. I asked Mickey Kantor to find a way to open the Japanese market more. Representatives of the fast-growing biotechnology industry told me that our research-and-development tax credit should be extended and made refundable for young firms, which often didn't make enough money to claim the full credit under current law. They also wanted stronger protection for their patents against unfair competition, and modifications in and acceleration of the product-approval process of the Food and Drug Administration. I told the team to analyze their proposals and make a recommendation. Finally, I authorized the development of the $20 billion one-shot stimulus proposal to increase economic activity in the short run.

I hated to give up the middle-class tax cut, but with the deficit numbers worse, there was no choice. If our strategy worked, the middle class would see direct benefits worth far more than a tax cut—in the form of lower home mortgages and lower interest rates on things like car payments, credit card purchases, and student loans. We also wouldn't be able to increase spending as much as I had proposed in the campaign, at least at first. But if deficit reduction brought interest rates down and growth up, tax revenues would increase, and I could still meet my investment objectives over four years. That was a big "if."

There was also another big "if." The strategy would work only if Congress adopted it. After Bush's defeat, the Republicans were more anti-tax than ever, so few, if any, of them would vote for any plan I put up with new taxes in it. A lot of Democrats who came from conservative districts would also be wary of tax votes, and liberal Democrats from safe seats might not support the budget if the cuts were too steep in programs they believed in.

After a campaign during which the economic problems of America were center stage, in a time when growth was lagging all over the world, I would begin my presidency with an economic strategy for which there was no precedent. It could bring enormous benefits if I could convince

Congress to pass the budget, and if it got the hoped-for response from the Federal Reserve and the bond market. There were compelling arguments for it, but the most important domestic decision of my presidency was still one big gamble.

While most of the transition was occupied by the cabinet and other appointments and the development of our economic program, a number of other things were going on. On January 5, I held a meeting leading to the announcement that I would temporarily continue President Bush's policy of intercepting and returning Haitians who were trying to reach the United States by boat, a policy I had strongly criticized during the election. After Haiti's elected president, Jean-Bertrand Aristide, was overthrown by Lieutenant General Raoul Cedras and his allies in 1991, Haitian sympathizers of Aristide had begun to flee the island. When the Bush administration, which appeared to be more sympathetic to Cedras than I was, began to return the refugees, there were loud protests from the human rights community. I wanted to make it easier for Haitians to seek and obtain political asylum in the United States, but was concerned that large numbers of them would perish in trying to get here in rickety boats on the high seas, as about four hundred had done just a week earlier. So, on the advice of our security team, I said that, instead of taking in all the Haitians who could survive the voyage to America, we would beef up our official presence in Haiti and speed up asylum claims there. In the meantime, for safety reasons, we would continue to stop the boats and return the passengers. Ironically, while human rights groups criticized the announcement, and the press characterized it as going back on my campaign pledge, President Aristide supported my position. He knew we would bring more Haitians to the United States than the Bush administration had, and he didn't want his people to drown.

On January 8, I flew to Austin, Texas, where I had lived and worked for McGovern more than twenty years earlier. After a reunion lunch with old friends from those days at Scholtz's Beer Garden, I held my first meeting since the election with a foreign leader, Mexico's president, Carlos Salinas de Gortari. Salinas was deeply committed to the North American Free Trade Agreement (NAFTA), which he had negotiated with President Bush. We were hosted by my longtime friend Governor Ann Richards, who was also a big supporter of NAFTA. I wanted to meet with Salinas early to make it clear that I cared about Mexico's prosperity and stability, and to make my case to him for the importance of labor and environmental side agreements to strengthen the treaty, and for greater cooperation against narco-trafficking.

On the thirteenth, my nominee for attorney general, Zoë Baird, got into hot water when it came out that she had employed two illegal immigrants as household help and had paid the employer's portion of Social Security taxes on them only recently, when she came into consideration for the Justice post. The employment of illegal immigrants was not that uncommon then, but it was a particular problem for Zoë, because the attorney general oversees the Immigration and Naturalization Service. With Zoë's early confirmation unlikely, the incumbent assistant attorney general for the civil division, Stuart Gerson, would serve as acting attorney general. We also sent Webb Hubbell, the associate attorney general–designate, over to the Justice Department to look after things.

Over the next two days, we announced several more White House staff appointments. Besides George Stephanopoulos as communications director, I named Dee Dee Myers the first female White House press secretary; put Eli Segal in charge of creating the new national service program; and made Rahm Emanuel the director of political affairs, and Alexis Herman director of public liaison. I was bringing several people up from Arkansas: Bruce Lindsey would handle personnel, including appointments to boards and commissions; Carol Rasco would be my assistant for domestic policy; Nancy Hernreich, my scheduler in the governor's office, would oversee Oval Office operations, with an office just outside mine; David Watkins would oversee the administrative functions of the White House; Ann McCoy, the

Governor's Mansion administrator, came to work in the White House; and my lifelong friend Vince Foster agreed to come to the counsel's office.

Among those who didn't come out of the campaign were my choice for White House counsel, Bernie Nussbaum, Hillary's colleague on the 1974 Nixon impeachment inquiry staff; Ira Magaziner, my Oxford classmate, who would work with us on health-care reform; Howard Paster, an experienced Washington lobbyist, who would manage our congressional relations; John Podesta, an old friend from the Duffey campaign, as staff secretary; Katie McGinty, Al Gore's choice for our environmental policy person; and Betty Currie, Warren Christopher's secretary in the transition, who would do the same job for me. Andrew Friendly, a young Washington, D.C., native would be the President's aide, going with me to every appointment and on every trip, making sure I read my briefing paper, and keeping in touch with the White House when we were away. Al had his own staff, with fellow Tennessean Roy Neel as chief of staff. So did Hillary, whose chief of staff, Maggie Williams, was an old friend of hers.

I also stated my support for David Wilhelm, my campaign manager, to succeed Ron Brown as chairman of the Democratic Committee. David was young and didn't have Ron Brown's public presence, but almost no one did. His strength was grassroots organizing, and our party badly needed revitalization at the state and local levels. Now that we had the White House, I figured Al Gore and I would have to shoulder the lion's share of the fund-raising and public pronouncements anyway.

Besides the appointments, I issued a statement strongly supporting the military action President Bush had taken in Iraq and, for the first time, said I would press for the trial of Serbian president Slobodan Milosevic for war crimes. It would take too long for that to happen.

During this period, I also hosted a lunch for evangelical ministers at the Governor's Mansion. My pastor, Rex Horne, suggested that I do it, and put together the invitation list. Rex thought it would be helpful to have an informal discussion with them so that at least I'd have some lines of communication into the evangelical community. About ten ministers came, including nationally known figures like Charles Swindoll, Adrian Rogers, and Max Lucado. We also invited Hillary's minister at Little Rock's First United Methodist Church, Ed Matthews, a wonderful man who we knew would stick with us if the lunch deteriorated into a war of words. I was especially impressed by the young, articulate pastor of Willow Creek Community Church near Chicago, Bill Hybels. He had built his church from scratch into one of the largest single congregations in America. Like the others, he disagreed with me on abortion and gay rights, but he was interested in other issues, too, and in what kind of leadership it would take to end the gridlock and reduce the partisan bitterness in Washington. For eight years, Bill Hybels came to see me on a regular basis, to pray with me, counsel me, and check on what he called my "spiritual health." We argued from time to time. Sometimes we even agreed. But always he would be a blessing to me.

At the beginning of my last week in Arkansas, with moving vans in the driveway, I gave a farewell interview to Arkansas reporters, confessing to mixed emotions of pride and regret at leaving home: "I've been happy and proud and sad almost on the point of tears a couple of times. . . . I love my life here." One of my final tasks before leaving for Washington was personal. Chelsea had a pet frog she had initially gotten for a school science project. While we were taking our cat, Socks, with us, Chelsea decided she wanted to free the frog so that it could lead a "normal life." She asked me to do it, so on my last day in Arkansas, I jogged down to the Arkansas River, took the shoebox the frog was in, climbed down a steep bank to the water, and let the frog go. At least one of us was returning to normal life.

The rest of us were excited about our new adventure, but apprehensive, too. Chelsea hated to leave her friends and the world she knew, but we told her she could have her pals come to stay with us often. Hillary was wondering how she'd feel without the independence of a paying job, but she was eager to be a full-time First Lady, both to pursue the policy work she loved and to perform the traditional duties of the office. She had surprised me with the amount of time she had already spent studying the history of the White House, the various functions she would be responsible for there, and the important contributions of her predecessors. Whenever Hillary undertook a new challenge, she was always on edge at first, but once she got the hang of it, she relaxed and enjoyed herself. I couldn't blame her for being a little nervous. I was too.

The transition period had been hectic and hard. In retrospect, we did a good job picking a cabinet and sub-cabinet officials who were able and who reflected the diversity of America, but I made a mistake in not appointing a prominent Republican to a cabinet post as a demonstration of my desire to build bipartisan cooperation. I also kept my commitment to put the economy first, with a first-rate team, the economic summit, and a decision-making process that was well informed and subject to thorough debate. And as I had pledged, Al Gore was a full partner in the incoming administration, involved in all the strategy meetings and the cabinet and White House staff selections, while maintaining a high public profile.

During and after the transition, I was criticized for not following through on my campaign commitments to cut middle-class taxes, halve the deficit in four years, and take in the Haitian boat people. With respect to the first two issues, when I replied that I was simply responding to the worse-than-expected deficit projections, some critics said I had to know the Bush administration was lowballing the deficit until after the election, and therefore I shouldn't have used official government figures in putting together my economic plan. I didn't take those criticisms too seriously. By contrast, I thought some of the criticism on the Haitian issue was justified, given the unqualified statements I had made during the campaign. Still, I was determined to bring more asylum seekers to the United States safely, and eventually to restore President Aristide. If I succeeded, my commitment would be fulfilled.

I was also being criticized for appointing Zoë Baird, for my tendency to want to know everything that was going on, and for taking too much time in making decisions. There was some merit to the hits. Zoë hadn't concealed the nanny issue; we had simply underestimated its significance. As for my management style, I knew I had a lot to learn, and I had used the transition to absorb as much about as many aspects of the President's job as I could. For example, I don't regret a minute of the time I spent coming to grips with the economy during the transition. It stood me in good stead for the next eight years. On the other hand, I had always had a tendency to try to do too much, which also contributed to physical exhaustion, irritability, and my well-deserved reputation for tardiness.

I knew that the transition was only a foretaste of what the presidency would be like: everything happening at once. I would have to delegate more and have a better-organized decision-making process than I had as governor. However, the fact that so many sub-cabinet positions had not been finalized had more to do with the fact that the Democrats had been out of power for twelve years. We had to replace a lot of people, we were committed to casting a wide net for diversity, and there were a great number of people with a claim to be considered. Moreover, the required vetting process had gotten so complicated that it took too much time, as federal investigators pored over every piece of paper and ran down every petty rumor to find people who were bulletproof in the face of political and press assaults.

Looking back, I think the major shortcomings of the transition were two: I spent so much time on the cabinet that I hardly spent any time on the White House staff, and I gave almost no thought to how to keep the public's focus on my most important priorities, rather than on competing stories that, at the least, would divert public attention from the big issues and, at worst, could make it appear that I was neglecting those priorities.

The real problem with the staff was that most of them came out of the campaign or Arkansas, and had no experience in working in the White House or dealing with

Washington's political culture. My young staffers were talented, honest, and dedicated, and I felt I owed many of them the chance to serve the country by working in the White House. In time, they would get their sea legs and do very well. But in the critical early months, both the staff and I would do a lot of on-the-job learning, and some of the lessons would prove to be quite costly.

We also didn't give messaging anything close to the amount of attention that we had in the election, though it's harder in government, even for the President, to get out the message you want every day. As I said, everything happens at once, and any controversy is more likely to dominate the news than a policy decision, no matter how important the decision might be. That's what happened with the Zoë Baird and gays-in-the-military controversies. Though they took up only a small part of my time, people watching the evening news could be forgiven for thinking I spent my time on nothing else. If we had thought more about this challenge and worked harder on it during the transition, I'm sure we would have handled it better.

Despite the problems, I believed our transition had gone reasonably well. So, apparently, did the American people. Before I left for Washington, an NBC News/*Wall Street Journal* poll gave me a 60 percent favorability rating, up from just 32 percent in May. Hillary was doing even better; 66 percent saw her as "a positive role model for American women," up from 39 percent in the earlier survey. Another poll taken by a bipartisan organization said that 84 percent of the people approved of my performance since the election. President Bush's job approval was up, too, nearly twenty points, to 59 percent. Our fellow citizens had regained their optimism about America, and they were giving me a chance to succeed.

On January 16, when Hillary, Chelsea, and I said goodbye to the friends who came to the Little Rock airport to see us off, I thought of Abraham Lincoln's moving farewell remarks to the people of Springfield, Illinois, as he left the train station on his journey to the White House: "My friends—No one, not in my situation, can appreciate my feeling of sadness at this parting. To this place, and the kindness of these people, I owe everything. . . . Trusting in [God], who can go with me, and remain with you and be everywhere for good, let us confidently hope that all will yet be well." I didn't say it as well as Lincoln, but I did my best to convey that message to my fellow Arkansans. Without them, I wouldn't have been getting on that airplane.

We were flying to Virginia, where we would begin the inaugural events at Monticello, Thomas Jefferson's home. On the flight, I thought about the historical significance of my election and the momentous challenges ahead. The election represented a generational shift in America, from the World War II veterans to the baby boomers, who were alternately derided as spoiled and self-absorbed, and lauded as idealistic and committed to the common good. Whether liberal or conservative, our politics were forged by Vietnam, civil rights, and the tumult of 1968, with its protests, riots, and assassinations. We were also the first generation to feel the full force of the women's movement, the impact of which people were about to observe in the White House. Hillary would be the most professionally accomplished First Lady in history. Now that she had resigned from her law practice and her boards, my income would be the sole support of our family for the first time since we married, and she would be free to use her enormous talent as a full-time partner in our work. I thought she could have a more positive impact than any First Lady since Eleanor Roosevelt. Of course, such activism would make her more controversial with those who thought First Ladies should stay above the fray, or who disagreed with us politically, but that, too, was part of what our generational change meant.

Clearly, we represented a changing of the guard, but could we meet the tests of these tumultuous times? Could we restore the economy, social progress, and the legitimacy of government? Could we blunt the rise of religious, racial, and ethnic strife across the globe? In the words of the *Time* magazine citation in its "Man of the Year" edition, could we lead Americans to "dig out of their deepest problems by reimagining themselves"? Despite our victory in the Cold War and the rise of democracy around the world, powerful forces were dividing people and tearing at the fragile fabric of communities, both at home and abroad. In the face of these challenges, the American people had taken a chance on me.

About three weeks after the election, I had received a remarkable letter from Robert McNamara, who, as secretary of defense under Presidents Kennedy and Johnson, had prosecuted the Vietnam War. He had been moved to write me by a news story he read about my friendship with my Oxford roommate Frank Aller, who had resisted the draft and had killed himself in 1971. This is what he said:

> For me—and I believe for the nation as well—the Vietnam war finally ended the day you were elected president. By their votes, the American people, at long last, recognized that the Allers and the Clintons, when they questioned the wisdom and morality of their government's decisions relating to Vietnam, were no less patriotic than those who served in uniform. The anguish with which you and your friends debated our actions in 1969 was painful for you then and, I am sure, the resurrection of the issues during the campaign reopened old wounds. But the dignity with which you met the attacks, and your refusal to draw back from the belief that it is the responsibility of all citizens to question the basis for any decision to send our youth to war, has strengthened the nation for all time.

I was moved by McNamara's letter, and by similar ones I received from Vietnam veterans. Just before the election, Bob Higgins, an ex-marine from Hillsboro, Ohio, sent me his Vietnam service medal because of my stand against the war and "the way you have conducted yourself in the bitter campaign." A few months earlier, Ronald Murphy of Las Vegas had given me his Purple Heart, and Charles Hampton from Marmaduke, Arkansas, had sent me the Bronze Star he earned for valor in Vietnam. All told, in 1992, Vietnam veterans sent me five Purple Hearts, three Vietnam service medals, a combat infantry badge, and my fellow Arkansan's Bronze Star. I framed most of them and hung them in my private hall off the Oval Office.

As my plane headed down into the beautiful Virginia landscape, which gave birth to four of our first five Presidents, I was thinking of those veterans and their medals, hoping that at last we could heal the wounds of the 1960s, and praying that I would prove worthy of their sacrifices, their support, and their dreams.

ACKNOWLEDGMENTS

I AM PARTICULARLY indebted to the many people without whom this book could not have been written. Justin Cooper gave up more than two years of his young life to work with me every day and, on many occasions in the last six months, all night. He organized and retrieved mountains of materials, did further research, corrected many errors, and typed the manuscript over and over from my illegible scrawling in more than twenty large notebooks. Many of the sections were rewritten a half dozen times or more. He never lost his patience, his energy never flagged, and by the time we got to the last lap, he sometimes seemed to know me and what I wanted to say better than I did. Though he is not responsible for its errors, this book is a testament to his gifts and efforts.

Before we began to work together, I was told that my editor, Robert Gottlieb, was the best there was at his craft. He turned out to be that and more. I only wish I'd met him thirty years earlier. Bob taught me about magic moments and hard cuts. Without his judgment and feel, this book might have been twice as long and half as good. He read my story as a person who was interested in but not obsessed with politics. He kept pulling me back to the human side of my life. And he convinced me to take out countless names of people who helped me along the way, because the general reader couldn't keep up with them all. If you're one of them, I hope you'll forgive him, and me.

A book this long and full requires a mammoth amount of fact checking. This lion's share of work was done by Meg Thompson, a brilliant young woman who carefully waded through the minutiae of my life for a year or so; then for the last few months she was assisted by Caitlin Klevorick and other young volunteers. They now have many examples of the fact that my memory is far from perfect. If any factual errors remain, it is not for lack of effort to correct them on their part.

I can't thank the people at Knopf enough, beginning with Sonny Mehta, the president and editor-in-chief. He believed in the project from the beginning and did his part to keep it going, including giving me an amazed look wherever and whenever I ran in to him over the last two years; a look that said something like, "Are you really going to finish on time?", and "Why are you here instead of at home writing?" Sonny's look always had the desired effect.

I also owe thanks to the many people at Knopf who helped. I am grateful that the editorial/production team at Knopf is as obsessed with accuracy and detail as I am (even with a book on a slightly accelerated pace as mine was) and especially appreciate the tireless efforts and meticulous work of managing editor Katherine Hourigan; noble director of manufacturing Andy Hughes; indefatigable production editor Maria Massey; copy chief Lydia Buechler, copy editor Charlotte Gross, and proofreaders Steve Messina, Jenna Dolan, Ellen Feldman, Rita Madrigal, and Liz Polizzi; design director Peter Andersen; jacket art director Carol Carson; the ever-helpful Diana Tejerina and Eric Bliss; and Lee Pentea.

In addition, I want to thank the many other people at Knopf who have helped me: Tony Chirico, for his valued guidance; Jim Johnston, Justine LeCates, and Anne Diaz; Carol Janeway and Suzanne Smith; Jon Fine; and the promotion/marketing talents of Pat Johnson, Paul Bogaards, Nina Bourne, Nicholas Latimer, Joy Dallanegra-Sanger, Amanda Kauff, Anne-Lise Spitzer, and Sarah Robinson. And thanks to the staffs at North Market Street Graphics, Coral Graphics, and Offset Paperback Manufacturers.

And my thanks to the folks at Vintage: Anne Messitte, Russell Perreault, Roz Parr, Stephen McNabb, Barbara Richard, Nicole Pedersen, Marla Jea, Daniel Gillespie, John Gall, Chris Zucker, and Quinn O'Neill.

Robert Barnett, a fine lawyer and longtime friend, negotiated the contract with Knopf; he and his partner Michael O'Connor worked throughout the project as foreign publishers joined in. I am very grateful to them. I appreciate the careful technical and legal review that David Kendall and Beth Nolan gave the manuscript.

When I was in the White House, beginning in late 1993, I met with my old friend Taylor Branch about once a month to do an oral history. Those contemporaneous conversations helped in recalling particular moments of the presidency. After I left the White House, Ted Widmer, a fine historian who worked in the White House as a speechwriter, did an oral history of my life before the presidency that helped me bring back and organize old memories. Janis Kearney, the White House diarist, left me with voluminous notes that enabled me to reconstruct day-to-day events.

The photographs were selected with the help of Vincent Virga, who found many that captured special moments discussed in the book, and Carolyn Huber, who was with our family throughout our years in the Governor's Mansion and the White House. While I was President, Carolyn also organized all my private papers and letters from the time I was a little boy to 1974, an arduous task without which much of the first part of the book could not have been written.

I am deeply indebted to those who read all or part of the book and made helpful suggestions for additions, subtractions, reorganization, context, and interpretation, including Hillary, Chelsea, Dorothy Rodham, Doug Band, Sandy Berger, Tommy Caplan, Mary DeRosa, Nancy Hernreich, Dick Holbrooke, David Kendall, Jim Kennedy, Ian Klaus, Bruce Lindsey, Ira Magaziner, Cheryl Mills, Beth Nolan, John Podesta, Bruce Reed, Steve Ricchetti, Bob Rubin, Ruby Shamir, Brooke Shearer, Gene Sperling, Strobe Talbott, Mark Weiner, Maggie Williams, and my friends Brian and Myra Greenspun, who were with me when the first page was written.

Many of my friends and colleagues took time to do impromptu oral histories with me including Huma Abedin, Madeleine Albright, Dave Barram, Woody Bassett, Paul Begala, Paul Berry, Jim Blair, Sidney Blumenthal, Erskine Bowles, Ron Burkle, Tom Campbell, James Carville, Roger Clinton, Patty Criner, Denise Dangremond, Lynda Dixon, Rahm Emanuel, Al From, Mark Gearan, Ann Henry, Denise Hyland, Harold Ickes, Roger Johnson, Vernon Jordan, Mickey Kantor, Dick Kelley, Tony Lake, David Leopoulos, Capricia Marshall, Mack McLarty, Rudy Moore, Bob Nash, Kevin O'Keefe, Leon Panetta, Betsey Reader, Dick Riley, Bobby Roberts, Hugh Rodham, Tony Rodham, Dennis Ross, Martha Saxton, Eli Segal, Terry Schumaker, Marsha Scott, Michael Sheehan, Nancy Soderberg, Doug Sosnik, Rodney Slater, Craig Smith, Gayle Smith, Steve Smith, Carolyn Staley, Stephanie Street, Larry Summers, Martha Whetstone, Delta Willis, Carol Willis, and several of my readers. I'm sure there are others I've forgotten; if so, I'm sorry and I appreciate their help as well.

My research was also helped greatly by many books written by members of the administration and others, and of course by the memoirs of Hillary and my mother.

David Alsobrook and the staff of the Clinton Presidential Materials Project were patient and persistent in recovering materials. I want to thank them all: Deborah Bush, Susan Collins, Gary Foulk, John Keller, Jimmie Purvis, Emily Robison, Rob Seibert, Dana Simmons, Richard Stalcup, Rhonda Wilson. And Arkansas historian David Ware. The archivists and historians at Georgetown and Oxford were also helpful.

While I was absorbed in writing for much of the last two and a half years, especially the last six months, the work of my foundation continued as we built the library and pursued our missions: fighting AIDS in Africa and the Caribbean and providing low cost drugs and testing around the world; increasing economic opportunity in poor communities in the United States, India, and Africa; promoting education and citizen service among young people at home and abroad; and advocating religious, racial, and ethnic reconciliation across the world. I want to thank those whose donations have made possible my foundation work, and the construction of the Presidential Library and the Clinton School of Public Service at the University of Arkansas. I am deeply indebted to Maggie Williams, my chief of staff, for all she did to keep things moving and for her help on the book. I want to thank members of my foundation and office staff for all they did to continue the work of the foundation and its programs while I was writing the book. A special word of thanks goes to Doug Band, my counselor, who helped me from the day I left the White House to build my new life and who struggled to protect my book-writing time on our travels across America and the world.

I also owe a debt to Oscar Flores, who keeps things going at my home in Chappaqua. On the many nights when Justin Cooper and I worked into the wee hours, Oscar went out of his way to make sure we remembered to have dinner and that we were well supplied with coffee.

Finally, I cannot list all the people who made the life chronicled in these pages possible—all the teachers and mentors of my youth; the people who worked on and contributed to all my campaigns; those who worked with me in the Democratic Leadership Council, National Governors Association, and all the other organizations that contributed to my education in public policy; those who worked with me for peace, security, and reconciliation around the world; those who made the White House run and my trips work; the thousands of gifted people who worked in my adminstrations as attorney general, governor, and President without whose dedicated service I would have little to say about my years in public life; those who provided security to me and my family; and my friends of a lifetime. None of them are responsible for the failures of my life, but for whatever good has come out of it they deserve much of the credit.

INDEX

The names of people who appear in the photograph insert are followed by *.

Aaron, Hank, 582
Abedin, Huma, 623
Abernathy, Ralph, 171
abortion issue, 302–4, 330, 418–19, 466, 537, 547, 565
Abrams, Creighton, 173
Acheson, Dean, 156
Adams, Eddie, 155
Adkins, Homer, 129
affirmative action, 270, 304
AFL-CIO, 289, 296, 470, 536
Agnew, Spiro, 171, 178, 185, 233
Aguilar, Luis, 105
AIDS/HIV, 416–17, 526, 539, 568
Aiken, George, 127
Alamo, Susan and Tony, 306–7
Albee, Edward, 194
Albright, Madeleine, 454, 504
    as UN ambassador, 600
Aldrin, Buzz, 205
Alexander, Kern, 345–6, 405
Alexander, Lamar, 420, 429
Alexis, Anik, 203, 221–2, 224
Alford, Dale, 108–9, 115
Alfred the Great, 184
Allen, Bill, 110
Allen, Charles, 536
Aller, Frank, *, 190, 193, 195, 211, 213–14, 228, 236, 237–8, 247–8, 619
Aller, Ulrich, 105
All-State Band, 72, 85
Alsdorf, Bob, 248
Altman, Roger, 595, 606–9
American Bar Association, 323
American Legion Boys State program, 23, 34, 68, 77–81, 84, 86, 88, 142
Anderson, Marian, 141
Anthony, Beryl, 412, 487
anti-Semitism, protective covenants and, 96
anti-war movement, 142–4, 198, 210, 215, 238
    1968 election and, 155, 156, 161–2
apartheid, 157, 469, 550
Apollo 11, 205
ARIAS (Alliance for Rebirth of an Independent American Spirit), 505
Aristide, Jean-Bertrand, 222, 611, 615
Arkansas:
    Democratic Party in, 341, 458, 539
    energy issues in, 322–3
    environmental issues in, 285–6, 545
    health care in, 296, 341, 458
    welfare reform in, 429

Arkansas, University of, 51–2, 87, 128, 204, 269, 409, 511
    BC on faculty of, 262–3, 267
Arkansas Advocates for Children and Families, 356
Arkansas attorney general election of 1976, 12–13, 376, 557
    BC's decision to run in, 311, 314
    black vote in, 315
    Bumpers's advice in, 316
    Moral Majority and, 316
    results of, 317–18
Arkansas attorney general's office, 321–40
    BC's accomplishments in, 340
    child-care centers issue and, 330–1
    gay rights and, 324–5
    Grand Gulf case and, 322
    Orange Bowl case and, 333–5
    Siamese twins case and, 327
Arkansas Baptist Convention, 68
Arkansas Business Council, 445
Arkansas Children's Hospital, 327, 351
Arkansas congressional election of 1974, 5, 41–2, 276–301
    BC's decision to run in, 277–8
    BC's first campaign trip in, 281–2
    BC's political proposals in, 296
    BC's speeches in, 289, 294–5
    black vote in, 280, 297
    chewing tobacco test in, 284
    Faubus interview in, 278–9
    finances in, 287, 300–1
    opponents in, 288
    organized labor and, 280, 296, 299
    primary in, 290
    results of, 290, 300, 304
    runoff in, 290
Arkansas congressional elections:
    of 1942, 129
    of 1958, 108–9
    of 1978, 113, 339, 376
Arkansas Democrat, 453, 494
Arkansas Democrat-Gazette, 494
Arkansas Democratic Convention of 1972, 251–2
Arkansas Education Association (AEA), 289, 346, 393, 408–9, 410–11, 419, 425, 472
Arkansas Energy Department, 350, 352–3, 379
Arkansas Energy Office, 352
Arkansas Gazette, 292, 297, 337, 350, 354, 380, 427, 430, 439, 460, 477, 494, 560

Arkansas gubernatorial election of 1978, 218, 332–40, 349, 376
  BC's decision to run in, 333, 335
  McClellan's encouragement in, 336–7
  results of, 339–40
Arkansas gubernatorial election of 1980, 217, 257, 330, 460
  BC's defeat in, 371–7
  car-tags issue in, 347–9, 363, 368–9, 371, 374–5, 376, 379, 382, 388, 395
  Cuban refugee crisis in, 360–7, 371–2, 374
  negative TV ads in, 371
  Panama Canal "give-away" in, 367, 372
Arkansas gubernatorial election of 1982, 257, 343, 387–400, 424
  BC's decision to run in, 382–5
  black vote in, 393, 396, 399
  candidates in, 389–90
  car-tags issue and, 395
  issues in, summarized, 388
  official announcement in, 388
  primary in, 395
  results of, 399
  runoff in, 396
  strategy of, 391–2
  TV-ad war in, 388, 390–2, 395–6
Arkansas gubernatorial election of 1990, 458, 467, 474, 483, 487, 506
  BC's decision to run in, 468–9
  candidates in, 467
  education issue in, 471–2
  primary in, 470–1
  results of, 474
  strategy of, 469–70
  union endorsement in, 470
Arkansas gubernatorial elections:
  of 1964, 107–9
  of 1966, 108–17, 123, 126, 192
  of 1970, 234
  of 1974, 113, 274, 283
  of 1984, 411, 414, 417
  of 1986, 424–8, 522
Arkansas Housing Development Agency, 404
Arkansas Industrial Development Commission (AIDC), 108, 355, 368, 379
Arkansas Law School, 207
Arkansas–Louisiana Gas Company, 78, 467
Arkansas Medical Society, 351
Arkansas Power and Light Company, 322, 352–4, 381, 388, 404
Arkansas Razorbacks, 49, 215–17, 271, 274, 333–5
Arkansas Science and Technology Authority, 404
Arkansas senatorial elections:
  of 1944, 129
  of 1968, 163–9, 187, 200
  of 1970, 184–5, 595
Arkansas State Press, 47
Arkansas–Texas football game, 215–17, 299
"Arkansas Travelers," 518
Armstrong, Bill, 177, 209, 511

Armstrong, Bob, 258
Armstrong, Neil, 205
Army Reserve Officers' Training Corps (ROTC), 204, 207, 209–12, 226, 511–12
Arnold, Cindy, 73
Arnold, Early, 88
Arnold, Truman, 496
Arrogance of Power, The (Fulbright), 132
Arsenic and Old Lace, 73
Ashby, Amy, *
Ashby, Kit, *, 140–1, 204, 230
Ashley, Eliza, 358
Ashley, Liza, *
Askew, Reubin, 255
Aspell, Bob, *
Aspell, Mauria, *
Aspin, Les, 565, 600
Associated Press, 5, 473, 576
Atkins, Ruth, 55
Atkinson, Dick, 270, 308
Atlanta, Ga., 517–18
Attlee, Clement, 184
Atwater, Lee, 453
Axelrod, David, 489

Babbitt, Bruce, 442, 601
Bachman, Dru, 189, 197
Baez, Joan, 243
Baird, Zoë, 601, 602, 612, 616, 617
Baker, Bobby, 179
Baker, James, 559, 578
Baker, John, 237, 263
Baker, Ralph, 273
Bald Knobbers, 330
Baliles, Jerry, 480
Ballmer, Steve, 580
Band, Doug, 622, 624
Banks, "Shug," 317
Barbieri, Arthur, 249–51
Barnes, Roy, 518
Barnett, Bob, 571, 577
Baron, Umberto, 6–7
Barram, Dave, 565
Barristers Union Prize Trials, 248–9, 262
Bartley, Anne, 287
Bassett, Marynm, 308
Bassett, Woody, 529, 623
Bates, Daisy, 47
Batista, Fulgencio, 105
Bayh, Birch, 126
Bayh, Evan, 126
Bay of Pigs, 71
Beauvoir, Max, 312–13, 328
Becker, Bob, 470
Becker, Ernest, 310–11
Begala, Diane, 559–60
Begala, Paul, 503–4, 516, 541, 552, 559–60, 565, 609
Begich, Nick, 261
Being Good: Women's Moral Values in Early America (Saxton), 179
Bekavac, Nancy, 235
Belgium, 198
Bell, Clarence, 346

Bell, Terrel, 405, 410, 442
Bellino, Joe, 48
Bennett, Bill, 442
Bennett, Victor, 150, 201
Bentsen, Lloyd, 258, 449, 454, 568–9, 594–5, 606–9
Berger, Sandy, 381, 438, 504, 591, 600–1
 background of, 504, 600–1
Bergman, Ingrid, 262
Berlin Wall, 465
Bernard, Charles, 165
Berrigan, Daniel, 161
Berrigan, Philip, 161
Berry, Orson, 350–1
Berry, Paul, 314, 315, 321, 623
Bersin, Alan, 180–1, 198
Biden, Joe, 441, 443
Bieber, Owen, 609–10
Biggers, Jan, 170
Bigham, Si, 281
Bilderberg Conference, 482–3
Billingsley, Bob, 98
Bishop, "Donkey," 169–70
Bishop, W. Hal, 169
Black, Charles, 262, 601
Black Power movement, 142
Blair, Dennis, 181
Blair, Jim, 275, 357, 623
Blair, Tony, 483
Blanchard, Jim, 441–2, 489
Blinder, Alan, 605–9
Bloodworth-Thomason, Linda, 170, 450, 452, 594
Blythe, Glenn, 48
Blythe, William Jefferson, Jr., *, 4–8
Bob Jones University, 124
Bogart, Humphrey, 262
Boggs, Hale, 261
Boggs, Lindy, 261
Bond, Julian, 174
Bond, Mary, 105, 150
Bookout, Jerry, 475
Boren, David, 469
Bork, Robert, 232–3, 237, 354, 443–4
Bosch, Juan, 132
Bosnia, Bosnia conflict, 559
Boswell, Ted, 169
Bourke-White, Margaret, 231
Bowen, Bill, 489
Bowens, Emily, 399
Bowie, Jim, 260
Bowles, Erskine, 294, 597–8
Bowman, Bertie, 120
Bradley, Bill, 547, 573
Brady, Pat, 117–18
Brady bill, 282, 459, 475, 502
Branch, Taylor, 208, 256–7, 259
Branson, Johanna, 308
Branstad, Terry, 462
Branstool, Gene, 556
Brantley, Ellen, 334
Brasel, Walter, 286
Bratton, Sam, 402
Breaux, John, 480
Breland, Keller, 33

Breslin, Jimmy, 527, 535
Brezhnev, Leonid, 214
Brinton, Crane, 134
Briscoe, Dolph, 258, 259
Broderick, John, 498
Brody, Ken, 496–7
Brooke, Edward, 127
Brooks, Cato, 319–20
Brown, Gordon, 483
Brown, Harold, 370–1
Brown, Jerry, 374–5, 498–9, 517, 519, 520, 522, 523–4, 528–9, 532–4, 535, 536, 539, 547, 550
Brown, Jesse, 599
Brown, John Y., 374
Brown, Ron, 481, 546–7, 568, 587, 596–7, 613
Brown, Sam, 208
Browner, Carol, 599
Brown v. *Board of Education*, 443
Broyles, Allen, 73
Broyles, Frank, 334
Brummett, John, 460
Bryan, William Jennings, 32
Bryant, Bear, 10
Bryant, Clifton, 53
BTU tax, 608–9
Buchanan, Pat, 178, 505, 516–17, 523, 562
Buck, Elizabeth, 74
Bucknell, Susan, 235
Bullock, Bob, 259
Bumpers, Dale, *, 47, 252, 277, 288, 294, 306, 316, 335, 336, 372, 437, 454, 487, 494
 1970 election and, 234
Bundy, McGeorge, 121
Burden of Southern History, The (Woodward), 236
Burkle, Ron, 538–9, 623
Burnett, Bill, 217–18
Burnett, Linda, 511
Burns, Jack, Sr., 305
Burroughs, Farris and Marilyn, 423
Bush, George H. W., *, 126, 216, 417, 453, 465, 543, 546, 593, 595, 603–5
 in 1988 campaign, 436, 441
 in 1992 campaign, 372, 478–9, 482, 483–5, 489, 497, 499, 505, 536, 539, 540, 542, 545, 553, 555, 559, 585–6, 588
 1992 Republican Convention speech of, 563, 566
 administration of, 551–2, 615
 BC's 1992 meeting with, 592
 Chelsea's encounters with, 412, 461
 Gulf War and, 478–9, 482
 Haitian refugee crisis and, 611
 Iran-Contra affair and, 441, 581, 602–3
 Iraq conflict and, 589, 590
 national debt and, 604–5
 "no new taxes" pledge of, 453, 462, 505, 577, 579
 pardons granted by, 602–3
 in presidential debates, 572, 573, 575–9

Bush, George W., 124, 191, 444, 539
Bush v. Gore, 444
Butler, Jim, 518
Butz, Earl, 297
Byrd, Robert, 125–6, 288

Cabe, Gloria, *, 373, 462, 469, 478
Calder, Alexander, 231
Califano, Joe, 341
California, 374–5, 479, 540
Campbell, Carroll, 455, 461
Campbell, Craig, 319
Campbell, Ernestine, 14
Campbell, Jude, *
Campbell, Patrick, *
Campbell, Tom, *, 93, 96, 140, 168, 193, 204
Camp David Accords, 374
Camp Yorktown Bay, 102–3
Canada, 569
capital punishment, 466, 472
Caplan, Mr. and Mrs., 163
Caplan, Tommy, *, 93–4, 140, 157, 162, 230, 344
Capps, John Paul, 457, 458
Carey, Hugh, 366, 489
Carey, Paul, 489
Caristianos, Mrs., 37
Carlisle, Lib, 458
Carlton, Kearney, 284
Carmichael, Stokely, 160
Carnahan, Mel, 520
Carr, Billie, 259–60
Carroll, John, 91
Carson, Johnny, 450–2
Carswell, G. Harrold, 130
Carter, Chip, 365
Carter, Jimmy, *, 117, 295, 305, 548, 562, 601
    accomplishments of, summarized, 374
    administration of, 351
    BC supported by, 534
    Cuban refugee crisis and, 360–7, 371–2, 374
    in election of 1976, 306, 311, 318–20, 437, 557
    in election of 1992, 534, 548
    HRC's appointment by, 306
    Iran hostage crisis and, 361, 365, 367
    Panama Canal returned by, 367, 372
    as southern Democrat, 124
Carter, Rosalynn, 507, 562
Carville, James, *, 251, 503–4, 510, 534, 559, 573, 602
    1992 election and, 503–4, 559–61, 583, 586
    on White House staff, 590
Casey, Bob, 503, 537, 544, 547
Cash, Clarence, 314
Cassidy, Edith Grisham (Mammaw), *, 11–12, 14, 22, 42–3, 44, 152, 154, 205
Cassidy, James Eldridge (Papaw), *, 11, 12–14, 22, 42–3, 44, 46, 154, 205
Castle, Mike, 434, 455
Castro, Fidel, 71, 105, 360, 361

Causey, Deloin, 363
Cauthron, Bill, 362, 363, 371
Cavazos, Lauro, 460
Cawkwell, George, 187, 201
Cecil, Ronnie, *, 68, 73
Cedras, Raoul, 222, 611
Central Intelligence Agency (CIA), 143, 222, 580, 601
Chamberlain, Neville, 135
Chamberlin, Alice, 201
Chambliss, Saxby, 213
Chaney, James, 124
Charles, Ray, 141
Chase, Chevy, 452–3, 540
Chennault, Anna, 185
Children's Defense Fund, 251, 265, 266
Chiles, Lawton, 480, 599
China, 100, 122, 132, 133–4, 225, 238
Chirelstein, Marvin, 245, 262, 263
Chisolm, Shirley, 253
Christian Coalition, 564
Christopher, Warren, 539, 544, 613
    named secretary of state, 600
    on transition team, 589–91
Churchill, Winston, 381
Church of God in Christ, 497
Cisneros, Henry, 589, 599
civil rights, 56, 71, 161, 236, 237
    anti-war movement and, 142
    Bork's views on, 443
    Branch's book on, 208
    busing issue and, 177
    Fulbright's stance on, 130
    Little Rock High School integration and, 46–8, 79–80, 152, 486
    murdered activists in, 124
Civil Rights Act of 1964, 122, 443
Civil War, 51–2, 55, 284, 285
Clark, Edith, 69
Clark, Jim, 69
Clark, L. W. "Bill," *, 384–5
Clark, Roy, 509
Clark, Steve, *, 45, 380, 392, 467
Clark, Wesley, 147
Clay, Eric, 235
Clean Water Act, 531
Cleaver, Eldridge, 195
Cleland, Max, 213
Clement, Frank, 44
Clifford, Clark, 156, 229
Cline, Patsy, 71
Clinton, Al, 39
Clinton, Bill:
    black-lung cases and, 304–5, 310
    campaign style of, 282, 392
    family tree of, 579–80
    Fayetteville house of, 307–8
    in first court appearance as attorney, 272–3
    first speech as elected official, 327–8
    HRC and, *see* Clinton relationship
    life goals of, 3
    Little Rock homes of, 321, 373
    musical interests of, 10, 37, 50–2, 57, 71–3, 82, 319, 344, 442, 452, 582

name of, 4, 67
personal and political philosophy of,
    101–2, 345, 430–1, 446, 463–4, 480–2,
    501, 554–5, 565, 586–7, 597–8
political interest of, 79–82
pro bono law work of, 272
reading interests of, 37–8, 121, 188, 195,
    197–8, 201, 203, 209, 218, 220,
    225–6, 227, 235, 236–7, 245, 247, 310
religious interests and activities of, 28–9,
    31, 38, 49–50, 87–8, 99–101, 194,
    205, 310–11, 312–14, 328–32, 386–7,
    565, 613–14
sports interests of, 24, 188–9, 215–18,
    333, 387
as teacher, 263, 267–70, 290–1, 302–4,
    307, 320

Childhood and Early Youth
autobiographical essay of, 75–6
at band camp, 51–2
baptism of, 38–9
birth of, 4–6, 9
in Boys Nation program, 68, 77–81
broken leg of, 23–4
Clinton family and, 39–41
Dallas trip of, 48
elementary schooling of, 23–6, 28–9
extended family of, 11–20, 39–41
first political experience of, 41
friends and acquaintances of, 34–5, 53
Georgetown decision of, 86–7
in high school, 71–8, 83–6, 87
Hot Springs homes of, 29–30, 64, 67–70
Hot Springs move of, 27–35
in junior high school, 49–55
King's "Dream" speech and, 83
in last boyhood summer, 88–9
legal name change of, 67
memories of father in, 5–8
Native Americans as interest of, 38
New Orleans visits of, 9–11
in student government, 81–2
television viewing of, 44–5
typical meals in, 18
Washington visit of, 79–81

Higher Education, Political Apprenticeship
anti-war movement and, 142–4
as foreign relations committee worker,
    118–22, 133–5
in Fulbright's 1968 senatorial campaign,
    163, 166–9
at Georgetown, *see* Georgetown
    University
1964 Arkansas election work of, 109–14
in 1968 voyage to England, 178
at Oxford, *see* Oxford University
in Project Pursestrings, 229
Quigley's influence on, 101–2
Rhodes Scholarship of, *see* Rhodes
    Scholarship
ROTC and, 204, 207, 209–12
school loans of, 263
student government activities of, 98–9, 104
and Vietnam War, 136, 158, 177, 186–7,
    195, 198–9, 203–4, 207–13, 226

Washington race riots observed by, 160
at Yale, *see* Yale University

Governor of Arkansas
assessment of first term, 345
Cuban refugee crisis and, 360–7, 371–2,
    374, 376
and decision to run in 1982, 382–5
disability benefits issue and, 412–13
DLC speech of, 480–2
Dukakis nomination speech of, 447–53
farewell address of 1980, 377
Governor's Mansion and, 342
in Grand Gulf case, 353–4, 425–6
health clinics issue and, 351, 379, 477
highways program and, 347–8, 372, 420,
    476, 477
inaugurations of, 344–5, 401, 475–6
on Johnny Carson show, 450–2
literacy initiative of, 456, 476
Little Rock Nine episode and, 46–8
lost election as viewed by, 371–4
missile silo explosion and, 372
natural disasters and, 359
1980 Democratic Convention addressed
    by, 369
1982 State of the State address by, 404
security measures and, 342–4
staff of, 402–3, 458–60
tag-fees controversy and, 347–9, 363,
    368–9, 371, 374–5, 376, 379, 382,
    388, 395
tax issues in, 409–10, 411, 457–8, 470
teacher-testing controversy in, 407–12,
    419
White's administration and, 378–81

President: First Term (1992–1996)
achievements of, 615
cabinet appointments in, 589, 594–7,
    600–1, 615
election of, *see* election of 1992
jogging habit of, 592
McNamara letter on Vietnam to, 619
national security appointments of, 600–1
negative press coverage of, 597
and preserving democracy, 611, 615
religion-related activities and, 613–14
staff appointments of, 589–91, 598–600
sub-cabinet appointments of, 591, 597,
    599–600, 615
transition period of, 589–94, 614–18

Clinton, Chelsea, 3, 15, 373, 374, 377, 392,
    412, 421, 425, 439, 440, 441, 475,
    584, 587, 617
BC's relationship with, 52, 182–3, 331,
    376, 378, 403–4, 440, 468, 492, 508,
    542, 585
birth of, 358
Bush's encounter with, 412, 461
early schooling of, 456, 483, 603–4
Mandela's encounter with, 550
naming of, 96
pet frog of, 614
senior thesis of, 528
at Stanford, 92

Clinton, Eula Mae Cornwell, 39

Clinton, Evelyn, 40
Clinton, Hillary Rodham:
    Arkansas bar passed by, 266
    background of, 241, 242
    and BC's 1988 presidential campaign
        decision, 440–1
    BC's relationship with, see Clinton
        relationship
    Buy American program and, 423
    Carter's campaign and, 320
    Chelsea's birth and, 357–8
    at Children's Defense Fund, 251, 265,
        266
    descriptions of, 240–1, 291
    dress and appearance of, 240–1, 249, 308
    on Education Standards Committee,
        406–9
    European trips of, 96, 318, 341–2, 444–5
    Fayetteville life of, 305–8
    legal practice of, 305–6, 483
    McRae confronted by, 471
    maiden name issue and, 336, 376, 388–9
    1974 election and, 295
    1982 election and, 385, 392
    1986 election and, 425
    1990 election and, 471
    1992 election and, 487–90, 504, 506–8,
        515, 516, 521–3, 525, 534, 547, 549,
        550, 556, 561–2, 581–2, 584, 587
    Nixon impeachment inquiry and, 291
    Rose Law Firm cases and, 321, 323
    transition period and, 593–4
    Virginia Kelley met by, 240–1
    Whitewater and, 529–31
    at Yale, 248–9
Clinton, Hillary Rodham, as First Lady,
        614–15, 618
    as role model, 615, 617
    staff of, 613
Clinton, Ilaree, 40
Clinton, Janet, 40–1, 52
Clinton, Karla, 27
Clinton, Marie, 288, 308
Clinton, Raymond, 21, 27, 28, 33, 41–2,
        88, 110, 117, 188, 287
Clinton, Raymond "Corky", Jr., 41
Clinton, Robert, 40
Clinton, Roger (stepfather), *, 21–2, 23–5,
        50, 54, 64–5, 71, 87, 88, 90, 103–4,
        119, 120, 137, 152, 227–8, 267
    death of, 149–50
    divorce and remarriage of, 65–7
    illness of, 137, 147–50
    in move to Hot Springs, 27–30
    shooting incident and, 24–5
    Virginia Kelley's relationship with, 24–5,
        58, 64, 65–6, 90
Clinton, Roger Cassidy (brother), *, 44, 58,
        61–2, 63, 64–5, 66–7, 70, 87, 90,
        103–4, 138, 148, 149, 163, 190, 192,
        212, 266, 293, 294, 308, 414–16,
        427–8, 441, 474, 493, 555
Clinton, Roy, 40–1, 52, 275, 288
Clinton Birthplace, 9
Clinton Birthplace Foundation, 25

Clinton Buick, 21, 27, 28, 34, 38, 88
Clinton relationship:
    Arkansas sojourn in, 266–7
    BC-HRC first meeting with, 238–40
    BC's marriage proposal in, 265
    California sojourn in, 242
    decision for Arkansas and, 265
    decision to live together in, 243–4
    first date in, 240
    first meeting in, 96–7
    honeymoon in, 310
    Kroft interview and, 507–9
    mutual love in, 3, 242, 265, 275–6, 507–8
    1972 campaign and, 242
    self-doubt in, 248
    seventeenth wedding anniversary and,
        571
    wedding in, 308–10
Clinton: The President They Deserve
    (Walker), 533
CNN, 452, 509, 571
Cocker, Joe, 452
Coe, Mr., 84
Coffin, William Sloane, 143
Cohen, Mike, 462
Cohen, Steve, 344–5, 438
Cold War, 147
Coleburn, Lila, 236
Coleman, Bill, 235, 240
Collins, Judy, 96
Collins, Michael, 205
Colombia, 315
Colorado, 517
Columbia, 205
Comeback Kid, The (Allen and Portis), 536
Commager, Henry Steele, 134
Communications Workers of America, 527,
    532
Conference of the Atlantic Community
    (CONTAC), 147, 198
Congress, U.S., 31, 113, 133, 134, 140, 160,
        323, 435, 489, 505, 589, 591
    BC's economic policy in, 610–11
    debate style of, 164
    ERA passed by, 338–9
    see also House of Representatives, U.S.,
        Senate, U.S.
Connally, John, 258
Connecticut, 230–4, 524
conservatism, 191, 264–5
Conservative Party, U.S., 93
Constitution, U.S., 338, 365, 380, 603
Constitution Hall, 141
Conway, Mike, 248–9, 278
Cooper, Gary, 26
Cooper, Glenda, *
Cooper, Justin, 621, 624
Coopersmith, Connie, 483
Coopersmith, Esther, 483
Cormier, Rufus, 236, 278
Cormier, Yvonne, 244
Cornwell, Mike, 289
Cotton, Paula, 319–20
Coulson, Mike, 50
Council of Economic Advisers, 596

Cox, R. L., 317
Cozzens, Arthur, 99
Craig, Greg, 344
Crain, Joe, 62
Crain, Louise, 62
Crane, Edie, 35, 54
Crane, Larry, 35, 54
Crane, Mary Dan, 35, 54
Crane, Rose, 35, 54, 288, 292
Crank, Marion, 169
Crawford, Gabe, 21, 22, 40, 41, 281, 287
Crawford, Nancy, 62
Crawford, Virginia, 21, 22, 40
Crazy Horse, 38
creation science, 379–80
Criner, Patty Howe, 498, 623
Crockett, Davy, 260
Cronin, Vincent, 244
Crowe, Bill, 567, 600
Crumbly, Jack, 393, 394
C. Turner Joy, USS, 144
Cuba, 185, 260, 375
Cuban refugee crisis, 360–7, 371–2
Cuomo, Mario, 438, 480, 485, 493, 500, 504, 532, 543, 550, 573
Currie, Betty, 613
Czechoslovakia, 224–5

Daiwa Steel Tools Industries, 422
Daley, Richard, 172, 174–5, 177, 495
Dangremond, Bob, *, 514
Dangremond, Denise Hyland, 102, 103, 178, 186, 203, 514, 623
Daniel, Charles, 282
Daniel, George, 282, 376
Daniel, James, 282
Daniels, Charlie, 223–4
Danner, John, 349–50
Darkness Visible (Styron), 247
Darman, Richard, 604
Daughters of the American Revolution, 141
Davids, Jules, 144–5, 150
Davis, Edward and Annie, 503, 516
Davis, Gail, 45
Davis, Gray, 374
Davis, Jeff, 336
Davis, Wade, 313
Davis, Wylie, 263, 279, 291
Dean, John, 208, 256
Dearie, John, 527
Debs, Eugene, 47
DeLay, Tom, 323
"Democratic Capitalism" (Clinton), 446–7
Democratic Governors Association, 369
Democratic Leadership Council (DLC), 161, 420, 447, 470, 474, 478–82, 486, 495–6, 500, 501–2
Democratic National Committee (DNC), 375, 487–8, 546, 596
Democratic National Convention of 1968, 171–6
  platform in, 173–4
  radical right reaction to, 175–6
  violent demonstrations and, 174–5

Democratic National Convention of 1972, 250–2
  California challenge in, 253–4
Democratic National Convention of 1980, 369
Democratic National Convention of 1988, BC's speech nominating Dukakis in, 447–53
Democratic National Convention of 1992, 546–55
  BC's acceptance speech in, 187, 551–5
  Cuomo's nominating speech in, 550
  Gore's acceptance speech in, 551–2
  keynote speeches in, 547–8
  platform of, 549
Democratic Party, U.S., 123–4, 155, 191, 233–4, 304, 341, 459, 540
  in Arkansas, 55, 279–80, 295
  BC's advocacy for change in, 369–70, 479–82
  see also specific candidates, conventions, and elections

Democrats for the 80's, 381–2
DeMolay, Order of, 57–8, 71, 85
de Montfort, Simon, 579
Denial of Death, The (Becker), 310
DeRoeck, Wally, 314, 376
DeRosa, Mary, 622
Deutsch, Jan, 245
Development and Finance Authority, Ark., 417–18, 427, 433, 473
Dickens, Charles, 55
Dierks, Jan, 206
Dinegar, Caroline, 263
Dinkins, David, 549
Dinneen, Father, 92
Dionne, E. J., 482
DiPrete, Ed, 444
Dirksen, Everett, 125
Dixon, Lynda, 402, 468, 484, 623
Doar, John, 262, 277–8, 291
Dodd, Chris, 126
Dodd, Tom, 126, 230–1, 233
Dokey, Verna, 52
Dokey, Vernon, 52–3
Dole, Bob, BC's relationship with, 592–3
Dominican Republic, 130, 132, 525
Donahue, Phil, 533
Donilon, Tom, 591
Donne, John, 215
"Do Not Go Gentle into That Good Night" (Thomas), 188
"Don't Stop Thinking About Tomorrow," 484
Douglas, Helen Gahagan, 56
Down and Out in Paris and London (Orwell), 201
Dozier, Phil, 120
Driver, Mike, 209, 438, 517
Drummond, James "Bulldog," 362, 363–4, 399
Dubček, Alexander, 224
Dublin, Ireland, 215
Duchac, René, 34
Dudley, Bob, 324

Dudman, Dick, 229
Dudman, Helen, 229
Duffey, Joe, 230–2, 233–4, 264–5, 287
Dukakis, Michael, 399–400, 442, 447, 449, 451, 453, 562, 600
Duke, David, 360
Duke, Steve, 237, 263
Duke University, 41, 137
Dumas, Ernest, 476–7
Duncan, Dick, 74
Duvalier, François "Papa Doc," 311
Duvalier, Jean-Claude "Baby Doc," 311–12
Dwire, Jeff, *, 172–3, 188, 189, 190–1, 205, 226, 230, 240, 266, 294, 315, 340
    background of, 172–3, 192
    BC's draft status and, 209–10, 211, 212, 511
    BC's eulogy for, 293
    illness and death of, 292–3
Dyke, Jim, 355

Eagleton, Tom, 254–5, 260
Eakeley, Doug, 180, 234, 240, 248
Earned Income Tax Credit (EITC), 502
Earth in the Balance (Gore), 545
Ebbert, Bill, 57
Ebeling, Betsy Johnson, 308
Ebeling, Tom, 308
Eckford, Elizabeth, 47
Economic Development Department, Ark., 355, 379
economic policy:
    in Arkansas, 345, 355, 388, 401–2, 404, 417–18, 421–4, 432–3, 445, 457, 464, 470, 481
    deficit-reduction goal in, 598, 604–11
    Little Rock summit on, 597–8
    in 1992 election, 514, 520–1, 543, 564, 565, 569–70, 586
    1993 federal budget debate and, 596, 610
    staff debate on, 604–9
    stimulus package proposal and, 608–10
    tax policy and, 607, 610
    trade policy and, 605–6, 612
Edelman, Marian Wright, 251, 265
Education Commission of the States, 429, 436
Education Department, Ark., 350
Education Department, U.S., 296
Education First, 479
education reform:
    in Arkansas, 345–7, 355, 366, 368, 388, 401–2, 404–12, 419, 423, 425, 432, 439, 457, 458, 469–70, 471–2, 476–7, 479, 481, 489
    Bush summit on, 460–3
    Nation at Risk report on, 405, 408, 461
    in 1990 election, 471–2
    teacher-testing controversy and, 407–12, 419
Education Standards Committee, 405, 408, 409
Edwards, David, 197, 202, 212, 215, 217, 228, 311, 318, 570
Egypt, 374

Ehrman, Sara, 293
Eidenberg, Gene, 360, 362, 363–4, 367
Eisenhower, Dwight D., 44, 47, 55, 56, 74, 198
Elders, Joycelyn, 458, 599
election of 1968, 41, 143, 229, 256, 264, 306, 437, 561
    Agnew nomination and, 171
    anti-war movement and, 154–7, 161–2, 177
    BC's absentee ballot in, 188
    BC's interest in, 157–8
    Democratic convention in, see Democratic National Convention of 1968
    feed-store incident in, 165–6
    Fulbright's senatorial campaign in, 163–9, 187, 200
    Humphrey's Vietnam War position and, 178, 184
    Jim Johnson in, 168–9
    King assassination and, 158
    L. B. Johnson's withdrawal from, 158
    Nixon's exploitation of peace talks in, 185–6, 191
    primaries in, 156–7, 159, 162, 249
    Republican National Convention in, 170–1
    southern Democrats and, 124
    Vietnam War and, 155, 163, 164, 173, 174
election of 1972, 184–5, 208, 272, 281, 306, 519, 546, 583
    BC-Barbieri encounter in, 249–51
    candidates in, 253
    Democratic Convention in, see Democratic National Convention of 1972
    Democratic volunteers in, 252
    Eagleton controversy in, 254–5
    L. B Johnson-McGovern meeting in, 258–9
    results of, 261
    Texas campaign in, 256–62
election of 1988, 436–54, 488, 505, 562
    BC's candidacy considered in, 436–41
    Dukakis nomination in, 447–53
    results of, 454
election of 1992, 8, 10–11, 46, 79, 85, 102, 161, 208–9, 257, 260, 344, 372, 446, 460, 464, 484–6, 490, 503–11, 516, 523–4, 531–6, 543, 555, 558, 560, 570–1, 572, 574, 576, 580–1
    abortion issue in, 537, 547, 565
    BC-Bush meeting in, 534
    BC's announcement speech in, 492–3
    BC's decision to run in, 475, 478, 482, 483–6
    BC's headquarters in, 493–5
    BC's staff in, 495–8, 503–4
    BC's victory speech in, 587–8
    BC's voice problem in, 574–5, 583–4
    black vote in, 497, 505, 519, 520–1, 535
    British involvement in, 570–1
    Bush-Perot conflict in, 543, 546, 569
    bus tours in, 556–9
    candidates in, 498–500, 584–6, 587

character issue in, 514–15, 520, 531–6, 570–1, 586
Democratic Convention in, see Democratic National Convention of 1992
draft issue in, 511, 518, 563–4, 567, 570, 572
economic policy in, 514, 543, 564, 565, 569–70, 586
endorsements in, 504, 510, 520, 529, 535, 536, 537, 547, 561, 564, 565, 567, 570, 571–2, 580
ethnic vote in, 497, 525–6, 527–8
family tree publicity in, 579–80
finances in, 496–7, 505–6
Georgetown speeches in, 501–4
Georgia campaign in, 517–18
Gore as running mate in, 544–6, 551–2
high-tech sector in, 565–6, 580
HRC's "tea and cookies" remark and, 522–3
Irish vote in, 527–8
labor unions and, 525–7, 529
Los Angeles riots and, 538
Michigan campaign in, 520–1
New Hampshire campaign in, 497–500, 502–3, 512–17
news media and, 539, 566–7, 571, 572–3, 581
New York campaign in, 524–7
1970 Moscow trip and, 225
Notre Dame speech in, 564–5
Perot's candidacy in, 537, 539–43, 551, 568–9
presidential debates in, 567–79
primaries and caucuses in, 516–18, 523–7
rapid-response teams in, 560–3
Republican Clinton-bashing in, 561–4
Republican Convention in, 561–3
results of, 585–7
Sister Souljah's remarks in, 541–2
strategy of, 558–60
Super Tuesday in, 518–20
tax issue in, 499–500, 505, 514, 520, 543, 563, 566–7
vice-presidential debate in, 573–4
War Room in, 560
Whitewater and, 529–31
election of 1994, 348, 459, 500
election of 1996, 486
election of 2000, 444
Nader and, 470
Supreme Court decision in, 444
elections, U.S.:
of 1836, 436
of 1852, 483
of 1912, 586
of 1948, 123, 563
of 1952, 45
of 1956, 44, 56
of 1960, 55, 56, 123, 157, 256, 259, 565
of 1964, 80, 92–3, 122, 123
of 1970, 546
of 1976, 295, 306, 318, 327, 367, 437, 504
of 1980, 360, 362–3, 367–8, 414, 546
of 1984, 416–17
of 1990, 462
of 2002, 124, 477, 539
see also specific state elections
"Elegy Written in a Country Churchyard" (Gray), 200
Elizabeth II, Queen of England, 579
Elliot, Cass, 95
Ellis, Carolyn, 241, 344
Emanuel, Rahm, 495, 612
Emerson, John, 597–8
Emerson, Tom, 237, 238
energy issues, 322
in Arkansas, 345, 352–5, 388, 395, 404
Enfield, Bill, 272
Engskov, Kris, 281
environmental issues, 285–6, 545
in Arkansas, 401, 459, 476, 477, 481, 530–1
Equal Rights Amendment (ERA), 338–9
Ernst, Don, 402
Ervin, Sam, 256, 276
Espy, Mike, 454, 480, 508, 601
Estonia, 221
Estrich, Susan, 454
Evans, Dianne, 329
Evans, John, 381
Evans, Sharon, 192

Fahd, King of Saudi Arabia, 590
Faisal, Turki al-, 144
Falwell, Jerry, 316
Family and Medical Leave Act, 359, 475, 502
Farenthold, Sissy, 259
Farmer, Bob, 487, 496
Farrakhan, Louis, 529
Faubus, Alta, 278
Faubus, Elizabeth, 278–9
Faubus, Orval, 43, 47, 79, 107–10, 123, 152, 169, 234, 272, 278–9, 336, 367, 424, 428, 464, 597
Faulkner, William, 245
Federal Bureau of Investigation (FBI), 570, 580
Federal Emergency Management Agency (FEMA), 564
federal student-loan program, 263
Ferraro, Geraldine, 416
Ferrer, Fernando, 527
fetal-tissue research, 597
Fields, Cleo, 331
Fields, Ron, 371
Finland, 220
First AME Church, 538
First Presbyterian Church, 41
Fisher, George, 350, 380, 381
Fisher, Jimmie Lou, *, 492
Fitzgerald, Reverend, 38–9
flag issue, 124
Flake, Floyd, 526
Flammang, Elizabeth, 594
Flaubert, Gustave, 201
Fleishner, Laura, 34
Fleishner, Marty, 34

Fletcher, Willie, 181
Flores, Oscar, 624
Florida, 504, 519, 520
Flowers, Gennifer, 473, 506–10, 516
Flynn, Ray, 528, 565
Foley, Tom, 591
Food and Drug Administration, U.S., 610
Food for Peace program, 238
Ford, Arch, 356
Ford, Gerald, 294, 320
Ford, Harold, 455
Ford Motor Company, 78, 470
Forney, Bo, 283–4, 286
Fors, Henry, 223–4
Fortas, Abe, 248–9
Fort Chaffee, Ark., 360–5, 366–7, 368, 371, 372, 399
Fort Polk, La., 331
Fort Roots, 282
Fort Smith, Ark., 280, 288, 296, 305, 325, 360, 368, 371, 474
Fosdick, Harry Emerson, 107
Foshee, Ed, 88–9
Foster, Lisa, 15
Foster, Vince, *, 314–15, 321, 323, 613
    BC's friendship with, 15
Fowler, Bill, 287
Fradon, Dana, 231
Franklin, Benjamin, 57
Frasers (neighbors), 69
Fray, Paul, 110
Frazier, George, 402
Freeman, Woody, 417
Freemasons, 57–8, 152
Frei, Terry, 216
French, Jim, *
Friendly, Andrew, 613
"Friends of Bill," 3, 513
From, Al, 591
Fulani, Lenora, 528
Fulbright, Betty, 129
Fulbright, J. William, *, 80, 125, 128–37, 140, 145, 150, 153, 157, 162, 186, 216, 251, 294, 295
    background of, 128–9
    BC as worker for, 118–22, 289
    and BC's 1974 congressional run, 277, 288
    BC's first meeting with, 80
    civil rights stance of, 130
    foreign affairs and, 131–3
    in 1968 senate race, 163–9, 187, 200
    Rusk and, 134–5
    Vietnam War stance of, 119, 122, 132–6, 163, 164
Fulbright, Roberta, 128, 129
Fulbright Resolution, 129
Fuller, Don and Betty, 378
Fuller, Millard, *, 562

Gaddy, Judy, 509
Game and Fish Commission, Ark., 272
Garcia, Franklin, 260
García, Márquez, Gabriel, 245
Gardner, Booth, 510

Gathings, "Took," 80
Gauldin, Mike, 451
Gautier, Aimée, 218–19
Gavin, James, 134
gay rights, 226, 324–5, 330, 526
gays in the military, 593, 617
Gearan, Mark, 591
George, Lloyd, 409
Georges, John, 421
Georgetown University, 91–106, 139, 287
    BC's academic studies at, 100–2, 104–6, 137, 144–7
    BC's Washington summer at, 140–2
    graduation from, 163
    New York City trips and, 96–7
Georgia, U.S., 320, 548, 582
    1992 election in, 517–18
    2000 senatorial election in, 548
Gephardt, Dick, 441, 495, 591
Gerard, Gil, 452
Germany, 134–5, 198, 566
Gerson, Stuart, 612
Giles, Walter, 105–6, 150
Gingrich, Newt, 455, 593
    budget issues and, 323, 459, 593
    conservatism of, 191, 593
    tax cuts and, 323, 593
Gist, Nancy, 235–6
Glascock, Darrell, 427
Glaser, Ariel, 549
Glaser, Elizabeth, 549
Glaser, Jake, 549
Glaser, Paul Michael, 549
Glass, David, 423
Gleckel, Jeff, 239
Glenn, John, 480
Glickman, Julius, 256–7
Glover, Mac, 110
Goggins, Will, 282, 290
Goldwater, Barry, 79–80, 123, 443
Gonzales, Henry B., 260
Goodman, Andrew, 124
Goodman, Steve, 398
Goodrum, Gail, *
Goodrum, Randy, *, 72, 344, 513, 555
Goodwin, Tommy, 414
Gorbachev, Mikhail, 483
Gore, Albert, III., 488
Gore, Albert, Jr., *, 44, 439, 470, 573–4
    economic policy and, 608–9
    environmental issues and, 323, 613
    at 1992 Democratic Convention, 480
    1992 election and, 480, 488, 550, 551–2, 556–9, 580, 583, 585, 587, 591
    selected as BC's running mate, 544–6
    transition period and, 615
    2000 election and, see election of 2000
Gore, Albert, Sr., 44, 126, 546
Gore, Pauline, 546
Gore, Tipper, *, 545–6, 547, 587
Gortari, Carlos Salinas de, 612
Governor's Mansion, Ark., 342
Governors' Task Force on Education, 460–3
Graber, Susan, 241

Graham, Billy, *, 49–50, 59
Graham, Bob, 385, 544
Graham, Katharine, 593
Graham, Ruth, 50
Grameen Bank, 432–3
Grand Canyon, 243
Grand Gulf nuclear project, 322, 353–4, 425–6, 444, 522
Grandmaison, Joe, 516
Grapevine, The, 218
Gray, Bill, 480
Gray, Boyden, 602
Gray, Francine du Plessix, 231
Gray, George, 37
Gray, Henry, 379
Gray, Thomas, 200
Great Britain, 135
  1992 U.S. election and, 570–1
Great Depression, 12–13, 55, 278, 285
Great Expectations (Dickens), 55
Great Society, 154
Green, Al, 344
Green, Ernie, *
Greenberg, Stan, 487, 534, 560, 581, 587, 609
Greening of America, The (Reich), 237
Greenspan, Alan, 594
Greenspun, Brian, 623
Greenspun, Myra, 623
Greenwood, Ark., 288
Greer, Frank, 487, 490, 496, 503, 505, 534, 579
Gregory, Dick, 175, 486
Grigsby, Ann, 48
Grisham, Lem, *
Grisham, Ollie, 16, 17, 18, 19, 42, 205
Grisham, Oren "Buddy," *, 16, 17–20, 205
Gruening, Ernest, 126
Grunwald, Mandy, 535, 560, 579, 609
Guantánamo, 361
Guardian, The, 199
Guinier, Lani, 236
Gulf War, 372, 475, 476, 478–9, 482, 484, 545, 574, 593
gun control, 477–8
  Brady bill and, see Brady bill
Gutierrez, Luis, 521

Habitat for Humanity, 562–3
Hackler, Hugh, 281
Hackley, Lloyd, 409
Hagel, Chuck, 213
Hahm, Albert, 34
Haines, Hank, 318
Haiti, 222, 311–14, 328
  refugee crisis in, 611, 615
Halberstam, David, 209
Haldeman, H. R., 216
Hall, Arsenio, *, 540–1
Hall, W. Q., 272
Hamill, Pete, 535
Hamilton, Arthur, 555
Hamilton, Lake, 33, 42, 169, 293
Hamilton, Lee, 544

Hammerschmidt, John Paul, 276, 281, 283, 290, 291, 292–3, 295, 298–300, 311, 315–16, 511
Hampton, Charles, 619–20
Harbour, Brian, 465
Hardgraves, Mike, 72
Hardin, Lillie, 435
Hardin, Lu, 418
Hargraves, Bobby, 288
Harkin, Tom, 488, 499–500, 516, 517, 519, 532, 547, 548
Harriman, Averell, 144, 185, 381
Harriman, Pamela, 381–2, 593
Harrington, Dave, 422
Harris, Maxine, see Jones, Maxine Temple
Harris, Oren, 80, 416
Hart, Gary, 74–5, 243, 252, 438
Hart, Hillary, 215
Hart, Peter, 371
Hassin, Gina, 69
Hassin, Guido, 34
Hatfield, Mark, 127
Hattoy, Bob, 549
Havel, Václav, 225, 600
Hawaii, 520
Hawke, Bob, 184
Hawking, Stephen, 184
Hawkins, Lefty, 210
Hawn, Goldie, 540
Hay, Jess, 259
Hayden, Carl, 125
Hayden, Tom, 175
Hays, Brooks, 108–9, 115, 143
Hazard, Geoffrey, 248
health-care reform, 296, 341
  in Arkansas, 345, 350–1, 356, 401, 419, 431–2, 456, 458, 476–7, 481
  1992 election and, 549, 586
Health Department, Ark., 350, 351
Health Department, U.S., 458
Healy, Patrick, 91
Healy, Tim, 495
Hearnes, Warren, 255
Hegel, G. W. F., 144
Helm, Levon, 536
Helms, Jesse, 334
Hendren, Kim, 390
Hendrix College, 294, 346, 415
Henley, Bill, 418
Henry, Aaron, 174
Henry, Ann, 274, 276, 309, 357, 623
Henry, Morriss, 274, 276, 309, 357
Henry III, King of England, 579
Hentz, Otto, 99–100
Herget, Dick, 367
Herman, Alexis, 546, 591, 612
Hernreich, Nancy, 612, 622
Hersey, John, 231
Heston, Charlton, 46
Hewlett-Packard, 566
Higgins, Bob, 619
High Noon, 26
Hightower, Maye, 28
Highway 60, 5
Highway Department, Ark., 379, 420

Hill, Henry, 54–5, 89
Hill, King, 48
Hills, Carla, 566
Hirt, Al, 10
Hitler, Adolf, 135
Hobbes, Thomas, 227, 228
Ho Chi Minh, 133
Ho Chi Minh City (Saigon), 156, 247
Hodges, Kaneaster, 338
Holbrooke, Dick, 504
Holiday, Jennifer, 555
Holly, Buddy, 71
Holmes, Eugene, 204, 207, 210–11, 215, 217, 226, 340, 511
Holt, Frank, *, 110–11, 113, 114–16, 150, 192, 202, 292
Holt, Jack, 110, 118, 119
Holt, Lyda, 111–12, 202
Holt, Mary, 111–12, 202
Holt, Melissa, 111–12
"Holt Generation," 110–11
Holtz, Lou, 333–5
Holum, John, 438
Homage to Catalonia (Orwell), 227
Home Instruction Programs for Preschool Youngsters (HIPPY), 432, 456
Hong Kong, 355
Hoofman, Cliff, *
Hoover, Herbert, 32
Hope Star, 112
Horne, Rex, 613–14
Horns, Hogs and Nixon Coming (Frei), 216
Horton, Willie, 453, 562
Hot Springs Convention Center, 294, 299
House of Representatives, Arkansas, 325–6
House of Representatives, U.S., 80, 122, 129, 391, 399
    See also Congress, U.S.
Housley, Charley, 70
Howe, Patty, 288, 308
Howell, Max, 352
How to Get Control of Your Time and Your Life (Lakein), 3
Hubbell, Webb, 321, 612
Huber, Carolyn, *, 357, 358, 488
Huckabee, Mike, 47
Human Services Department, Ark., 350
Humphrey, Hubert, 56, 123, 124, 126, 161, 162, 171, 173, 174–5, 177–8, 184–6, 191, 253, 255
Hunt, Jim, 366
Hurricane Andrew, 563, 564
Hussein, Saddam, 475, 578, 580, 589
Hussman, Walter, 494
Hutchinson, Asa, 416
Hybels, Bill, 614
Hyland, Chris, 525
Hyland, Denise, see Dangremond, Denise Hyland

Ickes, Harold, 489, 496, 526, 527, 534, 546
Ifshin, David, 465
"I have a dream" speech, 83, 207
Illinois, 488, 520, 521–4, 557
Immanuel Baptist Church, 386, 465

Immigration and Naturalization Service, 612
impeachment inquiry, in Watergate investigation, 212, 277
Imus, Don, 533, 535
Indyck, Martin, 504
Inouye, Daniel, 173
International Year of the Child, 356
Iowa, 488, 517
Iran, 367
Iran-Contra affair, 441, 455, 571, 581, 602–3
Iranian hostage crisis, 361, 365, 367, 539, 600
Iran-Iraq War, 580
Iraq, 574, 580, 589
Irish-Americans for Clinton, 528
Irish Issues Forum, 527
Irish Republican Army (IRA), 528
Irish Voice, 527
Irons, Edith, 87
Irving, Robert, 100–1
Isaacson, John, 195
Israel, 162, 374, 386, 387, 466, 497
Italy, 4, 7, 444–5
Iue, Satoshi, 422
Iverson, Ken, 423

Jackson, Andrew, 31, 436, 501
Jackson, Cliff, 505
Jackson, Henry "Scoop," 140
Jackson, Jesse, 441–2, 449, 480, 486, 519, 528–9, 534, 535, 538, 541–2, 547, 548–9
Jackson, Mahalia, 200
Jackson, Mauria, 88, 513
Jackson, Maynard, 518
Jackson, Reggie, 555
Jamison, Phil, *, 81
Jamison, Susan, *
Janklow, Bill, 418
Jann, Carlene, 141
Japan, 313, 355, 454, 566, 609–10
Javits, Jacob, 127
Jefferson, Bill, 331–2, 601
Jefferson, Thomas, 533–4
Jeffries, A. B. "Sonny," 38
Jeffries, Bert, 38–9, 193–4, 199, 208
Jeffries, Kathy, 199
Jenkins, Robert, 328
Jericho, 386
Jernigan, George, 314, 316–17, 550
Jerusalem, 386
John, King of England, 579
Johnson, Alston, 344
Johnson, Earvin "Magic," 568
Johnson, Jim, 109–10, 114–17, 123, 164, 168–9, 187, 192
Johnson, Luci, 98
Johnson, Lyndon B., 32, 56, 57, 93, 96, 105, 122–4, 130, 133, 137, 142, 143, 154–6, 162, 173, 174, 175, 179, 184, 185–6, 229, 258, 287, 619
    presidency assumed by, 85
    Tonkin Gulf Resolution and, 131–2, 144

Johnson, Roger, 497
Johnson, Virginia, 164, 169
Jones, Brereton, 510
Jones, Clint, 204
Jones, Fay, 266, 278
Jones, Hilary, 285–6, 349
Jones, Jerry, 467
Jones, Jimmy "Red," 375–6, 392
Jones, Margaret, 285–6
Jones, Maxine Temple, 33, 35
Jones, Odell, 521
Jones, Paula, 291, 509–10
Jones, Tom, 222
Jonesboro, Ark., 339
Jordan, Ann, 593
Jordan, Barbara, 547
Jordan, Vernon, 389, 482–3, 568–9, 589–91, 593, 601–2
Juan Carlos, King of Spain, 227
Julius Caesar (Shakespeare), 65, 75, 109
Justice Department, U.S., 134, 143, 185, 297–8, 362–4, 580

Kahn, Herman, 225
Kammer, Fred, 235, 344
Kant, Immanuel, 144, 311
Kantor, Mickey, 375, 438, 440, 484, 490, 534, 568–9, 589, 597–8, 601, 610
Karber, Jon, 69–70
Karber, Toni, 69–70
Katzenbach, Nick, 134
Kearney, Janis, 621
Keating, Kenneth, 127
Keene, N.H., 502–3
Kefauver, Estes, 44, 126
Kell, George, 383
Kelley, Dick, *, 387, 428
Kelley, Virginia Cassidy Blythe Clinton Dwire, *, 14, 46, 80, 87, 119, 120, 138, 147, 148–9, 152, 154, 162, 163, 190–1, 212, 227, 266, 287–8, 292–4, 308, 358, 365, 382, 441, 487, 493
    as anesthetist, 9, 28, 32, 62–3
    BC influenced by, 63
    cancer of, 474
    described, 61
    Dick Kelley's marriage to, 387, 427–8
    in divorce and remarriage to Roger Clinton, Sr., 65–7
    Dwire's marriage to, 172, 189, 192
    first marriage of, 4–5
    friends of, 62
    gardening hobby of, 29–30
    Georgetown visit of, 90–1, 92–3
    HRC and, 240–1
    memoir of, 21, 58
    New Orleans sojourn of, 9–11, 21–2
    Raymond Clinton's relationship with, 41
    Roger Jr.'s birth and, 44
    Roger Jr.'s drug problem and, 415–16
    Roger Sr.'s relationship with, 24–5, 58, 64, 65–6, 90
    shooting incident and, 24–5
Kelly, Grace, 26
Kendrick, Buddy, 120

Kennan, George, 134, 198
Kennedy, Edward M., 127, 162–3, 173, 174, 254, 255, 341, 365, 550
Kennedy, Jim, 622
Kennedy, Joe, 550
Kennedy, John F., *, 32, 44, 55–6, 68, 74, 80–1, 84–5, 93, 121, 123, 134, 157, 185, 189, 214, 255, 258, 259, 349, 501, 551, 565, 619
    assassination of, 84–5, 159
    BC's photo encounter with, 68, 80–1
Kennedy, Robert F., 127, 155, 156–7, 159–63, 171, 175, 180, 191, 215, 245, 259, 550
Kennedy Center, 73
Keohane, Nan, 41
Kerner, Otto, 142
Kerns, Barbara, 378, 402
Kerrey, Bob, 213, 437, 498–9, 500, 516, 517, 518, 519, 544, 547, 550, 567
Kerry, John, 213
Khomeini, Ayatollah, 367
Khrushchev, Nikita, 56, 214–15
Khrushchev Remembers (Talbott), 215
Kincaid, Diane, 274–5, 276, 338, 357
Kincaid, Hugh, 274, 276
King, Bruce, 510, 583
King, Coretta Scott, 56
King, Dick, 110
King, John, 98
King, Larry, 571
King, Mackenzie, 107
King, Martin Luther, Jr., 56, 141, 171, 191, 208, 419, 476, 486, 544
    assassination of, 158–63
    "Dream" speech of, 83, 207
King, Peter, 527
King, Rodney, 538
Kinnock, Neil, 571
Kissinger, Henry, 78, 185, 186, 216
Klaus, Ian, 622
Klevorick, Caitlin, 621
Kopold, Jan, 224–5
Koppel, Ted, 511–12
Korean War, 26
Kosygin, Aleksey, 214
Kovner, Victor and Sara, 527
Kroft, Steve, 507–9
Ku Klux Klan, 109, 360
Kunin, Madeleine, 589
Kuwait, 475, 578

Lader, Linda, 413
Lader, Phil, 413
Lady, Frank, 336, 339
Lake, Tony, 504
    named national security advisor, 600–1
Lakein, Alan, 3
Lamm, Dick, 517
Lancaster, Bob, 477
Landres, Sean, 484
Lane, Vince, 480
Larry King interviews, 541, 571
LaRue, Lash, 45
Lasater, Dan, 426–7

Latvia, 143–4
Lavelle, Avis, *
Leading with My Heart (Kelley), 21, 58
League of Conservation Voters, 564
League of Nations, 135
Lear, Norman, 375
Lee, Donald, 341–2
Lee, Harry, 11
Leflar, Helen, 271
Leflar, Robert, 270
Legal Services Corporation, 180, 258, 306,
    375, 406
Le Havre, France, 181
Lehrer, Jim, 572, 577
LeMay, Curtis, 185
Lenin, V. I., 220
Leopoulos, David, *, 34–6, 55–6, 68,
    227–8, 513, 623
Leopoulos, Evelyn, 34, 227
Leopoulos, George, 34
Leopoulos, Linda, *
Leopoulos, Thaddeus, *
Leopoulos, Thea, *
Leviathan (Hobbes), 227
Lewis, C. S., 184
Lewis, John, 518, 582, 601
Lieberman, Joseph, 480
Linares, Guillermo, 527
Lincoln, Abraham, 76–7, 81, 255, 439,
    533–4, 557, 574, 617–18
Lincoln Bedroom, 284, 286
Lincoln Memorial, 143
Lindsay, John, 253
Lindsey, Bev, 535
Lindsey, Bruce, 143, 451, 487, 495, 535,
    612
Lipton, John, 475, 487
Little Rock Central High, 46–7, 79, 108,
    152, 287, 336, 363, 424
Little Rock Nine, 46–8
Locke, John, 228
Long, Huey, 32, 226
Lorraine Motel, 159, 486
Los Angeles, Calif., 538
Los Angeles Times, 247
Louisiana, 454, 519
Louisville Courier-Journal, 571
Lovins, Amory, 322
Lowe, Lynn, 340
Lowe, Rudy, 198, 225
Lowenstein, Allard, 143–4, 155, 171, 174
Lower Mississippi Delta Development
    Commission, 454, 470–1
Lozano, Sarge and Louise, 378
Lucado, Max, 614
Luelf, Steve, 411
Lumpkin, James, 329
Lumumba University, 222, 224
Lyell, Van Hampton, 21
Lyons, Jim, 438, 517

Mabus, Ray, 454
McAfee, Carl, 223–4
McAllen, Tex., 261, 583
Macbeth (Shakespeare), 77

McCain, John, 213
McCarthy, Eugene, 126, 155, 156–7, 162,
    171, 174–5, 180, 184–5, 208, 229, 230
McCarthy, Joe, 130, 572
McCauley, Nathan, 74
McClellan, John, 80, 110, 127–30, 314,
    315, 332–3, 335–6, 373
McClellan, Norma, 128
McCoy, Ann, 612–13
McCurdy, Dave, 480, 550, 601
McDonald, LaVester, 318
McDonnell Douglas, Arkansas plant of,
    397–8
McDonough Gym, 160
McDougal, Jim (childhood friend), 84
McDougal, Jim (Whitewater associate), 165,
    529–30
McDougal, Larry, 71–2
McDougal, Susan, 418, 529–30
McEntee, Gerald, 527
McGee, Dean, 152
McGee, Linda, 314
McGee, Sister Mary Amata, 29
McGinty, Katie, 613
McGovern, George, 155, 171, 249–51,
    252–62, 264–5, 281, 283, 287, 611
McGovern-Hatfield amendment, 229
Machos, Rhonda, 549
Machos, Ron, 503, 516, 549
McIntosh, Robert "Say," 450
McKay, Buddy, 504
McKenna, Regis, 566
Mackey, Johnnie Mae, 74
McKinley, William, 438
McLarty, Mack, *, 78, 314–15, 376, 485
    BC's friendship with, 23, 25, 206–7, 315
    as chief of staff, 598
McLaughlin, Leo, 32
McMath, Sid, 32
McNamara, Ed, 489
McNamara, Robert, 156, 619
McPeake, Ellen, 189
McRae, Tom, 467–8, 469–70, 471
McSorley, Richard, 215
McWherter, Ned Ray, 510
Madame Bovary (Flaubert), 201
Madden, Owen Vincent "Owney," 32
Maddox, Ode, 419
Maddox, USS, 144
Madison, James, 91
Madison County, Ark., 272, 274, 280
Madison County Record, 278
Madison Guaranty Savings and Loan,
    529–30, 581
Magaziner, Ira, 565, 613
Mahone, Glenn, 206, 207
Mahoney, Jody, 325
Maitland, Sara, 200, 341
Major, John, 570
Malcolm X, 141
Malraux, André, 227
Manatt, Charles, 375
Manchester Union Leader, 512–13
Mandela, Nelson, 469, 549–50
"Man from Hope, The," 552

Mangun, Anthony, 329, 331–2
Mangun, Mickey, 329, 331–2
Mankiewicz, Frank, 252
Mankiller, Wilma, 597
Mansfield, Mike, 125, 156
Man's Hope (Malraux), 227
Manton, Tom, 526
Mao Tse-tung, 214, 254
Marcy, Carl, 120
Marines, U.S., 140–1
Marion County, Ark., 284
Markusen, Ann, 157–8, 161–2, 189, 190, 197, 198
Marshall, Burke, 244–5, 262, 263, 277, 278
Marshall, Capricia, 623
Marshall, Herb, 309
Marshall, Thurgood, 83
Martha's Vineyard, Mass., 208, 209, 256
Martin, Billy, 95
Martin, F. H., *, 288, 308
Martin, Mahlon, 402–3
Martin, Myrna, 308
Marx, Karl, 200
Maryland, University of, 77, 142
Mason Temple Church, 159
Massery, Hazel, 47
Matalin, Mary, 559
Matassarin, Mary, 52
Mathis, Randall, 336
Matsov, Peter, 220
Matsui, Doris, 589
Matter, Dave, 344
Matthews, David, 512–13
Matthews, Ed, 614
Mauro, Garry, 257
Mays, Richard, 325
Mears, Roger, 328
Medicaid, 123
Medicare, 123
Meet the Press, 442
Memphis Commercial Appeal, 428
Merck, Mandy, 226
Meri, Lennart, 220
Messinger, Ruth, 527
Mexican-Americans, 260, 519
Mexico, 260, 311, 569–70, 612
Michel, Bob, 593
Michigan State University, 577
micro-credit program, 433
Middle South Utilities (Entergy), 322, 353, 426
Miles, John, *, 192, 207, 387
Miles, Warren, 207
Miller, Arthur, 231
Miller, John, 397
Miller, Zell, 503, 504–5, 506, 510, 517–18, 582
Milligan, Jim "Red," 284
Millin, Douglas, 182
Mills, Wilbur, 80, 251–2, 311
Milosevic, Slobodan, 613
Mississippi County Nurse Midwife Program, 351
Miss Marie Purkins' School for Little Folks, 23

Missouri, 520
Mitchell, Bill, 169, 387
Mitchell, Bobby, 71
Mitchell, George, 591
Mitchell, John, 185, 186, 280
Mitchell, Joni, 95
Mitchell, Marge, 62, 169–70, 293, 387
Mixner, David, 208–9
Modglin, Terry, 139
Monaghan, Barney, 152
Mondale, Walter, 126, 370–1, 374, 399, 416, 417, 438, 558
Montgomery, Bernard Law, 181
Moore, Dorothy, 402
Moore, Henry, 240
Moore, Jane, *
Moore, Jim, *, 140–1, 163, 204, 230
Moore, Rudy, 276, 341, 349–50, 367, 373, 376, 623
Moral Majority, 316, 323–4, 336, 368
Morning Star Baptist Church, 328
Morris, Dick, 339, 371, 385, 387, 397, 425, 487
Morris, Willie, 178
Morrison, Bruce, 528
Morrison, Michael, 503, 515–16
Morse, Wayne, 126, 144
Moscow, 221–4, 465, 483, 570, 571
Moss, Ben, 246
Mount Nebo Chicken Fry, 111, 292
Moynihan, Pat, 455, 532
Mubarak, Hosni, 590
Mudd, Roger, 254
Munro, Don, 421
Murphy, Bill, 272
Murphy, Ronald, 619
Murray, Cecil "Chip," 538
Muskie, Edmund, 175, 185, 253, 255
Myers, Dee Dee, 496, 506, 612

Nabors, Peggy, 410
Nader, Ralph, 470
Naipaul, V. S., 184
Nash, Bill, 152
Nash, Bob, 392–3
Nashville Banner, 504
National Advisory Committee on Civil Disorders, 142
National Civil Rights Museum, 486
National Commission on Excellence in Education, 405
National Commission on HIV/AIDS, 568
national debt, 604–6
National Defense Education, 263
National Economic Council, 595–6
National Education Association, 419, 443, 497
National Governors Association, 357, 365–6, 412–13, 420–1, 429, 431, 436, 462, 487
National Guard, Arkansas, 212, 359, 362, 363, 375, 565
National Guard, U.S., 47, 160, 171, 172, 203
National Institute for Literacy, 69

National Liberation Front, 185
National Mobilization Committee, 172
National Park Service, 31
National Records Center, 570
National Rifle Association (NRA), 46, 459, 472, 477–8
National Security Council (NSC), 595
national service, 199, 481
National Student Association (NSA), 142–3
National Teacher Examination, 346, 407, 410
Nation at Risk, A, 405, 461, 463
Native Americans, 38, 439, 455
Naval Academy, U.S., 151, 319
Navy football team, 48
Nebraska, 468
"Necessity of Atheism, The" (Shelley), 184
Neel, Roy, 613
Nelson, Knox, 348
Nelson, Mary Jo, *
Nelson, Sheffield, 467, 471–2, 473–4, 530
Nelson, Willie, 258, 365, 398
New Alliance Party, 528
New Democrat philosophy, 430–1, 587, 597
New Hampshire, 497–8, 516, 547
1992 election in, 497–500, 502–3, 512–17
New Jersey, 582
Newman, Dub, 52
Newman, Joe, *, 52, 68, 72, 192
Newman, Paul, 231
Newman, Rae, 52
New Orleans, La., 9–11, 152, 322, 480
Newsweek, 152, 222, 487
Newton County, Ark., 76, 280, 285–6, 299
New York, N.Y., 96–8, 525
New York *Daily News*, 7, 452, 535
New York *Newsday*, 535
New York Post, 535
New York State, 143, 489, 532, 533
1992 presidential election in, 524–7
New York Times, 526, 529, 530, 531, 535, 566
Nichols, Larry, 473, 506, 509
Nightline, 511–12
Nixon, Freddie, 281
Nixon, Richard M., 55–6, 124, 130, 155, 156, 170–1, 173, 177–8, 209, 214, 216, 223, 228, 229, 254, 272, 274, 276, 281, 287, 490, 540
Ford's pardon of, 294
impeachment inquiry and, 212, 277
inaugural speech of, 194
Paris peace talks exploited by, 185–6, 191
resignation of, 292
see also Watergate scandal
Nixon, Vic, 281, 308
Nixon, Wally, 322
Nixon administration, 130, 251, 296, 297, 304
Nolan, Beth, 622, 623
Norman, Clarence, 526
North American Free Trade Agreement (NAFTA), 569, 612
North Atlantic Treaty Organization (NATO), 147, 465

Northern Ireland, 528
North Little Rock, Ark., 282, 328
North Toward Home (Morris), 178, 195
North Vietnam (People's Democratic Republic of Vietnam), 122, 133, 144, 161
Northwest Arkansas Times, 128
Norway, 219
Notre Dame University, 335, 564–5
Nunn, Sam, 480, 504–5, 510, 518, 582, 600
Nuremberg war crimes tribunal, 126, 230
Nureyev, Rudolf, 219
Nussbaum, Bernie, 613

O'Brien, Don, 259
O'Brien, William, 146
O'Cleireacain, Carol, 527
O'Connor, Mike, 622
Odessa (cleaning lady), 15–16
O'Dowd, Niall, 527
O'Dwyer, Paul, 527
Ohio, 556–7, 585
O'Keefe, Kevin, 438, 489, 495
Oklahoma, 369, 519
gubernatorial election of 1974, 469
Oklahoma State University, 333–5
O'Leary, Hazel, 599
Oliver, Henry, *, 460, 478
O'Neal, Tommy, 37
One Hundred Years of Solitude (García Márquez), 245, 315
O'Neill, Thomas P. "Tip," 326
Orange Bowl, 333–5
Organization for Security and Cooperation in Europe, 208
Organization of Petroleum Exporting Countries (OPEC), 352, 365
Orwell, George, 201, 227
Osenbaugh, Elizabeth, 270, 308
Overholser, Geneva, 41
Overholser, Reverend, 41
Overton, Bill, 380
Oxford Union debates, 194
Oxford University, 24, 150, 158, 169, 170, 177, 180, 192, 287
Arkansas-Texas football game and, 216–17
BC's academic studies at, 189, 225
BC's arrival at, 181–3
BC's rooms at, 182, 213
BC's switch of majors at, 187
Edwards's apartment at, 197
European trips and, 218–25, 227
first departure from, 201–2
Ireland trip and, 215
Union debates in, 194
university life at, 183–4
see also Rhodes Scholarship

Packard, Vance, 231
Paget, Debra, 45–6
Palestinians, 466
Panama Canal, 367, 372
Panetta, Leon, 605–9
OMB appointment of, 595

Paris, 201, 312, 318
Parish, Paul, 200, 226, 228
Parks, Charlie, 120
Parting the Waters (Branch), 208
Parton, Dolly, 306, 307
Paschal, Jan, 503, 515
Paschal, John, 170
Paster, Howard, 613
Patman, Wright, 261
Patricof, Alan, 527
Peace Corps, 258, 315
Pearl, Minnie, *
Pelczynski, Zbigniew, 189
Pell, Claiborne, 92
Pell, Nuala, 92
Peña, Federico, 601
Pennsylvania, 536–7, 556
Pentecostals, 329–32
People for the American Way, 375
Perot, H. Ross, *, 577–8, 580–2, 585–6, 593
    1992 election and, 537, 539–43, 546,
    551, 568–9
    in presidential debates, 572–6, 578, 579
Perry, Tavia, 36, 54
Peterson, Pete, 213
Pettijohn, Sharon, 6
Phillips, Emma, *
Phillips, Levi, 284
Picasso, Pablo, 318
Pierce, Franklin, 483
Piercy, Jan, 432
Pietrafesa, Nancy, 349–50
Plato, 101
Pledger, Jim, *, 459–60
Podesta, John, 232, 613
Pogue, Don, 235, 240
Poitier, Sidney, 479
Polk, Margaret, 23
Polk, Minor, 23
Polk, Mitzi, 23
Pollution Control and Ecology Department,
    Ark., 530–1
Poor People's Campaign, 161, 171
Port-au-Prince, Haiti, 312
Porter, Roger, 462, 484–6
Portis, Jonathan, 536
posse comitatus law, 362
Post, Markie, 31
Potomac River, 140
poverty, 142, 161, 592
Powell, Colin, 124, 331, 593
Powell, Dan, 296
Powell, Jody, 295
Powers, Francis Gary, 71, 223
Prague, 224
Preservation Hall, 11
Presley, Elvis, 45–6
Presley, Priscilla, 45
Princeton University, 151
Program for Effective Teaching (PET), 356
Project Pursestrings, 229
Pruitt, Ark., 285
Pryor, David, *, 47, 78, 113, 174, 333,
    335–6, 338–9, 368, 390, 487, 494
Pryor, Mark, 477

Public Service Commission, Ark., 322, 352,
    381, 388, 395, 404, 426
Puerto Rico, 525, 535
Purcell, Joe, 390, 392, 395–6, 399
Purvis, Joe, 25

Quayle, Dan, 542–3, 548, 559, 567, 573–4,
    587
Quayle, Marilyn, 561
Queens Democratic Committee, 526
Quigley, Carroll, 101–2, 482, 554

Rabin, Yitzhak, 590
race, racism, 71, 83, 157–8, 177–8, 206
    in BC's childhood, 14
    Billy Graham incident and, 49–50
    Housing bill and, 160–1
    Little Rock Nine episode and, 46–8
    1964 Arkansas election and, 109
    1968 election and, 155, 156
    in 1992 election, 520–1
    race riots and, 109–10, 123, 141–2
    Rodney King riots and, 538
    2002 election and, 124
Rainbow Coalition, 541–2
Rainer, Bill, 79
Rainwater, Gene, 288, 290
Raiser, Vic, 496
Rakito, Oleg, 222
Rapoport, Bernard, 259
Rasco, Carol, *, 402, 478, 612
Rasco, Hamp, 402
Rather, Dan, 450
Ratio Studiorum, 91
Ray, James Earl, 159
Rayburn, Sam, 7
Reader, Betsey, 206
Reagan, Ronald, 155, 170–1, 191, 233,
    365, 367, 372, 385, 413, 417, 420,
    443, 444, 455–6, 539, 553, 567, 593,
    594, 604–5
Reagan administration, 412, 446
Reagan Revolution, 441
Red Cross, 160
Red Star Over China (Snow), 214
Reece, Bo, 166
Reed, Bruce, *, 495–6
Rees, Mary Etta, 8
Rehnquist, William, 443
Reich, Charles, 237
Reich, Robert, 181, 182, 195, 235, 236,
    412, 591, 596, 606–7, 609
Reischauer, Edwin, 134
Renaissance Weekends, 413–14, 417, 603
Republic (Plato), 101
Republican National Convention of 1992,
    561–3
Republican Party, U.S., 124, 191, 272, 273,
    323, 369, 459, 480–1, 485–6, 501–2,
    523, 540
    BC's economic policy and, 605, 610
    political style of, 385–6
    rightward trend of, 155, 227, 303, 385
    *see also specific candidates, conventions,
    and elections*

Reserve Officers' Training Corps (ROTC), 204, 207, 209–12, 226, 511–12
Revere, Paul, 57
Rhine River, 198
Rhodes, Cecil, 150
Rhodes House, 181
Rhodes Scholarship:
  BC's interest in, 10, 147, 150–3
  essay for, 151
  interviews for, 152
  selection process for, 150
  see also Oxford University
Ribicoff, Abe, 174–5, 255
Rice, Condoleezza, 124
Rice, Donna, 75, 438
Richards, Ann, 612
Richardson, Nolan, 217
Riley, Dick, 510, 518–19, 591, 599–600
Ritzenthaler, Judy, 6
Ritzenthaler, Leon, 6
Rivera, Dennis, 528–9
River Valley Rally, 288
Riviere, Paul, *
Rivlin, Alice, 595, 609
Robards, Pat, 260
Robb, Chuck, 213, 480
Robbins, Liz, 452
Roberts, Don, 355–6
Roberts, Joan, 415
Robertson, Pat, 562
Robertson, Sandy, 566
Robinson, Jackie, 171
Robinson, Joe T., 56
Robinson, Tommy, 360, 467, 471
Rockefeller, Abby, 107
Rockefeller, Jay, 480, 537–8, 549
Rockefeller, Jeannette, 108
Rockefeller, John D., 107
Rockefeller, Nelson A., 170–1
Rockefeller, Winthrop, 107–8, 114, 116–17, 192–3, 234, 287
Rockefeller, Winthrop Paul, 192–3
Rockefeller Foundation, 107, 469, 471
Rodgers, Mary Jo, *
Rodham, Dorothy Howell, *
Rodham, Hugh (HRC's brother), *, 315, 504
Rodham, Hugh (HRC's father), *
Rodham, Maria, *, 504
Rodham, Tony, *, 504
Roemer, Buddy, 454, 584
Roe v. Wade, 302, 418, 489
Rogers, Adrian, 614
Rood, Tony, 248
Roosevelt, Eleanor, 32, 618
Roosevelt, Franklin D., 32, 55, 133, 286, 295, 439, 490, 501, 547, 548, 604–5
Roosevelt, Theodore, 32, 55, 260, 438–9, 586
Root, Paul, 74–5, 402
Rose Law Firm, 15, 323, 357, 426, 522, 529, 531
  HRC's joining of, 321
Rosenberg, Simon, 513
Rosensweig, Jeff, 206

Ross, Kate, 30–1
Ross, Michael, 31
Rostenkowski, Dan, 455
Rothko, Mark, 240
Rouse, Marty, 527
Roy, Elsijane Trimble, 305
Rubens, Kent, 325
Rubin, Bob, 497, 595–6, 605–6
Rude Pravo, 224
Rule, Herb, 115
Rural Health Advisory Committee, 351, 406
Rural Health Office, 350
Rush, Bobby, 521
Rusk, Dean, 134–5, 156
Russell, Bill, 208
Russell, Carl, 16–17
Russell, Carter, 17
Russell, Conrad, 17
Russell, Dwayne, 17
Russell, Falba, 17, 19
Russell, Myra, 17
Russell, Opal (Otie) Grisham, 16, 17, 48
Russell, Richard, 123–4
Russellville, Ark., 280, 288
Russia, 483, 542, 589, 603
Ruth, Babe, 582

Saigon (Ho Chi Minh City), 156, 247
St. Petersburg, Russia, 221
Sale, Debbie, 143
Sales, Roland, 335
Salisbury, Harrison, 134
Sánchez, Richard, 416–17
Sandburg, Carl, 197–8
Sanders, Dock, 36
San Jose Mercury News, 566
Sanyo, 422
Saudi Arabia, 563
Saxton, Martha, 179, 203, 215
Scalia, Antonin, 444
Scanlon, Jim, 288, 290
Schaer, Kathleen, 37
Schaffer, Archie, 529
Schaffer, Beverly Bassett, 529–30
Scharlau, Charles, 283
Schecter, Jerry, 214
Schlafly, Phyllis, 338
Schneider, Billie, 275
Schneider, Tom, 496
Scholtz's Beer Garden, 258, 611
Schumaker, Terry, 498
Schumpeter, Joseph, 147
Schwartz, Mitchell, 498
Schwartz, Tony, 385, 388
Schwarzlose, Monroe, 336, 362, 390
Schwerner, Michael, 124
Schwinden, Ted, 421
Scott, Marsha, 623
Sculley, John, 566
Searcy County, Ark., 280, 282, 290, 299
Seba, Dixie, 62
Seba, Mike, 62
Sebastian County, Ark., 299, 372, 474
Sebes, Joseph, 100, 150

Segal, Eli, 209, 495, 496, 510, 612
Selective Service System, 209, 210
Senate, U.S., 122, 123, 231, 391
  Bork nomination rejected by, 444
  Foreign Relations Committee of, 118–22,
    157, 208, 210, 212
  League of Nations rejected by, 135
  1966 makeup of, 124–7
  seniority system of, 80
  women in, 126–7
Sentinel-Record, 71
Serpent and the Rainbow, The (Davis), 313
Service Employees International Union
    Local 1199, 529
Severinsen, Doc, 452
Shackleford, Lottie, 535
Shakespeare, William, 65, 75, 77, 109,
    189
Shalala, Donna, 599
Shales, Tom, 449, 452
Shamir, Ruby, 623
Shanker, Al, 443
Sharabi, Hisham, 146–7
Shearer, Brooke, 237, 247, 623
Shearer, Lloyd, 237
Shearer, Marva, 237
Sheid, Vada, 281–2, 411
Shelley, Percy Bysshe, 184
Shelton, George, *, 288, 294
Shirer, William, 231
Show Coalition, 542
Shreveport, La., 4, 172, 173, 175
Shriver, Sargent, 255, 258, 261, 583
Shullaw, Richard, 220
Shumaker, Terry, 498
Shuman, Stan, 527
Sidwell Friends School, 604
silent majority, 171
Silicon Valley, 565–6
Silverman, Ricky, 34
Simmons, Bill, 473
Simmons, Ronald Gene, 472
Simon, Paul, 441, 495
Simpson, Carole, 575
Singer Plant, 401
Sinner, George, 510
Sirhan, Sirhan, 162
Sister Souljah, 541–2
60 Minutes, 507–9
Sjostrand, Janice, 331
Slater, Rodney, *, 392–3, 495
Slatkin, Leonard, 73
Smith, Al, 56
Smith, Craig, 495, 518, 532
Smith, Jane, 384
Smith, Jay, 295
Smith, Jimmy, 95
Smith, Leslie, 110
Smith, Margaret Chase, 126–7
Smith, Maurice, *, 383–4, 402, 469
Smith, Steve, 272–3, 276, 295–6, 314, 321,
    341, 349–50, 354–5
Smith, Wendy, 498
Smithers, Mary and Reese, 85–6
Smithers, Susan, 85–6

Smoot-Hawley Tariff Act, 135
Smyre, Calvin, 518
Snow, Edgar, 214
Snyder, Vic, 326
Soderberg, Nancy, 528, 591
Sofia, Queen of Spain, 227
Solarz, Steve, 480
Solien, Stephanie, 496
Solis, Danny, 521
Solis, Patti, 521
Somalia, 589, 603
Soto, Hernando de, 31
Soul on Ice (Cleaver), 195
South Carolina, 518–19
South Dakota, 517
Southern Baptist Convention, 109
Southern Baptists, 33, 56, 109, 465, 565
Southern Development Bank Corporation,
    433
Southern Manifesto, 126, 130, 134
Southern Regional Education Board, 411
South Shore Development Bank, 432
South Vietnam (Republic of Vietnam), 122,
    132–3, 185
Southwestern Proving Ground, 21
Soviet Union, 131, 133, 134, 135, 215, 225,
    297, 483
  BC's 1969–70 visit to, 220–4, 570
Spain, 227, 318
Spanish Civil War, The (Thomas), 227
Spanish Inquisition, 57
Special Alternative Wood Energy Resources
    (SAWER), 353
Spence, Roy, 257
Spender, Stephen, 184
Sperling, Gene, 543, 591, 607–9
Spock, Benjamin, 143
Spurlin, Virgil, 72
Sputnik, 74
Staley, Carolyn Yeldell, *, 68–9, 82, 160,
    192, 230, 344, 493, 513
Staley, Jerry, 69
Staley, Will, *
Stalin, Joseph, 214, 381
Stancil, Bill, 325–6
Standiford, Donna, 37
Star, 506–9
Stardusters (dance band), 71–2
State Department, U.S., 570, 601
Stearns, Rick, 180, 188, 198–9, 200, 208,
    213, 215, 226, 227, 238, 242–3, 252,
    253
Steenburgen, Mary, 452
Steinbeck, John, 195
Steinman, Neil, 241
Stennis, John, 124
Stephanopoulos, George, *, 495, 534, 560,
    583, 590, 609, 612
Stephens, Inc., 426–7
Stephens, Jack, 319, 333, 426, 428
Stephens, Witt, 319, 333, 426
Stern, Gerald, 589
Stevenson, Adlai, 44–5, 56, 155
Stewart, David, 288, 289–90
Stockdale, James, 573

stock market crash of 1987, 445
Stone, Ira, 199
Strauss, Bob, 366
Street, James, 216
Street, Stephanie, 623
Strickland, Pam, 453
Students for a Democratic Society (SDS), 142
Styron, William, 231, 247
Sullivan, Mike, 497, 510
Summers, Larry, 595, 606–8
Sununu, John, 441, 444, 462, 463
supply-side economics, 446, 605
Supreme Court, U.S., 96, 105, 106, 167, 272, 311, 380, 405, 418, 489, 500
    affirmative action upheld by, 270
    Bork's nomination to, 233, 354, 443–4
    busing decision of, 238
    right to privacy and, 325–6
    Roe v. Wade decision of, 303
Sutton, Eddie, 217
Sutton, Patsy, 217
Sweeney, Ruth, 77
Swindler, John, 472
Swindoll, Charles, 614
Swofford, Leon, 284
Symington, Fife, 94
Synar, Mike, 571, 577

Taiwan, 355, 429–30, 563
Talbott, Strobe, *, 180, 190, 195, 200, 209, 236, 237–8, 247
    Khrushchev book of, 214–15
Tallinn, Estonia, 221
Tamiroff, Akim, 61
Tatom, Sam, 370
Taunton, Larry, 78–80
taxes, tax policy:
    in Arkansas, 409–10, 411, 457–8, 470
    BTU, 608–9
    Bush's "no new taxes" pledge and, 453, 462, 505, 577, 579
    economic policy and, 607, 610
    in election of 1992, 499–500, 505, 514, 520, 543, 563, 566–7
Taylor, Ron, 284–5
Tennessee, 519
Tet offensive, 155–6
Texarkana, Tex., 4, 22
Texas, 256–62, 293, 519
Texas, University of, 216–17, 333, 335
Texas gubernatorial election of 1961, 126
Texas Longhorns, 216–17, 333, 335
Theofanis, Dimitrios, 513–14
The People, Yes (Sandburg), 197
Thieu, Nguyen Van, 185
Third Congressional District, Conn., 232
"Third Way," 502
Thomas, Clarence, 236
Thomas, Dylan, 188
Thomas, Helen, 578
Thomas, Hugh, 227
Thomas, Mike, 56, 209
Thomases, Susan, 232, 496, 534, 556
Thomason, Danny, 170, 450

Thomason, Harry, 170, 450, 452, 536, 552, 594
Thomasson, Jerry, 305
Thompson, Meg, 621
Thornton, Ray, 333, 335, 339, 487
3 Kings, 72, 344
Thurmond, Strom, 123, 271
Tillman, Seth, 125, 150
Time, 152, 180, 214, 222, 603, 618
Titan II missile silo, 370
Tonkin Gulf resolution (1964), 126, 131–3, 144–5
Tontons Macoutes, 312
Tony, 246
To the Finland Station (Wilson), 220
Tower, John, 126
Towns, Ed, 526
Trabulsi, Judy, 257
trade policy, economic policy and, 606, 612
Treuhaft, Walker and Burnstein, 241–2
Trimble, Jim, 80
Troy, Matty, 250
Trujillo, Rafael, 132
Truly Disadvantaged, The (Wilson), 447
Truman, Harry S., 16, 32–3, 55, 229, 274, 416, 465, 563, 564
Tsongas, Paul, 480, 499–501, 505, 510, 514, 516, 517, 519, 520, 522, 523, 524, 528, 535, 536, 547, 550
Tuchman, Barbara, 231
Tucker, Jim Guy, 272, 311, 314, 324–5, 333, 335, 339, 390, 391–2, 393, 395, 467, 469, 475–6, 487, 597
Tully, Paul, 568
Turner, Lonnie, 304, 414
Turner, Tina, 458
Tyer, Arlo, 324
Tyson, Don, 275, 297
Tyson, Laura, 596, 605–9
Tyson, Randal, 297
Tyson Foods, 279

Unfinished Odyssey of Robert Kennedy, The (Halberstam), 209
Uniform Child Custody Act, 356
United Auto Workers (UAW), 398, 536, 609
United Kingdom, see Great Britain; Northern Ireland
United Nations, 129, 550, 589, 600
United States Information Agency, 234
United Transportation Union, 527
Uruguay, 141
U.S. Agency for International Development, 433
U.S. News & World Report, 152, 452

Valens, Richie, 71
Van Buren, Martin, 436
Van Dalsem, Paul, 115
Vatican, 261
Vaught, W. O., *, 50, 386, 465–6
"Velvet Revolution" (Havel), 225
Versailles, Treaty of, 134
Veterans Administration, 503

Veterans Affairs Department, U.S., 564
Vietcong, 132
Vietnam, People's Democratic Republic of
  (North Vietnam), 122, 133, 144, 161
Vietnam, Republic of (South Vietnam), 122,
  132–3, 185
Vietnam Moratorium, 209, 210, 213, 215
Vietnam War, 56, 141, 144, 147, 154, 209,
  228, 281, 465, 546, 563, 575, 578,
  619–20
  Fulbright's stance on, 119, 122, 132–6,
    163, 164
  McGovern-Hatfield amendment and,
    229
  1968 Democratic Convention and, 173
  1968 election and, 155
  Paris peace talks in, 161, 185–6, 381
  Tet offensive in, 155–6
  Tonkin Gulf resolution and, 126, 131–3,
    144–5
Von Ihering, Dr., 99
voodoo religion, 312
Voorhis, Jerry, 56
Voting Rights Act, 122–3

Waco, Tex., 259
Wagner, Carl, 438, 440
Waihee, John, 520
Wales, 188
Walker, Jerry Jeff, 258, 583
Walker, L. T., 397
Walker, Martin, 533
Wallace, George, 41, 123, 124, 155, 156,
  164, 166, 177–8, 185, 186, 188, 253,
  399, 413
Wallace, Lurleen, 164
Wall Street Journal, 121, 511, 567, 617
Wal-Mart, 279, 422, 423, 445–6, 506
Walsh, Edmund A., 91
Walsh, Lawrence, 581, 602
Walters, Cora, *, 28, 61, 88
Walter Scott's Personality Parade, 237
Walton, Sam, 445–6
Wardlaw, Kim, 46
Warneke, Lonnie, 76, 196
War on Poverty, 109, 258
Warsaw Pact, 131
Washington, George, 57, 91, 533
Washington, Walter, 163
Washington Post, 5, 41, 121, 449, 541, 566,
  571–2
Washington Research Project, see Children's
  Defense Fund
Washington Star, 121
Watergate Committee, 256
Watergate scandal, 186, 208, 256, 268,
  276, 292, 306, 561
Waters, Maxine, 538–9, 550
Watkins, David, 391, 396, 425, 612
Watts, Duke, 199
Watts riots, 109, 123
Webb, Wellington, 584
Webber, Jim, 351
Webster case, 303
Weicker, Lowell, 233

Weinberger, Caspar, 581, 602
Weiner, Mark, 623
Weirton Steel, 556
Welch, Joseph, 131
welfare reform, 356, 429
  in Arkansas, 433–5, 455, 470, 481
Welfare Reform bill (1996), 356
Wellesley College, 41, 334
Welty, Eudora, 236
Westbrook, Parker, 165
West Virginia, 320, 556
Wexler, Anne, 233–4, 257, 460
Wheatley, Mr., 67–8
Whetstone, Martha, 623
Whillock, Carl, 274, 276, 281
White, Byron "Whizzer," 25
White, Frank, 367, 368, 372, 373, 381–2,
  388, 392, 393, 395–7, 400, 425–8,
  522
  administration of, 378–81
White, Gay, 428
White, James and Earlene, 88
White, Joe, 105
White, John, 258
White, Mike, 480
White, Randy, 374
White Citizens' Council, 49
White House staff:
  appointments to, 589–91, 612–13,
    616–18
  economic policy debate in, 604–9
White River, 266
Whitfield, Ed, 199–200
Whitson, Turner, 421
Whittington Park, 35
Whorton, Charles, 273, 274
Whouley, Michael, 498
Why Americans Hate Politics (Dionne),
  482
Widmer, Ted, 622
Wild and Scenic Rivers Act, 285
Wilder, Doug, 480, 499, 505, 547
Wilder, Thornton, 131
Wilhelm, David, 489, 495, 511, 556, 613
Will, George, 567
Williams, Alice, 22
Williams, Edgar "Bill," 181, 201
Williams, Edward Bennett, 365
Williams, Hank, 71
Williams, Lee, *, 118, 119, 120, 136, 150,
  165, 210, 211–12, 251
Williams, Maggie, 613, 623
Williams, Mrs., 201
Williams, Ned, 22–3
Williams, Paul X., 305
Williamson, Gaston, 152, 153
Williamson, Tom, 180, 188, 193, 198, 201,
  203, 215
Willis, Carol, *, 392–3, 495, 535
Wilson, Edmund, 220
Wilson, Harold, 184
Wilson, Jimmy, 393
Wilson, John (high school English
  teacher), 75
Wilson, John (judge), 12–13

Wilson, John Lee, 394
Wilson, Mary, 25
Wilson, Nick, 326
Wilson, William Julius, 447
Wilson, Woodrow, 111, 255
Winter, Bill, 508
Wirth, Tim, 584
Wirtz, Willard, 79
Witcover, Jules, 186
Wofford, Harris, 503, 544, 565
Wolfe, Thomas, 218, 236
women's issues, 97–8, 115, 178, 302
    HRC's "tea and cookies" remark and,
        522–3
Woodward, C. Vann, 236
Woodward, Joe, 336
Woolsey, John, 600–1
World War I, 134
World War II, 4, 32, 34, 135, 172, 181,
    182, 211, 238, 278, 285, 592, 595
World Wildlife Fund, 375
Wright, Betsey, *, 6, 257, 344, 373, 378,
    385, 387, 392, 396, 402, 403, 414–15,
    425, 426–7, 438, 459–60, 532
Wright, Lindsey & Jennings, 375, 378
Wright, Susan Webber, 291

Yale Child Study Center, 11, 432
Yale Daily News, 180
Yale Law Journal, 239
Yale Law School, 17, 226, 228, 234–5, 268,
    287
Yale-New Haven Hospital, 432

Yale University, 151, 226, 235, 277
    Barrister Union trials at, 248–9, 262
    BC accepted by, 228
    BC's academic studies at, 237, 244–5,
        248, 262
    BC's housemates at, 234–5
    BC's jobs at, 245–6
    law studies at, summarized, 263–5
    1970 Senate race and, 230–3
Yarborough, Glenn, 95
Yarborough, Ralph, 126, 258
Yates, Jack, 304–5, 414
Year the Dream Died, The (Witcover), 186
Yeldell, Carolyn, *
Yeldell, Kay, 68
Yeldell, Lynda, 68
Yeldell, Walter, 68
Yeldell, Walter, Jr., 68
Yellowstone National Park, 31
Yeltsin, Boris, 483, 589, 603
    BC's first meeting with, 542
York, Michael, 184
You Can't Go Home Again (Wolfe), 218
Young, John, 566
Young, Robert, 350–1
Young, Tommy, 136
Yunus, Muhammad, 433
Yusupov, Prince Felix, 184

Ziegler, Ron, 216
Zinnemann, Fred, 26
Zorub, David, 34
Zuckerman, Mort, 452